AQUARIUM

CORALS

Selection, Husbandry, and Natural History

Front Cover
Background: *Euphyllia ancora*. Photograph by Janine Cairns-Michael.
Left inset: *Stylophora pistillata*. Photograph by Janine Cairns-Michael.
Center inset: *Clavularia* sp. Photograph by Scott W. Michael.
Right inset: *Turbinaria mesenterina*. Photograph by Robert M. Fenner.

Back Cover
Top: *Acropora secale*. Photograph by Janine Cairns-Michael.
Center: 500-gallon reef aquarium. Photograph by Gregory Schiemer.
Bottom: *Scleronephthya* sp. Photograph by Janine Cairns-Michael

T.F.H. Publications, Inc.
One T.F.H. Plaza
Third and Union Avenues
Neptune City, NJ 07753
www.tfh.com

A Q U A R I U M
CORALS

Selection, Husbandry, and Natural History

ERIC H. BORNEMAN

With a Foreword by

DR. J.E.N. VERON

Principal Photographers

SCOTT W. MICHAEL, JANINE CAIRNS-MICHAEL

ALF JACOB NILSEN, PAUL HUMANN

MICROCOSM

tfh

PROFESSIONAL
SERIES™

T.F.H. Publications
One TFH Plaza
Third and Union Avenues
Neptune City, NJ 07753

This book has been published with the intent to provide accurate and authoritative information in
regard to the subject matter within. While every reasonable precaution has been taken in preparation of this book,
the author and publisher expressly disclaim responsibility for any errors, omissions, or adverse effects arising from
the use or application of the information contained herein. The techniques and suggestions are used at the reader's
discretion and are not to be considered a substitute for veterinary care. If you suspect a medical
problem, consult your veterinarian.

ISBN 978-1-8900-8747-0 (hardcover); 0-7938-2275-0 (softcover)

Printed and Bound in China
07 08 09 10 11   5 7 9 8 6 4

Library of Congress Cataloging-in-Publication Data
Borneman, Eric, 1965-
  Aquarium corals: selection, husbandry, and natural history /
Eric H. Borneman; with a foreword by J.E.N. Veron; principal
photographers, Scott W. Michael . . . [et al.].
    p. cm.
  Includes bibliographical references (p.). and index
  ISBN 0-7938-2299-8—ISBN 0-7938-2275-0 (pbk.)
  1. Corals. 2. Marine aquariums. I. Title
  SF458.C64 .B67 2000
  639.34'2—dc21   99-058676

Color separations by Pop Color, Burlington, Vermont
Designed by Eugenie Seidenberg Delaney

Co-published by

TFH Publications, Inc.
Neptune, NJ 07753
www.tfh.com

Microcosm Ltd.
Charlotte, VT 05445
www.microcosm-books.com

For my parents, Hugo and Eleanor,

who gave me the opportunity

to visit the far-off places

that have instilled in me a love of

tropical oceans and provided experiences

that imbued me forever

with the magnificence and wonders

of coral reefs.

Contents

Foreword

Dr. J.E.N. Veron

This book, coming from a self-taught aquarist, is extraordinary. Just as comets are now being discovered by amateur star-watchers rather than by professional astronomers, aquarists are now moving into an area of knowledge that was once the exclusive domain of marine biologists. It is a welcome development, and an exciting one for all those who choose to be part of it. Eric Borneman is clearly a scholar in his own right, but more than that, the essential message he sends in *Aquarium Corals* is: "This is a new field of discovery—come and be part of it."

When I look up from my computer screen I am confronted with about 10 meters of shelves full of publications about corals and coral reefs, all read, most defaced by my annotations. Those shelves hold a lot of knowledge. To my mind, they beg the question: Is our understanding of coral reefs changing and, if so, how, why, and does it matter? Many of the books on my shelves were written before the advent of scuba diving. These contain jargon-ridden descriptions of skeletal structures of "new species" or elaborate accounts of largely unknown reefs. They are hard to read and largely divorced from reality. The post-scuba publications are, understandably, somewhat dif-

> "Reefs, like forests, will only be protected in the long term if they are appreciated. Aquariums, both public and private, are playing a crucial role in this. They are helping to create interest for the general public, and it is not unreasonable to suppose that this interest, once embraced by a whole generation, will result in an active desire to conserve."

ferent. Most are not just written for a theoretical or technical purpose, but rather to make a point—or to convey information about some "reality" or other of reefs. Reality for coral taxonomy for example, may have less to do with skeletal details of museum specimens and more to do with how species vary according to light availability and where they are found.

We are now entering another historical phase of observation of corals. Because we now know how to keep corals in aquariums, we have the opportunity to observe them at any time of the day or night, in any weather and in microscopic detail. We can manipulate their environment as we choose. We can see how their feeding and reproductive behaviors change with water chemistry or temperature. We can see how different organisms interact with each other. We can make all sorts of experiments, just by moving specimens from one place to another. These are big changes in potential sources of knowledge and discovery. Perhaps a decade from now, most detailed observations about corals will come from aquariums rather than from the field. Obviously, field observations will continue to have a major role in information gathering, but that role will have a different focus and a different purpose. And the sum total of knowledge we have will be very much the greater for it.

In making these reflections, I am not supposing that everybody who keeps corals in an aquarium is an apprentice scientist! Far from it; most people who keep aquariums—like those who have gardens—have them because they are beautiful. This is important. Coral reefs, like forests, are being degraded everywhere. Only in the past decade has this issue moved into the international political arena, which at least has resulted in some reefs having a measure of legal protection. But reefs, like forests, will only be protected in the long term if they are appreciated. Aquariums, both public and private, are playing a crucial role in this. They are helping to create interest for the general public, and it is not unreasonable to suppose that this interest, once embraced by a whole generation, will result in an active desire to conserve.

A year ago, a colleague proposed that if we are to conserve coral communities we are eventually going to have to learn to "garden" them. At the time I thought this was absurd, but the novel notion of "coral gardening" keeps coming back to me. In fact, it does so every time I dive on yet another sick reef in yet another country. The unfortunate reality is that we are going to have to get active about preserving and rejuvenating reefs and better understanding reef management or we are going to lose most of our spectacular and diverse reef fauna some time this century. We need public awareness, we need to excite children, we need knowledge.

In his acknowledgments, Eric Borneman notes that it is remarkable that I take an interest in amateur aquarists:

now he knows why. We need them, in many thousands, around the world. When we have them, I believe we will then have the sorts of knowledge about corals that gardeners have about the plants in their gardens. And we will do our best to ensure that the pinnacle of Nature's achievement in the ocean realm—the coral reef—is ours to enjoy forever.

—*J.E.N. Veron*
Australian Institute of
Marine Science

Dr. J.E.N. Veron, known to colleagues worldwide as "Charlie," took up diving in the mid 1960s and has been working on corals ever since—work that has taken him to all the major coral reef regions of the world. Dr. Veron has three higher degrees, including a D.Sc. for his early work on coral taxonomy. For many years, he has been Chief Scientist at the Australian Institute of Marine Science, where he is responsible for the institute's multidisciplinary scientific initiatives. His professional interests are in conservation, evolution, education, and science communication.

He is principal author of 8 monographs and more than 70 scientific articles on the taxonomy, systematics, biogeography, and the fossil record of corals. He has published two popular guides to corals: Corals of Australia and the Indo-Pacific *(1986) and* Corals of Japan *(in Japanese, with Dr. M. Nishihira, 1995, Tohoku University Press). In 1995, he published the award-winning* Corals in Space and Time: The Biogeography and Evolution of the Scleractinia. *His* Corals of the World *(Australian Institute of Marine Science, 2000) is an end product of 30 years of research.*

Acknowledgments

When I began this project, my head and files were filled with information, I had a number of years of intensive hands-on coral husbandry under my belt, and I set to work thinking it would all be relatively easy to assemble—just make it a comprehensive coral reference for fellow coral-keeping aquarists. How long could it take?

As years ticked by, the manuscript began getting heavier and heavier. It threatened to become a tome, and I eventually realized that it would be impossible to pack everything I originally envisioned into a single volume. To study corals is a humbling experience—especially when you really delve into the various scientific disciplines that relate to coral biology and reef ecosystems. In the end, I learned why my idea for a truly "complete book of corals"—a thorough concatenation of cnidariology—is never likely to fit between two covers. I discovered that to explore the secret lives of corals in depth, including the multitude of exciting biochemical and reproductive findings that are emerging, deserves a full text of its own. I have also come away owing a great debt of gratitude to many many people who have generously aided and abetted my efforts over the past decade.

My sincere thanks to:

Dr. J.E.N. (Charlie) Veron, for his contributions to this work and his lifetime of pioneering research in coral biology and evolution. For one of the world's pre-eminent coral scientists to reach out and encourage aquarists and amateur coral experimenters is nothing short of remarkable.

Dr. Ronald Shimek, Rob Toonen, and Daniel Knop, who provided the inspiration to strive for excellence. They, along with Larry Jackson, Robert M. Fenner, Michael Paletta, and Thomas Frakes, gave me invaluable feedback on many parts of this book, and I am most grateful.

Scott W. Michael and Janine Cairns-Michael, for so many of the breathtaking photographs in this book. (Their work brings out pangs of envy in those of us who attempt our own underwater photography.) Also to the other photographers whose brilliant images are found in these pages: Alf Jacob Nilsen (Bioquatic Photo), Paul Humann, Norbert Wu, Kelvin Aitken, Greg Schiemer, Larry Jackson, Steve Tyree (Dynamic Ecomorphology), Jeff Turner (Oceans, Reefs & Aquaria), LeRoy and Sally Jo Headlee (Geothermal Aquaculture Research Foundation), and Wayne Shang.

John H. Tullock, who long ago helped my original unfinished manuscript take its first step toward reality and for his contributions toward ethical aquariology.

Allegra Small and Dr. Walter Adey of the Smithsonian Institution for the enlightening information they provided on the subject of calcification.

Dr. Esther Peters for her assistance in helping me understand the complexity of coral disease and, along with Dr. Harry McCarty, for providing access to their collection of disease photographs.

Book designer Eugenie Seidenberg Delaney, managing editor Alice Lawrence, editorial assistant Alesia Depot, illustrator Joshua Highter, my editor and publisher, James Lawrence, and all the other staff at Microcosm for their commitment to excellence and their incalculable talents.

All the fine folks at Wood's Hole, the Dauphin Island Sea Lab, and Rice University for letting me take up space, for refiling all those volumes, and for letting me burn up a copier or two in the process. Literally. (Yes, I was the one.)

In addition, sincere thanks to Douglas Fenner, coral taxonomist at AIMS, for his aid and input in the systematics of the Scleractinia; Morgan Lidster and everyone at Inland Aquatics; Stanley Brown at the Breeder's Registry; Perry Tishgart and everyone at Champion Lighting; Noel Curry at Scientific Corals; Don Dewey at *Freshwater and Marine Aquarium*; the editors at *Practical Fishkeeping*; Todd Kunkel, Tom Voytovich, Mike Kirda, J.R., Kirk Bierbauer, Russell Coy, Liz, Rick Martin, James Wiseman, Sanjay Joshi, Sam Gamble at John Pennecamp Coral Reef State Park, Tom Lang, America Online, everyone on the reefkeepers list and #reefs, and all those who gave me support, trust, opportunities, feedback, knowledge, and guidance.

Many thanks to my friends and colleagues:

Jan Burke, for her continuing support, and for letting me fly all around this country on buddy passes to go diving and researching to make this book better.

Deborah Lang, for her interest, suggestions, approval, disapproval, motivation, proofreading skills, and for listening to my worries and woes.

Jonathan Lowrie and Carl DelFavero, for their professional advice and unwavering friendship.

And, mostly . . . to my father, Hugo, who has taken me to so many wonderful places and given me the opportunity to visit so many others where I discovered my love of the tropical oceans. To my mother, as well, for tolerating our forays away from shore.

And finally, to Gaia, for providing the magnificence, the beauty, the awe, and the spectacle of coral reefs.

Aquarium Corals

Selection, Husbandry, and Natural History

Coming home from Woolworth's with my first 10-gallon fish tank, complete with undergravel filter and freshwater angelfish, I had no vision of the day when aquariums and aquarium literature would take over a large part of my life, occupying every available surface and shelf in my home and becoming a passionate fixation for most of my waking hours.

A child of the 1960s, I grew up in awe of coral reefs, and at an early age found myself formulating a life plan to visit as many of them as possible. I was as taken by marine aquarium fishes as the next person, but there was little connection between the indescribable beauty of a reef and the sterile boxes that were the saltwater tanks of that period. As a youthful aquarium keeper, I was nothing more than a freshwater dabbler, and for a time was guilty of maintaining a tank more for the amusement of my cats than anything else.

So it came as a bit of a shock on the day when I fell head over

> **"Through the window of my mask I see a wall of coral, its surface a living kaleidoscope of lilac flecks, splashes of gold, reddish streaks and yellows, all tinged by the familiar transparent blue of the sea."**
>
>
>
> Jacques Yves Cousteau,
> *Life and Death in a Coral Sea,*
> 1971

heels for a certain 240-gallon reef aquarium, replete with live colonies of *Acropora* corals. Instead of the typical saltwater tank of multicolored fishes doing laps in a stark aquascape of bleached, dead corals, here were carefully selected fish species swimming naturally among living branches, buttresses, and heads of coral on a reeflike mass of calcareous living rock.

I confess that it triggered an immediate "must have" response in me. In setting up and stocking my first system, I proceeded to do it like everyone else who was smitten by the reef aquariums of that era. Like a kid in a candy store, I bought specimens that caught my eye, not really knowing what they were, where they came from, or how to keep them alive. I mixed and matched with abandon, assembling my own unlikely aquascapes, plunking Florida gorgonians next to Indonesian stony corals, thinking they looked good together.

Why not? After all, live rock was a brand-new thing, books on the subject were nonexistent, and the World Wide Web, source of so much reef-keeping information today, wasn't even a glimmer in the public eye. The principles that were eventually so-

State-of-the-coral-keeper's art: a section of a 300-gallon reef system, designed by California aquarist Wayne Shang, exhibits vibrant corals and tridacnid clams.

Coral graveyard: typical early saltwater aquarium in a Panama bank, 1984.

Lush coral growth in a large, contemporary reef aquarium in Germany.

Exceptionally nice 180-gallon reef tank by Steve Tyree of Murrieta, California.

Huge tank-grown *Sarcophyton* sp. at Löbbecke Aquarium, Düsseldorf, Germany.

lidified by Charles Delbeek and Julian Sprung in their groundbreaking work, *The Reef Aquarium* (1994), were at the time considered to be just the mutterings and rumors of a handful of amateur experimenters.

Maintaining corals in an aquarium for any period of time was thought to be an extreme challenge, even by professional aquarists with access to good livestock and expensive equipment. Even as the reef aquarium hobby blossomed in the mid-1980s, stony corals were mostly doomed in terms of long-term survival. Success in keeping corals alive in captivity was all too often measured in days or weeks, with new specimens rotated in as the dead or dying were rotated out. As recently as 1992, some marine scientists were privately predicting that corals would prove impossible to sustain in captivity.

Today, of course, all that has changed. The use of new tech-

niques, more-appropriate equipment, and "natural" methods of reef keeping have allowed corals not only to be kept alive for years in home and public aquariums, but to grow, thrive, and even reproduce. Amateur aquarists have succeeded in growing massive colonies of corals in captive conditions—soft corals weighing as much as 34 kg (75 lbs.) and stony corals more than 50 cm (20 in.) in diameter that have to be pruned when they threaten to burst the bounds of their tanks. Many individuals and a growing number of enterprising companies are now successfully propagating both soft and stony corals in captivity. (Thousands of reef aquarium keepers are currently growing colonies of an *Acropora* species that for all intents and purposes has become a domesticated coral. It was cultivated from a coral imported on a piece of live rock by German aquarist Dietrich Stüber in the early 1980s. Growing rampantly in captivity, its descendants have provided huge numbers of staghorn fragments, which have been passed from tank to tank among marine aquarists throughout the world. After 20 years of cultivation, coral biologists are no longer sure what species it is.)

Much of this success can be attributed to the widespread use of more-intense lighting, enhanced water circulation and, most especially, the inclusion of live rock to maintain proper biologic diversity and natural forms of filtration. Once the basic requirements are met, with some simple, straightforward methods put in place, there is relatively little required for many corals to prosper. In fact, I consider most corals to be easier to keep than most fishes. (I know this last point is sure to spark debate, but it has been true in my experience, and I am not alone.)

LESS IS MORE

I have, over time, found most corals to have relatively few requirements to thrive much as they would on a natural reef. While many amateur reef keepers have taken a high-tech route to creating the proper micro-environment, I have found that less is more. Readers of this book will see that I do not advocate any single method of reef keeping. Indeed, many types of systems—both technically sophisticated and elegantly simple—can be made to work.

My own philosophy is uncomplicated: having a fundamental knowledge of corals and the environments they come from works as well as any commercial product or group of products off the shelf. Although I haven't written this book to recommend what I do in my own aquariums as "The Way," I do hope the reader will gain one critical lesson: the successful husbandry of corals does not reside in merely being able to identify them or in knowing what kind of light or water flow they need. It entails understanding what corals are, where they live, how they are nourished, and the many things they do to survive in a very competitive environment.

Many readers may choose to scan the chapters on coral biology and captive care in a cursory way. Some will simply flip to the beautiful photographs of family, genus, and species accounts and then use them to choose a coral or corals for their own systems. When things don't go well, they may wonder why. If so, then I will have failed.

Biochemists who keep reef aquariums tend to think that it's all about basic molecular changes and reactions. Biologists want to think that it's all about the function of the organism. Zoologists say that if you can't identify it, you can't know what it does. Ecologists invariably think that if you don't get the whole picture, the function of the individual is lost. They are all correct.

I have tried to encompass all these aspects (in a necessarily condensed and fundamental way), hoping to allow the reader to arrive at a bigger picture—a view of corals that I hope is harmonious and scientifically balanced. In my mind, that is precisely what will ensure the success and survival of these wonderful animals in the hands of marine aquarists.

Captive corals: once considered impossible to keep, many coral species are now thriving as aquarists learn to meet their essential physical requirements.

"**Stüber acropora**" Brooklyn-grown from a small fragment by Dr. Terry Siegel.

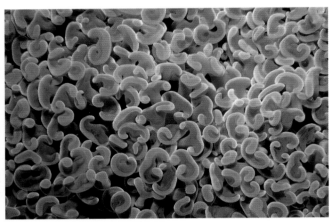

A well-known favorite among aquarists: *Euphyllia ancora*, the hammer coral.

Aquarists' challenge: this ***Siphonogorgia* sp.** is but one of many species and genera of corals whose husbandry requirements remain unknown.

ESSENTIAL EXPERIENCE

Who among us really can say they know what the captive requirements of some of these animals are?

For example, *Euphyllia ancora*, the hammer coral, is kept by many thousands of aquarists around the world with a high degree of success. Their cumulative reports count a great deal toward establishing the captive needs of this species. I have had two of these corals in my aquariums for many years, and coupling my own observations with the experiences of countless others, I think we have a pretty good picture of what this animal needs to thrive in captive settings.

That's easy enough. But what about a genus such as *Siphonogorgia*? I have seen these strikingly beautiful soft corals at aquarium retailers perhaps twice in all the stores I have visited across the country over many years. I have heard that they are difficult to keep alive. I don't personally know anyone who has had them survive in his or her aquarium. Even if I did, I would hesitate to publish a blanket recommendation based on the experience of one aquarist, however reliable. In this book, I strive to avoid exaggerating what we know about rarely kept corals, but I do hope that in future editions we will be able to fill in the blanks and upgrade the listings that are, of necessity, less than definitive today.

The reality is that our collective ignorance about corals and coral husbandry is still profound. In my mind, it's a simple matter of being confronted with so many corals and so little time. It is simply not possible for a single person to proclaim with any degree of accuracy the relative ease or difficulty with which a good number of these corals can be maintained. Many corals (or their natural clones) can easily outlive us, after all. How many generations of corals have any of us seen in captivity? Usually, not even one that reaches reproductive maturity. Can we claim success because we have maintained a certain coral for a period of months, or even a few years? In reality, we are just arriving at the frontier of captive coral husbandry. We barely know a thing about coral disease in the aquarium, much less how to treat it. We can't keep most aposymbiotic corals (those without photosynthesizing zooxanthellae) alive for very long, despite the large number of flamboyantly colorful species available.

A Simple Philosophy

I return to my basic philosophy: to be successful with corals, one needs to understand them, not merely follow a cookbook. There is no doubt in my mind that the recipes are going to change, in some cases dramatically, in the coming years, and I hope that readers will keep this in mind as they read this or any text on coral husbandry.

On the brighter side, we can easily provide ourselves with a working understanding of basic coral biology, and we do have easy access to the essential aquarium equipment needed to keep many hundreds of species alive and well. This knowledge has allowed a growing number of people to witness the splendor of the coral reef 24 hours a day through the keeping of coral reef aquariums. The ability to observe the behavior of animals freely, day and night, for months or years has also brought to many some real insight into and appreciation of life that was previously unknown or a great mystery.

Finally, I think a proper approach to the keeping of corals calls for all of us to have or adopt ethical and responsible attitudes toward the species in our care. I've tried to treat corals in my aquariums as the living animals that they are, not merely as art, ornaments, or transient display items. I know that this fundamental respect for all life is shared by many, many reef aquarists. I urge anyone who is either currently keeping live corals, or who is planning to do so in the future, to take great pains to learn about the many complexities and relationships that abound on coral reefs in nature. Visiting a coral reef in person, if at all possible, is a never-to-be-forgotten experience; it provides a whole new appreciation for the physical and biological dynamics we try to replicate in the aquarium.

It is not enough simply to purchase equipment and hope that these beautiful animals will live by good fortune and the advice of a single source. Education and knowledge are absolutely key to the privilege we have of co-existing with live corals in our homes. By so doing, we can make coral reef aquariums both aesthetically and functionally successful, while creating a more-accurate approximation of the look and interactions of a natural reef.

The incredible beauty and fascinating array of life in an es-

Residential reef: one of the world's ultimate home reef aquariums, a 35,000-liter (9,100-gallon) system built and stocked by German aquarist Klaus Jansen.

tablished reef aquarium can be so mesmerizing as to take one's breath away. I cannot even begin to count the hours I have spent blissfully staring into the crystal clear waters at the coral-encrusted pinnacles, nooks, and crannies of my own personal tropical reefs.

I hope that this book will aid the reader in his or her own exploration of the arts and sciences of keeping aquarium corals. I further hope—and trust—that all of us can use our enlightenment to support efforts to preserve the wild coral communities that fuel our imaginations, give us such pleasure, and are so in need of human protection.

CHAPTER 1

Reef Worlds

Beauty, Biodiversity, and Scientific Wonders of the Coral Realm

Some of my best memories are of the times spent drifting aimlessly over *Acropora* thickets in the Caribbean. Twenty-five years ago there was hardly an area in the West Indies where one couldn't take a mask and fins and paddle off a beach and see vast fields of staghorn coral, *A. cervicornis*, brimming with wild-colored reef fishes zipping in and out of a profusion of branches. Before arriving there, one necessarily swam over beds of turtle grass with countless conch gliding along the sandy substrate. Often, the water would become quite shallow, and vast fields of *Diadema* urchins would wave their spines menacingly below.

On one memorable day off a northwestern beach in Barbados, I found patch reefs rising haphazardly out to 152 or 182 m (50 or 60 ft.) of water. A storm had kicked the waves up from the night before, and the water was still surging quite a bit. As I swam in the shallows among the *Diadema* and *Acropora* fields, each wave would periodically lift and then drop me several feet. In the trough of the wave, the bottom would appear to come up suddenly, and the spines of the urchins came uncomfortably close. At one point, I realized I had to breathe shallowly and suck in my stomach, lest the spines actually find my skin. I quickly and carefully kicked around the staghorn thickets to deeper water, against the surging waves, to find myself, once again, in safer depths to enjoy the beauty of these reefs.

Such encounters were once common off many islands, but today they are increasingly rare. Mass mortalities of both *Acropora* and *Diadema* have occurred since I first began my explorations of coral reefs in Jamaica, Barbados, and elsewhere in the Caribbean. The conchs have become a threatened species in many areas. Today, I look with a great deal of wistfulness at the shelves of conch shells, urchin tests, and *Acropora* branches that I gathered for my private collections. Now I regret those lives I took as souvenirs. At the time, no one foresaw what would happen. I now use their presence as a reminder of the ecological change that can happen in the blink of an eye.

As a marine aquarist, I believe that understanding the biological complexity and some of the modern-day realities of coral reefs adds an important dimension to our keeping of captive corals. There is, in fact, a tangible link between our aquariums

> "Orange and speckled and fluted nudibranchs slide gracefully over the rocks, their skirts waving like the dresses of Spanish dancers."
>
>
>
> John Steinbeck,
> *Cannery Row*, 1945

One of Earth's most awe-inspiring ecosystems, the coral reef is a hotbed of biodiversity and home to myriad species, many still unidentified. (Indo-Pacific)

A huge mound of scroll coral (***Turbinaria reniformis***) provides shelter for an aggregation of Bigscale Soldierfish (*Myripristis berndti*) in Ulong Channel, Palau (Belau).

and the far-flung tropical reefs of the world, and anyone who undertakes the keeping of live corals is inevitably drawn into learning more about one of the most awe-inspiring environments in the world.

PARADISE IN A WATERY DESERT

Outside of tropical rainforests, coral reefs are the most biodiverse habitat on Earth. (Although the reefs have an even greater diversity per unit of area measured, the insect populations of the rainforests give them a numerical edge in the diversity of species per *volume*, given the great height of the trees.) Coral reefs house an overwhelming number of fishes, crustaceans, algae, plants, corals, sponges, benthic invertebrates, worms, plankton, and bacteria belonging to at least 38 separate phyla.

The sheer complexity of a healthy reef is astonishing and the number of species present is staggering, but the actual number of organisms is absolutely uncountable. Estimates of global reef diversity range from slightly over 1 million to more than 3 million species, and only about 10% of these species have yet been described (Wilson, 1988). Coral reefs are home to 1 in every 4 marine species on Earth, yet less than 10% of the vast Pacific reefs have been explored and catalogued by scientists.

The richness of this underwater fauna and flora is made even more amazing by the fact that these flourishing reefs exist in what has been commonly (though somewhat erroneously) termed "the marine equivalent of a desert." The crystal-clear, oxygen-rich waters in which corals typically thrive are relatively devoid of nutrients, and are known as oligotrophic. Observers have long wondered at the profusion of life in such a sterile medium. How such lush accumulations of strange and exotic creatures can exist in such a nutrient-starved, competitive world is a mystery that has endured for centuries and is still a scientific wonder. Yet corals thrive in these transparent waters—just as they have done since the first soft-bodied corals are believed to have evolved 650 million years ago.

FOSSIL RECORDS

From fossils of the very primitive rugose and tabulate corals, we know that cnidarians with skeletons have existed since the Paleozoic Era, before the appearance of dinosaurs and mammals. The initial development of true scleractinian (stony) corals occurred during the middle of the Triassic Period, approximately 230 million years ago. Many families of living corals developed in the favorable conditions of the Jurassic Period, from 210 to 140 million years ago. According to Dr. J.E.N. Veron in his landmark book, *Corals in Space and Time*, "Scleractinia . . . probably gained the greatest diversity the world has ever seen in the Jurassic; and they came to near-extinction at the close of the Cretaceous."

Following the event or events that led to the global mass extinctions that wiped out the dinosaurs and decimated life in the shallow seas at the end of the Cretaceous Period (65 million years ago), corals took millions of years to recover. The reef-building acroporids that are of great interest to aquarists today started to appear during the more recent Tertiary Period or beginning in the Eocene Epoch about 55 million years ago (Veron, 1995).

The impact of continental drift, wildly fluctuating sea levels and water temperatures, and the occurrence of Ice Ages has meant that all living reefs today are relatively young, although the

A mind-boggling profusion of life, including *Dendronephthya* spp. corals and numerous fishes, survives in the shelter of a protective ridge of *Porites* sp. coral.

genera that built them may be ancient. Our present reef systems are roughly 5,000 to 10,000 years old, based on geologic analyses of deep-reef core samples and coralline ridges. Remember that global sea levels have been as much as 6 m (18 ft.) above and as much as 135 m (439 ft.) below current levels over the past 130,000 years. The glacial ice and cold waters of the last Ice Age only retreated about 10,000 years ago, and our present sea level dates back just 6,000 years.

Throughout all the meteorological turbulence, the corals, as a

Favia fragum, the golfball coral, is a member of one of the oldest living genera of corals, dating to the Jurassic Period, 210-140 million years ago.

The Caribbean staghorn coral, *Acropora cervicornis*, is part of an ancient group that first appears in the fossil record after the disappearance of the dinosaurs.

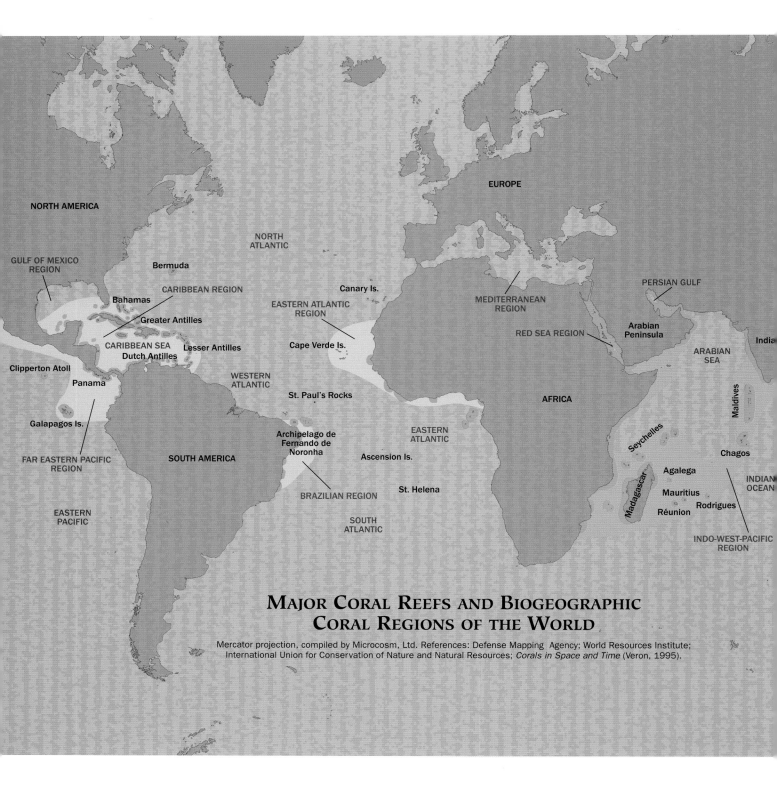

NORTH AMERICA

EUROPE

NORTH
ATLANTIC

GULF OF MEXICO
REGION

Bermuda

CARIBBEAN REGION

Canary Is.

PERSIAN GULF

MEDITERRANEAN
REGION

Bahamas

EASTERN ATLANTIC
REGION

RED SEA REGION

Arabian
Peninsula

India

Greater Antilles

CARIBBEAN SEA
Dutch Antilles

Lesser Antilles

Cape Verde Is.

ARABIAN
SEA

Clipperton Atoll

WESTERN
ATLANTIC

Maldives

Panama

St. Paul's Rocks

AFRICA

Galapagos Is.

Archipelago de
Fernando de
Noronha

EASTERN
ATLANTIC

Seychelles

Chagos

FAR EASTERN PACIFIC
REGION

SOUTH AMERICA

Ascension Is.

Agalega

INDIAN
OCEAN

BRAZILIAN REGION

St. Helena

Mauritius

Rodrigues

Madagascar

Réunion

EASTERN
PACIFIC

SOUTH
ATLANTIC

INDO-WEST-PACIFIC
REGION

MAJOR CORAL REEFS AND BIOGEOGRAPHIC
CORAL REGIONS OF THE WORLD

Mercator projection, compiled by Microcosm, Ltd. References: Defense Mapping Agency; World Resources Institute;
International Union for Conservation of Nature and Natural Resources; *Corals in Space and Time* (Veron, 1995).

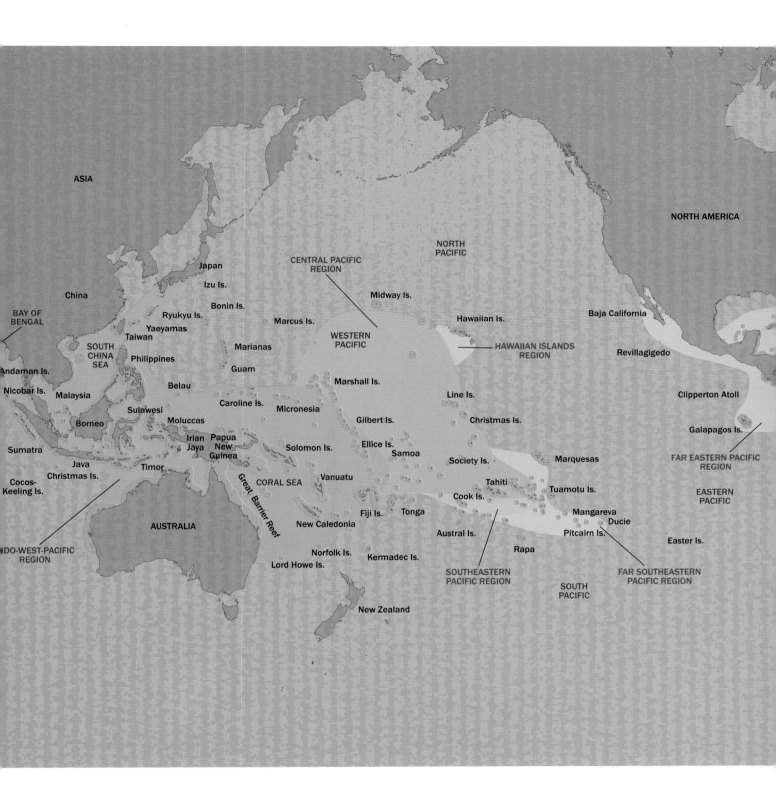

ASIA

NORTH AMERICA

NORTH
PACIFIC

CENTRAL PACIFIC
REGION

Japan

Izu Is.

Midway Is.

Hawaiian Is.

Baja California

China

Bonin Is.

Marcus Is.

BAY OF
BENGAL

Ryukyu Is.

Yaeyamas

Taiwan

WESTERN
PACIFIC

HAWAIIAN ISLANDS
REGION

Revillagigedo

Marianas

SOUTH
CHINA
SEA

Philippines

Guam

Andaman Is.

Belau

Marshall Is.

Line Is.

Clipperton Atoll

Nicobar Is.

Malaysia

Caroline Is.

Micronesia

Christmas Is.

Galapagos Is.

Sulawesi

Gilbert Is.

Borneo

Moluccas

FAR EASTERN PACIFIC
REGION

Sumatra

Irian
Jaya

Papua
New
Guinea

Solomon Is.

Ellice Is.

Samoa

Society Is.

Marquesas

EASTERN
PACIFIC

Java

Christmas Is.

Timor

Vanuatu

Tahiti

Tuamotu Is.

Cocos-
Keeling Is.

Great Barrier Reef

CORAL SEA

Cook Is.

Mangareva

Ducie

Pitcairn Is.

Easter Is.

Fiji Is.

Tonga

AUSTRALIA

New Caledonia

Austral Is.

Rapa

INDO-WEST-PACIFIC
REGION

Norfolk Is.

Kermadec Is.

SOUTHEASTERN
PACIFIC REGION

FAR SOUTHEASTERN
PACIFIC REGION

Lord Howe Is.

SOUTH
PACIFIC

New Zealand

Porites australiensis studded with Christmas Tree Worms *(Spirobranchus giganteus)*. Some massive *Porites* colonies are estimated to be 600-1,000 years old.

group, managed to adapt and survive. Caribbean corals represent the oldest living genera of corals, with an average age of about 60 million years. Corals of the Indo-Pacific region, by contrast, have fossil histories that take them back about 30 million years. Some of the oldest fossilized coral reefs are currently high and dry, found in such unlikely locations as the European Alps, west Texas, and northern New England. The top of Mt. Everest was once a reef.

IDEAL CONDITIONS

Living coral reefs are unique ecosystems in that they are geographically located within fairly definite demarcations of latitude: 30°N to 30°S. Only a few tropical genera can extend their range slightly beyond these latitudes, although there are cold-water corals, even deep reefs, in distant regions, such as Scandinavia.

Reef-building corals exist to some degree throughout most of the tropical and subtropical latitudes, but the main reef networks are found predominantly on the eastern sides of continents. The rotation of the Earth, and the prevailing currents imposed by this rotation, are responsible for this biogeologic anomaly. The tropical west coast of Baja California and Mexico, for example, is too cool for reef development because the California current brings cold water down the coast from more northerly regions. The tropical western coasts of both Africa and South America are likewise largely devoid of coral growth, owing to the temperature effects of ocean currents.

Reef-building coral polyps can only survive in water that fulfills the following general criteria: temperature and chemistry must remain fairly stable, and there must be large amounts of direct sunlight year-round. Temperature is an absolutely crucial factor, with a very narrowly defined range in which reef-building corals will thrive. Indeed, the calcification rate of corals slows at about 23°C (73°F) and stops at temperatures below about 20°C (68°F). Above 30-33°C (86-92°F), many coral animals may become stressed and expel their symbiotic algae in a process known as bleaching. Some will perish after prolonged exposure to temperatures 2-3°C (3-6°F) outside their normal water temperature—or the target range of 20-29°C (68-84°F). There are important lessons here for those of us with reef aquariums.

In addition, the water chemistry of the reef must remain stable. Flooding by freshwater runoff, silt from muddy streams and rivers, and effluent from human activities create water conditions that will fail to sustain corals. Similarly, if the plankton-rich waters of the northern and southern latitudes were constantly washed into the reef, the bright tropical sun would fuel the growth of huge beds and mats of algae and would obscure the clear water with microscopic plants and animals. The life-giving sun would fail to reach the organisms below, and the reef would soon expire in its entirety as its complex web of life would be destroyed, link by link.

SPECIES DIVERSITY

There are more than 2,000 species of living corals presently classified, with probably as many yet to be named. The greatest concentration of species occurs in the more recent reef systems of the Indo-Pacific, encompassing some 212 million km^2 (82 million sq. mi.). Despite being biologically "younger"—as measured by the age of living genera found there—the broad expanse of the Pacific with its numerous currents has allowed a greater proliferation of genera and species than has the comparatively isolated tropical Atlantic.

For example, about 35-40 true genera have been found in

the most-luxuriant areas of the barrier reefs of Belize and the northern coast of Jamaica (before natural and man-made ecological plights). By comparison, 88 or more true genera and more than 800 species (Veron, Fenner, pers. comm.) exist in and around the vast area of the Indo-Pacific, encompassing the Philippines, the northern Great Barrier Reef of Australia, New Guinea, and the island chains within the region known as the Coral Sea. Perhaps most astonishing is the fact that only 20 genera are common to the entire region, and that 6 genera (*Acropora, Montipora, Porites, Turbinaria, Pocillopora,* and *Fungia*) account for over half of all known reef-building coral species.

Coral reefs are by far the largest structures built by animals on the planet. A prolific reef can add from 12-24 tons of limestone per acre per year. Even a minimally productive acre of reef could produce the equivalent of more than 75,000 aquarium-sized small coral colonies in a year. The current estimate of total shallow-water coral reef areas worldwide is approximately 255,000 km^2 (more than 63,000,000 acres) (Spalding and Grenfell, 1997). (This estimate may be low, as the extent of deeper-water reefs is much more difficult to measure and map.)

A single coral colony can be more than 1,000 years old, and in many ways, through both hermaphroditic reproduction and its constant accretion of calcium carbonate, it is theoretically immortal. One well-known head of *Porites lobata* near Taiwan called "Big Mushroom," has more than 12 m (39 ft.) of vertical growth and an estimated age of 1,000 years (Soong et al., 1999). Coral colonies over 600 years old are common on some reefs. In fact, until very recently, corals were not thought to have the cells or genes that determine aging, or senescence. (Still, coral reefs are vibrant systems full of new growth rising atop older skeletons; the average age of living colonies of corals such as *Acropora* and *Porites* species on some Pacific reefs studied was just 4-11 years.)

Deep ocean upwellings, which bring nutrients from the depths of the sea, coupled with the bright tropical sun, allow tiny coral polyps to create formations that support bountiful fish and invertebrate life. As the coral animals die, are eaten, or are eroded by water forces, their limestone skeletons are ground into an aragonite and calcite sand. This substrate supports benthic micro- and meiofaunas and -floras that, in turn, are largely responsible for returning the nutrients and wastes produced by millions of animals and plants into a usable food source. Indeed, marine algae and bacteria provide for almost the entirety of the nutrition needed by reef inhabitants. This recycling of nutrients is the key to the success of coral reefs—an ability not just to survive, but to thrive gloriously in the comparatively barren waters and harsh environment of the Earth's tropical seas.

In view of their need for a very narrow range of habitats and environmental conditions, corals are frequently described as delicate or fragile. In fact, the cnidarians as a group, including the reef-associated corals, have managed to endure for hundreds of millions of years and through many periods of global environmental upheaval. As living communities, coral reefs are exceptionally durable and regenerative under normal conditions.

The most obvious aspect of a coral reef is the diversity of life that occurs there and the intense competition for food, space, and survival. As anyone who has had the good fortune to dive or snorkel in different tropical areas will know, coral reefs also vary dramatically from sea to sea, region to region, and even within the same locale.

There are numerous types of coral reefs, which are then further divided into zones, based on local conditions that shape coral growth. Within such zones, coral species and genera can be found to vary in abundance, and reef areas with the greatest diversity of zones and habitats will have the greatest diversity of corals.

The high productivity of coral reefs is also largely determined by the function of adjacent communities and sources of nutrients (adjacent ocean floor or abyss, lagoons, seagrass beds, mangrove swamps, estuaries, etc.), and by the "juxtaposition of high-activity, hard substrate zones with soft (regenerative) sediment zones" (Kinsey, 1991). Such high-activity, hard-substrate zones are where the preponderance of corals occur.

TYPES OF CORAL REEFS

Coral reefs are found in a number of natural formations. In 1842, Charles Darwin described the first three major reef types listed here, and several others have been added in later descriptions.

Barrier reefs are significant linear aggregations of coral and coral rock running parallel to and distant from the shoreline on the edges of continental shelves. A wide, deep channel typically separates the reef from the shore.

Atolls are ringlike reefs, usually enclosing (or partially enclosing) a lagoon area, formed as an island slowly sinks into the ocean during geologic events that span great lengths of time. Atolls are more frequent in the Pacific, where the volcanic "ring of fire" has resulted in more-pronounced Earth changes. In the tropical Atlantic, atolls are only found off Belize and in the Turks and Caicos island group.

Fringing reefs occur in tropical shallow-water areas surrounding islands and along continental shorelines. They are the most common type of reef development. While similar to barrier reefs in some cases, fringing reefs are less massive and tend to skirt the coastline closely, without a distinctively wide and deep channel running between reef and shore.

Patch reefs are those that develop independently of a main

Barrier reef: Ribbon Reef, part of the 1,900 km (1,140 mi.) Great Barrier Reef.

Fringing reef: coral growth comes up to the beach in Hanauma Bay, Hawaii.

Patch reefs: dotting the sandy lagoon of Aitutaki Atoll in the Cook Islands.

Bank/barrier-reef section: part of the 370 km (222 mi.) Florida Reef Tract.

reef framework. (Darwin and some others have included them under the fringing-reef category.) Reefs that have been destroyed, areas of debris (including artificial substrates like rubble, man-made reefs, shipwrecks, etc.), submerged rocky spots, and even stable sandy bottoms can provide just enough substrate for the attachment of a few coral species. Patch reefs are often scattered near shores or in shallow waters and are often dominated by a few key species at first, with larger numbers of settling and migrating species occurring as the framework grows. Often, patch reefs are either new areas of growth that may become large reef structures over time, the remains of a damaged reef (or dying reef), or are simply too isolated by local conditions to continue further growth.

Bank/barrier reef is a designation used by some to describe coastal coral formations of the tropical western Atlantic and the Caribbean (Kaplan, 1982). In the manner of classic barrier reefs, they run parallel to the coastline, but are less massive and are separated from the shore by a channel that is relatively narrow and shallow. (For example, the Great Barrier of Reef of Australia extends 1,900 km [1,140 mi.] from north to south with a lagoon that is up to 145 m [476 ft.] deep and more than 200 km [120 mi.] offshore in some places. It is indisputably a barrier reef. By contrast, the Florida Reef Tract, a bank/barrier reef running along the Atlantic side of the Florida Keys, is a 370 km [222 mi.] chain of reefs that average 6.5 m [21 ft.] in width, with a channel just 4-8 m [13-26 ft.] deep.)

CORAL DISTRIBUTIONS

On the windward side of islands, conditions tend to create a harsh environment of strong waves, winds, and the full brunt of storms. Corals from these areas tend to be much stronger and hardier, though they are also fewer in number and kind. Many coral reef life forms cannot adapt to these severe conditions. Leeward reefs are protected from the winds and pounding surf and have a generally less-tumultuous environment in which to exist. Consequently, there are a greater number of species found on leeward reefs, but they are also less rugged. Most corals for the aquarium trade come from leeward fringing reefs and their associated lagoons and shallows, where diversity is high and collecting conditions are generally best.

On the reef itself, different types and species of corals tend to thrive in different zones. Zonal distributions of corals exist because of the relative abilities of certain species to exploit certain niche environments. These locally unique areas of coral growth are important in coral reef communities because specific conditions lead to the proliferation and dominance of certain coral types over others. For example, branching and massive species can inhabit the reef crest because they are able to withstand the force of incoming waves and surges that would crush or dislodge other corals. To be sure, these branching species can also be broken by powerful waves and storms, but they exploit these natural pruning events as a primary means of asexual reproduction. The broken fragments can quickly reattach to the substrate and form new colonies, helping assure the proliferation and dominance of the species in its niche. Fragmentation of these species is also a simple and effective means of captive propagation for suppliers to the aquarium trade.

Laminar and encrusting species of corals, such as those found in the depths of the fore-reef slope, are much more efficient at collecting light than the branching types in the shallows and are better able to thrive in relatively dim conditions. Corals with soft bodies or large polyps are typically found in quieter waters, either in less-tumultuous zones on the fore or back reef or in lagoons.

Zonation has been defined as "a state of development where local ecological differences are reflected in the species association and signalized by one or more dominant species in an area" (Done, 1995). These zones are primarily affected by, but not limited to: depth of light penetration, temperature, exposure to air at low tide, salinity, water motion (including the removal of sediments from the water), and the amount of planktonic food available.

Sir Maurice Yonge described 17 distinct zones of coral reef growth, from the shore to the depths of the outer reef. In general, there is an increase in species richness and diversity with: a) increasing spatial heterogeneity (complexity of framework that results in a greater number of niche habitats); b) a depth to 30 m (98 ft.) or light intensity measuring 30-40% of subsurface irradiance. Species coverage and diversity is greater on steep slopes compared to flats (Done, 1995). In terms of size, smaller coral colonies tend to exist on reef flats and deeper slopes. Light also affects the upper and lower depth limits of the various species that can inhabit a given photic range, and colony size is generally greater in zones receiving higher intensity light. Species diversity, however, is not directly proportional to the amount of light received.

In addition to sunlight, one of the primary forces affecting coral populations is water motion. Water flow is sometimes described as lacerating, oscillating, unidirectional, or two-dimensional flowing. Waves, tides, and other currents are responsible for such flows. The force of waves attenuates with depth and can also be found losing energy in three phases (Done, 1995): presurf, surf, and postsurf. Bottom friction causes incoming waves to slow, concentrate energy, then break, releasing their energy. The variation of wave energy between various reef zones, and between leeward and windward shores can be dramatic—up to 80-fold on Grand Cayman, for instance (Roberts, 1974, in Done, 1995).

Easily accessed at low tides, shallow **fringing reefs** in the Indo-Pacific provide many of the corals available to reef aquarists (Bird Island, Viti Levu, Fiji).

Tidal changes can result in various and often dramatic differences in water height between high and low tide, dictating the coral species that can survive there. The greater the tidal flux, the greater the variation in species. These changes are classified as microtidal at 0.3-1.0 m (1-3 ft.), mesotidal at 1-3 m (3-10 ft.), macrotidal at 3-6 m (10-20 ft.), and supertidal at more than 6 m (>20 ft.). Sea level fluctuations and currents also affect coral zonation.

Reef wall: Myrmidon Reef in the central Great Barrier Reef complex, Australia.

Coral growth forms are also strongly affected by water movement. Higher flow rates tend to reduce spacing of both branches and plates. The amount of growth-form variation is naturally maximized to accommodate both food and light regimes. Flow rate can also modify the diameter of branching corals, with higher flow typically resulting in more robust, shorter, and thicker branches. Branch diameter and density tend to be inversely related to water flow; that is, the higher the flow rates, the greater the diameter and density of the skeleton. However, the stony coral *Madracis mirabilis* has been found to adopt thicker branches with flattened ends in lagoons, compared to its thin, cylindrical branches on the fore reef (Bruno and Edmunds, 1998). This finding has been occasionally made for other corals as well.

Sediments can shape zonation by affecting the amount of light reaching corals, and their distribution and persistence is modulated by the various water flows in an area. Another factor related to sediments is turbidity, caused by plankton and other light-diffusing material in the water column. (Where streams and rivers enter the sea, bringing both smothering sediments and nutrients that fuel plankton growth, coral growth is usually absent or limited.)

There are also biologic controls on zonation that frequently involve competition for space. Interactions and competition between corals and other corals, invertebrates, and algae all affect the relative distribution of corals in a zone. Furthermore, predation, boring, and bioerosion are other key influences on coral communities and their distribution. Coral growth forms may be influenced by biochemical communication signals, called isomones, secreted into the water to control growth patterns between and within species.

MAJOR REEF ZONES

Coral reefs are typically composed of distinct zones:

The **fore-reef slope or wall** is where the reef rises up from the depths of the ocean, often quite vertically and with great drama. The fore-reef slope faces the open ocean and is exposed to the harshest conditions of waves, wind, and currents near its upper limits, although the deep fore reef is comparatively unaffected by these factors. Upwellings from the ocean floor bring nutrients to corals and other reef organisms. There are often currents that drift along the reef wall, bringing constant supplies of "reef snow" (nutritionally rich plankton and detritus) to the animals living there.

At the **base or deep fore-reef slope**, one might see some nonreef-building corals at great depths, while most photosynthetic corals would only begin to appear with some frequency in

Upper-reef slope: with brilliantly clear waters and intense sunlight, this zone displays great species diversity, with soft and stony corals and masses of reef fishes.

waters around 30-40 m (100-135 ft.) deep. This is the approximate lower limit at which the zooxanthellae of most reef-building corals can begin harnessing the light from the sun. In this deep fore-reef region, most corals are laminar, large, and somewhat sparse in type and number. The great depth protects them from the majority of surge caused by the ocean waves and tides, but the lack of intense light prohibits the proliferation of many species. Many azooxanthellate corals and sponges also live here, feeding on the food brought in from the open ocean and from the settling particulate matter produced by the other reef flora and fauna above them. Caves are often cut or pocketed into the vertical surface, especially on windward reefs, and these are often lined with sponges and azooxanthellate corals.

The **shallow- or upper-reef slope** is exposed to clear oceanic water and strong light. Spatial heterogeneity is high, and although the coral coverage may be somewhat lower, species diversity is at its greatest. As the fore-reef slope rises, it peaks near the surface and is sometimes even exposed to the air at low tide.

Waves are seen to break over the reef that nears the water surface in an area known as the **reef crest**. The corals on the reef crest itself are constantly subjected to pounding waves, extremely high light levels, strong currents, UV radiation, and sometimes even the air itself. These corals are the most tenacious, often brightly colored and well adapted to the local conditions. Coral density

Deep-reef slope: soft corals, gorgonians, and *Halimeda* spp. calcareous algae at a depth of 20 m (66 ft.) on China Wall, North Boomerang Reef, in the Coral Sea.

Reef crest: a diversity of massive and sturdy branching stony corals adapted to withstand the fierce energy of incoming waves populates an upper-reef slope.

is often at its highest at the reef crest (often from 60-100% coral coverage), though the diversity of species may be low because not many can survive the harsh conditions. Small-polyped, encrusting, and robust branching corals are often dominant, as they are of a growth form that can withstand extreme water forces. Perhaps surprisingly, these growth forms are prone to desiccation if exposed to air, in contrast to the larger-polyped corals of the reef crest that are able to store water passively within the sulcus of the corallite, serving to keep their tissues moist. Still, all corals regularly exposed to air have heavy mucus coats to avoid the harmful effects of drying.

Where water motion becomes extreme, even the most rugged stony corals will fail to survive. In such cases, coralline algae form ridge communities, possibly with some encrusting forms of *Millepora* (fire corals).

Here too, the action of waves and tidal currents as they approach and move across the reef crest often creates channels of coral growth known as **spur-and-groove formations**. These shallow canyons can harbor rich assemblages of corals, fishes and other invertebrate life, and this diverse habitat is sometimes mimicked very effectively by advanced aquarists.

Leeward of the shallow reef crest is the **reef flat**, which may be relatively barren or covered with extremely durable corals that are sometimes exposed at low tides. Coral coverage becomes dense, but does not often reach its highest diversity of species. Where coral growth does proliferate on the reef flat, the area is sometimes referred to as a coral garden. Here, the waves have been completely broken by the outer-reef zones, and nutrients can be comparatively high, both from being washed over the

reef and from any land-based runoff. The shallow depth and calm waters allow tremendous amounts of light to penetrate, and many corals thrive. (On some reefs, the reef flat is sometimes referred to as a **rubble zone**, where beds of broken, dead coral skeletons have washed in from the reef crest or shallow fore reef.)

Some reef flats are dominated by relatively few coral species, while others show great diversity. On some reef flats, huge fields of soft corals (octocorals) compete with their stony counterparts (hexacorals). Despite the abundance of life here, the reef flat can also be a very hostile environment. Heavy rains may significantly dilute the salinity of the water. Temperature swings in the calm sea can also be significant, with the sun heating up the shallow water, only to be replaced quickly by cooler oceanic water at the next tide change. If the bottom is shallow enough, or if the reef formations are developed close enough to the surface, corals may be completely exposed at low tide. These corals must depend on their UV-protecting substances and heavy mucus layers to keep them from being burned by the sun or drying out. Aquarists who struggle to provide corals with perfect conditions and a narrow range of temperatures never fail to marvel at the sight of acres of beautiful coral colonies baking in the blazing sun—apparently unharmed—on a reef flat between tides.

Inshore from the reef flat, the reef again slopes downward, but is generally no deeper than 18 m (60 ft.) and, often, the bottom is less than 6 m (20 ft.) deep. This area is known as the **back-reef slope**. Here the diversity of species begins to increase because of the protection afforded by the outer reef crest and the buffer zone of the reef flat. More massive and hemispherical growth forms begin to occur, in addition to the many branching and

Reef flat: baking in the sun, corals in this shallow, exposed zone are exceptionally durable and form gardenlike assemblages of species. (Nananu-i-ra, Fiji)

Upper back-reef slope: although somewhat buffered from incoming waves, this is a zone with swirling currents and a great variety of coral forms and species.

foliaceous growth forms. The mixing action of currents and waves in these areas is also ideal for turbinate corals, as swirls of water twist the growth forms of many species.

Moving shoreward, the back-reef slope typically flattens into a sandy or sediment-covered bottom. Coral coverage thins, and a macroalgae or plant-dominated **lagoon** is most commonly found. Nutrient concentrations are comparatively high here, and this fosters the development of extensive plant and sedimentary growth (seagrass beds or "turtle fields"). Visibility in the lagoon waters is often lower, and a rich population of planktonic life thrives. Water temperatures can feel like bathwater at midday, with much lower water flows exaggerating the tepid calm. Corals may still be quite abundant, though their species diversity, composition, and growth forms change once again.

Several genera of corals thrive on the soft bottom of the lagoon, including *Catalaphyllia*, *Goniopora*, *Trachyphyllia*, and *Fungia*, along with corals that are tolerant of the high levels of nutrients concentrated here. This is not to say that many coral species, common to other areas, cannot proliferate as well. But in addition to the typical reef builders that happen to settle here, certain species are specifically adapted to the turbid lagoon conditions.

Still closer to shore, corals cease to occur as waves cross the sand flats that rise up to the shoreline and break on the beach. Small patch reefs may occasionally dot the lagoon and the sand flats. When no beach is present, waves may break directly onto a rocky shoreline called **ironshore**. Hardy encrusting and low-growing forms of coral can be found up to the water surface. Small massive and encrusting corals cling tenaciously as wave after wave pounds against them. I have seen ironshores where

the bottom slopes down quickly, or where a flat bottom occurs nearly 9 m (30 ft.) down. These areas can be quite fascinating, though the typical coral fauna is much reduced.

Corals can even be found in **tidepools** formed by the wave action on rocky shores. Organisms found here are able to exist in a stagnant hot pool of water at low tide, where life depends on the rising tide to bring in a "water change." The temperature in a tide pool can frequently exceed 38°C (100°F), with little to no water motion except that afforded by tiny ripples from offshore breezes. Unless waves break into the pool from time to time, evaporation can cause salt content to rise and dissolved oxygen levels to fall. The tenacious corals found here are crusted and attached to the walls and bottoms of these steamy pools. Although life is proposed to have formed in a tidepool, the question for me is simply how it could have survived in such harsh conditions once it appeared.

NEARBY COMMUNITIES

Of tremendous importance to the function and existence of coral reefs is their proximity to other communities. Reefs are exposed on one side to the vast open ocean, and, frequently, to land masses on the other. Atolls and barrier reefs, being isolated or existing large distances from land, may not be as affected. The influence of these communities can be substantial, allowing for the success or failure of the reef itself. Coral reefs depend to a large extent on oligotrophic conditions; that is, they thrive where ambient nutrient levels in the water are very low. The symbiosis of microscopic algae with calcifying organisms (such as corals) is often cited as the primary factor that allows for the continual

Mangrove swamp: a muddy, nutrient-rich shoreline on Nananu-i-ra, Fiji.

Estuary: freshwater meets the sea in a fertile, brackish habitat. (Samoa)

Seagrass area: life in the shallows on Green Island, Queensland, Australia.

growth and expansion of the calcifying reef framework. Without low nutrient levels, coral reefs become eutrophic; that is, they succumb to the faster-growing macroalgae. It is generally thought that an ecological shift from a coral-dominated reef to one taken over by algae can occur with seemingly minimal increases in nitrogen or phosphorus (1µM [micromole] of nitrogen and 0.1µM [micromole] of phosphorus) (Hay, 1999). Many coral reefs worldwide are now in a state of eutrophication caused by nutrients released into the water by human activities.

Some of the following communities typically found in the vicinity of coral reefs influence them by either importing or exporting nutrients.

Mangrove swamps are typically shoreline environments characterized by a mass of mangrove trees that forms a thick net-like forest. These trees, and the other terrestrial life forms that live there, are adapted to very harsh conditions that are neither fully marine nor fully terrestrial. Rather, they are adapted to survival in highly variable conditions, influenced by tides, rainfall, and other factors. Mangrove trees have been touted in the aquarium hobby as being extractors of nutrients from the water. Interestingly, this is not the case in the wild. Mangroves are indeed highly productive habitats, but they are largely self-sufficient communities and can exist far inland from the ocean itself. The sediments in which mangroves dwell are heavily enriched with organic matter that arrives from land-based runoff after rainfalls, as well as from bird droppings and the significant number of leaves that fall into the water and rot. Most of the nutrient production in mangrove areas comes from the microbial community, which provides a nice "compost" in the sediments in which the mangrove trees affix their roots. The roots, in turn, act as nurseries, homes, and shelters for a great diversity of marine life-forms, including juvenile fishes, mollusks, and sponges. Mangrove swamps are known to be areas of net export to reef communities. The rich organic material originating from these communities can be washed out to the reef where it is utilized as a nutrient source for the coral communities. Mangroves also act as a buffer between land and sea, trapping and utilizing much of the soil and runoff from land before it can be borne out to sea.

Estuaries are arms or inlets where freshwater rivers meet the sea, and they can also play a critical role in the development of coral reefs. These brackish habitats uniquely cater to life-forms capable of exploiting the variable salinities and nutrient levels found here. Typically, estuaries are also highly productive, with rich complexes of microbial communities. Like mangroves, estuaries can provide significant export of nutrients to coral reef communities. In cases of flooding, and where agriculture and other human activities cause the efflux of nutrients into river water, this nutrient export can be severely damaging. Many coral reefs are currently endangered or have been killed by the large amount of human-created (anthropogenic) waste regularly flushed into our rivers and streams and then into the sea via estuaries.

Seagrass beds are closer and more intimately related to coral reefs than are mangroves or estuaries. Found pandemically, seagrasses are true marine plants that grow entirely underwater, occasionally becoming exposed to air and sun at low tides in shallow waters. The plants form a benthic meshwork of interconnected stolons, much like the runners of terrestrial grasses. Perhaps more notably, these plants, like mangrove communities, provide habitat for a vast number of other life-forms. Also like mangroves, seagrass beds provide food, shelter, and nurseries for all matter of reef-associated life, including many species that dwell only in seagrass areas.

Patches of coral, along with prolific macroalgae, sponge, and mollusk populations, thrive in the nutrient-rich sediments. Cnidarians, including many types of anemones, also live here. Like mangroves, seagrass communities are nearly self-sufficient and may be influenced by terrestrial sources of nutrients. Unlike mangroves, however, seagrass communities, often encompassing areas 5 to 10 times greater than the reef itself, are frequently found in proximity to the coral reef, typically just inshore. Excess reef production of waste material, borings, flocculent detritus, coral mucus, and algal remains is deposited in these seagrass communities. Their productivity is due to the rich microbial flora found in their sediments, although the seagrasses trap these sediments, fostering the enrichment and productivity of the substrate. Although nutrient levels in waters above seagrass areas are typically higher than those found on the reef, the amount of plankton is also many times higher. Tide changes and wave flushing provide a constant back and forth flux between the production of both communities, with the seagrass areas thriving on nutrients from the reef and from land. As such, seagrass areas are considered to receive a net nutrient import from reef communities. It has been estimated that seagrass communities are well able to manage all of the excess production of the reefs. Because of this capability, seagrasses may be a valuable addition to coral reef aquarium systems, which can include them in special lighted sumps or refugiums.

Lagoons also have very important nutrient-processing abilities. Their sediments, like those of seagrass beds, are often enriched by the excess production of the reef community. The central lagoon of atolls is notable, as it maintains its function without the input of terrestrial nutrient sources. Fine silty sand enriched with organic material nourishes a highly productive microbial flora that acts as a sink for nutrients. As such, these areas contribute to the oligotrophic conditions found on the reef. Lagoons may be dominated by macroalgae, may support seagrasses, may be areas where little suprabenthic life exists other than the enriched sands, or may be almost indistinguishable from certain reef areas. Nonetheless, lagoons, with their slow water motion, foster the settling of organic material and so serve to process nutrients from the reef.

Many other environmental niches—pelagic communities, sand flats, deep ocean communities—exist adjacent to coral reefs and contribute to their function and development. The flux of nutrients, gametes, and larval organisms to, from, and within coral reefs is extremely interesting and complex. The understanding of nutrient dynamics, and how various communities act in harmony with each other, is information that can be advantageously applied to coral-containing aquariums.

One of the key lessons that aquarium keepers can gain from the reef is an appreciation of the very specific niche environments that set the conditions in which certain corals thrive while others fade or fail to establish themselves. Some coral species may adapt to a variety of aquarium settings, but they will respond best when the aquarist works to replicate the particular reef zone in which that coral has evolved to thrive, grow, and reproduce.

Coral-keeper's model: an Indo-Pacific reef scene worthy of aquarium replication.

CHAPTER 2

Anatomy Lessons

Polyps that Rule—and Build—the Reefs

C orals have fascinated and baffled curious humans for millennia, provoking puzzlement and long-standing debates about just what they were and how they came to be. At times in history, passionate arguments were made for and against their being part of the animal, vegetable, or mineral kingdoms. Even today, much confusion exists in the public mind about corals and coral biology.

Prior to the advent of scuba diving in the middle years of the twentieth century, living corals were difficult subjects for scientists, and most early studies were of necessity made on dead or dying specimens dredged from the sea or found washed onto the beach after storms. (Some of the early coral classifiers worked only with dead, bleached skeletons, and several who spent their entire lives in museums studying these remains are believed never to have seen or held a living coral.)

Anyone keeping corals in a marine aquarium has an unprecedented opportunity to watch these animals at very close

> **"For a gentleman should know something of invertebrate zoology; call it culture or what you will, just as he ought to know something about painting and music and the weeds in his garden."**
>
>
>
> Martin Wells,
> *Lower Animals*, 1868

range, day and night. To be successful—and to make the most of this experience—it is extremely useful to be able to recognize and understand the functional parts of corals. Without knowing the basic anatomy of different types of corals and having some familiarity with proper terms, hobbyists will find it difficult to recognize or describe their corals.

In my work, I encounter many people entranced with the life abounding in their home aquariums. But in communicating through cyberspace, we do not have the luxury of having the corals we are discussing available for inspection. Having such long-distance discussions when both parties aren't using the same standard terms can be very frustrating.

Part of the communications problem comes about because amateur or lay terminology—aquarium hobby usage—can be quite vague. The label "plate coral" can mean one thing to me and something entirely different to an aquarist or shipper thousands of miles away. It is in everyone's interest for all of us to possess some familiarity with proper anatomical and biological terms. One does not need a Ph.D.-level vocabulary to talk intelligently about corals. In this chapter, I offer an introductory his-

Typical coral polyps fringed with tentacles are displayed by this lovely cool-water corallimorpharian, **Corynactis californica**, at the Monterey Bay Aquarium.

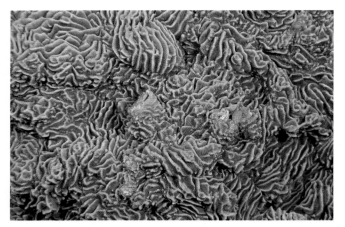

Pachyseris rugosa (elephant skin coral) with polyps embedded in the skeleton.

An encrusting *Montipora* sp. colony with tiny, contrasting polyps extended.

Plerogyra sinuosa (bubble coral) with grapelike, water-filled vesicles.

tory of corals, followed by what amounts to an elementary biology lesson, introducing the parts of corals and their functions, along with an overview of the common colony formations and growth forms.

ANIMALS OR PLANTS?

While corals have long played a role in human life in the tropics, our earliest written history dates back only to fairly recent Mediterranean cultures. In the fourth century B.C., the Greek philosopher Aristotle described the corals as animals and named them "cnidae," after *cnidos*, meaning "stinging nettle." This was a reflection of the stinging cells that unify this group. Hundreds of years later, the name of the group (phylum) to which corals belong would be changed from Coelenterata to Cnidaria, meaning, "to nettle."

The English word "coral" also comes from Greek, meaning "what becomes hard in the hand," "the maiden or nymph of the sea," or "the heart of the sea." The notion of corals hardening when out of water is attributed to the early collection of Mediterranean horny corals, which are flexible in the water but woody when dried. "Coral" may also have been used by the Celts to describe the precious coral, *Corallium rubrum* (formerly *C. nobile*), that varies from rosy pink to brilliant scarlet and has been treasured by jewelry makers for many centuries.

The word "polyp" was also coined by Aristotle, from the Greek word *polypous*, literally, "many-footed." The designation "polyp" temporarily lost favor at the beginning of the twentieth century, being replaced by "zooid"—a term still used today, albeit less so than "polyp."

In the intervening centuries, many early naturalists insisted that corals were plants, and as late as 1703 they were described as "plants without flowers, of a hard, almost stony nature." Even Linnaeus, the father of systematic classification, was confused: "The Zoophytes (animal plants) are not, like the Lithophytes (stone plants), the producers of their shells or trunks but the shells of themselves; for the stems are true plants which, being metamorphosed, change into animated flowers (true animalculae) completed by organs of generation and instruments of motion, in order that they may obtain motion which extrinsically they have not got."

A French ship's doctor, Jean André de Peysonnel, studied corals and gorgonians in the early to mid-1700s and made a number of important observations. By closely viewing the movement of tentacles on live, recently harvested corals, he became convinced that these polyps were exhibiting feeding behaviors and were obviously much more than flowers. When Peysonnel presented his findings to the Paris Academy in 1726, he found himself vigorously condemned by other scientists for trying to establish corals as animals, rather than plants. Peysonnel's reputation was restored only after some 25 years in limbo, but modern aquarists can applaud him for keeping his corals alive for extended periods of time using water exchanges and natural substrates in what is certainly one of the first known experiments in captive reef keeping.

Many others also grappled with the problem of classifying the corals. The German naturalist Peter Simon Pallas, by whom many corals were originally described in the 1700s, considered the corals to be zoophytes, wherein "Nature brought together the Animal and Vegetable Kingdoms." In 1755, the English naturalist J. Ellis offered this analysis:

"I own I am led to suspect that by much the greatest part of those Substances, which from their Figure have hitherto been reputed Sea Shrubs, Plants, Mosses, etc., are not only the Residence of Animals, but their Fabric likewise; and serve for the Purposes of Subsistence, Defence and Propagation, as much as the Combs and Cells fabricated by Bees, and other Insects, serve for similar Purposes."

He then added, in 1767…

"What and where the link is that unites the animal and vegetable kingdoms of nature no one has yet been able to trace out; but some of these corallines appear to come the nearest to it of anything that has occurred to me in all my researches; but then the calcareous covering, though ever so thin, shows us they cannot be vegetables."

Struggling to define the term "coral," English naturalist Sydney Hickson went on to say in 1924: " . . . the word as it is used by men of science and by the general public has some definite restrictions. It is not used for anything except certain animals and plants that live in sea-water or have lived in sea-water in prehistoric times. It is used principally for such animals and plants that produce a solid skeleton (or more accurately shell) structure of calcium carbonate which persists as such entire, after the death of the living organisms that produced it. The corals are, moreover, sedentary organisms, that is to say they are either fixed to some other hard substance at the bottom of the sea, or if free, are incapable of moving about from place to place."

Throughout the nineteenth century, naturalists and biologists began classifying the corals. Scientists such as J. Ellis, E.J.C. Esper, C. Lamarck, J.D. Dana, and J.V.F. Lamouroux studied the anatomy of coral polyps. Their names will be familiar to many aquarists, as they are frequently seen following the scientific name of corals in many references today. It was the German naturalist C. Gottfried Ehrenberg who, in 1831, finally asserted that many corals are colonies of animals representing many generations

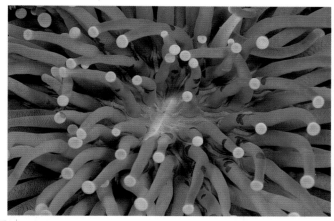

Heliofungia actiniformis (plate coral) with elongate tentacles. Note flatworms.

Anthelia sp. (waving-hand polyps) with tentacles contracted and fistlike.

Diploria labyrinthiformis (grooved brain coral) with tentacles retracted.

Characteristic octocoral feeding polyps on a sea pen (Order Pennatulacea).

and aggregating in a dynamic, organic union. Fittingly, Ehrenberg's name lives on attached to one of our most-admired aquarium species, the leather coral *Sarcophyton ehrenbergi*.

THE LIVING COMPONENT: THE POLYP

The small creature responsible for the phenomenal growth of coral reefs is a tiny sessile animal called a coral polyp. Through its constant labor of laying down bits of calcium carbonate, it has created literally mountains of limestone that support a vast and complex web of life.

The cnidarians we think of as corals are animals, many of them with a strong skeleton, living in a symbiotic union with microscopic algae. (The old arguments about whether corals were animal, vegetable, or mineral were all partly correct.) Corals, as an animal group, can be considered as having two distinct parts when referring to biologic and taxonomic information: a living component and a skeletal component.

The symbiotic algal cells that live in the tissues of many corals are known as zooxanthellae (see Chapter 3). These algae provide the coral polyps with tremendous nutritional advantages and are credited with giving the stony corals the amazing ability to construct massive reef structures.

The living coral polyp is an exceedingly simple—but phenomenally successful—organism, based primarily on the primitive hydroid body type. The polyp is a single living unit of a coral, and in most cases is a solitary animal with complete reproductive and biologic self-sustenance. In fact, some corals consist solely of single polyps and the calcareous skeletons they create. Two frequently encountered examples of single-polyped corals are *Scolymia* sp. and *Cynarina lacrymalis*.

However, most corals are colonial in nature, with many polyps growing together to create a coral colony. Frequently, the term "polyps" (e.g., "star polyps," "yellow polyps") is also used loosely in the aquarium hobby to describe the zoanthids—for example, *Protopalythoa* species. But because all corals consist of one or more polyps, using this term to describe any of the zoanthids is an oversimplification that aquarists should abandon.

Although coral polyps vary greatly in shape, color, and size, they all consist of a basic body form with common characteristics. A polyp has two principal layers of tissue that form a saclike shape. The polyp's exterior layer of tissue, called the **epidermis**, comes into direct contact with the water itself. The upper reaches of the epidermis have a variety of cell types, including those used for food capture, defense, excretion of mucus, and the movement of food particles toward the mouth, as well as the removal of debris from the coral. In stony corals, the lower epidermis also lies underneath the polyp structure, where it is in contact with the limestone skeleton of the colony. Termed the **calicoblastic epithelium**, it is also responsible for laying down additional calcium carbonate as the coral grows.

Lining the interior of the polyp's saclike body is the second cell layer, called the **gastrodermis**. In most corals, the gastrodermis is the tissue layer that contains the symbiotic algae known as **zooxanthellae**. It is separated from the epidermis by a very thin layer known as the **mesoglea**, which is important in immunologic and secretory functions. The mesoglea is also responsible for the **desmocytes**, which bind the living tissue to the skeleton.

Together, the epidermis, mesoglea, and gastrodermis make up the bulk of the tissue of a polyp. They may also connect to the corresponding layers of adjacent polyps in the colony. The outer tissue area that links, and lies between, all polyps in a colony is called the **coenosarc**. (The term **corallum** describes the entirety of a coral colony, including the skeleton and all the polyps.) Polyps within a colony have various degrees of interconnectedness. A system of **gastrovascular canals**, connecting the polyps of stony corals, octocorals, hydrocorals, and zoanthids, allows for exchange and transport of nutritional material within a colony. This system is particularly well developed in the hydrocorals and in some genera of stony corals, such as *Acropora*.

The upper part of the coral animal consists of a surface known as the **oral disc**, which surrounds the **mouth**. This provides passage to (and from) the **gastrovascular cavity** or **gut**, which serves both circulation and digestion functions for the animal. Depending on the size and shape of the polyp, the oral disc may be quite broad (as in members of the genus *Palythoa*) or almost nonexistent (as in members of the genus *Montipora*).

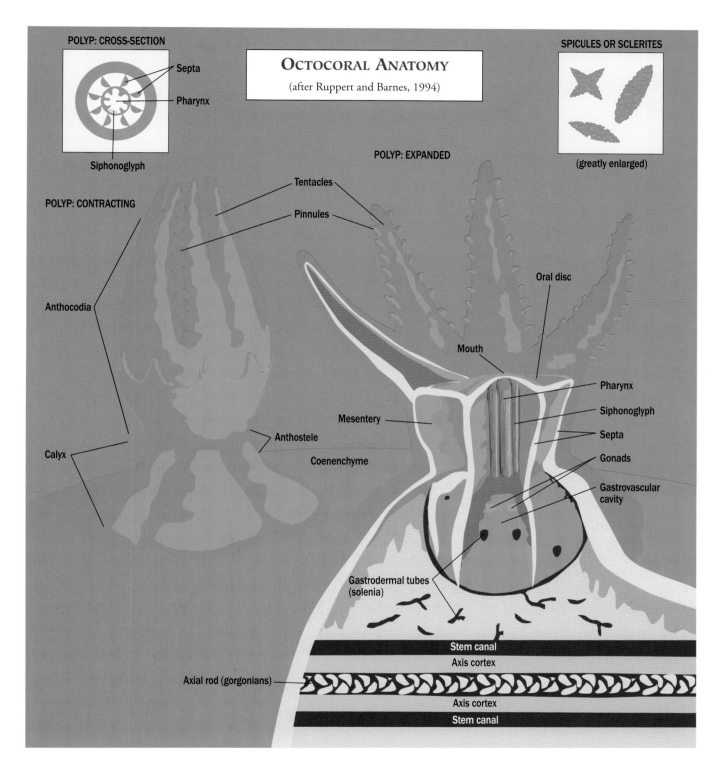

POLYP: CROSS-SECTION

Septa

Pharynx

Siphonoglyph

OCTOCORAL ANATOMY

(after Ruppert and Barnes, 1994)

SPICULES OR SCLERITES

(greatly enlarged)

POLYP: EXPANDED

POLYP: CONTRACTING

Tentacles

Pinnules

Oral disc

Anthocodia

Mouth

Pharynx

Siphonoglyph

Mesentery

Septa

Anthostele

Gonads

Calyx

Coenenchyme

Gastrovascular cavity

Gastrodermal tubes (solenia)

Stem canal

Axis cortex

Axial rod (gorgonians)

Axis cortex

Stem canal

The oral disc, because of its broad flat area, can act in some species as a significant light-gathering area where an expansive area of zooxanthellae are exposed to sunlight. Every polyp has a **mouth** that is a negative space, or opening, caused by the invagination of the oral disc into the gastrovascular cavity.

The mouth typically has a ring of muscle tissue, or **sphincter**, that allows the entrance to the gastrovascular cavity to be opened and shut like a purse string. In this way, the polyp can effectively control the movement of food and waste into and out of its gut. The gastrovascular cavity is further divided into sections, shaped like pie slices, by vertical curtains of tissue called **mesenteries**. These contain the **mesenterial filaments**, which are discussed in Chapter 5 (see page 70). Mesenteries are one of the principal areas where digestion takes place. The weakly muscular mesenteries are paired, and their function also includes an adaptive

role in that the polyp can be withdrawn completely into the skeleton. This action accomplishes an almost total elimination of water from the body, preventing the stagnation of water within the polyp and aiding in the elimination of waste material.

Surrounding the oral disc are rows of **tentacles** that aid in food capture, defense, and aggression. These tentacles are crucial to the survival of corals and allow them to compete for scarce food and space on the reef. The tentacles contain numerous batteries of cells called **cnidocytes** that, in turn, are packed with stinging organelles, the best-known of these in coral animals being **nematocysts**. They are like microscopic barbed harpoons with a toxic protein that is discharged through a connecting thread. More than 25 types of nematocysts have been described, with densities of up to 10,000 per square millimeter of tissue. Nematocysts are discharged by mechanical, neural, and/or chemical stimulation of the tentacles. The osmotic and/or ionic pressure built up by the coral to discharge these poison darts is astonishing, reaching levels up to 2,200 psi (140 atm).

Three types of nematocysts are typically present: **spirocysts** are common in the tentacle tips; **microbasic mastigophores** are used for penetration and adhesion, predominantly in day-feeding corals; and **holotrichus isorhizas** are most common in night-feeding corals. These microscopic coral harpoons can be deadly on planktonic food sources, and the intricate and complex structure and physiology of the tentacles and the many types of cnidocytes are the subject of entire books.

With nothing resembling a brain or spinal cord, coral polyps do have a simple nervous system, a loosely arranged web of nerve cells called a **nerve net**. These individual nets are interconnected, polyp to polyp, throughout a colony. The nerve net accounts for the reaction of an entire colony when only a few polyps are disturbed or excited by a stimulus.

COLORATION

The tissue of corals contains numerous pigment types that are partly responsible for their colors. (Other colors are related to the zooxanthellae and light, and are discussed in Chapter 3.) Invertebrates may contain more chemical forms of pigments than vertebrates, and they are largely involved in cryptic coloration or aposematic coloration adaptations. These defenses operate by camouflaging the corals or by warning predators not to come near or eat them, respectively.

Pigments create color via absorption, reflection, or diffraction of light. The color of corals is also modified under various conditions of tissue opacity and our own visual perception of them. Melanin is responsible for many colors from yellow to black. Sclerotins are responsible for brown pigment in some tissue, but are not responsible for the typical brown coloration in corals, a color which is largely a result of the endosymbiotic golden-brown zooxanthellae. Ommochromes are responsible for yellow, brown or red tissue pigmentation. Dietarily derived carotenoids, related to Vitamin A, can produce bright red, orange, and some yellow-orange coloration. Porphyrins and bilines produce some of the common green colors seen in coral tissue, while pterines, purines, and flavines contribute to blue, yellow, and red colors.

Chromolipid acids and various related esters and other chemical variants, often of unknown type, are also present in most coral pigment analyses of both tissue and skeletal material. There may also be iridescent colors caused by reflections and refraction of light on tissue surfaces and or specialized cell areas called iridophores (common in gorgonians of the Family Chrysogorgiidae). Bioluminescence, or the biological production of light, occurs in the sea pens, Order Pennatulacea. These pigment types, along with some others that may be associated with but not a part of the zooxanthellae, are either produced by precursors manufactured by zooxanthellae, or are acquired through dietary intake. Starvation or a carotenoid-free diet can result in the loss of pigment from coral tissue, at least for the many colors provided by carotenoids. There is also a large genetic component to the rainbow of colors that can occur on coral reefs (Chornesky, 1991; Fox and Pantin, 1944; et al.).

THE SKELETAL COMPONENT: THE CORALLITE

Because the soft-bodied octocorals do not usually secrete an external calcium skeleton, the remainder of this chapter refers primarily to the stony corals (Order Scleractinia). By far the largest number and most-recognized types of corals consist of intricate groupings of polyps that are linked together in often glorious limestone arrays, creating the colonial formations popularly thought of as corals.

The limestone skeleton secreted by the polyps is, in most cases, the identifying feature used by taxonomists to classify them. The intricate features of the skeleton must be examined and used for comparison with existing examples for accurate identification of many stony corals.

The basic skeletal unit of a stony coral is called a **corallite**, and it is within and around the corallite that the living polyp dwells. The area of the corallite that is visible and often protruding on the outside of the coral colony is called the **calice**. The calice may be raised from the colony surface, flat to the surface, or repressed.

Each corallite is like a tube, and in colonies each corallite is

Heavily reliant upon their ability to capture prey from the water column, **Tubastraea spp.** stretch from their skeletal cups with nematocyst-laden tentacles.

joined to others by plates and other calcium attachments called the **coenosteum** (plural: coenostea). (The fleshy coenosarc of the polyps covers the upper surface of the coenosteum.) The corallite is further divided by thin, radiating skeletal ridges called **septo-costae** that often give coral surfaces the appearance of being covered with stars, or turbines, of varying sizes. The **septa** (singular: septum) protrude inside the corallite wall, and the **costae** (singular: costa) extend outside the wall. The septa may have ridges on their top inner edges, called **paliform lobes**, or pali. The **columella** is the spindle, or columnlike structure, formed by the inner edges of the septa as they reach the center of the corallite. Some corals have septa that never meet in the center. In such cases, a columella is not present.

The skeletons of most, though not all, stony corals are white and unpigmented. However, many hydrocorals and octocorals have pigmented skeletons, including *Heliopora* species, *Tubipora* species, and others. Octocorals and gorgonians frequently incorporate skeletal pigments into their supporting calcium spicules. The pigments responsible for skeletal coloration are variable, but are mostly of similar types to those found in soft tissues. Carotenoids, astaxanthins, xanthophylls, and various other pigments are complexed and included during the calcification process.

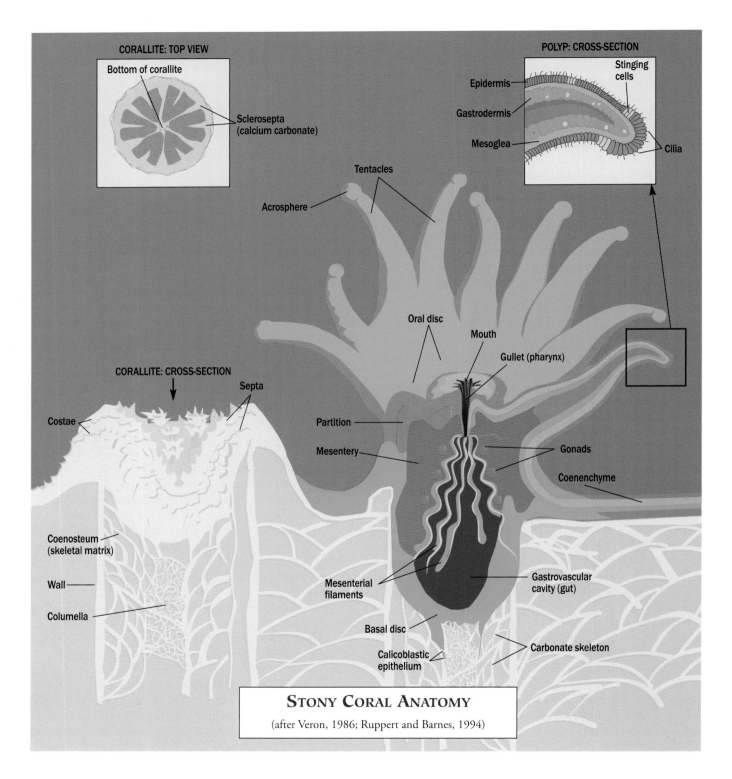

CORALLITE: TOP VIEW

Bottom of corallite

Sclerosepta (calcium carbonate)

POLYP: CROSS-SECTION

Epidermis

Gastrodermis

Mesoglea

Stinging cells

Cilia

Tentacles

Acrosphere

Oral disc

Mouth

Gullet (pharynx)

CORALLITE: CROSS-SECTION

Septa

Costae

Partition

Mesentery

Gonads

Coenenchyme

Coenosteum (skeletal matrix)

Wall

Columella

Mesenterial filaments

Gastrovascular cavity (gut)

Basal disc

Calicoblastic epithelium

Carbonate skeleton

STONY CORAL ANATOMY

(after Veron, 1986; Ruppert and Barnes, 1994)

COLONY FORMATIONS

Many coral polyps form colonial skeletal aggregations, which provide several advantages: 1) strength, stability, and protection; 2) cooperation and integration between polyps; and 3) asexual reproduction through budding, which can rapidly increase biomass (Coates, 1973). Corallites join together in many ways to become coral formations. Typical growth patterns can be divided into colony formations and growth forms. Colony formations start when a polyp divides and begins calcifying a new corallite. Together, all the corallites make a colony. Although most corals manifest a particular colony formation, there is some variability even within species. Therefore, identification of a species by colony formation is somewhat useful, but limited. The typical colony formations seen by aquarists are described by the following terms:

Plocoid corals have separated polyps with individual corallite walls, usually possessing raised and separated calices. The corallites may, in fact, touch each other, but their walls do not fuse. When viewed from above, a plocoid coral colony resembles the end-on look of a bundle of straws. (Example: *Favia* spp.)

Phaceloid corals also have individual corallite walls, but the polyps are very distinctly separated from each other by columnlike branches. In other words, each polyp dwells in a corallite on the end of a stalk or branch. (Example: *Blastomussa merleti*.)

Meandroid corals share common corallite walls and form valleys that are usually meandering and twisting. A meandroid coral looks like the top view of a medieval labyrinthine maze, with the hedges being the shared corallite walls. (Example: *Platygyra* spp.)

Cerioid corals also share common corallite walls, but do not form valleys and retain fairly obvious corallite distinctions. Here, corallites are packed so closely together that their individual walls become one. When viewed from the top, the cerioid structure resembles a honeycomb. (Example: *Goniastrea* spp.)

Flabellate, or flabello-meandroid, corals form skeletal valleys that do not share common corallite walls. Several figure-eight shaped bowls stuck together, side-by-side, in various ways could represent this variable formation. (Example: *Catalaphyllia jardinei*, elegance coral.)

Dendroid formations, which resemble phaceloid colonies in which the corallites are formed from a common branch, could be compared to a flower stem with buds. (Example: *Tubastraea micrantha*.)

Hydnophoroid is the name given to the characteristic colony formation of *Hydnophora* species corals, which have corallites arranged around raised skeletal bumps called hydnophores. (Example: *Hydnophora rigida*.)

PLOCOID CORAL (*Favia* sp.): note separated polyps in which individual corallite walls do not fuse.

PHACELOID CORAL (*Blastomussa merleti*): note polyps positioned at ends of stalks or branches.

MEANDROID CORAL (*Platygyra* sp.): note meandering corallite walls with twisting, mazelike valleys.

CERIOID CORAL (*Goniastrea* sp.): note joining corallite walls and honeycomb surface without valleys.

FLABELLATE CORAL (*Catalaphyllia jardinei*): note elongate, valleylike colony formation.

DENDROID CORAL (*Tubastraea micrantha*): note budlike corallites arranged on a stemlike branch.

Other uncommon and specific types of formations can also occur, with some corals forming variations of the above types, and some having more than one type of variation within the same colony.

GROWTH FORMS

Individual coral colonies display different and often distinctive growth forms, and these are the most obvious method of quickly identifying live corals on the reef and in the aquarium. However, there is considerable variance in growth forms among colonies, and even within a species. Water movement, lighting, nutrients, sediments, turbidity, predators, cryptofauna, competition, and other environmental conditions can all affect the shape and external appearance of a coral. Even within a single colony, several growth forms may be seen. Generally, hydraulic energy, in the form of currents, surge, tides, and the relative exposure or protection of a given habitat, is the key factor in determining growth forms.

Despite some formations being commonly adopted by a particular coral or group of corals, the use of growth form to identify coral species with certainty can be tricky—or even impossible. Growth forms are used in this book to describe the shapes that the majority of corals of a given type tend to form in the ab-

sence of specific environmental modifiers.

Massive corals are solid bodies, usually somewhat spherical or hemispherical, often resembling a boulder. Massive corals are usually found in shallow and mid-depth waters, as they are resistant to high water flow but are not dependent on it. They have linear extension rates averaging 1-3 cm (0.4-1.2 in.) per year and are generally very long-lived. Their skeleton is marked with yearly or semi-annual banding patterns of varying skeletal densities. Although they do not grow outward at a noticeably rapid rate, their overall rate of calcification, as measured by skeletal mass, is similar to other growth forms. (Example: *Diploria labyrinthiformis*, Caribbean grooved brain coral.)

Columnar corals form vertical pillars that do not branch, usually rising from a common massive base. Columnar corals are often found in mid-depth levels not exposed to extreme water flow. (Example: *Psammocora* spp. or *Dendrogyra cylindrus*, Caribbean pillar coral.)

Encrusting (or crustose) corals creep along the surface of the substrate where they have settled and cover it with sheet- or platelike growth, sometimes sending up short projections. Encrusting corals are found throughout the reef, though they are highly effective at exploiting areas with extreme water motion. Many corals may have an encrusting base, though the colony as a whole displays another growth form. Encrusting corals may also send projections outward to encompass other growth forms. (Examples: various *Montipora* spp. and *Porites* spp.)

Branching (arborescent, arboreal, or ramose) corals have growth forms that resemble a tree, with projections regularly occurring along the length of the other branches. They are usually anchored by a common base, or trunk. Branching corals are often found in water exposed to high wave action and surge. The pattern of branching is highly modifiable. They are most adapted to zooplankton capture, have faster linear growth rates, can withstand mechanical forces, and yet are easily reproduced by fragmentation. (Example: *Acropora formosa*.) Several distinctive variations exist

MASSIVE CORAL (*Diploria labyrinthiformis*): note boulderlike growth of this Caribbean brain coral.

COLUMNAR CORAL (*Dendrogyra cylindrus*): note unbranching pillars of this Caribbean species.

ENCRUSTING CORAL (*Montipora foveolata*): note irregular crustose growth on rocky substrate.

BRANCHING (arborescent) CORAL (*Acropora formosa*): note branchlike or "staghorn" structure.

FOLIACEOUS CORAL (*Leptoseris papyracea*): note upright sheets resembling formations of leaves.

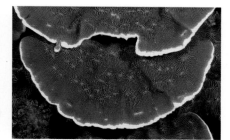

LAMINAR CORAL (*Leptoseris explanata*): note flat plate adapted to gathering sunlight in deep water.

TURBINATE CORAL (*Montipora capricornis*): note vaselike growth form with cone-shaped whorls.

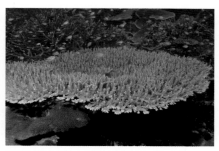

TABULATE (table) CORAL (*Acropora cytherea*): note platform of radiating, tightly spaced branches.

SOLITARY CORAL (*Fungia* sp.): note lone, self-contained formation (often unattached to substrate).

among the branching stony corals and are especially useful in describing the many types of *Acropora* species (see pages 221-233).

Foliaceous corals form thin plates and sheets that are commonly upright and folded in leafy formations. Typically found in areas of turbulent water flow, where mixing currents can bring food to polyps within the folds and effectively whisk waste and debris away. Shallow-water forms are more delicate and may depend on fragmentation, while deeper-water varieties are slow-growing and robust (Hughes and Jackson, 1985). (Examples: *Leptoseris* spp. and *Turbinaria* spp.)

Laminar corals form thin, flat plates, usually horizontal, sometimes terraced. Usually found in deeper water where the broad plates and upward-facing polyps can capture maximal sunlight. (Examples: *Leptoseris* spp. and *Pachyseris* spp.)

Turbinate corals have vaselike growth forms that somewhat resemble ice cream cones. They are usually found in quiet water at mid-depths, where the likelihood of debris collecting at the bottom of the folds is less prevalent. Brittlestars and other detritovores are often found dwelling at the base of such corals. (Example: *Montipora capricornis*.)

Tabulate (or table) corals are those that tend to form flattened, radiating platforms of tightly spaced branches suggesting tablelike formations. They are most frequently *Acropora* species,

but *Montipora*, *Merulina*, and a number of others may adopt this form. Initially encrusting, a young colony adopts a more-vertical orientation until mature, when it then decreases vertical growth almost entirely, spreading horizontally. Occasionally, tiers may form, and the tables have visible annual bands that appear as waves across their surface. These corals are predominantly from very shallow waters. (Example: *Acropora cytherea*.)

Solitary corals occur in many shapes and sizes, but are notable because they are lone corals often unattached to rock, substrate, or other coral colonies. Occasionally they are found in clusters but are not attached to each other. They frequently occur on sandy or rocky bottoms, in shallow to mid-depth water. Many solitary corals spend the early part of their life attached to substrate, becoming detached after a period of time. (Example: *Fungia* spp.)

The specific anatomy, biology, and growth forms of the various groups of corals are covered in more detail beginning on the following pages:

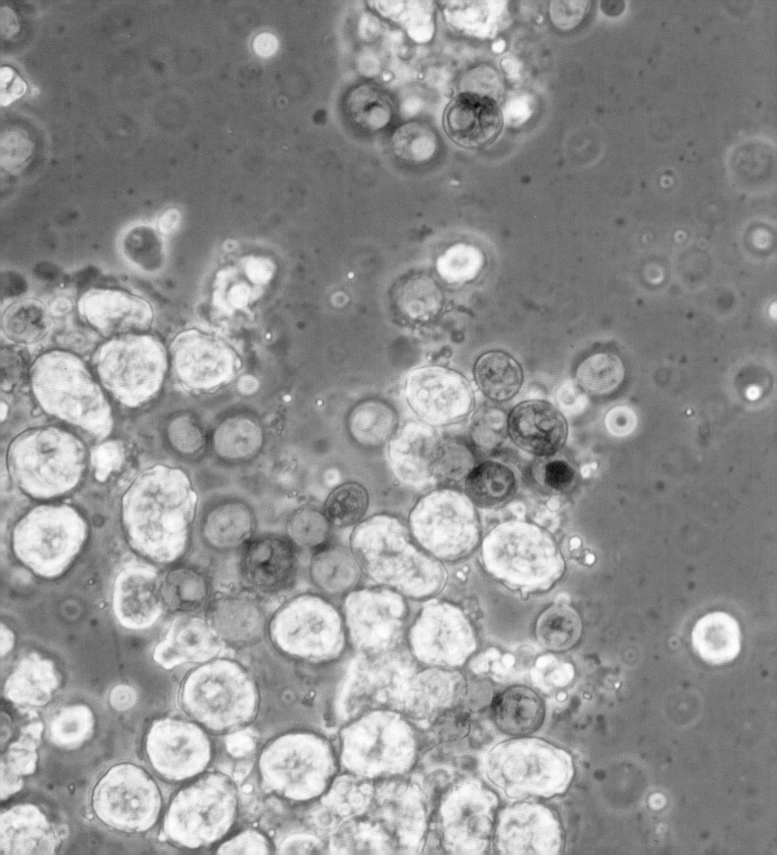

CHAPTER 3

Zooxanthellae

The Symbiotic Algae of Corals

Early in the life of a coral polyp, it may adopt—or, according to some, be "infected by"—a strain of single-celled algae known as zooxanthellae. (More correctly, they are dinoflagellates, photosynthetic protists considered to be algae.) These algal cells are exceedingly small. The number of zooxanthellae that dwell in the portions of a coral polyp exposed to sunlight is huge: about 10,000 would fit on the period at the end of this sentence. Even a small colony of coral harbors millions of zooxanthellae; for larger colonies, the count would quickly mount to the billions and beyond.

These microscopic cells allow corals to thrive and build tremendous reef structures in nutrient-starved tropical waters. Possessing chlorophyll, the zooxanthellae are able to synthesize oxygen and energy-rich products using sunlight, carbon dioxide, and water by means of photosynthesis.

The relationship between the algal cells and the coral polyp is highly complex. Simply put, a basic symbiosis exists that allows

> "Zooxanthellae . . . without which it is just possible that such immense aggregations of living matter which constitute a coral reef could not originate and flourish."
>
>
>
> C.M. Yonge, 1930
> *Studies on the Physiology of Corals*

the algae to exist in a stable environment with protection from predation in the open sea. The zooxanthellae benefit from the relatively constant physical and chemical conditions inside the cells of a living organism, where a beneficial exchange of nutrients and wastes is provided. Despite being somewhat sheltered from the sun, zooxanthellae are able to photosynthesize with nearly the same efficiency within coral tissue as they would if living free in the ocean. In addition to having the protection that the coral tissue provides, the zooxanthellae benefit directly from the dissolved nutrients that the polyp absorbs, especially nitrate and phosphate. Furthermore, the coral provides ammonia from its own metabolic processes to feed its population of algal partners.

In return, the zooxanthellae nourish the polyp with the energy-rich products of photosynthesis. (This type of give-and-take relationship is known as **mutualism**.) While the coral could, in theory, survive on the capture of zooplankton alone, in actual reef conditions this food source is limited and the zooxanthellae are needed to provide the nutrients for corals to grow and reproduce. (Stony corals experimentally screened from the sun in natural reef

Golden zooxanthellae cells from an aquarium specimen of *Euphyllia ancora* (hammer coral), magnified 400 times in a photograph by Alf Jacob Nilsen.

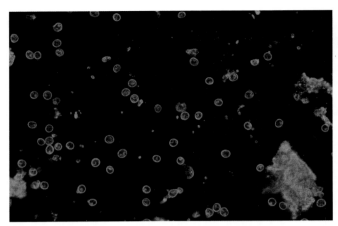

Zooxanthellae from *Heliopora coerulea* (blue coral), magnified 200 times.

Close-up of *Acropora cervicornis*, tinged with a golden cast from zooxanthellae.

conditions eventually expelled their zooxanthellae and died, despite the continued presence of zooplankton and dissolved nutrients in the water.)

The presence or absence of zooxanthellae is the characteristic used to divide all corals into two very different groups. It is a distinction with profound importance for anyone selecting specimens for the home aquarium: corals are classified as being **zooxanthellate** when they possess zooxanthellae in their tissues. These corals are also termed **symbiotic** or, by some in the aquarium trade, **photosynthetic**. In contrast, **azooxanthellate** corals lack zooxanthellae and can live in darkened conditions, relying not on sunlight but on their enhanced abilities to catch zooplankton or to absorb nutrients from the water. Such corals are also referred to as **aposymbiotic** or **nonphotosynthetic**.

In general terms, the symbiotic types will adapt much more readily to aquarium conditions and can often be expected to live for years. On the other hand, the aposymbiotic corals in captivity need to be fed regularly with planktonic foods. They are much more demanding of care and nutritional input, and many are very difficult to keep alive in the typical aquarium with the foods and equipment currently available. Some, such as the colorful *Dendronephthya* species, seem to require very frequent feedings of phytoplankton (microscopic water-borne algae) and have defied the best efforts of many aquarists to keep them alive.

Among the corals that build calcareous skeletons, two additional terms are commonly employed

Hermatypic refers to corals that are reef-building and make significant contributions of calcium carbonate to the reef structure. This group includes most zooxanthellate stony corals and a few octocorals that form calcareous skeletons, such as *Tubipora musica*.

Ahermatypic identifies corals that that do not contribute substantially to the reef structure. This group includes the soft corals and those without a significant stony skeleton, as well as some azooxanthellate, nonreefal stony corals.

Some disagreement surrounds these terms, with some using the word hermatypic interchangeably with zooxanthellate. This stems from the original definitions posed in 1933 by John W. Wells, and it has caused some long-standing confusion among biologists and geologists. To be sure, almost all reef-building or hermatypic corals contain zooxanthellae, but there are some vexatious exceptions. *Tubastraea micrantha*, for example, has no zooxanthellae but builds substantial calcareous skeletons. Many experts place it among the ahermatypes, because it is aposymbiotic and may be found in areas that are not part of the reef proper. On the other hand, a case can be made for its inclusion among the hermatypes, based on its abilities to create substantial stands of stony branches.

The proper use of the term hermatypic was suggested by Schumacher and Zibrowius (1985) and Fagerstrom (1987), restricting it to corals (and certain other invertebrates) that *contribute significantly to the reef matrix regardless of whether or not they contain symbiotic zooxanthellae.*

ZOOXANTHELLAE THEN AND NOW

In 1881, K. Brandt first described the symbiotic algae in coral tissues and proposed the name *Zooxanthellae nutricula* to describe them. The genus name suggested the alga's relationship to animals (*zoo*) and the typical yellow-brown color (*xanth* meaning gold).

The name changed several times over the next half century. R. Hovasse used the name *Endodynium* in 1922 to describe the symbiotic algae, which he believed to be parasites. In 1944, S. Kawaguti described the algae as being marine dinoflagellates of the genus *Gymnodinium*. In 1962, H.D. Freudenthal changed the name, once again, to *Symbiodinium microadriaticum*.

Today, the names *Gymnodinium microadriaticum* and *Symbiodinium microadriaticum* are used interchangeably, with the latter being generally more recognized. As D. Taylor (1974) notes, "most are content to refer to marine algal symbionts as 'zooxanthellae,' a term that lost all of its taxonomic significance before the end of the nineteenth century."

It was assumed, until nearly the present, that *S. microadriaticum* was the sole species that inhabited the tissues of certain corals and invertebrates, but there are now known to be at least four orders, seven genera, and many more species of symbiotic dinoflagellates. In all, more than 80 different strains have been isolated, many of which are separate species or subspecies. In fact, species of symbiotic algae have been postulated to be quite specific in terms of the coral species in which they dwell. For example, *Symbiodinium (Gymnodinium) kawaguti* is the species that dwells in the Indo-Pacific coral *Montipora verrucosa*, while *S. pilosum* is the species found in *Zoanthus sociatus*. These symbionts "are not just strains, but things as different as cows and rats" (Knowlton, 1999). Zooxanthellae species not only vary in their adaptability to different conditions, but even in their cell size, isozyme patterns, electrophoretic data, genetic composition at specific sites, etc.

The nutritional requirements of a coral, and the depths at which it is found, may play a role in the adoption of specific strains of symbionts. Even so, corals may be able to switch one species of zooxanthellae for other species that may be more adaptive to their specific conditions of lighting and location on the reef. This is especially true after bleaching events, where the previous strain may no longer be well adapted to prevailing conditions. Researchers have identified a number of large known pools (or **clades**) of zooxanthellae, some—but not all—of which are drawn upon by corals. Preliminary studies suggest that Caribbean corals harbor more species from different clades of zooxanthellae than do Pacific corals, which seem to harbor symbiotic algae only from a single pool. This clade is expected to be subdivided in the future. Its symbionts are often lost when exposed to unusually high temperatures or light levels (Knowlton, 1999).

It has been postulated that clade differences may be responsible for the more-frequent but milder bleaching episodes in the Atlantic, in contrast to less-frequent but more-severe bleaching episodes in the Pacific (Baker, 1997). Strain adoption may also be regulated during spawning events, as eggs and sperm fertilize in the water column. Usually, the newly formed planulae are initially aposymbiotic (azooxanthellate), and may preferentially choose from a pool of pelagic zooxanthellae.

One coral species, or even one coral colony, may possess numerous types of zooxanthellae. This tends to occur before the dominance of one strain over another is achieved, or if corals are exposed to significantly different conditions from one part of a colony to another. *Symbiodinium microadriaticum* appears to be one of the more highly photoadaptive zooxanthellae species. *Symbiodinium pilosum* seems strongly geared toward intensely lit, shallow reef areas, while *S. kawaguti* is intermediate in its adaptability.

To quote Iglesias-Prieto and Trench (1994): "There is a large body of evidence demonstrating that symbiotic dinoflagellates are more species diverse than previously recognized. Although it is very difficult to apply the Biological Species Concept to asexual microalgae, dinoflagellate symbionts isolated from different host species . . . consistently show morphological, biochemical, physiological, behavioral, and genetic differences."

ZOOXANTHELLAE AND CORAL METABOLISM

Generally, zooxanthellae are swallowed into the gastrovascular cavity of a new coral polyp and are transported into the gastrodermal tissues, where they begin to reproduce. A current theory is that specific cell-to-cell signals, perhaps with recognition molecules and cell surface events, may prevent the digestion of particular species or strains of zooxanthellae taken in by a coral. The zooxanthellae reside in specialized vacuoles within tissue cells in the gastrodermis. While this is the inner layer of cnidarian tissue, the zooxanthellae are nonetheless still well within reach of light energy. (Zooxanthellae can also be found in the tentacles of corals that expand during the day. Corals that feed only at night do not have zooxanthellae in their tentacles.)

As mentioned, it was once believed that only a single species of zooxanthellae existed, but it now appears that corals can and do selectively adopt the species and/or strains of symbiotic algae that suit them best.

In a few coral genera (e.g., *Litophyton, Porites, Montipora, Pocillopora, Efflatounaria*), the young polyp is brooded and provided with a small "starter culture" of zooxanthellae by its parent. Most corals, however, release their young planulae without zooxanthellae. The planulae acquire their symbionts from the water, after which the algal cells begin to multiply, dividing over and over until a very heavy density, often in multiple layers, is formed. Often, there is an almost solid blanket of zooxanthellae within the coral's cells.

Zooxanthellae are able to supply the coral with the high-energy natural products of photosynthesis, including carbohydrates and fats. The zooxanthellae, by themselves, can provide more than 150% of the metabolic carbon energy needs of some corals, and are generally able to provide at least 60% of the needs of other species. In fact, it has been found that from 78-99% of all **photosynthate** (the sum of all the products of photosynthesis) is normally passed on to the host animal in a process called **translocation**. Translocation results in the transfer of nitrogen and reduced carbon sources from the zooxanthellae to the polyp.

To date, the principal known products of translocation are glyceric acid, alanine, serine, glycine, glycerol, glucose, amino acids, and other carbohydrates and lipids. Lipids are stored by the polyp as reserve energy for sunless days, and can last up to a month in some species. The release of photosynthate is mediated by chemical host factors produced by the polyp, which allow for the selective release and leakage of the various photosynthetic products as they are needed. A low molecular weight compound, recently isolated and termed the **host-release factor (HRF)**, is responsible. It is not yet known if this is the only compound or if there are many compounds that selectively moderate the release of photosynthate.

ENERGY BUDGETS

The energy budgets for symbiotic corals can be summarized by the equation:

$$C + PS = (Pz + Pa) + (Rz + Ra) + F + U + G$$

Where:

C = consumption, or food intake;

PS = photosynthesis from the zooxanthellae;

P = production, as growth, of zooxanthellae (Pz) and animal (Pa);

R = respiration, as metabolic use, of zooxanthellae (Rz) and animal (Ra);

F = energy lost in feces;

U = energy lost as other excretion; and

G = energy used in gonad output.

This equation allows us to see the flow of energy as it is produced and consumed in corals. Energy comes in principally as food or as products of their symbionts, and is used or exits in various ways that sustain the corals. Energy budgets are especially interesting because corals live on the edge of metabolic fulfillment. Despite their potential ability to gain well over 100% of their nutritional needs through either food or zooxanthellae, rarely are conditions ideal.

The ability of corals to draw from multiple sources of nu-

Tiny *Fungia* sp. anthocaulus developing its first tentacles. Masses of energy-providing symbiotic algae are already present in the transparent coral tissue.

tritional energy is a large part of the explanation for their success over millions of years in exploiting oligotrophic (nutrient-poor) waters. If the sum of light and food availability is decreased, the balanced equation tells us either the photosynthesis, respiration, excretion, or reproduction of the coral will also decline. Generally, reproductive ability disappears first. The coral may well be able to survive even if lighting conditions are adequate but food availability is low—a typical situation in many reef aquariums. But if there is a significant combined deficit of light and food over a long term, growth rate and survivability can be affected, as well as the symbiosis itself.

LIGHT AND PHOTOSYNTHESIS

Symbiotic corals are found in their greatest densities in shallow, well-illuminated waters less than 18 m (60 ft.) deep, although some may be found with special light-gathering abilities in 137-152 m (450-500 ft.). *Leptoseris fragilis*, a deep-water plate coral, for example, has specialized photosynthetic machinery and is adapted to absorb light with wavelengths of 380-410 nm, the predominant wavelengths that penetrate to those depths.

The light-gathering and photosynthetic machinery of the zooxanthellae, including chloroplasts, chlorophyll, accessory pigments, etc., is known as a **photosynthetic unit** (PSU). Since the zooxanthellae are light-dependent, they are usually able to provide more photosynthate in higher light levels. This is especially true in the production of carbon-rich substances.

The rate of photosynthesis rises in corals with increasing light levels, up to a maximum rate at the so-called **saturation level** of light. The saturation level of most symbiotic corals in shallow waters is at least several times lower than the photosynthetically active radiation at the surface, or **PARS**.

This means that, above a certain level of irradiance, photosynthesis rates (and all the processes of a coral that are light-dependent, including metabolic rate, calcification, etc.) will not be increased by higher light levels. While many aquarists and writers have been concerned about the difficulty of replicating the intensity of sunlight on shallow tropical reefs, the fact is that many corals can reach their maximum rate of photosynthesis in light that is much less intense than that provided by tropical sunlight. In fact, studies have shown that some corals that depend on light to a greater extent, such as *Turbinaria* species, *Seriatopora* species, *Stylophora* species, and *Merulina* species, may have higher photosynthesis rates in moderate light than in strong light.

Coles and Jokiel (1978) also confirmed this in long-term studies with *Montipora* species, where light levels higher than those to which the corals were normally exposed caused not only reduced growth rates, but also increased coral mortality when combined with other stresses such as reduced salinity or heightened temperatures. Reduced calcification at very high light intensities was also found by Barnes and Taylor (1973). Other species that grow faster at intermediate depths are several *Porites* species, *Montastraea* species, and *Agaricia agaricites*, all from the Caribbean (Stimson, 1996). The point for coral keepers to remember is simple enough: more light is not always better.

Corals can, however, efficiently adapt to higher or lower light levels in several ways, over various time spans, in order to maximize the photosynthetic advantage. This ability is called **photoadaptation**, and it even occurs over the course of the average day. **Photoacclimation** is the term used for the actual changes that occur in the photoadaptive response. Though similar, these terms are frequently confused (Iglesias-Prieto, 1997).

The diurnal photoacclimation changes usually involve a change in the pigment content of the zooxanthellae. In sub-saturating light conditions, corals tend to change the PSU components, while in super-saturating light, they tend to increase the amount of photoprotective xanthophylls within the algal chromophores (cellular organelles that contain various pigments).

PHOTOACCLIMATION AND PHOTOADAPTIVE RESPONSES

In the ocean, despite the intensity of the sun and high irradiances even at moderate depths, only about 0.1% of sunlight between the wavelengths of 340 and 680 nm can penetrate both the water and the coral tissue to reach the zooxanthellae. Perhaps only 1% of the light of about 700 nm, and 2% of light energy above 720 nm, may actually reach the algae of many corals (Halldal, 1968). It is the unique photosynthetic abilities of the zooxanthellae and their pigments that allow for their ability to harness even relatively tiny amounts of light.

Not only are zooxanthellae adept at catching light, but the corals that harbor them have adaptive schemes as well. Corals can compensate (in the time-frame indicated below) for lower light levels by adjusting or changing the following parameters:

Stylophora pistillata in a German reef aquarium, displaying the typical brown coloration assumed by many captive colonies of stony corals.

Stylophora pistillata in Gregory Schiemer's aquarium, displaying a delicate pinkish hue. High nutrient levels may spur zooxanthellae to mask such colors.

A colony of *Acropora gemmifera* exposed to the air on a shallow reef flat in Fiji. Such corals often produce clear UV-blocking pigments and protective mucus.

- the amount of pigments in the algae PSUs (compensation takes place over a period of hours);
- the size of the PSUs (hours);
- the number of PSUs (days);
- the characteristics and number of zooxanthellae (days);
- dark respiration rates (hours to days);
- the sensitivity of the photosynthetic response (hours to days);
- the zooxanthellae respiration rate (minutes to days);
- enzyme characteristics (unknown);
- the pigment content of fluorescent reflecting or absorbing proteins (hours to weeks);
- the rate of feeding by prey capture or absorption (days to weeks);
- biosynthesis patterns (unknown);
- polyp expansion (minutes);
- polyp respiration rate (minutes to hours);
- polyp density (weeks to months); and
- the production of protective enzymes and pigments (days to months).

Over longer time periods, changes in the size or growth form of corals can occur in response to sustained light changes. Under nutrient-enriched conditions, or conditions of low light, the chlorophyll and accessory pigment concentrations may change (and especially increase). The result is an increase in photosynthesis, but an overall decrease in calcification rates.

Some corals rely more heavily on zooxanthellae to meet their energy needs: agariciids, poritids, pocilloporids, and xeniids. These more nearly autotrophic corals are also better at photoadaptation than those that depend more on heterotrophic feeding (Haramaty et al., 1997).

Despite the ability of the zooxanthellae to meet such a large portion of the energy needs of the polyp, it has been found that the carbon produced is used primarily as a quick energy source for coral metabolism and does not contribute significantly to growth. In fact, much of the carbon produced by the zooxanthellae is used in the production of excess mucus. In corals typically found in intensely lit conditions, carbon may also be lost directly as dissolved organic carbon (Muscatine et al., 1989a).

In order to grow, corals also need a nitrogen source. Although almost all the nitrogen-containing compounds produced by the zooxanthellae are translocated to the coral, this is not enough, and the coral must turn to outside feeding to meet its nitrogen needs for growth and other processes. In deeper water, even highly photoadapative corals become obligate heterotrophs, requiring supplemental nutrition from the environment (see Chapter 4).

ZOOXANTHELLAE PIGMENTATION

Zooxanthellae contain a large number of diverse photosynthetic pigments to harness the light of the sun. The pigments are very similar to those of dinoflagellates, in general, and absorb primarily between 300 and 720 nm wavelengths. The pigment primarily responsible for converting light energy into a food source that both the plants and animals can utilize is chlorophyll *a*, and it shows two light absorption peaks—at about 440 nm and 670-675 nm. Zooxanthellae, accordingly, also have two broad light-absorption peaks: the first at 430 nm (blue) with a range of 400-550 nm; the second at 670 nm (red) with a range of 650-700 nm.

Among the pigments found in zooxanthellae are chlorophyll *a* (blue-green), chlorophyll *c*$_2$ (light green), beta-carotene (orange), peridinin (brick red), diadinoxanthin (yellow), and other unknown pigments that are pale yellow, pale orange, and pink-orange.

Chlorophyll *a*, *c*$_2$, and peridinin are primarily the light-harvesting pigments, while the accessory pigments transfer the captured light energy (excitation energy) to chlorophyll *a* with nearly 100% efficiency. Accessory pigments are used to channel wavelengths of light that chlorophyll *a* is not capable of converting by itself into usable light energy. The xanthophyll zeaxanthin may be a particularly important pigment in dissipating excess excitation energy under high light conditions, in a photoprotective response called fluorescence quenching.

Corals also produce a number of "sunscreens" to protect themselves, and especially their zooxanthellae, from damaging ultraviolet (UV) radiation. Ultraviolet light easily penetrates clear tropical waters down to depths of about 30 m (100 ft.) or more, and corals must be able to deal with this potentially harmful radiation. These protective compounds were first described by the wavelengths they absorbed, but are now generally referred to as mycosporine-like amino acids (MAAs). Corals with thick tissue or deeply embedded polyps suffer the fewest negative effects of UV radiation and concomitantly show the lowest production of MAAs.

Coral animals produce these clear, non-light-blocking pigments, probably from precursors made by the zooxanthellae, to shield the algae from light-induced bleaching and to prevent UV light from inhibiting photosynthesis. The pigments are used in combination to absorb, reflect, or fluoresce UV light. They are also important in the photoadaptation of corals to different light intensities. Eleven different MAAs are now known to exist, the most common in corals being mycosporine-Gly, palythine, palythene, palythinol, and S-320. They absorb UV strongly in the range from 285-350 nm as a broad-band filter, with maximal absorption from 310-332 nm.

Despite their highly efficient and functional role, these UV-absorbing compounds are produced at an energy cost to the coral. Skeletal growth rates are lower in corals that must take away limited "energy funds" from calcification to produce UV protectants. Despite the premanufacturing of these compounds by the zooxanthellae, the coral concentrates them in its own epidermis. Even bleached corals maintain fluorescing and UV-blocking pigments, and MAAs have been found in coral mucus. UV does not appear to be the only trigger for the formation of these substances—increased stress, increased temperature, increased light intensity, increased production during breeding seasons, and diet have all been implicated as playing a role in their production.

Often, the color of a coral will change in the aquarium. It is likely that higher-nutrient water, along with the coral's photoadaptive response, are coupled in closed systems to induce this transformation. It occurs, to a large degree, by zooxanthellae pigment increases. It is not unnatural or unusual for previously bright-colored corals to turn brown. This is part of a normal response to certain ambient conditions. If an aquarium is well-maintained and provides proper light and water conditions, the bright colors of corals may or may not persist. Forcibly altering the captive environment to meet the aquarist's desire for bright colors may have repercussions in the health of the coral and the overall tank. It is best to concentrate on providing a high-quality environment conducive to the needs of all the species present, allowing the corals to "do what they do" in order to adapt to their new home. Considerable experimentation is ongoing in the aquarium hobby as aquarists seek the right combination of lighting and water conditions to elicit the most-attractive coloration consistent with good coral health and growth.

FLUORESCENT PIGMENTS

MAAs are very efficient at blocking harmful UV radiation, yet remain largely transparent to near-UV-a radiation, which the corals can use for photosynthesis by producing blue, cyan, green, and yellow fluorescent pigments. These pigments, present in coral polyp tissue and likely to have a photosynthetic role, are the **UV-reflecting and fluorescing proteins**. These compounds are responsible for some of the blue, green, and pink fluorescent colors found in so many corals of the reef. They do not seem to be part of the normal photosynthetic machinery, but rather dwell in the coral animal's epidermal cells in spherical granules, at least in some species studied. (The fluorescent granules of *Goniopora* species seem to lie in the gastrodermis.)

Fluorescent pigments are part of the chemical groups known as flavines, urobilines and pterines. The green fluorescing pig-

Green fluorescing pigments, as in this **Montipora** sp. colony in a California aquarium, are readily apparent under intense reef tank lighting.

ments are green in reflected light, but are pink in transmitted light, and fluoresce most strongly when activated by 380 nm light. In these conditions, the energy fluoresces back in a broad band from 450-530 nm, well within the ideal range for zooxanthellae photosynthesis. They absorb strongly at 320-330 nm, up to 400 nm, especially when corals are expanded and receiving strong irradiance. Many corals in the aquarium become fluorescent green under strong lighting, and it is likely that these pigments are the ones responsible for the color change. The red-orange fluorescence of some *Lobophyllia* species, *Leptoseris* species, and *Cynarina lacrymalis* may be of a different nature. Most recently, six new fluorescent proteins, including yellows and red-orange, have been found in corals such as *Discosoma* (Matz et al., 1999; Tsien, 1999). Both MAAs and fluorescing proteins, being localized in the animal tissue, persist after bleaching events. They are found only in epidermal cells, rather than the gastrodermis where the zooxanthellae are found. Their full functions are not known at present (Matz et al., 1999).

ULTRAVIOLET CONSIDERATIONS

Ultraviolet light has a bad reputation for being harmful to life. UV has been implicated in coral bleaching, reduced photosynthesis, cell damage, photoinhibition, reduced growth rates, reduced calcium uptake, increased mortality, decreased carbon fixation, and reduced pigment concentrations. Maintenance of UV-protective enzymes also comes at a metabolic cost to the coral.

Furthermore, UV-induced damage to resident microbial populations living in the **coral surface microlayer** (**CSM**) has been found, despite some MAA protection. This area exists near coral tissue in the mucus layer, and is the site of heavy bacterial productivity. UV radiation may affect the respiration and metabolism of a coral in many ways by reducing an important trophic resource, the bacterioplankton. However, many animals regularly exposed to high levels of UV, such as corals, have become remarkably adept at dealing with them. Primarily through the production of MAAs, corals can effectively shield their tissues and symbionts from damaging UV light. UV tolerance is somewhat species-related, and is also dependent on ambient levels of radiation.

On the positive side, UV is useful in photoadaptation, regulating zooxanthellae densities, exciting fluorescent coupling proteins, increasing larval production, controlling gene regulation, and increasing pigment adaptability. As well, there is the potential use of UV to drive photosynthesis under reduced-light conditions. UV may also prevent a degree of proliferation of other microalgae through photoinhibiton, giving a competitive edge to corals in high-nutrient conditions. Some corals even seem to display polyp expansion in response to UV light (e.g., *Goniopora* species), although the significance of this is yet unstudied.

Although the coral animal cannot rapidly adapt to changes in UV radiation, slow acclimation makes it possible for them to cope very effectively. The zooxanthellae themselves are extremely sensitive to UV. Although, the algae photoadapt to large and rapid changes in photosynthetically active radiation (PAR) easily, UV will cause problems if they are over exposed. Fortunately, the zooxanthellae are protected by their host corals and are largely unaffected by UV under normal conditions.

One recent study showed that corals acclimated to PAR and UV had higher photosynthetic rates than those acclimated to PAR only. It also showed that corals were not additionally stressed by UV radiation, and in fact "relaxed" as they became accustomed to the conditions to which they are normally adapted. They incurred little long-term metabolic cost to support their natural protection (Kinzie, 1993).

In summary, according to Jokiel and York (1982): " . . . UV is not clearly a harmful ecological factor. . . . UV has been present in significant amounts throughout the entire evolutionary history of life on our planet. . . . Therefore, we can only say that UV is an important environmental factor that influences the basic structure and function of these ecosystems."

PROBLEMS IN SYMBIOSIS

Despite what can be thought of as a beneficial relationship between the polyps and their zooxanthellae, this profitable mutualism comes at a metabolic cost to the coral. Under stressful conditions, the coral animal can expel its algal symbionts in a process known as **bleaching**. Bleached corals often appear white, simply because their tissue becomes more transparent and shows the white aragonite skeleton underneath. The tissue itself is not white. The loss of zooxanthellae involves significant intracellular changes that may also disrupt many of the coral's pigment components. (Some corals may bleach without showing visible signs. Losses of more than 50% of the zooxanthellae typically define bleaching, although some corals may lose the majority of their symbionts and appear unbleached because undisrupted pigments mask the loss.)

Most corals can adapt without much problem to regular short-term changes in local conditions without serious bleaching. Even under normal conditions, there is always a regular expulsion or digestion of "old" or dysfunctional zooxanthellae. Such regeneration is not bleaching, and the observation of strands of brown zooxanthellae being emitted from a coral are not necessarily indicative of a bleaching event. The normal rate of released zooxanthellae is from 1-6% of the total per day, usually at night

Healthy colony of **Meandrina meandrites** (Caribbean maze coral).

Alive but bleached, a **Meandrina meandrites** colony without its zooxanthellae.

and in the early morning.

However, prolonged exposure to stressful conditions may be more than the coral can tolerate. Although a coral's loss of its zooxanthellae is usually viewed as a maladaptive response, corals seem to do what is best for them. Often, bleaching is a last-ditch attempt by the coral to survive.

Under environmentally stressful conditions, glycoproteins may be released by the zooxanthellae and/or host polyp as chemical messengers of stress. In such situations, too much photosynthesis begins to occur, and the polyp becomes oversaturated with free oxygen and oxygen radicals. In response, a number of oxygen-destroying enzymes are produced by the animal. Superoxide dismutase (SOD) removes free oxygen, but produces dangerous hydrogen peroxide. Peroxide is then removed by enzymes such as catalase (CAT) and ascorbate peroxidase (AsPX). These enzymes then protect against the light-induced production of hydroxyl radicals. Without the action of these protective enzymes, and if photosynthesis continued at such a rate, the coral would literally digest itself or be poisoned by oxygen and free radicals. To prevent this occurrence, the algae are expelled.

Sometimes, the algae from bleaching corals are neatly expelled in a small pellet from the gastric cavity. Other times, the entire dermal cell containing the algae is expelled. Other defenses besides the toxic-oxygen-protecting enzymes may include thermal protection by heat shock proteins and the use of biochemically produced antioxidants, quenchers, and oxygen-scavenging molecules such as ascorbate, tocopherols, carotenoids, and urate.

In many cases, free-living dinoflagellates called swarmers (or pelagic zooxanthellae) are readmitted to the tissue, and the coral may survive. Bleaching may also be an adaptive way to swap one species or strain of zooxanthellae for another one more suited

for coping with new conditions—one likely to provide for enhanced adaptability and survival of the coral in the long term.

In recent years, news of mass coral bleachings has made media headlines. These events have implicated ozone depletion and global warming. The conditions found over the years to induce coral bleaching are prolonged exposure to increased temperature, increased exposure to ultraviolet radiation, increased light intensity (often brought about by cloudless days, still waters, or relocation of coral colonies by breakage), decreased light intensity, salinity changes, and chemical exposure (from dumping, spills, runoff, etc.).

More recently, a previously unidentified species of *Vibrio* bacteria, now known as *V. shiloi*, has been implicated as a causative agent of bleaching. Despite active research in this area, the exact reasons for bleaching are still unknown, but clearly seem to involve a combination of one or more of the factors listed above. It has also been theorized that coral mortality can result from a breakdown of the symbiosis between algae and coral. In such cases, less-tolerant corals, or possibly those having few strains of zooxanthellae (or those incapable of harboring more than one), may experience higher rates of mortality during bleaching episodes.

In sum, the zooxanthellae are the competitive edge that symbiotic corals have to ensure their dominance on the substrates of tropical reefs. The zooxanthellae provide nutrition to the coral and are the impetus for light-enhanced calcification. The complexity of this symbiosis is nothing short of a natural marvel. They further provide at least some of the many-hued color palettes that exist in the coral community. Without these tiny symbionts linked with their host polyps, the coral reef would be a vastly different place.

CHAPTER 4

Foods & Feeding

Nutrition on the Reef and in the Aquarium

Raised in Lower Alabama along the Gulf Coast, I grew up seeing the bountiful harvests of fish, shrimp, and crab not as luxuries but rather as staple foods of the "Redneck Riviera." Over the years, as we unscrupulous humans proceeded to pillage our maritime resources, the price of shrimp climbed from 49 cents a pound all the way up to around $4.00. (Still, considering the fishing pressures and the work involved, shrimp remains pretty darn cheap.)

Today, I've become an herbivore by choice, so when I go to the market and stand in the checkout lane with mounds of shrimp, crab, and Atlantic triggerfish, I often suffer more than a twinge of guilt. I sometimes feel I must explain to the clerks that these "seaflesh" items are for my pets. Yes, even in a vegetarian household there can be carnivores among us, and in my case they are cats, fishes, and corals.

There is a common belief, especially among aquarium keepers, that corals are **autotrophic**—requiring only light to survive. (Autotrophs manufacture their food from simple inorganic com-

> "Their power of destruction is not surprising once we see their method of obtaining food."
>
>
>
> Sir Aldous Huxley, on cnidocytes, 1965

pounds they extract from the environment, often using sunlight to synthesize it.) In fact, corals are also distinctly **heterotrophic** organisms. Simply put, heterotrophs are like humans, existing by consuming the organic products synthesized by autotrophs (or by ingesting the autotrophs themselves, as well as other heterotrophs). This means that corals depend at least partly, and in many cases exclusively, on active feeding or the absorption of nutrients from the surrounding water.

The confusion arises because most reef-building corals have autotrophic zooxanthellae in their tissues and obtain a significant portion of their nutrition by the intimate association they maintain with millions of these autotrophs (see Chapter 3). No symbiotic corals are fully autotrophic or heterotrophic, but are **mixotrophic**, utilizing both methods of feeding.

Armed with tentacles bearing countless tiny stinging organs, cnidarians are said to be unlike any other animals in having such a large portion of their bodies devoted to food capture. Reef explorer C.M. Yonge, writing in 1931 on the apparent feeding ability of corals, said, " . . . when an animal possesses an organ or set of organs which perform certain functions with perfect efficiency, it can be taken as axiomatic that such organs are used."

Reef snow: Pacific gorgonian (*Muricella sp.*) feeds on a storm of the particulate matter that provides essential nutrition. Note pygmy seahorse, center.

Augmenting the energy it derives from the sun, this *Millepora alcicornis* (fire coral) traps marine snow in its fine feeding hairs, or dactylozooids. (Florida Keys)

Certainly, corals can be voracious and effective predators, capturing and consuming prey in less than a minute. Hamner (1988) referred to the reef as a "wall of mouths," while Kinsey (1991) showed zooplankton input across 1 m (3.2 ft.) of reef to be on the order of 30 g (1 oz.) of carbon per day. (This is an enormous amount of food availability, far more than that provided in a typical home aquarium.) Despite the wide range of materials being supplied to the coral by the zooxanthellae, coral feeding must supply the remainder of necessary nutrients and vitamins for growth and metabolism.

Recent work with two species of *Pavona* has indicated that zooplankton may be even more important than light in supporting skeletal growth, even given the fact that this genus is known to be highly autotrophic. Along with many prior supporting studies, this confirms that feeding is of paramount importance to corals in the wild.

Some of the products required by corals and zooxanthellae that are not supplied by photosynthesis include vitamins (required by many marine dinoflagellates) and long-chain fatty acids (required by the coral animal). These compounds are supplied only by diet. Glycine is also a compound that many corals do not easily synthesize, and it, along with some carbon, may be obtained in the wild by living in proximity to the released photosynthetic products of certain macroalgae. Twenty years ago, it was thought that nonzooxanthellate nutrition only accounted for, at most, 25% of the total energy needs of corals. We now

believe that symbiotic corals, as a group, actually obtain anywhere from 20-50% of their nutrition from heterotrophic feeding, depending on average levels of plankton and dissolved organic matter. Some scleractinians are capable of meeting 200-300% of their basic energy needs by heterotrophic feeding, and most regularly meet more than 100% of their metabolic needs in such fashion. Zoanthids and octocorals can generally meet 10-100% of their needs through heterotrophy. (Intake in excess of an animal's basic energy needs is required for growth and reproduction.) Feeding also increases the respiration rate of the entire colony and leads to increased growth. Starvation has many consequences, not the least of which is the expulsion of zooxanthellae.

WHAT DO CORALS EAT?

Corals can utilize all of the sources of nutrition available to sessile invertebrates. They are largely carnivorous, mostly feeding on **zooplankton**, or small water-borne animals. Some of the more-abundant zooplankton items that corals commonly consume are copepods, polychaetes, chaetognaths, and all forms of larvae. Up to 85% of this foodstuff comes up at dusk and at night from within the reef where it is produced or dwells during the day.

Phytoplankton, or small water-borne plants (algae), are utilized extensively by some corals, but less so by most. Stony corals almost always reject plant material as food, although a few have been found to ingest it in relatively small amounts. Soft corals, zoanthids, and gorgonians are much more likely to feed on plant material, and some may be exclusively herbivorous. Most gorgonians and many soft corals are only weakly predatory; they are not found to capture significant zooplankton and seem to depend on floating plankton, weakly motile invertebrate larvae, and detritus.

Bacterioplankton consists of free-living bacteria, as well as the bacteria associated with particles in the water. Such bits of waste, mucus, dead plant material and other particulate matter is known as **detritus**, **particulate organic matter** (POM), **suspended organic matter** (SOM), and sometimes as **reef snow**, or **marine snow**. This nutrient-laden, drifting waste material, enriched with unicellular algae growth and bacterial aggregations, comprises the third important food source for corals. All corals studied feed heavily on bacterioplankton. **Pseudoplankton** is another term used to describe bits of material that includes detritus, floating eggs, and other debris.

Within the groupings of plankton, there are several subcategories that relate to the general size of the food items. In decreasing order, these are **macroplankton**, **microplankton**, **nanoplankton**, and **picoplankton**. Only the first category is visible without the use of a microscope. *Artemia* nauplii (baby brine shrimp), copepods, much of the detritus, and other zooplankton are considered relatively large sizes of food to be consumed by corals.

The final category of food used by corals includes the ciliate/mucosal transport (direct absorption across cell membranes) of **dissolved organic matter** (**DOM**). Bacteria and DOM are often lumped into the same category, though they are not similar, nor do they comprise a necessarily similar percentage of nutrition to any coral species. However, recent work suggests that the normal bacterial flora, perhaps even symbiotic, may play a role in the ability of corals to transform and uptake DOM (Ferrier-Pages et al., 1998).

Many corals with larger polyps, such as *Cynarina* and *Cataplaphyllia* species and some of the faviids and mussids, are capable of engulfing much larger items of food, including, occasionally, small fishes. In fact, many coral species (especially the soft corals and gorgonians) may choose appropriate prey items based more on the relative size of the plankton than on its composition.

It was suggested in the past that large-polyped corals, with more-aggressive tentacle formations, gained a larger percentage of their nutrition from feeding, rather than from the nutrition provided by their zooxanthellae. It is now apparent that small-polyped corals are equally, if not more, active heterotrophs, and studies over many years repeatedly show local conditions and species variances, rather than polyp size, to be of primary importance in degrees of prey capture. Despite their relatively benign-looking polyps, it is apparent that many small-polyped corals can be surprisingly aggressive feeders on plankton and particulate matter.

In general, faviids (and some aposymbiotic corals such as *Tubastraea* species) display greater levels of prey capture, while *Montipora* and *Porites* species have fairly low prey-capture rates. One leading coral propagator reports that *Favia* species, for example, must be fed in his systems to prevent tissue recession. Other corals that depend more heavily on light may not capture large quantities of zooplankton prey, but they may depend on other nonzooxanthellate modes of feeding. Nitrogen is needed for growth, and most small-polyped corals are among the fastest-growing species. Thus they have a large nitrogen requirement and must possess the means to fulfill it. In fact, even though almost all of the photosynthate produced by the zooxanthellae is translocated to the polyp, small-polyped highly photosynthetic corals, like *Acropora* species, may depend on particulate feeding and dissolved inorganic nitrate and ammonium for as much as 70% of their nitrogen needs and 60% of their carbon needs. The extra carbon is necessary for calcification. Since most respired carbon dioxide is used by the zooxanthellae, and most translocated carbon is used for metabolic needs and lost as mucus, the carbon source used for calcification is primarily dissolved bicarbonate from seawater. Nonetheless, the amount of carbon used and necessary for growth can vary depending on the species, the strain of zooxanthellae, and the ambient light conditions.

To further illustrate the importance of external food sources, the axial corallite (the specialized, distal, elongated corallite) of *Acropora* species contains few (if any) zooxanthellae, and yet it is the most rapidly growing part of the coral colony. The nutrition needed to sustain these active cells must come from intracolonial transport of organic material, and therefore from nutrition obtained by the feeding behavior of the coral. Concentration of cellular energy (ATP) is very high in the white tips, suggesting that the growth is fueled by a gradient that moves nutrients from the slower-growing mature branches to the faster-growing tips. Finally, rates of calcification occur in cycles, with the highest rates at sunrise and sunset, especially 2-3 hours after sunrise. Not coincidentally, these times happen to correspond with diurnal periods of highest plankton availability.

It has been suggested by Sorokin (1995), that corals are possibly "the most-selective heterotrophic feeders in the animal kingdom." Many corals *are* quite finicky, depending on chemical cues and light levels to capture prey. Studies have shown that certain species of *Sinularia*, *Eunicea*, *Paralemnalia*, *Plexaura*, and *Gorgonia* never consume zooplankton. Some corals, like *Dendronephthya* species, feed almost exclusively on phytoplankton, while others, like *Tubastraea* species, rely almost exclusively on

Contrary to popular belief, many photosynthetic corals, such as this **Acropora sp.**, derive a majority of their energy from feeding and nutrient absorption.

Daytime appearance of **Montastraea annularis** (Caribbean star coral), with polyps completely retracted, typical of many stony corals in the wild.

Nighttime appearance of **Montastraea annularis**, with polyps extended to catch zooplankters, which are available in much greater numbers after dark.

zooplankton. Other aposymbiotic corals have a diverse array of feeding choices, but DOM and particulate matter are very important for most.

Coincidentally, many aposymbiotic corals dwell at the openings to caves and overhangs where, compared to shallower reef waters, nitrate concentrations are up to 13 times higher, ammonia can be 2 times higher, and organic nitrogen 3 times higher. It would appear that aposymbiotic corals do not avoid the light-filled reef because they are "hurt" by light or cannot compete for space, but they exist instead where the nutrients are most likely to provide for their needs.

When Do Corals Eat?

Corals expand their polyps to feed depending on the optimal time of day, the temperature, the oxygen content of the water, the presence of food or sediment, and water movement conditions. Varying degrees of polyp expansion are common throughout the day and at night, depending on the relative abundance of food. Amino acids released by zooplankton seem to be the trigger that induces a feeding response in nature, and the amino acids proline, glycine, and glutathione will induce a feeding response in the majority of corals. Corals are exquisitely chemoreceptive and can detect food in dilutions as low as 1:10,000,000. Individual polyps feed until they are satiated, and this amount depends on their metabolic needs, the availability of food, and the species involved. In general, corals tend to feed at night in the wild when the planktonic sources are high. Feeding behavior may even be partly controlled by dusk, dawn, and nighttime irradiance levels. At night, their energy is not being used for a high rate of calcifica-

tion, since the zooxanthellae are less active in the photosynthetic processes. It is a fortuitous time for food capture.

The reverse is often true in captivity, where many normally night-feeding corals extend their polyps in feeding behavior during the day, retracting at night; normal diurnal patterns of feeding do occur in some species, however, even in the aquarium. I have theorized that regular daytime feedings utilized by most aquarists, which is in contrast to normal nighttime plankton availability in nature, has the effect of "training" corals to expand during the "daylight" rather than nocturnally. While charts have been made showing corals that expand during the day versus during the night, the availability of food in the water can change normal feeding behaviors, as can the level of dissolved organic matter, light levels, and polyp satiation.

Interestingly, light also seems to be a determining factor for the relative rates of heterotrophy in corals, as species accustomed to high-intensity light depend somewhat less heavily on heterotrophic feeding than do corals that exist in low-light conditions. High-light corals predominantly need to feed on zooplankton for their nitrogen content, since the zooxanthellae are already photosynthesizing adequate carbon and translocating it to them. Corals with polyps normally retracted during the day may remain in an expanded feeding state under low-light conditions to meet their carbon needs. This is also frequently observed in the aquarium. Further confirmation of the light-affected rate of heterotrophy comes from the fact that all symbiotic corals have reduced rates of food capture compared to those lacking zooxanthellae.

In order to capture prey effectively, and for a large absorptive surface to be present, the coral polyp and its tentacles must be expanded. Polyp expansion and the use of nematocysts mean an energy cost to the coral that may not be worthwhile in low ambient nutrient conditions. Yet if the polyps are not expanded in day-feeding corals, the zooxanthellae contained in the oral disc and tentacles are not as effective in gathering light and photosynthesizing. Such corals would then have to rely primarily on the reduced zooxanthellae densities of the coenosarc and/or direct absorption of nutrients from the water. Often, this may not be enough to meet their total energy budget. Therefore, the corals must balance the cost of expansion against the potential benefits of available food.

HOW DO CORALS EAT?

Corals are actually fairly efficient feeders, especially when the remarkably large surface area of the complex skeleton and the masses of mucus-covered, stinging, extended polyps are considered. To feed, corals extend their polyps and wait patiently for passing food sources. Captured food (prey and particulate matter) is moved along the surface of the coral toward the mouth by cilia. Once prey is captured and ingested, digestion is completed by the secretion of coelenteric fluid from the mesenteric filaments. The digested material is then absorbed.

Still, many types of zooplankton are elusive, and exhibit escape responses both prior to and during a capture attempt. They may also be able to sense the presence of their would-be captor through chemorecognition. Water-flow speed, zooplankton size/swimming ability, and the capture mechanisms employed by the coral will largely determine the success of the coral—or the misfortune of the zooplankton, as the case may be. Smaller and nonmotile food particles may be digested intracellularly after uptake into vacuoles. Most dissolved nutrients are not taken in through the mouth, but rather by uptake through the body wall using active and passive transport across the cell membranes.

Prey or particle capture can occur by several methods. LaBarbera (1984) outlined six that can be used alone or in combination. The first involves active movement by the coral to alter the flow of water to isolate a particle. This method, called **scan and trap**, is not common to corals, except perhaps in the pulsing xeniids. The second method is **sieving**, in which pinnules or other structures strain the water passively, trapping particles of a certain size. Most octocorals utilize this type of prey capture. Then, there are four **aerosol capture** methods: direct interception by nematocysts; inertial impaction, where water flow around the colony or polyp structure delivers a particle; gravitational deposition, where gravity rather than water flow delivers a particle; and diffusive deposition, in which the concentration of particles tends

to favor their interception. This last method commonly accounts for the uptake of dissolved organic matter. Most corals utilize at least one of the aerosol capture means of food uptake.

Mucosal capture occurs in several ways as well. Many corals form mucus webs and nets to trap particulate matter and free-floating bacteria that they can ingest. Normally clear mucus becomes opaque prior to being formed into a mucus web. The mucus is often extruded between septa and tentacles, where beating cilia "comb" it into a fine net. When the mucus net has captured enough food, the cilia reverse, pulling the food and mucus back to the mouth where it is ingested. Some corals (*Porites* species, pocilloporids) produce mucus flakes, which are then ingested when food has attached to them. These flakes aid in lumping particles together, immobilizing the prey or material facilitating the swallowing process. Agariciids, such as *Pachyseris* species, extrude mesenterial filaments coated in mucus, in addition to producing mucus nets.

Both tentacles and cilia can move captured prey and food toward the mouth for ingestion. *Hydnophora* species, and some other short-tentacled corals, extrude the mouth and mesenterial filaments in a "tube," engulfing and digesting prey on the exterior of the coral. Surface mesenterial digestion regularly occurs in *Galaxea*, *Montipora*, *Merulina*, *Stylophora*, and *Pachyseris* species, despite at least some of these having the ability to engulf prey through the mouth. Other corals may also occasionally engage in this type of behavior. Normal mesenterial digestion occurs when gland cells near the mesentery base secrete proteases and

Remarkable photograph of typical cnidarian feeding, showing an *Aiptasia* sp. polyp with a captured food particle being digested in its gastrovascular cavity.

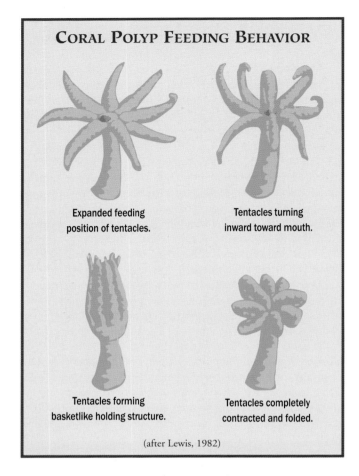

CORAL POLYP FEEDING BEHAVIOR

Expanded feeding position of tentacles.

Tentacles turning inward toward mouth.

Tentacles forming basketlike holding structure.

Tentacles completely contracted and folded.

(after Lewis, 1982)

other enzymes that lower pH and break down food. The filaments further the breakdown process by grinding the material into smaller particles. **Phagocytes** (engulfing cells) near their base then capture the smaller particles, moving them to the interior coral tissue for final digestion. The entire process takes 2-3 hours in stony corals and from 6-12 hours in most soft corals. Two final methods of capture and digestion can occur when 1. proteases are secreted by epidermal cells onto material trapped on the surface of the coral; or 2. very small particles of dissolved material are taken up directly from the surface itself (pinocytosis).

WHO EATS WHAT?

Coral colonies may alter their growth forms to maximize heterotrophic prey capture under various water flows. Skeletal protuberances may be formed to alter the turbulence over a colony to further "customize" and maximize heterotrophic prey capture. Corals that form upright plates tend to grow perpendicular to the water flow. Bifacial (two-sided) colonies tend to be found where water flow surges back and forth from wave action. Unifacial (one-sided) colonies tend to occur where laminar currents are more common. Branching corals tend to form colonies with tighter branch spacing in high-flow conditions to maximize prey capture.

Corals with flat, horizontal plates may depend more on the settling of particulate matter, so prey-capture efficiency is affected mostly by the water's velocity and the eddies that result as it flows over the coral surface. Both cylindrical and bifacial shapes tend to enhance food capture in lower-flow areas or where boundary layers are thick. Water velocities also determine which polyps of a colony are most likely to capture prey and may account for increased growth rates in these areas. Even the tentacles of the polyp may determine rates of prey capture; long tentacles and large polyps may be more proficient at the capture of larger sizes or quantities of prey, although they tend to bend and deform in high water flows, limiting their effectiveness.

Many soft corals, such as *Lobophytum* and *Sarcophyton* species, have reduced digestive structures, do not rely heavily on mucus nets, and have tentacles that are not as well adapted to prey capture. Instead, feathery pinnules on their tentacles sieve the water more effectively than the cnidocyte-laden tentacles of the stony corals. In addition, they can warp their upper surfaces or produce ridges to alter water flow and maximize prey capture. Soft corals tend to feed more heavily on bacterioplankton than on larger prey items. These corals have compensated for decreased predatory feeding with both increased direct nutrient uptake from the water and increased numbers of zooxanthellae in their tissues.

Corals from the Family Xeniidae, including *Anthelia*, *Xenia*, and *Cespitularia* species, and possibly many of the stoloniferans (*Clavularia* and *Pachyclavularia* species, etc.) possess highly reduced digestive zones. They depend almost entirely on absorption and zooxanthellae to meet their energy needs. Conversely, aposymbiotic corals, like *Dendronephthya* and *Tubastraea* species, must obtain all of their nutrition from heterotrophy. Symbiotic zoanthid heterotrophy varies from almost none to a large percentage that is comparable to stony corals. The degree to which zoanthids capture prey varies somewhat according to genus, more so according to species. In general, members of the genus *Zoanthus* are largely dissolved organic matter feeders, while the *Palythoa* species are more active prey-capture species.

Nutrients acquired by feeding (prey capture) are available to the coral first, whereas absorbed nutrients are available to the zooxanthellae first. Even so, corals seem to gain much extra-zooxanthellate nutrition from the direct absorption of dissolved organic matter, followed by ciliary uptake of bacterioplankton captured by filter feeding and mucus entrapment, and lastly from active feeding and capture of zooplankton. This order of nutrient sources also corresponds to the relative abundance of these nutrients on the reef and to the ease and energy expense needed for the coral to gain from these respective nutrition pools. In fact, the spaces between branches of certain corals are prime breeding grounds for bacteria that the coral can either ingest directly or use as a "lure" to attract and capture plankton that would normally feed on the bacteria. Even the extracellular products of these bacteria may be directly taken up by the corals to satisfy certain dietary requirements. It seems from these behaviors that corals are capable, to a degree, of actually "gardening" their own food.

SCARCITY VERSUS ABUNDANCE

It is often very difficult for corals to feed in the relatively pure waters of the reef, where all nutrients are so well disposed and recycled. Upwellings, groundwater, tides, seasonal changes, spawnings, and land-based runoff can all be sources of nutrients for corals, but a careful balance must be maintained in nature. Excess nutrients on the reef will stimulate algae, which can proliferate rapidly and overwhelm coral growth. Even within the coral itself, chronic exposure to high nitrogen levels can cause zooxanthellae to outgrow their hosts, causing the delicate balance between the symbionts to be lost.

Experiments with enriched ammonium environments have almost universally shown that the zooxanthellae will increase in density and number, but the amount of photosynthate released to the coral animal decreases, repressing calcification through competition for inorganic carbon.

Very low levels of nitrogen can satisfy the nitrogen needs of corals like *Pocillopora damicornis*. Concentrations above a certain level are not beneficial, and the coral can exert some degree of biochemical regulatory control over the influx and efflux of nitrogen from the surrounding water. Dissolved free amino acids can also be taken up from the water through transport across the cell membranes, although this appears to play a much reduced role in the nitrogen requirements of corals (Hoegh-Guldberg and Williamson, 1999).

Thus maintenance of the coral/algae relationship depends on low ambient nutrient levels with just enough external food sources to meet the corals' growth needs. Most corals, in general, have autotrophic nutrition from zooxanthellae and heterotrophic nutrition from feeding both potentially able to supply more than 100% of their daily needs under normal circumstances. On average, the hermatypic and symbiotic corals meet their total needs roughly as follows: 60-70% from zooxanthellae, 20-30% from feeding, and 10-20% from bacterioplankton and DOM, with each method taking up slack in the temporary absence of another.

Recent research has shown that in some situations, particulate matter, especially when highly enriched with free-living bacteria (35-45%), can provide up to 70% or more of the nitrogen requirements of corals, including *Acropora* species (Bak, 1998). Clearly this material plays a key role in supplying nitrogen for new growth and reproduction. Without question, the use of suspended detrital matter (and the avoidance of water sterility) are coming to be understood as crucial in maintaining the health of corals in aquarium settings.

EXCRETION

Comparatively little metabolic waste is excreted by corals. Most of the nitrogenous waste from coral polyps is taken up and recycled by the zooxanthellae. Corals may synthesize a number of other products not used by the algae, and these are released into the water. One such product is riboflavin. Apparently, corals release this vitamin into the surrounding water at an appreciable rate, where the vitamin is important to the health of surrounding microorganisms. Riboflavin is either obtained from the ingestion of phytoplankton, or it is manufactured by the zooxanthellae. Many corals also secrete a variety of unique chemical compounds that are used for competition, reproduction, immunity, and other functions.

Corals also produce mucus, composed largely of lipids, amino acids, carbohydrates, and nonprotein nitrogen components secreted by epidermal gland cells. The composition of coral mucus is highly variable between locations, coral species, and even within species. Up to 80% of carbon translocated to the polyp by the zooxanthellae is used to produce mucus. This substance has varying degrees of importance, depending on the species. For most corals, it serves as an important mechanical, chemical, and immunologic protective layer. For others, it is used as a way of feeding, as previously discussed. Some coral mucus, such as that of *Fungia* species, is highly specialized and is used both to capture zooplankton and to ensure competitive dominance. In fact, the mucus is an excellent medium on which many bacteria tend to thrive. Bacterial populations on coral mucus are very high in the ocean, comparable to those found in a bacteria-laden, silted, estuarine habitat. However, this rich nutrient base for bacterial growth may be a factor in some coral diseases seen by aquarists. Even normally nonpathogenic bacteria may create problems that cause the coral to become stressed (and even die) under the conditions commonly encountered between the time of collection and the final placement of a coral by the aquarist.

HOMEMADE CORAL RATION

The requirements for suitable coral foods are nutrients that will remain largely in suspension and contain a mix of particle sizes, compositions, and elements to sustain and enhance the requirements of a mixed coral tank. This recipe makes a large quantity of highly aromatic, nutritious food that may be used to nourish a wide range of corals. It is easily modified for smaller batches, but I prefer to make up a large quantity and freeze convenient serving-sized packets.

INGREDIENTS
Fresh Seafood
    6 whole fresh/thawed shrimp
    12 fresh mussels
    12 fresh clams
    12 fresh oysters

These foods contain blood components and blood, which are rich in nutrients, and are of a size easily taken up by many corals. If these products are not available, substitution of one for another (or similar seafoods) may be used. Canned seafood should not be used, and frozen seafood should only be used if it has no additional ingredients or preservatives. Precooked seafood is not recommended.

Frozen Aquarium Foods
    1 package frozen sea urchin (aquarium pack)
    1 package frozen fish roe (aquarium pack)
    225 gm (8 oz.) decapsulated *Artemia* nauplii (aquarium pack)

These products contain rich sources of nutrients. Many corals may swallow *Artemia* and then eject them undigested because of the presence of tough egg capsules. The decapsulated *Artemia* are ideal in this regard. If *Artemia* are not available, regular frozen brine shrimp can be used, but some corals may reject them because of their size or their carapace (shell).

Dried Seaweeds
    About ½ cup (120 ml) after soaking

A mix of brown, red, and green seaweeds is ideal. These can be obtained from pet stores, health-food shops, or stores selling Asian food ingredients. I use a mixture of nori, wakame, hijiki, dulse, ano, kombu, etc., whatever is available.

Seaweeds provide many trace elements and other nutrients, as well as providing some nutrition to those corals that feed on plant cells. Dulse is extremely rich in iodine. Roasted seaweed products or those containing spices or other ingredients should not be used.

Powdered Sea Greens/Antioxidants
    About 10 gm (0.3 oz.)

Health-food stores sell a number of products composed of phytoplankton and antioxidant compounds. I use a product called Aqua Greens that consists of a number of natural source antioxidants and various microalgae and blue-green components. Alternatively, commercial frozen or dried phytoplankton available in aquarium stores can be used.

Dried Aquarium Foods
    Marine flake food
    Tiny-pellet premium marine food

I use 1 small (approx. 85 gm [3 oz.]) container of each. Both of these products provide a number of additional food components that act as a substrate much like detritus or marine snow in the wild. Furthermore, certain small-pellet foods absorb well without disintegrating and are a good size for many corals to capture.

Liquid Vitamins
    30 ml (2 Tbsp.) Selco, Super Selco, or other marine vitamin/amino acid supplement.

A number of commercial vitamin mixes are available in liquid form in the trade. I use commercial Super Selco, which is highly concentrated and extremely aromatic.

Mucus composition under various environmental conditions can change, forming insoluble gel-like strings under stress.

Some corals, rather than secreting liquid or gel-like mucus, produce mucus sheets, or mucus tunics, which are characteristically formed and sloughed from their surface. The gorgonian genus *Briareum* and other gorgonians, soft corals of the genera *Alcyonium, Lobophytum, Sinularia,* and *Sarcophyton,* and the stony coral genus *Porites,* among others, all commonly form these tunics. During such formations, the coral polyps cease to expand, and a thin, waxy surface layer is formed and eventually released from the surface. It has always been assumed that this was a "regenerative" slough to rid the surface of contaminants, but the surface layer of the coral does not become fouled with algae, bacteria, and sediments until the tunic starts being produced.

PROCEDURE

1. Powder and mix the sea greens and antioxidant tablets, if used. (Use a mortar and pestle or other crushing implements.)
2. Add the liquid vitamins to the pellets, marine flake foods, and powdered micronutrients from step 1.
3. Thaw the fish roe, sea urchin, and *Artemia* nauplii in a separate bowl.
4. Soak the dried seaweeds in pure (nonchlorinated) water until soft.
5. Liquefy the fresh seafood and softened seaweeds in a blender or food processor. (All seafood shells are first removed and discarded, including those of the shrimp. I squeeze the heads and carapaces and retain all of the juices.)
6. Combine all ingredients in a large bowl and stir gently until well mixed.
7. Freeze in Ziploc-type plastic food storage bags in thin flats or in fish-cube flats.

FEEDING RECOMMENDATIONS

I feed about 20 ml (4 tsp.) of this food for 1,136 L (300 gal.) of system water every night.

Some experimentation may be needed as variances between tanks are likely. Reduce the amount being fed if water-quality problems result. This material remains in suspension for quite some time and provides a well-mixed group of nutrients. Many of the ingredients may have antibiotic and immune system-stimulating capabilities. (Oysters, for example, have been shown to possess anti-*Vibrio* properties.)

OPTIONAL/EXPERIMENTAL

Add small amounts of fresh produce items with a high pigment content, like eggplant skin, carrots, tamarillo, kale, etc. Whether or not such material contains usable forms of pigments for corals is unknown, but its addition is not harmful. Alternatively, powdered pigment complexes are available in health-food stores.

Thus, it does not appear that these formations are, in fact, regenerative in nature. The time required to produce and release a mucus tunic can last from a few days to up to several months before the layer is shed—up to 5 months in *Alcyonium digitatum*. During this time, the ability of the coral to feed is reduced or prevented. The reason these corals undergo such periodic sloughs remains a mystery (Coffroth, 1988, et al.).

FEEDING CORALS

The whole topic of providing our corals with food brings to mind the demanding creature in the film *Little Shop of Horrors* who repeatedly exhorted its owner: "Feed me, Seymour!"

Like Seymour, we are faced with the immediate question of *what* to feed. Despite the large body of information regarding coral nutrition and nutrient enrichment, there is little specific evidence to support the needs of symbiotic corals in captivity for supplemental nutritive inputs. Obviously, aposymbiotic corals must receive regular feedings, but there is some question as to the exact needs of those that contain zooxanthellae. Most captive reef aquariums, even if comparatively low in dissolved nitrogen and other nutrients, are many times higher in such measurements than those found in natural reef waters. Clearly, some corals have lived in aquariums—and grown—for very long periods of time (some more than a decade and still counting) without supplemental feedings.

But the question remains whether the nutrient content of aquariums is of the right quantity and quality to support the real needs of captive corals. It is highly probable that the nutrient availabilities in most aquarium systems are *not* entirely consistent with the heterotrophic needs of corals, and that increased feeding coupled with increased nutrient export is highly desirable.

Although many aquarists insist that supplemental feedings for most coral species are not required, it must be remembered that corals are actively heterotrophic animals. Most of them obtain a significant proportion of their daily energy needs from absorption or feeding from the environment. Yet many aquarists argue that food inputs tend to deteriorate water quality so that the advantages gained by their addition are offset by the reduced calcification and poor health of specimens resulting from nutrient-laden water.

Some aquarists, however, are finding that feedings (especially of live food) do not necessarily result in deteriorating water quality. In fact, many corals seem to be better nourished and more fully expanded when periodically offered external food sources. It is highly likely that they are, indeed, healthier. Some of the larger-polyped corals are especially responsive to feedings, and some may even fail to thrive without supplemental food in certain instances. *Catalaphyllia* is but one example of a coral that may begin to recede if not offered food. Unfortunately, it takes some experience for the aquarist to know which corals need the extra nutrition and which ones do not. Some experimentation is required to determine how best to administer food and manage the added nutrients in any particular system, in order to prevent deterioration of water quality. Certainly, heavy foam fractionation (protein skimming), other nutrient-export means (algal turf

Healthy wild colony of *Acropora gemmifera* in a high-current reef area, which is regularly flushed by tides, bringing zooplankton and other foods to the animal.

Aquarium-kept colony of *Acropora* sp. displaying tissue bleaching among the lower branches, possibly caused by a lack of current and food in the system.

scrubbing, macroalgae, other biological filters), and judicious use of activated carbon are all beneficial in this regard.

There are currently two predominant trends of thought regarding the feeding of corals in aquariums. The first, especially in those systems predominantly occupied by corals with few fishes, is to feed most corals nothing supplemental at all. This has been a widely established approach, and the long-term success of many corals without external food sources cannot be denied.

The newer view is to provide a larger nutrient input via external feeding, as long as there is a significant nutrient export or uptake system in place to extract excess nutrients physically, chemically, or biologically. The improvement of protein skimmers, algae turf scrubbers, biological modes of filtration, and the understanding of denitrification processes in captive systems has allowed many aquarists to handle relatively large biologic loads better. In systems with high-performance skimmers and/or algal or other efficient filters, it is possible to feed corals regularly and still maintain high-quality water conditions.

Because systems employing powerful foam-fractionation devices will be relatively free of particulate matter and planktonic elements in the water column, and because it is apparent that corals are distinctly heterotrophic to varying degrees, it is wise to employ at least occasional feedings to even the symbiotic corals in such an aquarium. Marine zoologist Dr. Ronald Shimek has made note that the feeding schedule for a 100-gallon tank, in order to maintain a quantity of planktonic food similar to that available to corals on the reef, would be 270 gm (9.5 oz.) of wet food per day (Shimek, 1997). (By way of comparison, a full "blister pack" of 24 typical cubes of frozen fish food weighs in at 100

gm [3.5 oz.], including water weight. It would take more than 60 of these cubes to match the natural availability of food suggested by Dr. Shimek.) It is clearly not possible to add this amount of material without polluting a typical home system, but we should acknowledge that corals in captivity may be desperately underfed. A challenge for those serious about coral husbandry will be to find ways to provide external food sources without compromising the overall health of captive systems.

In the actual mechanics of feeding corals, much depends on the size of the polyps. Some corals are easily fed chunks of fresh shrimp, shellfish, fish, and other marine carnivore-type food. Whole and fresh foods containing the whole animal, and not just the "meat" or muscle tissue, are likely to be far more complete nutritional sources. Smaller-polyped corals may be more adept at capturing food such as adult or newly hatched brine shrimp, *Mysis* shrimp, blenderized fresh marine fish, crustacean meat, and shellfish, pulverized flake foods and rotifers. These smaller foods are easily fed by direct application to the polyps with a syringe or baster-type device. Still other corals, including those with larger polyp sizes, can feed on much smaller particles directly administered to the tank.

There are a number of do-it-yourself invertebrate recipes available that include combinations of the blenderized foods listed above, perhaps combined with fish blood, *Spirulina* algae, fresh terrestrial and marine "greens," and vitamins. "Greenwater" or phytoplankton cultures of *Nanochloropsis* and *Isochrysis* may also be used. Live marine rotifers are an excellent cultured food, as are enriched newly hatched *Artemia* nauplii (brine shrimp). *Artemia* nauplii are inexpensive and simple to hatch in batch amounts.

Vitamins and antioxidants can be used as a "soak" to enrich frozen or prepared food, or as a food source for live cultures that will be fed to corals. The direct addition of vitamins to the tank itself will probably not provide any noticeable benefit to the corals. The vitamins are unlikely to be directly taken up by the corals unless they are in a colloidal suspension. Vitamins added directly to the water column will be rapidly removed by foam-fractionation devices, or they may become hydrophobic globules on the water surface. Of course, any supplemental food source added to the water may be lost by foam fractionation, which is why direct application of food to the coral polyps is always the best method.

Aquarists can expect to see a growing choice of commercially available frozen preparations formulated for corals and other filter-feeding invertebrates. Some that are becoming available include ocean zooplankton as well as phytoplankton. Unrefrigerated liquid food preparations have long been offered for the feeding of invertebrates, but these must be used with great care to avoid polluting the aquarium. Many of these invertebrate feeding formulas are not likely to benefit corals, but may dramatically affect the growth of problem algae.

I have, however, found that certain brands of high-quality dry marine food, available in tiny pellets, are especially suited to liquid vitamin absorption before being fed to corals, and are also an appropriate size for many corals to capture. Proline and reduced glutathione (GSH) are both compounds that can be added to the water to elicit a feeding response in many corals. The use of these substances may be of benefit in stressed animals and those that require "coaxing" to feed, such as *Tubastraea* species.

Gaining popularity with many aquarists, refugium tanks can hold deep sand beds and provide shelter for many species that do best in protected conditions.

There is precious little known about the specificity of foods on which corals normally feed, although a few studies have analyzed gut contents of various species. Some corals seem to have very specific prey targets that may be based on chemorecognition, although most seem to feed on any prey that meets a certain size requirement. Some are predominantly carnivorous, while some, such as *Dendronephthya* species, are primarily herbivorous. As with many aspects of coral care, feeding requires some degree of experimentation, as the exact requirements will vary between species, aquariums, and circumstances.

REFUGIUMS

In recent years, there has been a growing interest in refugiums. A refugium is a harbor—a haven or a safehouse—for all manner of plants and small organisms that would ordinarily be consumed by the fishes in a marine aquarium. It is a small tank within the tank (or attached to the tank) through which system water flows, but predators from the display aquarium, especially fishes and foraging invertebrates, cannot enter. Live sand, various macroalgae species, and cultures of small micro- and meio-fauna are often placed in the refugium as an ongoing natural food source for reef animals. It can be thought of as a breeding den for the likes of *Mysis* shrimp, various tiny crustaceans, worms, and other small reef organisms. Various aquaculture suppliers are beginning to offer invertebrate species ideal for propagation in refugiums, including appropriate crustaceans and mollusks whose gametes and/or larval forms will be conveniently swept into the display aquarium and readily consumed by corals and other predators.

Overall, a refugium can be a beneficial addition to any aquarium system, especially one housing corals, and is fascinating to observe in its own right. A refugium overcomes some of the shortcomings of natural plankton populations that are rapidly depleted in captive environments by filtration, centrifugal pumps, protein skimming, and predation.

In fact, I envision that the most-successful reef aquariums in the future will have multiple, separate habitats. The display tank, containing corals, fishes, and other invertebrates, will be linked to one or more large, multipurpose sumps—refugiums that, in many cases, may exceed the size of the display tank. In these we will see an increased use of macroalgae, marine grasses, and other flora and fauna for nutrient export. Such habitats will be able to provide nearly, if not all, of the necessary filtration and nutrient export and uptake. The larger water volumes will more easily sustain heavy bioloads, and the in-sump culture of large numbers of live food sources will not only result in aquariums that are healthier, more natural, and less expensive, but that are markedly easier to run and require little intervention.

CHAPTER 5

Secret Lives

Competition and Reproduction

Despite their breathtaking beauty, coral reefs may be one of the most fiercely competitive environments on the face of the Earth. Because they are limited geographically and by finite areas of substrate with the correct conditions and depths, the incredible biodiversity of life that assembles on and around the reefs is in a constant battle for space on which to live, grow, and reproduce.

Corals can cover up to 85% or more of the substrate on a reef and are thus very successful in claiming turf that would otherwise be taken by myriad forms of algae and other competitors. Not surprisingly, the corals have developed specialized and highly effective methods to secure and fill their own particular nooks. In reef environments, there is usually a mere 1-5% of exposed space on the hard substrate that is colonizable. Therefore, sessile organisms compete in what amounts to an all-out war in order to ensure their continued presence in an area.

Acquisition and maintenance of space can be gained by growth interactions, aggressive or cannibalistic interactions, feeding competition, and allelopathy (LaBarre et al., 1986b). Or-

> "It appears that the race is not necessarily to the most quickly growing species."
>
>
>
> C.M. Yonge
> *The Biology of Coral Reefs*, 1963

ganisms with rapid and effective reproduction have an added advantage.

Corals vie for space by using structures that hinder overgrowth by competitors, secreting anti-fouling agents, using escape mechanisms, and manifesting growth forms with a reduced susceptibility to disturbance. Some very subordinate corals, like *Porites* species, have an advantage in that they are able to tolerate damage from competitors and predators, surviving very well with localized dead areas on their skeletons. In fact, more corals are passive than aggressive, and they prefer to avoid encounters that sap their precious metabolic reserves. Active competition can be a significant energy cost to corals, and both growth and reproductive fitness are decreased during such encounters.

Even so, in nature, it is estimated that between 22 and 38% of all reef coral colonies are engaged in "combat" or are within reach to do so. Good defense is not always a winning strategy on the reef; most animals must also be aggressive to survive. Four levels of competition have been proposed (Rinkevich and Loya, 1985):

1. Behavioral: direct action by extracoelenteric digestion, sweeper tentacles, stinging nematocysts, acrorhagi, and mucus production;

Coral spawning: billowing clouds comprised of billions of tiny gametes rise in a mass release of eggs and sperm on a coral reef in Palau (Belau).

2. Morphological: overgrowth, oriented translocation, over-topping, movement, and retreat growth (in which the response to competition is growth in a different direction);

3. Chemical: colonies outside the coral's direct contact range are affected by the release of soluble compounds;

4. Energetic-physiological: energy is either gained or lost as a result of the encounter.

Once corals are engaged in a competition, several outcomes are possible:

• The subordinate coral is killed either by the competition or by having the dominant coral overgrow it.

• One coral or the other is overgrown or killed by disease, algal overgrowth/encroachment or other fouling organisms, or is preyed on as a result of its weakened state. Growth rates may be significantly reduced and gonadal development may be slowed or halted.

• There is a stand-off, with neither coral retreating or advancing.

• The competition is reversed over the long term, with the dominant coral becoming subordinate.

BEHAVIORAL COMPETITION

Extracoelenteric digestion: Within the gastrovascular cavity of the coral polyps are two types of digestive filaments, **septal** and **acontial**, collectively termed the **mesenterial filaments**. Corals can expel these digestive filaments (which contain cnidocytes), if they are chemically or mechanically stressed. If one coral detects chemicals released by a neighboring coral or comes in contact with the coral itself, it can literally "vomit" its insides onto the neighboring coral and digest the competitor's tissue. As such, the mesenterial filaments are very effective close-range aggressive and/or defensive structures that prevent other species from invading a coral's space. The dominance of one coral over another using these means is variable, with intraspecific hierarchies being present. The subordinate colony, even if initially extruding its mesenterial filaments, will usually withdraw them either to be overtaken or to engage in other competitive means (Romano, 1990, et al.). The dominance of one coral over another can depend on the species, the length of time in contact, the location and conditions of the encounter, other epifauna present, and the use of specialized aggressive structures. The quantity and length of the mesenterial filaments may also be important in establishing dominance.

Sweeper tentacles: Many corals have evolved specialized tentacles known as sweeper tentacles, or "catch" tentacles. These tentacles are much longer and thinner than other tentacles—more than 5 times the length, in some cases—and can reach

Deadly defense: a captive colony of *Oulophyllia sp.* (brain coral) protects its position with potent sweeper tentacles that can reach, sting, and kill nearby corals.

other corals some distance from the colony. The sweepers possess a larger **acrosphere** (swollen tentacle tip), more-numerous nematocysts, and contain a more-potent composition. These special nematocysts contain large **microbasic b-mastigophores**, whereas normal tentacles contain **microbasic p-mastigophores**. Some corals form random sweepers as a general defense mechanism, then localize them in the region where an interspecific encounter is occurring. They are, in a sense, "sniffing the water" for potential aggressors. Sweeper tentacles are formed from repeated mechanical or chemical contacts between neighboring coral colonies, including nematocyst discharge and **histoincompatibilities** (immune responses based on chemical recognition of species differences). Strong water flow also seems to induce their formation, although this may be a consequence of enhanced access to chemical cues. However, neither damage nor mechanical stimulation alone will result in sweeper tentacles—the presence of other competing corals must be sensed chemically. These spe-

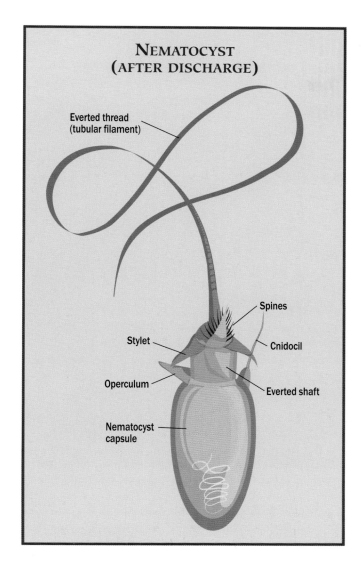

NEMATOCYST (AFTER DISCHARGE)

Everted thread
(tubular filament)

Spines

Stylet

Cnidocil

Operculum

Everted shaft

Nematocyst
capsule

in the aquarium is an effective way of preventing harm to other corals nearby, but because most tentacles have the capacity to become sweepers under competitive conditions, others will develop unless the competition is removed. Moreover, the resultant tissue injury from constant snipping can lead to infection. Cessation or decrease of water movement, however, will usually result in the retraction of sweepers; this is a more-effective way to limit their production.

Euphyllia and *Galaxea* species are well known for possessing particularly conspicuous, lengthy, and potent sweeper tentacles (they can be over a foot long), but even corals that would not seem to possess such aggressive modifications, such as *Pavona* and *Erythropodium* species, regularly form these deadly sweepers. Therefore, careful siting of sweeper-forming corals is necessary when placing them in the aquarium (see Chapter 10).

The nettling effect of some sweeper tentacles can be quite painful to humans. I once reached into one of my tanks to retrieve a dislodged lettuce clip. Previously, I had brushed my hand through a large *Euphyllia ancora* without incident. This particular time, however, a sweeper tentacle slammed right onto a small cut on the back of my hand: the pain was like the instant, electrifying sting of a wasp.

Stinging nematocysts: Often, the nematocysts of normal tentacles provide the most common interspecific aggression, as nearby corals sting each other repeatedly as they grow nearer, with one coral eventually (or quickly) showing dominance over the other. While this type of competition is not highly specialized, it is the most common form of aggression seen in areas of high coral density, such as in aquariums. The result is usually a defensive reaction by the subordinate coral, with growth stopping at the area of conflict and continuing off in other directions.

Another remarkable feature of corals, though more common in anemones, is the firing of long-distance nematocysts. Some corals periodically discharge their nematocysts into the water like a battalion of long-range missiles, allowing them to settle on and sting whatever they contact. This general aggression is a way of "clearing out the brush," so to speak. Corals up to several feet away can be stung as a rain of invisible nematocysts hail down on them, borne by water currents. More than once, I have put my bare arm into an aquarium and felt the unusual prickly sensation caused by the nettling of many waterborne nematocysts. Fortunately, this type of behavior is not as common as other forms of aggression, and may be a response to stress.

Acrorhagi: These specialized cnidocytes are found on both sweeper tentacles and column projections that also contain concentrated nematocysts. Acrorhagi require intimate contact with an affronting organism, but usually result in the complete death

cialized tentacles take from a few days to almost a month to form, but can remain present for up to 6 weeks. Repeat formation takes progressively shorter periods of time. The development of sweeper tentacles is considered to be both a defensive and an immunorecognition response, with specificity, memory, and persistence all being present.

While sweeper tentacles are certainly capable of feeding, their primary use is in aggressive competition. If a sweeper comes in contact with another coral, it usually "sticks" or breaks off onto the competing organism, then continues to discharge its nematocysts insuring that the other coral receives a damaging hit. Some sources have suggested that snipping off sweeper tentacles

Embattled turf: despite its calm beauty, a coral reef is the scene of constant battles among corals vying for precious space to attach and grow. (Indo-Pacific)

of all contacted tissue. Some corals use acrorhagi as they encrust or overgrow neighboring colonies. Acrorhagi are a specialized defensive response, since they will not be discharged by mechanical contact with nonliving articles such as metal and glass, nor will they discharge in response to prey animals. They only discharge in response to conspecific corals (corals of the same species) and certain other specific cnidarians that elicit a chemorecognition response.

Mucus: The production of either toxic or nematocyst-laden mucus can be an effective aggressive behavior, as water currents may allow it to drift some distance from a coral colony, causing a negative reaction, or even death, in other corals downstream. Some of the free-living corals, such as *Fungia* species, have copious nematocysts and other cytotoxic compounds in their mucus. If this mucus comes in contact with other corals, it can be very damaging because the contact time of mucus to coral tissue

is quite prolonged. This can be especially problematic with some of the solitary corals that have the ability to "walk" into neighboring corals. Some mucus contains enzymes, such as proteases, that are capable of tissue digestion. Fortunately, though, these enzymes are normally used only in phagocytic (feeding) or immunologic actions.

MORPHOLOGICAL COMPETITION

Overgrowth: Corals also effectively compete for space in their growth patterns. Many corals are encrusting, or at least partly encrusting, as they form firm anchorage on the substrate. Dominant species, even color morphs of the same species, can literally grow over the top of neighboring colonies. Often, there is a localized "war," as the polyps of adjacent corals grow within intimate contact range of each other. A denuded or bare line, representing the battle zone between colonies, is often seen. The victor continues its growth, literally pushing the weaker coral out of existence.

In one of my own reef tanks, a few colonies of a pink morph of *Montipora digitata* are currently engaged in overgrowing numerous colonies of a brown morph of the same species. Curiously enough, the brown morph is currently dominant, in that it grows much faster and has achieved spatial dominance of the habitat. Yet barring other influences, the tank could eventually be colonized predominantly by the overgrowing pink morph.

Overgrowth is also commonly employed by octocorals and stoloniferans that often fail to be detected as an "enemy" by stony corals. As such, these corals frequently grow right over the top of the stony corals with minimal effort. *Nephthea brassica* is well known to move across the surface of *Acropora hyacinthus*, leaving a trail of disfigured skeleton in its wake (LaBarre and Coll, 1982).

Oriented translocation: A further competitive edge given to corals that have fused, or at least grown together, is the oriented translocation of nutrients (Rinkevich and Loya, 1983). Dominant morphs can seize control of a weaker clone in at least some corals, in essence making the submissive clone its slave. The products of photosynthesis of the weaker coral can be directed to the stronger for their own use.

Overtopping: Faster-growing corals may grow over the top of slow-growing or small corals, blocking them from the sunlight like the trees of the rainforest canopy. Deprived of sunlight, the shaded coral's growth is slowed or stopped, and it often dies. Branching, tabular, and laminar corals, such as some *Acropora* and *Leptoseris* species, excel at this type of competition. Despite the long-established view that overtopping is an effective method of competition, a study of colonization under table *Acropora* species (Sheppard, 1981) showed that light under the corals was reduced by 95%, yet the density and number of coral species, and the associated flora and fauna, was not significantly different from that in surrounding areas. It appears that the reduced light is still above the values required for photoadapted colonies from the same area and is sufficient for the proliferation of species that are adaptable to reduced light. Furthermore, the overtopping corals actually help protect the understory corals from predation. Therefore, this may be a less-effective competitive method than has been commonly assumed. Instead, such corals may be only modifying the species composition, rather than eliminating competitors indiscriminately.

Movement: Specialized locomotion can also help achieve spatial superiority. Some *Xenia* species can actively "walk" across the substrate by a method of attachment, growth, and reattachment of their branches to the substrate. This is the method by which *Xenia* species initiate the primary settlement of new coral areas, and it is quite fascinating to watch these corals move across the aquarium. Like certain anemones and corallimorphs, they can also detach from the substrate to drift and resettle, thereby colonizing nonadjacent areas. Many of the fungiids move across the substrate by tissue expansion and contraction. Fungiid movement permits active colonization, as well as providing potential defensive action by means of tentacular and mucosal contact with nearby competitors. *Diaseris distorta* is actually capable of "tumbling" end over end by systematically turning itself over and then righting itself again (Hubbard, 1972). *Heteropsammia* and *Heterocyathus* species both settle on the back of the sipunculan worm *Aspidosiphon muelleri* in a mutualistic relationship that helps these free-living corals move across soft bottoms on their own private "taxi." The worm, in turn, is protected by the coral (Hoeksema and Best, 1991).

CHEMICAL COMPETITION

The last competitive method used by many corals is the production of toxic compounds in a process known as **allelopathy**. The primary known producers of these compounds are the alcyonarians (soft corals) and gorgonians. However, these corals have been studied more thoroughly in the past, and it is now being recognized that stony corals also produce terpenoids and other bioactive chemicals.

Goniopora species, for example, have been found to release toxic exudates, and recent work by Koh (1997) has shown that stony corals are also prodigious producers of bioactive compounds. *Acropora* species and pocilloporids produce terpenoid compounds, as do *Tubastraea* species. Chemical factors have also

Toxic compounds are produced by many corals to discourage predation and to force would-be competitors to keep their distance. (Ningaloo Reef, Australia)

CORAL TOXICITY TO FISHES

These experiments involved the testing of 68 coral species from the Great Barrier Reef, in which coral tissue was macerated in a blender and added to containers housing fish specimens. Overall, 52% of the corals studied were judged to be toxic.

Rating	% of Corals Tested	Fish Mortality
"Very Toxic"	15%	100% within 90 min.
"Toxic"	20%	83% within 12 hrs.
"Harmful"	17%	67% within 12 hrs.
"Nontoxic"	48%	48% within 24 hrs.*

*Test subjects were wild freshwater Mosquito Fish (*Gambusia affinis*), which tended to show high mortality when confined for 24 hours, and factors other than coral toxicity are assumed to have affected those in the "nontoxic" group.

(Coll, LaBarre, Sammarco, Williams, and Bakus, 1982)

been implicated in many studies of other stony corals, including *Stylophora*, *Montipora*, and *Montastraea* species. Studies done by Gunthorpe and Cameron (1990) showed variable and widespread toxicities of scleractinians, similar to those found in the soft corals. De Ruyter van Steveninck et al. (1988) and Bak and Borsboom (1984) even showed inhibitory effects of stony corals on algae. The possibility of toxins produced by the corallimorpharians, or mushroom anemones, is currently being investigated and seems likely to be of significant value. Observations of apparently toxin-mediated reactions involving other corals and invertebrates with the corallimorpharians are noted and reported with great frequency by aquarists.

In fact, virtually every sessile marine animal taxon utilizes some form of "chemical weaponry," including sponges, algae, tunicates, bryozoans—and corals. Sponges in aquarium experiments produce increased oxygen consumption, decreased photosynthesis, bleaching, and necrosis in exposed corals in as little as 8 minutes. Many researchers have pointed out increased metabolite effects in closed-system aquariums. Needless to say, such effects, whether from sponges or any toxic animal or plant (soft corals, algae, etc.), should be carefully heeded by the aquarist keeping corals.

Toxic compounds produced by corals are not only useful in aggressive competition for space, but are also excellent defensive measures to prevent predation and parasitism. Despite the fact that stony corals are often dominant corals on a reef, large areas in the Pacific and Indian Oceans can be found that are almost exclusively inhabited by soft corals, which are superior competitors in many ways.

Stony corals, for example, do not seem to be able to digest soft corals extracoelenterically. They are either chemically "fooled," or are genetically disparate enough that the normal self/nonself immunologic response is not triggered by the soft corals. This fact allows many soft corals simply to grow over their stony counterparts. Soft corals generally do not have strong nematocysts and are therefore not usually capable of "outstinging" their stony counterparts. However, they produce a bewildering array of toxic compounds that consist primarily of terpenes, but may also include: terpenoids, lipoids, brominated phenols, polyphenolics, fatty acids, diterpenes, peptides, alkaloids, sterols, wax esters, unusual amino acids, and others. Bromine is the element most often incorporated into these compounds. Although terpenes have previously been thought to be produced only by plants (and hence, the zooxanthellae), it came as a bit of a surprise to researchers who found that these corals were capable of producing classes of previously unknown terpenes. Almost half of all soft corals studied produce these toxins, with 15% of soft coral species considered very toxic (see box).

The genera *Sarcophyton* and *Lemnalia* are two of the most prolific producers of toxic compounds and contain some of the most-toxic species. *Sinularia*, *Nephthea*, *Lobophytum*, and *Cespitularia* species can also be highly toxic, although the toxicity of produced substances can vary greatly among species within the respective genera. In experiments, some toxin-producing soft

Many soft corals, such as this large aquarium-grown *Sarcophyton* sp., have been shown to release toxic compounds that can kill or stunt nearby stony corals.

Ichthyotoxicity of Some Soft Corals

Group	Toxic Species	Nontoxic Species
Alcyoniidae	**58**	**20**
Lobophytum spp.*	9	1
Sarcophyton spp.*	13	2
Cladiella spp.	8	1
Sinularia spp.*	28	15
Alcyonium sp.	0	1
Nephtheidae	**25**	**28**
Lemnalia spp.*	9	1
Nephthea spp.	12	7
Dendronephthya spp.	4	11
Capnella spp.	0	9
Xeniidae	**14**	**12**
Xenia spp.	6	1
Cespitularia spp.*	3	4
Efflatounaria spp.	4	6
Anthelia spp.	1	1

*denotes a genus with some very toxic species

(after Sammarco and Coll, 1987)

corals not only caused the death or stunting of all stony corals placed in contact with them, but were also able to cause harm to the same animals placed a significant distance away. They can affect both photosynthesis and respiration rates, as well as directly causing necrosis and/or mortality in as little as 1 day, with maximum effects after 4 weeks. Contact reactions are more acute than noncontact reactions, although the effects of such chemicals in a closed system makes such observations questionable in practice (home-scale aquariums may be considered basically contact situations because of the lack of dilution). Generally, response and/or avoidance to such allelopathy takes a minimum of 2 days, during which time significant damage may already have occurred. (In cases of physical damage to a soft coral, as when cuttings are being taken, toxic effects are sometimes much more rapidly seen, with fishes dying within hours of the incident.)

Concentrations of terpenes have been estimated in the wild at 1-5 ppm near some soft corals (Coll and Sammarco, 1983) with 5-10 ppm causing 100% mortality in some stony corals within 8 hours (Coll et al., 1986) and 10-20 ppm killing small fishes. The effects of dilution in the ocean are enormous, and it is likely that closed-system aquariums have significantly higher and prolonged exposure to levels at least this high in many cases. These secondary metabolites, or allelopathic toxins, are thought to act primarily by accumulating in the tissue of other corals. As the box on page 74 illustrates, soft corals can also produce lethal effects on fishes in closed systems.

CHEMORECEPTION

Corals utilize chemoreception in food procurement (Chapter 4), but it is also important in other ways. In order to survive a sessile life as a soft-bodied animal in a densely packed community, a coral must display a high degree of **immunological competence**. Immunity means more than solely the ability to fight off disease—although a coral is pretty good at this, too, under all but the most-stressful conditions. For these sightless animals, it is also essential to be able to detect "self" from "nonself." This competence exists for all living organisms, but true immunity requires several conditions:

1. that there be a mechanism and/or ability to recognize foreign agents and/or tissue (selective or specific reactivity);
2. that a mechanism exists for dealing with foreign agents and/or tissue (cytotoxic or antagonistic reaction); and
3. that the organism be able to recognize and respond to contact with the same or similar foreign agent and/or tissue in the future (inducible memory).

Corals possess all of these traits, and then some. A coral can discriminate between other coral genera, species, and even subspecies and genotypes of its own species with variable degrees of reactivity. The more closely related two species are, the less likely they are to respond to each other as enemies. This basic tenet of corals' ability to distinguish between species was once thought to be a useful tool for determining species—that is, if grafts of two samples of coral grew together and fused, they were considered the same species. Amazingly, a colony of coral can often detect the difference between itself and a same-species colony located a few meters away from it—even if both corals may have originated as fragments of the same parent colony at some point in the past.

New fragments of the same coral (isogeneic tissue) will always fuse both their skeletons and their tissue if they are in close proximity to each other. However, fragments of corals of the same species collected from different reefs near the same island are likely not to fuse. Putting together fragments of the same species collected from different islands would probably result in failure to fuse as well as clear incompatibility.

Responses can vary from simple fusion of skeletons without the fusion of living tissue to avoidance or all-out defensive action including the formation of sweeper tentacles, cytotoxic chemicals, and extracoelenteric digestion. The more distant the relationship in genetics, space, or time, the more severe the immunological reaction will likely be when the corals come in contact or near contact.

Various chemical messengers are known to exist in all corals studied thus far that do not require intimate contact to elicit a reaction. The more closely the corals grow to each other, the more likely the possibility of a defensive immune response based on such chemical recognition. This whole process is known as either **histocompatibility** or **histoincompatibility**. The exact methods, chemicals and reactions used will vary between species, but the response is universal. The time for various reactions to occur can be from as little as a few hours for direct contact situations to months (even up to a year) for full immune responses to develop in incompatible coral species. One common reaction is the formation of sweeper tentacles after the addition of a new coral to an aquarium.

Occasionally, corals may even display autolytic behavior, destroying their own tissue. This has been repeatedly observed in various stony corals, hydrocorals, and gorgonians. Histocompatability is an important aspect of coral behavior, and it is even likely to be involved in the recognition and acceptance of the various strains and species of zooxanthellae into coral tissue.

Even seemingly innocuous corals, such as these yellow **zoanthid polyps**, can harm corals within their reach, here killing the edge of a *Turbinaria* sp. colony.

SOME TYPICAL REACTIONS OF MARINE INVERTEBRATES TO BIOACTIVE COMPOUNDS

Tissue hypertrophy
Increased mucus secretion
Change in mucosal composition
Change in mucus-secreting cells
Initiation of feeding response
Polyp withdrawal
Formation of sweeper tentacles (stony/soft corals, gorgonians)
Formation of marginal tentacles (corallimorphs)
Formation of acrospheres
Change in growth rate
Change in growth form or direction
Change in nematocyst composition
Tissue necrosis (local or general)
Initiation of spawning
Cessation of gonad development
Change in metabolism
Change in behavior (nonsessile invertebrates)
Increased or decreased susceptibility to disease
Increased or decreased settlement of larvae
Increased or decreased fecundity
Bleaching
Mortality

Gorgonians, alcyonareans, and stony corals have all been reported to secrete antimicrobial substances. The type and amounts of substances seem to be highly species specific, and appear to vary depending on the needs of the coral and the potential threat of various pathogens. The gorgonians have long been known to produce general wide-range antibiotic substances, as have the soft corals. Some of these compounds prevent surface fouling by microalgae, cyanobacteria, and other microorganisms. More recently, the stony corals have also been found to produce antimicrobial substances, notably *Acropora, Tubastraea, Turbinaria,* and *Porites* species (Koh, 1997a, b).

The studies on the chemical ecology of stony corals is just beginning, and only limited work on species-specificity of both corals and microbes has begun. Even more interesting is the specificity and role that bacteria themselves may play in coral immunity. Normal coral bacterial flora found in the gastrovascular cavity and on the mucus may produce their own antimicrobial substances or antifungal substances not only to ensure their presence but to act as an agent of immunity for the corals. It is becoming more and more recognized that the normal bacterial flora associated with corals may exist in a symbiotic relationship (Kelman et al., 1998; Ferrier-Pages et al., 1998; and others). These species are commonly gram-negative strains such as *Pseudomonas* and *Vibrio* (Ritchie and Smith, 1995; Smith and Ritchie, 1995; Ducklow and Mitchell 1979; et al.).

Corals also produce and sense "olfactory" compounds, such as kairomones, allomones, and pheromones. Kairomones are chemicals released by one organism and used to advantage by another organism—for example, corals respond to the kairomones released by zooplankton. Allomones are those released chemicals that benefit the producer—for example, the defensive allelochemicals of soft corals. Pheromones are olfactory compounds that elicit a reaction in the receiver. Sex attractants are examples of well-known pheromones in other taxa.

DILUTION AND DIFFUSION

With the multitudes of known and unknown chemical cues and battles going on in reef communities, it should be little wonder that the concept of dilution and diffusion is frequently mentioned. Indeed, the fact that corals live in an ocean of great water volume and movement ensures that such reactions and chemical defenses are only effective over relatively short distances. This way, corals can adopt a behavioral variation of, "If it's not in my backyard, I won't let it bother me." This is, in fact, the case.

However, the dilution factor in aquariums is minimal. Effectively, all of a small- or average-sized aquarium is "the backyard," and over time, myriad chemical substances can accumulate. Many problems observed among captive corals may be related to chemical interactions, but very little research has been done in this area. To limit the very real possibility of toxic coral metabolites and chemicals becoming concentrated in an aquarium, some form of export of these toxic substances must be present.

Activated carbon and ion-exchange resins are both known to be effective in removing various organic acids, phenols, and terpenes. Water changes, obviously, serve to accomplish dilution, and are also effective. The use of foam fractionation devices and other types of water purifiers (ozone, etc.) are likely to be helpful, although their relative utility in the removal of these compounds is unclear.

It has also been found that a certain threshold limit must be exceeded to produce immune responses in corals, either in the concentration or amount of various signals. Habituation is also the rule, and the longer corals remain in each other's presence, the less likely they are to elicit such responses. An exam-

MARINE INVERTEBRATE TOXICITY		
	% Toxic	% Nontoxic
Gorgonians	100	0
Holothurians	100	0
Soft corals	88	12
Sponges (exposed type)	60	40
Echinoderms	50	50
Tunicates	0	100

(Bakus, 1981)

ple, again, is the common report of a group of corals co-existing in an aquarium without apparent incident until the sudden introduction of a new specimen causes all sorts of intratank havoc. In time, the habituation response occurs, and the corals become, once again, used to each other's presence. This typically takes from several weeks to a year or longer, with average habituation taking from 3 to 7 months. The exact nature, type, species, and levels of chemical tolerance have yet to be determined, and likely vary significantly from case to case.

REPRODUCTION AND GROWTH

Corals also compete for their place on the reef by multiplying themselves, and they do this in two ways: sexual and asexual reproduction. Both methods are very important in allowing for the continued presence of different species on a reef, with some corals depending more heavily on one means over the other. Typically, opportunistic species reproduce vegetatively through asexual means. Furthermore, various means of asexual reproduction are often specific to certain types of corals.

To distinguish between growth and true reproduction, it should be noted that there are methods of coral growth that are quasi-reproductive—they do result in more polyps, but do not ordinarily form new and separate colonies. This is exemplified by the growth of a stony coral colony: the polyps, grouped together in a limestone formation, are continually growing. They accomplish growth largely through calcification. However, if the polyps did not also divide, the colony would consist of an ever-increasing mass and surface area, with the polyps becoming more and more separated from each other. Yet this does not occur, and polyp sizes and densities remain relatively constant. (Polyp density can be modified according to various environmental conditions, and even within species, but they remain fairly uniform across the surface of an individual coral.) Polyps

Feeding frenzy: a feast for reef fishes comes during mass coral spawning events, as buoyant eggs rise from *Acropora* **spp.** at nighttime on the Great Barrier Reef.

accomplish this feat by dividing repeatedly within the colony. In general, polyps near the margins or edges of massive, laminar, encrusting, turbinate, and foliaceous corals tend to divide more often, while those in the center—the oldest polyps—divide less frequently. Polyps near the tips of branching corals divide most frequently, while those at the base divide the least, if at all. In one sense, this occurs because branch tips and margins are the fastest-growing areas. More often, there is simply no more room for the packed-in polyps in the center or base of a coral to divide.

It is also fortunate for the older parts of a colony that polyps do not become senescent under ordinary conditions. Senescence, however, has been shown in some of the rapidly growing genera, such as *Pocillopora* and *Acropora*.

Division of a polyp occurs in two ways, both representing types of **fission**. **Intratentacular budding** occurs when a polyp divides across itself, more or less, into two equal halves. **Extratentacular budding** occurs when a new polyp grows out, or buds, from the edges of an existing polyp. In both types, the halves or unequal buds of the parent polyp must pinch off the exposed margins of tissue that result from the dividing process. It is fascinating to think of the 3-dimensional changes that must occur in the skeleton after such an event.

ASEXUAL REPRODUCTION

Asexual reproduction results in the formation of new coral colonies that are genetic clones of the parent colony. No gametes are produced, and no new genetic material is present. In this way, many corals may be seen as theoretically immortal. Corals that depend heavily on asexual forms of reproduction are commonly found in large monospecific stands in the wild.

Fragmentation is common in highly branched corals or those with fragile and/or porous skeletons. In nature, the branching corals, typically sporting heavy mucus coats to help them survive damage to their skeleton, can be broken off parent colonies during storms and other physical disturbances. This is not only a common method of asexual reproduction, but can allow for colony dispersal of up to 50 m (164 ft.) from the point of breakage. Even so, studies generally find only about a 10-40% survival rate for fragments, with those least able to cement themselves quickly, and those with strong aversions to allelopathic effects, being the least likely to survive. Larger fragments, possibly because of their ability to withstand greater damage and to resist being tossed about and covered with sediments, have a significantly greater chance of survival—nearly 75%. Many *Acropora* species, despite their abundance and dependence on fragmentation for dispersal, also show relatively low fragment-survival rates. The process of fragmentation can, however, be utilized to great advantage under careful conditions in captivity to create new colonies.

Typically, corals that depend heavily on fragmentation have life histories distinct from those that do not. They tend to be broadcast spawners and not brooders, produce fewer viable larvae, spawn infrequently, reach sexual maturity at 8-10 years, have populations dominated by adults with few juveniles present, grow quickly, are morphologically plastic, do not form large, long-lived colonies, and are highly competitive (Highsmith, 1982).

Budding, or the formation of **polyp balls**, is a relatively common type of asexual reproduction in the stony corals and some octocorals in aquariums, although it is less frequently reported in the wild. In this process, small balls, or daughter colonies, grow outward from the parent colony like a growth or bud. Marginal areas of colonies are more likely to form buds. Sometimes, a bit of skeleton is present along with the budded polyp or daughter colony of stony corals. There are many variations seen in budding, but the end result is a small colony that grows off the parent colony, detaches by gravity, physical stress, or active separation induced by the parent, and begins to calcify. A new coral colony is formed, generally nearby or directly under the parent colony. If sufficient water motion is present, or if the slope or depth of the area below the colony is great enough, dispersal away from the budding colony can be much greater.

Certain corals, such as *Goniopora* species, tend to form budded daughter colonies more frequently than others. Many polyp balls can be produced at once, and may be as large as 25% of the parent colony before detachment. Because the budding mechanism is not known, it is not certain whether this is an innate ability of all corals, or whether it is a specialized ability of certain species. Observations of various corals forming buds in captivity have shown that species that have never been reported to engage in this behavior are capable of it. Budding tends to occur more frequently under certain conditions: corals in low light, or those exposed to inadequate light, tend to form buds more often. Stresses of various types, including sedimentation, temperature, and interspecific competition also result in more-frequent budding behavior.

Another type of budding is the most common means of reproduction for a host of soft coral species, stoloniferans, zoanthids, and corallimorpharians (mushrooms). These corals regularly reproduce by producing polyp buds at the base of the parent polyp near the site of attachment to the substrate. Each polyp (or bit of tissue) then grows larger and may then either remain attached to a common mat shared by all the polyps, or it may move and become separated from the parent polyp.

A few species, including some of the solitary fungiid corals, form **anthocauli** in a type of fission. Anthocauli develop from areas of localized damage to the skeleton. The coral begins a process known as **decalcification**, and intentionally dissolves part of its calcium skeleton to release a part of itself as a separate colony. In a sense, it "cuts off it's own arm." These segments of

Asexual reproduction: drooping flesh from this **faviid colony** will attach to substrate and form a new daughter colony that is a genetic clone of its parent.

the parent colony are capable of **regeneration** into a whole individual. Although this is somewhat like fragmentation, it is a process initiated and completed by the coral itself, principally as an advantageous response to frequently encountered environmentally stressful conditions. Many of the fungiids are constantly being buried by the sand and rubble on which they dwell; storms, waves, or even fishes knock them around on the bottom. They can use this fission response to prevent the erosion and tissue death that would happen to the buried parent. Some other stony corals seem capable of similar behavior under physical disturbances, but most do not employ it as a regular method of asexual reproduction.

Fission is also common in many corallimorphs, where individual polyps split lengthwise across the oral opening before dividing into separate polyps. This is the equivalent of intratentacular budding of a polyp, described earlier. However, the corallimorphs are not limited by a limestone encasement. In this process, a distinct bifurcation, resembling a raised line, forms and is visible across the oral surface of the polyp. Soon thereafter, the margins of the disc at the bifurcation begin to grow inward, and the polyp is soon divided. This does not seem to be a stress-induced response, but more of a normal reproductive method.

Corallimorphs also participate in a unique form of settlement, often after either dividing by fission or producing budded daughters. Frequently, the parent polyp, and sometimes a

Juvenile clones (anthocauli) that will become new colonies form on a **Fungia sp.** skeleton, after the parent coral died (tank kept by Dietrich Stüber in Berlin).

METHODS OF ASEXUAL REPRODUCTION IN STONY CORALS

Intratentacular budding ("fission")
Zooidal budding within colony (clonoteny)
Fragmentation/Regeneration
- accidental or traumatic
- nonaccidental (including longitudinal division and parricidal budding)
- partial colony mortality

Extratentacular budding
Zooidal budding within colony (clonoteny)
Fragmentation/Regeneration
- accidental or traumatic
- partial colony mortality (including polyp bail-out)
- polyp balls
- production of anthoblasts (bud shedding)

Asexual planulae

Transverse division (strobilation or programmed detachment)

(after Cairns, 1988)

---

daughter polyp, detaches from the substrate and drifts away. This has two positive effects: first, the process allows for dispersal of the species and settlement in new areas; second, the removal of the parent or daughter may be a means by which to avoid overcrowding or shading of the newly formed polyps, ensuring a higher chance of survival for the remaining polyp(s). The detachment process does seem to occur more frequently under stressful conditions and is polyp-mediated. That is, physical detachment by external factors is not normally involved. This voluntary release and resettlement may be quite common in some corals. Except for sick or dying polyps, the forced removal of a corallimorph from its substrate is almost impossible without destruction of the animal—they are tenaciously attached. *Palythoa* and *Xenia* species are also capable of detachment and resettlement under both normal and stressful conditions. As described next, even some stony corals may participate in a similar dispersal behavior.

Polyp bail-out is a behavior by which some stony corals may form new colonies asexually. The living polyps eject themselves from their skeleton to drift in the current, ideally finding a suitable settling place where they can attach and begin to calcify a new skeleton. During spawns, some pocilloporid coral polyps bail out, carrying active larvae, though the polyps soon disintegrate and release the larvae. Although this behavior may occasionally be a valid form of asexual reproduction under normal conditions, it is mostly seen as an escape response. Bail-outs are almost always seen in response to stress. This type of reaction is likely used as a last-ditch attempt for survival, rather than a normal method of asexual reproduction. *Seriatopora* and *Pocillopora* species are frequently reported to engage in bail-outs. I have witnessed another pocilloporid, *Stylophora pistillata*, perform a polyp bail-out. There are also reports of *Cataliaphyllia*, *Trachyphyllia*, and a few other genera of large-polyped stony corals releasing living tissue from their skeletons in captivity to drift and then begin the calcification of a new skeleton. Again, these incidents usually follow a period of stress. It is not known if this observed aquarium behavior is analogous to the true polyp bail-outs reported in the scientific literature.

Coral polyp expulsion is a recently described method of asexual reproduction observed in the Red Sea corals *Oculina patagonica* and *Favia favus*. In this type of behavior, individual polyps, along with their calices, detach and lift out of the colony skeleton. Obviously, the polyp engages in partial decalcification of its skeleton in order to detach with its calyx intact. Although this resembles polyp bail-out, the observed corals are ejecting from otherwise healthy colonies. Furthermore, no calcium skeleton is ever brought along in polyp bail-out as it is in this form of polyp expulsion. However, both behaviors seem to be triggered by physical disturbance and stress. The elongated polyps drift and settle, perhaps with a higher chance of success owing to their negative buoyancy and pre-formed calcareous base.

Asexual brooded planulae ("competent" larvae) can also be produced by budding in some corals, though this type of planulae release is much more frequently a sexual method of reproduction and is discussed below. *Tubastraea* and *Pocillopora* species may both produce asexual planulae with some regularity, even in captivity.

SEXUAL REPRODUCTION

When engaged in sexual reproduction, corals can be either **hermaphroditic**, possessing both sexes in the same colony and releasing eggs and sperm, or they can be **gonochoric**, having separate sexes in different colonies. In addition, corals can be divided into two groups with dramatically different reproductive strategies, the brooders and the broadcasters.

Ripening yellow gamete bundles signal readiness for spawning by this ***Montastraea annularis*** (star coral) on the Flower Garden Banks in the Gulf of Mexico.

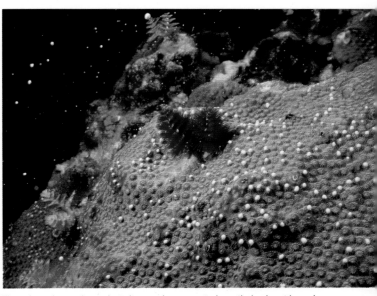

The colony shown above ejects its eggs in an event whose timing is set by various conditions, including water temperature and phase of the moon.

Brooders are usually hermaphrodites and self-fertilize within their gastrovascular cavity, releasing planulae into the water when they are ready. A minority, or approximately 25-40% of coral species, reproduce sexually by brooding larvae, and these corals typically release planulae multiple times during a year. Some corals, such as *Pocillopora* species, can produce and release brooded planulae from mature colonies each month. Brooders may be more likely to produce symbiotic planulae and eggs (oocytes) already stocked with zooxanthellae. In addition, some soft corals are external surface brooders. Typically having only one gametogenic cycle per year, these corals produce gametes that are brooded on the surface of the coral embedded in mucus, rather than developing within the gastrovascular cavity.

Broadcasters do not self-fertilize, but release both eggs and sperm into the water. The process is similar and analogous to the wind-pollination of terrestrial plants. Fertilization occurs in the water, and some genetic mixing may occur from the cross-fertilization of nearby same-species corals. Corals that reproduce by broadcast spawning can be hermaphroditic, but individual

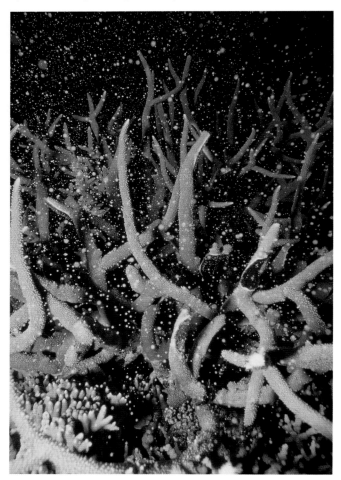

Blizzard of gametes: ***Acropora formosa*** takes part in the annual late spring coral spawning event that occurs five days after a full moon on the Great Barrier Reef.

colonies can also be gonochoric—distinctly male or female. Most corals, but not the vast majority, are hermaphroditic broadcast spawners. At least some (e.g., *Porites porites*) may be able to switch between gonochoric and hermaphroditic, depending on the environmental conditions. Hermaphroditic corals can self-fertilize at a 30-50% success rate, although this is not the preferred method (Gleason and Brazeau, 1999).

Depending on local conditions, reproductive strategies can vary; even within the same species, both brooding and broadcasting are possible for some corals.

Sexual reproduction on a reef can occur as infrequently as once per year or as often as several times annually. Spawnings are generally done *en masse,* with temperature, reproductive chemicals, lunar phase, photoperiod, and season all factoring into the moment when corals of many species from all over a reef release billions of their gametes into the water.

The spawn initiates a frenzied food feast for many reef inhabitants, but there is clearly a method in this synchronized ejection of gametes. By releasing in mass, corals have a statistically better chance of having some successful settlement of their fertilized eggs than if they spawned sporadically. In isolated spawn releases, the entire spawn of a single coral could easily be eaten by even a small school of fish.

Water temperature has been shown to be important in gonad maturation, with many spawnings occurring after lunar cues following the highest temperature of the year. Different regions have different temperatures, but there seems to be a critical temperature that prepares corals for a spawning event. It may be that latitude, the angle of the sun (seasonal periodicity), day length, and elevated water temperatures are all important factors in coral spawning. A note to aquarists: reduced salinity strongly retards invertebrate and coral reproduction and fertilization.

Moonlight levels do appear to be the actual timing trigger for the release of mature gametes in many corals. In other words, warming temperatures allow for the gonads of polyps to mature. As water reaches a critical ambient temperature, corals are ready to release, but many species depend on the exact moment to be determined by a given level of lunar light. The full set of conditions and the oddities involved in spawning events are yet to be fully understood. For example, unusually warm waters at the "wrong time of year" will not cause corals to vary from their annual spawning patterns. However, at least some corals studied can be induced to spawn using artificial moonlight. Aquarists attempting to encourage captive spawning must take into account the fact that tidal levels, day length, and lunar photobiology may all play a role in triggering the gamete release of sexually mature corals.

SETTLEMENT

The viable planulae of any spawn float to the surface and drift. Those that survive predation, beaching, being lost at sea, or other fates, finally settle to start new coral colonies. (Mortality rates for the larvae prior to settlement has been estimated in excess of 90%.) While tides and currents play the major role in transporting the spawn, coral planulae do exhibit swimming behavior, with rates varying from 7-15 cm/min. (3-6 in./min.). Most sexually released planulae settle in from 4 days to 3 weeks, and within 600 m (1,968 ft.) of their point of release. Settlement of asexual brooded planulae usually occurs within 3-5 days of release. Some planulae, lacking settlement opportunities or cues, may drift for hundreds or even thousand of miles on surface currents. Such long-distance scattering contributes to the astounding diversity of many reefs and accounts in part for the tremendous variability of coral species.

Even so, mass spawnings result in many nonviable hybrids, and huge surface "slicks" of gametes—sometimes stretching for miles—might be considered biologically wasteful. Obviously, though, the strategy works. *Pocillopora* and *Tubastraea* species have produced planulae that drifted for more than 100 days before settling into successful colonies, with various *Acropora* species showing settlement periods nearly as long.

A number of chemical cues present in the water induce the settlement of planulae, as well as biochemical and metabolic factors variably present in the larvae (Wilson and Harrison, 1998). It has been found that corals use red (coralline) algae as markers for settlement, drawn by chemical attractants called morphogens. It was once thought that coral settlement depended on various factors, including substrate texture, water column chemoregulation components, and signals emitted by biofilms—coatings of bacteria and other microbes that form a film on substrates. The bacteria were believed to exude various chemical signals, possibly sulfated polysaccharides, that induced settlement. However, it is now apparent that lactosamine sulfate from the cell wall of coralline algae is the "chemical flypaper" that attracts coral larvae. Thus far, all gorgonians, soft corals, and stony corals studied have been found to use coralline algae for settlement (Morse and Morse, 1991; Morse, 1999). There is a hierarchy of preferences among corals for different corallines. Depth also plays a role. Mass-spawning corals produce larvae that develop chemosensory competence over time, recognizing the coralline signals, and eventually settling on those located at their preferred depth levels (Morse, 1999).

There are other cues, too. Both light intensity and light spectral composition have been found to affect settlement and metamorphosis of coral planulae (Mundy and Babcock, 1998). These

Coral gametes caught in a web of mucus cast by an acroporid coral on the Great Barrier Reef. Of countless eggs released, very few survive to maturity.

factors allow planulae to determine the ideal depth, locale, and exposed/cryptic microenvironment best suited for their survival. Coral spat (larvae) most frequently settle on the undersides of plates, moving upward and outward as light becomes limiting. Vertical surfaces were preferred in the majority of species surveyed in one study (Carleton and Sammarco, 1987), while another reported that spat show no such preference (Morse, 1999).

Provided the larvae settle and attach, the road ahead is filled with bumps. Even once attached and growing, juvenile corals typically experience a 60-90% mortality during their first year of life. Another 30-40% of year-old corals will fail to reach maturity. Predation on juvenile corals and competition with other species both exact a heavy toll.

STRATEGIC APPROACHES

For corals, critical elements of sexual reproductive success include synchronization among individuals, egg-sperm interactions, embryological development, substrate selection, and recognition and acquisition of zooxanthellae by the new polyps (Richmond et al, 1999).

Corals can be divided into two groups, according to their strategy of sexual reproduction. The *r*-strategists are often pioneer species that reproduce frequently and in large numbers, but with a high rate of mortality for their offspring. They have shorter life spans, mostly forming small- to medium-sized colonies. Their prolific reproductive approach works toward frequent settling, increasing the odds that some planulae will survive. They are also frequently more dependent on asexual reproduction through budding or fragmentation. Among the corals that employ this

A successfully settled young coral (*Acropora loripes*) grows on a reef in Indonesia. Coralline algae acts as "chemical flypaper" to attract drifting larval corals.

type of strategy are most of the acroporids, pocilloporids, and *Psammocora* species.

The *k*-strategists frequently brood their planulae and funnel their energy into long-term growth. They form large, long-lived colonies with less-frequent sexual reproduction that relies on a lower mortality of offspring. They typically breed only once a year. Some corals that employ this strategy are *Porites* species and faviids. Most corals participate in reproductive strategies with characteristics somewhere between the *r*- and *k*-strategists.

The triggering of mass-spawning events may involve more than just the environmental factors listed above, and it has been suggested that **pheromones**, well-known for their reproductive roles in other phyla, are likely to be involved. In fact, spawning

can be induced in clams by grinding up the gonads and releasing the extract near other clams. Gamete maturation in sexually mature corals is highly variable between species. Once mature, stony corals typically take less than 12 months to develop their gametes, although some may take longer. Mature soft corals are similarly variable, with some xeniids and *Sarcophyton* species taking 1-2 years to produce mature gametes. It is also notable that many corals do not reach sexual maturity until they are several years old and of some considerable size. In most species, sexual maturity in stony corals is reached at 3-5 years of age. Octocorals tend to mature later—at 8-10 years. Some *r*-strategists tend to mature earlier, at 1-2 years, while *k*-strategists, like some *Porites* species, may take 16 years or more.

At least in corals, size really does matter. The average age for onset of reproductive activity and the first production of gametes is related to colony size, area, and branch length, depending on the species. The age may be related to the overall size of a mature colony and its life history/strategy. Corals that form massive, long-lived colonies typically become reproductive at a later age and larger size (Soong, 1993, et al.). Massive corals generally require 80-100 cm^2 (13-16 sq. in.) of polyp area, while in branching corals, branch length must be at least 10-20 cm (4-8 in.). If a coral is broken off from a mature colony, gonads disappear in the fragment, returning when the coral again reaches the required area, length, or number of polyps. Studies seem to indicate that, for at least some corals, energy budgets are also involved. Corals have a given amount of energy that must be used for metabolic processes, growth, and reproduction. Reproduction normally accounts from 0.5-10% of the total energy budgets of typical species (i.e., those that spawn annually or semi-annually and do not have unusual reproductive qualities and behaviors). Some studies indicate that the nutrition gained by feeding may be most important in maintenance of gonads and in sexual planulation. Corals that reproduce prolifically by asexual means, such as fragmentation, tend to use most of their energy budget toward growth. Therefore, it may be surmised that nutritional deficits, small sizes, immaturity, stress, type of reproduction (brooded versus broadcast), temperature, and moonlight are probably all interrelated in the successful sexual reproduction of corals, both in the wild and in captivity.

There appear to be specific chemical compounds in corals that can: cause planulation and egg release; function as sperm attractants and spawning release factors; enhance surface brooding and mucus sheet formation; and prevent predation of both eggs and planulae. Hormones or other chemicals appear to be responsible for the control over spawning and gamete maturation in soft corals. Chemical cues may also serve to curtail hybridization, as various genotypes of the same species may not be viable. It has been speculated that in local areas, a few "stud" corals may account for most of the colonies in an area (Toonen, pers. comm.), resulting in relatively few genotypes in that locale (Coffroth and Lasker, 1998).

Clearly, reproduction in the corals is both remarkable and complex, with great adaptability allowing survival of the species during times of threat or stress.

CAPTIVE REPRODUCTION: ASEXUAL

Aquarists determined to pursue captive reproduction have had great early success with asexual methods of propagation of both soft and stony corals, primarily by taking and nurturing cuttings and fragments.

In the aquarium, fragmentation occurs when a section or branch of the coral is accidentally or purposely broken from the parent colony. Each broken piece can then grow, becoming attached to substrate by its own means or by the aquarists' use of underwater epoxies or special glues. Heavy mucus production may occur in both fragmented branches and parent colonies after being broken. This is a normal adaptive response and facilitates survival and recovery. The broken regions of both the fragment and the parent colony quickly heal under good conditions, usually without incident. While very small pieces can be used to start new colonies, the optimum size for fragments seems to be 3-10 cm (1-4 in.), based on survival rates. Apical fragments (harvested from growing branch tips) show better survival than subapical or branch segments. Fragments reared in aquariums and those from high-energy zones tend to form basal encrusting attachments more quickly.

Fragmentation works extremely well in most cases. Still, any time there is tissue trauma, an opportunity exists for viral, bacterial, or protozoan infection, algae overgrowth, or opportunistic encroachment by other organisms. This is usually a result of localized dying, necrotic, and/or healing tissue. Yap and Gomez (1985) and others have shown the effects of stress involved in transplantation, remarkably akin to those in captive propagation, to have significant negative effects on growth. Thus fragmentation is not without risk, even if the success rate is high for many corals.

An easy method of fragmentation is possible with soft corals. Most can simply be sliced with a razor blade or sharp scissors to produce cuttings, which are then loosely but securely reattached

Farmed fragments: new **Acropora sp.** colonies started by coral propagation pioneer Dick Perrin grow in his Tropicorium greenhouses in suburban Detroit.

New frontier: sexual reproduction of aquarium corals is a goal of many advanced aquarists. Here, a male *Fungia* colony ejects sperm in a reef aquarium.

Although it is possible to fragment corals with more solid and massive skeletons by cleaving the colonies using saws, chisels, or other equipment, this process is difficult and more traumatic to the coral. The most current methods of captive propagation may be found through other sources, including the Breeder's Registry (see Contacts, page 406) and Knop (1997, 1998). Most aquarists will find it worth experimenting with propagation to create entirely new coral colonies.

Both cyanoacrylate and epoxy glues work well for attaching fragments to substrate. Corals that secrete heavy mucus or those too "soft" (including some soft corals and corallimorpharians, which are very slippery and are prone to "shrinkage" as they expel water from their tissue), may be more easily attached using a binding method, such as tying or pinning the fragment to the substrate. If left in a relatively calm area on a small bed of gravel, not subjected to direct water flow, most cuttings and fragments will attach on their own under normal circumstances. After cuttings reattach to substrate, the original growth form of the parent colony is soon reestablished.

Following attachment, coral fragments shunt energy into healing soft tissue and adhering to the substrate, rather than growth. Normal growth will resume up to several months after initial attachment. It is important that conditions remain as stress-free as possible during this initial period.

Budding also frequently occurs in captivity, mostly among those corals likely to produce buds in nature. *Goniopora*, *Euphyllia*, *Cataliaphyllia*, and *Sarcophyton* species are among the corals that can almost always be expected to produce buds. Most of the nephtheids, as well as other branching soft corals, frequently drop branchlets to produce new juvenile colonies in a similar fashion. If a particular coral is producing buds, the tiny new colony can be carefully placed so that its growth and success is favored once separation is complete. It is usually not necessary to assist with the separation process.

The other corals that use budding as a normal method of spread (zoanthids, stoloniferans, corallimorpharians, xeniids, etc.) may also show this behavior in captivity. Corallimorpharians will occasionally detach and drift in the tank until settling some distance away from the parent to begin forming a new remote colony. This type of budding is very common in many species available to the reef hobby, and such reproduction in healthy tanks is almost certain. Vast fields, mats, and accumulations of regularly budding polyps may soon occur even in newly established tanks.

Both fission and the production of true anthocauli will also occur in captivity, under the same conditions that produce them in the wild. Similarly, polyp bail-outs of the pocilloporids are a

to substrate with a rubber band, needle and thread, plastic strap, or adhesive. Again, there is some risk with this procedure, but it is an easy and successful method of propagating soft corals, a process that can be likened to the grafting of a plant. Although this seems like a very casual procedure, propagating most soft corals is quite literally that simple.

Many branching-type stony corals are just as easy to fragment, simply by snapping or cutting off a branch, then gluing the branch to a rock. For stony corals, efforts made in cooler water temperatures with the fragments affixed in an upright orientation on natural substrates or pieces of acrylic aged in seawater seem to have the best success rates both in practice and in studies. Good lighting and water circulation is essential.

frequent occurrence. Bail-outs are especially common upon introduction to a tank, or if there is a sudden change in water conditions. Provided that they are not destroyed by pumps or protein skimmers, numerous juvenile pocilloporids may begin growing throughout the aquarium, much to the delight of the aquarist who discovers them.

CAPTIVE REPRODUCTION: SEXUAL

Sexual reproduction in captivity is perhaps the ultimate complement to the success of a coral keeper. Coral spawnings in captivity are still rare events, though they are becoming more frequent. In the aquarium, spawning has been successfully induced through careful temperature and dimmable "moonlight" control. Although spawning is not yet predictably inducible, a mature, stable, healthy tank is likely to see at least some sexual reproduction, given enough time and proper care. At the very least, the brooded planulae of *Pocillopora* species may be a reasonably common occurrence.

Single spawns, to date, seem more frequent than mass spawnings. Perhaps the stress of collection and the small size of many captive and wild-collected specimens reduces their functional sexual maturity so that only the older or long-established species are likely to spawn. Indeed, in many reports of mass spawnings in private aquariums, the systems were quite mature with long-term resident corals present.

Most hobbyists who have observed spawnings at night—and they almost always occur at night, as in the wild—have noted that the spawning corals seemed unusually "bloated," "inflated,"

Successful settlement of a **Tubastraea sp.** (stony coral) in a reef aquarium.

or "puffy" for a day or more before the release. Immediately prior to one release in my tank, the corals adopted strange configurations, and many had extended sweeper tentacles. It may be possible in some cases to see ripe planulae nearing the surface of the oral opening or to see ripe gonads through the coral tissue.

Unfortunately, because most spawnings go unnoticed, the vast majority of fertilized eggs are removed by the protein skimmer or other filtering devices before they can settle. The rest will most likely be eaten by fishes that seize the opportunity for a most delectable midnight snack. Spawnings can also produce a bit of a paradox. The amount of spawn released into the water by even a single coral can be substantial, and visibility in the tank can be reduced dramatically. The eggs of female colonies can also contain toxic metabolites. Oxygen levels, redox, and other water parameters may be affected quite rapidly. An important decision must be made by the aquarist: worry about the spawn or worry about possible effects of the spawn on the other tank inhabitants? In my opinion, the spawn should be removed with a very fine net (plankton mesh) and transferred to a separate tank, if possible, for settling.

A simple and inexpensive device for capturing spawn is described in Styan (1997) using an air bubbler, a plastic jar, a plastic bag, a piece of tubing, and a small valve. Substrates of various compositions can be utilized to attract the planulae when they settle, including live rock, acrylic, sand, etc. It seems that coralline algae are a preferred substrate for many corals, although work with settlement in jellyfish planulae has shown considerable interspecific variations, with strong species preferences for some materials over others. It is quite possible that corals have similar specificities for settlement, perhaps also depending on chemical cues. There may be a certain amount of genetic programming in some corals that allows them to recognize key signals.

What might be done to induce sexual reproduction in captivity? A combination of these efforts should be considered: moving the aquarium hood or bulb position by even a few degrees to affect the relative position of the "sun" and "moon" over the tank (the azimuth); making precise temperature modulations to follow readings taken from actual areas where corals have been collected; slightly varying the photoperiod that corresponds to any seasonal differences for the area; and using artificial moonlight on a dimmer switch to "trigger" the spawning event.

Even without such intentional manipulations, sexual reproduction does occur in aquariums, but very little practical information is yet known about how to initiate and manage such events successfully. Nevertheless, it may not be too optimistic to anticipate the day when future aquarists will boast of having huge crops of "baby corals" sexually produced in aquarium settings.

CHAPTER 6

Taxonomy

Coral Classification—and Its Limitations

A s a young scuba diver, I often carried a small waterproof species-ID card purchased at the local dive shop. It attached to a mesh collection bag that dangled around my waist. I was on a mission back then, not only to possess everything I could get my hands on (especially shells), but also to know the names of the corals and fishes I came across in my explorations of various coral gardens off the north coast of Jamaica.

The problem was that the 6 x 8 illustrated card had a very limited number of animals, and thus I was constantly confronted with species I could not identify. Asking the local divers was sometimes an exercise in frustration.

"What are the big round corals that look like a maze?" I asked on one occasion.

"Yah mahn, dat's de brain coral," the Jamaican replied.

"Well," I went on, "then what's the other big round one that looks different and has the other kind of grooves?"

"Dat's brain coral, too."

Sigh. This was no great help to the impatient curiosity of a

> ## "To a very significant extent, the complexities of coral taxonomy are man-made."
>
>
>
> J.E.N. Veron,
> *Corals of Australia and the Indo-Pacific,*
> 1986

10-year-old. For the majority of casual divers, snorkelers, and marine aquarists, knowing the term "brain coral" is enough, even if it encompasses a number of different species. For those of us who are drawn more to the scientific side of identifying and keeping corals, however, a brain coral is no longer just a brain coral.

Enter taxonomy, the science of classifying, describing, naming, and identifying organisms. (Looking back, I now know that my Jamaican acquaintance and I were talking about boulder brain coral, *Colpophyllia natans,* and grooved brain coral, *Diploria labyrinthiformis.*)

SCIENTIFIC NAMES

Taxonomy is a biological classification system based on the increasing similarity within and between groupings of living things. A Domain, for example, is the broadest grouping of similar organisms, which are subdivided into Kingdoms. The species is the most-basic unit of classification. In classical taxonomy, members of a species can breed with each other, but not with members of other species. (As we shall see, however, this rule does not work well for many corals.)

Taxonomic classification follows the main hierarchical

Source of confusion: many genera and species are known as "brain corals," including this **Diploria labyrinthiformis** (grooved brain coral). (Cayman Islands) groupings, or taxa, shown in boldface. The individual organism is usually described by its genus and species name, a naming convention called **binomial nomenclature**. For example, the diminutive golfball coral of Florida and the Caribbean has the following taxonomy and would be called *Favia fragum*:

Kingdom: Animalia
Subkingdom: Metazoa
Phylum: Cnidaria
Class: Anthozoa
Family: Faviidae
Genus: *Favia*
Species: *fragum*

Naming confusion: ***Colpophyllia natans*** (boulder brain coral) has also been called the giant brain coral and closed valley brain coral. (South Florida)

Note that the genus name is capitalized and the species name is not capitalized. Both are written in italics. When writing about numerous species of the same genus, the genus name is frequently abbreviated (e.g., *F. fragum*). The plural of genus is genera, and the terms **generic** and **specific** refer to genus and species, respectively. For example; intrageneric means within a genus, while interspecific means between species.

In the taxonomy of organisms, Latin names are traditionally used. This should not be intimidating. Almost everyone already knows more Latin taxonomic names than will be provided in the entirety of this book, though they may not realize it. Consider these common genus names: *Salmonella* for a group of common bacteria, *Rhododendron* for a group of well-known shrubs, *Homo* for the human race. When the genus and species is followed by a name and year, this is the name of the scientist who first described the species and the year it was described. If this information is in parentheses, it means that the species was originally assigned to a different genus. For example, *Montipora digitata* (Dana, 1846) was described by U.S. geologist and mineralogist James Dwight Dana in the mid-nineteenth century but was originally put in a different genus.

Practice and usage make scientific name pronunciation and recognition second nature. In fact, learning scientific names is really easier than learning common names, even if the words look and sound strange at first. Many names describe physical characteristics. For example, the name *Montipora digitata* tells us that this species is typically digitate or fingerlike; *Distichopora violacea* tells us that this species is violet-colored.

The common names of corals can vary from country to country, region to region, and even aquarium shop to aquarium shop. In addition, many corals of different genera are given the same common name, leading to confusions. Consider the internationally popular aquarium coral *Catalaphyllia jardinei*, which a British aquarist might know as comb or wonder coral, but which most North Americans call elegance or elegant coral. Some shopkeepers, however, refer to this same species as meat coral—a nondescriptive label that is also used with various other fleshy corals of different genera. Thankfully, there is a growing trend in aquarium circles today to use Latin genus names, such as *Acropora* and *Xenia* as common names. In order for coral enthusiasts to communicate effectively, they must steer clear of common names and use scientific designations, even if they are unsure of the pronunciation.

I often use the family group name as a descriptive when describing characteristics of the group as a whole; for example, a faviid or pocilloporid is a member of the Family Faviidae or Family Pocilloporidae, respectively.

SPECIES AND OTHER DEFINITIONS

A **species** is defined as the largest unit of reproductive capability. This means that a member of a species can breed successfully with other members of the same species, but cannot produce viable offspring with other species. It is the basic unit of biologic classification.

Unfortunately, this definition works well with many life forms, but seems somehow less than adequate with corals. To confuse the usual distinctions between species, interspecific hybrids are common in corals. Furthermore, corals have classically been sorted taxonomically according to their skeletons. In other words, a living coral is denuded of its polyps, the elements of its limestone skeleton are compared, and proper classification is then established. Up to 60 different skeletal characteristics are used to identify a stony coral species. Because it is now recognized that coral skeletal formations can be influenced by environmental factors, many modern taxonomists will not even attempt to classify corals without the use of DNA testing and gene sequencers.

With soft corals, tiny calcium spicules within the tissue are the only solid elements on which to base taxonomy. There is an obvious drawback to this methodology for the aquarist. Since there may be no way to identify a coral accurately without skeletal or spicule identification, and since the animal (or part of it) must be sacrificed for such classification to occur, what use is it? Practically, very little for the aquarist. The average aquarist is not likely to donate a scrap of coral tissue to a DNA laboratory for an expensive analysis just to ascertain the identity of a specimen. Fortunately, this is not always required because enough skeletal elements may be observable in a living coral to be able to know its species. There are also some species in which the living soft tissue of the coral does indeed contribute to its classification as a distinct species.

Coral taxonomist and author J.E.N. Veron has suggested the following coral-appropriate definition of species: "Species in corals are the most clearly identifiable discontinuities in continuous morphological and/or genetic variation from the population to the genus." Veron makes clear that we are working with human-defined, arbitrary classifications, and he offers this explanation: "Species are operational morphotaxonomic units, that is, units that are recognized by taxonomists and users of taxonomy." In other words, the corals themselves might not agree with the way we slot them into species groups, but without classification there would be chaos.

Though less precise than we might wish, these definitions will be adopted for use within this book. The taxonomy of most corals is based on the work of very early reef explorers and scientific organizations of the eighteenth, nineteenth, and early twentieth centuries. Soft corals, especially, have remained in a remarkable state of confusion, and recent papers suggest that it is indeed time for a review and possible overhaul of the current taxonomy of many species based on modern findings and knowledge.

Stony coral taxonomy is also struggling with its antiquated past. Original species, often based on small collected fragments from early expeditions, were described with abandon, with separate species being named when even slight variations between skeletal specimens were found. Communication and records involving ecological data, collection location, and other pertinent data were often missing or inaccurate. Important microhabitat descriptions were (and to some degree still are) almost totally lacking, as the prolific classifiers of the nineteenth century worked primarily with specimens brought up by dredging, rather than hand-collection.

Over time, these methods have lost credibility with the realization of the variability of coral forms and distributions, including factors such as: sedimentation, light, water flow, temperature, depth, salinity, subtotal immersion, physical damage, disease, substrate variability, and genetic disparity. Finally, most collected soft coral specimens were hideously distorted by preservation in embalming-type fluids. To look at the lumpy mass of gray tissue in soft coral taxonomy papers is roughly the equivalent of classifying a wad of chewing gum by appearance.

Taxonomy today is rapidly changing in many ways. With only a fraction of the total reef biota classified, massive and unprecedented environmental changes are taking place, creating pressure to speed the work before mass extinctions occur. At the same time, science is increasingly aware of the physical variability of corals and the limitations of traditional taxonomic approaches.

Using molecular probes with actual samples of genetic material from corals and their zooxanthellae, modern taxonomists are able to establish relationships between groups based on their phylogeny or common evolutionary history. This is known as cladistics, with genetically related organisms grouped into **clades**. This methodology, while not yet perfected, may prove to be a better way to organize corals. Unfortunately, it is also proving that there can be many species where we once thought there were few—and, conversely, few where it was once thought there were many.

With all this in mind, one must realize that the exact identification of corals with any degree of accuracy by aquarium hobbyists (or even professionals) is simply not possible for many species. Even the world experts are often unable to identify a

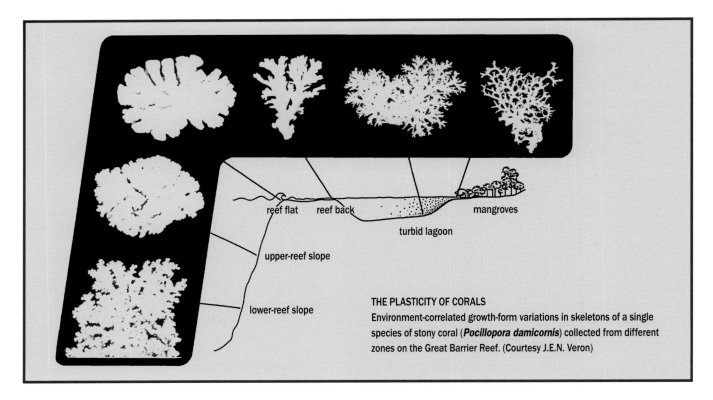

THE PLASTICITY OF CORALS
Environment-correlated growth-form variations in skeletons of a single species of stony coral (*Pocillopora damicornis*) collected from different zones on the Great Barrier Reef. (Courtesy J.E.N. Veron)

species from external appearances alone. Nor is knowing the species altogether of paramount importance to aquarists.

With a recent push to adopt new taxonomic standards, some of the classifications in this book may soon be changed in favor of new ones. Many corals have been reclassified in recent years, so that readers of this text may wonder what species other books are even referring to in light of many now-extinct terminologies. Furthermore, there are likely to be as many unknown and unrecorded species as those actually known to exist.

Aquarists attempting to identify a "mystery coral" must face the fact it might be nothing more than a morphological variant of a known species. On the other hand, it may be a rarity or even an entirely new species. Adding to the confusion, it is possible that a coral may have been sold as a particular species, when in fact it is outwardly similar but an entirely different species.

The presence of ecotypes and ecomorphs are common in stony corals. **Ecotypes** are variants of species that differ in appearance due to some degree of genetic variation and varying degrees of environmental modification. These are sometimes described as "subspecies," a term with only limited use in describing corals. **Ecomorphs** are corals that are genetically similar, yet have strongly divergent appearances based on environ-

mental influences. Over time, ecomorphs may become isolated enough, or divergent enough, to become new species.

Some additional terms and concepts are useful in understanding and discussing taxonomy:

Phylogeny describes the evolutionary history of a particular group of organisms. **Ontogeny** refers to the developmental history of an individual organism.

Divergent organisms are related genetically, but show differences in their anatomical structure caused by different environmental pressures. **Convergent** organisms are not genetically related but show similarities of anatomical structure caused by similar environmental pressures.

Genotype is the genetic makeup of an organism or group of organisms, as evidenced by a trait or complex of traits. **Phenotype** is the observable makeup of an organism, or its appearance, as a result of the interaction of its genotype and the influences of its environment.

VARIABILITY ABOUNDS

One of the major problems with coral taxonomy is the **plasticity** of species. What is meant by plasticity? Corals are inherently variable and adaptive organisms. Within a single species, the external form and appearance of a coral can differ dramatically. The classic demonstration of this is a collection of skeletons of six specimens of *Pocillopora damicornis* assembled by Dr. J.E.N. Veron in his book *Corals in Space and Time* (see illustration on facing page). To the untrained eye, these skeletons appear to represent a number of very different species. In fact, they are all *Pocillopora damicornis* but with significant differences in form attributed to where they happened to grow on or near the reef.

A coral's appearance can vary significantly from region to region. Even within a single reef, a species may have further degrees of variability based on ambient light levels, water flow conditions, available foods, and so forth. Even within a single species found in virtually identical locations within the same reef, high degrees of apparent differences can be found. Species differences can be seen in the variations between corallites and in overall colony growth forms. These differences can be found within biotopes, within the same reef locale, within regions, within entire geographic locations, and over geologic time. Determining the species identification of many corals by gross external appearance is therefore exceedingly difficult; in many of the soft corals it is simply impossible.

Yet the remarkable ability of corals to adapt is what accounts for their inherent variability of appearance and also their success. As with other animal groups, even within a single species of coral there can be considerable genetic disparity, with a range of physical appearances. The variability of genetic material between differing subsets of a species may account for some of the differences in morphology or external appearances seen, and some species exhibit astonishing plasticity of form. However, corals from the genera *Pavona*, *Acropora*, and *Montipora*, which depend to a large degree on asexual fragmentation or self-cloning for reproductive success, may be less likely to show significant genetic differences and may express less plasticity.

Hybridization resulting from crossbreeding between species may result in reproductively viable colonies, which are, by long-standing definition, new species. *Montastraea annularis* (the lobed star coral of the Caribbean) is a highly plastic species that until recently was thought to have several morphotypes. Two of these, *M. franksi* and *M. faveolata*, are now believed to be valid "sibling species" based on the study of hybrid crosses (Szmant et al., 1997). As the authors of this work state: ". . . in most all scleractinian cases examined, there is a common finding that morphological and ecological distinctness do not correlate with genetic or reproductive distinctness." Such unpredictability in the corals makes the taxonomic waters all the more murky and mysterious—and a great source of fascination for all who take a serious interest in the complex lives of these reef animals.

Montastraea annularis (lobed star coral): see "sibling species," below.

Montastraea faveolata (mountainous star coral): see species above and below.

Montastraea franksi (boulder star coral): see "sibling species," above.

CHAPTER 7

The Corals

Families, Genera, and Species of Special Interest to Aquarists

Although some may dream of a truly complete photographic guide to the corals of the world, the reality is that such a compilation would be a mammoth undertaking. There are some 2,000 coral species identified and living today, with new discoveries constantly being made. The real challenge comes in the phenomenal differences found within these species. It has been estimated that many species would require 50 or more individual photographs just to represent the known variations in form and color. Clearly, the forces of evolution have played themselves out in a fantastic diversity of corals that defies compilation in a single volume.

The selection in this book will focus on those families and species of particular interest to reef aquarists. They are arranged primarily by order then family (taxonomically), then by genus and species (alphabetically). While this collection of aquarium corals and photographs is among the most extensive yet published for the marine hobbyist, it is far from complete. In general,

> **"We are astonished to see how slight and how few are the differences, and how manifold and how marked are the resemblances."**
>
>
>
> Charles Bonnet,
> *Contemplation de la Nature,* 1764

there are simply too many species to show in a work of this scope, and a representative sample of typical variations is presented wherever possible.

In some cases, morphological variations are shown to emphasize the chameleonlike variability of certain corals. For most, very typical specimens are shown to provide familiarity with a genus or species. Comparisons of similar genera or species are sometimes shown to compare or contrast features. In large part, the photographs were taken in natural settings on the reef without disturbing the corals. This provides a realistic view of the settings in which these animals establish themselves as well as appearances that haven't been modified by captive conditions. In terms of availability of species to aquarists, these are the mainstays and potentially available choices of today, but there is really no telling what others will become available.

Not found here are the sea anemones, whose dismal record of survival in captive systems for the past three decades should restrict them to the care of advanced and determined marine aquarium keepers.

Also omitted are the cnidarian oddities such as jellyfishes, along with rare species that are extremely uncommon and have

Turbinaria reniformis (yellow scroll coral) with smaller colonies of *Pocillopora eydouxi* (brush coral) and a Darkfin Hind (*Cephalopholis urodeta*). (Fiji)

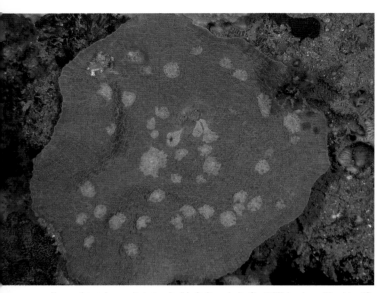

Unusual specimen photographed in Indonesia by Scott Michael: positive identification of corals from photos, without skeletal analysis, is often an impossibility.

little or no history of captive coral husbandry. The *Corynactis* species, for example, are quite beautiful but rarely encountered. At this point, I feel that too little is known about the requirements of these species to warrant their being included in a book of husbandry. In time, this may change. Until then, the aspects of the biology and ecology of such species is best left to the descriptions of what is known about the corals in nature. I have, however, listed the representative genera of many uncommon groups within the descriptions of each family, so that the reader gains an appreciation for the diversity of these groups, and perhaps to inspire further investigations by those who are so inclined.

Novice aquarists sometimes draw the conclusion that a label of *"Acropora* sp." or *"Acropora* spp." (meaning an unidentified *Acropora* species or group of *Acropora* species, respectively) is an indication that the author or photographer didn't take the time to make a clear identification. In fact, identifying many corals from photographs alone is impossible in many cases, even for professional coral biologists. Field identification of living corals is tenuous, even with a hand lens. True identification usually involves laboratory analysis of tissue and/or skeletal material. Aquarists who wish to dissect their corals and carry out microscopic examinations are urged to do so using information from the scientific literature. Wherever there was doubt about the identity of a particular coral pictured in these pages, I have opted to go no further than identifying it to the genus level.

For most marine aquarium enthusiasts, I hope this guide will serve as a reliable identification and care resource; some may use it as something of a "wish book" to plan future coral acquisitions. However, as appealing as many of these specimens are, I think the most important information to be gained from these pages is an understanding of what it will take to allow a particular coral to have a reasonable chance of survival (and even reproduction) in a home aquarium. The corals we choose to own deserve no less, for not only are they tremendously beautiful additions our reef aquariums, they are the precious jewels of the sea.

THE CORALS: PHYLUM CNIDARIA, PART 1

Order Milleporina
e.g., *Millepora*

Order Stylasterina
e.g., *Distichopora*

Class Scyphozoa
e.g., *Aurelia*

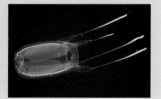

Class Cubozoa
e.g., *Cubozoa*

Class Hydrozoa
    Order Milleporina (fire corals)
    Order Stylasterina (lace corals)
Class Scyphozoa (jellyfishes)
Class Cubozoa (sea wasps)

KEY: Covered in this text.   Not covered in this text.

Millepora complanata (blade fire coral): the fire corals are interesting and undemanding aquarium specimens when provided intense light and strong water motion.

to the rest of the colony. Dactylopores house the retractile **dactylozooids**. These tiny hairs regularly protrude from the skeleton, giving it a fuzzy appearance, and are responsible for prey capture. They contain strong nematocysts that can release a proteinaceous toxin, causing a painful sting or burn if handled. This may not be surprising, as the fire corals are more closely related to jellyfishes and hydroids than to corals. In feeding, dactylozooids remain stationary; once prey is captured, the gastrozooid swells outward. Then the dactylozooids bend inward, like the tentacles of stony corals, bringing the prey to the gastrozooid, which then extrudes its mouth over the prey. The only other pores found on the surface of the *Millepora* skeleton, are the special **ampullae**, which produce the sexual **medusae**.

Identification: The species of *Millepora* adopt many growth forms including laminar, branching, encrusting, and massive colonies. Other descriptions of colonial growths refer to the highly variable forms of *Millepora*: lacelike, leaflike or bladed, and boxlike. *Millepora* will likely adopt any growth form based largely on water flow. Encrusting colonies are found in turbulent water conditions, but are also the initial form of a new colony in other areas. Lacelike growth forms are vertical (**apical shooting**) arising from an encrusting base under low water flow. Infilling of the

Millepora alcicornis (branching fire coral): note hairlike structures called dactylozooids, responsible for prey capture and containing stinging nematocysts.

Millepora dichotoma (fire coral): fanlike colony with *Xenia* sp. (Red Sea)

Millepora platyphyllia (fire coral): species forming vertical plates. (Maldives)

skeleton occurs if a lacelike growth form receives stronger water movement, and it may then take on the leaflike or bladed growth form. Boxlike forms commonly result when leaflike growth forms suffer repeated damage from strong water motion.

In general, *M. complanata*, *M. dichotoma*, and *M. platyphyllia* are typically leaflike species subjected to wave surge. *Millepora tenella* and *M. exaesa* commonly form heavy branches or lumpy protuberances throughout reef zones. *Millepora alcicornis* is a branching species found in variable areas. Though 13 species are currently recognized (Boschma, 1948), it appears that the species of *Millepora* are on a convergent evolutionary path.

Natural Location: Found worldwide, *Millepora* are particularly conspicuous in areas of high current and light, common from sea level to 40-m (130-ft.) depths. They are one of the first colonizers of new reef areas and one of the last to go in dying reef zones. Clearly, they are highly adaptable and quite hardy. *Millepora* are so abundant that they are the third-largest contributor to reef growth worldwide, typically covering about 10% of the reef, but up to 50% in some areas. Their tolerance of physical disturbance and their resilience on damaged reefs make their increased presence in the future likely, despite a low rate of sexual reproduction. *Millepora dichotoma* is most common in distinct zones in less than 3 m (10 ft.) of water.

Colors: *Millepora* are strongly photosynthetic, with a uniform mustard yellow to dark brown color, rarely pink or green. *Millepora squarrosa*, an Atlantic species, tends to be pink to cream-colored. The tips or edges of colonies are regularly white or lighter-colored. The combination of stark brownish skeleton, no visible polyp or corallite structure, and white margins is usually a clear indicator of this genus.

Captive Care: *Millepora* species are capable of encrusting living tissue and may take over the skeletons of other corals and gorgonians. In fact, *Millepora* may grow faster in the direction of nearby corals in order to overgrow them. They are quite hardy, but definitely prefer their natural conditions of strong light and water movement. *Millepora* are not extremely fast-growing, typically extending their linear growth from 4-20 mm (0.18-0.8 in.) per year. In the aquarium, these corals are not subject to many diseases, predators, or parasites, but they do tend to bleach fairly easily. Some common predators and parasites of *Millepora* are *Pyrgomatina* barnacles, carnivorous and commensal polychaetes, nudibranchs of the genus *Phyllidia*, and several filefishes (*Aluterus* and *Cantherhines* species).

Small bubbles of oxygen are frequently released from brightly illuminated specimens as the zooxanthellae exude surplus oxygen. This may be an indication of excessive light levels. Once colonies begin to encrust the substrate, it is very difficult to stop their growth. Consideration of this fact is notable when placing such corals in an aquarium. Despite being strongly photosynthetic (approximately 75% of their carbon needs are provided by photosynthesis in shallow water), all species are also eager plankton feeders. They may also actively culture excess zooxanthellae to be digested. They do not have the coordinated feeding methods of *Stylaster* and depend largely on aggressive nematocyst capture and intracolonial transport through their canals.

In reproduction, *Millepora* (and all hydrocorals) do not release planulae but have free-swimming medusae. The medusae are short-lived, and their release occurs synchronously with many other fire corals, but they are not dependent on lunar cues. Gametes develop quickly—in 20-30 days, rather than in the months or years that it takes for stony corals (Soong, 1998).

Millepora tenella (fire coral): can compete aggressively with other corals.

Millepora alcicornis (encrusting fire coral): completely covers a gorgonian stalk.

Special Information: Hawkfishes are often seen perched atop these corals. Because their pectoral fin extremities are not covered by tissue, the sting of the coral doesn't affect them and they gain *Millepora*'s protection in the process. In the wild, *Millepora* are not subject to attack by *Acanthaster planci*, the Crown-of-Thorns Starfish. Even these predators must feel the "flame" when they approach fire coral. *Millepora* can give the reef keeper a quite annoying burning/itching sensation, although the perceived pain varies from individual to individual. (Tender skin, as on the underside of the wrist, is more susceptible to the stinging effects.) Ammonia (in whatever form is most convenient) or a powdered meat tenderizer may be effective in alleviating the pain or itching.

Millepora are capable of chemically detecting gorgonians, such as *Plexaura* species, toward which they then increase their growth, eventually overtaking and encrusting them.

Collection Impact: *Millepora* collection has an exceptionally low impact on natural reef communities. They are excellent candidates for captive reproduction—even a small chip of *Millepora* can form an interesting colony quickly, if provided with proper conditions. It is hoped that they will be propagated commercially to a greater extent in the near future.

ORDER STYLASTERINA

FAMILY Stylasteridae Gray, 1847

Genera: *Distichopora*, *Stylaster*, and others.
Unlike the Milleporidae, Family Stylasteridae has many genera and species, which are divided into three subfamilies: Stylasterinae (Gray, 1847), Distichoporinae (Stechow, 1921), and Errininae (Hickson, 1912). Most are tropical, but not all. Some live in very deep water and are found in all the oceans. Nonetheless, and despite the many beautiful corals in the Family Stylasteridae, only two genera are available with some regularity to reef aquarists: *Distichopora* and *Stylaster*. Another Stylasteridae genus, albeit rarely from tropical waters and unavailable in the aquarium trade, is the blue *Allopora*. These are mostly temperate and may be suitable for cool-water aquariums.

GENUS *Distichopora* Lamarck, 1816
(dis'-tih-kop'-oh-rah)
Common Species: *D. anceps, D. coccinea, D. gracilis, D. irregularis, D. nitida, D. violacea.*
Common Names: lace coral, ember coral.
Identification: Beautiful and often lacy, *Distichopora* species are easy to identify. Their skeletons branch ornately in one plane, like *Stylaster* (see below), but their branches are thicker and have blunt ends. Unlike *Stylaster* and *Millepora*, *Distichopora* have no recirculating canal systems and the dactylopores align next to the gastropores laterally along the branches. A middle row of gastropores has a row of dactylopores on each side of it. *Distichopora irregularis* is likely to have a massive skeleton with odd protuberances. *Distichopora violacea* is the most common species and adopts a lacy, uniplanar, branching formation. Colonies are typically quite small.
Natural Location: Like *Stylaster*, *Distichopora* are ahermatypic and aposymbiotic hydrocorals found in shaded and usually higher nutrient conditions. The often-lacy colonies are found growing in crevices and under overhangs, in and among the reef structure.
Colors: Common colors are purple, salmon, and yellow, with other bright hues found in nature but rarely imported. Zeaxanthin and astaxanthin skeletal pigments are present in *Distichopora*

Distichopora sp. (lace coral): note fanlike shape and blunt branch tips.

Distichopora spp. (lace corals): vividly colored but very difficult to feed.

Distichopora violacea (lace coral): young colony. Note extended dactylozooids.

Distichopora sp. (lace coral): lacks zooxanthellae, often found in shaded spots.

in even greater quantities than in *Stylaster*.

Captive Care: *Distichopora* are not regular aquarium offerings, though they are becoming more available. At least one group is using them in captive-propagation efforts (Curry, 1996-7, pers. comm.). They do not have the powerful sting of *Millepora* species and are dependent on plankton and absorption of nutrients for all their energy needs. Aquarium care is the same as for *Stylaster*— it is likely that these hydrocorals will also succumb to dietary insufficiencies. They are perhaps even more difficult to maintain than *Stylaster*, owing to their lack of a circulatory system for nutrients.

Special Information: *Distichopora*, like *Stylaster*, have skeletons composed of aragonite and/or calcite.

Collection Impact: Collection is limited by low demand and there is little impact on reefs from the taking of these specimens.

GENUS *Stylaster* Gray, 1831
(sty-lass'-ter)

Common Species: *S. elegans, S. roseus, S. sanguineus,* and many others.

Common Names: lace corals, fire corals.

Identification: *Stylaster* are closely related to *Millepora*. They were long ago presented as belonging to a separate order of the Subgroup Filifera, characterized both by their long, tapering, filiform-type tentacles, and also by their formation of temporary ampullae. These ampullae produce gonophores that remain attached to the colony during reproduction, in contrast to the free-swimming medusae of *Millepora*. The stinging cells of *Stylaster* are not potent as in *Millepora*, and the colonies are ahermatypic. (*Millepora* skeletons are composed of aragonite, while *Stylaster* may be at least partially composed of calcite.)

Although occasionally encrusting or heavily arborescent, *Stylaster* are usually quite delicately branched, with fine, lacy networks of brightly colored calcareous skeletons. Their skeletons are less porous, and consequently harder, than those of their relatives. Colony branches are thin and pointed and tend to grow in a single plane. Their growth forms are much more fragile than those of *Millepora* and *Distichopora*, and they usually form smallish colonies.

Stylaster are aposymbiotic (azooxanthellate), depending entirely on tiny planktivorous prey capture for feeding and nutrient absorption. The cyclosystems of *Stylaster* are so prominent and well organized that they may take on the appearance of corallites in some species.

Natural Location: *Stylaster* are found predominantly under overhangs and in caves, under rocks and corals, almost always in shaded conditions. They are often found in areas of strong current where their lacy growth form serves them well in the capture of drifting plankton.

Colors: *Stylaster* are commonly pink, with white margins and branch tips. Orange, yellow, white, and other variations, usually quite bright in hue, are also common. The bright coloration of the skeleton is due to the presence of dietarily acquired carotenoids, notably astaxanthin and zeaxanthin.

Captive Care: In captivity, *Stylaster* have a very poor record of survival, though unskimmed, Jaubert, and algal-turf-scrubber-style tanks may have a higher likelihood of supporting their needs. It is likely that these corals fail to thrive due to dietary insufficiencies. They need a steady, moderate current and are most natural-looking in dimly lit conditions, though exposure to light is not likely to be harmful. Ultraviolet bleaching of their skeletal pigments may be likely in an exposed location. Laminar currents and regular feeding with natural or substitute plankton is likely to be required in order to achieve success with these hydrocorals.

Special Information: *Stylaster* have a cyclosystem in which a single gastrozooid is surrounded by at least two to three dactylozooids, often more. There may be two types of dactylozooids present: one that is a "sweeper," the others being normal rigid hairs typical of the taxon. The longer, thicker sweeper polyps actively patrol the water for prey. *Stylaster*'s skeletons are composed of aragonite and/or calcite. The name *Stylaster* comes from the calcium column at the base of the pores, called a style.

Collection Impact: *Stylaster* are not hermatypic and can be easily collected by breakage from parent colonies. These corals are neither as common as *Millepora* nor as successful in captivity, but the small number of imports does not pose a significant threat to reef populations.

***Stylaster* sp.** (lace coral): often grows from overhangs in the wild. (Sulawesi)

***Stylaster* sp.** (lace coral): demands special care and feeding in the aquarium.

Stylaster roseus (rose lace coral): common Caribbean species with sponge.

The Octocorals

Soft Corals, Stoloniferans, Gorgonians, and Sea Pens

Living proof that a stony skeleton is not required for success on the reef, the Subclass Octocorallia includes some of the most vividly colored, alluring, and numerous cnidarians on the reef. Although the casual term "soft coral" is widely used as a synonym for "octocoral," this group is actually composed of several distinctive groups.

From an aquarist's perspective, the Subclass Octocorallia consists principally of the soft corals (Suborder Alcyoniina) and the gorgonians (Suborders Scleraxonia and Holaxonia). Other members of the subclass include the blue coral (Order Helioporacea), the mat polyps (Suborder Stolonifera), and the sea pens (Order Pennatulacea).

The majority of octocorals are characterized by having soft bodies without a limestone skeleton and polyps with eight tentacles. The well-known blue coral (*Heliopora coerulea*) is an exception, as it does have a calcareous skeleton, but it is the only member of its taxon. Organ-pipe coral (*Tubipora musica*) is another nonconformist, with a red calcareous skeleton, though it shares many traits with other stoloniferans. The gorgonians derive structural strength from **gorgonin**, a stiff but flexible proteinaceous substance that is related to mammalian horns—and that gives the group the sometimes-heard vernacular label of "horn corals."

Dendronephthya **spp.** soft corals emblazon an Indo-Pacific lagoon pinnacle, **left.** Classic eight-tentacled polyps on a *Minabea* **sp.** octocoral, **right.**

Rather than depending on a calcium carbonate skeleton, the form and shape of the majority of octocorals is maintained by tiny calcium skeletal pieces embedded within the body called **sclerites** or **spicules**. Except for some of the spicules of gorgonians, these supporting elements are composed of calcite, not the aragonite common to the skeletons of their stony coral relatives. It appears that these spicules are manufactured in epidermal cells, then migrate internally from the epidermis. They eventually reside mostly in internal formations or within the mesoglea. Some octocorals also generate calcified holdfast structures to anchor themselves to the substrate while others produce rodlike internal supports to hold the colony erect.

DISTRIBUTION OF OCTOCORALS

Despite large fields of octocorals on reefs throughout the Indo-Pacific, most of these corals are not hermatypic and are usually not dominant. Several species of *Sinularia*, however, are considered to be reef-building, and there are some areas where *Xenia*, *Sarcophyton*, *Lobophytum*, and *Cespitularia* can occasionally be dominant. Generally, soft coral diversity and total coverage is greatest at depths below the maximum density of stony corals (Dineson, 1983). Soft corals are rarely found in areas of high wave action, excepting certain sturdy encrusting forms. Most of their coverage occurs more prolifically throughout the inner-reef zones. They are often dominant over scleractinians where high sediment conditions predominate. Along the east coast of Africa, soft corals may exceed the scleractinian corals in number and mass, with 84 endemic genera and an estimated 200 species present. Sixty percent or more of the coral coverage of many reefs of Africa is by soft corals, consisting mainly of *Sarcophyton*, *Sinularia*, and *Lobophytum* species (Williams, 1993). The Red Sea also has prolific numbers of soft corals (including abundant growths of xeniids), and the Caribbean has extensive populations of gorgonians.

Though octocorals are mostly ahermatypic by definition, they do contribute greatly to reef sediments because the calcium carbonate content of their spicules is released to the surrounding reef following their death. Amazingly, the spicule content on some reefs is as great as 12 metric tons/hectare (5.38 tons/acre). This amount of calcium carbonate is certainly contributory to the reef mass, even if it is not immediately incorporated into the hard structure of the reef.

ANATOMY, BIOLOGY, AND ECOLOGY

Like the stony corals, most octocorals are **polytrophic** (mixotrophic), meaning they obtain nutrition from multiple sources and are therefore flexible in their adaptation to various energy sources. Because the polyps of most octocorals do not possess many nematocysts compared to stony corals, prey capture is mostly restricted to microplankton. The entrapment and consumption of such tiny prey is likely to be aided by mucus secretion and ciliate transport, although the epidermis of octocorals often has fewer cilia than that of stony corals. However, octocorals do have extremely well-developed epidermal microvilli, structures generally associated with high rates of absorption across biologic surfaces. Trapped particles can be carried from the highly efficient filter-feeding tentacles into the polyp mouth by ciliary action. Octocoral polyps can be of one or two types, autozooids and siphonozooids.

Autozooids are the primary feeding polyps, with eight feathery tentacles at the ends. The tentacles are always hollow, with the cavities continuing into the feathery **pinnules**, or pinnae. Autozooids are also responsible for the production of gametes.

Siphonozooids are reduced polyps that aid in water circulation throughout the colony and may not be present in all species.

Octocorals with only autozooids are termed **monomorphic**, while those with both autozooid and siphonozooid polyps are termed **dimorphic**. When most polyps arise from a localized or distinct area of the coral, this area is often called the **polypary**, or polyparium—or sometimes the **capitulum**, or "head."

The ends of octocoral polyps containing the eight tentacles and mouth are called **anthocodiae**, which may be on the end of stalks (**anthosteles**) that can retract into raised hillocks, if present, called **calyces** (*sing.* **calyx**). The calyx is part of the **coenenchyme** that acts as a shelter and, sometimes, a pedestal for the polyp on the coenenchyme surface. The coenenchyme is often supported by sclerites buried within. The interconnected gastrovascular canals of the polyps are also embedded in the coenenchyme. The anthocodiae are often referred to as the upper part of the autozooid, which may or may not be retractile, depending on the species (see illustration, page 39).

The **introvert** is the basal part of the polyp that connects to

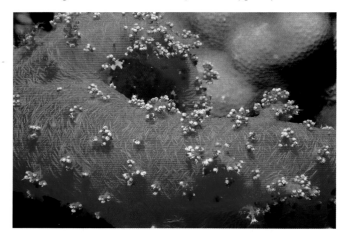

 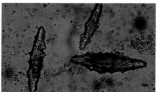

Close-up of supporting sclerites in the flesh of a *Dendronephthya* sp. coral, **top**. Sclerites from *Alcyonium* sp. magnified 100X, **bottom left**, and 400X, **bottom right**. Microscopic examination is essential in identifying many soft corals.

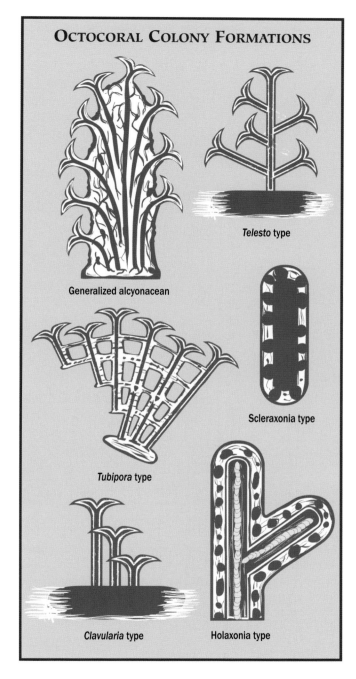

OCTOCORAL COLONY FORMATIONS

Generalized alcyonacean

Telesto type

Tubipora type

Scleraxonia type

Clavularia type

Holaxonia type

traction is complete. Polyps are interconnected by interior canals called **solenia**. These canals allow nutrient and possibly chemical communication.

FEEDING AND PUMPING

Octocorals are capable of adapting to different water flow rates to maximize the capture of food particles. The inherent plasticity of the soft corals allows them to bend or warp their surfaces to allow their polyps to take prey more effectively through various filtering techniques. Fingerlike colonies are generally found in areas of slower water flow, while lobed and rounded types are seen more commonly in faster water flow. Change in morphology, even within a species, is a common response to different prey capture and flow situations. Despite the common belief that the soft and leather corals do not require food, their planktonic inputs are substantially similar to the stony corals, the most notable difference being the smaller size of the prey. The polyps of a colony "sieve" the water and ensnare particles with as much tenacity as aggressive stony corals, even though most alcyonaceans do not possess penetrating-type nematocysts. Prey size seems to be very important in most soft corals, with typical zooplankton often being too large or active to be caught. Therefore, bacterioplankton, nanoplankton, particulate matter, and phytoplankton may play a more important role than larger zooplankton in their heterotrophic needs.

One of the most fascinating behaviors of corals is the ability of some species of soft corals, notably the Family Xeniidae, to pulse their tentacles rhythmically—even when not in the act of catching visible prey. In fact, this behavior may not be as strange as it seems. The typical soft coral feeding response following prey capture involves the tentacles pulling together toward the mouth, either singly or in unison. Soft corals also show various degrees of neuromuscular polyp contraction that, in a less-dramatic way, are basically the same as the pulsing of the xeniids.

Even so, absorption of nutrients from the water is likely to be a more significant source of nutrition to these corals than prey capture. Octocorals are quite capable of substantial uptake of nutrients directly from the seawater into their cells. Many are symbiotic and have large numbers of zooxanthellae in their tissues. Despite sometimes higher algae densities, their photosynthetic efficiency is not as great as for most stony corals. Coupled with their generally deeper depth distribution, this means that they may be more dependent on heterotrophy through feeding and, most probably, direct uptake of organic matter and bacterioplankton. Soft corals reach their highest densities at about 15-25 m (50-80 ft.) in depth, where light intensity is only about 15-20% of surface values.

the anthostele and lies inside the calyx, which contains the mesenterial filaments. Polyp contraction and retraction occurs as follows: the tentacles fold inward over the polyp mouth, shortening. Then the anthostele becomes flaccid and collapses until re-

Soft corals dominate some reefs, as in this shallow area in the Coral Sea, festooned with many colonies of **Sarcophyton spp.** and the bushy gorgonian **Isis hippuris**.

Only the most photoadaptive species, such as *Efflatounaria*, *Briareum*, and some *Sarcophyton* and *Sinularia* species can meet their energy needs (even theoretically) without feeding at these depths, though they are prolific here. The common brown to green coloration of many soft corals is due to their zooxanthellae, although gorgonians and some soft corals may have colored pigments in their tissues as well. Other brightly colored aposymbiotic soft corals (*Dendronephthya* species, many gorgonians, etc.) may even incorporate pigment into the sclerites themselves; their coloration is acquired solely by diet.

Many other organisms are commonly found living with the octocorals. Some, such as fire corals (*Millepora* species), are entirely parasitic on the octocorals they slowly encrust. Others, such

as the surface-foraging ovulid gastropods and certain copepods that dwell in the gastrovascular cavities—seem to have a commensal relationship: the octocorals are not harmed, but the other organisms rely entirely on them for their survival. This attribute of commensalism is far more pronounced with the octocorals than with the scleractinians.

SPECIES IDENTIFICATION

For the aquarist determined to identify soft corals to the species level, a rich and frustrating experience lies ahead. In fact, aquarium amateurs will quickly find little straightforward guidance from the work of marine zoologists, whose own work on this large group is incomplete—and often confusing. "All octocorals thus far examined have been identified to genus, but only two are positively identified to species level," said Gary C. Williams in *Coral Reef Octocorals* (1993), referring to African octocorals.

It has been estimated that only about 50% of the total number of species of octocorals is presently known. Perhaps more astonishing is the estimate that 40% of octocoral species from southern Africa (where much of the research has been done) are incorrectly identified or are not valid species (Williams, 1993). Thus taxonomy in the octocorals is often an exercise in futility. It is amusing to see books and people proclaiming the genus and species names of many soft corals based on a photograph or a visual sighting while diving or visiting an aquarium shop. To do so accurately, given the facts of octocoral biology and their flexible morphologies, is nearly impossible.

Because there is no limestone skeleton to use in identification, the taxonomy of the octocorals is based on the colony growth form, the polyps (kind, distribution, and structure), and the sclerites. It is the distinct appearance of the sclerites (spicules) that allows for the accurate identification of most soft corals, although the shape of the colony is also important in the identification of many genera and species (Verseveldt, 1980, et al.). Within the coral, the sclerites are sometimes adorned with protuberances called **tubercles**, and the shapes are described according to certain nomenclature. Sclerites are often identified by removing a piece of tissue and dissolving it in household bleach to extract them. The small calcium pieces are then compared to existing records in order to identify the coral. Of course, to those keeping these corals in their aquariums, this procedure is of limited value and of questionable importance—identification to the genus level is all that is normally possible for many octocorals. It is unlikely that there are as many true species of soft and leather corals as are currently thought to exist, and it is also likely that many true species are as yet unrecorded.

Most coral research has revolved around the more prolific and obvious stony corals. With the host of ecological and anthropogenic imbalances currently taking place with coral reefs, octocorals have been, proverbially, "swept under the rug." Soft corals were first described in the mid to late nineteenth century, with another large description of species taking place in expeditions to the Great Barrier Reef in the early twentieth century. Since that time, there have been only a handful of works that describe octocoral species, especially the soft corals. The 1950s and 1980s saw occasional research and taxonomy work, and recently the subject has been coming into focus again. Occasionally, new species are reported, but even notable soft coral researchers and scholars are in favor of a complete revision of most taxa of the octocorals.

PATTERNS OF GENERAL TOXICITY IN SOME SOFT CORALS

Sarcophyton

Dendronephthya

Anthelia

Regularly highly toxic
- *Sarcophyton* spp.
- *Lobophytum* spp.
- *Lemnalia* spp.

Variably highly toxic
- *Cladiella* spp.
- *Paralemnalia* spp.
- *Sinularia* spp.
- *Heteroxenia* spp.
- *Nephthea* spp.
- *Efflatounaria* spp.
- *Cespitularia* spp.

Occasionally highly toxic
- *Xenia* spp.
- *Briareum* spp.
- *Dendronephthya* spp.

Rarely highly toxic
- *Anthelia* spp.
- *Capnella* spp.

This "call to arms" is being partly fueled by the discovery of many unknown and undocumented chemical compounds known to be produced by octocorals. Among these are isoprenoids, phenols, terpenes, diterpenes, carotenoids, prostaglandins, and steroids. Economically valuable prostaglandins are prevalent in species of *Plexaura*, which have become a valuable natural resource for many islands. Of course, immediate interest focuses on potential pharmaceuticals that could benefit humanity. Recent findings of pharmaceutical agents derived from gorgonians seems to be fueling the drive to isolate more "wonder drugs" from other groups. But the tremendous variability of the little-studied octocorals, along with a bewildering number of compounds that can be produced by even a single species, makes such endeavors a daunting research assignment. Ensuring that already-endangered reef habitats are not overharvested in these pursuits is a further challenge.

Aquarists have a much longer history of success with the octocorals than with the scleractinians. "Leather" corals became quite popular in the early Berlin systems in Europe, as they were among the first corals to be successfully maintained. Peter Wilkens wrote about these "lovely flower animals," and began bringing them back with him from the wild to raise in captivity. They proved to be quite hardy, growing into impressive, beautiful specimens even in the relatively primitive aquarium conditions at that time. As the reef hobby spread to the U.S., these were among the first corals to become readily available. They remain very common today, and are often hailed as "starter" corals. Most new hobbyists begin their experience of captive corals with some sort of soft coral, and they are usually available and heartily endorsed by stores, hobbyists, magazine articles, books, and suppliers.

Lovely unidentified member of the Family Nephtheidae in Lembeh Straits, Indonesia. Although beautiful, such corals present difficult husbandry challenges.

HUSBANDRY CONSIDERATIONS

It has also been found that some genera of soft corals are inherently more toxic than others, with a degree of variability between species (see box, page 111). Soft corals that already have some physical defenses to predation, such as sharp spicules and retractable polyps, generally prove less toxic (or as toxic) as those without physical defenses. Still, exceptions are common, with *Lemnalia* and *Sarcophyton* species consistently very high in toxicity and *Cladiella*, *Capnella*, and *Anthelia* species being consistently low. *Lobophytum* and *Sinularia*, along with many other corals, have species representatives that are both highly toxic and barely toxic. Still, at least half of all known soft corals produce toxic compounds. Furthermore, some soft corals seem to maintain high levels of toxic compounds in their tissues, while others release them into the surrounding water. This difference is probably a result of various functions of the chemicals, and at least partly determined by the needs of the particular species.

All of this should at least serve as a warning to aquarists: soft corals can be a threat to other organisms in a home-scale aquarium. Given the obvious complications that can arise in a small, closed system, it should not be surprising that there are many reports of mysterious and inexplicable recessions of stony corals in tanks housing large specimens or many types of soft corals. Such anecdotal observations are becoming numerous enough that it is possible to see some trends.

Some stony corals seem infinitely more sensitive to the chemicals produced by certain octocorals. Others seem comparatively unaffected. The obvious zonations that occur in the wild should be carefully considered, and it is in the coral keeper's interest to have soft corals and hard corals minimally intermixed, if at all. The soft corals are all beautiful and hardy in their own right, but as we begin to learn about the habitats, physiology, and biology of our captive corals, we must also bear the responsibility of maintaining proper conditions for them. It should be decided, in advance, if an aquarium will house a relatively easy-to-keep and quite beautiful display of soft corals, or if it will contain predominantly stony corals. Mixed displays should be researched beforehand, with consideration of potential incompatibilities. Many octocorals are exceptionally appealing—fast-growing, hardy, and reproducible. This makes them highly desirable, but just as we would not keep a parrotfish with our stony corals, many soft corals deserve similar respect for their biochemical weaponry.

In fairness, there are some advanced aquarists who disagree with this view, and who feel that soft and stony corals can be intermixed in systems that are properly set up and managed. Foam fractionation or skimming and activated carbon are generally

GUIDE TO THE OCTOCORALS

Helioporacea
e.g., *Heliopora*

Stolonifera
e.g., *Tubipora*

Alcyoniina
e.g., *Sarcophyton*

Scleraxonia
e.g., *Briareum*

Holaxonia
e.g., *Swiftia*

Pennatulacea
e.g., *Ptilosarcus*

Phylum: Cnidaria
Class: Anthozoa
Subclass: Octocorallia
Order: Helioporacea (blue coral)
Families: Lithotelestidae, Helioporidae
Order: Alcyonacea (stoloniferans, soft corals, gorgonians)
Suborder: Protoalcyonaria
Families: Taiaroidae
Suborder: Stolonifera
Families: Cornulariidae, Clavulariidae, Tubiporidae, Coelogorgiidae, Pseudogorgiidae
Suborder: Alcyoniina
Families: Paralcyoniidae, Alcyoniidae, Asterospiculariidae, Nephtheidae, Nidaliidae, Xeniidae
Suborder: Scleraxonia
Families: Briareidae, Anthothelidae, Subergorgiidae, Paragorgiidae, Coralliidae, Melithaeidae, Parisididae
Suborder: Holaxonia
Families: Keroeididae, Acanthogorgiidae, Plexauridae, Gorgoniidae, Ellisellidae, Ifalukellidae, Chrysogorgiidae, Primnoidae, Isididae
Order: Pennatulacea (sea pens)
Family: Veretillidae

---

acknowledged to be good tools for removing or diminishing the toxins. (Carbon must be changed regularly to afford a consistent level of protection. Some aquarists always add fresh carbon when introducing a new specimen or trimming a coral.) Still, less-experienced aquarists are advised to use caution in mixing stony corals with soft corals, especially those that are known to be highly toxic. Even advanced aquarists might be well advised to watch closely for the chemical impact that certain soft corals may be having on their systems, especially as toxicity can change over time.

ORDER HELIOPORACEA

The Order Helioporacea consists of two families: the Lithotelestidae and the Helioporidae. Both are highly unusual for Octocorallia because they are externally calcifying—the polyps form an external skeleton of aragonite. (The Family Tubiporidae has the only other genus in the octocorals with an external skeleton.) The Family Helioporidae, the familiar blue coral, has a massive skeleton, whereas Family Lithotelestidae does not.

FAMILY Lithotelestidae (Bayer, 1992)

This family contains a single genus, *Epiphaxum* Lonsdale, 1850. The genus, like *Heliopora*, is calcifying. The four *Epiphaxum* species form mostly aragonite corallites connected by stolons. The corals are white, and the polyps contain sclerites made of calcite. They are very infrequently available to the aquarium trade. A complete coverage of the genus can be found in Bayer (1992).

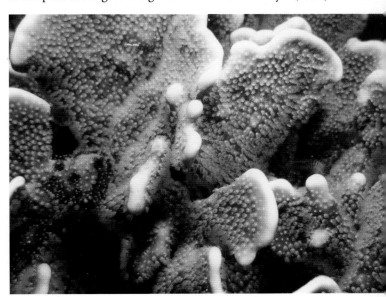

Heliopora coerulea (blue coral): one of the few reef-building octocorals.

FAMILY Helioporidae Mosely, 1876

In the time of the Tethys Sea and worldwide warmer ocean temperatures, Helioporidae was among the most dominant families of corals in the ocean. However, the family didn't fare well when the seas cooled during the last Ice Age, and all but one genus consisting of a single species have become extinct. *Heliopora* is thus considered something of a living fossil. Even today, it maintains abundance only in a narrow equatorial band of the tropical oceans, where its preference for higher temperatures is a reminder of the loss of its less-tolerant kin. With warming ocean temperatures likely in the future, it may again become a more competitive coral, with the possibility of more species appearing over time.

GENUS *Heliopora* de Blainville, 1830

(heel'-ee-oh-pohr'-ah)

Common Species: *H. coerulea.*

Common Names: blue coral, ridge coral.

Identification: Although technically an octocoral, *Heliopora* is hermatypic and has as much in common with stony corals and hydrocorals as with octocorals. Despite having an aragonite skeleton, the polyps are connected by ribbonlike stolons contained within a massive, common coenosteum. Its growth forms are branching, platelike, columnar, or encrusting. Often all growth forms are displayed within the same colony; the shape is, surprisingly, not primarily environmentally induced. Polyps are quite long and thin and dwell within a canal system of tubes throughout the skeleton. The lack of corallites on the surface, combined with the obvious eight-tentacled polyps, make *Heliopora* unmistakable.

Natural Location: This very common species thrives in a brightly lit and high-energy environment, being most abundant from depths of 6-9 m (20-30 ft.). It can, however, occur in a wide variety of environments and may be the dominant coral on some reefs. *Heliopora* is found most commonly in equatorial regions.

Colors: The skeleton color is greenish gray to light brown on the outside, with the characteristic blue pigment hidden within the skeleton. The inner coral skeleton is from pale to deep blue with gray-white to olive polyps.

Captive Care: *Heliopora* prefers strong lighting and currents, though it is quite tolerant of moderate light and current. They will occasionally shed an outer "skin"; this behavior is seen among many octocorals and is completely normal. Because it is uniquely attractive, common in nature, quite hardy, and fast growing, *Heliopora* makes an excellent addition to any aquarium. It used to be only infrequently available to the trade but is now quite common. This coral prefers a higher temperature than most, optimally around 29°C (84°F).

Special Information: A unique coral comprising the only species of its genus and family, *Heliopora coerulea* is most well known for its dried blue skeleton, sold commonly as a souvenir or curio. When broken, the skeleton reveals veins and crystals of a dark blue pigment. Originally called helioporobilin, the pigment was later found to be a type of biliverdin. To produce the pigment, the coral has the extraordinary ability to strip the surrounding water of iron, then oxidize the iron to a blue salt that is deposited in the skeleton. The skeleton itself appears to be formed by an invagination of basal tissue. In contrast to gorgonians, which secrete their skeletal elements interiorly, *Heliopora* secretes "inside out," forming a hard external skeleton.

Collection Impact: This is a common, highly successful, and easily harvested coral; its collection should not pose any significant threat to wild populations. Furthermore, the volume of imports

Heliopora coerulea (blue coral) in a shallow lagoon. (Maldives)

Blue coral growing on glass-bottom tank with blue skeleton visible in reflection.

Cornularia sp. (mat polyps), with individual polyps sheathed in horny material.

is quite low compared to many other coral species. *Heliopora* is easy to grow in captivity and should have popular appeal. At least one commercial source is already offering captive-grown colonies.

ORDER ALCYONACEA Lamouroux, 1816

This order is composed of numerous suborders of highly variant taxa: Protoalcyonaria, Stolonifera, Alcyoniina, Scleraxonia, and Holaxonia. Together, these comprise the leather corals, soft corals, mat polyps, and gorgonians. With the exception of members of the Family Xeniidae, they are characterized by being "firmly attached to solid substrate by a spreading holdfast" (or coenenchyme) or by being "anchored in soft substrate by rootlike projections of the axial skeleton or of colonial coenenchyme" (Bayer, 1981). Polyps can be monomorphic or dimorphic.

SUBORDER PROTOALCYONARIA
FAMILY Taiaroidae

This small family consists of just two genera of unobtrusive octocorals, but the family is distinct enough to warrant its own taxon. The two genera, *Taiaroa* Bayer and Muzik, 1976 and *Hartea* Wright, 1864, are separated by the size of their polyps and sclerites. *Taiaroa* has larger polyps. These are solitary octocorals, consisting of a single polyp, that do not form colonies asexually by budding. Not normally collected for the aquarium market.

SUBORDER STOLONIFERA
Mat Polyps

The stoloniferans are octocorals that share a common trait of having many tall or short individual retractile polyps connected by runners, known as **stolons**. The combined stolons of the corals form either a network or a solid mat of polyps that are usually en-

crusting, occasionally forming vertical or flaplike elements. *Tubipora musica*, of the Family Tubiporidae, which forms a calcium skeleton, is an exception. Although most stoloniferans have poorly developed mesentaries and are not likely to capture prey, at least some may be more likely to feed actively, including *Sarcodictyon* spp. (Ocana et al., 1992).

There are five families: Cornulariidae, Clavulariidae, Tubiporidae, Coelogorgiidae, and Pseudogorgiidae.

FAMILY Cornulariidae Dana, 1846

Consisting of a single primitive Pacific genus, *Cornularia* Lamarck, 1816, this is a group of small stoloniferans with separate polyps, no sclerites, and a less "rubbery" mat. The polyps are connected only at their bases, and the basal part of the polyps is sheathed in a horny material. This genus is occasionally represented in the aquarium trade, where it is frequently incorrectly identified as *Clavularia*. Those I have seen have all had very large polyps, most of which were in the process of dying. Most of their sheaths were already empty of polyps, looking like semirigid brown tubes.

FAMILY Clavulariidae Hickson, 1894

Clavulariidae consists of four subfamilies (Clavulariinae, Sarcodictyiinae, Telestinae, and Pseudocladochoninae). These contain numerous genera

The Clavulariidae are a fairly diverse family of corals, although the exact number and descriptions of the species are somewhat limited. In some colonies, tall polyps arise from well-separated calyces that, in some way, resemble the tubes of polychaete feather duster worms. Polyp appearance is similarly diverse, with polyp tentacles that can be feathery and pinnate—or stark and bare; long and thin—or flat and wide, and so on. As the taxonomy of the Clavulariidae is already scientifically "loose," identification of collected species is difficult and often inaccurate. The polyps have small sclerites for support, as does the coenenchyme. The coenenchyme is a gelatinous or horny substance in which the lower parts of the polyps are embedded. This substance forms the supportive structure of the mat and helps to lend rigidity to the polyps, allowing them to remain upright. The mats can be heavy, thick, and encrusting, or as simple as thin, almost nonexistent runners connecting widely separate polyps. These layers can build upon each other, forming a fibrous mat that encrusts and anchors the polyps to the substrate. Stolons, which give rise to the colonies, are generally not divided into two layers, except in *Pseudocladochonus*, *Pachyclavularia*, *Telestula*, *Rhodelinda*, and *Scyphopodium*. Most members of this family have a very limited

Clavularia sp. (clove or glove polyps) note typical feathery or pinnate tentacles.

Family Clavulariidae: unidentified stoloniferan mat polyps. (Indonesia)

Family Clavulariidae: may rely heavily on uptake of dissolved nutrients.

Family Clavulariidae: very hardy if provided adequate light and water motion.

uptake of nutrients through nematocysts or other prey capture, and tend to depend more heavily on the uptake of dissolved organic material, the products of their zooxanthellae, and photosynthesis. Most studies have failed to isolate prey of any type in their gastrovascular cavities. They have significantly reduced nematocysts, and may even culture excess zooxanthellae that are then digested for their nutritional content. The degree to which bacteria and microplankton are important to these corals is not well established, though the pronounced pinnae along their tentacles appear more than vestigial.

SUBFAMILY Clavulariinae: This is the subfamily of the Clavulariidae most familiar to marine aquarists from exposure to the genus *Clavularia*. Other genera are: *Bathytelesto* Bayer, 1981; *Rhodelinda* Bayer, 1981; and *Scyphopodium* Bayer, 1981.

GENUS *Clavularia* de Blainville, 1830
(klav'-yoo-lahr'-ee-ah)
Common Species: *C. hamra*, *C. inflata*, *C. viridis*, and perhaps 40 others. There is a single Atlantic species, *C. modesto*.
Common Names: clove or glove polyps, palm tree polyps, fern polyps.
Identification: *Clavularia* are encrusting soft corals that form mats and clumps connected by stolons: rootlike growths that adhere to the substrate. The stolons are flat, unlayered, and bandlike, and they interconnect to form a meshlike network supported by unfused sclerites. Many cylindrical tubelike calyces, about 1-5 cm (0.5-2 in.) tall, rise up uniformly from the mat. The autozooid solitary polyps of varied colors arise from the calyces and can retract completely into the base of the calyx. Many species have very attractive, feathery tentacles, with numerous long pinnae.

Clavularia sp. (clove polyps): hardy corals that will spread in reef aquariums.

Clavularia sp. (clove polyps): note similarity to palm tree fronds or leafy ferns.

Family Clavulariidae: unidentified mat polyps with tubular tentacles.

When fully extended, the polyp can resemble a palm tree or leafy fern because of its pinnate nature. Daughter polyps do not arise from the parent, but from the ends of the stolons. Identification of these corals is not easy, even for experts, and it is possible that many stoloniferans sold as *Clavularia* actually belong to other genera.

Natural Location: *Clavularia* grow predominantly in the recesses of fore- and back-reef slopes and in rubble zones, although they may be found throughout the reef. Despite their abundance, certain species have a narrow depth distribution.

Colors: The mats of *Clavularia* are usually cream, brown, or gray. The polyps are varied colors, including green, purple, yellow, white, brown, and cream.

Captive Care: These are generally very hardy corals that prefer moderate to bright light and moderate to strong current for rapid growth and encrustation of substrate. Of course, the diversity of the genus makes the potential for more specific requirements entirely possible, especially concerning light, since the depth distribution of certain species may be narrow. Observation in the aquarium will be the determining factor as to whether or not their requirements have been met. All species are subject to detritus collection and the concomitant proliferation of filamentous algae amongst the stolons. Good water flow and regular "blasting" of the colony with a turkey baster, syringe, or small powerhead is an effective precautionary measure to prevent this problem. *Clavularia* will probably not feed on typical food items that are offered. Like xeniids, they are poorly suited for prey capture, they lack well-developed digestive mesenteries, and they are known to overproduce zooxanthellae for digestion.

Some species have a unique form of planulae formation, with

Carijoa riisei (white telesto): azooxanthellate Caribbean species.

Telesto fruticulosa (orange telesto): rarely seen western Atlantic species.

Polyps of *Carijoa riisei*: requires fine particulate foods and planktonic prey.

the young being brooded on the surface of the colony.

Special Information: *Clavularia* are unusual corals in that they are not easily damaged by the stings of other corals and do not themselves attack other corals. In fact, they possess only rudimentary nematocysts (mostly in the gastrovascular cavity), but seem to have efficient chemical defenses to discourage potential grazers.

Both *Clavularia* and *Pachyclavularia* are sensitive to the aluminum oxide in some phosphate-removing sponges.

Green star polyps are often called *Clavularia viridis*. This is incorrect; see *Pachyclavularia* (page 119).

Collection Impact: *Clavularia* grow in small to large mats that typically must be taken with a piece of the substrate to avoid damaging the colonies. Colonies attached to small pieces of rubble are inherently better suited to collection than those that must be chipped free, not only because of reef impact, but for ease of

collection. They ship reasonably well, and like most stoloniferans, fare well in captivity. They can also be propagated in captivity by allowing them to spread and encrust new pieces of substrate.

SUBFAMILY Sarcodictyiinae: Consists of five genera: *Cyathopodium* Verrill, 1868; *Sarcodictyon* Forbes, 1847; *Scleranthelia* Studer, 1878; *Tesseranthelia* Bayer, 1981; and *Trachythelia* Forbes, 1847. None are offered for sale (at least intentionally) to the aquarium hobby.

SUBFAMILY Telestinae: Consists of four genera: *Carijoa*, *Paratelesto*, *Telesto*, and *Telestula*. None are regularly available to the aquarium hobby, although the first two are fairly well known both in nature and in numerous field guides.

Carijoa F. Muller, 1867: White colonies superficially similar to *Telesto*. Bushy colonies with tall, thin axial polyps, which bud daughter polyps. Pacific species has retractile polyps, tapering bushy branches connected by stolons and frequently covered by a red sponge. *Carijoa riisei* has densely branched, bushy colonies with large white polyps, including a terminal polyp, and white to pale pink stalks. Epizooic growth present. These are pioneer species of new hard substrate in various locations. (Azooxanthellate, it must be fed fine particulate foods and tiny planktonic forms.)

Paratelesto Utinomi, 1958: Similar to *Telesto* but axial polyp has multiple solenia rings.

Telesto Lamouroux, 1812: Polyps retractile into anthosteles and without mesogleal intrusion tissue. Simple unlayered stolons without fused sclerites. Axial polyps have a single ring of solenia. *Telesto fruticulosa* (orange telesto) is found in varied hard substrates in the tropical western Atlantic. *Telesto sanguinea* (red telesto) is a bright red deep-water Atlantic species.

Telestula Madsen, 1944: White to brown colonies of layered stolons with fused sclerites. Mesogleal intrusion tissue present. Polyps retractile into stolons.

SUBFAMILY Pseudocladochoninae: Consists of a single Pacific genus, *Pseudocladochonus* Versluys, 1907. Not available to the aquarium hobby.

FAMILY Tubiporidae Ehrenberg, 1828

The Tubiporidae are best known for the genus *Tubipora*, a familiar octocoral that forms a dark red calcium skeleton that suggests a neatly arranged mass of tiny organ pipes. This family also includes the genus *Pachyclavularia*, the very familiar group known commonly as the star polyps. Both are widespread in the Indo-Pacific, but neither genus is represented in Atlantic waters.

GENUS *Pachyclavularia* Roule, 1908

(pak'-ee-klav'-yoo-lahr'-ee-ah)

Common Species: *P. purpurea, P. violacea,* and others.

Common Names: star polyps, green star polyps, daisy polyps.

Identification: Some *Pachyclavularia* species have growth forms that are very similar to *Clavularia*. However, the flat stolon mats are quite rubbery in texture and less fibrous than those of *Clavularia*—a result of irregularly layered stolons. The polyps that emerge from the stolons are completely retractile, but they are much less featherlike, and lack the lush pinnules typical of *Clavularia*. Instead, they have 8 thin, smooth tentacles that surround a polyp center and oral opening that is often a contrasting color.

As a source of ongoing confusion for aquarists, Green star polyps are often called *Clavularia viridis*. This is incorrect, with

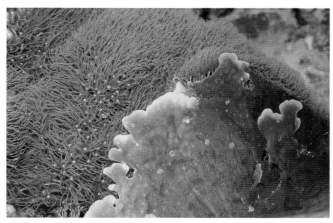

Pachyclavularia violacea (green star polyps): note purple mat on glass.

Pachyclavularia violacea (green star polyps): colors vary from green to white.

Pachyclavularia violacea (green star polyps): encrusting coral skeleton in wild.

Pachyclavularia violacea (green star polyps): hardy and fast-spreading.

Pachyclavularia sp. (star polyps): often sold as "*Clavularia*."

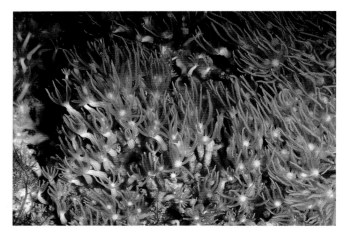

Pachyclavularia sp. (star polyps): note red mat that is typical of this genus.

Unidentified stoloniferan: note retracted polyps.

the proper identification being *Pachyclavularia violacea*. Disagreement about the correct placement of this species has a long history. Quoy and Gaimard in 1833 described two species, *C. viridis* and *C. violacea*. But Gohar (1940) says that *C. viridis* was also described by Hickson in 1894 and then states, "Owing to the inaccuracy of their original description, Hickson (1894, p. 330) suppressed the genera *Anthelia* Savigny, *Rhizoxenia* Ehrb, *Sarcodictyon* Forbes, *Gymnosarca* Kent, and *Cornulariella* Verrill, and included them in *Clavularia*." Following some other taxonomical blunders that resulted mostly from confusion between *Anthelia* and *Clavularia* (which, admittedly, look superficially similar), things were more or less straightened out. Even taxonomy has its scientific scandals—and cover-ups.

Even today, there are some who suggest that *Pachyclavularia* may be synonymous with *Briareum* (page 157), and some sources

list "green star polyp" as an unidentified species of *Briareum*. However, mucus studies with *Briareum* species have shown that they regularly shed mucus "sheets," a trait not shared with *Pachyclavularia*. Furthermore, *Briareum* are known for sending up vertical projections from their mats that contain a medullar axis, whereas *Pachyclavularia* seem capable only of loose folds. *Briareum* are also reported to produce sweeper tentacles. Since *Pachyclavularia* are described only from the Pacific, it may be that this genus shares a common evolutionary progenitor with *Briareum* but has remained separate in space and time. Chemotaxonomic studies have shown that the types and functions of their secondary metabolites are also quite different. Further research may clarify the relationship—some species of either genus may actually belong to the other. Still, most of the literature, including work based on chemotaxonomy, recognizes separation of the two genera (Dineson, 1983; Gerhardt, 1983; Bayer, 1981; Verseveldt, 1977; Mather and Bennett, 1993; Sammarco and Coll, 1992; et al.). Whether or not they should be placed in the Family Briareidae is another question.

Natural Location: *Pachyclavularia* are found, along with *Xenia*, *Clavularia* and other alcyonarians, from fore-reef slopes to lagoons. They are most common on inshore and submerged reef flats in environments with somewhat reduced water flow.

Colors: Purple to reddish-violet mats are a hallmark of the genus. The polyps are normally brown or bright green (*P. violacea*), but other variations may occur. White, yellow, or green polyp centers may contrast with the polyp tentacles.

Captive Care: *Pachyclavularia* are exceptionally fast-spreading corals that are tolerant of both low-level and intense lighting and varying current conditions. Like *Clavularia*, they have mats that should be occasionally blown free of accumulated detritus to prevent filamentous and slime algae from gaining a foothold. Although these corals do not possess any significant numbers of tentacular nematocysts, they can overgrow neighboring corals. Unlike *Clavularia*, however, they can be stung. Some corals with potent stings (e.g., *Catalaphyllia* and *Euphyllia*) will prevent the polyps from emerging from their mats when they are located too near each other. Furthermore, *Aiptasia* anemones can settle among the polyps and prevent localized areas from opening. The pedal attachment of these nuisance anemones may also cause degeneration of the mat. When the mat becomes necrotic, it falls apart like a wet bread crust. This breakdown, though fairly uncommon in these hardy corals, can spread even in a healthy colony. In such cases, it may be necessary to excise the area by cutting into the healthy tissue and then scraping and/or siphoning off the injured area. The remaining healthy areas should soon regrow onto the exposed substrate. *Pachyclavularia* species brood their planulae on the surface of the colony.

Special Information: There are many reports of iodine additions (in the form of Lugol's solution) causing an adverse reaction in these colonies, often leading to a lack of expansion or even colony death. It is not yet known why this occurs, though the strong oxidizing properties and reactivity of elemental iodine may be involved.

As mentioned under *Clavularia*, *Pachyclavularia* species are sensitive to the aluminum oxide in some phosphate-removing sponges.

Pachyclavularia violacea (and likely other *Pachyclavularia* species) possesses significant terpenoid and diterpenoid compounds, presumably as predator deterrents, and competes for space on the reef mostly by overgrowth.

Collection Impact: Removal of large sections of a colony by chipping loose the substrate leaves the reef with temporary scars, but smaller specimens found on loose pieces of rubble can be taken with little impact. Captive propagation is a simple matter with these corals.

GENUS *Tubipora* Linnaeus, 1758
(too'-bih-pohr'-ah)

Common Species: *T. musica*.

Common Names: organ-pipe coral, pipe-organ coral.

Identification: *Tubipora* is an atypical octocoral genus that builds a dark-red skeleton composed of fragile, thin tubes of calcite attached lengthwise to one another. These hardy stoloniferans are unfortunately more frequently sold in souvenir shops and as empty skeletons for aquarium and household decorations than as living specimens. The tubes are actually secreted and fused sclerites, rather than being the normal calcareous skeleton of a stony coral. Retractile polyps that vary significantly emerge from the tubes, displaying the eight feathery, pinnate tentacles that characterize their taxa. The externally fused, calcareous sclerite tubes are further partitioned by horizontal plates called **stolon plates** (tabulae). Once the whole colony of polyps is expanded, the skeleton is totally obscured (unless visible from the sides), and the resultant mass of polyps looks very much like a mat of *Clavularia*. (Oddly, they are more closely related to *Pachyclavularia*.) The size, length, and diameter of the tubes and tentacles vary considerably, though there is only one valid species recognized.

Natural Location: *Tubipora musica* prefers calmer protected wa-

Tubipora musica (organ-pipe coral): surrounded by encrusting blue sponge.

Tubipora musica (organ-pipe coral): note brittle red tubes of calcite.

Tubipora musica (organ-pipe coral): typical appearance with polyps expanded.

Tubipora musica (organ-pipe coral): colony appearance with polyps retracted.

Unusual organ-pipe coral variant: requires brisk water movement to thrive.

ters that are also frequently inhabited by other soft corals, but may be found over a wide range of habitats.

Colors: *Tubipora* has a distinctively bright to dark red skeleton with green, gray, cream, or white polyps.

Captive Care: The skeleton is very fragile, and most *Tubipora* brought to market are broken from large colonies. However, the polyps are mostly isolated from one another except for the layered tabulae that connect the tubes. Therefore, any broken pieces are quite able to survive and grow. Unusual brown-jelly-type infections are somewhat common in this species, though the coral is still hardy. I have found that *Tubipora* is mostly very light tolerant, though bright light is always desirable. Water movement should be brisk, but direct laminar forces may blow the ultra-lightweight colonies from their position and damage them. If not placed carefully, *Tubipora* may have its fragile tubes crushed, re-sulting in the demise of the entrapped polyps. Overall, *Tubipora* thrives in somewhat nutrient-laden, turbid conditions, so aquarists employing heavy foam fractionation may have a more difficult time sustaining this coral. It is also observed to catch prey with its polyps (Lewis, 1982, et al.).

Special Information: The half-broken or empty tubes make excellent burrows for many creatures, and tiny bristleworms seem fond of them. Commensal sponges found within empty tubes of the colony may die and decay, causing local damage to the coral.

Collection Impact: *Tubipora* musica is fairly common, occurring in diverse habitats and growing in large colonies. The colonies are susceptible to considerable damage in the collection process, and this exposes both collected pieces and the parent colony to a greater-than-normal chance of demise. However, it is unlikely that the collection of live specimens poses a significant threat to *Tubipora* in the wild. The mass collection of this coral for aquarium decorations and dried decorative coral skeletons—sometimes huge pieces—is generally considered a greater threat. Thankfully, many aquarists and pet stores are moving away from encouraging trade in these dead skeletons.

FAMILY Coelogorgiidae

This family, similarly, consists of a single genus, *Coelogorgia* Milne, Edwards, and Haime, 1857. It is an interesting twiglike coral that is not frequently available to the aquarium trade. Fosså and Nilsen (1998) discuss its husbandry and report that it is photosynthetic and hardy in captive conditions. Bayer (1981) gives its key as having nonretractile polyps with an oral region of infolded tentacles when contracted, richly arborescent, white, and with very short polyps.

FAMILY Pseudogorgiidae

Consisting of the sole genus *Pseudogorgia* Kolliker, 1870, these stoloniferans are generally unavailable to the aquarium trade. Bayer (1981) gives its key as having colonies with a single dominant axial polyp with a long gastrovascular cavity; thick, coenenchymal walls with numerous short, lateral polyps embedded; unbranched, flattened capitulum on a thin sterile stalk; and attached to annelid tubes or small objects.

SUBORDER ALCYONIINA

This suborder contains at least six distinct families found almost exclusively in Pacific waters, the Indian Ocean, and Red Sea. These are: Paralcyoniidae, Alcyoniidae, Asterospiculariidae, Nephtheidae, Nidaliidae, and Xeniidae. Alcyoniidae, Nephtheidae, and Xeniidae are regular imports to the aquarium trade, although many genera are infrequently represented on both reefs and in the trade. A few species may be found in the tropical Eastern Atlantic. None are present in the Western Atlantic or Caribbean Sea in shallow waters.

FAMILY Paralcyoniidae

Genera: *Carotalcyon, Maasella, Paralcyonium,* and *Studeriotes.* None are especially or commonly available in the aquarium trade or in nature. None are reported from the Atlantic. The only common import is *Studeriotes.*

Carotalcyon Utinomi, 1952: Rarely available; a bright orange, carrotlike soft coral with long, thin, translucent-white, dimorphic polyps appearing across the surface. Polyps are at the end of several partially retractile lobes that are, themselves, at the top of a stalk. Reported as difficult to maintain in captivity.

Coelogorgia palmosa (twiglike octocoral): rarely seen, but aquarium-hardy.

Paralcyonium Milne, Edwards, and Haime, 1850: Widely spaced, retractile, dimorphic polyps arise from the ends of thin branches that make up a somewhat divided "head" or polyparium. The stalk is soft and the branches are retractile.

Maasella Poche, 1914: Colonies consist of short coenenchymal stalks joined in series by a stolon. Clusters of dimorphic polyps arise from the stalks and are somewhat retractile.

GENUS *Studeriotes* Thomson and Simpson, 1909
(stuh-dehr'-ee-oh'-tees)

Common Species: *S. longiramosa* and possibly others.

Common Names: Christmas tree coral, medusa coral, snake locks coral.

Identification: These unusual corals are seen with some frequency in the aquarium hobby. They have the unique behavior of withdrawing their branches completely into the base, in an anemone-like manner, at night. During the day, they unfold and are said to resemble a Christmas tree with drooping branches. Polyps are monomorphic. The appearance of these corals is consistent and remarkable, with little confusion as to identity at the gross level except perhaps to other family members.

Natural Location: Typically found in shallow to mid-depth water, on soft sand or rubble bottoms.

Colors: These octocorals are normally brown to gray, of uniform coloration, or with a pale base. Polyps are often darker than branches and the base.

Captive Care: Despite the brownish coloration, these corals are aposymbiotic and require feeding. Along with a number of soft corals, they send out rooting tendrils from the base to anchor themselves in the substrate. Because of this propensity, a coarse rubble bottom or soft substrate is often the best location for them. Preferring a moderate to strong water flow to supply enough nutrition, they are not particularly easy to keep success-

Studeriotes longiramosa (Christmas tree coral): an unusual species that tends to collapse without good currents, proper substrate, and plankton-type foods.

fully. Accepted foods include live baby brine shrimp and other small plankton-type fare. Starvation and poor water flow are the usual causes of decline, and without good currents and feeding, they tend to collapse and then fail to reexpand. (Buying specimens in such a deflated condition is not recommended, as some do not recover.)

Special Information: These corals are likely to be incorrectly identified, often as *Sphaerella* species. Little is known about their reproduction, and they have not been reported to be amenable to captive propagation via cuttings.

Collection Impact: The unpredictable appearance of *Studeriotes* species in the hobby suggests that they are not subject to heavy or constant harvesting. However, a poor record of survival in captivity because of their nonphotosynthetic nature, along with their requirements for specialized care, make these soft corals less appropriate for collection than most octocorals.

FAMILY Alcyoniidae Lamouroux, 1812
Leather Corals

Genera: *Acrophytum, Alcyonium, Anthomastus, Bathyalcyon, Bellonella, Cladiella, Lobophytum, Malacacanthus, Metalcyonium, Minabea, Nidaliopsis, Parerythropodium, Sarcophyton,* and *Sinularia.* Verseveldt and Bayer (1988) revised the family to include *Eleutherobia,* formed from 16 species formerly part of *Alcyonium, Nidalia* (Family Nidaliidae), and *Bellonella.* Also formed was a new genus, *Inflatocalyx* (an Antarctic species).

Known for their thick and encrusting forms and their leathery skin, these octocorals often form lobed or arborescent colonies with polyps embedded in a heavy coenenchyme. The five genera known to aquarists (*Alcyonium, Cladiella, Lobophytum, Sarcophyton, Sinularia*) of the Family Alcyoniidae form the vast majority of octocoral coverage throughout the world, except in the Atlantic where only a few deep-water species exist (in the genus *Alcyonium*). They are mostly dimorphic with spindlelike sclerites, although many other types can be found.

Many grow very large and can also form large colonial and/or clonal aggregations of individual colonies. These genera have both monomorphic and dimorphic members.

GENUS *Alcyonium* Linnaeus, 1758
(al'-see-oh'-nee-uhm)

Common Species: *A. complanatum, A. digitatum, A. fulvum, A. molle, A. sidereum,* and perhaps 30 others.

Common Names: finger leather coral, encrusting leather coral, colt coral, seaman's hand coral.

Identification: The growth forms of *Alcyonium* are extremely variable, though they are most often described as encrusting and lo-

Finger leather (possible *Alcyonium* sp.): difficult to identify, even for experts, and one of many species sold to aquarists under the general label of "colt coral."

Finger leather (possible *Alcyonium* sp.): close-up of the specimen at left, with lushly feathered polyps. Will thrive and grow quickly with reasonable care.

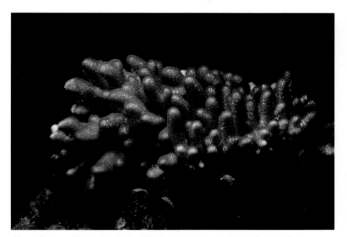

Alcyonium sp. (finger leather): will adapt to many reef aquarium settings.

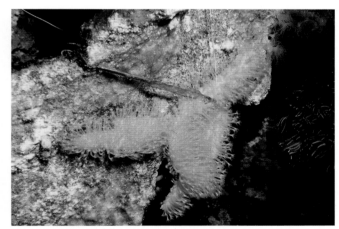

Parerythropodium fulvum fulvum: aquarium propagation of a cutting.

bate species. A stalk for a basal attachment may or may not be present, and the colonies may be fingerlike, globular, lobed, or possess other variations. Most often, they are simply lobed with short projections. Color is not a valid indicator of the species (see below). Even the sclerites are highly diverse between species. However, most species have a somewhat encrusting base and are smaller colonies—not massive. Their polyps are completely retractile and consist only of the feeding autozooid type (monomorphic). The most available species, frequently called *A. fulvum* or *A. fulvum fulvum*, is always encrusting, usually hav-

ing lobed fingers projecting outward from the colony. It is now known that this species is from the genus *Parerythropodium*, a group composed of mainly encrusting forms. *Alcyonium* tends to be upright with or without a stalk (Bayer, 1981), although Williams (1993) describes "membranous" species (*A. membranacea*). Some deep-water species may be aposymbiotic, though most offered in the hobby are photosynthetic.

Natural Location: *Alcyonium* species are common in calm turbid water, along with other soft corals. Some species are from temperate waters, and these are likely to be aposymbiotic. Such ex-

Cladiella sp. (finger leather coral): note short stalks and stubby "fingers."

Cladiella sp. (finger leather coral): showing typical gray-white color.

Cladiella sp. (finger leather coral): easily kept with moderate light and current.

amples tend to form small colonies through fission in order to enhance food uptake. *Parerythropodium fulvum fulvum* occurs between 3-40 m (10-130 ft.) in depth and is a common species.

Colors: Color in *Alcyonium* is highly variable, as yellow, green, red, orange, and brown are all possible. *Parerythropodium fulvum fulvum* contains the yellow pigment fulfulvene, which is responsible for this symbiotic coral's color (Kelman, 1998).

Captive Care: If lighting and water flow are at all adequate, these corals should thrive and grow very quickly. Stronger currents accelerate their encrusting nature, if present. They are also easy to propagate through cuttings. Common problems for *Alcyonium* are the same as for *Sarcophyton*. *Alcyonium digitatum*, and perhaps all *Alcyonium*, rarely capture zooplankton but are known to feed on phytoplankton (Sorokin, 1995, et al.).

Special Information: This genus may be found for sale as "colt coral," but the aquarist should know that this is a notoriously vague common name—and one that exemplifies the troubles of common names. I have seen corals sold with the "colt" label that could possibly be assigned to *Alcyonium*, *Cladiella*, *Litophyton*, *Capnella*, *Nephthea*, or *Lemnalia*. Without sclerite identification, and because of the great diversity and similarity regarding outward appearances, true identification is difficult.

Delbeek and Sprung (1997) assign "colt" to *Alcyonium*, citing a "slimy feel" as an identifying marker. Indeed, the "colt" corals commonly sold tend to be quite slimy. However, *Cladiella* is also routinely considered a synonym of "colt" in the aquarium trade, and this genus is also known for its slippery quality. (At one time, *Alcyonium* was part of the *Cladiella* genus.)

The classic appearance typical of the aquarium "colt" coral includes multiple branches with polyps that show as a feathery ornate plumage, usually cream, off-white, or tan in color. Unfortunately, many *Alcyonium* and *Cladiella* species are very tough and leathery, sometimes encrusting, and rarely show the branching and bushy polyp display of the standard colt coral. Just exactly what genus constitutes the "real" colts is open to debate, but the aquarist should be aware that there are at least four separate genera to which the designation "colt coral" is assigned.

Collection Impact: Abundant in nature and easily collected without damage to the reef. Easily propagated from cuttings.

GENUS *Cladiella* Gray, 1869

(klad'-ee-ell'-ah)

Common Species: *C. australis, C. humesi, C. hunisi, C. sphaerophora,* and perhaps 40 others.

Common Names: finger leather coral, colt coral.

Identification: *Cladiella* species are similar to *Alcyonium*, but they usually have shorter-lobed projections. Often encrusting with a very short stalk, colonies look heavy and lumpy, especially when in a retracted state at night. Their projections are many, forming round to cone-shaped masses of projecting lobes. One of the major corals of most wild soft coral "galleries," along with *Sarcophyton* species, *Lobophytum* species, and *Sinularia* species, these alcyonians are abundant inhabitants of the reef. Although color is a poor indicator of coral identity, almost all of the *Cladiella* species are a cream to gray-white color, whereas *Alcyonium* species are often seen in brown or yellow. The base of most *Cladiella* are a pale white, and the colonies have a heavy mucus coat. However, the colony itself is not terribly soft, but quite thick and durable. Solely autozooid polyps (monomorphic) without calyces are completely retractile. The sclerites tend to be heavy spiked dumbbells (double heads) and robust tuberculated rods.

Natural Location: Wide ranging from back reefs to reef slopes and flats, *Cladiella* are usually found in the company of other family members.

Colors: Usually cream to gray-white, often with contrasting brown or greenish brown polyps. (See Identification section, above, for more details.)

Captive Care: *Cladiella*, like the other common soft corals listed above, are all hardy and adaptable to most conditions of lighting and water movement. Most are reportedly found in mid-depth water, so moderate lighting and current is usually optimal.

Special Information: Most *Cladiella* species that have been investigated are quite nontoxic in terms of chemical defense.

Collection Impact: This is an appropriate group of soft corals for collection or propagation.

GENUS *Lobophytum* Marenzeller, 1886

(low'-boe-fy'-tuhm)

Common Species: *L. crassum, L. pauciflorum,* and perhaps 43 others.

Common Names: finger leather coral, lobed leather coral, devil's hand coral, cabbage leather coral.

Identification: A very common and often dominant genus of soft coral, *Lobophytum* species usually form low, encrusting, dimorphic colonies with thick, heavy, lobed projections. They may also be dish-, or bowl-shaped, or stalked and erect. Colonies can exceed 1 m (3 ft.) in diameter. The capitulum differs from that of *Sarcophyton* in that it tends to form crowded, plated, or fingerlike folds across its upper surface. Stalks are low, wide, and short. The lobed projections are generally present, but can be quite variable in size and number. Both autozooid and siphonozooid polyps are present, though the latter are usually not conspicuous. The polyps are not well-stalked calyces, but mere tufts of tentacles (or reduced stalks) that are completely retractile.

Lobophytum **sp.** (lobed or finger leather): wild colony with polyps retracted.

Lobophytum **sp.** (finger leather or devil's hand coral): polyps extended.

Lobophytum **sp.** (finger leather): extremely hardy, but a threat to stony corals.

Lobophytum **sp.** (lobed leather): unusual colony in Lembeh Strait, Sulawesi.

Lobophytum pauciflorum (devil's hand): a species highly toxic to stony corals.

Lobophytum spp. (lobed leathers): two color morphs, possibly two species. (Fiji)

Lobophytum **sp.** (finger leather): excellent polyp extension in a captive colony.

Primary sclerites are predominantly club-shaped tuberculate spindles, though other types may exist even within the same colony. *Lobophytum* tissue is made somewhat brittle and grainy by an abundance of sclerites. *Lobophytum crassum* is one of the more distinct species, with vertical stalks and retractile polyps equally distributed over the surface, often arising from a convoluted, ridged top edge. The disc-shaped body has lobed projections from its top edge. *Lobophytum pauciflorum*, known as Devil's Hand, is usually mustard to brown with white polyps arising sporadically from the slightly dimpled surface of its smooth and often handlike shape. Species identification of other *Lobophytum*, as well as distinguishing between look-alike genera, will likely require sclerite identification.

Natural Location: *Lobophytum* species are very common on reef flats and in near-shore shallow water, where they may be exposed at low tide. They do inhabit much more diverse locations, but the flats are their primary areas of prolific growth. *Lobophytum pauciflorum* is known to form large tracts on reef crests, competing with the stony corals, though it is found in other locations as well. They frequently expand into large monospecific stands in shallow water and can be a dominant species.

Colors: *Lobophytum* colors are somewhat species-specific, but range from mustard to pinkish, brown, cream, gray, green, and all shades in between. Dull gray, pink, green, cream, and brownish colors typify the common specimens seen in the aquarium hobby.

Captive Care: *Lobophytum* are regular shedders of mucus tunics, and care should be taken to avoid letting the waxy shed material come in contact with other corals. Like most of the other members of the Family Alcyoniidae, they are very hardy corals that adapt well to almost all light and current regimes. The colonies grow rapidly and can attain very large sizes. Common problems of *Lobophytum* are generally the same as those of *Sarcophyton* (see below). Slicing sections of these corals and reattaching them to pieces of hard substrate is a common, easy, and successful method of propagation.

Special Information: Many *Lobophytum* species can cause significant damage to stony corals even without actual contact taking place. Many are considered to be in the "most toxic" category, with more than 20 different terpenoid compounds isolated from various species. *Lobophytum pauciflorum* is considered particularly toxic.

Lobophytum arboreum often provides refuge for juvenile damselfishes who hide among the lobed branches.

Lobophytum crassum, and perhaps other *Lobophytum* species, don't have recognizable gonads until they are over 18 cm (7 in.) across, 2 years old, and weigh about 83 g (3 oz.). This type of size maturity before sexual development is also common in the Scleractinia (stony corals), although less is known about specific development requirements of other soft corals. All polyps of a single colony of *L. crassum* are the same sex.

Collection Impact: These are appropriate soft corals for collection or propagation.

GENUS *Sarcophyton* Lesson, 1834
(sahr'-koh-fy'-tahn)

Common Species: *S. ehrenbergi, S. elegans, S. glaucum, S. trocheliophorum,* and perhaps 33 others.

Common Names: toadstool coral, leather coral, mushroom leather coral, trough coral.

Identification: *Sarcophyton* species are a very hardy group of dimorphic soft corals and one of the predominant octocorals in

Sarcophyton sp. (leather coral): note attractive, elongate autozooid polyps.

Sarcophyton elegans (leather coral): bright yellow color denotes this species.

Sarcophyton sp. (mushroom leather coral): polyps completely retracted.

Dividing *Sarcophyton* sp. colonies: new colonies are easily grown from cuttings.

Sarcophyton sp. (mushroom leather coral): large aquarium specimen.

Sarcophyton sp. (mushroom leather): can easily outgrow a small aquarium.

most areas. There are thought to be at least 36 species worldwide, all characterized by a distinct sterile stalk and a broad, flared, smooth, mushroom-shaped top called a **capitulum**. The capitulum is sometimes folded or funnel-shaped, and it is the area from which the polyps emerge; both autozooid and siphonozooid polyps are present, and they are completely retractile. Tissue is generally soft and firm but easily torn. All known *Sarcophyton* are symbiotic and have large numbers of zooxanthellae in their tissues. They are quite distinct and easily recognized to a genus level. Young colonies tend to have the mushroom-shaped capitulum, with the upper surface becoming more lobed and folded as the colony grows larger. They can also morph their shape to maximize prey capture and under various other conditions. A complete taxonomic review of *Sarcophyton* can be found in Verseveldt (1982).

Natural Location: *Sarcophyton* are commonly found on reef flats and in lagoons, often in the company of both hard and soft coral species. *Sarcophyton elegans* is more abundant in slightly deeper water than *S. trocheliophorum* 2 m vs. 5 m (7 ft. vs. 16 ft.). They frequently form large monospecific stands in shallow water and can be a dominant species. They are both common aquarium species.

Colors: Although many octocorals are brightly colored, members of this group of leather corals are often quite drab by comparison. They are usually brown or cream-colored, owing to the large number of symbiotic dinoflagellates contained near their surface. Some species may be yellow or lemon-cream-colored (*S. elegans*), and these are most often reported to be collected from the waters around the island kingdoms of Fiji and Tonga. Occasionally, the polyp tentacles may be green, although shades of white, cream, and brown are most common.

Captive-bred leathers: two daughter colonies grown from large parent, top.

Sarcophyton sp. (leather coral): small, developing colony on an Indonesian reef.

Captive Care: *Sarcophyton*, like most alcyonians, are extremely hardy in the aquarium and are capable of substantial uptake of nutrients directly from seawater into their cells. They adapt well to most current regimes, although they are not fond of heavy currents. *Sarcophyton* are very photoadaptive and tolerate many lighting schemes. They grow quickly and can become very large in captivity in a short period of time. All shed a surface layer of dead waxy tissue from time to time. This is apparently not a regenerative action but does serve to rid the surface of accumulated algae and waste. Stronger currents in the aquarium will help limit the frequency of this process. During the shedding, many aquarists observe a sick-looking and withdrawn *Sarcophyton* and assume that the coral is dying or that something is drastically wrong in the tank. After the shed, however, the coral reexpands to full glory and appears larger and healthier than ever.

Several species of planaria, nudibranchs, and parasites tend to feed on the coral tissue. A simple 5-minute dip of the coral in freshwater of the same temperature and pH is usually all that is required to remove the parasites and predators. Alcyonians, in general, tolerate such dips very well. Some species of crustaceans may also feed on the tissue. There are occasions when the tissue of *Sarcophyton* degenerates (starts to deteriorate and become "cheesy"). This is normally caused by poor tank conditions, heavy sedimentation, the presence of a toxin, or improper lighting. Affected areas can be trimmed off with a razor blade. I once treated a necrotic and fragile yellow *Sarcophyton* with an extended dip of 10 drops of Lugol's solution to 1 L (1 qt.) of water. I accidentally forgot to remove the coral for 4 hours, but it seemed to be restored by the dip and healed within 24 hours of being put back in the tank. During shedding, and in aquariums where water currents are low, cyanobacteria tend to form on the surface of these (and all) alcyonians. This coating can cause tissue degeneration and may even be toxic in some cases. To avoid problems, the cyanobacteria can be blown off with water currents or lightly brushed away.

Sarcophyton are extremely "cuttable." All sections of the coral are **totipotent**, meaning that a slice of the colony attached by glue or banding to a substrate can reattach and form another complete colony fairly quickly. There is very little risk involved, and almost any type of slicing is possible to create new colonies. The coral can be divided along the length and across the top like a pie, or the capitulum can be sliced off and reattached to a new substrate base. Much of the captive propagation of soft corals is accomplished in this manner—it is simply as easy as "cut and paste."

Sarcophyton reach sexual maturity quite late, with male colonies becoming mature at 6-8 years and female colonies at 8-10 years. Males are also smaller, but must be about 11x11x11 cm (4x4x4 in.) in size, with females having a size requirement of about 61x61x61 cm (24x24x24 in.) for sexual maturity (Benayahu and Loya, 1986). They may also reproduce asexually by fragmentation, budding, and stolons (Tentori et al., 1997).

Special Information: As previously mentioned, *Sarcophyton* species are producers of more than 50 different chemical compounds, many of them unknown and of uncertain chemical makeup. The most well-known, prevalent, and dangerous is sarcophytotoxide. Some predatory nudibranchs even store the toxins from

Sarcophyton elegans (leather corals): blanketing a shallow section of reef in the Coral Sea. Collection impact on the reef is low for this genus.

S. trocheliophorum and other soft corals in their cerata (tubular projections on their backs) for their own defense systems.

Certain clownfishes may adopt *Sarcophyton* as a surrogate anemone. This may be detrimental to the coral as it often becomes irritated, fails to expand fully, and may eventually perish.

Sarcophyton may be capable of some limited movement, like *Nephthea*, by a slow release and reattachment of its base.

Collection Impact: *Sarcophyton* are easily obtainable from the reef. They are quite widely available, both in nature and to the aquarium hobby. Considering the ease with which these corals can be divided and propagated, wild-collected specimens may not even be required in the near future. Simply by cutting sections from parent colonies and attaching them to small bits of coral rubble, large quantities of these alcyonians could be "farmed" in an appropriate and conducive environment—either in captivity or in protected tropical waters—leaving the parent colonies intact and practically untouched.

GENUS *Sinularia* May, 1898
(sin'-yoo-lahr'-ee-ah)

Common Species: *S. asterolobata, S. brassica, S. densa, S. dura, S. flexibilis, S. fungoides, S. gibberosa, S. graye, S. leptoclados, S. macropodia, S. minima, S. polydactyla,* and around 84 others.

Common Names: cabbage leather coral, finger leather coral, knobby leather coral, flexible leather coral, flat leather coral.

Identification: *Sinularia* is one of the largest and most predominant genera of all soft corals, forming low, flat, fingered, and encrusting colonies. Stalks are either vertical and well developed or virtually absent. The corals may form lobes, fingers, or crests with solely autozooid and retractile polyps. The same species may take different forms, as in *Sinularia nanolobata*, which may appear with large spherical or flattened lobes or an aberrant morph with small, rough-surfaced lobes (Benayahu, 1998). The numerous autozooid polyps do not have calyces and appear as tufts. Colony shapes are used in differentiating species, but many resemble *Cladiella* with a heavy, leathery skin. *Sinularia dura* is one of the most common imports, and is easy to recognize with its furled, broad, blunt branches on a prominent stalk. Most *Sinularia* tissue feels dry, tough, and leathery and is not easily torn. If degenerating, sclerites are released like snowflakes falling from the well-supported tissue. *Sinularia flexibilis*, in contrast, along with a few other species, is much more flexible and is slimy to the touch.

Natural Location: Many *Sinularia* species are found in diverse locations and are often a major component of soft coral coverage. They are frequently the most common soft coral in the shallowest waters, possibly because of their strong, supportive sclerites and their ability to withstand strong water movement. They fre-

Sinularia brassica (finger leather): note presence of autozooid polyps only.

Sinularia notanda (finger leather): a hardy species with a stiff stalk.

Sinularia **sp.** (finger leather): unusual colony. (North Sulawesi)

Sinularia **sp.** (knobby leather): unidentified white encrusting specimen. (Fiji)

Sinularia flexibilis (flexible leather coral): note long, flowing lobes.

Sinularia **sp.** (finger leather): aquarium specimen. (Note seahorse, foreground.)

Sinularia dura (cabbage leather coral): a distinctive, extremely hardy species.

Sinularia sp. (finger leather): wild colonies can grow to several meters in width.

Sinularia asterolobata (knobby leather): an unusual species with stubby lobes.

quently form large monospecific stands in shallow, turbid waters and can be dominant species in that location.

Colors: Cream, brown, pinkish, gray, green, and purple.

Captive Care: These corals grow very large and go through periodic shedding of their top layer. *Sinularia* are subject to the same parasites and problems as *Sarcophyton*, but are equally hardy. They are very tolerant of different light and current conditions, though bright light and moderate to strong water motion seem appreciated in most cases. Some experimentation with positioning may be necessary for maximum expansion and growth. Some species, such as *S. dura* and *S. flexibilis*, may reproduce by fragmentation and/or branch dropping. Colony fission also occurs, taking from 3 to 4 months for completion, on average.

Special Information: *Sinularia flexibilis* is a particularly toxic species to other reef inhabitants, with strong terpenes called flexibilide and dihydroflexibilide (also called sinularin and dihydrosinularin) being acutely detrimental to (at least) some species of *Acropora* (*A. formosa*) and *Porites* (*P. andrewsii*). In fact, many *Sinularia* species are classified as being in the "most toxic" category. Studies have repeatedly shown them to inhibit or stunt the growth of stony corals, potentially causing mortalities. Anecdotally, it seems that this is even more pronounced in aquariums, where repeated reports of stony coral demise (especially large-polyped corals such as *Catalaphyllia*, *Euphyllia*, and *Plerogyra* species, etc.) occur regularly in the presence of multiple, large, nearby, or even isolated *Sinularia* specimens.

Some *Sinularia*, such as *S. polydactyla*, *S. leptoclados*, and *S. minima*, form large, heavy accretions of fused carbonate spicules and are considered to be hermatypic in this regard. These formations of cemented sclerites near the base of colonies may be several meters across in colonies that are over 100 years old, and their density is greater than the skeletons of many stony corals (Schumacher, 1997). In *Sinularia polydactyla*, the female colony remains erect during spawning, while the male colonies become flaccid and retracted.

Collection Impact: *Sinularia* are abundant in nature and can be easily and harmlessly collected.

FAMILY Asterospiculariidae Utinomi, 1951

This is a small family consisting of one Pacific genus: *Asterospicularia* Utinomi, 1951. They are not known in the aquarium trade. These are low-growing, bushy, heavy-stalked soft corals with multiple-lobed polyparies, monomorphic, retractile polyps, and stellate spicules that, according to Bayer (1981) resemble those found in some tunicates. Their stalks are sterile, tentacles lack pinnules, and their coenenchyme has honeycombed chambers within it. They are typically greenish brown.

FAMILY Nephtheidae Gray, 1862
Tree, Cauliflower, and Carnation Soft Corals

Genera: *Capnella, Coronephthya, Daniela, Dendronephthya, Drifa, Duva, Gersmania, Lemnalia, Litophyton, Morchellana, Neospongodes, Nephthea, Paralemnalia, Pseudodrifa, Roxasia, Scleronephthya, Spongodes, Stereonephthya,* and *Umbellulifera* (Bayer, 1981).

These bushy or treelike soft corals are generally much more delicate than the heavy-lobed alcyonarians. The nephtheids are almost all stalked and branched, with most having nonretractile monomorphic polyps and a sterile stalk. They have less coenenchyme, and their stalks and branches are filled with large gastrovascular canals that allow them to collapse when water is expelled. The siphonozooids of dimorphic species may play a large role in the transport of water into and out of these sometimes large species and colonies. Their sclerites are generally abundant and clustered in small groups, giving the outer layer a smooth appearance, though a rough feel. These corals are not encrusting and can grow quite large. Branch dropping is a common form of asexual reproduction in most species. They are generally not easy to maintain in captivity, tending to collapse. Their tissue is generally soft and quite elastic. Many genera and species in this family are observed to feed on phtoplankton, particulate matter and/or weakly motile and very small zooplankton (Fabricius, 1995 and pers. comm.). The species are all ahermatypic, split fairly evenly between zooxanthellate and azooxanthellate members. Some genera may have both types of species. Nephtheids are both temperate and tropical, with species living from surface level depths to more than 325 m (1,000 ft.). The taxonomy of the genera is loose and identification is difficult, even to the genus level.

The following descriptions are for the seven genera known to make their way into the aquarium trade (*Capnella, Dendronephthya, Lemnalia, Litophyton, Nephthea, Scleronephthya,* and *Stereonephthya*):

GENUS *Capnella* Gray, 1869
(kap-nell'-ah)

Common Species: *C. imbricata.*

Common Names: Kenya tree coral, tree coral, cauliflower soft coral.

Identification: *Capnella* form small lobed and arborescent capitate colonies. Small, nonretractile polyps arise from a rounded caplike polypary, with many clustered polyps near the terminal ends of branches or atop lobes. In branching forms, they arise along the length of the terminal branches. Long stalks and secondary branches tend to be sterile. Identification to species depends on sclerite identification, with large, numerous sclerites present in the stalk and canal walls. Even recognition to the genus level can be difficult. A key to the genus and species is given in Verseveldt (1977). It may be difficult to distinguish between *Capnella* and *Litophyton*, the primary difference being the presence of leaf-shaped clubs in the coenenchyme of *Capnella*.

Natural Location: Like other nephtheids, *Capnella* tend to grow in clear water with stronger currents on deeper reef slopes. They can also be found in more turbid areas.

Colors: *Capnella* are typically cream to brown, occasionally tinted green, with brown polyps.

Captive Care: *Capnella* seem to be able to receive less nutrition through zooxanthellae than many corals, relying more heavily on heterotrophy. Consequently, adequate food sources from dissolved materials must be present to meet their needs. They reproduce by branchlet dropping, like other family members, as well as by colony fission. The fission process in *Capnella* is not quick, often taking several years to occur. Colonies may be capable of

***Capnella* sp.** (Kenya tree coral): a hardy genus and good beginner's octocoral.

***Capnella* sp.** (Kenya tree coral): note short branches arising from thick stalk.

Capnella imbricata (Kenya tree coral): easily multiplied from colony cuttings.

some amount of movement. Collapsing is common, though reportedly less common than with some other family members.

Special Information: The relative toxicity of *Capnella* has been found to be generally low in the species examined. They seem more prone to be affected or disturbed from contact or near-contact interactions with both stony and soft corals.

Collection Impact: *Capnella* are easily reproduced corals that are moderately common in nature.

GENUS *Dendronephthya* Kukenthal, 1905
(dehn'-droh-nef'-thee-ah)

Common Species: *D. aurea, D. gigantea, D. hemprichii, D. mirabilis, D. rubeola,* and perhaps 250 others.

Common Names: carnation coral, cauliflower soft coral, tree coral, strawberry soft coral.

Identification: The members of the genus *Dendronephthya* are easily some of the most beautiful corals in all the world. Like *Tubastraea*, they appear in nearly every coffee table book on coral reefs. They can exist in spectacular arrays of color; when expanded, they present a gaudy array of spiky polyps. Colonies are somewhat broccoli-like, with strong upright stalks and branches with bushy or ball-shaped bunches of polyps at the terminal ends. Only nonretractile autozooid polyps exist, and the sclerites may even extend outside the polyp tissue. The sclerites of *Dendronephthya* are particularly needlelike, quite long, and often brightly colored. They are easily visible through the translucent coenenchyme tissue of an expanded specimen. It has been supposed that the sclerites, which protrude from the coral in the collapsed state, may help facilitate gas and water exchange.

Natural Location: Though *Dendronephthya* are found in the wild under ledges, overhangs, and in caves, many can also be found on reef slopes in full sunlight. The one commonality is their location in a constant current that provides adequate planktonic input from the surrounding water. They are almost unknown in flow rates less than 5 cm/sec. (2 in./sec.), and tolerate much higher flow rates than other corals. In *D. hemprichii*, polyps are found contracted at flow rates less than 3 cm/sec. (1 in./sec.) and greater than 25 cm/sec. (10 in./sec.), with polyp expansion only occurring at values between these levels (Dahan and Benayahu, 1997).

Colors: *Dendronephthya* are found in vibrant reds, greens, purples, pinks, whites, oranges, and yellows—no doubt they are some of the most flamboyantly colorful of the octocorals.

Captive Care: *Dendronephthya* are entirely aposymbiotic. In nature, they are voracious feeders, directly absorbing many nutrients, and almost constantly feeding on phytoplankton and/or zooplankton. According to one study with *D. hemprichii*, zooplankton comprise only an incidental part of their diet (Fabricius, 1995). However, Sorokin (1991) found another *Dendronephthya* species to be among the most active predators of aposymbiotic octocorals he had studied, throwing into question the popular assumption that all members of this group feed on algal plankton. They have actually been observed producing sweeper tentacles in the wild.

With such glorious colors, it is no wonder that they appear with such frequency in aquarium stores across the country. Their allure of color and beauty, however, will lead to disappointment. All members of *Dendronephthya* are extraordinarily difficult to keep, and all but the most experienced and dedicated aquarists should resist purchasing them. Most collapse upon introduction to an aquarium, never to reinflate. An almost constant drip of phytoplankton and/or zooplankton is necessary to keep them well fed, and a strong, consistent current is mandatory. The need

Dendronephthya sp. (carnation or tree coral): a heartbreak for aquarists because of its demand for heavy, specialized feeding. Note spiny, brightly colored sclerites.

for large amounts of food makes it all but impossible to maintain high water quality within a typical marine reef tank. As with *Goniopora* species, there are cases of aquarists who have maintained these corals successfully, but the incidence of success is low and the reasons are not consistent enough to warrant their continued importation. There are also a number of predatory snails that are "dendro-vorous."

Dendronephthya commonly reproduce asexually by dropping branchlets, through longitudinal fission, and by stoloniferous-type budding. This last method is not a truly correct term, since this coral doesn't really form stolons. However, rootlike growths move outward from the base attachment, each producing 2-15 small colonies, with as many as 200 baby *Dendronephthya*s with

4-12 polyps each produced by a single colony in a week (Dahan and Benayahu, 1997). Probably related to adequate food availability, *D. hemprichii* has been found to release both sperm and eggs almost continuously throughout the year, although this may be water-flow related, because release only occurs if polyps are expanded. Sexual maturity is reached early in these corals, at less than a year for male colonies and less than 1.5 years for female colonies (Dahan and Benayahu, 1997).

Special Information: *Dendronephthya* seem to contain a fairly strong concentration of toxic compounds, despite their prolific sclerites that are also used to discourage predation.

Collection Impact: *Dendronephthya* are in the same category as *Goniopora* in that their record of survival is currently too poor to jus-

***Dendronephthya* sp.** (carnation or tree coral): Indonesia

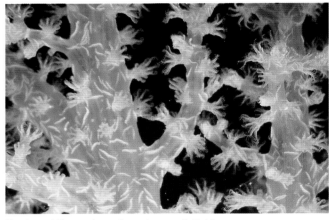

***Dendronephthya* sp.** (carnation or tree coral): Maldives

***Dendronephthya* sp.** (carnation or tree coral): Indonesia

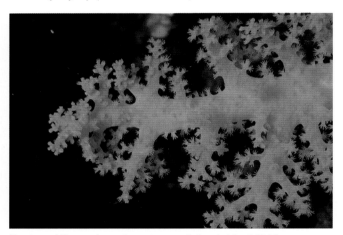

***Dendronephthya* sp.** (carnation or tree coral): Kuredu Island, Maldives

***Dendronephthya* sp.** (carnation or tree coral): Great Barrier Reef

***Dendronephthya* sp.** (carnation or tree coral): Red Sea

Dendronephthya **sp.** (carnation or tree coral): Madang, Papua New Guinea

Dendronephthya **sp.** (carnation or tree coral): Red Sea

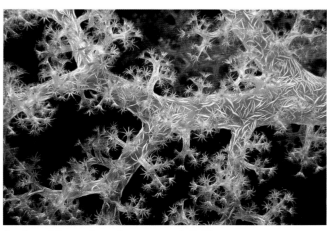

Dendronephthya **sp.** (carnation or tree coral): Red Sea

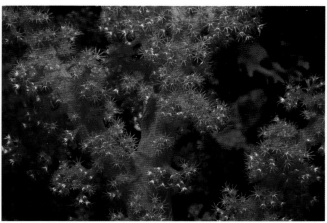

Dendronephthya **sp.** (carnation or tree coral): Red Sea

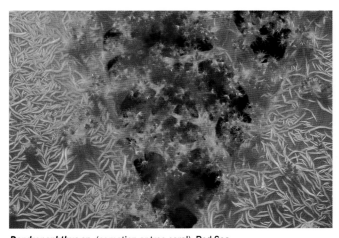

Dendronephthya **sp.** (carnation or tree coral): Red Sea

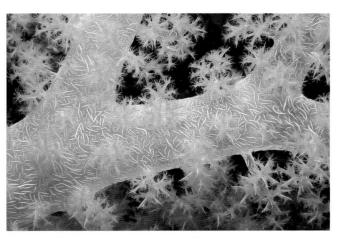

Dendronephthya **sp.** (carnation or tree coral): Fiji

tify their commercial collection except in minimal numbers. Although they are common in many areas of the Red Sea (where it may be the dominant genus present in some areas) and the Indo-Pacific, the process of collection, holding, and transport seals the fate of the majority of these fragile soft corals. These aposymbiotic corals are notoriously difficult to provide for in captivity even when healthy specimens are obtained, and they should not be bought unless the aquarist is willing and able to provide the extraordinary care they demand.

GENUS *Lemnalia* Gray, 1868
(lehm-nal'-ee-ah)

Common Species: *L. africana, L. bournei, L. cervicornis, L. rhabdota*, and others.

Common Names: cauliflower coral, tree coral, branch coral.

Identification: *Lemnalia* are part of a group of common nephtheid soft corals, along with *Nephthea, Capnella*, and *Litophyton*, that may be indistinguishable at the gross level. *Lemnalia* are notable for their numerous needlelike sclerites in the branches and stalks, but without supporting sclerites in the polyps. If polyp sclerites are present, they are tiny and transparent. The tall, thin stalk does not produce polyps, and the primary and secondary branches (also long and thin) are also sterile. The smaller branchlets bear scattered polyps with small lobed scales on the tentacles. With retractile polyps, similar colors, and an arborescent growth pattern resembling their relatives, *Lemnalia* are far from unique in appearance. The closely related *Paralemnalia* have branches that emerge from an encrusting base.

Natural Location: These soft corals, like *Nephthea*, prefer less turbid conditions than many soft corals. They are common on fore-

Lemnalia sp. (cauliflower or tree coral): profusion of branches, sparse polyps.

Lemnalia sp. (cauliflower or tree coral): in turf war with *Favites* sp. brain coral.

Paralemnalia sp. (finger coral): note branches emerging from encrusting base.

Paralemnalia sp. (finger coral): good water flow is needed to prevent collapse.

and back-reef slopes exposed to moderate surge conditions and sometimes strong currents, although flow rate has been found to be negatively correlated with the growth of *Lemnalia* (Fabricius, 1997).

Colors: Commonly white, cream, brown, or pinkish brown.

Captive Care: Available literature indicates that most, if not all, *Lemnalia* are symbiotic, and may thus be fairly well suited to captivity. Still, these corals are not as durable as many of the non-Nephtheidae members. Like other family members, they have a habit of collapsing for no apparent reason, and they rarely recover. Most of the *Lemnalia* species need a moderate to strong water flow to help prevent such a collapse, and they also seem to prefer a coarse gravel-type substrate for attachment. They grow well under moderate to bright light, since they are commonly found on reef flats in the wild. *Lemnalia*, as well as other Nephtheidae members, may be prone to parasites. They may also be irritated by certain crustaceans that pick at their surfaces. As in *Nephthea*, asexual reproduction by longitudinal fissure and branchlet droppings is common.

Special Information: *Lemnalia*, along with *Sarcophyton*, are categorized as being in the "most toxic" category in terms of their chemical defenses. Extracts from *Lemnalia* species, including the sesquiterpenes lemnalan and lemnalactone, have been shown to be 100% lethal to fishes within 12 hours.

Collection Impact: Not subject to heavy harvesting, natural populations are not likely to be diminished by collection for the aquarium trade.

GENUS *Litophyton* Forskal, 1775

(lee'-toe-fy'-tahn)

Common Species: *L. acutifolium, L. arboreum, L. viridis.*

Common Names: tree coral, cauliflower soft coral, colt coral.

Identification: Most imported *Litophyton* species form treelike or bushy colonies, with the tall stalks totally lacking polyps. Branches are often cascading and tapered. Only the thinner secondary branches have the autozooid polyps (monomorphic), usually extended day and night, although nighttime closure is also common. These are not retractile polyps, leaving characteristic warty protuberances on the stalks when they deflate. These are not very soft or "squishy" corals, owing to their considerable skeletal support. Reproduction occurs through stalk fission, and also from branchlet buds that frequently fall from the parent colony. It is possible that at least some of the corals sold commonly as "colt" corals are *Litophyton,* but these corals are generally rougher, stiffer, and more "spiky" looking.

Litophyton species are difficult to identify in many cases, and this is made worse by their highly variable appearance in different tank conditions. A colony that was mostly brown and very spiky-branched in one of my aquariums has turned more lobular and pink in another—in gross appearance, they would not be recognizable as the same coral.

Natural Location: *Litophyton* are found in diverse locations throughout the reef, from reef slopes to turbid lagoons, accompanying other soft coral fauna. They frequently form large monospecific stands in such areas. *Litophyton viridis* forms easily dislodged attachments and is found in sheltered areas.

Colors: Creamy white to pinkish brown and green in color, *Litophyton* species are not notable for their vibrant hues.

Captive Care: *Litophyton* thrive under almost all lighting conditions but prefer a moderate to strong current. Unlike many members of the Family Nephtheidae, these soft corals are symbiotic and are consequently much more adaptable and hardy than the many others that lack zooxanthellae. In fact, they contain some of the highest densities of zooxanthellae in the octocorals. Still, they will bleach and/or fail to expand if acclimation to a new tank is not done cautiously. All species are very sensitive to rapid changes in light, temperature, pH, and salinity. Just putting a hand in the tank water can cause a rapid and nearly complete contraction response. Most *Litophyton* grow very quickly once acclimated to ambient conditions, and they may grow very large. Despite appearing flexible and soft, *Litophyton* are quite rough and solid. They are subject to bristleworm attack if species with such tendencies are present. Reportedly, they occasionally fail to thrive in tanks housing large numbers of stony corals, though the reason for this is unknown. Conversely, some stony corals may fail to thrive in proximity to *Litophyton*, a much more logical outcome as *Litophyton* can be quite toxic. These corals frequently drop branchlets to form new colonies. They may also propagate vegetatively, like some

***Litophyton* sp.** (tree coral): a hardy, fast-growing, potentially large soft coral.

Nephthea sp. (tree coral): easily confused with **Lemnalia** and other genera.

Nephthea sp. (tree coral): requires good water motion and particulate foods.

Nephthea sp. (tree coral): colors can vary under different aquarium conditions.

xeniids, by having their branches bend, touch, and then attach to nearby substrate, finally breaking free from the colony.

Special Information: *Litophyton* produce a toxic terpene called palustrol, and certain species of damselfishes (*Abudefduf* species) may retreat to its branches for safety when threatened. The damsels have an immunity to this noxious compound, which repels other fishes and predators, and the production of palustrol is stimulated by repeated direct contacts by the fishes. This particular relationship is analogous to the well-known clownfish-sea anemone duo, and the *Litophyton*-damselfish symbiosis is possible to arrange in captivity—perhaps even more easily—and is equally endearing.

Litophyton are known to infect their planulae with zooxanthellae during the brooding process and prior to their release.

Collection Impact: These are fairly common corals whose collection should not ordinarily influence local populations. However, *Litophyton* (and most of the nephtheids) are reported to ship poorly. Many are lost unnecessarily to poor collection, shipping, and holding facilities. Captive-propagated colonies appear to have a clear advantage.

GENUS *Nephthea* Audouin, 1826
(nef'-thee-ah)

Common Species: *N. brasilica, N. charbrolli, N. cornuta,* and others.

Common Names: tree coral, cauliflower soft coral.

Identification: *Nephthea* form upright bushy and treelike formations that are generally more squat than *Litophyton*. They are monomorphic, with only nonretractile autozooid polyps. Robust sclerites are mainly present in the polyps, not in the main stalks. The few sclerites in the stalk are very near the surface. When contracted, the corals adopt a cauliflower-like appearance. They are characterized by having polyps that arise in lappets, or catkins. These are areas in which each polyp is given support by a bundle of sclerites. This has been mentioned as a distinguishing characteristic of the Family Nephtheidae, but most family members have bundled polyps and sclerites throughout. The main stalk(s) and secondary branches are generally sterile, with polyps arising in groups from the terminal branchlets.

Natural Location: *Nephthea* are common in reef zones that receive surge, back-reef slopes, and occasionally reef crests. Stronger flow conditions and exposure to deeper clear oceanic water are preferred. They are found in the largest sizes and greatest abundance on steep slopes at mid depths.

Colors: *Nephthea* are usually uniformly dull cream to brown-colored, although there are occasionally brighter-colored specimens available. One of the most common *Nephthea* in the trade is called the "neon green tree" coral (species unknown). It nor-

Scleronephthya sp. (tree coral): strikingly attractive, with a less-conspicuous stalk than *Dendronephthya* but the same demand for planktonic foods.

mally turns brown under intense lighting, indicating the presence of zooxanthellae.

Captive Care: *Nephthea* are notoriously delicate to ship and have a fairly poor record of survival in the aquarium. Feeding is reported to be imperative in these corals: small particulate foods should be regularly blown across their extended polyps. *Nephthea* may be unable to feed on *Artemia* nauplii, as they are often too large and motile. Current flow around these corals should be moderate to strong, though not so strong as to displace the unsupportive stalk. Although the literature on *Nephthea* is somewhat scarce, it would appear than some species have zooxanthellae and others do not. If so, it is likely that those with bright colors, and which do not "brown up" under lighting, are most likely to be aposymbiotic—and therefore more difficult to keep.

Special Information: *Nephthea* are one of the more toxic genera of soft corals in terms of their chemical defenses, producing some of the most diverse and unusual compounds of all soft corals. Some *Nephthea*, such as *N. brasilica*, are able to move their colonies in

the same way as *Xenia*, in order to colonize new areas. LaBarre and Coll (1982) found that the movement of *Nephthea* over *Acropora* species caused an infilling of the stony coral, leaving a "paved trail" where the *Nephthea* moved at a rate of about 5 cm (2 in.) per week.

Collection Impact: Widespread, common, and abundant in nature, natural populations are not likely to be diminished by collection for the aquarium trade.

GENUS *Scleronephthya* Studer, 1887
(sklare'-oh-nef'-thee-ah)

This genus may have a close resemblance to *Dendronephthya* (page 136) and they are often sold under the same common names. *Scleronephthya*, although brightly colored, have a generally shorter stalk, and sclerites are not present to any degree in the polyps themselves. They tend to be less highly branched as well. According to some reports, they may be slightly more likely to survive in the aquarium if adequate

Scleronephthya sp. (tree coral): growing in typical upside-down position.

Scleronephthya sp. (tree coral): sclerites are primarily found in the branches.

Scleronephthya sp. (tree coral): may feed on phytoplankton. (Indonesia)

Stereonephthya sp.: new species collected by K. Alderslade in the Maldives.

plankton or a plankton-substitute is provided on a regular basis—at least one species (and likely more) is herbivorous.

GENUS *Stereonephthya* Kukenthal, 1905
(stare'-ee-oh-nef'-thee-ah)

Common Species: *S. bellisima, S. cordylophora, S. imbricans, S. inordinata, S. macrospiculata, S. unicolor.*

This genus is usually not brightly colored (gray to brown shades), with nonretractile polyps uniformly spaced along the stiff branches and sparsely along the stalk. The sclerites are similar to *Nephthea*; corals may even resemble *Nephthea* in overall appearance. *Stereonephthya* have mostly unbranching treelike colonies, with polyp-bearing branchlets appearing directly off the main stalk(s). The supporting sclerites are prominent, sometimes making the colony "spikier" than *Dendronephthya*. Closely related to *Neospongodes*, this genus differs in the lack of sclerites in the inner canal walls. At least some *Stereonephthya* may be symbiotic and thus possible to maintain in the aquarium.

FAMILY Nidaliidae Gray, 1869
The Nidaliidae are only occasionally seen in the aquarium trade and they are mostly, if not totally, aposymbiotic. With no zooxanthellae, they are very difficult to keep because of their largely unknown food requirements. Not a wise choice for inclusion in aquariums until it can be determined how and if their needs can be met in captivity. This family is comprised of two subfamilies:

SUBFAMILY Nidaliinae: Consisting of the genera *Nidalia, Agaricoides, Nidaliopsis,* and *Pieterfaurea.* None are common in the aquarium trade.

Siphonogorgia sp. (china coral): a handsome soft coral with characteristic red branches; resembles a gorgonian but with poorly understood husbandry needs.

SUBFAMILY Siphonogorgiinae: Consisting of *Chironephthya, Nephthyigorgia,* and *Siphonogorgia.*

Siphonogorgia species, commonly called china corals, form large, tall colonies with many brittle, thin branches. Their polyps are retractile into calyces and their coenenchyme separates spicule-packed canals that run longitudinally. Once thought to be an exclusively Pacific genus until *S. agassizi* was described from the West Indies (Verseveldt, 1978). Considered synonymous with *Chironephthya* by Bayer (1981), *Siphonogorgia* resemble many Pacific gorgonians in outward appearance, frequently forming beautifully colored fans and delicate formations. They are rigid, anastomosing, arborescent colonies, typically having reddish branches with white to yellow contrasting clustered polyps. They are occasionally seen in aquarium shops.

Chironephthya can be distinguished by polyps that retract to form a calyx, according to Gosliner et al. (1996). They are quite spiky in appearance. I currently have what appears to be a *Chironephthya* species in one of my aquariums; it feeds day and night, with notable polyp extension after the addition of phytoplankton. Care for these seldom-imported corals is experimental; they cannot be recommended to the average reef aquarist.

FAMILY Xeniidae Ehrenberg, 1828
Pulse Corals

Genera: *Anthelia, Cespitularia, Efflatounaria, Fungulus, Heteroxenia, Sympodium, Xenia.*

Members of this family are considered unique in the coral kingdom. At least five of the genera are known to possess the ability to pulse their polyps rhythmically. The basis of the pumping is likely related to their heavy dependence on dissolved organic ma-

Chironephthya **sp.**: note longitudinally aligned sclerites and blunt-tip branches.

Nonphotosynthetic *Chironephthya* **sp.** hangs from the roof of a cave. (Maldives)

Chironephthya **sp.**: polyps may feed heavily on phytoplankton.

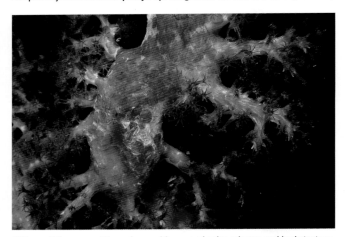

Chironephthya **sp.**: wild specimen with unusual color scheme and body texture.

terial for nutrition, supplemental to a strong dependence on their zooxanthellae. They also produce copious amounts of mucus.

Species identification is difficult because of their uniformity and lack of spicule elements. As such, color, pulsatility, retractility, breeding season, larval characteristics, and the form, dimensions and arrangements of the stalk, anthocodiae, tentacles, pinnules, and spicules must all be considered. The xeniids are all symbiotic; none are hermatypic. Most grow in small colonies or large aggregates of individual colonies. They are extremely soft corals, sometimes totally lacking in skeletal support with small sclerites present only in the epidermis, if at all. In captivity, collapse of these animals is common, and they ship poorly.

All family members studied so far are brooders; many species are surface, or external, brooders, with variations possible between species and locations. Depending on the genus, asexual reproduction may occur by budding, transverse fission, and/or pinnitomy (pinnules fall from the polyps, attach to the substrate, and begin a new colony). Captive-propagated xeniid colonies have a much greater success rate in captivity.

GENUS *Anthelia* Lamarck, 1816
(an-thee'-lee-ah)

Common Species: *A. fishelsoni, A. flava, A. glauca,* and others.
Common Names: waving-hand coral, glove coral, pulse coral.
Identification: *Anthelia* is a common genus of the Xeniidae family, comprised of species with individual monomorphic polyps that are joined to a common membranous and encrusting base.

The polyps of *Anthelia* always arise directly from the basal encrusting mat, this being the key to genus identity. (Compare to the typical *Xenia* form, which has a stalk and branches.) They

Anthelia sp. (waving-hand coral): note polyps arising from encrusting base.

Anthelia sp. (waving-hand coral): tend to be more hardy than *Xenia* spp.

Anthelia sp. (waving-hand coral): some specimens may exhibit pulsing behavior.

Anthelia sp. (waving-hand coral): captive-bred colonies fare better for aquarists.

have small oval- or oval-rod-shaped sclerites, if any are present at all. The polyps are tall and cylindrical and are solely nonretractile autozooids. *Anthelia glauca* has very long polyps, up to 13 cm (5 in.) or longer. This is the most common species of the genus and is reported from most Indo-Pacific reefs, forming small, clustered colonies. Gohar (1940) reports this to be a nonpulsatile genus, although I have seen pulsing behavior in *Anthelia* species. It is possible that this inconsistency is due to Gohar's reports being solely from the Red Sea.

Natural Location: Many *Anthelia* species come from somewhat more protected waters than other xeniids. They are rarely on the reef flat with other xeniids, which outcompete them for space, but are more common on dead coral skeletons and the undersides of hard substrate. *Anthelia glauca* is reported at depths of 8-22 m (26-72 ft.).

Colors: *Anthelia* species are normally cream, ivory, gray, or brown; *A. flava* is bright blue.

Captive Care: *Anthelia* can have pulsing species, but they are even less likely to pulse in captivity than *Xenia*. Feeding behavior, care requirements, and conditions for the success of *Anthelia* are the same as for *Xenia*, although they are somewhat hardier and less prone to crashes. Bright-colored xeniids tend to come from the shallowest waters, and light should be adjusted correspondingly. Pinnitomy is a common form of asexual reproduction in *Anthelia* species (Gohar, 1940).

Special Information: Almost all species of *Anthelia* have been shown to be relatively nontoxic to other nearby corals. Their chemical defenses seem to be minimal, and they are less able to compete successfully with other corals.

Anthelia glauca is an external surface brooder, active in warm months, with a 4-5-month season of reproductive activity. A special pharyngeal extension, called a **brooding pouch**, is present in this coral (Kruger et al., 1998). Planulae are symbiotic.

Collection Impact: Common and abundant in nature, but suffering high mortality in the collection and shipping process. Captive-bred colonies fare much better.

GENUS *Cespitularia* Milne, Edwards, and Haime, 1850
(sess-pit'-yoo-lahr'-ee-ah)

Common Species: *C. infirmata* and others.

Common Names: None.

Identification: *Cespitularia* are xeniids with stalks, forming small, branched colonies that resemble a cross between a soft coral and a *Xenia*. Small platelet sclerites are found throughout the stalks and branches. Nonretractile and evenly distributed autozooid polyps occur along the branches, but may also arise directly from the digitate or lobed stalk. Some species may have colored sclerites, though these are rarely imported or seen in the hobby. *Cespitularia* are reported to be totally nonpulsatile.

Natural Location: Similar to other xeniids and can form large assemblages in areas of less soft coral coverage, predominantly in the inshore areas of reduced water clarity and motion. There has been a tendency to group *Cespitularia* and *Efflatounaria* together, but they are very distinct in both morphology and location.

Colors: The stalks are normally white to cream-colored, with cream-, blue-, green-, and brown-tentacled polyps. Interior sclerites can be pigmented and produce some vivid shades.

Captive Care: Similar to *Xenia,* with good lighting and moderate currents.

Special Information: Some species of *Cespitularia* have highly toxic chemical defenses.

Collection Impact: Very rarely imported for the aquarium hobby. Captive propagation promises to provide some beautiful stock in the near future.

GENUS *Efflatounaria* Gohar, 1934
(eff-flat'-oo-nahr'-ee-ah)

Common Species: *E. infirmata* and others.

Common Names: None.

Identification: *Efflatounaria* have monomorphic polyps that are completely retractile, and the colonies form upright digitate lobes. Stalks are sterile and generally quite short, with rounded, bulbous, or tapered tentacle tips. Stolons are generally less than 5 mm (0.25 in.) wide, but may be 8-10 cm (3-4 in.) long. *Efflatounaria* are much less "*Xenia*-like" in appearance, more closely resembling other soft corals.

Natural Location: Most common in mid-shelf to outer-shelf reef slopes, *Efflatounaria* can be the dominant soft coral in some areas. As such, they seem to grow best when receiving some surge and current and clear oceanic water.

Colors: The stalks are normally white to cream-colored, with cream-, blue-, green-, and brown-tentacled polyps. Others can be very colorful, incorporating pigment into their sclerites.

Captive Care: *Efflatounaria* reproduce asexually by the formation of daughter colonies from stolons that arise from the base of a branch or the stalk. They are capable of rapidly colonizing substrate and grow quickly, with new colonies forming in less than 2 months. Some amount of colony thinning by mortality may occur when too many daughter colonies crowd a given area of substrate. Fission also occurs, with splits occurring over times ranging from a week or two up to several months. Sexual reproduction occurs by external surface brooding (Benayahu, 1998). Generally their care should be similar to that required by other xeniids. In nature, these corals prefer moderate to strong currents. They are quite photoadaptive and should be able to adjust to a wide range of lighting regimes.

Special Information: Some species of *Efflatounaria* are considered toxic, though these corals are known to have predators. Some fishes or turtles may nip off the branch tips, and colonies cannot always tolerate extensive damage.

Collection Impact: These soft corals are less likely than other xeniids to have their populations affected by collection because they are very rarely imported for the aquarium hobby. Captive propagation possibilities appear promising.

GENUS *Heteroxenia* Kolliker, 1874
(het'-er-oh-zee'-nee-ah)

Common Species: *H. fuscescens* and others, not well documented.

Common Names: pom-pom xenia, pulse coral.

Identification: *Heteroxenia* are similar to *Xenia* in that the polyps arise from a capitulum (or syndete) on a stalked base. However, *Heteroxenia* have short, distinctive siphonozooid polyps between the longer, nonretractile autozooid polyps, and the colonies are, therefore, dimorphic in nature. Siphonozooid tentacles are almost nonexistent and may only be present during breeding. These short polyps are clearly visible on a usually rounded ball-like capitulum with the extended autozooid polyps giving the colony the look of a cheerleader's pom-pom. Tentacles are well feathered with pinnules. Colonies usually do not branch at all. Sclerites, if present, are like those of *Xenia*. It is believed that all *Heteroxenia* species are pulsatile.

Natural Location: *Heteroxenia* are, along with *Xenia*, one of the first colonizers of new reef areas, and they are found in similar habitats. They are abundant on shallow inner reefs, commonly in-

Efflatounaria sp.: attractive rarity photographed on the Great Barrier Reef.

Cespitularia sp.: an uncommon genus, resembling *Xenia* on a tall stalk.

Heteroxenia sp. (pom-pom xenia): a fast-pulsing rarity in the aquarium world.

fluenced by tides and subjected to strong lighting *Heteroxenia* are much more common in the Red Sea.

Colors: Similar to *Xenia*, *Heteroxenia* are usually found in cream-colored to white colonies.

Captive Care: The behavior, care, and conditions required for successful growth of *Heteroxenia* are similar to those of *Anthelia* (page 146) and *Xenia* (page 150). As with other family members, these corals derive most of their nutrition from dissolved organic matter and from their zooxanthellae. Particulate food can be captured but is of highly reduced importance. *Heteroxenia* are much rarer and more often misidentified than other xeniids in the aquarium hobby, despite their abundance in nature. They reproduce sexually in a unique manner: planulae are brooded in specialized pouches externalized in the mesoglea after internal brooding in the gastrovascular cavity. They also reach sexual maturity in less than a year, giving this coral a good chance of reproducing in captivity, if conditions are right.

Special Information: The polyps of most *Heteroxenia* are among the fastest pulsing varieties, often contracting 30-45 times per minute. Most *Xenia* species contract an average of 8 times per minute.

Heteroxenia seem to be "fast" in everything they do: the planulae of *H. fuscescens* settle on coralline algae and metamorphose within 8 hours, acquire zooxanthellae by day 3, and have mature polyps in just 1 month (Benayahu et al., 1989).

Collection Impact: Common and abundant in nature, but suffering high mortality in the collection and shipping process. Captive-bred colonies fare much better.

Xenia sp. (pulse coral): easily among the most captivating of aquarium corals, the members of this genus are capable of rhythmically pulsing their tentacles.

GENUS *Xenia* Lamarck, 1816

(zee'-nee-ah)

Common Species: *X. elongata, X. macrospiculata, X. mucosa, X. multipinnata, X. stellifera, X. umbellata,* and perhaps 60 others.

Common Name: pulse coral.

Identification: *Xenia* species make up a large group of fleshy, stalked, soft corals with very small oval or plate-shaped sclerites, if any are present at all. Most species have a thick, short, smooth, unbranched stalk, although some branching may occasionally occur. The stalks are normally translucent or white with greenish, brown, or cream-colored polyps. Polyps are nonretractile (but they do contract) monomorphic autozooids on dome-shaped branch ends that form a distinct capitulum. Tentacles are pinnate, although the degree of "feathering" is variable. The polyps of *Xenia* differ from those of *Anthelia* in that *Xenia* polyps arise from a definite capitulum at the terminal end of a stalked base. They form generally smallish colonies, some rarely taller than a few inches. Within a species, there may be large differences in the size of the stalks, anthocodiae, tentacles, and pinnules that may reflect environmental conditions or age. Colonies collected from deep water or low irradiance tend to have long anthocodiae with thin tentacles and pinnules, while those from strong lighting are more robust. Size differences in colonies are mostly due to age (Benayahu, 1990). Not all *Xenia* species are pulsatile.

Natural Location: *Xenia* are noteworthy corals. They are among the first colonizers of a reef area, and are able to "walk" to new sites by the systematic attachment and detachment of their branches and stalks to adjacent locations. This ability allows them to move rapidly (relative to other corals) into new areas, and they may even encrust living corals and algae in the process. They are capable of competitively excluding other early colonizers, like *Stylophora*, *Pocillopora*, and *Heteroxenia* species by dense overgrowth. They may inhabit varied locations throughout the reef, forming large, monospecific gardens—covering up to 70% of the substrate in some locations. Perhaps most notable is the prolific growth of *Xenia* and other family members near the effluent discharge of hotels and sewage pipes on near-shore reefs.

Colors: Cream, white, ivory, brown, and light green are the most common colors for *Xenia*. They are fairly uniform in coloration with little contrast between stalks and polyps.

Captive Care: *Xenia*, along with other xeniids, have a capacity to pulse their polyp tentacles rhythmically. They are also capable of bending and twisting single tentacles. This behavior is unique among coral families. Its function was originally thought to be related to enhancing nutrient uptake, but later work seemed to target respiration and gas exchange. There are personal observations of a *Xenia* colony that pulses at night but not during the day. This corroborates Gohar's work (1959), in which he found the polyps of *Heteroxenia* to pulse at night, with spaced breaks in pulsing during the day: polyp contraction occurred regularly near dawn, dusk, and midday. The function of pulsing is still not certain, although large colonies can cause substantial local water agitation during the contractions. The contraction movement is stronger than the extension, resulting in a net water flow away from the oral disc rather than mere turbulence. It has been suggested that xeniids depend to a great degree on dissolved organic compounds, and the action of pulsing influences their uptake across cell membranes by renewing the water source around the colonies. Pulsing has also been shown to be a likely substitute for the virtually nonexistent ciliary action on the coral surface.

Captive-bred colonies seem to pulse to a greater extent than wild-caught species, but many *Xenia* cease to pulse once they have been introduced to an aquarium. Though the polyps may be inactive, they seem to retain their pulsing potential. Changes in water chemistry seem to modify the pumping action; initiation, cessation, and rates of pulsing are all affected. It has been suggested that the use of small amounts of granular activated carbon or a higher pH may help retain this behavior (Curry, pers. comm.). I have found no universal rules for maintaining the pulsing behavior. Certainly the use of carbon would decrease the amount of dissolved organic material present, and the coral colony might then be expected to pulse, based on its need to supply itself with enough dissolved organics in a nutrient-poor situation. There is also quite a bit of variability in the coordination, strength, and speed of the pulse. Factors vary widely between genera and species, but also vary according to unknown water-quality parameters. It is not known whether the presence

Xenia sp. (pulse coral): colonies at the surface of a shallow Indonesian tidepool.

Xenia sp. (pulse coral): polyps attach to thick stalk, unlike *Anthelia* (page 147).

Xenia sp. (pulse coral): colors vary from light green to snow white.

Xenia sp. (pulse coral): pulsing is neither fully understood nor predictable.

Xenia sp. (pulse coral): these wild colonies do not ship as well as captive-breds.

Xenia sp. (pulse coral): strong lighting and good water motion are required.

or absence of certain nutrients or trace elements in the water may be partly causative. Indeed, species that may not have pulsed for years may suddenly start to pulse under new tank conditions. There have been several chemical substances found that stimulate pulsing behavior: one is methanol, which is clearly not something that should be deliberately added to aquariums. Electrical stimulation also works, probably by stimulating the neurons responsible for the contraction process. The cell energy source, adenosine triphosphate (ATP), also stimulates pulsing. Surprisingly, exposure of *Xenia* to the extracts of soft corals, predominantly *Sarcophyton* species, isolated to any of several common terpenoids, will cause *Xenia* to pump (Pass et al, 1989). Other factors that affect pulsing are water flow (some flows promote it; strong flows cause cessation), temperature (a dome-shaped curve), drugs, hormones, chemicals, and various mechanical stimulations (Gohar, 1959). Interestingly, calcium chloride has a depressant effect (Gohar, 1959).

In tanks that support their growth, the rate of reproduction and spread of *Xenia* can be astonishing. *Xenia* reproduce asexually mostly by colony fission (a process taking only about 10-14 days), with rapid spread possible. They are naturally found quite often in areas of high nutrients, so that reef tanks with very low nutrient levels housing large populations of stony corals are often not conducive to the success of *Xenia* and other family members.

Despite their hardiness in the wild, *Xenia* species ship poorly and are quite fragile (at least initially) in captivity. They are very prone to "crashes," in which an entire colony will stop pulsing, wilt, deflate, and degenerate rapidly. This crash can occur in colonies that have been dividing and thriving for long periods of time. Without any noticeable change in conditions, the colonies fail rapidly, almost as though they had exhausted some as-yet-undiscovered factor in the water. Also, they do have short lifespans on the reef, some only 1-2 years, but generally 3-7 years. Wild-collected specimens seem much more fragile and prone to "crashing" than captive-raised *Xenia* specimens. Iodine is anecdotally reported within the aquarium hobby and among some propagators to be important to these soft corals. Regular—if not daily—additions are often reported necessary for their health and growth. The actual iodine concentrations in the water are also said to be important, and readings should be checked with an iodine/iodide test kit for an assessment of proper levels (Curry, pers. comm.). Although some hobbyists report great success using Lugol's solution with *Xenia*, others have noted that the addition of this strong iodine product has caused the demise of entire colonies. The risk of such loss should be carefully weighed before using Lugol's with *Xenia*. I have not found iodine to play a role in the success of *Xenia*, nor is its need or uptake documented, though I have found it to be detrimental in some, but not all, of my experiences with these corals.

Xenia, and other xeniids, do not possess many or potent nematocysts, well-developed cilia, or complete digestive structures. Therefore, they are almost entirely dependent on direct nutrient uptake from the water and photosynthesis. It has been wrongfully asserted in some sources that these corals do not feed. It is more accurate to say that their feeding is highly reduced. Prey items have been repeatedly found in *Xenia* species in feeding studies, especially in the wild. In addition to the large uptake of dissolved organic matter in this family, these corals seem to have a larger turnover of zooxanthellae, which they may use for supplemental nutrition. Some mesenteries, nematocysts, and cilia do exist, primarily in the gastrovascular cavity. These reduced structures may be used for microzooplankton and are used for digestion of the zooxanthellae. As can be imagined, good water circulation around the colony (without forceful currents directly blowing at the polyps) and strong lighting is highly recommended.

Xenia tend to grow on vertical surfaces in the wild, and such placement may be the most natural position for them in captivity. With their soft bodies and lack of sharp sclerites, *Xenia* are preyed upon by by a variety of predators, including some polychaete worms and crustaceans. There is also a nudibranch that preys on *Xenia* and that is an astonishingly good mimic of the *Xenia* polyp. Other predators include small crabs, indigenous to live rock, that may prune entire colonies like loggers clear-cutting a forest. The detachment often causes them to die (if they are not already eaten by the crab).

Xenia are hermaphroditic and reach sexual maturity at about 2 years of age. They have a very short planula stage, settling and metamorphosing quickly after being released. Planulae develop in brooding pouches among the polyps and below the anthocodiae (Benayahu, 1998).

Special Information: A few species of *Xenia* produce chemical substances that can cause significant damage to stony corals. In general, they are considered to be one of the less-toxic genera, but likely have significant terpenoid defenses to prevent predation. (Some reef aquarists do allow *Xenia* species to spread on the rock among their colonies of stony corals without apparent harm.)

Xenia are also capable of detachment from the substrate to drift into possible colonizable areas. This ability, similar to that of some anemones and corallimorphs, may cause problems in the aquarium if the detached colony affixes itself too near other corals, resulting in overgrowth. Such detached offspring should be either carefully placed to facilitate attachment in a suitable spot or removed to a separate tank until attachment is completed.

Like *Litophyton arboreum* and *L. viridis*, *X. umbellata* broods

Spreading across a wall of aquarium glass, Red Sea *Xenia* sp. reproduce prolifically by colony fission in a small system maintained by Julian Sprung.

planulae that are endowed with zooxanthellae before they are released.

Collection Impact: The poor survivability of *Xenia* is a cause for concern in the collection of wild specimens, even though they are a common and rapidly reproducing species. Many colonies do not survive the collection and shipping process. Those that do have a substantial risk of not surviving in their final captive environment because of the unknown aspects of their care. While certain aquarists have success with *Xenia* (to the extent that they reproduce asexually like weeds), others will watch as colony after colony melts or crashes in their tanks. Fortunately, these beautiful and fascinating corals are being commercially bred in captivity, where much shorter shipping periods are needed and there are fewer variables involved in their transfer and holding. Captive-bred *Xenia* not only spare natural populations, they are unquestionably easier to care for and are often highly successful in captivity.

***Acalycigorgia* sp.** (Pacific gorgonian): one of a huge group of semirigid octocorals, some photosynthetic and easily kept, others demanding special feeding and care.

THE GORGONIANS (SUBORDERS SCLERAXONIA AND HOLAXONIA)

The gorgonians in this book are grouped as suborders of the Order Alcyonacea. However, many texts assign them to a separate order, the Gorgonacea. Natural history information about the gorgonians, especially the Caribbean species, is remarkably greater than with other taxa of the Subclass Octocorallia. Fortunately, these are also the ones most likely to be encountered within the aquarium trade, as well as those most likely to be successful in an aquarium.

Gorgonians are distinct from the soft corals in that they have fairly rigid structures or branches composed of calcite spicules and/or a horny protein substance known as **gorgonin**. They are normally erect and branching, whiplike, or bushy, although a few encrusting species exist. These octocorals are often brightly colored. They can be highly variable—even displaying different coloration within a species—with growth-form variability frequently occurring as a function of the depths at which they are found and the type of water flow to which they are exposed.

Gorgonians may be symbiotic or aposymbiotic, and those containing zooxanthellae typically have brownish-colored polyps. In general, gorgonians seem to respond most strongly to light from 350-500 nm. Those without zooxanthellae normally have white or brightly colored polyps and are much more difficult to maintain as they require frequent and regular feedings. Although many gorgonians have been noted to capture and ingest baby brine shrimp (*Artemia* nauplii), they are frequently not digested in several species and are later expelled. It is fairly well established that gorgonians feed heavily on particulate matter, and zooplankton capture may comprise a relatively small part of their diet. The reasons that some species have proved difficult to keep are likely to be related to nutrition.

The stems and branches of gorgonians have a very strong central **axis**, **core**, or medulla made of either calcareous or horny material (Suborder Holaxonia), or tightly grouped spicules (Suborder Scleraxonia). In the Families Plexauridae and Gorgoniidae, a central **chord** lies in the center of the axis, a hollow tube divided into sections by partitions along its length, its chambers filled with stranded hollow fibers. Most gorgonian groups have solid axial skeletons or cores made of fused sclerites, with collagen as the primary supporting material. The horny material of the Holaxonia group of gorgonians, gorgonin, contains significant amounts of bromine, iodine, and tyrosine. Iodine uptake is established in several gorgonian genera, as is a metabolic pathway and deposition (Goldberg, 1977, et al.), although this does not necessarily indicate the need for iodine supplementation in the aquarium. Surrounding this core is a tissue layer called the **rind**, or cortex, from which polyps may originate from openings in the surface called **apertures**. As with other corals, the **calyces**, if present, are the raised areas of the rind around the apertures from which the polyps emerge. The cuplike attachment that the main trunk or branch has with the substrate is called a **holdfast**. A ciliated canal system allows for intercolonial transport of food between polyps. These **solenia** (also called stem canals) run parallel around the axial skeleton, with transport of nutrients running in either direction. Common branching patterns of gorgonians are classified as pinnate (feathery branches), dichotomous (random Y-shaped branches), lateral (side branches extending off of another main branch), interconnected netlike (forming a web of interlaced, connected branches), or unbranched (single stalks arising from a base).

Gorgonian identification is based on colony shape and size, branching pattern, polyp distribution, polyp dimorphism (presence of autozooids and siphonozooids), axis structure (including sclerites and spicules), and color. More promising for gorgonians, and all octocorals for that matter, is classification based on chemotaxonomy. This field establishes taxonomic data based on the terpenoids and other chemical substances produced by these corals. It appears that for most gorgonians, colony shape and orientation are largely determined by water flow, with fan-shaped colonies oriented perpendicular to the prevailing currents predominating in areas of strong tidal flows and wave surge. By contrast, thinner-branched patterns, spindly shapes, and whips predominate

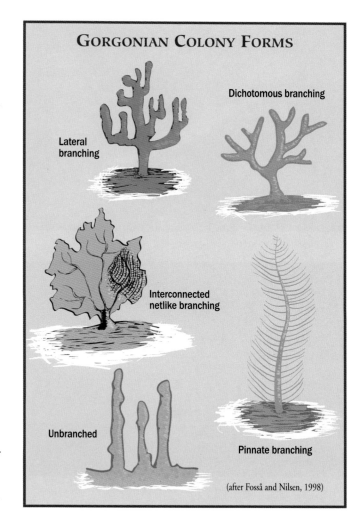

GORGONIAN COLONY FORMS

Lateral branching

Dichotomous branching

Interconnected netlike branching

Unbranched

Pinnate branching

(after Fosså and Nilsen, 1998)

in deeper environments with lower-flow regimes. Gorgonians with stiff branches are generally from deep water, flexible branches from moderate surge, and intermediate stiffness from shallow areas of high water motion. Such characteristics can be used to aid in placement of colonies in the aquariums.

It is notable that gorgonians, many of which are quite tall, will potentially reach from the bottom to the top of some aquariums. They can, therefore, be exposed to a rather large variation in light intensity, which may have relevance to their success. Fortunately, this does not seem to be of great importance in the majority of cases, as even tall specimens will grow uniformly in captivity. The implications of this are interesting in terms of what is known about light penetration, photoadaptation, and photosynthesis. Of course, the aposymbiotic gorgonians are not de-

Pacific gorgonian: Sulawesi.

***Acalycigorgia* sp.** (Pacific gorgonian): Indonesia.

***Acanthogorgia* sp.** (Pacific gorgonian): Sulawesi, Indonesia.

Unidentified Red Sea gorgonian.

Unidentified Red Sea gorgonian.

Pacific gorgonian: New South Wales, Australia.

pendent on light, and many are found in quite deep water—some species at several thousand feet. Gorgonians can also be the primary corals in temperate and even Arctic waters.

Gorgonians, in general, are found to be less tolerant than stony corals to high temperatures and elevated salinity. Many gorgonians shed a waxy surface layer like other octocorals, and the event usually lasts a week or so. Most gorgonians produce prostaglandins, sterols (gorgosterol, hippurin, and others), and more "conventional" terpenes and phenols that are not only effective in preventing predation and competing for space, but often give gorgonians a very strong and distinctive smell when removed from the water. The foul-tasting lipoid compound crassin-acetate is found in many species of *Eunicea* and *Pseudoplexaura*. Briantheins are found in *Briareum* species, and lophotoxin is common to the Pacific *Lophogorgia* species. Furthermore, many of the chemical types found in soft corals are also produced by the gorgonians. Additionally, gorgonians are well known to secrete antimicrobial substances that act on a variety of marine bacteria and potential pathogens. Such substances have been found in other corals, too, but they are somewhat better studied in the gorgonians. It has been theorized that each coral may, in fact, produce antimicrobial substances specific to the potentially harmful bacteria to which it is most exposed (Kim, 1994; Jensen et.al, 1996).

Although gorgonians exist in the Indo-Pacific, they are much more prevalent in the mix of coral species on Caribbean reefs. Reproduction is generally only described as sexual, although branch fragments can survive and grow into new colonies. The Pacific sea whip, *Junceella fragilis*, reproduces vegetatively like many soft corals—by branchlet dropping (Walker and Bull, 1983). The degree to which this mode of spread can occur with other gorgonians has not been established in the wild and may be uncommon, though it seems quite plausible, based on efforts at captive propagation of various species. Consequently, and since octocorals are still legal to collect in some parts of the Tropical Atlantic, most species available in the hobby are Atlantic, rather than Pacific, species.

PACIFIC GORGONIANS

Although not entirely rare on Pacific reefs, gorgonians of the Indo-Pacific are rarely imported to the aquarium trade for several reasons. Unlike their Atlantic counterparts, most Pacific gorgonians are aposymbiotic, which makes most of them largely unsuitable for success in captivity. Consequently, there is comparatively little known about their care requirements and their success in captive systems. It would have to be assumed, in the absence of more elaborate data accumulation, that the "rule of

thumb" which suggests that thicker-branched species are easier to maintain than thinner-branched species, holds true for Pacific varieties also. The fact that species with brown polyps are photosynthetic and are easier to keep than the nonphotosynthetic white or colored polyp species also holds true for Pacific varieties. Aposymbiotic gorgonians would require large planktonic inputs to meet their energy needs. Many Pacific gorgonians are found in fairly deep water, and the particulate "reef snow" that drifts in currents and upwellings is likely to be an important trophic resource to these corals.

SUBORDER SCLERAXONIA

The Scleraxonia gorgonians are characterized by having fused, or mostly fused, sclerites within their central core or axis and other sclerites contained in their rind. Occasionally, sclerites may also be found in the polyps that arise from the rind. Few of the many genera and species are available to the aquarium trade, and fewer still are really suitable for captivity as they are frequently azooxanthellate (aposymbiotic). There are seven separate families (Bayer, 1981): Briareidae, Anthothelidae, Subergorgiidae, Paragorgiidae, Coralliidae, Melithaeidae, and Parisididae. Most are Pacific groups, although the Anthothelidae, Briareidae, and Paragorgiidae have Atlantic representatives.

FAMILY Briareidae Gray, 1859
The family consists of a single genus, *Briareum*. Species are found in both Atlantic and Pacific Oceans.

GENUS *Briareum* de Blainville, 1830
(bry-ayr'-ee-um)
Common Species: *B. asbestinum, B. stechei,* and others.
Common Names: corky sea fingers, deadman's fingers, moss coral.
Identification: *Briareum* are normally encrusting gorgonians with long "grassy" polyps arising from raised calyces. Polyps are normally expanded continuously, unless disturbed. The polyps are fully retractable (although slow to retract) into a smooth mat, occasionally nodular from slightly raised calyces. In fact, they superficially resemble the stoloniferan *Pachyclavularia*. However, these gorgonians may form short, upright fingers or lobes from their encrusting base, a feature not common to *Pachyclavularia*. Two distinct morphs commonly occur, erect or encrusting, and these growth forms are genotypically distinct. They will encrust other living corals, especially other gorgonians. Sclerites are straight or curved spindles and tripods, purple in the medullar core, purple or white in the rind. The solenia penetrate both layers.

Briareum are easily recognized, as they are the only Atlantic

Briareum stechei (Pacific encrusting gorgonian): note mat color. (Indonesia)

Briareum asbestinum: encrusting form.

Briareum asbestinum (corky sea fingers): erect form. (Caribbean)

gorgonian genus that remains unbranched from an encrusting base, with single erect branches rising from the base up to 1 m (39 in.) in height. *Briareum* are also found in the Pacific, and their phylogenetic lineage and similarity are apparent.

Natural Location: *Briareum* are found in varied locations in all reef habitats; from bays to deep-reef slopes, in areas of strong water movement and little water movement, in areas of turbid nutrient-rich water to clear oceanic regions. Most collected specimens will come from shallow, protected waters with strong illumination and moderate wave surge. Colonies from shallow, high-flow areas have short, fat vertical projections, and may even have a few reduced, lateral branches. Those from deeper or calmer waters, or reduced illumination, are tall, thinner, and unbranched. They are one of the most common Caribbean gorgonians, found from about 1-40 m (3-130 ft.).

Colors: Polyps are typically brown or occasionally greenish. The mat or rind is usually purplish gray.

Captive Care: *Briareum* are highly photosynthetic and easy to keep. They are quite photoadaptive, tolerant of most lighting conditions, and grow rapidly with strong currents and bright light. *Briareum* may occasionally slough a mucus sheet from their surface. In nature, this occurs about every 10 days. Turbid water that allows for more accumulation of bacteria or sediments on their surface will increase the frequency of this shedding. Consideration of the encrusting nature of these corals when placing them near other corals is required, as they are hard to stop once they begin to spread—growing at a rate of about 4-10 cm (2-4 in.) per year. They do not feed on zooplankton to any degree, have relatively few nematocysts, and rely on mucosal capture of particulate matter as the primary method of food capture. This coral propagates by both pseudo-runner/stolon growth and by fragmentation of the stolon or, more frequently, the vertical projections. The unusual structure of its inner and outer layers allows for its propensity toward fragmented spread. In the former type of vegetative reproduction, *Briareum* can produce branches that appear runnerlike, which then attach to the substrate, forming a new colony before separating from the parent colony. *Briareum* are also unusual in that they brood planulae on the surface of the colony.

Special Information: *Briareum asbestinum* is one of the most toxic gorgonians known, secreting a number of terpenes and acetogenins. (The primary terpenoid compound is briarane, which is supplemented primarily by asbestinane.) The depth at which the coral is collected allows for variable toxicity, with deeper water colonies showing stronger terpenoid characteristics than shallow-water species. This characteristic is not known to be universal, but may be somewhat specific to this species. Perhaps more surprising is the fact that the terpenoid group of briantheins, also present, are apparently quite good insecticides.

Collection Impact: *Briareum* are common and fast-growing corals found in diverse locations. They are easily propagated through training them to encrust rubble, and are very successful in captivity. The only significant deleterious aspect to the reef is that colonies are often collected attached to substrate that is forcibly broken free from the reef with commensal organisms. However, it is a simple enough matter to avoid this destruction by taking colonies that have totally encrusted loose pieces of substrate, harvesting vertical elements only, or undertaking *in situ* propagation.

FAMILY Anthothelidae Broch, 1916

This family is divided into three subfamilies, Anthothelinae, Semperininae, and Spongiodermatinae. Only the last, with the Atlantic genera *Diodogorgia* and *Erythropodium*, is normally found in the aquarium trade.

SUBFAMILY Anthothelinae: Consists of a single tropical genus, *Anthothela* Verrill, 1879.

SUBFAMILY Semperininae: Consists of 3 genera: *Iciligorgia* Duchassaing, 1870 (Atlantic); *Semperina* Kolliker, 1870 (Pacific); and *Solenocaulon* Gray, 1862 (Pacific).

Iciligorgia is very common. *Iciligorgia schrammi* is known as the deep-water sea fan, and it occurs mainly below 18 m (60 ft.) in clear water with a current. Paul Humann (1993) reports it may be found down to 365 m (1,200 ft.). I mostly see this beautiful gorgonian on steep outer-reef slopes—areas on the eastern or windward side of Grand Cayman Island are dense with *Iciligorgia*. Unfortunately, this species is aposymbiotic, very large, and unavailable to the aquarium trade. It is, however, pictured and discussed in many works describing reef corals.

SUBFAMILY Spongiodermatinae: Consists of the genera *Diodogorgia* and *Erythropodium* (detailed below); *Alertigorgia* Kükenthal, 1908; *Callipodium* Verrill, 1869 (W. Central America); *Homophyton* Gray, 1866; the brilliant sea fingers or *Titanideum* Verrill, 1863 (Florida); and *Tripalea* Bayer, 1955 (E. South America).

GENUS *Diodogorgia* Kukenthal, 1919
(dy'-oh-doh-gore'-gee-ah)

Common Species: *D. nodulifera* and perhaps two others.
Common Names: colorful sea rod, red or orange tree gorgonian.
Identification: These aposymbiotic gorgonians are found in small, sparsely branched colonies. Sclerites support the very stiff and smooth branches. Their identification is quite obvious, using the bright colors, the contrasting calyces, and distinctive appearance. Only *Titanideum* resembles this genus, and is occasionally sold as *Diodogorgia*, but its calyces are not raised or contrasting.
Natural Location: *Diodogorgia* are one of the most frequently of-

Diodogorgia nodulifera (colorful sea rod): unfortunately for aquarists, these corals are aposymbiotic (lacking zooxanthellae) and are a challenge to feed.

Diodogorgia nodulifera (colorful sea rod): orange-branch type, polyps extended.

Diodogorgia nodulifera (colorful sea rod): red-branch type, polyps retracted.

Diodogorgia nodulifera (colorful sea rod): orange-branch type, polyps retracted.

fered gorgonians in the aquarium hobby, despite the fact that they are collected from predominantly deep-water areas and overhangs.

Colors: Snow white polyps arise from the raised calyces. Branches are either deep red with darker red or orange calyces, or orange to yellow with red- or purple-shaded calyces.

Captive Care: Demand for these beautiful, slow-growing gorgonians is high, and there is no denying that they are remarkably attractive. Unfortunately, all too often they become covered in algae and soon degenerate into tiny stumps. Without proper feeding, *Diodogorgia* do not survive in the aquarium. Lighting intensity is irrelevant because they do not have zooxanthellae. Frequent light brushing of the outer rind to prevent microalgae from forming, along with strong currents and frequent feedings of small, planktonlike food, may extend their lives in captivity. Although strong currents are not always present in their deep-water habitats, the low-nutrient, low-light oceanic water where they are commonly found prevents algae overgrowth in the wild. This can be somewhat compensated for by the use of currents in captivity. As with most of the aposymbiotic species, it is best to avoid these gorgonians.

Special Information: For those aquarists who are successful in feeding and keeping *Diodogorgia*, the brittle branches are easily broken and may be used to propagate new colonies.

Collection Impact: Although fairly common in the wild, these gorgonians have a poor record of survival in captivity. The demanding care required to keep them should mandate a more-limited collection of these species in the interest of their conservation. Only aquarists willing to devote the time and care necessary for their survival should attempt to keep them.

GENUS *Erythropodium* Kolliker, 1865
(eh-rith'-roh-poh'-dee-um)

Common Species: *E. caribaeorum, E. polyanthes,* and others.

Common Name: encrusting gorgonian.

Identification: These commonly seen encrusting gorgonians are quite distinct from *Briareum*, forming smooth mats that rarely have calyces. The retractable autozooid polyps are very fine in texture, and appear from pinhole, star-shaped apertures in the mat. Their tentacles are fine and "hairy," and quite long. Their stolon is never purple-gray like *Briareum*, and they never form vertical outgrowths. There is really no question as to the identity of this coral as it is quite distinct from any gorgonian or stoloniferan.

Natural Location: *Erythropodium* are versatile gorgonians, inhabiting many patch reef areas in various levels of light and water movement. I have seen them from intertidal areas to protected mid-depth waters on all types of reefs. There are both Atlantic and Pacific species. *Erythropodium caribaeorum* is the most common, and it is an Atlantic species. Pacific species are reported from similar reef locations.

Colors: *Erythropodium* form tan to toffee-colored mats with polyps that are cream or light brown shades. The coenenchyme of the internal supportive medulla may be purplish red.

Captive Care: Because of the varied natural locations in which *Erythropodium* are found, they can be considered very hardy gorgonians for the aquarium. They adapt well to most lighting and water flow conditions, although strong currents may induce the formation of sweeper tentacles (see Special Information, below). They grow quite fast and are one of the most dominant, if not the most dominant, encrusting organism on the reef. There are no corals yet studied that *Erythropodium* do not or cannot encrust and overgrow. Their mats are extremely tenacious, and removal is difficult if they begin to threaten neighboring colonies. Careful placement is advised in the aquarium, as they can and will kill other corals.

Special Information: This genus of gorgonian can form elongated nonpinnate sweeper tentacles along the edge of the expanding mat that contain prominent stinging acrospheres. In fact, they are more numerous than those found in most scleractinian corals, allowing for these gorgonians to be considered highly aggressive. The use of sweeper tentacles is of great significance in *Erythropodium* because of their propensity to overgrow other living corals, including other colonies of *Erythropodium*. It seems they do not recognize other colonies as being "self" and treat any encroaching colonies as an aggressor. This indicates either a lack of produced chemical cues for self-recognition, or an inability to recognize them. These gorgonians also contain strong deterrents to predators, including chlorinated diterpenoid compounds, such as erytholide.

Collection Impact: Can be harvested on loose pieces of substrate with little harm, and are ideal subjects for propagation efforts.

FAMILY Subergorgiidae Gray, 1859

This family is composed of the single Pacific genus *Subergorgia* Gray, 1857.

The species in this genus, commonly referred to as Pacific sea fans, are large, bushy, arborescent or reticulate (netlike) fan-shaped gorgonians with a gorgonin-containing core. Some species branch dichotomously with monomorphic polyps in one or two rows along the edges of the branches. Colors are normally red to orange, brown, and yellow. These common gorgonians form large colorful, dense fans. They do not show the fine, tightly interconnected, lacelike structure typical of the

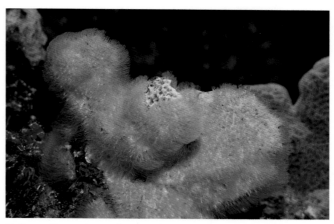
***Erythropodium* sp.** (encrusting gorgonian): blue-hued colony. (Cayman Islands)

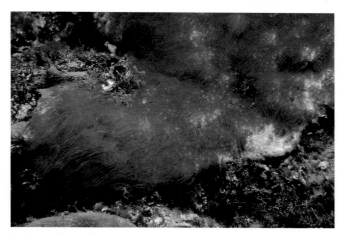
Erythropodium caribaeorum (encrusting gorgonian): rapid-spreading species.

Subergorgia mollis (Pacific sea fan): large-growing species. (Coral Sea)

Melithaea sp. (Pacific sea fan): note characteristic swollen nodes. (Indonesia)

Melithaea sp. (Pacific sea fan): delicate beauty but very difficult to maintain.

Caribbean *Gorgonia* species, rather forming primarily from extensive lateral, planar branching. A longitudinal groove may be present along the branches. Some significant degree of anastomosis (joining of branches) is present. The main branches are heavier and distinct, forming the primary "veins" of the fan. Secondary branches remain quite heavy as well. This genus is aposymbiotic and rarely available in the aquarium trade.

FAMILY Paragorgiidae Kukenthal, 1916

This family consists of two genera: *Paragorgia* and *Sibogagorgia*. Neither is available in the aquarium trade.

Paragorgia Milne, Edwards, and Haime, 1857: Represented in the Atlantic (*P. arborea*), Arctic, and Pacific. Colonies are massive, and arborescent with thick branches. Dimorphic polyps with calyces. Cortex with pink/red sclerites not separated from the medulla by canals.

Sibogagorgia Stiasny, 1937: Reported from the East Indies. Similar to *Paragorgia*, but the medulla and cortex are separated by canals.

FAMILY Coralliidae Lamouroux, 1812

Corallium Cuvier, 1798: *Corallium rubrum*, precious pink (red) coral, has been used in trade, jewelry, and other human artifacts for thousands of years. It was the first coral species ever described. Found in the Mediterranean, it is not available for aquariums and is a protected and threatened species.

Colonies are arborescent or bushy with dimorphic polyps, a stiff skeleton of fused sclerites, and characteristic "opera glass" sclerites. Other species are Pacific.

Pleurocorallioides Moroff, 1902: Similar to *Corallium*, but cortical sclerites differ.

FAMILY Melithaeidae Gray, 1870

This family consists of several Pacific genera of beautiful, colorful aposymbiotic fans, characterized by having internodes between the branches that look like contrasting disks. The internodes are composed of sclerites and gorgonin and allow the branches to flex (hinge) somewhat. These fans are likely to be very difficult to maintain. The genera are: *Acabaria*, *Clathraria*, *Melithaea*, *Mopsella*, and *Wrightella*. They are rarely, if ever, available to the aquarium trade.

FAMILY Parisididae Aurivillius, 1931

Consists of the genus *Parisis* from the Pacific. These species are unavailable to the aquarium trade.

Parisis Verrill, 1864: Colonies form large, white, planar, arborescent fans, much like *Melithaea*. Internodes are rigid, calcareous, flat, and radially grooved.

SUBORDER HOLAXONIA

The Holaxonia are durable gorgonians with a strong central core formed by calcareous or horny material—unlike the Scleraxonia with their skeletons of fused sclerites. This is a large suborder of gorgonians that encompasses many families in both oceans. The families are: Keroeididae, Acanthogorgiidae, Plexauridae, Gorgoniidae, Ellisellidae, Ifalukellidae, Chrysogorgiidae, Primnoidae, and Isididae. The families containing genera common and appropriate to aquarium keeping are primarily the symbiotic members in the Caribbean families Plexauridae and Gorgoniidae.

FAMILY Keroeididae K. Kinoshita, 1910

The family consists of three genera, none of which are usually available to the aquarium trade. They are characterized by a hol-

Eunicea mammosa (knobby candelabrum): challenging to feed and keep.

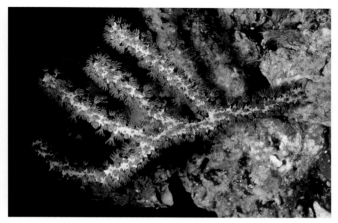

Eunicea sp. (knobby sea rod): genus is noted for its foul odor out of water.

low, chambered central chord surrounded by unfused skeletal elements. The outer spicular layer of the axis and the axial epithelium, formed by smooth sclerites joined together by a horny sheath, makes this family a bridge between the Holaxonia and the Scleraxonia. The genera are: *Ideogorgia*, *Keroeides* (Atlantic, Pacific), and *Lignella*.

FAMILY Acanthogorgiidae Gray, 1859

This family consists of several genera, none of which are commonly available in the aquarium trade. They are characterized by a purely horny axis without sclerites (may have unformed calcareous deposits) and a wide, well-chambered central chord. Simple, undifferentiated polyps are nonretractile, but contract within the coenenchyme by folding their tentacles inward. The rind is typically thin. They tend to inhabit moderate-depth waters. Genera are: *Acalycigorgia* (Pacific), *Acanthogorgia* (Atlantic, Pacific), *Anthogorgia* (Pacific), *Calcigorgia* (Pacific), *Cyclomuricea* (Pacific), *Muricella* (Pacific), and *Versluysia* (Pacific).

FAMILY Plexauridae Gray, 1859

This is, by far, the largest family of tropical gorgonians and is composed of two subfamilies, each having many genera. They may be very difficult to tell apart and are found in widely variant ranges. They generally have thick branches and polyps with retractile anthocodiae. The central chord is chambered. The rind tends to be thick with stem canals and bifurcates the cortex into two layers. All gorgonians of the Family Plexauridae have a large amount of magnesium carbonate in their axial skeletons.

SUBFAMILY Plexaurinae: Composed of the tropical and subtropical Atlantic genera *Eunicea*, *Euplexaura*, *Muricea*, *Muriceopsis*, *Plexaura*, *Plexaurella*, *Psammogorgia*, and *Pseudoplexaura*. Many are common to the aquarium trade.

GENUS *Eunicea* Lamouroux, 1816

(you-niss'-ee-ah)

Common Species: *E. asperula*, *E. calyculata*, *E. fusca*, *E. knighti*, *E. laciniata*, *E. mammosa*, *E. palmeri*, *E. succinea*, *E. tourneforti*, and perhaps 27 others.

Common Names: knobby sea rod, candelabrum.

Identification: *Eunicea* is a large genus of gorgonians most easily recognized by the raised warty calyces (except in *E. knighti*) that are evenly spaced along branches of colonies that usually resemble a candelabrum. Branches grow laterally and are normally uniform, hard, and moderately thick. Identification to the species level requires sclerite examination.

Natural Location: *Eunicea* are found in varied locations throughout the reef, but are most common where other gorgonians are found—in areas receiving strong lighting and wave surge in shallow to mid-depth waters.

Colors: The appearance of *Eunicea* is highly variable, with many colors within a single species. However, gray and brown shades are the ones most commonly seen in the aquarium trade.

Captive Care: It does not appear that all species are symbiotic, and *Eunicea*, in general, have a reputation of being difficult to maintain in captivity. Certainly this is true for any aposymbiotic species. *Eunicea* are predominantly shallow-water corals, so strong lighting is necessary for the photosynthetic species, with strong indirect water flow for all species.

Special Information: *Eunicea* are known to have a distinctively bad smell when removed from the water due to their abundant production of phenols. *Eunicea mammosa* produces the chemical compound mammosin, which resembles penicillin, has antibacterial effects, and is toxic to fishes—thus deterring predation and increasing resistance to potential pathogens. *Eunicea palmeri* and *E. succinea* produce the chemical compound crassin, which has similar functions.

Collection Impact: *Eunicea* are widespread and common; overharvesting by the aquarium trade is unlikely.

GENUS *Muricea* Lamouroux, 1821
(myoor-iss'-ee-ah)

Common Species: *M. atlantica, M. californica, M. elongata, M. fructicosa, M. laxa, M. muricata, M. pendula, M. pinnata,* and perhaps 9 others.

Common Names: spiny sea fan, spiny sea rod, spiny sea whip.

Identification: *Muricea* is a small genus of distinctive gorgonians with tall, upward-pointed, rough calyces that resemble some *Acropora* stony corals. The calyces are supported by projecting spindle-shaped spicules. The overall appearance of the branches, even with extended polyps, is very spiny. Most *Muricea* colonies are quite short and stout and do not grow to much more than 60 cm (24 in.) in height. They normally exist with tightly spaced branches that may be lateral or pinnate.

Natural Location: *Muricea* are predominantly shallow to mid-depth gorgonians, but occur in diverse habitats.

Colors: Mostly grayish white, orange-brown, or brown.

Captive Care: Many *Muricea* species are available in the hobby and are, almost without exception, very hardy aquarium specimens. Several captive-bred *Muricea* gorgonians are available; these show tremendous tolerance of varied lighting and water-flow conditions. Nonetheless, moderate flow and moderate to bright light will benefit these corals.

Special Information: *Muricea* have been known to produce sweeper

Muricea elongata (orange spiny sea rod): very hardy in the aquarium and distinguished by its rough, upward-pointed calyces and overall spiny appearance.

Muricea pinnata (long-spine sea fan): hardy choice for a Caribbean biotope.

Muricea laxa (delicate spiny sea rod): can be propagated from cuttings.

Muricea pendula (pinnate spiny sea fan): colorful Florida-Caribbean species.

Muriceopsis flavida (rough sea plume): color varies from yellow to purple-grey.

tentacles, though not to the extent of *Erythropodium*. It has also been established that they incorporate iodine into their skeletons.

Collection Impact: Abundant in the wild, *Muricea* are not likely to be overharvested for the aquarium trade and are good prospects for propagation efforts.

GENUS *Muriceopsis* Aurivillius, 1931
(myoor-iss'-ee-op'-sis)

Common Species: *M. flavida*.

Common Names: rough sea plume, Lamarck's gorgonian, feather gorgonian.

Identification: The most common and familiar species, *M. flavida*, forms tall colonies with plumelike branches. Other species, often forming low bushy colonies or occurring in deeper waters, are much less common and are not typically harvested for the aquar-

ium trade. The thin, cylindrical side branches are pinnate, having numerous small apertures and small fuzzy polyps randomly distributed along and around the branches. The axial sheath houses slender acute spindles, with spiny and often purple-colored spindles in the rind. Besides *Pseudopterogorgia* these are the only plumelike Atlantic gorgonians. *Muriceopsis*, however, has cylindrical branchlets.

Natural Location: Found commonly in shallow to mid-depth water, though they may occur in various reef habitats.

Colors: Can be found in brown or yellow hues, though purple or purple-gray is the most common color.

Captive Care: *Muriceopsis* are not reported to be as easy as other photosynthetic gorgonians to maintain in captivity, although I have not found them to be particularly demanding. They commonly shed their outer layer, but also tend to lose their rind

Plexaura homomalla (black sea rod): easily kept with good light and current.

Plexaura homomalla (black sea rod): rich source of human drug ingredients.

Plexaura flexuosa (bent sea rod): note dichotomous branching and tan color.

from the branch tips inward, leaving a thin axial core exposed on the branch like a dead twig.

Special Information: *Muriceopsis petila*, known as the deep-water sea plume, is found in depths of 30 m (100 ft.) or more in South Florida and the Bahamas (Humann, 1993).

Collection Impact: *Muriceopsis* contains common species whose wild populations should not be impacted significantly by the aquarium hobby.

GENUS *Plexaura* Lamouroux, 1812
(pleks-ohr'-ah)

Common Species: *P. dichotoma, P. flexuosa, P. homomalla, P. nina,* and perhaps 18 others.

Common Name: sea rod.

Identification: *Plexaura* is a large genus of gorgonians having flat formations of branches in numerous planes. They are bushy, but fairly short, rarely growing taller than 36 cm (14 in.) in height. The thick branches of *Plexaura* feel comparatively dry and rough compared to the usually heavily mucus-covered branches of some other genera. If present at all, small calyces are minimally raised from the rind surface with pore or pitlike apertures. Polyps are retractile. *Plexaura* species, unfortunately, are definitively identified by their sclerites. Therefore, species-level identification will not be possible for the hobbyist, and even genus identification is difficult because of *Plexaura*'s similarity to other gorgonian genera. *Plexaura flexuosa* is dichotomously branching and variable in color (often tan), and *P. homomalla* has a normally dark brown or black rind with less color variability and lateral branching, forming somewhat bushy colonies. Other species differences are mainly in the diameter and length of the end (terminal) branches.

Natural Location: Found from surface waters to over 60 m (200 ft.) in depth, these are photosynthetic gorgonians of great range, most of which can be expected to be reasonably tolerant specimens in the aquarium. *Plexaura nina* is generally found in deeper waters. *Plexaura homomalla* is characteristically from shallow to mid-depth waters.

Colors: Varied, but most *Plexaura* species are shades of purple, brown, and purplish gray.

Captive Care: *Plexaura* are tolerant of a wide variety of lighting and current requirements. No specific needs must be addressed in maintaining them. However, most collected specimens will come from areas of strong illumination and surging water movement. They commonly reproduce asexually by fragmentation, with over 90% of colonies in the wild produced in this manner (Lasker, 1983). Growth rates in some species can be up to 20 cm (8 in.) per year for some branches, although 9-20 mm (0.33-0.75 in.) per year seems about average. Like some other corals, *P.*

flexuosa is likely to feed on phytoplankton (Kim and Lasker, 1997).

Special Information: *Plexaura* species have received substantial media coverage in the past decade because they produce large amounts of prostaglandins (especially *P. homomalla*), chemicals known to have a wide variety of well-established pharmaceutical benefits. In contrast to many soft coral compounds produced by the zooxanthellae, prostaglandins are produced by the animal part of the gorgonian. The antibiotic effect of these substances makes many gorgonians resistant to disease, as well as discouraging predation. Concentration of prostaglandin A_2 in *P. homomalla* is a million times greater than that of most other invertebrates (Bakus et al., 1986).

Collection Impact: *Plexaura* contains common species that reportedly do not tolerate transport well. As with most gorgonians, specimens attached to substrate with their holdfast tend to be more adaptable to captivity than those without the attachment. Unfortunately, removal of the substrate piece is not usually in the best interest of the reef community. Although fragmentation or "branch snipping" is a far less invasive means of collection, the branches often die as they lie on substrate or bottoms in collection and holding facilities, as well as in wholesaler and retailer tanks. It would be most beneficial to allow branch trimmings to attach to small pieces of rubble in the ocean and then collect them once they have become attached.

GENUS *Plexaurella* Valenciennes, 1855
(plecks-or-ella')

Common Species: *P. dichotoma, P. fusifera, P. grisea, P. nutans, P. plumilla,* and perhaps 22 others.

Common Name: slit-pore sea rod.

Identification: *Plexaurella* species are distinguished easily by their normally slitlike or elliptical apertures from which a dense number of large, fuzzy, retractile polyps emerge. Calyces may or may not be present. They are often tall and bushy, with thick, sparse, cylindrical branches. Colonies show primarily dichotomous branching forms. Identification of their highly variant internal sclerites is necessary in identifying most species.

Natural Location: This genus consists of mostly mid-depth gorgonians, although they can be found in a diversity of habitats.

Colors: Yellow to brown; purple-gray.

Captive Care: Most species accommodate fairly well to aquarium conditions, preferring a regime with moderate current and light.

Special Information: As with other gorgonians, *Plexaurella* is a good candidate for aquaculture efforts.

Collection Impact: Overcollection is not perceived as a threat to natural populations.

Plexaurella nutans (giant slit-pore sea rod): distinguished by the slit-like apertures from which polyps emerge, this genus is hardy and grows quite large.

GENUS *Pseudoplexaura* Wright and Studer, 1889
(sood'-oh-plecks-ohr'-ah)

Common Species: *P. flagellosa, P. porosa, P. wagenaari,* and perhaps two others.

Common Name: porous sea rod.

Identification: *Pseudoplexaura* are not easily distinguished from *Plexaura.* They almost never have calyces around their gaping polyp apertures, which are numerous, round to oval in shape, and porelike. They also do not have spicules in their completely retractile polyps. They are normally dichotomously branching with thick main trunks and long tapering end branches. *Pseudoplexaura wagenaari* is a small colony, while *P. porosa* grows large and is often more than 1 m (3 ft.) across when mature.

Natural Location: Most common in shallow reef flats on substrate

Pseudoplexaura sp. (porous sea rod): durable and fast-growing.

Swiftia exserta (red-polyped gorgonian): poor aquarium survival prospects.

exposed to direct light and constant water movement, *Pseudoplexaura* are usually subject to the moderate surge of passing waves. *Pseudoplexaura porosa* is common to shallow back-reef areas.

Colors: Color is highly variable and includes colonies in hues of purple, yellow, brown, and gray.

Captive Care: All species are most common in shallow reef environments, so moderate to strong current and light is most beneficial in captivity. They are very hardy, although the rapid growth and mature size of some species makes small specimens (or very large tanks) a requirement.

Special Information: Most species are very slippery or slimy, owing to their heavy production of mucus.

    Pseudoplexaura crassa, *P. flagellosa*, and *P. porosa* produce the chemical compound crassin, which resembles penicillin, has antibacterial effects, and is toxic to fishes. These features are responsible for both deterring predation and increasing resistance to potential pathogens.

Collection Impact: *Pseudoplexaura* contains common species whose wild populations should not be impacted significantly by the aquarium hobby.

SUBFAMILY Stenogorgiinae: Composed of more than 20 tropical and subtropical azooxanthellate genera from the Atlantic, Indo-Pacific, and Mediterranean: *Acanthacis, Astrogorgia, Bebryce, Calcigorgia, Dentomuricea, Echinogorgia, Echinomuricea, Heterogorgia, Hypnogorgia, Lepidomuricea, Lytreia, Menella, Muriceides, Nicaule, Paracis, Paramuricea, Placogorgia, Pseudothesea, Scleracis, Swiftia, Thesea, Trachymuricea,* and *Villogorgia.* Of these, only *Swiftia* is seen with any regularity in the aquarium trade.

GENUS *Swiftia* Duchassaing and Michelotti, 1864 (swift'-ee-ah)

Common Species: *S. casta, S. exserta, S. kofoidi.*

Common Names: red-polyped gorgonian, orange tree gorgonian, orange sprite, orange sea fan.

Identification: The beautiful bright orange dichotomously branching colonies of *Swiftia* have showy and delicately pinnate red polyps with a spiky appearance. *Swiftia* are unlikely to be confused with other species, and gross appearance is usually all that is required to identify them. They are mostly planar, with scattered or biserial polyps and prominent conical calyces.

Natural Location: These are aposymbiotic corals, usually found at depths below 15 m (50 ft.) in caves and under overhangs.

Colors: Bright orange branches with red polyps.

Captive Care: Although not common in the wild, *Swiftia* species appear in aquarium stores with some regularly. Unfortunately, these corals have proved very difficult to maintain over the long term, and even frequent feedings are not usually enough to keep them alive. It is possible that highly specialized tanks provided with intentionally high nutrients, cooler water, a cavelike habitat, and a constant feeding schedule might be able to sustain them. Otherwise, *Swiftia* species are better left in their natural habitat.

Special Information: These gorgonians seem to be capable of substantial iodine uptake. The degree to which this plays a role in their survival and health is not known.

Collection Impact: The poor record of survival in captivity and intensive care required for these gorgonians should discourage their collection and sale. Only aquarists willing to devote the time and care necessary for their survival should attempt to keep them.

FAMILY Gorgoniidae Lamouroux, 1812

The Gorgoniidae are characterized by a horny axis with a minimally chambered central chord. Their polyps are retractile and the rind is composed almost entirely of gorgonin. They grow in diverse forms in varied locations (both Atlantic and Pacific genera exist). The genera are: *Adelogorgia, Eugorgia, Eunicella, Gorgonia, Hicksonella, Leptogorgia, Lophogorgia, Olindagorgia, Pacifigorgia, Phycogorgia, Phyllogorgia, Pseudopterogorgia, Pterogorgia,* and *Rumphella*. Those found in the aquarium trade are described below:

GENUS *Gorgonia* Linnaeus, 1758

(gor-go'-nee-ah)

Common Species: *G. flabellum, G. mariae, G. ventalina,* and perhaps 49 others.

Common Name: sea fan.

Identification: Quite possibly the best-recognized gorgonians in the tropical seas and once one of the most common purchases by curio-hunting tourists, these gray- and purple-veined sea fans with brown polyps make up a well-known genus with several members. Adult colonies form medium to large fans with interconnected netlike structures composed of small branchlets fused in a tightly woven mesh. (*Gorgonia mariae* and some others may lack the tight-mesh spacing, becoming slightly more open, with branchlets not always interconnecting.)

These sea fans always branch in single planes, although new fans may begin growing out of the primary plane. In such cases, perpendicular "plane-lets" can be seen, usually near the base of the colony. Branchlets are typically flattened perpendicular to the fan blade in *G. flabellum*, and are flattened parallel to the fan plane in *G. ventalina*. Polyps extend from the inner surfaces of the branchlets toward the voids in the fan meshwork.

Natural Location: *Gorgonia flabellum* is common to outer-reef zones, while *G. ventalina* is more common on inshore and patch-reef areas. Sea fans are most common from the surface downward to about (15 m) 50 ft. They can be found both in great abundance and as sparse populations. Those near the water's surface and exposed to higher water movement tend to be smaller and more sturdy.

Colors: Most *Gorgonia* are purple to lavender and gray, with primary veins being more distinctly purple. Brown polyps tend to cast a golden tone over the fan. Occasionally, sea fans are bright yellow or shades of yellow to brown.

Captive Care: Sea fans have not always done well in aquariums, and in the past they were reported to deteriorate over time. In recent years, however, many aquarists have had better success with some sea fans by providing bright lighting and more vigor-

Gorgonia mariae (wide-mesh sea fan): requires strong light and water motion.

Gorgonia ventalina (common sea fan): collection is prohibited in many areas.

Gorgonia flabellum (Venus sea fan): must be oriented perpendicular to current.

Leptogorgia miniata (carmine sea spray): requires extraordinary care.

Leptogorgia virgulata (violet sea whip): note marine snow, a key food source.

ous circulation. They should be placed so that the fan is perpendicular to the water flow. The base must be firmly attached to a rocky substrate with underwater epoxy or a cable tie until the sea fan anchors itself in place. Water movement should be oscillatory and surging against the broad face of the fan, and lighting should be quite intense (they are photosynthetic animals). The fanlike branching pattern is a highly effective filter-feeding pattern that can become clogged with debris and hair algae without adequate water movement. Small colonies, especially, can do well for experienced reef aquarists.

Special Information: Polyps of *Gorgonia* species produce many terpenoid compounds and may adversely affect other corals in captive systems.

Collection Impact: The two most common species, *G. flabellum* and *G. ventalina*, are now both illegal to collect in Florida waters and many—but not all—Caribbean locations. This is a good limitation, as overharvesting for the souvenir market has been a serious problem and large numbers of sea fans have been lost to the sea fan disease *Aspergillosis*. Concerned hobbyists should be careful to acquire only legally collected specimens. Propagation of sea fans, both in captive systems or in aquaculture tracts, is a possibility.

GENUS *Leptogorgia* Milne, Edwards, and Haime, 1857
(lept-oh-gor'-gee-ah)

Common Species: *L. californica, L. cardinalis, L. caryi, L. euryale, L. hebes, L. medusa, L. miniata, L. punicea, L. setacea, L. stheno, L. virgulata,* and perhaps 12 others.

Common Names: sea spray, sea whip.

Identification: These thin and sparsely branched gorgonians are either pinnate or dichotomously branched, usually in a single plane. Polyps are arranged in rows on either side of the branches, sometimes in a single row or, more frequently, in double rows. Calyces are subdued, except in *L. hebes* where they are notably raised. Colony shape depends largely on water flow, with whiplike specimens in low-flow areas, and fanlike shapes in areas of tidal flow and back-and-forth wave action. *Leptogorgia virgulata* forms colonies typically less than 45 cm (18 in.) tall. Bayer (1981) and Cairns (1991) assert that *Leptogorgia* and *Lophogorgia* are separate genera. In contrast, Humann (1993) and Grasshoff (1992) claim that *Leptogorgia* has absorbed the *Lophogorgia* genus. In this text, we follow the latter convention.

Natural Location: These aposymbiotic gorgonians are very common throughout the reefs of the tropical Atlantic, with a range that extends to the western Pacific and Indian Oceans and the mid-Atlantic coast of the United States. *Leptogorgia* is even found in my old stomping grounds of the northern Gulf coast outside of Mobile Bay (Mitchell et al., 1993), although I'm not eager to brave those mucky waters to look for it. (Down the road along the Florida Panhandle is a much better place to go *Leptogorgia* hunting.)

Colors: White, yellow, orange, and red are the most common.

Captive Care: *Leptogorgia* reportedly fare very poorly in the aquarium. The polyps must be fed frequently and, even so, may tend to lose their rind tissue and degenerate until nothing is left but the hairlike axial centers. In the wild, tests have confirmed that these corals quit feeding when as few as 10% of the polyps have captured food. In the aquarium, this presents obvious difficulties. They are also easily overgrown by algae and are very difficult to maintain under even the best aquarium conditions.

Special Information: *Leptogorgia* secrete homarine, a substance known to inhibit diatom growth.

Pseudopterogorgia americana (slimy sea feathers): good aquarium choice.

Pseudopterogorgia bipinnata (bipinnate sea plume): popular and hardy.

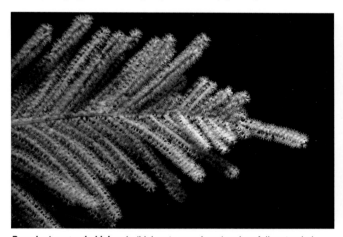

Pseudopterogorgia bipinnata (bipinnate sea plume): polyps fully extended.

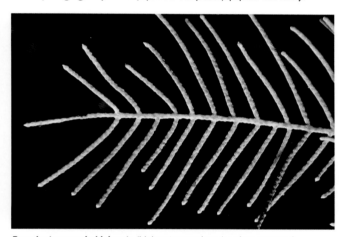

Pseudopterogorgia bipinnata (bipinnate sea plume): polyps retracted.

Collection Impact: The poor record of survival in captivity and demanding care required for these gorgonians mandates a more-limited collection in the interest of their conservation. Only aquarists willing to devote the time and care necessary for their survival should attempt to keep them.

GENUS *Pseudopterogorgia* Kukenthal, 1919
(sue-dop'-tare-oh-gor'-gee-ah)

Common Species: *P. acerosa, P. americana, P. bipinnata, P. elisabethae, P. kallos, P. rigida,* and perhaps 13 others.

Common Names: sea plume, sea feathers, purple frilly gorgonian.

Identification: Most gorgonians of the *Pseudopterogorgia* genus are not offered to the aquarium trade because of their large size, but some appealing smaller species are often available. Many *Pseudopterogorgia* are very slimy (except for *P. acerosa*) and some

grow to the height of small trees—up to 2 m (7 ft.). All species have pinnate plumelike branches with long evenly spaced secondary branches that grow in single planes. Although they share the small slitlike apertures of *Plexaurella*, the apertures are neatly lined up in single or staggered double rows on each side of branches and stiff branchlets, instead of being uniformly and randomly spaced. *Pseudopterogorgia americana* has small polyps with short tentacles, and colonies usually less than 1 m (39 in.) tall.

Natural Location: *Pseudopterogorgia* occur in varied locations, habitats, and depths. Most are found where there is significant water current and surge. *Pseudopterogorgia americana* is most common in shallow patch-reef environments.

Colors: The most commonly available aquarium species is *P. bipinnata*, often a bright purple or bright yellow. *Pseudopterogorgia elisabethae* is a photosynthetic gorgonian that is almost always

Pterogorgia citrina (yellow sea blade): note distinctive flattened branches.

Pterogorgia sp. (purple sea blade): photosynthetic, but somewhat demanding.

Rumphella sp. (Pacific sea rod): a likely aquarium candidate but seldom seen.

purple with polyps that appear white, though they are actually a very pale brown.

Captive Care: *Pseudopterogorgia* are symbiotic (photosynthetic) and highly adaptable. They are quite tolerant of varying light conditions and prefer moderate current and lighting. The most common problem seen with these corals is the loss of rind tissue from the branch ends. Snipping the tip of the denuded core slightly ahead of the branch recession sometimes allows the coral to stop losing the rind, and the cut end can heal rapidly. These gorgonians also seem to fare better when purchased while still attached to a clutch of substrate by their holdfast. Once acclimated, they become quite tolerant to most tank conditions. These gorgonians, along with many, are susceptible to cyanobacterial band diseases (Chapter 11). *Pseudopterogorgia* have also been shown to have fairly sharp lethal temperature limits at about 31°C (88°F) (Goldberg, 1973).

Special Information: *Pseudopterogorgia* produce high levels of terpenoids, including curcuquinone and pseudopterolide, that function as antimicrobial agents, feeding deterrents, and cytotoxins. Pseudopterosins are being investigated as potential painkillers.

Collection Impact: *Pseudopterogorgia* are common, widespread gorgonians whose wild populations should not be impacted significantly by the aquarium hobby.

GENUS *Pterogorgia* Ehrenberg, 1834

(tare-oh-gor'-gee-ah)

Common Species: *P. anceps, P. citrina, P. guadalupensis*, and perhaps 12 others.

Common Names: sea whip, sea blade.

Identification: An easy genus to identify, *Pterogorgia* have flattened, bladelike, or triangular branches with polyps extending from rows of apertures along the flat edges. Apertures are normally slit-like with raised calyces or grooves along the branch edge. Colonies are mostly heavily and dichotomously branched. Although white polyps in some species normally indicate a non-photosynthetic gorgonian, members of this genus are photosynthetic. Other species have the more-typical tan to brown polyps. *Pterogorgia anceps* has three- or four-flanged flattened branches that look like an X or a Y in cross section, with polyps extending from each of the three or four edges. They are usually dark purple, though other colors are occasional. *Pterogorgia citrina* is often bright yellow, orange, or brown with contrasting white polyps, although its olive-colored morph is most commonly collected.

Natural Location: Predominantly shallow-water inshore corals.

Colors: The colonies are quite variable in color from purple to gray, olive, brown, yellow, or orange.

Ellisella elongata (long sea whip): tall, deep-water species that is part of an azooxanthellate genus.

Pacific sea whip, possibly *Ellisella* sp.: apparently healthy specimen growing in a European aquarium.

Nicella schmitti (bushy sea whip): a deep-water Caribbean beauty that defies easy captive care.

Captive Care: These are considered to be difficult gorgonians to maintain in captivity, and they often become covered in microalgae. After a while, they may refuse to open and will waste away. Strong currents and a regular feeding schedule may offer a higher chance of success. Strong illumination, particularly for *P. citrina*, is very important.

Special Information: *Pterogorgia* are copious producers of unusual pharmaceutically beneficial compounds. Among them are lactones like ancepsenolide.

Collection Impact: *Pterogorgia* contain common species whose wild populations should not be impacted significantly by the aquarium hobby.

GENUS *Rumphella* Bayer, 1955

(rum-fell'-ah)

Common Species: *R. aggregata.*

Common Name: Pacific sea rod.

Species of these typically bushy, brownish gorgonians contain very high numbers of zooxanthellae and may be successful in the aquarium if they are available. They have a continuous axis with sclerites of symmetrical clubs and spindles. Commonly brown, the lateral branches are fairly thick and uniform, forming unremarkable growth patterns of often twisted, flexible branches.

FAMILY Ellisellidae Gray, 1859

This family consists of seven genera, none of which are commonly available in the aquarium trade. All are azooxanthellate (nonphotosynthetic) and those that have been imported are reported to be very difficult or impossible to keep alive. They are characterized by a highly calcified axis. The central chord is neither soft nor chambered. Growth forms are variable and are found in both Atlantic and Pacific Oceans. The genera are: *Ctenocella* (Pacific lyres or candelabra), *Ellisella* (Atlantic, Pacific, and Mediterranean sea whips), *Junceella* (Pacific sea whips), *Nicella* (Atlantic and Pacific deep-water fans and whips), *Riisea* (Atlantic gorgonians), *Toeplitzella* (Pacific gorgonians), and *Verrucella* (Pacific gorgonians).

FAMILY Ifalukellidae Bayer, 1955

This family consists of two genera, neither of which are commonly available in the aquarium trade. They are characterized by arborescent colonies with a highly calcified axis. The central chord is neither soft nor chambered. Polyps look like *Tubipora* and the sclerites like *Xenia*. The genera are *Ifalukella* and *Plumigorgia*.

FAMILY Chrysogorgiidae Verrill, 1883

Genera: *Chalcogorgia, Chrysogorgia, Distichogorgia , Helicogorgia, Iridogorgia, Isidoides, Metallogorgia, Pleurogorgia, Radicipes, Stephanogorgia, Trichogorgia,* and *Xenogorgia.*

The family consists of 12 genera, none of which are commonly available in the aquarium trade. They are characterized by a highly calcified, glossy, iridescent or metallic axis. Their scales reflect metallic or iridescent colors with polarized light. They have either a large, branched calcareous root for attachment to soft sub-

Ctenocella pectinata (Pacific candelabrum): distinctive and rare. (W. Australia)

Isis hippuris (Pacific bushy gorgonian): photosynthetic and reef tank suitable.

strate or a small holdfast for hard substrate. Most are found on soft bottoms. Colonies adopt unbranched or highly regular linear, spiral, or dichotomous branching patterns. They are mostly found in deep water, and their twisting, regular branching patterns, as well as their coloration, make some spectacular formations.

FAMILY Primnoidae Gray, 1857

Genera: *Ainigmaptilon, Amphilapsis, Armadillogorgia, Arthrogorgia, Ascolepsis, Callogorgia, Callozostron, Calyptrophora, Candidella, Dasystenella, Narella, Ophidiogorgia, Paracalyptrophora, Parastenella, Plumarella, Primnoa, Primnoella, Primnoeides, Pseudoplumarella, Pterostenella,* and *Thouarella*

This family consists of 21 genera found throughout the world's oceans, but none are commonly available in the aquarium trade. Colonies are typically highly branched, characterized by a highly calcified axis without a chambered or soft chord. Their base is calcified and disclike, rarely branched and rootlike. The sclerites are scales. Polyps are heavily armored and are always nonretractile and noncontractile. The tentacles can only fold over the oral opening, but they are protected by eight scales that form an operculum. They are typically pinnate and are prone to becoming infested with epizoic life, other parasites, and associated commensal organisms.

FAMILY Isididae Lamouroux, 1812

This family consists of four subfamilies, with very few available to the aquarium trade. They are characterized by an axis of alternating nodes and internodes; the nodes are purely horny and the internodes calcareous. They may have a calcareous holdfast or calcareous rootlike bases (for soft substrate).

SUBFAMILY Isidinae: Characterized by having fully or partly retractile anthocodiae. The genera are *Chelidonisis* and *Isis*.

Chelidonisis Studer, 1890: Colonies dichotomously branch in one plane from the nodes, rather than from the internodes. The rind is thin and the polyps are fully retractile (Atlantic, South Africa).

Isis Linnaeus, 1758: This may be one of the better genera to keep in aquariums, because at least some species are photosynthetic. These are unique gorgonians with rigid fused sclerites for inner support. However, polymeric materials make up "joints" that allow for flexibility and food procurement in ocean water movement. Colonies are planar or bushy, branching from the internodes, with a thick rind and fully retractile polyps. Typically yellow-brown. The most common species is *Isis hippuris* (Pacific).

SUBFAMILY Muricellisidinae: Characterized by fully retractile polyps with prominent, separated, and well armored calyces. Branching occurs from the hollow internodes. The genus is *Muricellisis* (Pacific).

SUBFAMILY Keratoisidinae: Characterized by the sclerites and by having nonretractile polyps. The genera are: *Acanella* (Atlantic, Pacific), *Isidella* (E. Atlantic, Mediterranean), *Keratoisis* (Atlantic, Pacific), and *Lepidisis* (Pacific).

SUBFAMILY Mopseinae: Characterized by nonretractile polyps and branching from the internodes. The genera are: *Chathamisis, Circinisis, Echinisis, Minuisis, Mopsea* (Pacific), *Peltastisis* (Pacific), *Primnoisis* (Antarctic).

Ptilosarcus gurneyi (sea pen): rare and beautiful, but demanding deep substrate and heavy feeding.

Cavernulina or *Cavernularia* sp. (sea pen): will feed on suspended detritus and zooplankton-like fare.

Pteroeides sp. (sea pen): some members of this genus grow to 60 cm (24 in.) in the wild.

ORDER PENNATULACEA Verrill, 1865

FAMILY Veretillidae

Sea Pens

The final group of octocorals that are occasionally available in the aquarium hobby are the sea pens, or pennatulaceans. There has been virtually no work done in the study of these curious octocorals, so knowledge about them is limited at best. The reasons for this relative obscurity include the lack of good characteristics with which to evaluate them, a poor fossil record owing to their lack of a true skeleton, a shortage of available specimens for study, and a high degree of variability between individuals.

Aquarium Genera: *Cavernularia, Pteroeides, Virgularia,* and others.

Common Species: *Cavernularia obesa.*

Common Names: sea pen, pennatulacean, sea plume.

Identification: Current classification depends on axis development, body symmetry, sclerite characteristics, polyp type and arrangement, secondary polyp appendages, presence of adjacent polyp fusion, degree of dimorphic polyp zonations, and growth form. Clearly, identifying the sea pens is no easy task.

Natural Location: Sea pens inhabit soft sand or mud bottoms and are solitary corals with unbranched colonies that look very similar to an old quill pen buried to the plume in the sand. The lower portion of the body is the primary polyp or muscular **peduncle** that buries into the bottom and helps to anchor the animal in substrate. A feathery group of feeding polyps, an apparatus

called the **rachis**, is then unfurled directly above the substrate into the water column. Sea pens usually have both autozooid and siphonozooid retractable polyps on leaflike extensions of the main polyp axis, called the **oozooid**. All species have a calcified central axis with needlelike or platelike sclerites. Polyp sclerites are mostly ovals and rods.

Colors: Sea pens are highly variable in appearance, with white, purple and grayish white being most common.

Captive Care: Sea pens require, at the very least, a good supply of particulate food in the water and a deep substrate—at least 8-10 cm (3-4 in.)—in which to sink their "feet." They are primarily nocturnal and are filter-feeding specialists. They will capture small particles of detritus stirred up from the substrate and should be given regular feedings of zooplankton-like fare (enriched brine shrimp and other high-protein marine rations of small particle size). They tend to move around in the soft bottom and may even occasionally "float" out of the substrate into trouble. These unique corals do not have a good history of survival in the aquarium. The lack of sufficient and proper food sources may be the reason for their usually short life in captivity.

Special Information: Many sea pens are phosphorescent/bioluminescent and may emit sparks and waves of glowing greenish or bluish light at night. The flashing likely serves as a warning to potential predators, often fishes and gastropods.

Collection Impact: Pennatulaceans are not heavily collected for the aquarium trade.

The Zoanthids

Colonial Anemones and Button Polyps

Forming thick blankets or billowy masses of polyps that resemble miniature anemones, the zoanthids can make appealing and sometimes very colorful additions to a reef aquarium community. They are among the hardiest of all cnidarians and can add interest and beauty to any reefscape, although some are aggressive colonizers that can overtake other aquarium corals.

The 60 or so described species of zoanthids, otherwise known as button polyps or colonial anemones, are not always thought of as corals at all, but these small, soft-bodied, noncalcifying organisms are typically grouped with the corals within the aquarium hobby. Although there are some solitary species, most that make their way into aquariums tend to form large aggregations in nature, encrusting hard substrates and superficially appearing to be large coral colonies. Some are epizoic—living on sponges or other sessile invertebrates in a relationship that can be a challenge to sustain in captivity.

ANATOMY AND BIOLOGY

Like some of the octocorals (*Clavularia* species and other stoloniferans), button polyps are often connected by runners, called **stolons**. Others are encased in a mat called the **coenenchyme** or **mesoglea**. A number of species incorporate bits

Parazoanthus **sp.** (yellow polyps): although a challenge to identify, many zoanthids are attractive, easily kept, and justifiably popular with marine aquarists.

of sediment, sand, and rock into the coenenchyme that add rigidity and support to the colony. Many have flattened, smooth oral discs that are often quite broad, with no tentacles on the disc surface. Instead, two rings of tentacles, often alternating, encircle the disc.

Zoanthids are described by their internal anatomical differences as being either **brachycnemic** or **macrocnemic**, depending on the arrangement of their mesenteries. The brachycnemic zoanthids have a fifth incomplete mesentery in cycles where the septa do not reach the center of the column. Macrocnemic zoanthids have a complete fifth mesentery. This arrangement, along with other characteristics, is used in the systemic classification of the group. DNA work appears necessary to make further subdivisions, especially to the species level.

A single **siphonoglyph**, or mouth, leads into the gastrovascular cavity, which has vibrating cilia that assist in both feeding and water exchange within the polyp. Zoanthids have a leathery skin, the **cuticle**, which covers the soft-bodied creatures like a protective outer shell. It is composed partly of chitin. Most are very heavy mucus producers and are found bathed in heavy, sticky secretions.

Colonial anemones vary dramatically in their morphology, according to their location on the reef. Some species are found in normal mid-level reef environments, while others are found covering the rocks where waves break. Colonies from areas of higher water movement show expectedly reduced polyp profiles, usually having a dense encrusting mat, short tentacles, inflexible body columns, and lowered mucus production. Those from deeper and calmer waters show taller growth forms, larger oral discs, more flexible body columns, higher mucus production to aid in sediment rejection, and longer tentacles to assist in prey capture/filter feeding.

Although some zoanthids feed preferentially either at night or during the day, most feed continuously and only close in response to physical disturbances. Zoanthids may also occasionally undergo surface cleansing. At such times, the polyps close up for a week or so while surface mucus and tissue layers are sloughed off, ridding the colonies of surface algae, sediments, and wastes.

Many colonial anemones live in association with sponges and other invertebrates, and such species were at one time considered to be parasitic (*Parazoanthus* species, *Epizoanthus* species, and others). However, it now seems that although the zoanthids do gain nutrition when they grow on the surface of living organisms (usually sponges), they also tend to protect their hosts from predation. In turn, the sponges, which are apparently immune to zoanthid toxins, gain some nutritive value from the waste material and mucus community of the zoanthids. Many species are **aposematic**, having bright coloration as a warning to discourage predators. Dull-colored zoanthids do not usually have the protection of toxic compounds and may gain protection from sponges with which they associate. These sponges not only provide warning coloration, but also contain toxic compounds these zoanthids lack. Thus, the relationship is more commensal than was previously thought.

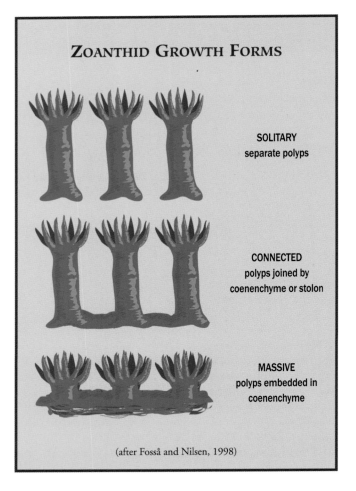

ZOANTHID GROWTH FORMS

SOLITARY
separate polyps

CONNECTED
polyps joined by
coenenchyme or stolon

MASSIVE
polyps embedded in
coenenchyme

(after Fosså and Nilsen, 1998)

Masses of zoanthid colonies (*Palythoa* sp.) at low tide on the Great Barrier Reef.

Most zoanthids encountered are symbiotic and contain dense populations of zooxanthellae. Zooxanthellae can even be found in the mesoglea and epidermal layers of some species of *Palythoa*. However, heterotrophy and direct absorption of nutrients from the water can play an important role in their nutrient acquisition. In fact, most species are very active feeders on plankton and particulate food, closing rapidly on bits of material that drift through their tentacles. Studies have shown that even under very bright illumination, species that do not actively capture prey still must supplement their energy needs; light alone is not enough to sustain their metabolism. Starvation results in a rapid reduction in polyp size and filamentous algae overgrowth.

Despite their strong anemone-like feeding response, it does not appear that the colonial anemones have a very strong sting. Most nearby corals are usually dominant over colonial anemones in this respect. As such, these animals rarely cause significant harm to their neighbors. However, the zoanthids are frequently dominant in their ability to overgrow and smother other colonies. Some studies have shown a "dead zone" in competitive encounters, and the more actively heterotrophic species may exhibit a chemical or stinging-type ability in competitive encounters. Zoanthids are known to produce the highly potent toxin **palytoxin** (see page 182), and the pharmacologically active substance **seratonine**. Because they are very hardy and quite tolerant of comparatively poor water quality, colonial anemones are often found thriving in areas where the reef has been damaged by pollution and excess nutrients. Little is known about most zoanthids' reproductive abilities, but most seem to be hermaphroditic.

TAXONOMY

"Zoanthid taxonomy is currently in a state of chaos, with many described species, very few of which can be reliably identified," wrote W.J. Burnett et al. in 1997. Predictably, identification of the colonial anemones to the species level is difficult because of the inherent variability of the colonies and polyps, lack of skeletal characteristics, and an overall lack of experience with their relative abundance in nature. Revision of all the genera is likely in the near future.

Some recent aquarium literature states that *Palythoa* has been mostly absorbed by *Protopalythoa*, and that taxonomic revisions are in place (Delbeek and Sprung, 1997; Fosså and Nilsen, 1998). However, while Burnett et al. (1997) affirm that revisions are likely, they also show phylogenic charts and proposals that do not support the information presented in these other works. Using genetic studies, new findings show that *Palythoa* and *Protopalythoa* are actually more distinct than some authors have suggested.

The work of Burnett et al. has indicated that genetic data and morphological characters are not in agreement and should be reassessed. They doubt the current validity of the *Protopalythoa* genus and note that the incorporation of sand into the coenenchyme (the bed of tissue from which the zoanthid polyps arise) and/or the degree to which polyps are embedded in this connecting tissue are not the only distinguishing characteristics between the two. The number of tentacles, as well as the presence or lack of zooxanthellae in the ova of *Protopalythoa* and *Palythoa*, respectively, may be other distinguishing characteristics in some species. To avoid total chaos, I will use this currently accepted taxonomy (Burnett et al.) until such reclassifications are actually established.

A number of zoanthid genera are not covered here because of the relative unavailability of such species in the aquarium trade. For example, the Family Neozoanthidae (which consists

GUIDE TO THE COLONIAL ANEMONES

Zoanthidae
e.g., *Palythoa*

Epizoanthidae
e.g., *Epizoanthus*

Parazoanthidae
e.g., *Parazoanthus*

Phylum: Cnidaria
Class: Anthozoa
Subclass: Hexacorallia
(Zoantharia)
Order: Zoanthidea
(Zoanthiniaria)
Suborder: Brachycnemina
Family: Zoanthidae
Family: Neozoanthidae
Suborder: Macrocnemina
Family: Epizoanthidae
Family: Parazoanthidae

of the single genus *Neozoanthus*) is never commonly available to the hobby.

SUBORDER BRACHYCNEMINA

FAMILY Zoanthidae Gray, 1840
Genera: *Acrozoanthus, Isaurus, Palythoa, Protopalythoa, Sphenopus,* and *Zoanthus.*

Only *Zoanthus, Palythoa, Protopalythoa,* and *Isaurus* are available in the aquarium trade, with only the first three occurring with any regularity. *Acrozoanthus* may occasionally be available. This family is characterized by having brachycnemic mesenteries and tentacles. This means that the fifth pair of mesenteries is incomplete. Furthermore, the tentacles are arranged in two rows around the periphery of the oral disc. Most are symbiotic (except *Sphenopus,* and perhaps species of *Acrozoanthus*).

GENUS *Acrozoanthus*
(ak'-roh-zoe-an'-thuss)
These are the fairly common aquarium imports called "stick polyps" that grow on the outer covering of certain tube-dwelling polychaete worms or fanworms. Most frequently, these show up, *sans* worm, with a few zoanthids spaced apart

Acrozoanthus sp. (stick polyps): captive colony growing on a tubeworm casing.

Isaurus tuberculatus (tube polyps): occasionally arrive on pieces of live rock.

on the empty tube. I have found them to survive reasonably well, but there is a problem: The outer tube of these worms is a tough organic material, but one that the worm must consistently rebuild using its own secretions. Without this constant repair work, the vacant tube becomes food for various organisms and microbes. Soon, the tube is gone, and the zoanthids wind up drifting away.

Acrozoanthus have long tentacles and have mistakenly (and understandably) been grouped with the Family Parazoanthidae in the past. They are small and attractive, gray to brownish, occasionally dark brown. If they can be affixed to more permanent accommodations, they may survive—if adequate food is available. Their natural attraction to the polychaete tube, however, seems to indicate a nutritional preference, but more research is needed to clarify the nature and importance of the relationship.

GENUS *Isaurus* Gray, 1828

(i-sahr'-us)

Atlantic Species: *I. duchassaingi, I. spongiosus, I. tuberculatus.*
Pacific Species: *I. cliftoni, I. maculatus, I. tuberculatus.*
Common Names: snake polyps, tube polyps.

Isolated colonies of the upright tubular polyps of *Isaurus* may occasionally be seen for sale, or they may be found attached to live rock as incidental organisms. These small colonies usually occur naturally either on the reef crest or on sediments. They have reduced tentacles and longer cylindrical body columns that often remain partially buried in substrate. Individual polyps may remain separate or attached by stolons. Like some *Palythoa* and *Protopalythoa* species, they contain zooxanthellae in both their gastrodermis and epidermis. They are typically seen in shades of gray, brown, or green. *Isaurus tuberculatus* is named for the

Isaurus sp. (tube polyps): zoanthids can fill various niches in a reef aquarium.

Palythoa sp. (sea mat): polyps extended. Will encrust live rock in the aquarium.

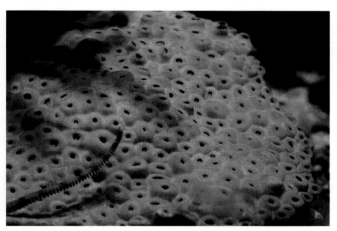

Palythoa sp. (sea mat): polyps retracted. Grows best under bright lighting.

rows of protuberances along its column, called tubercles. Other *Isaurus* possess these features as well, but they may be variable and typically are less pronounced. *Isaurus* species are rarely available to the aquarium hobby.

GENUS *Palythoa* Lamouroux
(pal'-ee-thoe'-ah)

Common Species: *P. caesia, P. caribaeorum, P. complanata, P. mammillosa, P. psammophila, P. tuberculosa,* and many others.

Common Names: sea mat, button polyps.

Identification: *Palythoa* is a very common genus of colonial anemones that often cover large tracts of reef. Usually found on reef flats and lagoons, the polyps have a coenenchyme that incorporates debris and small reef elements that can comprise up to 45% of their total weight (Haywick and Mueller, 1997). Sedi-

ments are ordinarily removed from the surface, but finer material is transported by cilia into the mesoglea to be added to the coenenchyme, where it may reside for several years before being expelled. It appears that the material is selected on the basis of size, not composition. The colonies often grow in convex or hemispherical shapes and usually remain less than 30 cm (12 in.) across. The polyps are broad, flat discs with knoblike, short, tapered or long, thin tentacles surrounding the disc rim. Tentacles are generally fewer than in *Protopalythoa.* Some species also incorporate zooxanthellae into their eggs. Not only do *Palythoa* species bind and incorporate sediments, but they are also capable of rudimentary aragonite crystal formation in a type of light-induced biological mineralization (Haywick and Mueller, 1997).

The following are the common species with their descriptions as currently known and accepted:

Atlantic Species:

Palythoa caribaeorum: Forms large and small encrusting mats of short tan, white, or coffee-colored polyps; polyps very densely packed and touching each other; often seen with some polyps closed while others remain open. This coral aggressively overgrows almost all known sessile life (except a tunicate and *Erythropodium* species) and has a very high growth rate—up to 4 mm (0.125 in.) per day; found generally in shallow areas of higher water movement.

Palythoa mammillosa: Forms small hemispherical colonies, less than 15 cm (6 in.) across; forms encrusting mats of yellow to golden brown polyps; encrusting base looks very "coral-like" with definite demarcations between individual polyps that do not touch when expanded; polyps have a large oral disc with short round tentacles; common in shallow areas of strong water movement and intense lighting.

Pacific Species:

Palythoa caesia: Forms encrusting mat of small ovoid blobs less than 10 cm (4 in.) across; sediment-encrusted polyps are buried in a thick coenenchyme; polyps are dark brown to white; prefers high water movement and light as it is found subtidally and on reef crests.

Palythoa psammophila: Forms encrusting mat of light brown to green polyps, often with fine radiating lines on the oral disc;

Palythoa caribaeorum (white encrusting zoanthid): may overgrow other corals.

Palythoa caesia (Pacific mat polyps): handle all zoanthids with great care.

fine hairlike tentacles surround rim; oral disc often fluorescent under actinic light. This is a common import with heavy attachment of sand and debris in the coenenchyme; polyps often partially buried in sand.

Palythoa tuberculosa: Small, single-layered, hemispherical encrusting colonies of milk-chocolate-colored polyps; colonies are coral-like with polyps distinctly separated on an organic solid coenenchyme, yet individual polyps appear attached to the substrate. Colonies split frequently, appearing initially adjacent like the honeycomb patterns of some stony corals and then fusing together. Many polyps may be closed at one time. This is predominantly a nighttime feeder. Found in diverse habitats from shallow surge zones to deep water; rarely changes its color.

Natural Location: *Palythoa* zoanthids grow frequently among the company of other corals. They are normally found in high-energy shallow-water areas where certain species can form large colonies that cover vast areas of substrate. They are most often found shoreward from the reef crest in diverse habitats, although I have frequently seen *P. caribaeorum* on outer-reef slopes at depths of 15-18 m (50-60 ft.) in the Lesser Antilles. (See species descriptions, above, for specific habitat information.)

Colors: Found in cream, brown, yellow, and other shades, the coenenchyme color is more or less continuous up the column of the embedded polyps. The oral discs may contrast somewhat, typically being darker than the coenenchyme ground color, occasionally with notes of greenish brown, but rarely highly colored.

Captive Care: *Palythoa* species are very light tolerant, but grow rapidly with bright light. However, these zoanthids will bleach, and, in fact, *P. caribaeorum* is one of the first corals to expel its zooxanthellae in Caribbean reefs and may even serve as an indicator of bleaching episodes. Water flow should be moderate to strong, depending on the species. *Palythoa* species are well known to be competitive with and dominant to almost all other corals, capping their supremacy by overgrowing their victims. Reef keepers should keep this fact in mind, as any sessile life near a growing colony will almost certainly die eventually, becoming covered in *Palythoa*.

Special Information: See "Neurotoxin Warning," page 182.

Collection Impact: *Palythoa* divide and spread rapidly and are usually abundant in nature. However, their collection can be difficult, and also incidentally damaging, in that the substrate must usually be removed to obtain an intact colony. Occasionally, the mat can be cut and lifted or peeled from the substrate. These colonies are rarely offered as captive-propagated colonies, although they should be an easy group to multiply on pieces of rubble or artificial substrate.

Palythoa sp. (Pacific mat polyps): with *Caulerpa racemosa*. (Fiji)

Protopalythoa sp. (solitary Pacific zoanthids): competing for space. (Maldives)

Protopalythoa vestitus (green zoanthids): can dominate other corals. (Fiji)

Protopalythoa grandis (sun zoanthid): large-polyped Caribbean species.

Protopalythoa sp. (unidentified zoanthid polyps): spreading aquarium colony.

GENUS *Protopalythoa*

(pro'-toe-pal'-ee-thoe'-ah)

Common Species: Many apparently different species are seen, but most are unclassified.

Common Names: button polyps, sea mat.

Identification: *Protopalythoa* is a genus that is often considered to be part of *Palythoa*. However, the polyps are usually not embedded in the base mat (coenenchyme), remaining crowded but separate, with conspicuous stalks that are often connected at their bases. They generally have more tentacles than *Palythoa* as well. There have been some discrepancies describing this genus in aquarium literature, and the correct differences should be noted. Colonies are usually not large, with some even existing as predominantly solitary animals. Brown or dark green polyps with short and sometimes knobbed tentacles are often encrusted with sediments and particles. The tentacles and oral opening may contrast in color with the rest of the animal. Oral discs are broad and flat, and spokelike striations are common patterns on the discs. Though not readily apparent, numerous internal mesenteries (more than 60) are a conspicuous characteristic. *Protopalythoa grandis, P. caribbea,* and at least some other species are somewhat unique in that they possess zooxanthellae in both their tissue layers and in the mesoglea.

Pacific Species:

Protopalythoa mutuki: Heavily sediment-encrusted polyps joined only at the base that are found intertidally on reef flats and rocky shores. Large polyps are normally dark green with a white mouth. This zoanthid commonly arrives in the aquarium as a survivor on live rock.

Protopalythoa toxica: Noted for abundant production of palytoxin, this large polyp may be the same species as the Atlantic species *P. grandis.* Large, mottled brown-and-white oral disc is solitary or in small colonies; edges often curled upward.

Protopalythoa variabilis: Does not form mats, but has brown leathery polyps connected by stolons at the base; fairly long polyp tentacles feed predominantly on zooplankton and particulate matter at night. It is often found buried in the sand, not encrusting rocks. Typically grows in areas with quieter water flow.

Protopalythoa vestitus: Small polyps forming large colonies; polyps connected by stolons; very delicate with white rounded perimeter tentacles and deep brown oral disc; white radiating stripes on disc. This is a shallow-water species that prefers high water movement and strong lighting. The mucus layer occasionally peels off toward the base.

Atlantic Species:

Protopalythoa grandiflora: Large-polyped; polyps connected by stolons, forming small colonies; does not form mats. Brown oral disc with lighter-colored tentacles.

Protopalythoa grandis: One of the largest zoanthids; green-to-brown mottled oral disc, often somewhat iridescent, giving rise to its common name, moon polyp. Often solitary or in small colonies; does not form mats; polyp disc and tentacles often curved inward like a cup. Normally found in deep water or shaded areas; low lighting and moderate currents should be used. This zoanthid is clearly a *Protopalythoa* species (Trench, 1974; Ryland and Babcock, 1991), and there is no coenenchymal mat present. Nonetheless, most aquarists still call this a *Palythoa* species.

Natural Location: In general, if the polyp is squat and stubby, with short, nontapered tentacles, it is from a higher-flow region; those that are larger, more separated, and possessing longer, tapered tentacles are from more-protected waters. (See species description, above, for specific habitat information.)

Colors: Although some may be more colorful, most *Protopalythoa* are brown or dark brown with sometimes fluorescent elements incorporated into the tentacle tips. They may also have mottled or striated patterns on the oral disc.

Captive Care: Some of these zoanthids feed on large food items, rapidly enclosing and swallowing prey in the manner of an anemone. Budding is common and frequent, with polyps becoming very dense in substrate-limited colonies. Occasionally, strong lighting may alter their color to a more-uniform brown shade. At other times, strong lighting may bring out fluorescent highlights. Experimentation with different lighting regimes is recommended. Those with longer tentacles and broad oral discs, usually with a deeper fluted "throat," are more likely to get a significant portion of their diet from active feeding. There may be several diseases, unreported in the literature, that affect these and other colonial anemones.

Special Information: See "Neurotoxin Warning," page 182.

Collection Impact: *Protopalythoa* divide and spread rapidly and are usually abundant in nature. However, their collection can be difficult, and also incidentally damaging, in that the substrate must usually be removed to obtain an intact colony. Occasionally, the mat can be cut and lifted or peeled from the substrate. Fortunately, these animals are very successful in captivity, and their rapid multiplication through budding or other asexual means is a prolific method being used in captive-propagation efforts.

GENUS *Zoanthus* Cuvier, 1800
(zoe-an'-thuss)

Common Species: *Z. coppingeri, Z. danae, Z. mantoni, Z. pacificus, Z. pulchellus, Z. sociatus, Z. solanderi, Z. vietnamensis,* and many others, mostly unclassified.

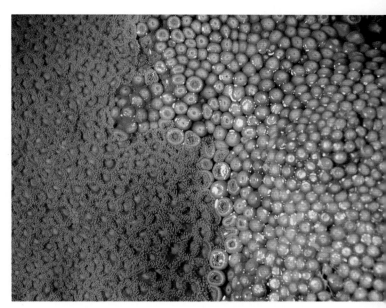

Zoanthus sociatus (sea mat): large mass of polyps at low tide in Florida.

Common Names: sea mat, button polyps.

Identification: *Zoanthus* are very common and fast-reproducing colonies occurring throughout various reef zones. Their polyps are rarely larger than 125 mm (0.5 in.) across the oral disc. The polyps do not incorporate sediments and particles into their bases or mats. Although species identification may be difficult from external observation, they do have a divided sphincter muscle surrounding the oral opening that is their distinguishing anatomical characteristic. *Zoanthus* species normally reproduce by buds that are attached at their base to the parent colony, whereas many *Palythoa* species reproduce by buds of their stolons.

Atlantic and Pacific Species:

Zoanthus pacificus: Small to large clumped colonies of short-tentacled polyps that vary in color; usually found in shallow areas of high water movement. The oral disc is often a contrasting, lighter color.

Zoanthus sociatus: Forms elaborate piecemeal mats of normally green to turquoise polyps. They are often found on reef flats exposed to high light intensity and intermittently strong currents. Stolon-connected polyps normally have 30 short tentacles; polyps are extended continuously day and night and feed predominantly on detritus, not zooplankton. Colonies can grow quite large and some can be partially submerged in sand.

Atlantic Species:

Zoanthus pulchellus: Forms an encrusting mat so dense that polyps crowd and press against each other when expanded.

Large button polyps (**Protopalythoa vestitus**) with smaller, bright green **Zoanthus sp.** polyps with golden centers that sometimes take on a brilliant orange color.

Polyps are variable in color (but often brown) and have short, blunt tentacles. When unexpanded, colonies are usually hemispherical and suggest *Favia*-esque coral heads. This species is found in variable light and current conditions, with deep-water colonies occasionally fluorescent orange.

Zoanthus solanderi: Forms large, dense, fast-growing colonies primarily on reef flats and back-reef areas. They are aggressive competitors and are usually able to overgrow nearby sessile life.

Pacific Species:

Zoanthus coppingeri: Small polyps are not encrusted with sediment; forms large colonies on coral rubble and on colonies of *Montipora digitata*; found in bright colors, including orange, red, yellow, and green. Light and current-loving colonies are found on rocky shores and reef flats.

Zoanthus mantoni: Dark brown and green, grayish blue, or bright green polyps form a mat that is usually buried in silt and substrate up to the oral disc, and is often found along with *Protopalythoa*. The oral disc shows white, distinct patterns that can be quite pretty and that contrast with the tentacles. This is a lagoon species that prefers low current and bright light but is very tolerant of varying aquarium conditions.

Zoanthus vietnamensis: Forms extensive, sheetlike mauve or blue rubbery, thinly encrusting mats; the polyps are completely buried in the coenenchyme. Numerous short tentacles usually contrast in color with the rest of the colony; light blue or blue-green oral discs are common. Found in areas of rough shallow water where it may occur with *Palythoa* and/or *Protopalythoa*.

Natural Location: Various reef zones. (See species descriptions above, for specific habitat information.)

Colors: *Zoanthus* species are often brightly colored, or at least more so than the palythoids, and their oral discs and tentacles are much more likely to be seen in contrasting colors. They may also be a zonating species, with several differently colored species occurring together. They regularly increase or decrease their zooxanthellae populations in response to lighting changes, and may thus darken considerably in certain light environments. This adaptability makes them less likely to bleach than other zoanthids. The zooxanthellae studied in *Zoanthus* are known to be a different species that is adapted to strong light and depends on the substantial production of protective xanthophylls to cope with high irradiances.

Captive Care: *Zoanthus* colonies are highly dependent on their zooxanthellae—rather than active feeding on zooplankton—for energy, and should always be placed in the aquarium where they will receive bright lighting. *Zoanthus sociatus* is highly autotrophic, containing very dense populations of zooxanthellae and feeding minimally.

Many reports both in scientific and hobby literature claim that *Zoanthus* species do not exhibit feeding responses to any prey. This is mostly true for typical zooplankton prey, but I have found that the right kind of food will elicit a standard prey-capture response.

For example, *Z. sociatus* will not capture *Artemia* nauplii, chopped squid, or copepods. However, it will seize and swallow sea urchin eggs like a typical voracious, carnivorous coral. Without the presence of specific food, some zoanthids will simply ignore many types of prey items until something triggers their specialized feeding responses. (Unlike some of its relatives, *Z.*

Zoanthus pulchellus (zoanthid button polyps): attractive Caribbean species.

Zoanthus **sp.** (zoanthid button polyps): urchin eggs may elicit feeding response.

variabilis has a much stronger feeding response to zooplankton.)

The aquarist may not have to be overly concerned with feeding these animals, as the zoanthids have been found to feed largely on bacteria, algae, and dissolved organic material. Some of the zooxanthellae may depend on the animal rather than the environment for key nutrients. In fact, the metabolic by-products of the bacteria that *Zoanthus* species culture within their gastrovascular cavities may be important in providing inorganic nutrients used in lipid and protein synthesis.

Special Information: *Zoanthus sociatus*, and perhaps other zoanthids, have an unusual larval "crawling" stage, in which larvae metamorphose into a form that crawls on the substrate before attaching near the edges of overhangs.

Collection Impact: *Zoanthus* occurs in abundance, and harvesting effects should be inconsequential unless substrate is chipped away to free portions of colonies.

SUBORDER MACROCNEMINA

FAMILY Epizoanthidae

This family consists of just two genera, *Epizoanthus* and *Thoracactis*, neither being seen with any regularity in the aquarium trade, with the latter especially uncommon. Many species in this family are known to be nonphotosynthetic and require regular feeding with zooplankton-type items.

GENUS *Epizoanthus*

(ehp'-ih-zoe-an'-thuss)
This genus may prove to include many species, but these are currently undocumented in most cases. They are frequently associated with specific commensal organisms and are hardly distinguishable from many *Parazoanthus* species. Many, and possibly all, are aposymbiotic. Like *Parazoanthus*, these animals may

Unidentified zoanthid, possibly ***Epizoanthus* sp.**: with sometimes complex natural histories and often requiring planktonic foods, they can be difficult to keep.

not survive without their associated organism, depending on the nature of the relationship. Many are from mid-depth to very deep water.

FAMILY Parazoanthidae

This family is composed of the genera *Gerardia*, *Isozoanthus*, and *Parazoanthus*, but only the latter is commonly available in the aquarium trade.

Epizoanthus species are almost always found growing on the surface of various living and dead substrates. *Parazoanthus* may also adopt similar pairings with other sessile life. By definition, an **epizoon** is an animal living on the exterior surface of another animal, while a **parazoon** is an animal parasitic on another organism. In the case of these zoanthids, neither *Parazoanthus* nor *Epizoanthus* are likely to parasitize their host, and occasionally may be found without a host at all. (*Parazoanthus* is thus a misnomer.)

GENUS *Parazoanthus*

(pare'-ah-zoe-an'-thuss)

Common Species: Possibly many, mostly unclassified or wrongly identified (e.g., "*Parazoanthus gracilis*").

Common Names: yellow polyps, colonial yellow polyps.

Identification: *Parazoanthus* is a common genus of the zoanthid group, and species are usually found living either on bare rock or growing on living organisms such as hydroids, gorgonians, and sponges. They usually form small colonies, reproducing by budding from the base of the parent polyp. A system of canals, including a well-developed ring canal, is found in the mesoglea of colonies. These function in allowing nutrient and water exchange between polyps. The mesoglea of *Parazoanthus* species does not normally incorporate sand or other particles. Their mat is usually membranous if it is present. The polyps are frequently yellow, cinnamon, or brown, with fluted bodies and long, thin tentacles. Polyps usually contrast sharply in color with their host organism, probably to warn off any potential predators. In fact, studies have shown the compounds released by the *Parazoanthus* species to be quite toxic to fishes. The individual polyps look quite anemone-like and seem much less coral-like than other zoanthids. Most of the Pacific parazoanthids are not commonly identified to the species level, and are usually described by their color, tentacle number, or host organism.

The familiar aquarium species usually called "yellow polyps" or "*Parazoanthus gracilis*" is the most recognizable of this group, yet several noted sources have protested that this species name is certainly wrong. For the time being, this zoanthid should be recognized as *Parazoanthus* sp. as it is unknown in the scientific

Unidentified yellow polyps: dubbed "*Parazoanthus gracilis*" by aquarists.

Parazoanthus sp. (colonial polyps): note typical association with live sponge.

Parazoanthus sp. (colonial polyps): growing with red sponge on black coral.

Parazoanthus swiftii (golden zoanthid): commensal with live encrusting sponge.

Parazoanthus sp. (colonial polyps): Lembeh Strait, Sulawesi.

Parazoanthus parasiticus (sponge zoanthid): polyps dot a Caribbean sponge.

literature. While the taxonomic and morphologic vagueness of the zoanthids as a group makes any current classification difficult, at least one of the commonly imported yellow zoanthids from the Atlantic (Mediterranean and tropical Atlantic), has been classified as *P. axinellae*. It is possible that it also occurs in Pacific waters. *Parazoanthus axinellae* is frequently found unassociated with other organisms, hence its good record of captive survivability.

Atlantic Species:

Parazoanthus axinellae: These commonly recognized "yellow polyps" are found encrusting rock, old worm tubes, and other dead matter in various locations throughout the reef; prefers a moderate current and moderate light; individual fluted colonies with unconnected polyps. Mediterranean, Atlantic, and possibly Pacific species. (Mediterranean and Atlantic specimens may be more orange, representing different color morphs or possibly different species.)

Parazoanthus catenularis: Brown to yellow-brown polyps with 20 pointed tentacles.

Parazoanthus parasiticus: Brownish to yellow or greenish brown polyps with a white body column that is encrusted with sand and 28 thin tentacles. This species, often called "clove polyps," occurs singly or in very small groupings on red boring, loggerhead, and tube sponges.

Parazoanthus puertoricense: Dark red to wine-colored polyps; somewhat translucent. Common on Pipes of Pan, tube, and volcano sponges.

Parazoanthus swiftii: Bright orange, gold, or yellow polyps with 26 tiny tentacles; normally found on living or dead sponges. Colonies grow in winding bands and rows across living rope, finger, and tube sponges.

Parazoanthus tunicans: Small orange, pale yellow, brown, or green polyps with sand-encrusted body columns. Normally grows on living and dead hydroids of the genus *Plumularia*, in dimly lit areas.

Pacific Species:

Parazoanthus dichroicus: Small, slightly sediment-encrusted beige polyps with yellow or orange tentacles and ridges on the surface of the oral disc. Commonly seen growing on hydroids.

Parazoanthus dixoni: A commonly imported species of "yellow polyps." Superficially indistinct from *P. axinellae*. This can be one of the species mislabeled as "*Parazoanthus gracilis.*"

Captive Care: *Parazoanthus* care is similar to that of other colonial polyps, but some species may require a certain substrate to thrive. Not all species contain zooxanthellae, and most will respond to feedings of zooplankton-type foods. Those found on dead or dying commensal organisms may fail to survive for long, depending on the nature of the association. If living with a

Parazoanthus swiftii (golden zoanthid): living in intimate association and taking advantage of the constant water flows created by its host sponge. (Caribbean)

sponge that fails to adapt to the aquarium, the parazoanthids may have little chance of survival. Obviously, those species that are not photosynthetic must receive food to survive. Many of them will feed heavily if given the opportunity. The common "yellow polyps" seem highly indiscriminate in their food preferences, and yet they often seem to survive well without direct feedings. There is obviously much work to be done on the ecology of these zoanthids.

Special Information: As mentioned, these colonial polyps were once thought to be entirely parasitic as it appeared that they derived nutrition from the animals on which they were found. However, the host animal is also likely to derive some protection from potential predators through the toxic compounds released by the zoanthids. The *Parazoanthus* species are usually concentrated near the inhalant openings of sponges and are thought to benefit from the passage of oxygenated and plankton-laden water before it reaches the sponge.

The parazoanthids have many complex associations with other sessile invertebrates. Some choose palatable sponges to colonize; in this case, either the sponge or the zoanthid may display warning or cryptic coloration to avoid being preyed upon. In other cases, such as that of the maroon zoanthid, *Parazoanthus* n. sp., the coral does not contrast with its maroon sponge host. In this case, the sponge is toxic and shows a remarkable antibiotic activity against 82 different species of marine bacteria. Hence, the commensal relationship is probably one of mutualism. Quite often, a sponge and a parazoanthid will both colonize the skeleton of a gorgonian, black coral, or stony coral, creating unusual and very attractive formations.

Collection Impact: Parazoanthids do not normally form the large masses seen among other colonial anemones, and their resultant collection may be somewhat easier. However, the removal of their commensal host may be of some consequence and must be evaluated on a case-by-case basis. Otherwise, *Parazoanthus* are similar to the other zoanthids in terms of captive success, rate of reproduction, and the potential for propagation.

The Corallimorpharians

Mushroom Corals

With a multitude of colors, graphic stripes, blotches of iridescence, and fluorescent hues, the mushroom corals are eye-catching, hardy, and often the first cnidarians a new reef aquarist acquires. Also commonly known as mushroom anemones, disc anemones, or corallimorphs, this diverse group of corals is generally easy to keep and most will readily reproduce. On the other hand, they are part of a taxonomic nightmare and difficult to identify with any degree of accuracy. The Order Corallimorpharia is largely unstudied and the subject of much current scientific controversy and revision. The aquarist can be forgiven for being confused, as even the taxonomic experts are in disagreement. What is known for certain is that almost all corallimorpharians adapt nicely to aquarium conditions and can even be maintained very successfully by beginning reef aquarists.

Quite literally corals without a skeleton, the mushroom corals are an anomaly. Often referred to as "false" corals, they possess virtually the same internal structure as stony corals (Order Scleractinia), but lack the typical long predatory feeding tentacles with which to capture larger and more motile plankton. In the corallimorpharians, tentacles are reduced to bumps or stubby protrusions and are not retractile.

Corallimorphs consist of rapidly budding, single, unfused

*Actinodiscus (= **Discosoma**) **striata*** (striped mushroom coral): durable and often beautiful, corallimorphs are a favorite first coral for many new reef aquarists.

polyps. Their attachment site is called the **pedal disc**, and their stalked (often highly reduced) body is called the **column**. Their upper surface is, not surprisingly, the **oral disc**. Most other anatomical features are very similar to the features of the stony corals. Their tentacles can have acrospheres (round nematocyst-laden ends), and tentacles are usually of two morphologic types: those found at the margin of the disc, and those on the surface of the disc. Some species are armed with atrich-type nematocysts (spirocysts) that are sticky, rather than penetrating. Atrichs are nematocysts without barbs, without a differentiated basal shaft, and with a smooth appearance. In general, corallimorphs have at least several of the major types of stinging cells, although many do not seem to use them the way the stony corals do; that is, they do not possess the tentacle length necessary for aggressive feeding except to capture small food particles that contact the animals' surface.

The Family Discosomatidae, for example, are partly identified by their total lack of spirocysts—the nematocysts that exist prolifically on the prey-capturing tentacles of scleractinians. However, the potent "sting" of some corallimorphs when in contact with other corals leaves little doubt that these seemingly innocent corals are far from defenseless. In fact, there is not a significant difference in the composition of the nematocysts between most corallimorphs and stony corals. The degree to which nematocysts and/or chemicals play a defensive role is not fully established. Instead, greatly reduced tentacles often appear on the

Rhodactis inchoata (bullseye mushrooms): most corallimorpharians do well with moderate lighting and gentle currents, and are often forgiving of water quality lapses.

surface as round bumps in radial rows. Some species' tentacles are slightly longer, and though recognizable as tentacles, usually are not efficient at prey capture. These reduced tentacles both radiate outward from the center and form concentric circles from the center. The small pimples and other protuberances that adorn the surface of most *Actinodiscus* (= *Discosoma*) species are vestigial tentacle knobs called **papillae**, whereas slightly lengthened fuzzy tentacles formed by evaginations of the oral disc are known as **verrucae**. Corallimorphs often have extended or protruding mouths (**hypostomes**), in contrast to the normally flat or inward projecting mouths of true anemones and most true corals. Most feed by direct absorption and ciliary transport of trapped particulate matter across their heavy-mucus-coated surface.

Some larger species (*Amplexidiscus*, numerous *Rhodactis* species, etc.) are capable of quickly infolding their edges into a saclike shape, trapping slow-moving animals—including fishes—and other food sources inside. These corals may be very soft or rigid, depending on the development of their mesoglea. It seems that as many corallimorphs are symbiotic as aposymbiotic. Fortunately, most of the species in the aquarium trade are symbi-

otic and able to live on the products of photosynthesis. But to what degree? Some of the mushroom anemones are found in shallow water and are obviously fairly typical zooxanthellate corals. However, just as many are not—especially those commonly available, like *Actinodiscus* (= *Discosoma*) species. Very little is known about the zooxanthellae that inhabit these animals.

The ability of some of these mushroom corals to exist without direct sunlight is somewhat puzzling, given that they are often considered largely autotrophic, with poor prey-capture capabilities. Tropical symbiotic corallimorphs are frequently found in brightly lit shallow water, but are even more frequently found in shaded areas. I have seen many "symbiotic" corallimorphs dwelling vertically under the shade of other corals, completely hidden from downward-cast or upwelling light. In fact, it is well known that many types of corallimorphs do not thrive in captivity under powerful metal halide lamps, expanding and reproducing better under much-reduced lighting. It is highly unlikely that these animals could be anywhere near "autotrophic," unless they possess specialized photosynthetic apparatus like some of the deep-water corals (*Leptoseris fragilis* et al.).

As mentioned in Chapter 4, photosynthesis provides, optimally, a large portion of the carbon needs of corals, but nitrogen still must be acquired through feeding. Yet the corallimorphs are, largely, not good at prey capture, lacking spirocysts, the specialized penetrating nematocysts found in stony coral tentacles. Both the presence of such structures in stony corals and the lack of them in corallimorphs is a hallmark of each taxon, respectively.

However, the corallimorphs are morphable and flexible. They possess surface structures that disturb hydrodynamic flow, are readily capable of mesenterial extrusion, and have a broad oral surface. Furthermore, they have a heavy mucus coat, well developed ciliate transport mechanisms, and tend to exist in low-water-movement environments. Finally, they grow well in captivity where higher nitrate levels are present. These traits are well established in other taxa as indicative of animals that feed by gravitational and flow-dependent deposition of particulate and flocculent material, as well as by direct absorption.

den Hartog (1980) notes that the warpable surface of corallimorpharians may be used to capture light. Delbeek and Sprung (1994, 1997) have also described the trumpetlike shape taken on by some mushroom corals in response to inadequate light levels. However, this shape change occurs frequently and sporadically in captivity with no variance in the corallimorph's light field. While expansion of the polyp has been shown to influence the exposure of zooxanthellae, this trumpeting trait in the soft-bodied symbiotic corals has been shown repeatedly to be an accommodation to maximize prey capture and modulate water flows across the coral surface (Sebens, Patterson, et al.). In fact, deposits of detritus on the surface of many corallimorphs are usually moved inward toward the mouth by the trumpeting (up-folding) of the edges. While certainly unproved, it is my estimate that this may be a significant, if not primary, contributor of energy to these animals.

Reproduction will usually be observed by anyone keeping mushroom corals. While it is certain that genetic mixing and long-distance spread of species is accomplished by sexual reproduction, there are almost no reports of such events among the tropical species in the wild. Asexual reproduction, however, is well recorded. Not surprisingly, aquarists are among those who have most often observed this reproductive behavior. Chen et al. (1995) found that asexual reproduction increases with temperature. This makes sense because the metabolism of animals increases with increasing temperature, and reproduction in other corals follows similar trends. Furthermore, den Hartog (1980) found that colonial groupings of corallimorphs occur in shallow (warmer) water, while solitary individuals grow in deeper (cooler) water. Budding is a common form of asexual reproduction that occurs when parent polyps lose small bits of their column, sometimes by an injury or tear. The **totipotent** tissue allows even a small piece to grow and take on the form of the parent. In another process known as **laceration**, healthy specimens move slowly over the substrate, leaving behind tiny pieces of tissue from the pedal disc, which will then begin to adopt the characteristics of a new corallimorph.

Fission (or fissure) is another method of asexual reproduction, where the parent colony divides across the entirety of its surface the way single cells divide in mitosis. Common to anemones, this process begins as the margins of the oral disc pinch inward across the oral surface, typically across the mouth, until two more-or-less-equal halves exist. In **transverse fission**, the animal pinches off across its stalk, with the upper section eventually coming loose to drift and settle elsewhere.

These types of asexual growth are also common to anemones and make it apparent that the corallimorpharians have as much in common with sea anemones (Order Actiniaria) as they do with "true corals" (Order Scleractinia). Thus they are somewhat of an enigma and a possible link between the taxa.

Inverse budding is a more recently described method of reproduction in a *Rhodactis* species, in which the pedal disc of the parent lifts up, rolls together, and forms a bud attached to the parent by its oral disc. The attached bud then folds downward to become reattached as a daughter colony. It is not known to what degree this method of reproduction is common in other

Mixed group of mushrooms (**Actinodiscus = Discosoma spp.**) at the base of an aquarium reefscape: metal halide lighting is often too strong for corallimorphs.

Rhodactis sp. (hairy mushroom): a common and easily maintained aquarium subject, but capable of eating unwary fishes that venture too close (see below).

The same specimen shown above, now closed after trapping a Banggai Cardinalfish (*Pterapogon kauderni*) in Gregory Schiemer's New York aquarium.

corallimorphs (Chen et al., 1995).

Competition in the corallimorphs is also atypical. While some species can develop nematocyst-loaded acrospheres in the marginal tentacles that often become whitish or opaque near the active edges (Delbeek and Sprung, 1997), many lack this ability. Often the margins of corallimorphs fold against and adjacent to competing organisms. Rarely is contact initiated. Over time, a necrotic area may develop on the noncorallimorph, or the corallimorph will withdraw the near-contact margin. In the latter case, the tissue of the corallimorph becomes somewhat mottled and withdrawn. While undocumented in the literature, this appears to be a clear example of competitive dominance hierarchies.

Like other noncalcareous corals, the corallimorphs seem to have developed effective chemical defense systems. Despite their soft, vulnerable tissue, they are rarely preyed upon, and they seem to be able to cause significant passive destruction to nearby corals. In fact, most corals will not be able to settle near these animals. Numerous reports and personal observations by aquarists who have placed corals in contact or proximity to corallimorphs describe significant damage, necrosis, or even death to the neighboring coral. It has been suggested that toxins and allelochemicals secreted by the mushroom corals can kill nearby invertebrates, even causing an otherwise inexplicable failure to thrive and pronounced general recession of stony corals throughout the aquarium. The mucus of some corallimorphs is highly aromatic, suggesting the presence of volatile organic compounds. *Amplexidiscus*, a notorious aquarium-fish eater, has also been postulated to possess a narcotizing agent (Hamner and Dunn, 1980).

Although there is no direct evidence to support the presence of widespread use of allelopathy or chemical warfare on nearby competitors, it is hard to imagine that it does not exist. If so, protein skimming and regular use of activated carbon may be wise in tanks housing significant corallimorpharian populations in order to avoid any toxic response in other inhabitants. On the other hand, protein skimming reduces the amount of organic matter on which these animals may be feeding, and aggressive skimming has been anecdotally reported by a number of aquarists to be detrimental to corallimorph success. What to do? These corals can expand tremendously, so allowance for the growth, division, and expansion of colonies should be taken into consideration. The use of activated carbon, which must be replaced on a regular basis to be effective, is probably warranted in all reef systems containing corals of any kind. Algal scrubbers and other biological refugium filters, run without a foam fractionator, can also sidestep the problem of overskimming.

Occasionally, individual polyps of mushroom corals, especially parents, may become detached from their substrate. In such cases, it is possible to glue, pin, or sew them onto a new base. To allow for their natural reattachment, they should be placed in an almost motionless area of the tank (or in a separate tank), and left to settle on their own. Magnesium has been shown to promote pedal adhesion in anemones (Robson, 1976). This study found that adhesiveness is due to an "active state of the pedal ectoderm which can be excited or masked by suitable stimuli." Produced by the secretion of an unknown material, adhesiveness persists in the presence of magnesium ions.

Iodine is anecdotally reported as important in maintaining the coloration and health of all mushroom corals; weekly additions of potassium iodide seem to be the safest way to add this element. There is no firm evidence that I am aware of to support this observation, however, and I have had corallimorphs grow, reproduce, and remain brightly colored even in the absence of specific iodine additions.

Taxonomy

It is hard to imagine a more taxonomically tenuous group of organisms than the corallimorphs. Few investigations have been done, many of them are now highly dated, and all too many are now regarded as of dubious value or simply incorrect. Traditionally, a fossil record is used to establish phylogeny or the evolutionary history of organisms, and, from that, their taxonomy. The soft corals, at least, possess sclerites that can be used in such work. The corallimorphs have no fossil record.

Classical taxonomy uses various features to establish lineage and taxonomic position. Perhaps most accurately, the **cnidom**, or type and number of nematocysts present, is a distinguishing characteristic. Unfortunately, it is not infallible. Other aspects used in the taxonomy of corallimorphs are the relative thickness of the mesoglea, the distribution of tentacles, the number and pairings of mesenteries, the color, etc. Unfortunately, none have proved very reliable. The newer—and more reliable—methods entail DNA/RNA testing, as the phylogeny of the organism can be deduced by the sequence of genes in the DNA. Unfortunately, research funds to study and learn about corallimorpharians are hard to come by. As aquarists, we may have to accept that the correct taxonomy of this group is somewhere off in the future. Anemone expert Daphne Fautin is working on a worldwide revision of corallimorph systematics (Fautin, 1999, pers. comm.), while Chen continues to work on phylogeny.

Even amid the controversy, the corallimorphs are currently thought to belong to four families: Sideractidae, Corallimorphidae, Ricordeidae, and Discosomatidae. (Note that the cor-

rect term is not "Discosomidae," an imperfect name found here and there even in scientific literature.) Actinodiscidae (*Actinodiscus* species), is currently thought to be an invalid name according to the Copenhagen rules.

Other genera may be considered to be substituted (e.g., *Actinodiscus* = *Discosoma*, *Rhodactis* = *Discosoma*, etc.) or transferred in the future. With exceptions of the Ricordeidae and *Amplexidiscus fenestrafer*, all of the corallimorphs commonly available in the aquarium trade would be considered to be *Discosoma* species. Do we trust Carlgren, who was the first (and, to some degree, only) one to describe Pacific species, or do we trust den Hartog, whose excellent survey was limited to Caribbean corallimorphs and suggestions of taxonomic change? Clearly, a better understanding is warranted. It is unfortunate that so little information is available about these remarkable creatures.

They are extremely hardy, multiply easily, and have become staple organisms in the marine aquarium hobby, yet they seem to have the potential to create at least as much intertaxic and interspecific aquarium chaos as many of the soft corals.

The classic taxonomy of the Corallimorpharia described two families (Carlgren, 1949): the Actinodiscidae and the Corallimorphidae. However, den Hartog (1980) did not feel that the Actinodiscidae genera were separable or correct, and proposed they all be considered part of the Family Discosomatidae. In addition, the large piscivorous mushroom coral discovered that year by Dunn and Hamner, *Amplexidiscus*, was put into the Actinodiscidae, even as den Hartog was saying that grouping should no longer exist. This is frustrating for anyone who cares about neat and clean taxonomic placements. None of this would really be a problem today, except that Chen et al. (1996), using very ac-

Guide to the Mushroom Corals

Ricordeidae
e.g., *Ricordea*

Discosomatidae
e.g., *Actinodiscus* (= *Discosoma*)

Phylum: Cnidaria
Class: Anthozoa
Order: Corallimorpharia
Family: Sideractidae
Family: Corallimorphidae
Family: Ricordeidae
Family: Discosomatidae

Pseudocorynactis sp. (white ball corallimorph): unusual and anemone-like.

Pseudocorynactis caribbeorum (orange ball corallimorph): nocturnal genus.

Pseudocorynactis sp. (white ball corallimorph): seen on a night dive. (Sulawesi)

curate genetic probes, showed that the *Actinodiscus* of Carlgren appeared to be distinct and quite separate from *Rhodactis* and *Amplexidiscus* genera, which appear more closely related to each other. Pires and Castro (1997) studied the cnidom of the Discosomatidae and found them to be clearly separate from both the scleractinians (stony corals) and the other corallimorpharians. They found them to be most closely related to the scleractinians of the Family Caryophilliidae and also to the genus *Fungiacyathus* of the Family Fungiidae.

What I have done in the following text, in light of all this, is provide double names of genera where needed until the matter is resolved.

FAMILY Corallimorphidae

Genera: *Corallimorphus*, *Corynactis*, and *Pseudocorynactis*.

The Corallimorphidae are mostly composed of temperate and deep-water species. The remaining few species that are tropical are sometimes available to aquarists, but little is known about their care requirements. Occasionally, they may be attached to live rock. The one species of *Pseudocorynactis* (*P. caribbeorum*, the orange ball corallimorph), is especially beautiful. It has an orange column with clear tentacles tipped by bright orange balls. It is nocturnal and from sandy or rocky areas near reefs. For those interested in such animals, Delbeek and Sprung (1997) and Fosså and Nilsen (1998) cover them in some depth and suggest feeding with fish flesh at night when the tentacles are extended.

FAMILY Ricordeidae

GENUS *Ricordea* Duchassaing and Michelotti, 1860 (rih-kohr'-dee-ah)

Common Species: *R. florida*, *R. yuma*, and others (*Discosoma fungiforme?*).

Common Name: None.

Identification: *Ricordea* species have randomly pimpled, polka-dotted surfaces with the dots (verrucae) often of a contrasting color. Lengthened tentacles may occur around the edges of the disc. These are laden with several types of nematocysts that are not capable of aggressive action except with intimate contact. Many individuals are polystomatous, and the mouth opening is oval, rather than round. These mushrooms are not motile and do not contain acrospheres. Neither the tentacles nor the body can withdraw. *Ricordea* grow very low against the substrate (commonly on rubble or dead coral), rarely showing a visible stalk and blanketing the rocks on which they are attached. They become less community oriented and more solitary as depth increases. *Ricordea* are also found living with massive corals like *Montastraea* species, which they can "burn." The true *Ricordea*

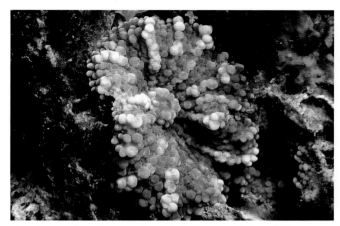

Ricordea yuma: knobby or berrylike tentacles are characteristic of this genus.

Ricordea yuma: *Periclimenes* spp. shrimps may associate with this corallimorph.

Ricordea florida: note two mouths, possibly a prelude to division of the polyp.

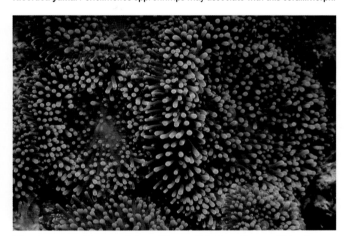

Ricordea yuma: this genus thrives with more light than other corallimorphs.

species from the Indo-Pacific, *R. yuma* Carlgren, 1900, is much less colorful than its Atlantic counterpart but is otherwise nearly identical; commonly has verrucae on the raised oral opening.

Natural Location: *Ricordea* are found in diverse locations, often growing vertically on dead coral and rocky substrate in both shallow and deep waters. Some are found attached to colonies of Lister's Tree Oysters (*Isognomon radiatis*). They are more prolific in turbid waters, but can also be found elsewhere. *R. yuma* is apparently also from shallow, often turbid water.

Colors: *Ricordea* mushrooms can be subtly or brightly colored in iridescent red, green, yellow, orange, or blue toward the margins, becoming more muted toward the center, and with a green protruding mouth (hypostome). Marginal tentacles may contrast in bright or muted colors with those of the disc tentacles. Their bases, if visible at all, may be a contrasting color, typically brown

to purple. *Ricordea yuma* is found predominantly in muted pink, brown, or green with less contrast of the verrucae.

Captive Care: While not as hardy as some mushrooms, these corals tolerate brighter light but do not seem to thrive under direct metal halide lighting. Pink and orange *Ricordea* are commonly from shallower water. They are also more tolerant of greater water movement around the colony, probably due to their low hydrodynamic profile. Both species have a tendency to extrude their mesenterial filaments when stressed chemically or mechanically. Grows to 2.5-4 cm (1-1.5 in.).

Special Information: *Periclimenes* commensal shrimps may often associate with *Ricordea* species.

Some Indonesian and African *Actinodiscus* (= *Discosoma*) mushrooms are mistakenly offered for sale as a type of *Ricordea*. While somewhat similar in color and appearance, these mush-

Actinodiscus (= Discosoma) sp. (spotted mushroom)

Actinodiscus (= Discosoma) striata (striped mushroom)

Discosoma sp. (fuzzy mushroom)

rooms have short but pronounced tentacles in place of the distinctively rounded dots that grace the surface of true *Ricordea*. Furthermore, the *Actinodiscus* (= *Discosoma*) disc is much softer than the firmer and more well-developed mesoglea of either *R. florida* or *R. yuma*.

Collection Impact: The current ruling covering collection of soft-bodied corals in Florida is that they may be attached to substrate roughly the size of a quarter (slightly less than 2.5 cm or 1 in.) area around their base, holdfast, etc. (Herndon, pers. comm.). The collection of larger pieces of hard substrate is illegal. My own belief is that aquarists should help enforce this ban and ought to report retailers who still mysteriously—and knowingly—sell illegal *Ricordea florida* on large pieces of rock. A friendly chat with the store owner or manager is a start. If they fail to see the wisdom of obeying a law that is in everyone's best interest, call the U.S. Department of Fish and Wildlife or a local marine police/fisheries agency. As aquarists we need to police ourselves if we don't want greater policing by government inspectors or total bans on all collecting (see Chapter 12).

Captive-bred colonies and single polyps of *Ricordea* species are now becoming available. Asexual reproduction is usually by longitudinal fission of a parent colony, so propagation (although not difficult) is slow.

FAMILY Discosomatidae den Hartog, 1980
(FAMILY Actinodiscidae Carlgren, 1949)

Genera: *Actinodiscus* (= *Discosoma*), *Amplexidiscus, Discosoma, Metarhodactis, Orinia, Paradiscosoma, Rhodactis.*

These corallimorpharians are all solitary polyps, though frequently colonial in nature. Size varies greatly among the species, from 2.5 cm (1 in.) to well over 30 cm (1 ft.) across. Similarly, their aggression and feeding behaviors are variable. Most are fairly easy to maintain in captivity, and they reproduce asexually with great regularity. Classification beyond the genus level is difficult, and the lack of supporting elements compounds the taxonomic challenge.

Rhodactis is included with the other genera of this family in some recent works, but classic taxonomy deems it a separate genus, and DNA work again suggests it is distinct. Contrary to some recent revisions, I am also leaving it separate based on the work of Chen et al. (1995, 1996).

Actinodiscus has sometimes been considered separate and distinct and sometimes synonymous with *Discosoma*. For the purposes of this text, I have listed the *Actinodiscus* species under the genus *Actinodiscus* (= *Discosoma*). It is my belief, based on current genetic studies by Chen et al., that the *Actinodiscus* name, rather than *Discosoma*, will prove valid for many of these species.

Actinodiscus (= *Discosoma*) *cardinalis* (red mushrooms): attractive group of corallimorphs spreads in a rocky niche in the lower reaches of a New York reef aquarium.

GENUS *Actinodiscus* Carlgren, 1949 = *Discosoma* Rüppell and Leuckart, 1828
(ack-tin'-oh-disk'-us) (dis'-koh-soh'-mah)

Common Species: Unknown number of true species, many variants seen by aquarists.

Common Names: mushrooms, mushroom corals, mushroom anemones, disc anemones.

Identification: The mushrooms of this genus vary greatly in color, texture and pattern. Their actual anatomical attributes, however, are quite similar. Surfaces can be smooth, rough, dimpled, pimpled, and frilly. Colors can be solid, mottled, metallic, striped, patterned, spotted, and more. Some species can change their surface texture and coloration depending on ambient light and nutrient characteristics of their environment. It is likely that using such morphologic characters to assign species is not a helpful methodology. The taxonomy of the corallimorpharians is dated, confused, and in need of revision, and the genus and species names applied here may well change in the near future. (*Those marked with an asterisk may not be valid species.)

Actinodiscus (= *Discosoma*) *cardinalis:* Dark red; pimpled and radiating grooved striated surface is common. Prefers very dim light;

Actinodiscus (= *Discosoma*) *coeruleus:* Metallic, shiny blue; mainly smooth surface with low pimples and somewhat ruffled edges.

Actinodiscus (= *Discosoma*) *ferrugatus:* Red-brown to rust-brown; often with a pimpled surface.

Actinodiscus (= *Discosoma*) *malaccensis:* Light to beige-brown, sometimes gray or green; bumpy surface in radiating patterns. Tolerates brighter light.

Mixed mushrooms (*Actinodiscus* (= *Discosoma*) **spp.**) in a U.S. reef tank.

Mixed mushrooms (*Actinodiscus* (= *Discosoma*) **spp.**) in a European reef tank.

Actinodiscus (= *Discosoma*) *coeruleus* (metallic blue mushroom).

Actinodiscus (= *Discosoma*) *marmoratus* (marbled mushroom)

Up-reaching mushrooms display stalks that are typically contracted and hidden.

Actinodiscus (= *Discosoma*) *mutabilis* (speckled mushrooms)

Actinodiscus (= Discosoma) mutabilis (speckled mushrooms)

Actinodiscus (= Discosoma) striata (striped mushrooms)

*Actinodiscus (= Discosoma) marmoratus: Commonly fluorescent green with a mottled or marbled pattern; pimpled surface.

*Actinodiscus (= Discosoma) mummiferus: Pink, reddish brown, or brownish purple; ruffled edge with grooved striations and pimpled surface common.

*Actinodiscus (= Discosoma) mutabilis: True to its name, it changes colors: light brown to green and often speckled or iridescent; sometimes burled.

*Actinodiscus (= Discosoma) neglectus: Reddish brown to brown, with faint white stripes radiating from center; textured, raised surface.

Actinodiscus (= Discosoma) nummiforme: Rüppell and Leuckart, 1828: Green to reddish brown; mottled and textured surface, often velvety with large nodules common around outer edges. Prefers shelter from light and current. Can grow to 10-13 cm (4-5 in.) across. (As *Discosoma nummiforme* has been recently examined from the Red Sea, this may prove to be a correct name and valid species.)

*Actinodiscus (= Discosoma) punctatus: Blue and red; obvious and contrasting pimpled surface.

*Actinodiscus (= Discosoma) ruber: Fluorescent red mushroom sometimes called "metallic red." Prefers dim light.

Actinodiscus (= Discosoma) striata: Strong dichotomous, fluorescent, blue-green stripes radiating from center (Matz, 1999).

Natural Location: These mushrooms are widespread, but found mostly in mid-depth waters and usually in somewhat shaded areas of the reef, often between coral heads or among pieces of rubble. They may also be found in shallower water.

Colors: Red, green, blue, metallic hues, stripes, and other colors and patterns. Highly variable and changeable.

Captive Care: These varieties of *Actinodiscus (= Discosoma)* species

are normally characterized as being smallish, nonpredatorial feeding animals that gain nutrients through direct uptake from the water, from ciliary mucus transport of trapped particulate matter, and from their zooxanthellae. They do contain nematocysts, although these are rudimentary and incapable of anything much more than the capture of the smallest particulate matter. There is sometimes a bare zone between the marginal and disc surface papillae (tentacles), but they are hardly different in form.

These mushrooms do not respond well to intense lighting or strong currents. In fact, fluorescent lighting and low currents seem to allow for maximal expansion and reproduction. If keeping these corals in brightly lit systems, it is best to place them low in the tank or under overhangs in the rockwork. Otherwise their colors tend to fade as the zooxanthellae overwhelm the natural pigmentation of the animals themselves. This results in an abundance of brown-colored animals. As with all Discosomatidae, these corals should not be placed immediately near any other stony corals, soft corals, or sessile animals because of their potential detrimental effect. Most of these species grow to 5-8 cm (2-3 in.) in diameter, depending on lighting and flow conditions. The need for iodine supplementation to maintain the health of these animals has never been proved, yet continues to have strong support based on anecdotal experiences of some hobbyists. I have never noticed any positive effect from its use, and regular water changes may make its supplementation unnecessary.

Special Information: Although commonly hailed as extremely easy animals to maintain in captivity, these mushrooms can have a finicky nature in some aquariums. Tanks with lower light levels and current seem to make them expand, grow, and multiply. Yet as tanks mature, and in tanks of virtually identical conditions, the same mushrooms may fail to thrive. Unfortunately, there is vir-

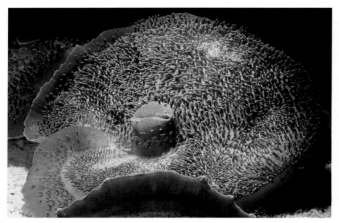

Amplexidiscus fenestrafer (giant cup mushroom): open position.

A. fenestrafer (giant cup mushroom): beginning purse-string closure.

tually nothing known about the diseases or physiology of these mushrooms, and what could be a relatively simple explanation is still a puzzle. Their active feeding needs must be great because their light needs are quite low.

Collection Impact: The collection of these mushrooms from reef communities is not an especially easy task. The substrate on which they are attached must be detached from the reef structure, unless they are found on loose rubble. Thus their collection involves some collateral damage to the reef and the loss of incidental organisms. However, mushroom anemones grow and divide very easily under good conditions, and many are being captive bred. This should be supported to limit pressures on wild stock (local populations are not reported to be especially abundant and are thus subject to overharvesting).

GENUS *Amplexidiscus* Dunn and Hamner, 1980
(am-plex'-ih-disk'-us)

Common Species: *A. fenestrafer.*

Common Names: giant cup mushroom, giant elephant ear mushroom.

Identification: Although it is possible that more species exist in this genus, *A. fenestrafer* is by far the most common import and the only described species. (One can only guess where this genus may end up. Is it going to be part of its originally described Actinodiscidae or part of its den Hartog-ish Discosomatidae?) First described as a new genus in 1980, these enormous mushrooms are usually 20-30 cm (8-12 in.) across and have pronounced beadlike verrucae spaced sparsely across their surface. Occasionally lengthened verrucae form short, lobed tentacles around the margins of the disc that lengthen when the animal contracts. *Fenestrafer* means "windowbearer" in Latin and refers to the almost translu-

cent bare border area without verrucae near the edges of the oral disc. (This margin helps distinguish this species from the somewhat similar hairy *Rhodactis* species or *Discosoma* species.) Grows to 45 cm (18 in.) or more.

Natural Location: *Amplexidiscus* are typically found in shallow waters in subtidal coral reef lagoons, often in turbid and quiet waters throughout the Indo-Pacific. They are often vertically attached and may be found in clusters.

Colors: These ivory, brown, or greenish gray mushrooms are not flashy, though they are quite distinct. Their color fades to a lighter shade from the oral disc to the base. The oral opening may be orange.

Captive Care: The *Amplexidiscus* mushrooms are capable of capturing and eating small fishes by forming the purse-string configuration of many of the *Discosoma* species. *Amplexidiscus* means "embracing" or "enfolding plate," and *Amplexidiscus* are capable of closing very quickly (within 3 seconds) and usually feed at night. They can enclose 4 L (1 gal.) of water upon closure (Hamner and Dunn, 1980). Their mouth only opens when the cup is fully formed, and recloses when the disc opens again after swallowing prey. Possible extracoelenteric digestion may be initiated upon capture of prey, including a unique characteristic of effecting a narcotizing influence on its prey prior to capture. Many "mysterious" disappearances of aquarium specimens have been linked to *Amplexidiscus*. This particular mushroom may also form mucus nets that could be toxic to other corals downstream. *Amplexidiscus* does have an appreciable number of nematocysts and may rely upon these and other prey capture methods for its survival. Unlike many mushroom corals, *Amplexidiscus* is tolerant of bright light even though it exists well in low to moderate light conditions. Contrary to some reports, it does possess zooxanthellae. Slow to moderate water flow is preferred. Asexual cloning is likely by longitudinal fission.

Special Information: *Amplexidiscus* may be a lethal mimic of the anemone *Stoichactis* sp., using its similarity to lure anemonefishes to their death when they engage in commensal behavior. *Amphiprion* and *Premnas* fish species will show an interest in *Amplexidiscus*, but generally avoid rubbing in and on the surface of its tentacles. If contact is initiated, usually at night, the fishes will be swallowed.

I suspect that, contrary to the initial descriptions (Dunn and Hamner, 1980; Hamner and Dunn, 1980), mechanical stimulation is not the only thing that is required to initiate this corallimorph's contraction. Stroking lightly, heavily, or with various motions of a finger across the disc of an *Amplexidiscus* will not necessarily trigger a closure. Other tactile or chemical cues must be necessary.

Collection Impact: Similar to *Actinodiscus* (= *Discosoma*), although *Amplexidiscus* are often solitary and not as common.

GENUS *Discosoma* Rüppell and Leuckart, 1828
(dis'-koh-soh'-mah)

Contrary to the previously listed group of *Actinodiscus* (= *Discosoma*), this group of *Discosoma* species is and has been fairly continuously known as *Discosoma*. No major or recent changes in their nomenclature have occurred—at least not since the late 1800s or so. (Unfortunately, Chen et al. [1996] alludes to the possibility that *D. sanctithomae* may be a *Rhodactis* species. Also, at least a couple of the Caribbean *Discosoma* species may be *Paradiscosoma* species.)

Common Species:

Discosoma carlgreni Watzl, 1922: Commonly called the forked tentacle mushroom, this corallimorph has short, widely spaced, square to forked marginal tentacles, short knobby disc tentacles, and a fairly rigid oral disc. Normally green to brown, occasionally translucent and more colorful, with a mottled surface pattern, brown, or purple. Tentacles usually not contrasting, but occasionally bright white, green, yellow, gray; usually solitary or in small colonies in secluded dimly lit areas. Grows to 5-8 cm (2-3 in.).

Discosoma neglecta Duchassaing and Michelotti, 1860: Caribbean species that looks like an inverted umbrella; tentacles around rim; brown to dark green with possible white streaks, or a mottled pattern of greens, browns, creams, and occasionally blue to purple; tentacles usually not contrasting; flattened and rigid oral disc; capable of capturing small fishes and crustaceans as prey. Thick, short, and square-shaped irregular peripheral tentacles may sting and are capable of forming a type of "sweeper"

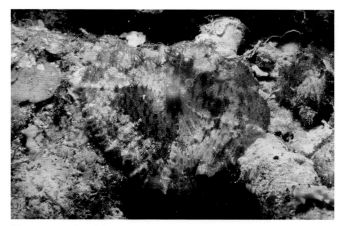

Discosoma carlgreni (forked tentacle mushroom) (Caribbean)

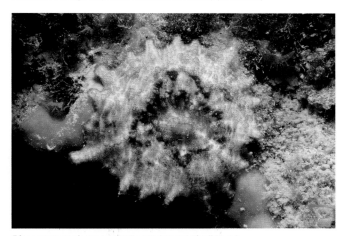

Discosoma neglecta (umbrella mushroom) (Caribbean)

Discosoma sanctithomae (bubble or warty mushroom) (Caribbean)

tentacle; reduced oral disc verrucae with disc edges form lengthy protrusions used in defense; no bare marginal zone; prefers dimly lit environments and is usually solitary; occurs in areas of rapidly growing corals and is capable of relocation. Commonly called the umbrella mushroom. Grows to 10 cm (4 in.).

Discosoma sanctithomae Duchassaing and Michelotti, 1860: Translucent green, blue, yellow, or brown body with tentacles that may contrast and/or be iridescent; small, forked, fuzzy tentacles are spaced sporadically on soft-bodied oral disc; tapering, short, unbranched tentacles surround the collarlike disc edges. These marginal tentacles have a potent sting, as they enlarge with acrospheres much like the sweeper tentacles of stony corals. It prefers dim light and usually occurs in small colonies or singly in areas of rapid coral growth among *Porites* and *Agaricia* corals, often in shallow water. Individuals are capable of relocation and movement. This mushroom inflates noticeably, imparting a thickness to the oral disc and stalk alike that gives rise to its common name, the bubble mushroom (also known as the warty mushroom). This a Caribbean species that, although beautiful and legal to collect, is infrequently available to the aquarium trade. Grows to 10 cm (4 in.).

Common Names: disc anemone, metallic mushroom, umbrella mushroom, bubble mushroom, warty mushroom, forked tentacle mushroom.

Natural Location: *Discosoma* are widely variant, in terms of light, water movement, and depth found. See individual habitat descriptions in identification section, above.

Colors: Green is a common color among the numerous species, but many hues are possible. The tentacles are often contrasting in color and may also have contrasting tips.

Captive Care: Many *Discosoma* mushrooms fold upward, forming a purse-string-like enclosure, and they may do so spontaneously and for no apparent reason. Most often, it is a feeding response elicited by tactile and chemical stimulation of the oral disc. Simply touching the oral disc lightly will not evoke the reaction. Many species can ensnare small prey, sometimes even small fishes, using this purse-string closure. It is likely that the predisposition of the mushroom to fold in this way is an attempt to lure prey into hiding in the almost-enclosed mushroom. Then, instead of sanctuary, it finds capture.

These mushrooms are generally hardier than other mushrooms and can usually tolerate much greater light intensities. However, they still seem to prefer the typical conditions of indirect light and reduced currents. It may be necessary to experiment with different positions in the tank to ensure that the mushroom is in a location conducive to good coloration, expansion, growth, and reproduction.

Special Information: *Discosoma* spp. have a cnidom with exceptionally large holotrichus-type nematocysts (Pires and Castro, 1997).

Collection Impact: Many of these species exist as solitary individuals or small colonies and are uncommon. They may be less appropriate to collect, although they are uncommon in the trade.

GENUS *Rhodactis* Milne, Edwards, and Haime, 1851
(***Discosoma*** Rüppell and Leuckart, 1828)
(roe-dak'-tiss)

Common Species:
(*Those marked with an asterisk may not be valid species.)

Rhodactis inchoata Carlgren, 1943: Purple to blue mushroom, often with green highlights/margins; it may have a red mouth, and other colors are possible. Often sold as Tonga blue mushroom or bullseye mushroom. Marginal tentacles are lengthened and torpedo-shaped. Cauliflower-like papillae with bare areas of oral disc are distinct. Prefers dim to moderate light and low water flow. Typically 4-5 cm (1.5-2 in.) in diameter, but grows to 8 cm (3 in.). Rare in the literature though somewhat common in the hobby, this species often hails from Tonga for the aquarium trade, though it is described elsewhere.

Rhodactis indosinensis Carlgren, 1943: Colors vary greatly and encompass pinks, rust, brown, green. The oral disc and tentacles frequently contrast markedly in color. One of the hairy mushrooms, this species is highly variable in the type and amount of prolific verrucae adorning its upper surface. Marginal tentacles are present and can be quite long. Oral disc tentacles may be bifurcated, single and tapering, or with multiple branched ends. den Hartog describes an "intermediate" naked zone between marginal and discal tentacles. This *Rhodactis* species has a soft body, thick disc, and heavy aromatic mucus. Typically 10-13 cm (4-5 in.) across, but grows to 20 cm (8 in.). It is a typically shallow-water species that thrives under bright light, but also tolerates reduced light. May exist singly or, more commonly, in large colonial associations. Reproduces by fission and laceration. I have noticed that nearly fully formed lacerates are capable of movement away from the parent after detachment, although they become fixed over time. This may be the inverse budding described by Chen et al. (1995). Will feed extensively, multiply quickly, and quite often draws up in a purse-string closure.

*Rhodactis (= *Discosoma*) *meandrina*: Dark brown to green, this large elephant ear mushroom has thin, ruffled edges; prefers dim light despite apparent density of zooxanthellae. Grows to 25 cm (10 in.). Probably the same species as *R. mussoides*. *Discosoma viridis* from aquarium literature is also likely *R. mussoides*.

Rhodactis mussoides Carlgren, 1943: Olive green or brown with a large folded surface and a white or pink mouth. The tis-

Rhodactis **sp.** (hairy mushroom): note longer tentacles on margin.

Rhodactis **sp.** (hairy mushroom): note forked tentacles.

Rhodactis inchoata? (bullseye mushroom): colors range from purple to green.

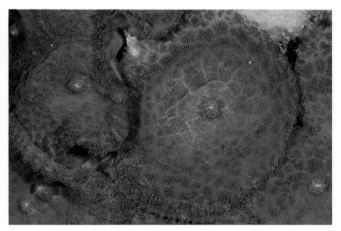

Rhodactis inchoata (Tonga blue mushroom): delicate, pale-blue variants.

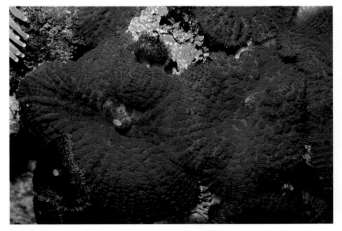

Rhodactis inchoata (Tonga blue mushroom): vivid-blue specimens.

Rhodactis **sp.** mushrooms (Lembeh Strait, Sulawesi)

Unidentified hairy mushroom (**Rhodactis sp.**): unusual multi-colored specimen photographed by Janine Cairns-Michael in Lembeh Strait, Sulawesi, Indonesia.

sue is very leathery with ruffled edges, reduced verrucae, and no marginal tentacles. It has multiple mouths (polystomatous). Typically 20-25 cm (8-10 in.), but grows to 38 cm (15 in.). Does not capture prey to any noticeable extent, but it can warp its margins considerably and can pull into a purse-string formation, usually at night or after a tank feeding, although this is a rare occurrence. Divides by longitudinal fission and typically occurs in limited colonial associations of several individuals. Prefers low to moderate water flow and reduced light, although it tolerates strong light. Called elephant ear mushroom.

Rhodactis (= *Discosoma*) *plumosa:* Very hairy to fuzzy-surfaced elephant ear mushrooms in all shades of green and brown, often with white striations underneath the abundant verrucae. Grows to 15 cm (6 in.). This species tolerates more intense light than other species. This may be the same species as *R. indosinensis* or *R. rhodostoma*.

Rhodactis rhodostoma Ehrenberg, 1834: Green, rust, brownish purple, or brown with (sometimes) pink mouth; very hairy with surface entirely covered with fine, branched tentacles that are spaced apart and in cauliflower-like arrangements. Typically brown discal tentacles may be tipped in contrasting colors and

may contrast markedly with oral disc surface. Thinner oral disc than similar *R. indosinensis*. Marginal tentacles present and well developed; acrospheres may be present. Prefers reduced lighting and water flow. Lives individually or, more commonly, in small associations of several individuals. Grows to 13 cm (5 in.).

Common Names: elephant ear mushroom, hairy mushroom, metallic mushroom.

Identification: The *Rhodactis,* formerly *Discosoma,* formerly *Rhodactis,* mushrooms seem to have reclaimed their original taxonomic genus. These mushrooms are normally much larger than those in other genera, often growing more than 30 cm (12 in.) across. Their surface is usually covered with comparatively short, split-ended or single (dendritic) tentacles called verrucae, radially arranged, giving them a fuzzy or hairy appearance. Marginal tentacles are lacking or reduced with occasionally small acrospheres. They are characterized by a lack of spirocyst-type nematocysts. Other species have tentacles that are large, round, warty knobs that dot their surface heavily. Some form elongate oval shapes with ruffled edges that give rise to the common name elephant ear mushroom.

Natural Location: Varies from deep water, where solitary specimens are typical, to more shallow locations, where colonial groups tend to form. Can be found vertically or horizontally in dim light or full sun.

Colors: See species descriptions, above.

Captive Care: Many *Rhodactis* species are among the hardiest of the corallimorphs. Some can grow quite large, especially *R. mussoides*, with several—if not all—capable of slow, purse-string-type closure behaviors. Most are quite tolerant of full lighting, unlike the *Actinodiscus* (= *Discosoma*) species, which mostly thrive in reduced light. (*R. inchoata* is an exception to this rule, preferring lower light levels.) However, strong lighting does not seem to be a requirement of the group.

Some species have a very strong odor when removed from the water, indicating the presence of volatile organic components. These mushrooms tend to be somewhat more aggressive in their ability to overtake other corals, either through chemical ecology or their ability to use nematocysts for competition.

Water motion, in general, should not be strong. These corallimorphs are not susceptible to many problems, other than those directly attributable to aquarium lighting, water motion, and water quality. They are quite tolerant of relatively high nutrient levels and have few known predators.

Special Information: Clownfishes may use hairy mushroom corals as surrogate hosts. Note carefully, however, that the somewhat similar giant cup or giant elephant ear mushroom (*Amplexidiscus fenestrafer*) will trap and eat fishes.

Collection Impact: Unknown, but similar to other corallimorphs. These are not common corals, with little known about their taxonomy and much less about their relative abundances and ranges in the wild. Overcollection may be a problem in some areas.

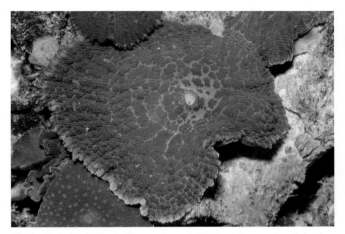

Rhodactis inchoata (Tonga blue mushroom): this genus is exceptionally hardy.

Rhodactis mussoides (elephant ear mushroom): leathery texture.

Rhodactis rhodostoma (hairy mushroom): note characteristic pink mouth.

Rhodactis indosinensis (hairy mushroom): if well-fed, will multiply rapidly.

The Scleractinians

Stony Corals

Stony corals are the primary builders of the great reef structures of the tropical seas—and the animals the world thinks of as "true corals." They range from massive domes of boulder brain coral (*Colpophyllia natans*), to thimblelike *Caryophyllia* species and other tiny, solitary corals that live in near darkness at depths down to 1,000 m (3,000 ft.) or more. In between are thousands of species that can appear as vast, impenetrable thickets of staghorn-type *Acropora* corals, fields of leafy *Pavona cactus*, or even corals hidden in obscurity, such as the delicate, brittle little colonies of *Anacropora* that survive in the turbid waters of muddy, shallow areas.

Belonging to the Subclass Hexacorallia, the stony corals, or Scleractinia, are characterized by having polyps with tentacles that number six or multiples of six, as well as a solid calcareous skeleton secreted by the polyps.

Although highly variable, stony corals often possess distinctive growth patterns, shapes, and colors, with the polyp itself sometimes displaying unique characteristics. Taxonomy to the species level in the stony corals can be quite apparent, given sometimes obvious skeletal clues that are clearly visible despite the polyp's tissue. In other stony corals, species-level distinctions can be cryptic at best, and the use of tissue samples, microscope examination or even DNA analysis may be needed to make a positive identification. In many cases, identifying stony corals to the genus level will be the best that aquarists can hope to do.

"SPS" AND "LPS" CORALS

In this text, the stony corals are not split, as is often the case in aquarium literature, into "small-polyped stony" (SPS) corals and "large-polyped stony" (LPS) corals. While these terms are commonly used within reef-keeping circles, there is little objectivity to such a classification or division.

Unfortunately, there is no real correlation between polyp size, where corals occur on the reef, and how they should be main-

Stony corals vary dramatically in size and shape or morphology: **left**, huge colony of **Colpophyllia natans** (boulder brain coral) in the Caribbean; **right**, a diminutive deep-water **Caryophyllia sp.** with a one-polyp, thimblelike skeleton.

Phylum: Cnidaria
Class: Anthozoa
Subclass: Hexacorallia
(Zoantharia)
Order: Scleractinia
(stony corals)
Families: Astrocoeniidae,
Pocilloporidae,
Acroporidae,
Poritidae,
Siderastreidae,
Agariciidae,
Fungiidae,
Oculinidae,
Pectiniidae,
Meandrinidae,
Mussidae,
Merulinidae,
Faviidae,
Trachyphylliidae,
Caryophylliidae,
Dendrophylliidae,
Rhizangiidae,
Flabellidae

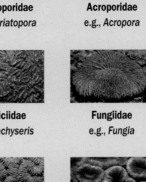

Pocilloporidae
e.g., *Seriatopora*

Acroporidae
e.g., *Acropora*

Poritidae
e.g., *Goniopora*

Siderastreidae
e.g., *Siderastrea*

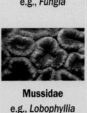

Agariciidae
e.g., *Pachyseris*

Fungiidae
e.g., *Fungia*

Oculinidae
e.g., *Galaxea*

Pectiniidae
e.g., *Mycedium*

Meandrinidae
e.g., *Meandrina*

Mussidae
e.g., *Lobophyllia*

Merulinidae
e.g., *Hydnophora*

Faviidae
e.g., *Favites*

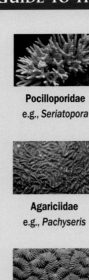

Trachyphylliidae
e.g., *Trachyphyllia*

Caryophylliidae
e.g., *Euphyllia*

Dendrophylliidae
e.g., *Tubastraea*

Rhizangiidae
e.g., *Phyllangia*

tained in captivity. Some species of so-called SPS corals have polyps as large or larger than other species not usually mentioned in or thought of as belonging to the SPS group. Conversely, corals of a predominantly large-polyped family, or even genus, may have species with very small polyps, yet these are not usually thought of as belonging to an SPS designation. Several families and genera of corals have species that contain both large- and small-polyped varieties. The genus *Turbinaria*, for example, contains species with polyps large and small.

Furthermore, many aquarists think of SPS corals as fast growing and colorful but difficult to care for, requiring intense light, lots of water movement, and low-nutrient conditions. This is a serious oversimplification. Many corals designated as SPS are slow growing, dull-colored, easy to maintain, and very adapt-able to different tank conditions. In fact, many small-polyped branching corals are not only more photoadaptive than other corals, but are more capable of alternating between autotrophy and heterotrophy (Haramaty et al., 1997), giving them a more flexible nature. There are also just as many that do not fit this description. Although some of the large-polyped varieties *are* relatively undemanding in their care requirements, this characteristic is not without exception.

The scientific community has used the term "micropolypal" to designate corals with polyps 1-2 mm in diameter, while "macropolypal" refers to those with polyps 10-40 mm in diameter. By far, most corals found throughout the reefs of the world have polyps that fall somewhere between these two definitions, with diameters from 2-10 mm.

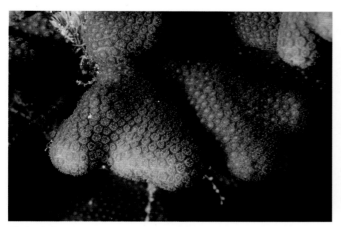

Madracis formosa (finger or cactus coral): a genus ripe for captive propagation.

Palauastrea ramosa (finger coral): Pacific species rare in the aquarium trade.

By placing the stony corals into basic taxonomic families, then sorting between symbiotic and aposymbiotic species, and noting groups with different growth patterns, we have much more valid information for reef keeping than artificially lumping them into polyp-size categories. Thus, segregation by family has been adopted in this book for reasons of important biological similarity—reasons that, I hope, will be infinitely more useful in the husbandry of these animals.

However we organize them, the scleractinians offer both challenge and incredible beauty, making more than average demands on one's skills and dedication as an aquarist but returning the incalculable satisfaction of growing a coral reef in the confines of a home aquarium.

FAMILY Astrocoeniidae

Genera: *Madracis* and *Palauastrea.*
Madracis is found in both Atlantic and Pacific Oceans in clear, deeper waters. *Palauastrea* is a Pacific genus.

GENUS *Madracis* Milne-Edwards and Haime, 1849
(mad-rah'-sis)
Commonly called finger, pencil, or cactus corals, these are some of the more beautiful corals in the Atlantic. Common in Caribbean waters, they are seen in bright yellow, blue, pink, green, and violet hues, in addition to brown. These are primary reef-building species in many areas, especially in the Lesser Antilles. Despite collection bans, some fragments may become available for captive-breeding efforts. They would be highly suitable candidates, likely to be quite tolerant of various captive conditions. The Pacific species, *M. kirbyi*, is both uncommon and somewhat unattractive. Nonetheless, it too shows potential for captive propagation.

GENUS *Palauastrea* Yabe and Sugiyama, 1941
(pal'-ow-ass'-tree-ah)
This Pacific genus includes but a single species, *Palauastrea ramosa*, which somewhat resembles a cross between *Porites cylindrica* and *Stylophora pistillata*. It is a beautiful, blunt-ended, branching coral that can be somewhat common in more-turbid waters on sandy bottoms (Veron, 1986). It has star-shaped corallites and may be a cream color with contrasting polyps. Rare in the aquarium trade, it is likely to become a candidate for captive-propagation efforts, thus providing an uncommon coral to the aquarist without depleting natural populations.

FAMILY Pocilloporidae Gray, 1842

Pacific Genera: *Pocillopora*, *Seriatopora*, and *Stylophora*.

The pocilloporids are the second-largest contributors to reef formations, despite having relatively few species. There are three exclusively Pacific genera. Pocilloporids are most active and in their greatest abundance in shallow, high-energy environments. They produce planulae (free-swimming larvae) year-round. Pocilloporids are found in most reef zones and form medium-sized colonies subjected to asexual fragmentation that survive stress well. Pocilloporids are tolerant and adaptive, with polyps that remain open day and night. While growth forms may vary, most are somewhat digitate (fingerlike) or ramose (branching).

GENUS *Pocillopora* Lamarck, 1816
(poh-sill'-oh-pohr'-ah)
Common Species: *P. damicornis, P. danae, P. eydouxi, P. ligulata, P. meandrina, P. verrucosa,* and others.
Common Names: cauliflower coral, bird's nest coral, brush coral, cluster coral.

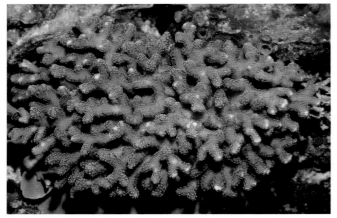

Pocillopora damicornis (cauliflower coral): a highly variable, adaptable species.

Pocillopora damicornis (cauliflower coral): note warty skeletal verrucae.

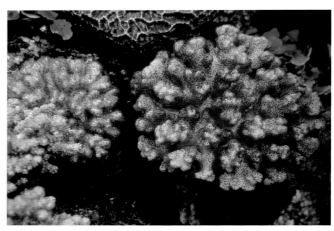

Pocillopora damicornis (cauliflower coral): extended polyps provide a fuzzy halo.

Pocillopora damicornis (cauliflower coral): grows rapidly in good conditions.

Pocillopora damicornis (cauliflower coral): colors range from pink to dark brown.

Pocillopora damicornis (cauliflower coral): wild, green-tipped colony. (Indonesia)

Identification: Fairly young on the evolutionary scale, *Pocillopora* species are characterized by having submassive or ramose skeletons with bladelike or arborescent branches. They may occasionally be encrusting or massive, though these are rarer growth forms. The presence of warty growths on the skeleton, called **verrucae**, is the hallmark of this genus. The corallites are immersed in the skeleton. *Pocillopora* polyps in nature only appear at night, sometimes remaining opened day and night, though the reverse is usually true in captivity. Their polyps are small, but very prominent and fuzzy. They account for one of *Pocillopora's* common names—cauliflower coral—because of the appearance that colonies take on with their polyps expanded.

Also unusual is the skeletal matrix of *Pocillopora,* which contains large amounts of chitin, a trait shared only with *Fungia.* The significance of this is unknown. *Pocillopora damicornis* is a branching species with a high degree of variability among colonies. It is, however, the most common *Pocillopora* species to be offered within the hobby. The verrucae may be less raised than on other species—they look more like "eyes" on the skeleton. *Pocillopora verrucosa* normally has decidedly larger verrucae than *P. damicornis,* making it resemble a head of cauliflower even when the polyps are not extended. The branches of *P. verrucosa* are heavier and more blunt and are uniformly bumpy. *Pocillopora meandrina* is very similar to *P. verrucosa,* though the verrucae are somewhat smaller. The branches may have a meandering pattern to them not present in *P. verrucosa,* though there are many exceptions. *Pocillopora eydouxi* is recognizable from its flattened, platelike branches and uniform verrucae.

Natural Location: *Pocillopora* are second only to *Acropora* as significant contributors to reef structures in the world. They are called the "coral guinea pigs," for they are easily kept in captive or laboratory conditions and are one of the most well-studied coral groups in the world. This enormously common genus is found throughout the Pacific, and for good reason. *Pocillopora* have tremendously polymorphic growth patterns. *Pocillopora damicornis,* for example, is capable of surviving and thriving in high and low currents, being exposed to the sun at low tide or hidden in shaded conditions, thriving in shallow or deep water, and existing in all shades of brown, pink, and green. The variability expressed by this genus is so remarkable that it would be hard for an untrained person to believe that the different patterns, colors, and shapes of this coral could possibly be the same species (see page 92). *Pocillopora meandrina* is commonly found in areas of the reef crest exposed to very strong water flow and wave action.

Colors: Most *Pocillopora* are brown, although a large number are pink. Other colors occasionally seen in aquarium specimens are

Pocillopora eydouxi (brush coral): colorful violet-tipped colony provides shelter for a Blue Surgeonfish (*Paracanthurus hepatus*). (Seychelles, Indian Ocean)

green, blue, and cream. Some species may have fluorescent halos on the polyp tips. *Pocillopora verrucosa* is less commonly found as a brown morph in the wild; it is normally pink.

Captive Care: Though found in widely varied environments in nature, *Pocillopora* can be considered somewhat less tolerant in captivity. They need good water quality to thrive, even though many can be found in quite "dirty" water in nature. They also

Pocillopora sp. (brush coral): natural siting in a shallow, high-surge area.

Pocillopora sp. (brush coral): wild colony with intense pink coloration.

Pocillopora sp.: unidentified colony photographed in North Sulawesi, Indonesia.

do best in strong, turbulent water with strong lighting, conditions that bring about rapid calcification, yet they are tolerant of lower light levels. Because they can grow quite rapidly, space should be allowed for such expansion. *Pocillopora damicornis* is found over a greater range of conditions than any other coral. *Pocillopora meandrina*, in contrast, is typically found in high-energy environments and requires strong water flow in the aquarium. Without it, it may die. Small examples are more adaptable in the aquarium, because the highly branched nature of most colonies creates shade on lower branches that cannot be overcome by artificial lighting. Once adjusted to ambient tank conditions, *Pocillopora* become quite hardy and "magically" become more adaptive to less-than-optimal conditions. For this reason, captive-bred colonies are much easier to maintain than those collected from the wild. Polyps on *Pocillopora* retract immediately when disturbed and quickly reappear when the stimulus is removed. Sweeper tentacles are common, though they are comparatively short—less than 2.5 cm (1 in.) long. Still, nearby submissive colonies may be affected by them.

Pocillopora gonad development and growth rate seem to be sensitive to temperature variations—changes and high temperatures seem to affect both negatively. It appears that the multiple and prolific methods of reproduction are of major importance to this coral, possibly a dominant method of competition over those with faster extension rates. Despite being thought of as a fast-growing coral, *Pocillopora* from various locations were found to grow at very different rates, ranging from less than 0.5 cm to almost 6 cm (0.25 in.-2.5 in.) per year in linear extension. This is also observable in captivity, where *Pocillopora* colonies can sometimes seem to grow much more slowly than other branching small-polyped corals. However, despite slower linear extension rates, the growth form of *Pocillopora* colonies hides much of their rapid calcification and increase in colony volume.

Problems with these corals are not uncommon in wild-harvested colonies. Certain commensal shrimps and crabs dwell in the branches. While most are symbiotic associates, some feed on the polyps and can closely mimic benign species. *Pocillopora* can be troubled by recession, bleaching, and virtually all of the diseases that affect corals. Their tissue layer is very thin and easily damaged, making them difficult to save once a problem starts.

Both sexual and asexual brooded planulae are found in the polyps of *Pocillopora damicornis* in nearly all lunar phases, indicating that reproduction, at least in this species, occurs regularly and frequently. Prolific reproduction has been reported in captivity. Fragmentation, sexual reproduction, and polyp bail-out are all methods of captive propagation. Colonies reach sexual maturity within 2-3 years, fairly young by coral standards. Perhaps this is because *Pocillopora* rarely live longer than 7-8 years in the wild (Richmond, 1987, 1988).

Special Information: The pigment responsible for the pink morphs of *Pocillopora* and other family members—pocilloporin—is an anomaly. Normally present in shallow-water colonies, its presence is an energy cost to the corals, and pink morphs calcify more slowly. Yet the pocilloporin-containing colonies are competitively superior to other color morphs. The function of pocilloporin is a mystery—it does not seem to act in photosynthesis, as a UV- or photo-protectant, as a fluorescing coupling pigment, or in any other obvious role. It may be a type of antipredatory chemical defense or play a part in the immune system, as pink morphs are dominant over brown morphs where both exist together.

Like similar branching corals, *P. damicornis* is notable for the number of fauna associated within and around the colony. A study in 1980, for example, discovered 951 individual faunal components representing 101 species in just 40 specimens of *Pocillopora*. These were symbionts, parasites, commensals, and other associated animals, all making use of an amazing microniche. Even within a coral head, space is precious.

Pocillopora planulae, in addition to their monthly production and overall vigor, have the ability to drift pelagically (in the open ocean) for long periods. They have another unique attribute—they are morphogenically reversible. A planula that has settled and begun corallite development can reverse its development for up to 3 days after settling if the location is stressful. It will detach, morphing back to a planktonic stage to resettle in another location (Richmond, 1985).

Collection Impact: *Pocillopora* may be considered an ideal group of stony corals for aquarists. Their widespread abundance, ease of collection by simple breaking of branches, high rate of asexual and sexual reproduction, and diverse geographic habitat make them exceptional corals for the aquarium. Poor survivability of some wild colonies seems the only drawback. Captive-propagation efforts are already well underway commercially, and at-home propagation is very easy.

GENUS *Seriatopora* Lamarck, 1816

(sehr'-ee-at'-oh-pohr'-ah)

Common Species: *S. caliendrum, S. hystrix.*

Common Names: bird's nest coral, needle coral, brush coral.

Identification: *Seriatopora* species have an appearance that is distinctive among corals. Extremely thin branches with needlelike tips intertwine and connect to form a nest of a skeleton. The colonies grow as small bushlike formations, with corallites neatly aligned in rows on the branches. Polyps extend at night in nature, but usually show themselves both day and night in captivity. *Se-*

Pocillopora verrucosa (cauliflower coral): note typical blunt, bumpy branches.

Pocillopora verrucosa (cauliflower coral): easily fragmented for propagation.

***Pocillopora* sp.**: this genus is highly amenable to captive propagation efforts.

Seriatopora hystrix (bird's nest coral): colony in Indonesia. Note sharp tips.

Seriatopora hystrix (bird's nest coral): colony in aquarist Wayne Shang's reef.

Seriatopora hystrix (bird's nest coral): note polyp alignment. (Red Sea)

Seriatopora caliendrum (bird's nest coral): note blunt-tipped branches.

riatopora hystrix is unmistakable with its needlelike tapered branches that are often dangerously sharp. _Seriatopora caliendrum_ has heavier branches than _S. hystrix_ (although still quite thin compared to most corals) and they are not quite as sharply pointed or tapered.

Natural Location: Found in diverse locales from lagoons to the reef crest, _Seriatopora_ are most common on sheltered reef slopes where they form smaller, more-isolated colonies. They are also found at the interface of hard substrate and the sand or soft bottom.

Colors: Common colors are brown, pink, and pale yellow with cream intermixed, and occasionally with green tints and highlights. Being a pocilloporid, the pink morphs are colored by the light-induced pigment pocilloporin.

Captive Care: These lovely corals grow very quickly, with branches rapidly sprouting off and often fusing with others nearby. The place where branches grow together is called an **anastamosis**. Colonies thrive under moderately strong light and somewhat reduced water flow. Similarly, in nature, colonies are generally found in protected areas of the reef, under other coral colonies, and in nooks and overhangs where both lighting and current are lower. They can be sensitive to poor water quality and fall victim to many of the same problems as _Pocillopora_. _Seriatopora_ are easily fragmented as one means of asexual reproduction, and polyp bail-out may also occur in this genus. Although not as variable in the wild, the same conditions that allow for _Pocillopora_ to thrive in the aquarium should make _Seriatopora_ grow equally well.

Special Information: Certain commensal crabs are unique to _Seriatopora_. In one species, the female intentionally traps herself in

Stylophora sp. (club finger coral): fast-growing and highly adaptable.

Stylophora sp. (club finger coral): thinner branches in a low-energy zone.

Stylophora sp. (club finger coral): colors vary in different environments.

Stylophora sp. (club finger coral): young colony on a reef in New Guinea.

a cagelike cavity formed by live *Seriatopora* branches and awaits smaller males to crawl in and mate with her.

Collection Impact: While not as widespread as the prolific *Pocillopora*, the abundance of *Seriatopora* in nature makes collection impact practically insignificant. Captive breeding is well under way at local and commercial levels, with *S. hystrix* as the most-common species propagated.

GENUS *Stylophora* Schweigger, 1819
(sty'-loh-for'-ah)

Common Species: *S. mordax, S. pistillata, S subscriata.*

Common Names: finger coral, cluster coral, brush coral, club finger coral.

Identification: *Stylophora* is another genus of remarkably well-studied corals—their fast growth and adaptation to varying condi-

tions make them excellent research subjects. Colonies are branching, with branches that are thick, occasionally flattened, and normally with round, blunt ends. Colonies from calmer water are more highly branched. The corallites are usually immersed and may be hooded, and the **coenosteum** (the calcareous skeleton) has small conical spines called **spinules**. Polyps are uniformly small, though clearly visible, as in all the pocilloporids. The polyps extend at night on the reef, though they are usually extended day and night in captivity.

Natural Location: *Stylophora* are found in widely diverse locations, but are most common on reef fronts where they are subject to high light and water motion. In such areas, they may be the dominant coral. *Stylophora mordax* is typically a high-energy-environment coral. *Stylophora pistillata* is found in highly diverse regions.

Colors: *Stylophora* can be very colorful, found in bright shades of pink, green, blue, purple, and cream. The branches are often solid-colored, and the polyps may be contrasting in fluorescent colors. Pale brown to darker brown, depending on ambient nutrient and light levels, may predominate. Branch tips may be paler or contrasting in color.

Captive Care: Found in many locations throughout the reef, *Stylophora* are quite adaptable to light and currents. Strong lighting tends to bring out their naturally bright colors, while strong water flow encourages rapid calcification. Nonetheless, *Stylophora* can be one of the most light-adaptable colonies in the wild, and shaded colonies can exist at 0.5-1% of subsurface irradiance levels. In the aquarium, duplicating their preferred reef locations in areas subject to intense surge and wave action, as well as high irradiance levels, is not required.

Sweeper tentacles are common, especially at night and at the tips of branches. These sweepers are like those of *Pocillopora*—effective, but comparatively short at 2.5 cm (1 in.) or less. Sweepers are a surprising feature, because these corals rank exceedingly low in aggression hierarchies, usually achieving dominance through rapid colonization or oriented translocation. They are "nettled" by almost all other corals in immediate proximity. Perhaps more interesting is that *Stylophora* have been found to produce allelopathic chemicals. They have been extensively studied in immunological research, and have been reported to engage in autolytic (self-digestion of tissue) behavior in response to exposure to certain other corals.

Like their relatives, *Stylophora* can be quite hardy and successful in captivity, though they are susceptible to recession, common coral diseases, and bleaching. Polyp bail-out is likely in cases of stress, though fragmentation of branches is the most common method of asexual propagation.

Special Information: *Stylophora* are not markedly affected by lunar cycles in triggering spawning. Damselfishes, such as *Dascyllus marginatus*, may have a mutualistic relationship with *Stylophora*. The damselfish gains protection in the branches, and the coral benefits from the fish's waste material. In fact, growth rates are significantly higher in *Stylophora* corals inhabited by damselfishes.

Collection Impact: Although fragmentation is commonly used to propagate new colonies, fieldwork has shown that survivability of *Stylophora* fragments is quite low, indicating that they are somewhat less suitable than other small-polyped corals for regular branch-breaking cultivation, even though they are easily collected. Nevertheless, if the somewhat demanding conditions are provided for the successful captive care of this genus, they are excellent choices for the hobby and their collection has an insignificant impact on natural populations. *Stylophora pistillata* is a common species found in very wide geographical ranges that has the added advantage of having sexually and asexually produced larvae that are "famous" for prolific and long-distance settlements. *Stylophora* are also being captive bred with some degree of success at several commercial facilities.

FAMILY Acroporidae Verrill, 1902

Genera: *Acropora, Anacropora, Astreopora,* and *Montipora.*

This family is the largest and most important contributor to coral reef formations in the world. The two primary genera—*Acropora* and *Montipora*—together account for almost one-third of all hermatypic (reef-building) coral species. The other two genera, *Astreopora* and *Anacropora*, are less important, though not uncommon.

Highly adaptive corals—opportunistic, fast growing, highly successful in both asexual and sexual reproduction—they are predominantly found in the Pacific. There are only three species of *Acropora* in the Atlantic, with no other genera represented. Not long ago, *Acropora* were once common and the primary reef builders in these waters, but their populations have been severely damaged by disease, storms, and anthropogenic (human-created) influences.

Natural, shallow setting for **Stylophora pistillata** (different color forms, **foreground**) and **Pocillopora eydouxi, rear,** on a reef flat in Bunaken, North Sulawesi.

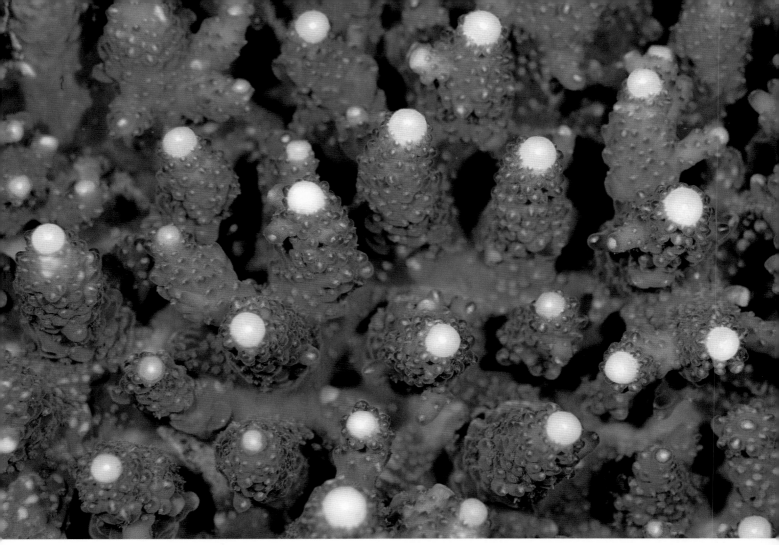

Fantastically successful reef builders, **Acropora** species have fast-growing axial corallites, seen here as pink tips on an unidentified colony. (Lembeh Strait, Sulawesi)

GENUS *Acropora* Oken, 1815
(ah-crop'-or-ah OR ak'-roh-pohr'-ah)

Common Species: *A. abrolhosensis, A. aculeus, A. aspera, A. austera, A. bushyensis, A. carduus, A. cerealis, A. clathrata, A. cuneata, A. cytherea, A. digitifera, A. divaricata, A. echinata, A. elseyi, A. florida, A. formosa, A. gemmifera, A. horrida, A. humilis, A. hyacinthus, A. kirstyae, A. latistella, A. loripes, A. lovelli, A. lutkeni, A. microclados, A. microphthalma, A. millepora, A. nana, A. nasuta, A. nobilis, A. palifera, A. pulchra, A. samoensis, A. secale, A. selago, A. tenuis, A. tortuosa, A. valida, A. verweyi, A. yongei,* and many others.

Atlantic Species: *A. cervicornis, A. palmata,* and *A. prolifera* are currently under collection restrictions and are not generally available to amateur aquarists.

Common Names: There are various vernacular descriptions based on color and growth form: staghorn coral, cat's paw coral, bottlebrush coral, table or tabletop coral—each of these names is used (often confusingly) with a variety of different species.

Identification: These darlings of the reef hobby easily deserve a book of their own, but despite their popularity there is still an ongoing argument about the pronunciation of the genus name. To set matters straight, both "ah-crop'-or-ah" and "ak'-roh-pohr'-ah" are acceptable pronunciations. The variation is mostly one of culture, not correctness. Typically, Americans say the latter, although it grates on the ears of old-school marine biologists.

The skeletons of all *Acropora* species are very porous and

ACROPORA SPECIES GROUPED BY GROWTH FORM

BRANCHING
e.g., *A. nobilis*

BUSHY
e.g., *A. cerealis*

CLUSTER
e.g., *A. gemmifera*

Branching (Arborescent)
Staghorn types: *A. abrolhosensis,*
A. formosa, A. nobilis,
A. pulchra, A. yongei*
Other branching types: *A. austera*,*
A. florida*, A. horrida*,
A. microphthalma, A. yongei*

Bushy (Caespitose)
A. austera*, A. cerealis*,
A. divaricata*, A. horrida*,
A. kirstyae, A. loripes*, A. lovelli*,
A. selago*, A. tortuosa*, A. valida*

Cluster (Corymbose)
A. aculeus, A. aspera, A. cerealis*,
A. digitifera*, A. gemmifera,
A. humilis, A. latistella*, A. lutkeni*,
A. microclados*, A. millepora,
A. nana, A. nasuta, A. samoensis,
A. secale, A. selago*, A. tenuis,
A. valida*, A. verweyi, A. yongei*

BOTTLEBRUSH
e.g., *A. granulosa*

FINGER
e.g., *A. digitifera*

TABLE
e.g., *A. hyacinthus*

Bottlebrush
A. carduus, A. echinata, A. elseyi,
A. granulosa, A. loripes*, A. lovelli*,
A. lutkeni*, A. tortuosa*

Finger (Digitate)
A. bushyensis, A. digitifera*,
A. monticulosa

Tabular (Table or Tabletop)
A. clathrata, A. cytherea,
A. divaricata*, A. hyacinthus,
A. latistella*, A. microclados*

Plates, Columns, Other
A. cuneata, A. palifera*

COLUMN
e.g., *A. palifera*

***Species marked by an
asterisk commonly take
more than one growth
form or intermediate
growth forms.**

---

lightweight—at least near the branch tips. The presence of an axial (terminal) corallite is a recent evolutionary advantage by which all but a few species can be identified. This specialized corallite lacks zooxanthellae, yet it has a rapid growth rate, being fed by other areas of the colony. This arrangement allows for

Rampant-growing staghorn (***Acropora* sp.**) showing light-colored axial corallites that lack zooxanthellae and are fed by the rest of the colony. (Fiji)

the genus to have a distinct advantage in being able to outgrow other corals and rapidly colonize the reef. Fast-growing *Acropora* branches are easily spotted with their light-colored tips, which may be almost white or brightly hued.

There are 13-15 basic growth forms in *Acropora* (Randall, 1981), with variations according to the size and shape of the axial and radial corallites, the size and shape of the branches, the number and position of secondary branches, the number of corallite septa, and the nature of the coenosteum. All species have distinct raised corallites with (normally) 48 septa that are not visible to the eye. The axial corallite is tubular with other radial corallites being pocket-shaped, possibly less tubular and more circular. The radial corallites arise from the base of axial corallites and are indeterminate, perhaps forming another axial corallite if conditions permit. Other than species like *A. palifera* or *A. cuneata*, which have thick, blunt branches with small, round calices, speciation outside general growth forms is difficult.

The most commonly available aquarium species tend to fall within these growth forms: branching (arborescent), bushy (caespitose), cluster (corymbose), finger (digitate), bottlebrush (short side branches), and, more rarely, tabular (with tabletop formations). (See box, above, for species grouped by growth form.)

Acropora sp. (staghorn acropora): young colony with intertwined crinoid.

Acropora formosa (staghorn acropora): a widespread favorite of reef aquarists.

Acropora austera (branching acropora): an unusual and highly variable species.

Acropora yongei (staghorn acropora): exposed thicket at low tide. (Fiji)

Acropora grandis (staghorn acropora): large colonies are typical in the wild.

Acropora nobilis (staghorn acropora): colors vary from tan to green and blue.

Acropora cerealis (bushy acropora): note neat, pillowlike colony appearance.

Acropora valida (cluster acropora): variable species with odd-sized corallites.

Acropora austera (branching acropora): assumes a range of colors and forms.

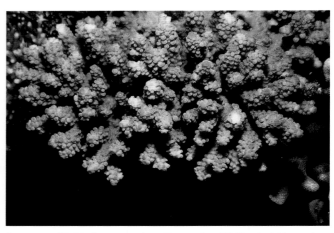

Acropora valida (cluster acropora): a widespread and highly adaptable species.

Acropora lutkeni (cluster acropora): sturdy with irregular radial corallites.

Acropora sp. (cluster acropora): unidentified species. (Sulawesi, Indonesia)

Acropora verweyi (cluster acropora): plump axial corallites are typical.

Acropora valida (cluster acropora): will grow with great speed in the aquarium.

Acropora verweyi (cluster acropora): note nariform (nose-shaped) corallites.

Acropora secale (cluster acropora): popular species among coral farmers.

Acropora nasuta (cluster acropora): tight branches need flushing water surges.

Acropora nasuta (cluster acropora): upside-down nose-shaped corallites.

Acropora sp. (cluster or corymbose acropora): unidentified species, Indonesia.

Acropora sp. (cluster acropora): strong light and water flow recommended.

Acropora sp. (cluster acropora): unidentified species, Lembeh Strait, Sulawesi.

ium. In nature, these corals are the most significant contributors to reef formations in the world. They are the fastest growing corals on the reef and have an extremely high metabolism. Over 300 named species exist in the Pacific alone. Growth patterns, colors, and shapes are nothing short of staggering.

Highly adaptable, *Acropora* can exist in turbid lagoons, wave-pounded reef crests, and calm reef flats. Many species are regularly out of water at low tide, relying on their UV-absorbing substances and heavy mucus coat to survive until the water levels rise again. They tolerate huge differences in light intensity, water movement, and even salinity, as shallow, protected reefs become exposed to tremendous downfalls and land-based rainwater runoff. The amount of research and description on the *Acropora* genus alone could fill a small library, and their forms intrigue both underwater observers and aquarium hobbyists alike.

Given the recent evolutionary success of these corals in demanding reef conditions, it would be expected that one could virtually ship them in an envelope across continents, place the corals in a pitcher of saltwater, and have them grow. Yet nothing could be further from the truth. In fact, they are very demanding in captivity. By the same token, they are consistently found in dozens of studies to be some of the most sensitive species in tolerating temperature change, sedimentation, and other chemical and environmental stresses that are outside of their normal conditions. However, once a certain critical acclimation period has passed, and if stable conditions are present, *Acropora* will thrive.

When selecting wild *Acropora*, the presence of axial corallites should be noted. This will signify that the coral is or was from a rapidly growing area of the colony and has not been removed from an interior area of the colony where growth rates were limited. Brown tips, where the axial corallite has become indistinguishable from the radial corallites, do not grow as well in terms of branch extension, though infilling and radial growth may still occur. A new axial corallite can develop under favorable conditions, but at a metabolic cost to the coral that may not be feasible with newly placed specimens; many such examples fail to thrive in their new environment.

In general, *Acropora* species with thick branches are reported to be more difficult to keep than those with thin branches, probably due to an inability of the captive environment to provide enough water flow. Furthermore, many thick-branched species seem more prone, initially, to problems. Brown specimens, bottlebrush types, and thin-branched types seem to be somewhat more "tolerant," as they are typically from lower water flow and light conditions. Tabletop-type *Acropora* species are among the most difficult to keep, with the traditional staghorn varieties somewhere in between.

Captive-bred specimens are generally healthier and much easier to care for than wild-caught colonies. Nonetheless, all *Acropora* seem to prefer a strong, random, mixing-type current for maximum health and growth, high levels of calcium and (anecdotally) strontium, and intense lighting. Very few species, except perhaps captive-bred colonies, will tolerate moderate lighting and water flow. Water parameters should also be excellent. It is not advisable to keep *Acropora* in new tanks, as the stability of a mature tank (well in excess of a year old) offers a much higher chance of success. *Acropora* typically reach sexual maturity at 3-5 years of age, after having attained a branch diameter between 4-7 cm (1.5-2.75 in.) (Fitzhardinge, 1988).

Acropora suffer from many maladies, including certain predatory animals they harbor within their branches. Others harbor commensal crabs and shrimps, which are sometimes symbiotic in offering protection to the coral from predation. Quite a number of fishes and other animals prey exclusively on acroporid tissue. *Acropora* need careful acclimation so that they are not shocked by light or water-parameter changes, yet they must be placed in their final positions quickly enough to avoid stress or unfulfilled metabolic needs. Such stresses include low light and water current, as well as movement from position to position. *Acropora* do not tolerate any sudden changes in tank conditions, and they may bleach, die, recede, or rapidly waste if stability is not maintained. Field observations show that up to 5-6 months is necessary under ideal conditions for transplanted *Acropora* to regain normal growth rates.

In many studies, as well as in practice, *Acropora* seem to be one of the least tolerant corals to temperature flux. They are also subject to virtually every known coral malady including white-band disease, black-band disease, various types of tissue necrosis (RTN et al.), bleaching, recession, etc. In summary, *Acropora* are extremely demanding though not at all impossible to keep if their needs are met.

Special Information: *Acropora* has a particular susceptibility to rapid tissue necrosis (RTN), the aquarium-hobby term for the syndrome of rapid tissue sloughing or "peeling" often encountered in this genus (see Chapter 11). Wild-collected *Acropora* are much more likely to exhibit this contagious and often-fatal condition than other coral species, yet another reason to support propagation facilities by purchasing captive-bred colonies (which have a markedly reduced incidence of this malady). It is highly probable that many aspects of this *Acropora* "disease" are related to stresses that take place between collection and final establishment in a reef aquarium.

Acropora skeletons vary in strength and density—even within the same colony. The outer and upper branches of many species

Acropora longicyathus (bottlebrush acropora): with Yellowtail Blue Damselfish.

***Acropora* sp:** young specimens offer perplexing identification challenges.

***Acropora* sp:** lovely lime-green unidentified species. (Lembeh Strait, Sulawesi)

Acropora tortuosa (bushy acropora): unusual species with irregular growth.

Acropora granulosa (bottlebrush acropora): note tapering, tubular corallites.

Acropora caroliniana (bottlebrush acropora): upcurving corallites are typical.

Acropora sp. (bushy acropora): unidentified species. (Indonesia)

Acropora sp.: unidentified young colony with indeterminate growth form.

Acropora sp. (bushy acropora): may morph dramatically in the aquarium.

Acropora cytherea (tabletop acropora): table-forming species are abundant on upper-reef slopes in the wild, but very demanding of strong currents in captivity.

may be porous, but the densities of the skeletons at the base of the staghorn corals *A. cervicornis* and *A. formosa* are among the highest ever recorded among the stony corals (Hughes, 1987). *Acropora pulchra* is one of the fastest-growing corals known in nature. It has a linear skeletal extension rate that can exceed 22 cm (8.5 in.) per year.

Nonetheless, boring sponges (clionids) are active, primarily at the base. The sponges may help the asexual reproduction of *Acropora* in the wild by eroding the skeleton and causing branches to fall and recolonize on the substrate. Certain commensal crabs and shrimps, as well as decapod crustaceans (*Cymo* spp. et al.) may modify the growth of branches, preventing or accelerating branch fusion, or causing other skeletal changes. These do not seem to harm the corals and may be effective in preventing actual predators from approaching the colony.

An unusual morph of a normally tabulate *Acropora* species was reported from the Red Sea by Riegl et al. (1996). This is *A. anthocercis*, a free-living so-called corallith, a veritable basketball of rolling *Acropora*.

Collection Impact: *Acropora* are fast growing, highly reproductive, and abundant, and new, small colonies are easily collected with minimal reef impact. They are highly successful as captive-bred specimens, and are being cultured commercially with great success. Their only pitfall is their high rate of mortality due to stress, disease, and improper captive conditions. The potentially endangered *Acropora palmata*, *A. prolifera*, and *A. cervicornis*, all Atlantic species, would be wonderful candidates for captive propagation, should they become available. *A. palmata*, however, is an extremely large coral with potentially demanding requirements.

Some of the most common *Acropora* species, the tabletops (*A. hyacinthus*, *A. cytherea*, *A. latistella*, *A. clathrata*, etc.), are known as difficult to ship and acclimate, yet they are among the most highly desirable species. Small colonies have a much-improved survival record over fully formed tables, and captive-propagated specimens are becoming available. Some patience is required as the distinctive table begins to take shape from a small colony, but growth tends to accelerate, and the whole process is fascinating to witness.

Acropora anthocercis (table acropora): young, developing colony. (Indonesia)

Acropora valenciennesi (table acropora): note characteristic upturned branches.

Acropora clathrata (table acropora): horizontal branches can form table. (Fiji)

Acropora clathrata (table acropora): fusing or anastomosing branches.

Acropora sp. (table acropora): underside of a large table. (Papua New Guinea)

Acropora latistella (table acropora): note damselfishes taking refuge.

Acropora cytherea (table acropora): colony forming above large *Montipora* sp.

Acropora palmata (elkhorn coral): Caribbean species forms massive branches.

Acropora latistella (table acropora): daytime polyp extension in wild colony.

Acropora palifera (columnar acropora): can form pillars, ridges, or branches.

Acropora hyacinthus (table acropora): note tiered spirals. (Papua New Guinea)

Acropora palifera (branching acropora): young branched colony in a lagoon.

Anacropora sp. (briar coral): thin, brittle branches can form stony thickets.

Astreopora sp.: rarely collected, but care requirements are easily met.

GENUS *Anacropora* Ridley, 1884

(an-ak'-roh-pohr'-ah)

Common Species: *A. forbesi, A. spinosa,* and others.

Common Name: briar coral.

Identification: Until recent years, *Anacropora* were virtually unheard of within the reef hobby. However, they have become more readily available and are well worth knowing. *Anacropora* are actually more closely related to *Montipora* than to *Acropora,* both in terms of their evolutionary and taxonomic similarities. The colonies grow in a formation like those of *Acropora,* with thin and obviously tapered branches. They do not have the fast-growing axial corallites that distinguish the *Acropora* genus, but have widely spaced tiny corallites that stand apart on the skeletal branches. The polyps often emerge from corallites at the base of conical spines (spinules). These corallites will bud to form new growth. *Anacropora* also tend to grow in colonies that are less organized than most *Acropora,* resembling a thicket of twisted branches.

Natural Location: *Anacropora* formations can be found in very turbid conditions on muddy substrates and also in quiet lagoons and patch reefs without current. They are comparatively uncommon in the aquarium trade.

Colors: Common colors are reported to be quite drab, ranging from brown to cream. Branch tips may be lighter in color, though they do not seem to display the attractive colored tips and margins common in this family. They can be very pale to almost white, having fewer zooxanthellae.

Captive Care: Because of their location in such extreme conditions, these corals are reported to be quite hardy—tolerant of high-nutrient water, various light intensities, and variable water movement. Not much is known about the problems common

to this genus, but any coral capable of significant silt rejection is probably fairly resistant to common coral maladies.

Special Information: The brittle skeleton makes this genus difficult to ship without breakage.

Collection Impact: Not enough is known about the abundance of *Anacropora* at this time to make valid assessments of the impact of aquarium-related collections on wild populations. It is likely, because of their fairly slow growth rate and reported rarity in the usual reef harvesting zones, that they may not be as suitable for collection as related family members. They should make admirable candidates for captive-propagation efforts, however, and some progress has been made in this regard.

GENUS *Astreopora* de Blainville, 1830

(ass'-tree-oh-pohr'-ah)

Common Species: *A. listeri, A. myriophthalma,* and perhaps 16 others.

Common Names: None.

Identification: *Astreopora* were once thought to be part of the genus *Turbinaria,* which some species can resemble, especially when forming plates. They are similarly variable in their morphology. The hemispherical-to-flattened colonies superficially resemble *Turbinaria, Echinopora,* and *Cyphastrea* species and some other round, massive corals. However, *Astreopora* colonies are quite porous, appearing less solid in their shape, with corallites evenly spaced and conical. Upon close examination, the lack of perforating septa make the corallites quite recognizable as belonging to the Family Acroporidae. There is no columella. The outsides of the calices and coenosteum are quite rough and feathery, like *Acropora* skeletons. The coral surface appears pebbled. New corallites appear in the coenosteum between existing coral-

Montipora digitata (velvet finger coral): an ideal beginner's stony coral.

Montipora sp. (velvet coral): fast-growing and exceptionally hardy.

lites, whereas in other family members, they frequently appear as buds of the parent polyp. In nature, *Astreopora* polyps are generally expanded at night, though I find them to be expanded day and night in captivity. Polyps have 24 tentacles that are flat and petal-like, arranged in two cycles. Some species can be free-living.

Natural Location: *Astreopora* are quite common in nature, found at all depths and on almost all reefs, though not nearly as common as *Acropora* or *Montipora*. They are most often found in clear waters with strong currents. Rare to reef flats, they do not tolerate exposure at low tides.

Colors: *Astreopora* are typically cream or brown, although dull to rich reds, greens, bright blue, and orange occur. Margins can be intensified or contrasting. Although they can resemble *Turbinaria*, *Astreopora* are never mustard-colored.

Captive Care: *Astreopora* are difficult to include in a reef aquarium as they are (unfortunately) rarely offered for sale. Preferring moderate to strong current, clear water, and intense lighting, their care requirements are very similar to those of *Acropora*. They are not usually encroached upon by other corals. Fragmentation is a method of asexual reproduction. Polychaete worms and pyrgomatid barnacles occasionally infest these corals (Lamberts, 1982). Colony growth occurs by extratentacular budding. Decalcification seems common in these corals. *Astreopora* seem to be intermediate in difficulty to maintain—easier than *Acropora*, more difficult than many *Montipora*.

Special Information: *Astreopora* may be the evolutionary precursors of the acroporids. According to fossil records, their unique porous skeleton gave rise to *Acropora*, *Montipora*, and finally *Anacropora*.

Collection Impact: Seldom sought out by collectors, but where they occur in abundance, small colonies may be taken without significant disturbance.

GENUS *Montipora* de Blainville, 1830
(mahn'-tih-pohr'-ah)

Common Species: *M. capricornis, M. crassituberculata, M. danai, M. digitata, M. foliosa, M. patula, M. spongodes, M. spumosa, M. stellata, M. tuberculosa, M. verrucosa,* and others.

Common Names: velvet coral, velvet finger coral, velvet branch coral.

Identification: *Montipora* is one of the largest genera of corals, judged by the number of species. It is a vastly divergent group that encompasses almost every type of coral growth form known, including laminar, foliaceous, encrusting, and branching. Most species are even capable of displaying two or more forms within the same colony.

Their corallites are tiny, making them distinct from all other corals except *Porites*. However, the corallites of *Montipora* have inward-projecting septa, even if they are almost microscopic. In many cases, corallites are immersed within and between a well-textured corallum, with tiny openings and polyps barely visible in and around the coenosteum. Various skeletal characteristics can be used in identifying different species of *Montipora*, although it can be extremely difficult for anyone not skilled in such identifications. Skeletons are very lightweight and porous. Polyps are tiny, uniform, and fuzzy, and give rise to the common name velvet coral. It is my opinion that this vernacular label suits some species, while others simply look stony, with almost no observable polyps at all.

Although specific tank conditions may change its growth form, *M. digitata* is generally a branching species and can resemble both *Palauastrea* species and *Porites cylindrica*. However, its branches tend to be much thinner, especially in captivity. *Montipora stellata* has rough, irregular, upright plates. *Montipora*

Montipora sp. (encrusting montipora): many arrive on live rock.

Montipora spumosa (encrusting montipora): may develop projecting columns.

Montipora verrucosa (encrusting montipora): surface pattern is characteristic.

Montipora foveolata (encrusting montipora): will grow across aquarium rock.

Montipora efflorescens (encrusting montipora): note mounding formations.

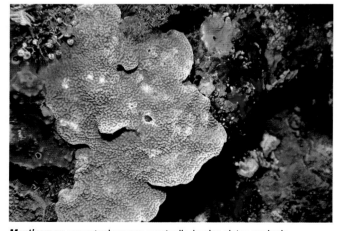

Montipora sp.: young colony may eventually develop plates or whorls.

capricornis is noted for having a pretty spiraling vase shape in the mature colony. There are many species of *Montipora*, although the aforementioned species are the most common types currently available. The encrusting or submassive growth forms of many *Montipora* species make their collection difficult, although some are already being propagated and others appear on wild-collected live rock.

Natural Location: *Montipora* are found from deep water to the reef crest, from clear oceanic reefs to turbid lagoons. *Montipora digitata* is commonly found in turbid lagoons and shallow areas, and many other species available to the hobby, such as *M. verrucosa* and *M. capricornis*, are also more common to lagoonal-type shallow-water habitats. Growth form is a decent indicator of the conditions a species requires: those with smooth surfaces are generally from calmer water; textured surfaces and convoluted shapes are from higher-flow conditions; and platelike forms are from deeper water.

Colors: Various species of *Montipora* can be found in almost every hue of the rainbow, but green, pink, purple, and brown seem to be the most common. *Montipora* polyps are frequently brown or green, tending to be in contrast to the sometimes more brightly hued coenosarc. There are examples, especially those subjected to intense illumination, with green polyps. I have also seen morphs with purple polyps on a purple skeleton. Branch tips of ramose species are often lighter-colored, even white, reflecting areas of more rapid growth similar those seen in many fast-growing corals. Laminar, foliaceous, and turbinate colonies are often ringed around the growing margins by a lighter or contrasting hue. Curiously, the recently popular *M. capricornis* may be a dull brown when collected and imported, but can transform itself into glowing green, pink, purple, and blue colors under artificial lighting.

Captive Care: *Montipora* are generally quite hardy with many fast-growing species. The deep-set polyps are unusually resistant to total bleaching and disease, which is surprising, considering they are in the same family with the finicky *Acropora* group. Once established and found to be free of recession or disease, *Montipora* grow very easily and soon begin rapidly calcifying and encrusting the substrate.

Montipora are submissive corals and do not possess strong defensive or aggressive structures. Care must be taken to place them away from other corals to allow room for growth, since they will almost always lose a territorial battle. Despite a preference of some species for strong lighting and water movement, they are surprisingly adaptable. In fact, *Montipora* grow quite well in lower light conditions, although they may become substantially "brown" in color as the zooxanthellae proliferate and photo-

***Montipora* sp.** (plate montipora): pleasing growth in a California reef tank.

Montipora tuberculosa (plate montipora): colors vary from drab brown to blue.

***Montipora* sp.** (plate montipora): captive colony with bright pink margin.

Montipora sp. (plate montipora): on a Solomon Islands fore reef.

Montipora capricornis (whorled montipora): uniform color is characteristic.

adapt—often quickly. Fragmentation is extremely easy with branching and foliaceous species, making this genus ideal for at-home propagation efforts.

Special Information: One researcher has called *Montipora* polyps "busy": at any given time they are, singly or in groups, expanding and contracting. Their small size makes it likely that the regular retraction and expansion is used in procuring larger particulate food sources.

The popular aquarium coral *M. capricornis* may be confused with *M. foliosa, M. tuberculosa,* and others.

Collection Impact: Because of their abundance in nature, diversity of species, easy collection through fragmentation (leaving the mother colony intact), hardiness, and ease of captive propagation, *Montipora* are one of the most appropriate and desirable groups of corals for the aquarium hobby. Captive-breeding efforts are well underway at both commercial and local levels. As more species become available, aquarists will be able to move beyond the most common species, *M. digitata,* which many regard as an ideal beginner's small-polyped stony coral.

FAMILY Poritidae Gray, 1842

Genera: *Alveopora, Goniopora, Porites, Poritipora,* and *Stylaraea.*
As the third largest contributor to coral reef formations, mostly by members of the *Porites* genus, Poritidae encompasses 3 primary genera and approximately 120 species. The common genera are *Alveopora, Goniopora,* and *Porites.* Members of *Stylaraea* and *Poritipora* are rare. *Porites* form large, long-lived, mostly massive species in widely variant locations. *Goniopora,* in contrast, are opportunistic species and early settlers of new areas. All genera are Pacific, but *Porites* can also be found in the Atlantic.

GENUS *Alveopora* de Blainville, 1830
(al'-vee-oh-pohr'-ah)

Common Species: *A. allingi, A. catalai, A. fenestrata,* and others.
Common Names: daisy coral, ball coral, flowerpot coral.
Identification: *Alveopora* closely resemble *Goniopora.* They usually have round, massive, or sometimes branching skeletons. As with other family members, the skeleton is lightweight and porous. A distinction between the two is that *Alveopora* polyps have only 12 tentacle tips and their corallites have 12 septa (*Goniopora* have 24 of each). *Alveopora* tentacle tips frequently have slightly bulbous or flattened ends and contrasting centers that give the polyp end the appearance of a daisy. Their polyps are normally shorter and smaller than those of *Goniopora,* and their calices are smaller, with thin, narrow corallite walls. Like *Goniopora, Alveopora* extend their polyps during the day, partially retracting them at night.

Alveopora sp. (daisy coral): note 12 tentacles per polyp; *Goniopora* has 24.

Alveopora catalai (daisy coral): colonies tend to waste away slowly in captivity.

Alveopora sp. (daisy coral): rare species, photographed in North Sulawesi.

Natural Location: The occurrence of *Alveopora* in nature is wide ranging, but sporadic. Their availability in the aquarium trade is likewise not predictable or common; occasionally, they are regularly offered for sale, at other times they are impossible to locate. The species most commonly seen in the aquarium trade (*A. catalai*) is usually from the same soft substrate bottom as many species of *Goniopora* , though other species can come from lagoons or the reef slope in deeper water.

Colors: *Alveopora* are commonly light brown, cream, or green, although shades of whitish pink, yellow, or blue can occur in some species.

Captive Care: *Alveopora* are considered similar in their care requirements and as difficult to maintain as *Goniopora*, and they are not likely to survive in most home aquariums. Low current and low to medium lighting with, perhaps, a slightly higher nutrient content seem to fit their most common locations in nature. *Alveopora* are naturally adapted to living in both high-light and low-light environments and are one of the more-tolerant corals, at least in this respect.

Special Information: None.

Collection Impact: As with *Goniopora,* this genus can't be recommended to most aquarists, and its collection should not be encouraged as long as its care requirements remain a mystery.

GENUS *Goniopora* de Blainville, 1830
(goh'-nee-oh-pohr'-ah)

Common Species: *G. columna, G. djiboutiensis, G. lobata, G. minor, G. pandoraensis, G. stokesi, G. tenuidens,* and others.

Common Names: flowerpot coral, ball coral, daisy coral.

Identification: *Goniopora* usually have highly porous round, massive, or columnar skeletons. Rarely, they are encrusting or branching. The polyps of most *Goniopora* are exceedingly long (up to 30 cm [12 in.] or more) and graceful, and can be easily identified as having 24 tentacle tips. Polyps are almost always extended by day, and partially to completely retracted at night. Corallites have 24 septa. Examination of the underside of a skeleton may be useful for distinguishing between *G. stokesi,* a common import which is normally free-living, and other *Goniopora* species, which are usually attached. These other species may bear marks on the undersides of their skeletons, called attachment scars, where they have been detached from substrate. Identification of attached species requires corallite examination and knowledge of colony growth forms.

Natural Location: Some specimens are free-living on soft bottoms in turbid water (*G. stokesi*), while others can be attached to substrates or form large colonies composed of many individuals. Lagoons with high sediment content are common collection

Goniopora sp. (flowerpot coral): eye-catching red specimen. (Indonesia)

Goniopora djiboutiensis (flowerpot coral): note 24 tentacles per polyp.

Goniopora sp. (flowerpot coral): wild colony with brown flatworm infestation.

Goniopora stokesi (flowerpot coral): genus has poor captive survival.

areas, along with other shallow areas, patch reefs, reef flats, and rubble zones. *Goniopora* can be found in clearer waters, but areas with some amount of runoff or high plankton counts (even enough to cloud the water) are often where they thrive. As with many corals having long tentacles, *Goniopora* species prefer water motion that is usually somewhat becalmed.

Colors: Colors range from the more common green or brown shades to shades of pink, cream, yellow, or gray. Often, the extended polyp column contrasts with the tentacles and oral disc.

Captive Care: For currently unknown reasons, *Goniopora* have a long history of failing to survive in the aquarium, often going into a slow demise for no apparent reason. The novice aquarist often buys a *Goniopora* coral and then boasts of its "long-term" survival after 6 months. However, *Goniopora* frequently thrive for up to a year or more before declining. Typically, they gradually fail to expand their tentacles and eventually either waste away or "shut down" (the polyps no longer open). Often, brown jelly infections occur that rapidly destroy all the coral's living tissue (see Chapter 11).

Recent research suggests that almost half the food taken by *Goniopora* in the wild is phytoplankton, and the rest very small zooplankton. These prey items are in very short supply in the typical reef aquarium. Tanks using algal turf scrubbers seem to have some success with *Goniopora*, and there is some speculation that this is due to the increased microfauna associated with those systems. Jaubert-style tanks (without protein skimmers) may also have better long-term success with *Goniopora* as there is no mechanical removal of suspended matter, trace elements, or plankters from the water. The availability of cultured phytoplankton and other commercially packaged planktonic fare may also allow more appropriate keeping of these corals.

Goniopora are strongly aggressive corals and can easily sting nearby specimens with their long, flowing polyps. They normally prefer medium current flow and medium to bright light, as they are often found in lagoons in the wild. Brightly colored specimens tend to be from shallower, brighter environments. Feeding *Goniopora* is likely to be required, because the energy provided from photosynthesis is not adequate for their daily energy needs. Many *Goniopora*, however, have not been seen to capture prey in captivity, so absorption of nutrients or unknown food sources may be their primary method of heterotrophy. (Paradoxically, the fairly strong "sting" associated with some *Goniopora* is a characteristic usually indicative of active and capable prey capture.)

Because of the hydrodynamic drag of the long polyps, *Goniopora* should be firmly attached if placed up on the rockwork, lest they become victims of "falls" caused by water motion or other disruption. This is especially true in small, light colonies. *Goniopora* are fragile enough without subjecting them to further stress and injury that could easily result in infection.

Relatively high nutrient levels do not pose a serious problem for these corals, but their almost inevitable decline make them poor choices for home aquariums until the reason(s) for their failure can be ascertained and/or accommodated.

Special Information: Certain clownfishes may adopt a *Goniopora* specimen as a surrogate anemone. This may be detrimental to the coral; incapable of full expansion, it will become irritated, fail to open, and then perish. The commensal shrimp *Hamopontonia corallicola* may reside within the long polyps of *Goniopora*.

Goniopora have been found, along with other scleractinian corals, to release allelochemicals much like octocorals (Gunthorpe and Cameron, 1990). One chemical isolated was bioactive and toxic to other species of *Goniopora*.

Collection Impact: Because of their poor survival in captivity, *Goniopora* cannot be recommended for ongoing collection and sale. Despite their dismal track record, many suppliers continue to import them in large numbers. Removal from the reef environment usually entails the removal of the entire free-living coral resulting in one less parent colony with which to repopulate the area. To be sure, these corals are widespread and often found in large numbers, but the practice of taking corals that are so likely to perish prematurely is questionable.

One positive collection feature is the propensity of these corals to produce polyp balls of baby daughter colonies, which could prove to be a fairly prolific method of asexual reproduction in captivity. *Goniopora* are not candidates for captive breeding at this time, but breakthroughs both in propagation and husbandry may improve the situation.

Goniopora sp. (flowerpot coral): tanks without skimmers may improve survival.

Goniopora djiboutiensis (flowerpot coral): common species in turbid lagoons.

Goniopora sp. (flowerpot coral): this genus readily spreads daughter colonies.

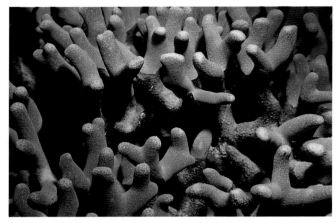

Porites porites (finger coral): polyps retracted. (Caribbean)

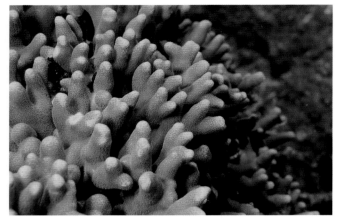

Porites cylindrica (jeweled finger coral): prefers bright light, high currents.

Porites cylindrica (jeweled finger coral): branches can fuse in some situations.

Porites nigrescens (jeweled coral): similar to *Montipora*; note pitted surface.

GENUS *Porites* Link, 1807

(pohr-eye'-tees)

Common Species: *P. compressa, P. cylindrica, P. lichen, P. lobata, P. lutea, P. rus, P. solida,* and others.

Common Names: finger coral, jeweled coral, Christmas tree worm rock, boulder coral, plating jewel coral.

Identification: *Porites*, like *Montipora*, can be very difficult to identify not only because of their astounding variety of growth forms and number of species, but because their identifying features are so small. Colonies are usually encrusting and/or massive with lobes, but may also be flat or branching. Corallites are very small and septa are abundant, giving them the appearance of having tiny jewels across their surface. They are distinct from *Montipora* in that *Porites* have outward-projecting septal teeth and generally less coenosteum between the coralites. Skeletal density varies, but most are lightweight and porous. Differentiating species of *Porites* is a difficult task that must be done under magnification. *Porites* are also extremely modifiable by prevailing environmental conditions, with corallites having many intermediate forms—sometimes there are traits of two or more species in the same colony. For practical purposes, colonies may be delineated by growth form: massive or encrusting, branching, or flat plate. Most *Porites* specimens for the aquarium are a branching type, usually *Porites cylindrica,* but various encrusting species may appear on live rock.

Natural Location: *Porites* are found in some of the most diverse locations of any group of reef corals. *Porites lutea* is commonly seen at the base of coral mounts on flat or gently sloping sandy areas, or it may form entire pinnacles on sandy areas or reef flats following decalcification, a common result of the action of boring animals. *Porites* can be quite tolerant of local conditions, growing well in turbid areas and even surviving in locations subjected to low salinity.

Colors: Colors are generally muted, but green, blue, mustard, yellow, purple, and pink are all common and sometimes quite bright and eye-catching. Colors of *Porites* are often due to chromophores and a lipofuscin-type pigment.

Captive Care: Growth rates can be impressive with *Porites*, and high current seems to make them thrive. They can be very tolerant of light conditions, but bright light is usually optimal. Brighter colors usually imply a preference, and perhaps requirement, for high illumination. Collected *Porites* do not always succeed in captivity, but if they do become acclimated, they are very durable. Good-quality live rock often has small *Porites* colonies on its surface, usually of a massive or encrusting type. These indigenous colonies seem to be much hardier than those collected alone, and their polyps are extended day and night. Many species are predominantly autotrophic and have greatly reduced capacities for zooplankton capture.

Porites are also quite well known for the colorful fanworms and Christmas Tree Worms (*Spirobranchus giganteus*) that bore into their skeletons. These worms obtain nutrition from their commensal relationship with the coral, and the worms are usually offered for sale with the attached *Porites* colony considered an "incidental." This is misleading, because the coral colony must usually remain alive for the worms to survive—the worms are actually the "incidental" organisms, despite their beauty.

All *Porites* species occasionally shed their surface layer with a waxy peel, called a mucus tunic, to rid themselves of algae and wastes. These sheets are produced with lunar periodicity, being formed around the time of the full moon, and consist of carbohydrate-rich mucus fouled with "sediment, fecal pellets, debris, bacteria, ciliates, nauplii, ostracods, diatoms, and filamentous algae" (Coffroth, 1990, 1991).

Porites are subject to white-band disease, black-band disease, algae encroachment, bleaching, and other problems. Nonetheless, they are a resilient group of corals that will likely survive most diseases, despite showing local areas of damaged skeleton. In fact, it is their ability to live on despite damage that allows for their prolific presence on most reefs, often becoming a dominant species in some areas, despite a lack of aggressive adaptations.

Special Information: The other notable members of this family are the large-polyped genera *Goniopora* and *Alveopora*. They have some of the longest polyps, while *Porites* have some of the smallest, a reminder that morphologic appearances are not always a good basis for taxonomy in most corals. Furthermore, *Goniopora* are highly aggressive, while *Porites* are quite possibly the most-submissive corals. (An encrusting colony of *Porites* in one of my

Porites porites (finger coral): note furry appearance with polyps fully extended.

Porites porites (finger coral): rarely seen lavender morph. (Caribbean)

Porites nigrescens (jeweled coral): encrusting base gives rise to branches.

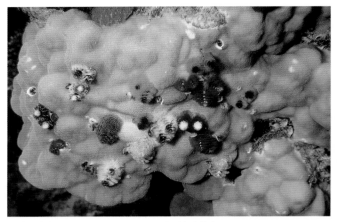

Porites lobata (boulder coral): note embedded Christmas tree worms.

Porites sp. (boulder coral): intense light may bring out bright coloration.

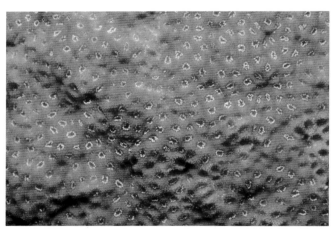

Porites sp. (boulder coral): bright colors are more common in shallow water.

Porites vaughani (boulder coral): new colonies may arrive on live rock.

Porites sp. (boulder coral): this genus produces some of the largest corals seen.

Porites astreoides (mustard hill coral): common in Florida and the Caribbean.

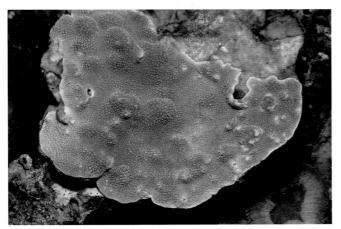

Porites lichen (plating jewel coral): may form sheets, nodes, or projections.

Porites lichen (plating jewel coral): encrusting a hard substrate. (Sulawesi)

aquariums has actually proved to be dominant over *Montipora digitata*—certainly an all-out war of the meek.) *Porites* survive and thrive on the reef by being able to survive aggressive attacks by growing and calcifying, despite dead areas on their skeletons. The strategy is certainly successful: some coral heads of *Porites* are over 1,000 years old.

Some species of *Porites* in some locations may incorporate zooxanthellae into their planulae.

Collection Impact: The sheer number of *Porites* colonies in the wild makes normal collection impact fairly insignificant, though many *Porites* colonies are not of a growth form that allows easy collection. The branching specimens commonly seen for sale are easily harvested. Other types of *Porites*, including the Christmas tree worm rock, must be cleaved from the substrate. The poor survival rate of collected *Porites* in aquariums is a downside for collection. Captive-bred *Porites* should be more widely available in the near future and will probably be better suited to captivity.

FAMILY Siderastreidae Vaughan and Wells, 1943

Pacific Genera: *Anomastrea, Coscinaraea, Horastrea, Psammocora,* and *Pseudosiderastrea.*

Atlantic and Pacific Genus: *Siderastrea.*

This family is composed of five Pacific genera and one Atlantic-Pacific genus. The latter has a species, *Siderastrea radians,* that may be the only tropical pandemic coral, found in both Atlantic and Pacific Oceans. All are characterized by fanlike or starlike corallites formed as the septa fuse at the center. Uniform coralla are the rule. Oddly, none of these genera are regularly seen in the aquarium trade, although some are common throughout the Indo-Pacific region.

GENUS *Psammocora* Dana, 1846

(sam'-oh-kohr'-ah)

Common Species: *P. contigua, P. digitata, P. superficialis.*

Common Name: pillar coral, cat's paw coral.

Identification: A diverse assemblage of growth forms, species of *Psammocora* often form pillars or flattened branches, hence their common names. However, they may also be encrusting, platelike, foliaceous, or massive. Small, even corallites cover the corallum, often with granulations apparent across the surface, resulting from the upper margins of the septa. With the tissue retracted, the skeleton, with its tiny flush-to-the-surface corallites, looks like small flowers have been drawn across its surface (petaloid). Encompassing one or more corallites are raised areas, mostly shallow dome-shaped rises in the surface, called **collines**. Short polyp tentacles expand during the day in the common species. *Psammocora*

polyps, agariciids are found in both Atlantic and Pacific Oceans. They could be "poster children" for the term "stony coral" as most look very much like intricately carved solid, colored limestone. In the Pacific, the genera are *Pavona, Leptoseris, Pachyseris, Gardineroseris,* and *Coeloseris. Pavona* is the only

tive propagators. In the future, we can hope to see the lovely Sunray lettuce coral (*Leptoseris cucullata*) from south Florida, the Bahamas and Caribbean available to coral farmers. In keeping with the *Leptoseris* habitat (and available aquarist reports), dim light and slow water flow are advised for this genus.

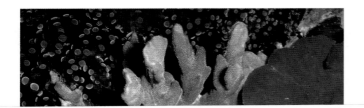
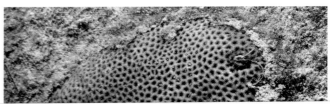

GENUS *Pachyseris* Edwards and Haime, 1849
(pak'-ee-seh'-ris)

Common Species and Names:

P. rugosa: elephant skin coral, corduroy coral, castle coral.

P. speciosa: phonograph record coral.

Identification: Displaying the common ridged and uneven skeletal surface of most of the Family Agariciidae, *Pachyseris* have no visible polyps or tentacles, only thin, ciliated tissue. They form frilly branching or laminar colonies with parallel septa and no visible corallite centers. The ridges and valleys are parallel to the growing edge of the coral, and the tissue layer is astoundingly thin. *Pachyseris rugosa* forms ridges on the corallum, rough meanders that can curve and interact to make a highly textured, ruffled surface. *Pachyseris speciosa* meanders, by contrast, are mostly in parallel and give a neat, ordered appearance to the surface.

Natural Location: *Pachyseris* are most common in deep-water environments according to most surveys, though Veron (1986) reports them as common to shallow lagoons, on reef slopes, and in surge channels. They often form vast tracts of large colonies. Judging by their relative abundance in the aquarium trade, it is likely that these came from shallower environments. Growth form is a good indicator of the general area of collection, with stout colonies likely being from high water motion, while more foliaceous colonies probably originated in protected areas.

Colors: Normally found in shades of brown, both cream and green examples are also common. A light-inducible green fluorescent pigment may turn brown colonies to a fluorescent green-brown under strong lighting conditions.

Captive Care: These corals obtain all their nutrition from direct absorption, photosynthesis, and possible mucosal capture of

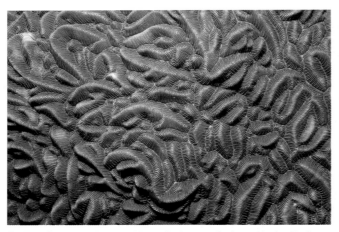

Pachyseris rugosa (elephant skin coral): close-up of colony with platelike form.

Pachyseris rugosa (elephant skin coral): colony with gnarled branches.

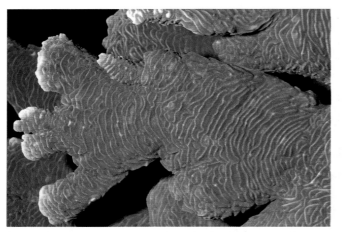

Pachyseris rugosa (elephant skin coral): requires excellent water conditions.

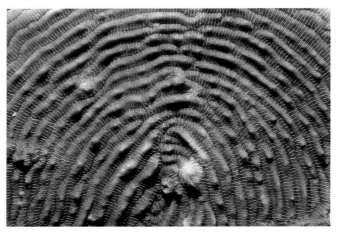

Pachyseris speciosa (phonograph record coral): often forms rounded plates.

Pachyseris speciosa (phonograph record coral): curiously contorted colony displays the plasticity of form seen in stony corals. (Muiron Islands, Western Australia)

particulate matter and therefore prefer high water movement, strong light, and fairly high nutrients. *Pachyseris* have also been found ingesting their own zooxanthellae. They are susceptible to white-band disease and other necroses and do not usually tolerate treatments to remedy such problems. Local application of antibiotics may be the only course of action, as the tissue will peel off rapidly under stress. They are also one of the first corals to bleach in nature, possibly due to their high dependence on zooxanthellae to meet daily energy needs.

These are difficult corals to maintain in less-than-optimal conditions. Their normally slow growth rate and lack of polyp expansion makes it difficult to assess their health and well-being.

Providing there is no tissue recession, it can be assumed that the coral is doing well.

Special Information: *Pachyseris,* along with some Atlantic *Agaricia* species, are unique in having have no tentacular development at all. They have only well-developed cilia across their surface and into their gut.

Collection Impact: *Pachyseris* are common corals that can be collected from larger formations without threat of sacrificing the entire colony. They are not terribly common imports, so aquarium-related collection should have minimal reef impact. They are not yet widely available through captive propagation, though they may be in the near future.

GENUS *Pavona* Lamarck, 1801

(pa-voh'-nah)

Common Species: *P. cactus, P. clavus, P. decussata, P. explanulata, P. frondifera, P. praetorta, P. speciosa, P. varians,* and others.

Common Names:

P. cactus: cactus or lettuce coral.

P. clavus: star column coral.

P. decussata: leaf coral.

P. praetorta: bark cloth coral.

Identification: All members of this family are well known for having very fine tentacles, and *Pavona* are no exception. Colonies are often leafy, with poorly defined corallites separated by ridges that give the skeleton a fine and intricate linear pattern. The leafy species are commonly **bifacial**, meaning polyps extend from both sides of the plates or leaves. (Similar-looking *Leptoseris* species are typically **unifacial**.) *Pavona* also have very spindly

Pavona clavus (star column coral): columns are typical, but may form plates.

pointed tentacles that give the coral the appearance of being covered with short spines. *Pavona cactus* has thin wavy plates, remarkably thinner than those of *P. decussata,* whose plates are thick and planar. However, the plasticity of *P. cactus* is remarkable. While it is influenced by lighting and flow conditions, the variations of *P. cactus* even within the same environment may make it easily confused with congenerics. One study has shown *P. cactus* to consist of many separate clones of slightly different genetic composition, each of which has little morphologic variability (Ayre and Willis, 1988). Other works have noted that *Pavona* show little phenotypic plasticity, perhaps supporting the prevalence of genotype diversity (Willis, 1985). *Pavona varians* is submassive and/or encrusting, occasionally sending out angular folded sheets. Most often, the colonies of *P. speciosa* and *P. frondifera* seen in the hobby are unusual angular folded shapes, somewhat resembling *Hydnophora rigida* in growth form. *Pavona frondifera* has "fluffier" polyps. The presence of low walls between the calices distinguishes *P. clavus. Pavona explanulata* is encrusting and erect.

Natural Location: *Pavona* are found predominantly in shallow-water areas, although they maintain a strong photoadaptive ability that allows them to thrive in deeper water as well. Colonies of *P. praetorta* are apparently capable of exclusively autotrophic existence at depths greater than 25 m (80 ft.), even on cloudy days.

Colors: Most examples are commonly brown to green with cream or white margins. Delicate green shades may often appear over the brown hues, probably due to green fluorescing proteins.

Captive Care: *Pavona* are all quite hardy and excellent "starter SPS" species. They are, in fact, a good example of the relative uselessness of the "SPS" designation and the notion that all such corals are hard to keep.

Pavona cactus (cactus coral): hardy, easily transplanted, and an excellent "starter" genus for aquarists. Fronds are bifacial and thinner than *P. decussata.*

Pavona explanulata (encrusting star coral): surface pattern is distinctive.

Pavona varians (encrusting pavona): grows well in most reef aquarium settings.

Pavona decussata (leaf coral): Red Sea colony just beginning to show fronds.

Pavona clavus (star column coral): plasticity of growth is a *Pavona* hallmark.

These corals are mostly fond of strong random currents and bright direct lighting. However, they are tolerant of less-than-intense light (even living well at 10 to 30% of surface irradiance), grow well under most adequate aquarium conditions, and are fairly resistant to diseases. The deeply embedded corallites probably shield the polyps from external stressors and pathogens to a large degree. Their tentacles are highly reduced, and they gain a larger percentage of their daily energy from photosynthesis than other corals. Therefore, lighting, rather than food, is most important in their success.

Pavona clavus is an especially easy-to-care-for species, as it may have an increased ability to compensate for lowered amounts of either light or food. *Pavona* do form sweeper tentacles that are surprisingly effective in the immediate local environment when the corals begin attaching to and encrusting substrate.

These sweeper tentacles can extend several inches and be quite numerous. They are also capable of forming uncalcified tissue buds that appear on the surface like small spiny balloons but are not released. The significance of these buds is not known, and they do not seem to be a form of asexual reproduction.

Special Information: Asexual reproduction by fragmentation is common in *Pavona*, and is often facilitated by the presence of the boring sponge *Cliona* sp., which may even influence the coral's growth form. Accordingly, the apparent dissolution of a branch or plate of a *Pavona* colony may not be entirely indicative of a failing specimen.

Pavona can be found to be quite aggressive, sending off numerous sweeper tentacles from all over the colony. One fascinating report described a colony of *P. decussata* that was sending sweeper tentacles over 15 cm (6 in.) long during a particularly ag-

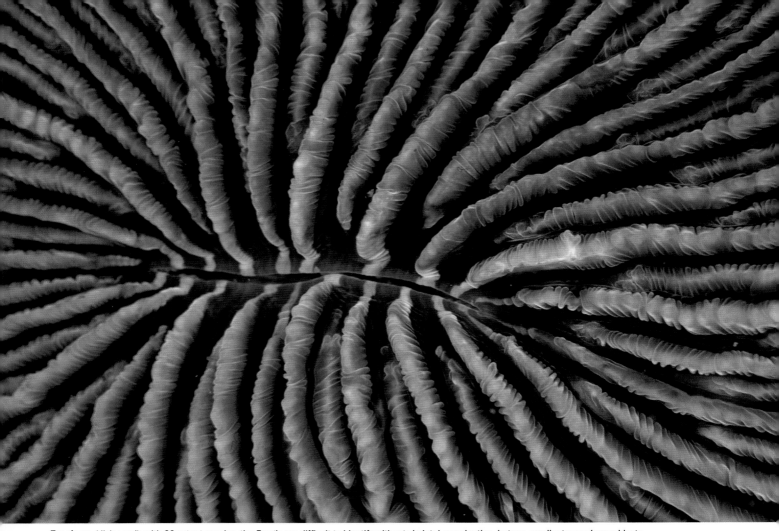

Fungia sp. (disk coral): with 33 extant species, the *Fungia* are difficult to identify without skeletal examination, but are excellent aquarium subjects.

gressive stage—the sweepers were responsible for new colony formations where they "stuck" to substrate, much like the reports about *Euphyllia ancora*. This anecdotal account may, in fact, be a landmark observation of *Pavona* reproduction.

Collection Impact: *Pavona*, provided they are collected with care, can be easily broken off their parent colonies. As common corals, their populations are unlikely to be impacted significantly by aquarium-related collections. They are hardy in the aquarium and are easily fragmented for asexual propagation. *Pavona* have repeatedly been shown to have extremely high success rates in transplantation studies. Their rates of mortality following fragmentation are exceptionally low—they are excellent corals for captive breeding. Such efforts are well underway for numerous species, both commercially and on local levels.

FAMILY Fungiidae Dana, 1846

Fungiids are all solitary corals and ahermatypic, although they are abundant on coral reefs and their skeletons eventually add to the mass of calcium carbonate in such environments. There are fourteen primary genera: *Cantharellus, Ctenactis, Cycloseris, Diaseris, Fungia, Fungiacyathus, Halomitra, Heliofungia, Herpolitha, Lithophyllon, Podabacia, Polyphyllia, Sandalolitha,* and *Zoopilus*. Veron (1986) considers the genus *Ctenactis* to be a subgenus of *Fungia*, which would then also include the questionable genus *Herpetoglossa*, herein known as *Fungia simplex* (Veron, 1986; Hoeksema, 1989).

Almost all are found living together in turbulent areas on soft or rubble-covered bottoms of lagoons, reef flats, and reef edges, most commonly from 3-9 m (10-30 ft.) in depth (Hoeksema,

1989). *Fungiacyathus* is typically not from reef areas, though it is tropical. Only three of the genera remain fixed to the substrate as adults: *Lithophyllon* and *Podabacia* are fixed and colonial; *Cantharellus* is fixed and solitary (Hoeksema and Best, 1984). One characteristic of the fungiids, because of their location, is their ability to reject sediments either by allowing them to fall off (dome-shaped species), by mucus and ciliary removal, or by polyp inflation. In general, those fungiids with sharp septal spines and flat morphology are less able to rid themselves of sediment. These species are common to rocky or rubble bottoms rather than soft substrates and are readily available in the aquarium trade. As such, the customary tendency to place fungiids on a soft sandy bottom exposed to significant sedimentation may be problematic. Fungiids also have the ability, to some degree, to right themselves if flipped over. However, large fungiids, generally those greater than 900 g (2 lbs.) or 25 cm (10 in.) across, are unable to do so.

Fungiids will often surprise aquarists by moving around the tank. I once babysat a *Polyphyllia* that belonged to Jonathan Lowrie, a friend and professional aquarist, in one of my own aquariums. This particular coral had apparently been through every conceivable horrid experience possible and was obviously a "survivor." It arrived at my house by overnight delivery in a shredded, dripping box, devoid of water—but alive and well. This coral had once made its way across the length of a tank, then upward more than 46 cm (1.5 ft.) to the top of some live rock. Jonathan jokingly told me I could send it back to him just by pointing it down the road. These corals can be survivors, with some extraordinary behaviors, considering they are stony corals.

GENUS *Fungia* Lamarck, 1801
(fun'-jee-ah)
Common Species: *F. concinna, F. danai, F. echinata, F. fungites, F. horrida, F. repanda, F. scutaria,* and others.
Common Names: disk coral, mushroom coral, plate coral, tongue coral, fungus coral, chinaman hat coral.
Identification: *Fungia* corals are unique, beautiful, and characteristic of the solitary fungiid family. They are usually saucer- to dome-shaped corals, but may be dented or elongated. In nature, the polyps usually remain retracted or semiretracted during the day, barely visible among the many bladelike septa that radiate from the central mouth. Although commonly green and purple, the disk corals are often available in a rainbow of colors. Species identification is difficult and depends on skeletal analysis. (See Veron, 1986, or Hoeksema, 1989.) They are single-polyped, single-mouthed (monostomatous) corals with a chitinous skeletal matrix. Several *Fungia* species (including *F. echinata* and *F. simplex*) are elongated, have central furrows, and have septa sim-

ilar to *Herpolitha limax* (see page 260).

Note: *Cycloseris cyclolites* (see page 254) is another common fungiid coral found on sandy flats, but is usually not seen or properly identified in the aquarium trade. It is less "tinted" than most *Fungia* species, and is usually found in cream, white, and light green shades. It is also usually much smaller, often less than 5 cm (2 in.) across when mature. Without reference to skeletal cues, *Cycloseris* may not be recognized as being a separate genus when small *Fungia* are offered. *Cycloseris*, coincidentally, is the evolutionary predecessor of *Fungia*. *Diaseris* species are also somewhat common, but the underside of their skeletons are divided into pie shapes from which daughter colonies arise through decalcification of a "slice" (see page 254). This trait makes all *Diaseris* easily distinguished from members of *Fungia* and *Cycloseris*.
Natural Location: *Fungia* are found on reef slopes and on flats between lagoons and the reef. They are commonly located on rubble or soft bottoms because of their behavior and shape, and are found in areas protected from strong wave motion. The juvenile *Fungia* are often attached to rock or coral, becoming detached and free-living as they grow. Such corals bear attachment scars on their undersides. Because the family members do not "sting" each other, areas are often littered with fungiids of many genera and species. *Fungia echinata* and *F. repanda* are from somewhat deeper-water environments. *Fungia fungites* has a predominantly shallow-water distribution.
Colors: *Fungia* are some of the most colorful corals to be found on the reef. Commonly seen in shades of bright purple, red, and green, there are also those with markings of pink, blue, brown, orange, and yellow.
Captive Care: Overall, these corals are quite successful in the aquarium, provided they are properly handled and placed. They

***Fungia* sp.** (disk coral): free-living wild colonies are often found in groups.

Diaseris distorta (mushroom stony coral): note pie-shaped daughter segments.

Cycloseris cyclolites (disk coral): related genus, much smaller than *Fungia*.

Fungia fungites (disk coral): natural habitat is rubble bottoms. (Indonesia)

***Cantharellus* sp.** (disk coral): note relatively smooth edges on septa.

Fungia klunzingeri (disk coral): eye-catching red specimen. (New Guinea)

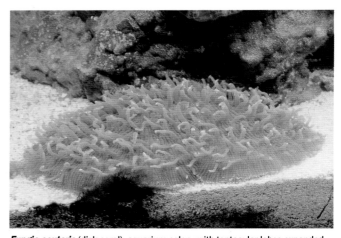

Fungia scutaria (disk coral): aquarium colony with tentacular lobes expanded.

Fungia sp. (disk coral): feeding with bits of fish or crustacean meat is advised.

Fungia paumotensis (disk coral): elongate species with prominent central arch.

Fungia sp. (disk coral): avoid direct currents or coverage by sandy substrates.

Fungia scutaria (disk coral): polyps are often retracted during the day.

should be located on a soft or rubble bottom to prevent damage from falls, which are quite likely given their propensity for movement. Certain species are more able to reject sediments than others. Those that are strongly dome-shaped, capable of polyp expansion, and have broad, flat septa will be able to be placed on sandy bottoms. Species such as *F. danai, F. fungites, F. klunzingeri, F. echinata, F. horrida,* and *F. scutaria* are all common to rubble bottoms. Small bits of live rock to elevate them may be beneficial in aquariums with high sedimentation from sand-sifting fishes or those with strong water movement and fine substrates. In any event, sedimentation is a metabolic stress and physically irritating, and it may eventually result in tissue loss, especially in locally anoxic areas. Care must be taken to avoid having *Fungia* move too near other corals as this can result in the injury or death of one of the corals. The damaged coral is almost never the *Fungia*. In fact, *Fungia* cause unilateral damage to over 94% of other corals by depositing thick mucus on them, causing necrosis. Yet they do not seem to harm each other or other free-living fungiids.

Delicate handling is necessary when moving these corals as they are easily damaged. Like all corals, they should not be removed from the water while expanded (the weight of the water can cause tearing). Allowing the coral to retract before lifting it out of the tank is advised. *Fungia*, despite containing prolific zooxanthellae, also have a large carbon requirement because of their mucus coat. Therefore, feeding these corals is recommended, if only to provide essential trace nutrients. Starvation will typically result in tissue regression and/or expulsion of zooxanthellae.

Fungia produce anthocauli, or daughter colonies, that often

Fungia somervillei (disk coral): this genus is immune to many coral diseases.

Fungia **sp.** (disk coral): note formation of small, secondary mouth.

Fungia repanda (disk coral): pink colony photographed in the Solomon Islands.

Fungia echinata (tongue coral): previously placed in genus *Ctenactis.*

Fungia simplex (tongue coral): several mouths are present in long axial furrow.

Fungia **sp.** (disk coral): this genus will damage other corals within its reach.

stem from receiving an injury or becoming buried in substrate. These corals are known for their ability to decalcify parts of their skeleton in order to generate such progeny. Fragmentation is also a method of asexual reproduction. In *Fungia*, and all fungiids, fragments that include at least one-sixth of the corallum can regenerate to form new colonies. Juvenile *Fungia* species, if still attached by a short stem to rock, may detach and settle to the bottom. In some cases, the stem remains viable, generating more juvenile corals. *Fungia* may produce new budded polyps on either their oral or aboral surface.

In the aquarium, most *Fungia* prefer low to moderate current and bright light. They are best placed on the bottom of well-lit tanks. Extremely deep tanks or those with moderate illumination may not be able to support these bottom-dwelling specimens. *Fungia* are one of the few coral genera not susceptible to most common coral diseases.

Special Information: Most species feed minimally during the day, relying on their slightly exposed tentacles to capture prey. At night, the corals tend to swell markedly and extend their tentacles completely. Rarely are *Fungia* in the aquarium completely retracted during the day as they are in nature, where living animals can resemble dead skeletons. Their heavy mucus coat was once thought to contain powerful nematocysts that were used to paralyze zooplankton that became entrapped in the viscous layer. The mucus has recently been found to contain cytotoxic molecules that are secreted in response to rough handling or contact with other corals. Therefore, it may be incorrect to assume that prey capture is more than simple mucosal or tentacular capture, with the damage exerted by *Fungia* on other corals being a result of their cytotoxic secretions.

Fungia are capable of considerable movement through systematic tissue inflation/deflation, and are phototaxic (move toward light). Short-distance migration is possible—up to 30 cm (12 in.) per day—and they can climb up to a 30° slope. Furthermore, they are able to right themselves if flipped upside down, are capable of "unburying" themselves from sand, and can easily rid their surfaces of debris.

Fungiids are fairly resistant to bleaching, which is generally not lethal (Hoeksema, 1991).

Collection Impact: Because the entire colony must be removed for collection, *Fungia* are theoretically vulnerable to overharvesting. However, many species are abundant, producing offspring readily, both sexually and asexually. The number of species and the widespread diversity throughout the tropical Pacific makes them a minimal risk for loss of significant numbers to the hobby. Fungiids are reproducible in captivity by several natural asexual means, and fragmentation by physical splitting is possible.

GENUS *Halomitra* Dana, 1846
(hal'-oh-my'-trah)

Common Species: *H. clavator, H. pileus.*

Common Names: helmet coral, dome coral, Neptune's cap coral.

Identification: *Halomitra* belong are solitary corals, much less common in nature than most other fungiids, but occasionally available to the hobby. Their disclike skeletons are similar to *Fungia* and vary from highly arched to flat in profile. The typical dome shape, more-numerous and uniform fuzzy polyps, and secondary mouths surrounding a primary mouth may be distinctive. They are polystomatous (multiple-mouthed). The top edges of the septa tend to be smooth, distinguishing them from *Sandalolitha*.

Natural Location: *Halomitra* are found in lagoons, usually in deeper water than other fungiids; *H. clavator* is found in quiet, murky water; it does not appear to occur in clear water.

Colors: These corals are usually ochre-brown or cream-colored, often with pink or purple margins. Tentacles tend to be translucent, and mouths tend to be white.

Captive Care: *Halomitra* have the same behavioral traits as the other solitary corals, and their care in the aquarium is also similar. They can tolerate, and perhaps should be exposed to, stronger water movement than the flatter fungiids. Their body shape, when it occurs as a thicker, heavier, and more solid form, may be suited to a habitat with some wave motion. Shorter tentacles are also indicative of this type of habitat.

Special Information: None.

Collection Impact: Because they are much less abundant in nature, *Halomitra* may be subject to local overharvesting. However, collection and availability of *Halomitra* is fairly rare, and therefore probably only poses a small risk to wild populations.

Halomitra pileus (helmet coral): aquarium rarity with multiple mouth openings.

GENUS *Heliofungia* Wells, 1966

(heel'-ee-oh-fun'-jee-ah)

Common Species: *H. actiniformis.*

Common Names: plate coral, long tentacle plate coral, disk coral, mushroom coral.

Identification: Despite the skeletal and shape similarities to many *Fungia*, *Heliofungia* are obviously distinct, with remarkably longer and larger tentacles with knobbed tips. When fully expanded so that the skeleton is obscured, these solitary corals could easily be mistaken for an anemone. Unlike in *Fungia*, the tentacles are extended during the day (except during planulation), and their tissue expansion, especially at night, can be remarkable. They are free-living and monostomatous, circular to oval, and flat to slightly arched in profile.

Natural Location: Similar to *Fungia*, although found only in the central Indo-Pacific.

Colors: *Heliofungia* are usually not as colorful as *Fungia* and are commonly seen in brown or brownish green with white tentacle tips. Brightly colored morphs of green with yellow radial stripes and yellow tentacle tips or pink to grayish violet with pink tentacle tips are occasional. Almost all individuals have a striped oral disc or mouth. Although most *Heliofungia* are brown with white-tipped tentacles in nature, the collectors for the aquarium hobby tend to seek out those somewhat uncommon examples with green- or pink-tipped tentacles and colorful bodies. Regardless of the base color (olive, brown, dark purple, green), the tentacle tips are usually contrasting to some degree.

Captive Care: *Heliofungia* are more delicate than *Fungia* and can die quickly from nettling (by other corals' nematocysts), injury, or infection. Other than those limitations, the conditions for their success are similar to *Fungia*. Placement on a soft or rubble bottom with low to medium current and good lighting is best. These corals also require food, perhaps to a larger degree than *Fungia*. Their tentacles are certainly indicative of a strong reliance on heterotrophic

Heliofungia actiniformis (plate coral): despite knobbed tentacles suggestive of an anemone, this single-species genus has a *Fungia*-like skeleton. (Indonesia)

nutrient acquisition. *Heliofungia* do not form anthocauli, but do reproduce asexually by budding, and they are strongly regenerative (like all fungiids) if fragmented. Also, in contrast to other *Fungia* species, *Heliofungia* are brooders rather than broadcast spawners.

Special Information: The commensal shrimp *Periclimenes kororensis* is known to be an associate of *Heliofungia*. Other members of *Periclimenes* may adopt this and other fungiids as surrogates or natural hosts. Other common commensals to these corals are *Metapontonia fungiacola*, *Hamopontonia corallicola*, *Periclimenes holthuisi*, and *P. tenuipes*.

Heliofungia show a pronounced immunity to bleaching (Hoeksema, 1991).

Collection Impact: Similar to *Fungia*, except for their reproductive capabilities (see Captive Care section, above). Their range is also somewhat more restricted.

Heliofungia actiniformis (plate coral): genus has largest polyps of all corals.

Heliofungia actiniformis (plate coral): polyps withdrawn, showing skeleton.

Heliofungia actiniformis (plate coral): more delicate than *Fungia*. (Maldives)

Heliofungia actiniformis (plate coral): may grow to 50 cm (20 in.) in diameter.

Heliofungia actiniformis (plate coral): will feed on pieces of fish or crustacean.

Herpolitha limax (tongue coral): largest of the solitary corals.

Herpolitha limax (tongue coral): colonies may form V, Y, or X shapes.

Polyphyllia sp. (slipper coral): Y-shaped colony with typical white-tipped polyps.

GENUS *Herpolitha* Eschscholtz, 1825

(her'-poh-lee'-thah)

Common Species: *H. limax.*

Common Names: tongue coral, slipper coral, mole coral.

Identification: *Herpolitha* comprise one of two common genera of elongated free-living corals, with shapes that suggest an extended human tongue. Although they commonly bend, bifurcate, and/or branch, forming V-, Y-, and X-shaped colonies, this shape is often a result of regeneration and is not the original, natural colonial form. Although several species of *Fungia* may grow quite large, *Herpolitha* are the largest of the solitary corals. They can grow to 1 m (39 in.) or more in the wild, although they average 46-61 cm (18-24 in.) in length. Their skeleton almost invariably has a deep central groove, or furrow, running the entire length of the coral, and they are flat to arched in profile. Numerous mouths appear along the surface of the furrow—making them polystomatous. Secondary or lateral centers, with mouths, may appear outside the central furrow. Tentacles and skeletal septa are widely spaced and distinct like those of *Fungia*. Tentacles are actually not true tentacles, but inflations of the tissue membrane around the mouths (Lamberts, 1984). *Fungia echinata* and *F. simplex* may both superficially resemble *Herpolitha*, though both of these *Fungia* species have sharp ridges on the top edges of their septa, while those of *Herpolitha* are rounded and interspaced. The central furrow of *Herpolitha* generally has rounded ridges lateral to the groove that are more prominent. Further, *F. echinata* has a single mouth.

Natural Location: *Herpolitha* are widely distributed throughout the Pacific and the Red Sea. They are usually found among other fungiids, but are more common on semiprotected and protected reef slopes. They are also typically from slightly deeper water.

Colors: Usually seen in brown, cream, or green tones, *Herpolitha*'s translucent tentacles do not usually contrast significantly in color from the rest of the coral, occasionally becoming white or green. Dana in 1846 described them as "umber with a sprinkling of bright green" (Lamberts, 1984).

Captive Care: *Herpolitha* are among the hardier solitary corals and have most of the same requirements and characteristics as other fungiids; that is, they prefer a soft bottom, gentle currents, and bright light. Fortunately, their nematocysts (or mucus secretions) do not seem to be as powerful or dangerous to nearby corals as those of *Fungia*.

Special Information: Like *Fungia*, *Herpolitha* produce true anthocauli as a common form of asexual reproduction.

Collection Impact: Abundant and widespread, *Herpolitha* are apparently at minimal risk from overcollection for the aquarium trade.

Polyphyllia talpina (slipper coral): moplike tentacles extend during the day.

Sandalolitha sp. (dome coral): uncommonly imported, but a typical fungiid.

GENUS *Polyphyllia* Quoy and Gaimard, 1833
(paw'-lee-fill'-ee-ah)

Common Species: *P. novaehiberniae, P. talpina.*

Common Names: slipper coral, tongue coral, mole coral.

Identification: Strongly resembling *Herpolitha* when their polyps are out, *Polyphyllia* can be differentiated, in most cases, by the lack of a prominent central groove. While an axial furrow is typically present, more numerous and "hairy" tentacles cover the surface and obscure the furrow. Tentacles are typically horn-shaped and about 2 cm (0.75 in.) long. Polyps are extended during the day, and the tentacle ends are usually tipped in white and may occasionally have forked ends.

Colonies are flat to arched in profile. Their skeletal septa are also arranged like petals, rather than like the radiant blades of *Herpolitha*. They are polystomatous, having many mouths spread across the corallum surface; the larger mouths may be aligned with the central axis or furrow. The skeletal septa are not as distinct as those of *Herpolitha*. True anthocauli do not form, but survivable fragments from mechanical breakage are common.

Lithactinia is a genus that has been grouped together with *Polyphyllia* by both Veron and Pichon. However, Lamberts (1984) describes *Lithactinia* as a separate genus, citing typically rose-colored and bronze species with a thin corallum. They are almost round, with abundant tentacles, a central calice with a central furrow, and no secondary centers. Furthermore, their geographic range is separate and nonoverlapping.

Natural Location: Usually found among other fungiids, although most common on soft, muddy bottoms. *Polyphyllia* are also found on sandy bottoms, rubble, and among other corals in shallow water 1-4 m (3-13 ft.) deep in protected areas.

Colors: *Polyphyllia* are usually brown, occasionally with cream or green shades. The basal tissue can become fluorescent green to teal. Tentacles are typically brown with white tips.

Captive Care: Like *Herpolitha*, these corals are easily kept in the aquarium under the same basic conditions as other solitary corals: soft or rubble bottom, slow gentle current, and bright light. *Polyphyllia* seem to be the most light tolerant of all the fungiids and are quite hardy.

Special Information: *Polyphyllia* are regarded by some as colonial, rather than solitary, corals because of their numerous mouths.

Collection Impact: Abundant and widespread, *Polyphyllia* are apparently at minimal risk from overcollection for the aquarium trade.

GENUS *Sandalolitha* Quelch, 1884
(san'-da-loh-lee'-thah)

Common Species: *S. dentata, S. robusta.*

Common Names: dome coral, helmet coral, plate coral.

Identification: These thick corals strongly resemble *Halomitra* in that they are typically rounded or dome-shaped. They are heavier, more ruggedly built, and often have a more ruffled, bumpy surface to the skeleton. This appearance is due to serrated spines along the top edge of the septa, which alternate in a thick and thin pattern. They are free-living and have a large detachment scar on the underside. Tentacles are short and fuzzy like *Halomitra*. *Sandalolitha* have multiple mouths (polystomatous) across the corallum surface.

Natural Location: Found principally on patch reefs, lagoons, and barrier reef slopes and in rubble areas subject to slightly higher water motion than that preferred by most fungiids.

Colors: *Sandalolitha* are mostly found in brown tones with translucent tentacles. Colonies sometimes have alternating green and brown tones, with occasional purple or bluish brown accents and tentacles.

Captive Care: Though more common than *Halomitra*, these solitary corals are rarely available in the aquarium hobby. Their care requirements are similar to those of other fungiids.

Special Information: The commensal shrimp *Metapontonia fungiacola* may associate with *Sandalolitha*.

Collection Impact: *Sandalolitha* may be subject to local overharvesting, but collection is limited and therefore probably only poses a small risk to wild populations.

FAMILY Oculinidae Gray, 1847

Genera: *Acrhelia, Archohelia, Cyathelia, Galaxea, Madrepora,* and *Oculina.*

The Oculinidae are composed of two tropical symbiotic Pacific genera, *Galaxea* and *Acrhelia*. There are Atlantic species (*Oculina*), and also aposymbiotic species that do not live near coral reefs or tropical regions. *Acrhelia* species are rarely available to the aquarium trade, although at least one propagator is attempting to make this unique genus available. They are perhaps most well known for their unmistakable, distinctive septa that create ornate skeletons. Nonreef-dwelling but tropical Pacific genera also include: *Archohelia, Cyathelia,* and *Madrepora* (Veron, 1986). *Cyathelia* closely resemble some species of the Atlantic genus *Oculina.*

GENUS *Acrhelia* Edwards and Haime, 1849
(ak-reel'-ee-ah)

This family member is rarely offered to the aquarium hobby, although it is occasionally available. At least one group is trying to culture *Acrhelia* in waters near their home reefs for the aquarium trade. It is uncommon in many areas of the Pacific, but may be more common in others. *Acrhelia* forms distinctive branching colonies that are widely spaced or bushy. Each branch bears spiky corallites that are notably similar to those of *Galaxea* (perhaps having even more exsert septa), spiraling around the delicate branches. They are typically shades of ivory, yellow, gray, or green and found in clear, highly illuminated water.

GENUS *Galaxea* Oken, 1815
(gal-ax'-ee-ah)

Common Species: *G. astreata, G. fascicularis.*

Common Names: galaxy coral, crystal coral, star coral, brittle coral, durian coral.

Identification: *Galaxea* form extensive wild colonies with separate, long-branching, fluted corallites and a fragile, easily broken skeleton. The corallites are joined by thin, light, bumpy plates that are obscured deep in the colony. Septa are tall and thin, projecting well above the corallite wall. Colonies form generally small, rounded configurations, although large spires, plates, encrustations, and branches can occur. Even with their various growth forms, the tubular corallites and septa are pronounced and distinctive. The tissue layer that covers them is very thin. *Galaxea astreata* can be recognized from *G. fascicularis* by its smaller corallites with fewer inward-projecting septa.

Natural Location: *Galaxea* colonies can be found in widely variant conditions. However, inshore reefs or areas of somewhat protected water movement and turbid conditions tend to be where *Galaxea* occur in greatest abundance.

Colors: *Galaxea* are commonly seen in green, gray, pink, and brown. Their tentacles, clear to translucent, often have white tips.

Acrhelia horrescens (bush coral): a spiky, branching relative of *Galaxea*.

Galaxea fascicularis (galaxy coral): notorious for its stinging sweeper tentacles.

Galaxea astreata (galaxy coral): often suffers transplant injury.

Galaxea astreata (galaxy coral): colonies spread rapidly in good conditions.

Galaxea fascicularis (galaxy coral): colors vary from red to brown and green.

There is typically an increase in contrast and opacity from the outer tissue margins toward the oral disc.

Captive Care: These colonies often do not survive well in the aquarium. They easily succumb to brown jelly infections, necrosis, and recession, often resulting from breakage of the parent colony to obtain specimens small enough for the aquarium. However, if healthy, *Galaxea* are fairly tolerant of water conditions and prefer a brightly illuminated area of the tank with low to moderate water flow that helps reduce their tendency to form sweeper tentacles.

Because of the colony growth form, the protected spaces between adjacent corallites are an ideal home for many small cryptic animals, including mussels, crabs, and shrimps. Delbeek and Sprung (1994) note that because these corals are commonly found with a variety of commensal animals and sponges, the death of these commensals during collection and shipping may result in localized fouling that can result in the infection and possible decline of the coral. Often, *Galaxea* are seen in stores with fairly large areas of empty corallites. Fortunately, the nature of the well-separated polyps somewhat limits further spread of problems, as adjacent corallite contact is limited.

In addition to being fragile, *Galaxea* pose another problem in the aquarium. All species produce very long stinging sweeper tentacles. Some larger colonies have produced sweepers that extend well over 30 cm (12 in.) in length. Such tentacles can jeopardize corals quite a distance from the colony. Low water flow is effective in minimizing sweeper tentacle formation, but they can still pose a problem. It is always advisable to provide a colony of *Galaxea* with ample perimeter space to allow for growth and to prevent damage to other corals by its sweepers. (For this reason, these corals make poor choices for small or crowded reef aquariums.)

Special Information: The thin and easily broken skeletons of *Galaxea* can be a significant contributor to reef sediments.

Galaxea fascicularis colonies have a unique reproductive attribute. They are composed of two types of colonies: a female colony that produces red eggs, and a hermaphrodite colony that produces viable sperm and "fake" white eggs. These white eggs help float the sperm to facilitate their success in fertilizing the positively buoyant and "real" red eggs (Harrison, 1988).

Collection Impact: *Galaxea* specimens are easily broken off larger colonies, which are left to multiply. But the specimens have fragile skeletons that do not ship well, and they may have problems adapting to captivity. Captive-propagation efforts are in their infancy, although the easily fragmented skeletons and fairly fast growth rate may make them an attractive coral for such efforts in the future.

GENUS *Oculina* Lamarck, 1816

(ahk'-you-lee'-nah)

Despite being an Atlantic coral, hence not available via commercial collection, several *Oculina* species are extremely common in nature. Because of this, these small mustard to brown colonies are frequently attached to pieces of rock, rubble, or the base of sessile organisms that are collected from some Florida and Caribbean areas. These areas are often highly turbid or sedimented, and *Oculina* tend to be hardy survivors. They are typically branching—bushy or with widely spaced branches. Corallites are arranged as in *Acrhelia*—widely spaced and separate, although they tend to have fewer exsert septa.

Oculina species seem to be very tolerant of conditions in captivity and may be good candidates for future captive-breeding efforts. Their tissue is very thin, as with *Galaxea*, although foul-ing and total colony loss is infrequent, with tissue rapidly recovering exposed skeleton. *Oculina* species are also unusual in that they can be zooxanthellate (in shallow water) or azooxanthellate (in deep water).

FAMILY Pectiniidae Vaughan and Wells, 1943

Genera: *Echinomorpha, Echinophyllia, Mycedium, Oxypora, Pectinia,* and *Physophyllia.*

Pectinia, Mycedium, and *Oxypora* species are fairly common aquarium imports. Many in this family form plates or encrusting masses, and they tend to be colorful and unique. All feed at night with long, transparent tentacles. *Mycedium, Oxypora, Physophyllia,* and *Echinophyllia* species can be difficult to identify, especially as their tissue is fairly heavy and obscures the skeleton. All are Pacific species.

Oculina diffusa (diffuse ivory bush coral): tropical western Atlantic genus.

Oculina varicosa (large ivory coral): deep-water, azooxanthellate Florida rarity.

Echinophyllia sp.: unusual but easily maintained genus.

Echinophyllia pectinata?: a fleshy and oddly contorted coral.

Mycedium elephantotus (elephant nose coral): coloration varies wildly in this genus, and this small colony in the Maldives exhibits exceptionally delicate hues.

GENUS *Echinophyllia* Klunziger, 1859

(eh-kine'-oh-fill'-ee-ah)

This genus is occasionally available in the aquarium trade. Species tend to be very heavy-tissued and can be quite colorful. They are naturally found over a wide range of habitats, and tend to form encrusting plates and folds, with the surface often showing rounded ridges. Corallites are raised and warty, pointing at different angles. Like other Family Pectiniidae members, *Echinophyllia* are quite tolerant and surprisingly aggressive. Sweeper tentacles do occur, and the transparent feeding tentacles occur primarily at night. The species I have maintained is extremely tolerant of light and water flow, and maintains its bright orange and red coloration under all conditions.

GENUS *Mycedium* Oken, 1815

(my-see'-dee-um)

Common Species: *M. elephantotus, M. robokaki, M. tenuicostatum, M. umbra.*

Common Names: elephant nose coral, peacock coral.

Identification: *Mycedium* are dubbed elephant nose corals because of their prominent corallites—raised and angled tubular calices that protrude from the surface of the skeleton. They may actually look more like human noses, but perhaps their common colors influenced the "elephant" appellation. The corallites are typically angled outward toward the perimeter of the colony, making these corals distinguishable from *Oxypora* species. In addition, the skeletons of *Mycedium* do not have a pitted coenos-

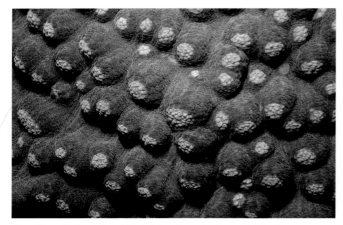

Mycedium elephantotus: delicately hued young colony. (Maldives)

Mycedium elephantotus (elephant nose coral): note outward-angled "noses."

Mycedium sp.: colors may be drab or vivid.

Mycedium? sp.: note "no competitor zone" surrounding wild colonies.

Mycedium elephantotus: feeding polyps often stay retracted during the day.

Mycedium elephantotus: may use sweeper tentacles, toxic agression.

teum between their variably spaced corallites. The many marginal septa may be visible when the corals are unexpanded, and have many sharp spines along their entire length. The colonies are laminar or foliaceous, occasionally semi-encrusting. Many are well "folded." As with *Oxypora*, sizable and highly translucent tentacles extend at night from the sparsely distributed polyps. *Mycedium robokaki* is brown with a bright pink oral disc, while *M. elephantotus* has a green or brown oral disc. *Mycedium tenuicostatum*, a predominantly deep-water species, can be distinguished by a more-granular coenosteum.

Natural Location: Most collected *Mycedium* are probably from shallow fore reefs, although they are more often found in deeper water, where they become quite platelike and are commonly found on overhangs and steeply sloped drop-off areas.

Colors: The corals are usually brown, gray, or green, although oral discs of the polyps may be contrasting in red or green. A lighter-colored circumferential band often contrasts with the main corallum color at the margins. While typically not a showy coral, the occasional specimen can be gaudy. An example in my own tank is bright red with blue highlights.

Captive Care: *Mycedium* are found throughout the reef zones and seem exceptionally tolerant to varying degrees of light and current. However, they seem to expand more and show better marginal calcification when exposed to strong irradiance. The unique appearance of these corals, along with their general hardiness, make them an excellent choice for the reef aquarium. In keeping with their habitat, vertical placement is probably correct. Feeding tentacles are normally extended at night, although the presence of food in the water during the day may allow them to "peek out" occasionally.

Special Information: While perhaps seeming innocuous, *Mycedium* can produce sweeper tentacles. They are also anecdotally reported to be capable of some amount of toxic aggression. Corals placed near *Mycedium*, even in the absence of any noted tentacular or aggressive action, have exhibited an acute and rapid loss of their adjacent tissue area. I have also noticed a pronounced decline in the spread and growth of soft corals near *Mycedium*. This can occur up to 5 cm (2 in.) from contact areas.

I have had the good fortune to witness a *Mycedium* species spawning in captivity. This coral spawned within approximately two hours of "sundown," after having been established for a little over a year in one of my aquariums. The duration of the release was about 30 minutes, during which a considerable quantity of sperm was released. Unfortunately, there was no successful settlement.

Collection Impact: Collection of a small section of *Mycedium* from a larger colony should be relatively benign, with the remaining colony free to continue its growth. They are also a fairly uncommon offering in the hobby, so that those colonies which are found are not likely to represent a significant loss to natural populations. Some captive-bred fragments are occasionally available.

GENUS *Oxypora* Saville-Kent, 1871
(ahk'-see-pohr'-ah)

Common Species: *O. glabra, O. lacera.*

Common Names: scroll coral, chalice coral.

Identification: These corals are commonly laminar or foliaceous in growth form, often spiraling outward with thin plates facing upward at an angle. Other areas of the colony, especially toward the center, may be thick and irregular. The corallites in *Oxypora* colonies are always visible and can be very large, walls are indefinite, and adjacent corallites may be linked together. The

Oxypora lacera (scroll coral): quite hardy, but not often available to aquarists.

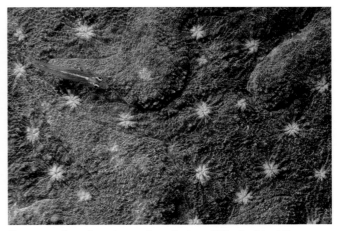
Oxypora sp.: tiny goby rests on surface of colony off Sipadan Island, Borneo.

septo-costae, if obscured by tissue near the center, may frequently be seen near the colony edge as thinner, closely set blades that radiate outward, perpendicular to the margins. The plates are often quite thin, and may not be strongly attached. Small examples available to aquarists may not yet have these features and frequently look like an encrusting growth form or small flat "chunk" of amorphous skeleton covered by tissue. A great deal of brown coenosarc is exposed on most species, with a pitted, bumpy surface occasionally and irregularly punctuated with brown or green calices. Calices may be fairly small and are not usually angled, but face more or less upward. In *Oxypora*, the corallum is distinguished by having slits or pores on its surface, though heavy tissue in living corals will obscure this identifying aspect. Polyps generally appear only at night, and their tentacles are transparent and fairly long. *Oxypora glabra* has smooth-edged septo-costae, while those of *O. lacera* are spiny.

Natural Location: *Oxypora* are most commonly found on reef slopes in shallow water. As such, a vertical or somewhat vertical orientation is common.

Colors: *Oxypora* are usually pale brown, cream, or green, with brown, green, pink, and occasionally red centers. The corals are often elegantly shaded in several muted hues.

Captive Care: Fairly common in the wild, these corals are usually protected from wave action and thus appreciate low to moderate current and bright light. They seem to be quite hardy in the aquarium, though are unfortunately not frequently available. If *Oxypora* are fed at night, tentacles from the unusual, irregularly spaced corallites appear on their surface. This is often quite surprising, because the corallum does not always indicate the place from which one would expect to see these tentacles emerge. *Oxy-*

pora, as well as *Mycedium*, have a strong "sting"—other corals that contact even their flesh are usually damaged extensively.

Special Information: Members of this genus may be confused with *Mycedium* species. The latter generally have corallites that angle outward toward the perimeter of the colony, rather than being perpendicular or randomly facing as in *Oxypora*.

Collection Impact: *Oxypora* are common corals that may or may not be broken from larger colonies. Collection of a small section of *Oxypora* should be relatively harmless, and the remaining colony is free to continue its growth. They are also a fairly uncommon offering in the hobby, so their collection is not likely to represent a significant loss to natural populations. Some captive-bred fragments are occasionally available, usually at local levels.

GENUS *Pectinia* Oken, 1815
(pek-tin'-ee-ah)

Common Species: *P. alcicornis, P. lactuca, P. paeonia.*

Common Names: lettuce coral, plate coral, antler coral, palm coral, hibiscus coral.

Identification: *Pectinia* species are striking corals that form frilly lettucelike sheets and formations in the wild. Their colonies sometimes present a cross between laminar vertical sheets and pillarlike branches, with thin walls and wide valleys between the sheets. Some of the platelike walls have spires that project upward from the top edge, making these corals appear even more elegant. Septa are thin, long, and parallel across the valleys and up the walls of the corallum. Costae are present on the underside of the colony. The calices, from which the polyps emerge, are spaced around the walls and valleys without much order. The large polyps rarely extend, and do so only at night with long, thin, tube-shaped tentacles projecting from mouths spaced randomly

Pectinia lactuca (plate coral): mature colonies develop long, deep valleys.

Pectinia lactuca (juvenile): wonderful aquarium corals, but not rapid growers.

Pectinia ayleni: (lettuce coral): note clusters of fluted laminae or "leaves."

Pectinia alcicornis (antler coral): fragile skeleton suggests moose antlers.

Pectinia paeonia (lettuce coral): may prefer reduced water flows.

Pectinia lactuca (hibiscus coral): maturing colony with ruffled, petallike walls.

around the corallum. The corals swell in the aquarium day and night, giving an almost gel-covered look to the skeleton, with their bright colors easily visible below the expanded tissue. As all three common species are available to the hobby, it is fortunate that they can be differentiated.

Initial identification can be difficult in small specimens, though mature colonies develop fairly distinct growth patterns: *P. lactuca* forms elongated walls and valleys in a somewhat maze-like pattern. The fluted walls are of roughly the same height, and spires on the walls are rare. The valleys are quite wide and usually meet in the center after some twists and turns from the margins, giving a deep labyrinthine appearance. *Pectinia paeonia* does not have lengthy valleys, but the fluted walls seem clustered from the center and project outward. The walls usually have spires at their outer margins and give a distinctly antlerlike ap-

pearance to the individual walls of the lettucelike colony. *Pectinia alcicornis* is even more extreme, and its columella walls are very steep and tall. Spires are distinct and bifurcate the walls, making the coral appear to be of a branching type. The effect produced is more "chaotic," and the colony looks less "uniform." The valleys are so deep as to be almost obscured by the tall, clustered walls, and the overall growth form vaguely resembles a mass of antlers.

Natural Location: *Pectinia* are commonly collected in turbid waters and seem to respond to less-vigorous water flows in the aquarium. They are found in both shallow- and deep-water habitats, though specimens for the aquarium, especially highly colored ones, are likely to have been found in shallower regions. *Pectinia lactuca* is generally from deeper water on reef slopes, and *P. alcicornis* from shallow areas, inshore, on flat substrate.

Colors: Found in beautiful fluorescent greens, deep reds, and unique shades of cream and brown, *Pectinia* offer wonderful choices for the aquarium. *Pectinia lactuca* is the most drab, but commonly has an unusual blue-gray to brownish green tone.

Captive Care: Though tolerant of intense lighting, *Pectinia* seem to grow best in moderately strong light. *Pectinia lactuca* is normally found in deeper water and may therefore prefer slightly less light. Sometimes prone to recession and decalcification, *Pectinia* are neither extremely difficult nor easy to maintain. If anything, they tend to fail over long periods of time. I have

Dendrogyra cylindrus (pillar coral): imposing tower in a Caribbean setting, where it and other scleractinians are currently off-limits to collection.

found *Pectinia* to prefer reduced water flows. They do not seem to grow rapidly in the aquarium, and this is unfortunate because much of their beauty is in their colony formations. Small colonies have not had time to develop these features completely. They will succumb to protozoan jelly infections quite readily, and are prolific producers of mucus. Because of this, shipping *Pectinia* seems to extract a heavy toll, as the shipping water may become fouled. Despite possessing long and seemingly potent feeding tentacles at night, *Pectinia* are unaggressive and are easily overcome by many other corals.

Special Information: *Pectinia* skeletons are very weak, thin, and fragile. Some references even consider them to be ahermatypic (nonreef-building), along with other stony corals with fragile skeletons, such *as Euphyllia* species.

Pectinia, like other corals with prolific mucus, should be rinsed or flushed well with running seawater after shipping to avoid fouling their new system.

Collection Impact: *Pectinia* are quite simple to collect without degrading the reef. The colonies are often large enough that smaller pieces may be broken off, leaving the parent colony to survive and reproduce. They are fairly common in the wild, from diverse reef zones, and not terribly common in the hobby, so that any amount of collection to supply aquariums probably has minimal impact on natural communities. Captive propagation should be possible, although a slow growth rate may limit their commercial potential.

FAMILY Meandrinidae Gray, 1847

Pacific Genus: *Ctenella.*
Atlantic Genera: *Dendrogyra, Dichocoenia, Goreaugyra,* and *Meandrina.*

In the Atlantic, the meandrids are prolific and significant contributors to reef formation. *Dendrogyra, Meandrina,* and *Dichocoenia* are quite abundant. *Dendrogyra cylindrus,* the pillar coral, is an unusually dramatic coral in the formations it creates. The Meandrinidae are noted for having typically fused or nearly joined corallites that form intricate meanders across the corallum surface. Septa and costae tend to be large, smooth, and prominent; *Meandrina,* in particular, are unmistakable in this regard. *Dichocoenia* may be the least conformist in appearance, not forming meanders and somewhat resembling certain members of the Faviidae, but still distinct. They consist of smallish colonies of elliptical, round, or amoeboid and disorganized calices with very prominent septo-costae, with many in various stages of intratentacular division. Unfortunately, none of these Atlantic/Caribbean genera are currently available to the aquarium trade because of import restrictions.

FAMILY Mussidae Ortmann, 1890

Pacific Genera: *Acanthastrea, Australomussa, Blastomussa, Cynarina, Lobophyllia, Micromussa,* and *Symphyllia.*

Atlantic Genera: *Isophyllastrea, Isophyllia, Mussa, Mussimillia,* and *Mycetophyllia.*

Atlantic and Pacific Genus: *Scolymia.*

The mussids are a group of mostly large, heavily tissued, often massive hermatypic corals with large corallites. The single-polyped *Cynarina lacrymalis* and *Scolymia* sp. are the only noncolonial forms.

Although not available to the aquarium trade, the Atlantic mussids closely resemble their Pacific counterparts. They are similarly common and conspicuous in many reef areas. Heavy tissue, cerioid to meandroid valleys, prominent corallite walls, and toothed septa are hallmark characteristics. Some *Mycetophyllia* species very closely resemble the wide-valleyed species of *Symphyllia*. Likewise, some *Mussa* species bear a strong resemblance to *Lobophyllia*. The interoceanic *Scolymia* are also very similar in appearance, behavior, and habitat.

GENUS *Acanthastrea* Milne-Edwards and Haime, 1848
(ack'-an-thass'-tree-ah)

These are fairly common mussid corals in the wild, especially *A. echinata*. They resemble some faviids, but have heavier tissue. Typically cerioid, but rarely meandroid, and found in shades of green, brown, burgundy, and gray, these corals may actually be fairly common in the aquarium trade, although often misidentified. Care requirements should be very similar to other mussids. Other species are more common in high-latitude reefs and temperate waters.

GENUS *Blastomussa* Wells, 1961
(blass'-toe-muss'-ah)

Common Species: *B. merleti, B. wellsi.*

Common Name: pineapple coral.

Identification: Although these corals are sometimes sold as "open brain" or even "moon" corals, *Blastomussa* neither resemble them nor is their skeleton similar. They have a phaceloid skeleton, with separate corallites extending out from a common center. Each corallite continues to grow outward from the center until it is no longer considered a common colony. Veron (1986) notes that these individual clones may then compete with each other. Each polyp is very fleshy and highly expansive. When extended fully, the polyps easily obscure the skeleton. In such a state, the clustered individual polyps can somewhat resemble a colony of *Actinodiscus* species (mushroom anemones). The septa are toothed, a common characteristic of the mussids. *Blastomussa*

Meandrina meandrites (maze coral): attractive tropical Atlantic species.

Dichocoenia stokesii (elliptical star coral): forms plates and rounded heads.

Acanthastrea echinata (pineapple coral): common in wild, often misidentified.

Blastomussa merleti: easily propagated by separating long, tubular corallites.

Blastomussa wellsi (pineapple coral): exceptionally hardy in subdued lighting.

Blastomussa wellsi (pineapple coral): fleshy polyps completely hide skeleton.

wellsi can be easily distinguished by its corallites and polyps, which have a much larger diameter, up to 10-13cm (4-5 in.), more than twice the size of *B. merleti* in a mature colony. *Blastomussa merleti* develops long, tubular corallites that are brittle and easily broken from healthy specimens to form new colonies.

Natural Location: Although widespread in their distribution, these corals are somewhat rare in the wild, *Blastomussa* are not frequently encountered for sale. They are found on lower reef slopes and in turbid water where collection is difficult.

Colors: *Blastomussa* are commonly available in two distinct color morphs: dark red and various shades of brown, usually with green centers or markings.

Captive Care: Because *Blastomussa* are found in deep or protected waters, they prefer fairly low water current and moderate lighting. In fact, strong light is commonly reported to prevent their polyps from fully expanding. (Some aquarists have cemented *B. wellsi* to vertical walls of rock with excellent results.) Outside of these basic conditions, they are very hardy corals for the aquarium. Asexual reproduction is fairly common in captivity through budding.

Special Information: Commensal sponges, mollusks, other sessile invertebrates, and even other corals may frequently find a cryptic safe haven within the branches of *Blastomussa* corals. Occasional inspection to prevent fouling is important.

Collection Impact: Growing outside easy collection zones, *Blastomussa* species appear only in small numbers in the aquarium trade. They are easily harvested by breakage while leaving the mother colony intact, and their survivability in captivity is quite high. Furthermore, they readily form extratentacular budded daughter colonies, and captive propagation is underway.

GENUS *Cynarina* Bruggemann, 1877
(sigh'-nah-ree'-nah)

Common Species: *C. lacrymalis.*

Common Names: button coral, cat's eye coral, doughnut coral, meat coral, tooth coral.

Identification: *Cynarina* are glorious corals, especially considering that each specimen is a lone polyp with a single corallite. They are one of the largest single-polyped corals in nature, are always solitary, and are usually attached to substrate (rarely free-living). They have a circular or oval skeleton. The toothed septa are very large, with prominent paliform lobes near their inner margins, and are found in a cyclical pattern in which large primary septa have several less prominent septa between them. The tissue of *Cynarina* expands outward in a lobed doughnut shape around the oral disc. The coenosarc tissue, though it may be pastel-colored,

Cynarina lacrymalis (button or cat's eye coral): an unmistakable solitary coral that occurs in a range of colors and displays large, water-filled lobes during the day.

is very translucent, and the skeleton can usually be easily seen beneath it. Feeding tentacles typically appear at night, although daytime expansion is also fairly common if food is detected in the water.

Natural Location: *Cynarina* are found attached to rock substrates on overhangs and reef slopes, usually facing upward. They may occasionally be free-living on muddy bottoms, as well.

Colors: *Cynarina* are available in many colors, from drab browns to bright reds, pinks, and greens to pastel colors with contrasting centers. They also have the unusual capability of exhibiting either a dull, mottled appearance or a glossy finish to the polyp tissue. They can change this appearance regularly, and often in accordance with prevailing ambient tank conditions. The significance of this chameleon-like ability is uncertain. Some authors

have assumed that the lobes serve a light-gathering function, though their ability to become and remain opaque without obvious consideration to prevailing light conditions makes this explanation questionable.

Captive Care: These are generally hardy corals for most aquariums, though they do seem to be prone to filamentous algae encroachment around the margin of the tissue. Their inflated tissue is also prone to being torn by accidental mishandling or mishaps. Anecdotally, they are also very sensitive to the presence of some soft corals. For example, a specimen that is fully inflated at the store can be placed in a new location with mushroom anemones and some octocorals and never expand, assumedly from allelopathic compounds released by the other organisms. Death can result in a few weeks or sooner. In healthy specimens, a ring of

Cynarina lacrymalis (button coral): hardy and a good indicator of water quality.

Cynarina lacrymalis (button coral): usually grows attached to rocky walls.

Cynarina lacrymalis (button coral): will accept feedings of marine fish flesh.

feeding tentacles is expanded at night, capable of capturing and engulfing fairly large food items. They are tolerant of low light, though upward-facing placement with low to moderate light is optimal for the photosynthetic bubble-shaped lobes of the polyp to be truly well adjusted. Current should be low to allow for full expansion of the highly inflatable coral tissue.

Special Information: *Cynarina* can be excellent bio-indicators of water quality. Their degree of expansion seems to be a fairly good measure of the overall health of the aquarium, with superb water conditions being indicated by a ring of feeder tentacles that appear from a very swollen polyp, even during the day.

The species referred to in the aquarium literature as *Cynarina macassarensis* is *Indophyllia macassarensis* and is found free-living on sandy bottoms near the reef base, in moderate depths, on the leeward side of islands. *Cynarina deshayesiana*, also in the aquarium literature, is regarded as fitting within *C. lacrymalis* (Best and Hoeksema, 1987; Veron, pers. comm.).

Collection Impact: Because they are solitary, the entire coral must be collected, and localized overharvesting may be a problem. They are not known to be particularly abundant in nature in the first place. Fortunately, *Cynarina* are hardy in captivity, and therefore frequent replacement should not be necessary.

GENUS *Lobophyllia* de Blainville, 1830
(low'-bow-fill'-ee-ah)

Common Species: *L. corymbosa, L. hataii, L. hemprichii.*

Common Names: lobed brain coral, flat brain coral, open brain coral, meat coral, modern coral, large flower coral.

Identification: Available in many growth forms and somewhat muted colors, these corals have a typically flabello-meandroid or phaceloid colony form typical of many brain corals. However, they are usually quite flat and less spherical than other brain corals. The polyp tissue is heavy and prominent, leading to one of their common names, meat coral. Single "sections" of *Lobophyllia* may easily be confused with *Scolymia*, and the meandroid pattern is often unrecognizable or not present in some species. The twisted circular and oval-shaped broken pieces are not necessarily sinuous and can remain as separate, closely-set polyps. In time, colonies adopt a more typical shape, become polycentric, and no longer of questionable identity. *Lobophyllia hemprichii* is the most common species, and its colony size and colors are its primary distinction from other species, unless examination of its septa and calices are carefully considered. It may form flat, massive colonies or have polyps on the ends of branches that can be up to 30 cm (12 in.) long. (Despite their length, these branches are often effectively hidden by the expanded mass of polyps above.) *Lobophyllia corymbosa* is easily confused with *L.*

Lobophyllia robusta? (lobed brain coral): an adaptable and very hardy genus.

Lobophyllia sp. (lobed brain coral): unusual specimen seen in North Sulawesi.

Lobophyllia hemprichii (lobed brain coral): color and appearance are variable.

Lobophyllia hemprichii (lobed brain coral): most-common offering in this genus.

Lobophyllia hemprichii (lobed brain coral): note two color morphs, side-by-side.

Lobophyllia hemprichii (lobed brain coral): feeds readily if offered meaty items.

Lobophyllia sp. (lobed brain coral): shown with tentacles partly extended.

Lobophyllia hemprichii (lobed brain coral): very common on Indo-Pacific reefs.

Lobophyllia hemprichii (lobed brain coral): two color morphs in a reef aquarium.

Lobophyllia hemprichii (lobed brain coral): daytime appearance may be smooth.

Lobophyllia hemprichii (lobed brain coral): coarse texture is frequently seen.

hemprichii, especially with aquarium-sized specimens. *Lobophyllia hataii* is the most easily recognized species, being distinctly more meandroid, with all meanders converging at the center. Its valleys are quite shallow when compared to other species. *Lobophyllia* are also easily confused with *Symphyllia*. However, corallites of most collected species of *Lobophyllia* remain separate, while *Symphyllia* corallites have fused common walls. This trait is clearer when the coral is not fully expanded, because the heavy tissue tends to obscure skeletal features.

Natural Location: *Lobophyllia* are found in diverse habitats, but are most common on upper-reef slopes and fore-reef slopes. They are found both vertically and horizontally in both shaded and well-lit environments. Most often, they are in somewhat protected areas.

Colors: These corals are typically olive, dark red, green, brown, and gray, though other color morphs are available in combination or in uniform patterns. *Lobophyllia hemprichii* may be the most colorful species, widely variant, often with contrasting peripheral (marginal) and oral disc tissue. Blue, white, gray, green, orange, and red are all common color morphs. *Lobophyllia corymbosa* and *L. hataii* are normally greenish brown with light-colored centers.

Captive Care: *Lobophyllia* are common Indo-Pacific corals in the aquarium trade—very hardy, tolerant, and highly recommended. Their polyp tissue expands greatly in captivity, and feeding tentacles are usually visible at night, running sinuously along the prominent meandroid grooves, or from the margins between the oral and peripheral tissue. The tentacles occasionally extend during the day. These corals readily take food offerings. If minimally adequate light and water movement is offered, they should grow well throughout the tank. Bright di-

rect light and calm currents are optimal. Because *Lobophyllia* are heavy-bodied corals, growth rates are not apparent, but photographs taken several months apart will prove that they do grow significantly. *Lobophyllia* are fairly submissive to other corals (despite their feeding abilities), and recession is their most likely problem. There are reports of sweeper tentacles being formed when *Lobophyllia* come in contact with adjacent corals.

Special Information: None.

Collection Impact: Many *Lobophyllia* specimens are collected from large formations by breakage, although healing of the remaining colony can be rapid. Collection from phaceloid colonies is likely to cause less collateral reef damage. Because these are very common and widespread corals in nature, the aquarium trade is unlikely to have any significant impact on natural communities.

GENUS *Scolymia* Haime, 1852
(skahl'-ee-my'-ah)

Common Species: *S. australis*, *S. vitiensis,* and others.

Common Names: doughnut coral, button coral, disk coral, mushroom coral, flat brain coral, meat coral, tooth coral.

Identification: *Scolymia* are another group of single-polyped and normally solitary corals similar to *Cynarina*. Some forms may be colonial. Their skeleton is usually monocentric, meaning a single oral opening is normally present. However, multiple openings may occasionally be present near the center. The septa are less pronounced than in *Cynarina*, and they are closely spaced and slope outward. Septa do not have paliform lobes, and the margins usually have numerous small, sharp, spiny teeth. The limestone skeletons of mature colonies are also larger, heavier, and more dense than those of *Cynarina*. Polyp expansion of *Scolymia* is nor-

Scolymia vitiensis (doughnut coral): solitary coral with a single fleshy polyp.

Scolymia vitiensis (doughnut coral): beautiful example on dark volcanic gravel.

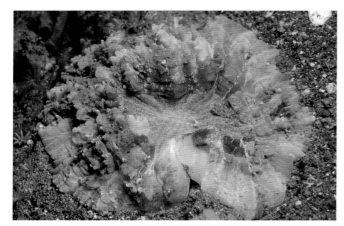

Scolymia vitiensis (doughnut coral): note lack of clear bubbles as in *Cynarina*.

Scolymia vitiensis (doughnut coral): highly prized red morph in an aquarium.

Scolymia vitiensis (doughnut coral): may expand best in gentle currents.

Scolymia vitiensis (doughnut coral): green morph with *Tridacna* clam.

mally much less dramatic than *Cynarina*, and usually occurs in a flat outward way that conforms to the skeleton, rather than in the puffy enlargement of *Cynarina*. The septa of *Scolymia* are not nearly as apparent as those of *Cynarina*, whose translucent polyps allow for their actual presence to be noted. Moreover, the tissue of *Scolymia* is more opaque and heavier. Feeding tentacles normally emerge at night in a ring shape from within a groove running circumferentially, approximately midway between the coral margins and the oral opening. This groove in the tissue is generally obscured except during feeding expansion. Some species of *Scolymia* can be confused with juvenile colonies of *Lobophyllia*, but *Lobophyllia* are flatter and have reduced costae. *Scolymia australis* is normally cup- or saucer-shaped, while the more commonly available *S. vitiensis* is more flat- or dome-shaped. However, both are variable.

Natural Location: These corals are found predominantly on reef slopes in protected water, often under overhangs, but can also be found in other diverse reef areas, often in those that do not have extensive coral coverage.

Colors: *Scolymia* are typically seen with more muted dull colors of dark green or red. Mottling is typical across the tissue, and numerous rounded pimples may be seen in some species. These raised and radiating bumps correspond to skeletal features beneath the tissue.

Captive Care: *Scolymia* seem to expand most in lower currents and moderate light and are tolerant of lower light levels than most corals. However, they are easily overrun by filamentous algae, may be prone to cyanobacterial growth on their surfaces (especially near the oral opening), and are easily stung by other corals. Under less than ideal conditions, they tend to recede from their margins and succumb to infections. Despite these few problems, *Scolymia* are relatively hardy and easily kept corals overall.

Special Information: At least in Atlantic species, aggressiveness in *Scolymia* is correlated with skeletal surface features. Those species with rougher and larger septa are dominant and more-aggressive feeders than those with smoother, flatter surfaces (Lang, 1971).

Collection Impact: Because they are solitary, the entire coral must be collected and localized overharvesting may be a problem. Fortunately, *Scolymia* are hardy in captivity, so frequent replacement should not be necessary.

GENUS *Symphyllia* Edwards and Haime, 1848
(sim-fill'-ee-ah)

Common Species: *S. agaricia, S. radians, S. recta,* and others.

Common Names: closed brain or dented brain coral, meat coral, brain coral, Pacific cactus coral.

Identification: The genus *Symphyllia* is recognized by its prominent and wide valleys and dome-shaped or flattened meandroid growth shapes. These are heavy, massive corals that have a distinctly more sinuous appearance than *Lobophyllia*, though their polyp tissue is similarly "meaty." They are often referred to as dented brain corals because of a prominent groove that often runs the length of the corallite walls, usually visible even in well-expanded specimens. Another difference between *Symphyllia* and *Lobophyllia* is a lateral fusion between the corallite walls of the former. Some species have extremely wide valleys with prominent walls. Feeding tentacles appear day and night in captivity when food is present.

Natural Location: *Symphyllia* can be found in many reef areas, though are most common on protected reef slopes in fairly shallow water. They are generally less common, though, than *Lobophyllia*.

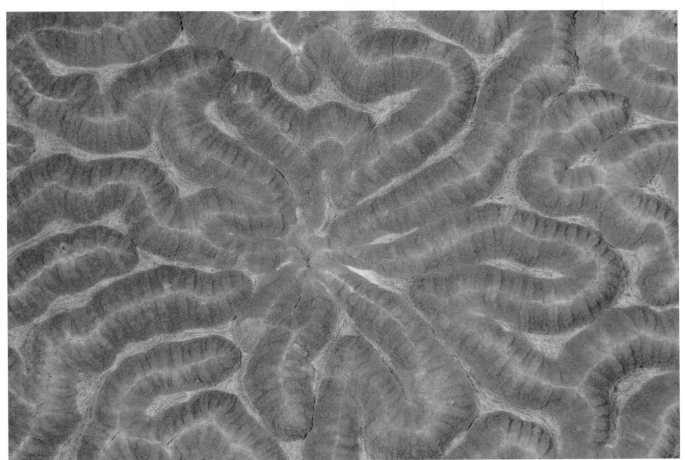

Symphyllia recta (dented brain coral): exceptionally handsome and usually successful in captivity, this genus is characterized by grooves atop the meandering walls.

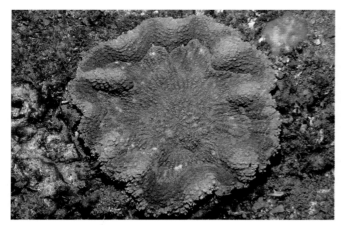

Symphyllia sp. (brain coral): a rarity with a large central valley.

Symphyllia radians (brain coral): straight valleys may form in flatter colonies.

Symphyllia recta (brain coral): may react to the toxins of certain soft corals.

Symphyllia radians (brain coral): note typical sinuous valleys.

Colors: Though found in muted dull browns, greens, reds, and creams like *Lobophyllia*, the normal colors of *Symphyllia* tend toward pastel and creamy hues with contrasting valleys. Less frequently, richer-colored examples of contrasting greens and whites may be found.

Captive Care: These corals grow very large and heavy and are highly successful in captivity. Their great tolerance of different light and current conditions is similar to that of *Lobophyllia*. Bright, indirect light and low to moderate currents seem to be best. *Symphyllia* seem to be less likely to recede or be stung by nearby corals than the similar *Lobophyllia* species. In my own observations, *Symphyllia* seem somewhat more sensitive to the presence of certain soft corals, notably *Xenia* and *Litophyton* species.

Special Information: *Symphyllia* tend to be very reactive to food present in the water. In healthy tanks, the appearance of a *Symphyllia* species in "feeding mode" is quite astonishing, with tissue that seems almost to turn inside out. As frequently, the polyp tissue may retract for a day or so, pulling very tight against the skeleton and then, as suddenly, reinflating. Although this looks like a mode of excretion, I have never noticed foreign material being ejected. The *Symphyllia* sp. in my own tank also reacts very quickly to phytoplankton or algae in the water, quickly responding by expanding its feeding tentacles, possibly indicating some herbivorous tendencies.

Collection Impact: *Symphyllia* can be a challenge to harvest, because colonies are not easily separated from the substrate or from mother colonies without collateral damage. However, it is unlikely that collection will have any significant impact on the natural populations of the more common species.

Hydnophora exesa (horn coral): note prominent hydnophores or stony hillocks.

Hydnophora rigida (horn coral): will respond to direct feeding in the aquarium.

Hydnophora rigida (horn coral): prefers bright lighting and moderate currents.

FAMILY Merulinidae Verrill, 1866

Genera: *Boninastrea, Hydnophora, Merulina, Paraclavarina,* and *Scapophyllia.*

Found only in Pacific regions, merulinids are all quite beautiful, interesting corals. Five genera are present, though only *Hydnophora* and *Merulina* are common in nature or in the aquarium trade. Their growth forms are highly variable, as are their sometimes striking colors. All are symbiotic and typically from protected lagoonal and reef-slope areas.

GENUS *Hydnophora* Fischer de Waldheim, 1807
(hide'-no-for'-ah)

Common Species: *H. exesa, H. grandis, H. microconos, H. rigida.*
Common Names: horn coral, velvet horn coral, knob coral.
Identification: *Hydnophora* are best known to aquarists as two common species, *H. rigida* and *H. exesa*. A unique skeletal characteristic, called a **hydnophore**, is present in all species. A hydnophore is formed where adjacent corallite walls meet and fuse into small, conical mounds, or hydnae. In nature, the polyps are normally extended at night, though the opposite is true in captivity. The growth forms can somewhat resemble *Australogyra* in that dramatically chiseled, angular branches are common, but other obvious skeletal differences make the two distinct. *Hydnophora* have short, blunt tentacles that arise from the base of the hydnophores and protrude between the septa. *Hydnophora exesa* forms encrusting flat or branching growth forms and is found in most reef habitats; *H. rigida* is thinly branching with small, pointed hydnae; *H. grandis* is flat or forms thick branches with broad hydnae and is found in sheltered deep-reef areas; *H. microconos* forms massive round to flat colonies with

Hydnophora sp. (horn coral): unidentified plating species. (Sulawesi)

Hydnophora microconos (horn coral): note uniform hydnophores.

Hydnophora exesa (horn coral): this common species typically forms encrusting sheets, from which thickened projections or branches can develop.

Paraclavarina triangularis (horn coral): often confused with *Hydnophora*, but lacks hydnophores and has branches that are triangular in cross-section.

very small and regular hydnae. Numerous growth forms may exist within the same colony.

Natural Location: *Hydnophora* are found in large tracts in equatorial lagoons and murky, protected areas, although they may occur in other areas.

Colors: Colors are normally cream or green, and the fluorescence of many species is striking. The polyp tentacles may contrast slightly with the coenosarc color, with dashed highlights of brown or burgundy occasionally occurring.

Captive Care: Because they are subject to bleaching, recession, and other maladies, *Hydnophora* can't be regarded as especially easy corals to keep, but they are relatively tolerant of captive conditions. Most will thrive with bright light and moderate current. Under such conditions, their tissue may swell to an almost balloonlike state in the aquarium, effectively masking the hydnophores (and

most other skeletal aspects). Fragmentation is a common method of asexual reproduction, and broken branches heal and attach to substrate rapidly. *Hydnophora rigida* is not reported to form an encrusting base in nature, although it will attach to substrate where tissue is in contact. I have encountered numerous colonies of this species that do, in fact, encrust under many circumstances in captivity. These corals are capable of sending out sweeper tentacles, though it is not a frequent occurrence. They can deliver a powerful sting to other corals and are usually the dominant species in contact encounters, which usually involve acrorhagi or mesenterial filament attack. Surprisingly, *Hydnophora* will accept fairly large food items. They eat quite willingly, digesting large prey externally on the coral surface. *Hydnophora* are actually quite unlikely to suffer from many diseases, probably in part due to their production of a heavy and thick mucus layer that forms mucus nets. Bleaching is one of the more common maladies and is usually caused by inadequate light. Brown jelly infections may also occur, and these will consume the *Hydnophora* tissue rapidly. Recession may also take place, primarily from the basal areas.

Special Information: The commensal shrimp *Metapontonia fungiacola* may associate with *Hydnophora* species.

Collection Impact: *Hydnophora* are well suited to collection because of the ease of noninvasive collection methods, relative abundance in nature, tolerance to varying stresses and water conditions, and reasonably high survivability. Captive-bred colonies are available from a number of sources.

GENUS *Merulina* Ehrenberg, 1834
(mehr'-yoo-line'-ah)

Common Species: *M. ampliata, M. scabricula.*

Common Names: ruffled coral, lettuce coral, ridge coral, cabbage coral.

Identification: *Merulina* species are some of the most beautiful corals in the world. They form fantastic ruffled plates and fans, with sometimes laminar or branching meandroid forms. Multiple growth forms within a colony are the rule. *Merulina ampliata*, common in sheltered reef areas, is foliaceous, arborescent, or nodular, with different growth forms occurring in the same colony as a result of varying environmental conditions. *Merulina scabricula* forms branching or sub-branching colonies and is much rarer. All species have readily apparent corallites forming intricate valleys and ridges that meander across the colony surface, radiating from the center. Septa are prominent and contribute to the ruffled appearance of the skeleton as they arch over the corallite walls. The polyp tentacles are rarely visible, but if food is present at night, they arise from the surface and extreme edges of the colony. Small colonies of *Merulina* can superficially resemble other corals, including *Goniastrea pectinata*, though *Goniastrea* are typically massive and folded while *Merulina* are foliaceous. *Merulina* tend to be encrusting as small colonies, forming flattened, ruffled leaves as they grow larger.

Natural Location: Most often found in lagoons, but may also occur throughout the reef; they are common, though not abundant.

Colors: Colors can be vibrant or subtle shades of green, pink, lavender, violet, blue, brown, and cream. Several of these colors may be evident in one colony.

Captive Care: *Merulina* swell outward in captivity, much like *Pectinia*. The tissue is overlying and obviously present, but rarely hides the intricate skeleton below. These corals are not at all easy to keep in the aquarium, despite being predominantly lagoon-based corals (normally indicating relative ease of maintenance). They tend to decalcify and fail to thrive in many cases. Reces-

Merulina ampliata (ruffled coral): note characteristic texture of valley walls.

Merulina scabricula (ruffled coral): fantastic variations in form are the rule.

Merulina ampliata (ruffled coral): not an especially easy aquarium subject.

sion with unknown cause is common, as is bleaching. They lose tissue quickly by necrosis where contact with other corals or sedimentation occurs. They seem to prefer strong lighting and moderate water flow. They are heavy mucus producers, but it is not known whether stronger currents would be beneficial or detrimental, as reports of captive conditions are widely variant in this regard. My own experience indicates that these corals should be left alone and untouched, distant from potentially aggressive corals and other animals/algae that may tend to produce allelopathic toxins. The growth patterns and colors of the specimen may not be indicative of the conditions it is accustomed to receiving, since various growth forms within a colony are common. *Merulina* grow quite slowly.

Special Information: *Merulina* seem to be very passive corals, despite their formation of very long sweeper tentacles. Sweeper tentacles generally emerge when food is in the water and currents are stronger. They appear mainly from around the peripheral margins, occasionally from the corallum surface, and can extend well over 8 cm (3 in.).

Collection Impact: One drawback to the collection of *Merulina* is the relatively high failure rate among captive colonies using currently known care methods. Other aspects of their harvest from the reef are similar to *Hydnophora*, as is their potential likelihood of being captive-bred in the future.

FAMILY Faviidae Gregory, 1900

Faviids are the fourth largest contributor to reef formations in the world, and include more than 20 genera from the Atlantic and Pacific regions. This family is second only to Acroporidae in number of species. All members are symbiotic and hermatypic.

Australogyra zelli: a unique, branching faviid that is seldom imported.

Pacific Genera: *Astreosmilia, Australogyra, Barabattoia [Bikiniastrea], Caulastrea, Cyphastrea, Diploastrea, Echinopora, Erythrastrea, Favites, Goniastrea, Leptastrea, Leptoria, Moseleya, Oulastrea, Oulophyllia, Platygyra,* and *Plesiastrea.*

Atlantic Genera: *Cladocora, Colpophyllia, Diploria, Manicina,* and *Solenastrea.*

Atlantic and Pacific Genera: *Montastraea* and *Favia.*

Faviids are a distinctive coral family—frequently massive, hemispherical to round, and often strikingly fluorescent. Their skeletons are very dense and nonporous. *Erythrastrea* is one of the "odd" genera, as it has a fleshy polyp on a flabello-meandroid skeleton that more closely resembles *Nemenzophyllia* (fox coral) of the Family Caryophylliidae (see page 309).

GENUS *Australogyra* Veron and Pichon, 1982

(oss-tral'-oh-jie'-rah)

Common Species: *A. zelli.*

Common Names: None.

Identification: This beautiful branching faviid is absolutely unique, and readily distinguished from other faviids. The corallites are meandroid and sometimes cerioid, with branches chiseled in angular and sculptural patterns. The polyp tissue is velvety, and does not expand greatly from the skeleton. Although at a glance they somewhat resemble some *Hydnophora*, the recessed corallites and inward-protruding septa make these corals unmistakable.

Natural Location: *Australogyra* are relatively uncommon corals found in turbid areas of the reef around "high islands" (islands composed of rock from nonreef origins) off northeastern Australia (Veron, 1986). Comparatively little other information is available regarding their location in other Pacific areas, though their distribution extends into the Solomon Islands, where they may enter the aquarium trade.

Colors: Colors commonly seen in *Australogyra* are brown and gray-green, although fluorescent green and ivory colors are possible, resembling those seen in *Favia* and *Favites.*

Captive Care: Once almost unheard of in aquarium circles, *Australogyra* are now occasionally available. They are not impossible to keep, although they demand high water quality. Tissue recession seems fairly common, and they may have a tendency to decalcify in captivity. It is not known if this skeletal loss is a result of boring worms and algae or the coral's own behavior. They are found in turbid waters in nature, indicating that light and current levels should both be moderate. Bright but indirect light seems justified, and though turbid water usually implies a tolerance of higher nutrients, *Australogyra* seem quite finicky in captivity.

Special Information: This coral's rarity and branching growth habit may make it an ideal candidate for captive propagation.

Collection Impact: Seldom collected, with some collateral damage typical during harvesting.

GENUS *Caulastrea* Dana, 1846

(kaw'-lass-tree'-ah)

Common Species: *C. curvata, C. echinulata, C. furcata.*

Common Names: trumpet coral, torch coral, candy cane coral, candy coral, bullseye coral, cat's eye coral.

Identification: These common aquarium imports are among the most easily recognized stony corals. A lightweight and phaceloid skeleton gives rise to plump, circular polyps clustered on the end of branched stalks. The septa are distinct and well developed, usually showing through the translucent green or brown polyp tissue as clean, bright stripes.

Caulastrea furcata is by far the most commonly available species, with bright colors, smaller corallites, and a slightly less-packed array of polyps. *Caulastrea echinulata* has densely packed polyps, substantially larger and more oval-to-meandering-shaped corallites, and is rarely as colorful as *C. furcata*. The polyp tissue expands more in this species, often forming trumpetlike extensions from the skeleton. *Caulastrea echinulata* tends to resemble some faviids when expanded, because of the compactness of the corallites. However, there is usually space around each polyp that hints at the length of the long phaceloid branches. *Caulastrea curvata* is much more open in its configuration, with skeletal stalks sprawling outward. Greater space lies between the phaceloid stalks, and individual stalks often divide as they grow upward.

Natural Location: These corals are found primarily in protected waters with a sandy bottom in shallow to mid depths. *Caulastrea echinulata* is an exception, frequently seen in lagoons and in slightly deeper water.

Colors: Although some recent *Caulastrea* imports, principally from Fiji, are a beautiful uniform and noncontrasting translucent green to teal, *Caulastrea* are normally brown, pale brown, or cream. The centers of the polyps, at the oral disc, are usually a contrasting white or green color. The overall color pattern makes *Caulastrea* resemble a peppermint, with white stripes of septal banding patterns—hence the common name candy cane coral. *Caulastrea echinulata* is more drably colored in brownish pinks to grays, and typically shows less contrast between the outer tissue and the oral disc.

Captive Care: Indirect bright light and moderate current will allow for the best expansion and health of *Caulastrea*. They seem quite sensitive to direct metal halide lighting and to strong water flow. Recession is sometimes seen in these corals,

***Caulastrea* sp.** (trumpet coral): plump polyps are clustered on stalks.

Caulastrea furcata (trumpet coral): popular and usually successful species.

***Caulastrea* sp.** (trumpet coral): stalks are easily separated for propagation.

Caulastrea furcata (trumpet coral): growing colony in a reef aquarium with a very rare Resplendent Pygmy Angelfish (*Centropyge resplendens*) from Ascension Island.

Caulastrea furcata (trumpet coral): often sold as "candy cane coral."

Caulastrea sp. (trumpet coral): note tubeworms growing between polyps.

especially on a single polyp or more. The loss of a polyp does not usually imply any colony susceptibility, nor is it necessarily deleterious to the other polyps. The fragile skeleton may be prone to invasion and dissolution by boring worms, sponges, and algae. Thriving colonies of *Caulastrea* can easily be fragmented to form new daughter colonies. Budding of individual corallites occurs frequently as the coral grows. I have noted that a surging current seems to bring a very positive response, and that polyp division increases greatly under such a flow regimen.

Special Information: The striped pattern of *Caulastrea* may disappear without adequate lighting or in high-nutrient conditions, possibly as a result of increased densities of zooxanthellae populating the formerly whitened area.

Commensal sponges, mollusks, other sessile invertebrates, and even other corals may find a cryptic safe haven within the branches of *Caulastrea*. Detritus should not be allowed to collect within the colony, and inspection to remove dying cryptofauna is important.

Collection Impact: *Caulastrea* are easily fragmented corals that are relatively abundant in the wild and have an excellent history of success in captivity. They also reproduce readily by budding and are already being actively propagated.

GENUS *Diploastrea* Matthai, 1914
(dip'-loh-ass-tree'-ah)

Common Species: *D. heliopora.*

Common Name: moon coral.

Identification: *Diploastrea* is composed of a single species with a unique and beautiful appearance. It is one of the easiest corals to identify—composed of geometrically perfect, even, dome-shaped, plocoid corallites. No other Pacific faviid resembles it. Each dome is radially striated by even and conspicuous septocostae. Colonies form large flat to dome-shaped encrustations, rarely becoming rounded and massive like so many other faviids. They extend their feeding tentacles at night, but may also do so occasionally during the day in captivity, especially if food is present. The septa arch sharply downward toward the oral opening, creating, in effect, a rounded, volcano-like appearance to the tissue-covered corallites. Colonies may grow to more than 7 m (21 ft.) in diameter, and 2 m (6 ft.) in height.

Natural Location: Infrequently encountered in the wild and in the aquarium trade, *Diploastrea* is highly prized for its beauty. It is typically found in areas protected from strong wave action, but may occur within several reef zones. It is widely distributed throughout the Pacific.

Colors: Most commonly brown, gray, tan, and occasionally green from the corallite wall outward, the overall color scheme of *Diploastrea* is quite uniform, serving only to highlight an already extremely organized surface. The oral disc is contrasting in white or a lighter shade, fading sharply as it moves outward to match the ground color of the rest of the corallum.

Captive Care: There are few reports on the care of this lovely coral, but other faviids are quite tolerant of variable light and flow regimes and have similar competitive and behavioral adaptations. Those who have kept this coral for extended periods have reported that it is quite undemanding.

Special information: This species' dense skeleton makes it resistant to attack by boring organisms. Apparently, it is also resistant to grazing by fishes and *Acanthaster planci*, the Crown-of-Thorns Starfish (Veron, 1986).

Collection Impact: Rarely collected for the aquarium trade.

Diploastrea heliopora (moon coral): forms huge domes up to 7 m in diameter.

Diploastrea heliopora (moon coral): rarely imported but reportedly quite hardy.

Echinopora lamellosa (plating echinopora): tiered plates—one of many forms.

Echinopora lamellosa (plating echinopora): colony with whorls and tubes.

Echinopora horrida (hedgehog coral): note encrusting base, twisting branches.

Echinopora mammiformis: note smooth coenosteum, typical of the species.

Echinopora sp. (plating echinopora): seldom seen in aquarium trade.

Echinopora lamellosa: requires adequate currents to flush away sediments.

GENUS *Echinopora* Lamarck, 1816

(eh-kie'-no-pohr'-ah)

Common Species: *E. lamellosa, E. mammiformis, E. pacificus,* and others.

Common Name: hedgehog coral.

Identification: *Echinopora* species are not commonly available in the aquarium trade, and when they do appear, misidentifications are the rule rather than the exception. The genus is characterized by great variability in growth forms. Adopting branching, encrusting, massive, and foliaceous forms, all species have plocoid corallites, usually widely spaced, with a broad coenosteum between them. The corallites are hemispherical, measuring 3-10 mm, like small domes on the flat surface of the corallum. The centers of the corallites are usually quite distinct and often contrasting in color from the rest of the polyp tissue. Aquarists will need to consult taxonomic references to identify unknown examples, as there are many species and morphs of *Echinopora,* making them fairly difficult to recognize—at least for the amateur. Veron (1986) notes that they "are not difficult to identify." While this may be so with a good view of the skeleton, living corals are not so obvious. They can superficially resemble *Mycedium, Oxypora, Echinophyllia,* and a host of related but usually unavailable faviids of the genera *Cyphastrea* and *Diploastrea.* Perhaps most notable is the pattern of berrylike corallites across the surface, which appear as small, rounded, bumpy hillocks. In this regard, they may resemble *Astreopora,* though a simple touch will distinguish the thin-tissued *Astreopora* from the more fleshy *Echinopora. Astreopora* corallites have openings that resemble the axial corallites of *Acropora* when looking down on them. *Echinopora's* corallite openings are normally well closed by visible tissue and are larger. The polyp tentacles extend at night, and polyp tissue rarely swells substantially.

Natural Location: *Echinopora* are normally found in shallow water, often in turbid conditions. Foliaceous growth forms are most common on reef slopes, branched forms are predominantly found on reef crests and rims, and solid and encrusting (with or without projections) forms are more common in protected areas.

Colors: Color variations are wide, but brown, green, cream, and pink are most common. One well-known source of captive-raised *Echinopora* reportedly has specimens of a lovely sky blue color.

Captive Care: Because of their common collection location in shallow, turbid waters, these corals can be expected to enjoy moderate to strong currents with fairly bright light. Despite their abundance in nature, *Echinopora* are somewhat of a rarity in the aquarium trade. This is unfortunate, as they are unusual, attractive, and durable. The growth form of the colony, if apparent in the typically small aquarium specimens, should be indicative of the captive conditions that would be conducive to its growth.

Special Information: None.

Collection Impact: The more frequently collected examples are quite prolific and can usually be easily collected by fragmentation from a mother colony. Captive-breeding efforts are beginning, and they are fairly successful.

GENUS *Favia* Oken, 1815

(fay'-vee-ah)

Common Species: *F. favus, F. matthaii, F. pallida, F. stelligera,* and others.

Common Names: moon coral, green moon coral, pineapple coral, brain coral, closed brain coral, star coral. (See *Favites,* page 293.)

Identification: *Favia* are among the most common and prolific species of coral in the world. Comprised of a wide number of species and colors, all *Favia* display a fairly common skeletal morphology. They are massive and usually domed or round-shaped colonies, seldom staying flat or encrusting in form. The feeding tentacles emerge at night in a characteristic circle inside each corallite. The polyp tissue swells substantially during the day in the aquarium and obscures the skeleton. However, even the tissue retains most of the markings and distinct shape of the corallites below.

Favia sp. (moon coral): very common shallow-water coral with distinctly separate corallites. Contrast to *Favites* spp., with shared walls between corallites.

Favia pallida (moon coral): species is noted by dark calices and light body.

Favia **sp.** (moon coral): easily maintained in most reef aquariums.

Favia **sp.** (moon coral): will respond to direct feeding at night.

Favia **sp.** (moon coral): note three polyps dividing, each with a pair of mouths.

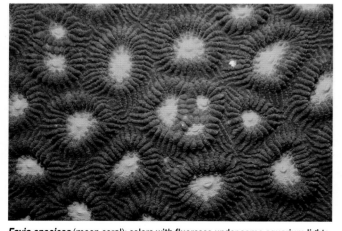

Favia speciosa (moon coral): colors with fluoresce under some aquarium lights.

Favia **sp.** (moon coral): unknown species seen in Lembeh Strait, Sulawesi.

Favia **sp.** (moon coral): compare separate corallites with *Favites* sp., **right**.

Favites **sp.** (moon coral): compare shared corallite walls with *Favites* sp., **left**.

Nonetheless, identification to a species level is barely possible using a taxonomic reference to match skeletal features of the corallites and associated structures in living examples. Because of the many species of *Favia* commonly available and found in nature, and owing to their variability, it is not possible to provide such identification information here. However, individual corallites that do not share common walls is the easiest way to distinguish *Favia* from related *Favites* and *Goniastrea*, both common aquarium imports. (See photographic comparisons.)

Natural Location: *Favia* occur in a wide range of depths and habitats. The great abundance of species on the reef makes any type of useful generalization impossible.

Colors: These corals are broadly and commonly known in the aquarium hobby as moon or green moon corals, partly for the beautiful greens that fluoresce blindingly under actinic light. The round-shaped colonies, coupled with the craterlike corallites, green colors, and highlights certainly lend credence to this name. Pineapple coral is the name that many give to *Favia* morphs that do not have the green polyps and are strictly brown, or have variations of other colors. *Favia* can be found in yellow, cream, brown, green, rarely orange/red tones, and in combinations thereof. They can be exceedingly colorful.

Captive Care: *Favia* are hardy corals tolerant of most tank conditions. While generally preferring bright light, they will typically tolerate much lower levels. They are also quite tolerant of water motion, though extremely strong current prevents full polyp expansion in many species. Some *Favia* can attach to the substrate by forming a bond from the underside of the skeleton. Before attachment, it would seem impossible that these corals could accomplish such a feat, as the underside of their skeleton is quite solid with no visible tissue showing. Yet, these occasional colonies can attach if left undisturbed for several months. Many species send out long, thin, transparent sweeper tentacles at night, so care must be exercised in their placement. They can also be fed, and an occasional gentle current of brine shrimp at night seems to be well appreciated. Polyp buds can occur in captivity as a means of asexual reproduction. *Favia* tend to suffer from recession and jelly-type infections, though they tolerate anti-protozoan dips (see Chapter 11). Proper feeding and water flow limits these problems.

Special Information: There are many genera in the Family Faviidae. Such corals are often sold under the catch-all genera of *Favia* and *Favites*. Other faviid genera that may resemble each other, but are often wrongly identified include *Montastraea*, *Oulastrea*, *Barabattoia*, *Plesiastrea*, *Leptastrea*, and *Cyphastrea*. Interested reef keepers may consult taxonomic reference books and perhaps find that the faviid they have had for years may be a rarity in the aquarium world.

Collection Impact: Because *Favia* are widely distributed and comprise such a tremendous group of species and numbers, even the fact that a few species are relatively uncommon does not change the fact that any collection of *Favia* for the aquarium hobby (unless drastically overcollected in local areas, or from areas already compromised by other factors) will unlikely have any notable effect on wild populations. The collateral damage to the reef itself from the invasive methods needed to sever *Favia* from their attachments is a downside to their collection, though it is no greater than for many similar corals.

Favites **sp.** (pineapple coral): although rather slow-growing, the faviids are highly regarded by many aquarists for their hardiness and eye-catching appearance.

Favites **sp.** (pineapple coral): colors vary under different water, light conditions.

Favites abdita (pineapple coral): feeding tentacles are usually retracted by day.

GENUS *Favites* Link, 1807
(fah-vie'-tees)

Common Species: *F. abdita, F. complanata, F. flexuosa,* and others.

Common Names: pineapple coral, moon coral, brain coral, closed brain coral, star coral. (See *Favia,* above.)

Identification: *Favites* are very closely related to *Favia* and are confusingly labeled with many of the same common names. As with *Favia,* colonies are usually massive and are dome-shaped or rounded. They are also similar in their coloration, feeding habits, locations, and diversity. In fact, the most notable differences between the two genera are often purely skeletal taxonomic features. The corallites of *Favites* are cerioid, meaning they share common walls. When the polyps are fully expanded in some species, this distinction is not always readily apparent, and the two genera can be easily confused. In other species, it is quite obvious. With practice, distinguishing between the two becomes easier. *Favia* polyps are commonly seen as figure-8 shapes as they are in the process of dividing, and this can also help distinguish them from other faviids. *Favites* do share this trait, but dividing *Favites* polyps are usually seen around the circumference of the coral, rather than being equally spaced around the colony. Furthermore, *Favites* polyp divisions are extratentacular, rather than intratentacular. The corallite walls of *Favites* are often more raised than in *Favia,* can be quite uneven, and tend to adopt a slightly more polygonal shape. A combination of the above attributes may allow for proper generic classification. Species-level identification of living individuals will be very difficult.

Natural Location: *Favites* occur in a wide range of depths and habitats.

Colors: May be even more brightly colored than *Favia,* but are generally similar in coloration. Quite a number of *Favites* with large corallites imported from Fiji have a pretty yellow to cream color, rather than the more typical greens and browns.

Captive Care: Many specimens are commonly available to aquarists, all excellent and beautiful additions to the reef tank. Care requirements are identical to *Favia,* above.

Special Information: The Family Faviidae includes many genera that are easily misidentified. Many faviid corals are confusingly sold under the catch-all genera of *Favia* or *Favites.* Other genera that may resemble each other, but are often wrongly identified, include *Montastraea, Oulastrea, Barabattoia, Plesiastrea, Leptastrea,* and *Cyphastrea.* Interested reef keepers may consult taxonomic reference books and perhaps find that the faviid they have had for years may actually be from an unusual genus.

Collection Impact: *Favites* are widely distributed. Collection is unlikely to have any notable effect on wild populations. See *Favia,* above.

GENUS *Goniastrea* Edwards and Haime, 1848
(goh'-nee-ass-tree'-ah)

Common Species: *G. aspera, G. pectinata, G. retiformis,* and others.

Common Names: honeycomb coral, star coral, wreath coral, moon coral, pineapple coral, brain coral, closed brain coral.

Identification: *Goniastrea* are massive, dome-shaped, or rounded, with cerioid to meandroid corallites that are often distinctly honeycomb patterned. They are distinguished from *Favites* by having distinct paliform lobes extending above the corallite top that impart a more distinctly ridged skeletal pattern visible beneath the tissue. This characteristic also separates meandroid examples of *Goniastrea* from some species of similar *Platygyra.* If meanders exist, they are generally less sinuous than most *Platygyra,* yet more so than most *Favites.* While corallite walls may be rough, the overall effect is a normally even, smooth corallum. *Goniastrea pectinata* can bear a resemblance to *Merulina,* and I have often found it sold as such. Closer examination of the skeleton and colony shape should make the distinction between the two obvious. (See *Merulina,* page 283.). *Goniastrea pectinata,* the most common species in the Indo-Pacific, forms flat to rounded colonies in all reef zones.

Natural Location: These very hardy corals are often exposed to the air at low tide on the reef in conditions intolerable to most other species. Many are also found on "ironshore," where waves break onto the shore. Predominantly shallow-water corals, they often endure violent water movement and intense sunlight.

Colors: Although their coloration is similar to *Favites, Goniastrea* are less commonly found in the highly fluorescent green tones. Shades of brown, green, pink, yellow, and cream are common, with valleys frequently in a lighter shade than the walls. *Goniastrea pectinata* is often seen in pink tones.

Goniastrea retiformis (honeycomb coral): among the most hardy stony corals.

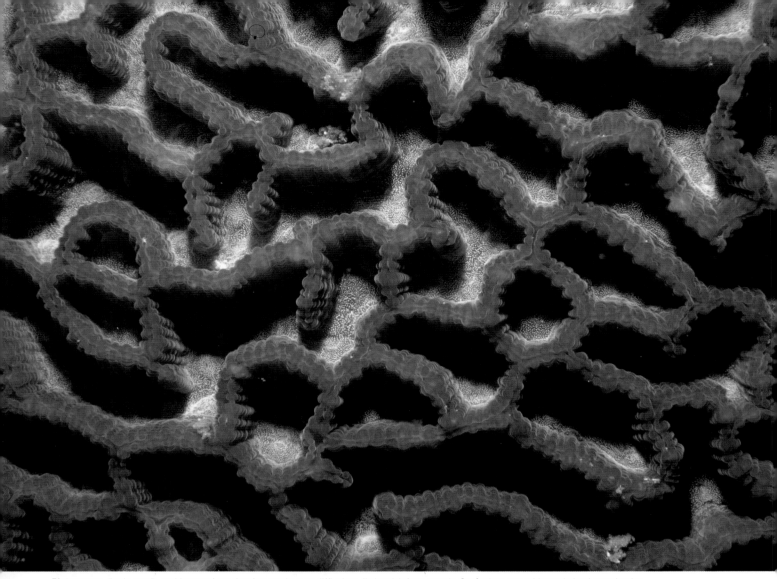

Platygyra sp. (brain coral): a widespread species that can be very difficult to distinguish from certain *Goniastrea* spp. without skeletal examination.

Captive Care: Because of their natural location in extreme conditions, *Goniastrea* thrive under strong water flow and bright lighting. Those with brighter colors and more-flattened forms will likely have been collected from shallow-water areas; the more rounded forms and darker colors are from somewhat deeper, quieter waters. Tolerant of less-than-natural conditions in the aquarium, they are among the most durable stony corals available.

Special Information: If one finds a colony of *G. pectinata* being sold as *Merulina* sp., it may be that the source is either wrong or being deceptive. In this case, silence is golden. Although *Merulina* may be regarded as more desirable by some, *G. pectinata* is equally beautiful, especially in rich pink tones, and is likely to be far more durable in captivity than *Merulina*.

The commensal shrimp *Metapontonia fungiacola* may associate with *Goniastrea* species.

Collection Impact: Unlikely to affect reef populations under typical collection pressures. (See *Favia*, above.)

GENUS *Leptoria* Edwards and Haime, 1848
(lep-tohr'-ee-ah)

Common Species: *L. phrygia.*

Common Names: maze coral, brain coral, closed brain coral, labyrinth coral.

Identification: The genus *Leptoria* consists of one strikingly beautiful true species that can form massive skeletons with even, uniform surfaces and ripples of intricate meandroid corallites. The colonies can become quite large, somewhat lobed, and generally flattened with rounded edges. In many ways, it appears similar to certain *Platygyra* species. However, *Leptoria* is even more meandroid and has very wall-like columellae. Its septa are very regularly spaced, smooth, and even. Corallite walls are thinner than similar *Platygyra*. As in other faviids, feeding tentacles appear at night. In general, however, *Leptoria* specimens are quite distinctive.

Natural Location: Although a rare jewel to find in an aquarium shop, *Leptoria* are fairly common in nature. This may be because they form large colonies, primarily on the reef front and shallower reef slopes, typically in areas exposed to clear oceanic water. These colonies are not easily divisible without damage. They are uncommon in turbid or sheltered locations.

Colors: *Leptoria* are green, cream, or brown with noticeably contrasting fluorescent white, greenish, or cream valleys, but any simple color description does not do justice to their beauty.

Captive Care: *Leptoria* are similar in care to the other faviids, although they may be slightly more sensitive to water conditions—the fact that *Leptoria* are found in areas mostly receiving clear oceanic water makes their tolerance to high nutrients lower than that of similar genera. *Leptoria* are exceptionally defensive, and will readily digest neighboring corals. Be sure to give *Leptoria* ample space in the aquarium. They produce large amounts of clear, runny mucus and are fairly efficient at sediment rejection. However, they are also intolerant of persistent or heavy sediments; place them vertically if detritus is common, as the gravitational deposit of such particulate matter can cause mortality in *Leptoria* more easily than in other corals. *Leptoria* grow very slowly.

Special Information: *Leptoria* have become an almost "mythical" coral in the reef hobby. They are rarely found, yet many stories are told of retailers selling *Platygyra* and other similar corals as *Leptoria* to command a higher price.

Leptoria, like other corals with prolific mucus, should be flushed well with running seawater after shipping to avoid fouling the aquarium.

Collection Impact: *Leptoria*, because of its perceived higher value and relatively less-abundant nature, may be the target of overcollection in local areas where it can be found. However, it is very widely distributed in the Indo-Pacific and common in many areas. The relatively few specimens that make their way into the trade are unlikely to have any effect on wild populations.

Goniastrea palauensis (honeycomb coral): unusual species, similar to *Favites*.

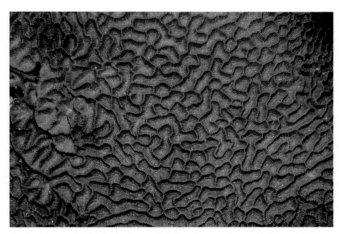

Goniastrea australensis (brain coral): thrives in strong currents, intense light.

Leptoria phrygia (maze coral): a rare jewel highly prized by reef aquarists.

Montastraea annuligera (boulder coral): this genus is similar to Favia, forming large spheres or mounds, and is relatively hardy with good light and water motion.

GENUS *Montastraea* de Blainville, 1830

(mahn'-tass-tree'-ah)

Common Species: *M. annularis, M. cavernosa, M. curta,* and others.

Common Names: boulder coral, great star coral, brain coral, closed brain coral, pineapple coral.

Identification: *Montastraea* are known as massive spherical or dome-shaped corals, yet they also create platelike formations at greater depths. They are one of the most common and widely studied genera of reef-building corals in the Atlantic and Caribbean (*M. cavernosa* and *M. annularis*), yet their presence in the Pacific is somewhat less prolific. There are four Pacific species (*M. annuligera, M. curta, M. magnistellata,* and *M. valenciennesi*). *Montastraea curta* is the most common of the Pacific species and is likely to be the only species imported for the aquarium trade (Wijsman-Best, 1977). *Montastraea multipunctata* is an unusual encrusting species that is often buried in sediment and closely resembles a colony of co-occurring zoanthids or *Blasto-mussa merleti* (Hodgson, 1985). *Montastraea* closely resemble *Favia* in that all their corallites have distinct walls and are plocoid. However, each corallite is separated from adjacent corallites by a thin margin of coenosteum, making them even more individualized than those of most *Favia*. (There are exceptions, of course.) This may be the result of the extratentacular budding characteristic of the asexual growth of a colony, where small corallites may be found wedged between mature ones.

Natural Location: *M. curta,* occurs predominantly on reef flats. Other less-common species are found in varied environments.

Colors: *Montastraea* are normally cream or brown, with contrasting shades of both colors often found within a single colony.

Captive Care: *Montastraea* are easy corals to maintain in captivity and are typical of the faviids in that they do best with reasonably bright lighting and good water motion. Because they are common on reef flats, most collected specimens would likely benefit from somewhat stronger lighting than other faviids, and would likely be more tolerant of even stronger currents. Polyp tissue expansion is noticeably less than with related genera. Flat, platelike growth forms are collected from deeper water and require subdued light, at least initially. They tend to produce a lot of clear mucus, like *Leptoria*.

Special Information: *Montastraea* are known for forming long, potent sweeper tentacles at night when the normal feeding tentacles are extended. The sweeper tentacles often form in patterns that do not indicate any apparent or likely future encounter with other corals and thus seem to be purely defensive. It is only when they are involved in an encounter that the sweepers become localized and more numerous. This seems to be common in a number of faviids, though there have not been formal studies to confirm this observation.

Collection Impact: While *Montastraea* are not uncommon, neither are they particularly abundant in most locations in the Pacific. At the same time, they are not widely available in the aquarium hobby. Their collection procedures are similar to *Favia*, which is to say, somewhat invasive. It is my hope that the beautiful, fast-growing, and prolific Caribbean species, *M. cavernosa* and *M. annularis*, may one day be available for captive breeding. (Following the loss of Atlantic acroporids in the Caribbean, *Montastraea annularis* has become a primary reef builder in many areas and is currently a coral research "guinea pig" species.)

GENUS *Oulophyllia* Edwards and Haime, 1848
(oo'-loh-fill'-ee-ah)
Common Species: *O. aspera, O. crispa.*
Common Names: ejection-seat coral, brain coral, maze coral, closed brain coral.

Identification: *Oulophyllia* are massive and meandroid like some other Faviidae genera, but their valleys are much wider and more V-shaped, resulting from their sloped corallite walls. Some corallites may be cerioid as well. The upper ridges of the walls are also V-shaped, making the large coral heads look as if they are covered by winding, miniature mountain ranges.

The nightly extended polyps are larger than in other related genera, as might be expected from the wide valleys. *Oulophyllia crispa* should not be confused by name with a much rarer family member, *Oulastrea crispata*, which has much smaller and cerioid corallites and a brown-pigmented skeleton (a rather unique feature).

Natural Location: *Oulophyllia*, like *Leptoria*, are fairly common in nature but are only rarely seen in the aquarium trade. Like many faviids, they occur in several reef zones, but are usually found in protected areas like lagoons, where they can thrive using their innate capacity for sediment rejection.

Colors: *Oulophyllia* are normally brown, grayish green, or cream, with cream or pink fluorescent valleys.

Captive Care: These corals are quite hardy and beautiful, and have a pronounced ability to reject surface sediments. They can also form sweeper tentacles, like other faviids. Otherwise, *Oulophyllia* are not notably different in their care, requirements, or behavior from *Platygyra* and similar corals.

Special Information: Reproduction by ejecting pieces of tissue in a type of bail-out, similar to the polyp balls of *Goniopora*, is a notable feature and gives rise to one of *Oulophyllia*'s common names—ejection-seat coral.

Collection Impact: Similar to *Leptoria*, because they are relatively uncommon.

Oulophyllia crispa (brain coral): note broad, V-shaped valleys and large mouths.

Oulophyllia bennettae (brain coral): may reproduce by ejecting polyp balls.

Platygyra lamellina (maze or brain coral): not commonly seen in the aquarium trade, but eye-catching and hardy when given adequate lighting and water motion.

GENUS *Platygyra* Ehrenberg, 1834

(plat'-ee-jie'-rah)

Common Species: *P. daedalea, P. lamellina, P. pini, P. sinensis, P. verweyi.*

Common Names: brain or closed brain coral, maze coral.

Identification: *Platygyra* seem to be recent corals in evolutionary terms, and species differences may be made all the more vague by this knowledge. Like many corals, *Platygyra* show more than a little morphologic variation between and within species. They share many similarities with some of their faviid relatives, yet may appear remarkably different due to their often highly sinuous skeleton. The colonies are massive, and either dome-shaped or flattened. Their corallites are almost always meandroid, with oc-

casional cerioid examples intermixed. They can be occasionally confused with meandroid *Goniastrea* species, but the absence of protruding paliform lobes above the corallite walls distinguishes *Platygyra*. (See comparative photographs, pages 293-295.) *Platygyra* is also, in general, much less sinuous than *Leptoria*, and has wider meanders with rougher septal teeth and rougher, heavier corallite walls.

Platygyra daedalea and *P. lamellina* are similar-looking but can be distinguished from each other by noting the smoother, rounded septa of the latter. *Platygyra daedalea* is the most common species of *Platygyra* and is also the one most likely to be imported. It shows considerable variation in appearance, and the variances appear to be relatively independent of either environmental or genetic influences. The implications of such morphologic plasticity are still largely unknown in this coral.

Natural Location: Like *Favia*, *Platygyra* are found in a diverse array of reef habitats, but can be abundant on reef flats and back reefs accessible to collectors. *Platygyra daedalea* occurs in all reef zones, although typically in deeper waters. They are common reef inhabitants, though not often available in the aquarium trade.

Colors: *Platygyra* are found in various shades of green, brown and gray, often with contrasting valleys that are white, cream, pink, or gray. Frequently, the valleys are fluorescent and beautiful under actinic light.

Captive Care: *Platygyra* are hardy corals, but perhaps less so than the *Favia*, *Favites*, and *Goniastrea* genera. They have been noted to bleach more easily, and seem to have necrotic tissue loss in response to stress before many other hermatypic species. *Platygyra*

typically feed at night. Sweeper tentacles are thin and quite long and tend to occur slightly more often than on some of the other faviids. They are especially localized near adjacent corals. *Platygyra* secrete copious amounts of mucus.

Special Information: As with other corals that produce prolific mucus, *Platygyra* should be flushed well with running seawater after shipping to avoid fouling.

Collection Impact: Unlikely to affect reef populations under typical collection pressures. (See *Favia*, page 289.)

OTHER FAVIIDS

There are many genera in the Family Faviidae, but the identification of genera and species may be difficult even for professional taxonomists, much less the untrained. The identification of living corals is especially problematic. Fortunately, the faviids, al-

Platygyra daedalea (maze coral): note contrasting valleys and walls.

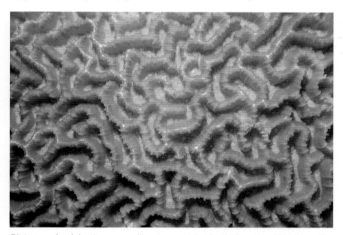

Platygyra daedalea (maze coral): note exsert (projecting) septa within the walls.

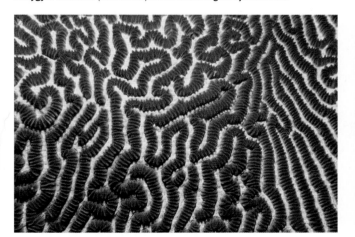

Platygyra daedalea (maze coral): copious slime producer during shipping.

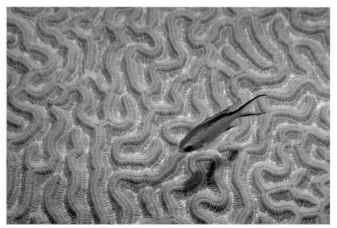

Colpophyllia natans (boulder brain coral): Atlantic species with Blue Chromis.

most without exception, are fairly tolerant and hardy in captivity and share enough similarities that detailed descriptions are not mandatory. Often, there isn't the availability of specimens or the captive experiences to warn of any unusual requirements of some of the less-common types. Several excellent taxonomic references, including Veron (1986), may aid in the more specific identification of faviid genera and species.

Atlantic Species: While unavailable to the trade at this writing because of restrictions banning the importation of stony corals from Atlantic waters, the Faviidae of the Caribbean are as prominent and important to reef formations as they are in the Pacific. They are also widely distributed and, for the most part, easily recognizable—at least to the genus level. Caribbean faviids tend to be somewhat muted in their coloration compared with their often gaudy Pacific counterparts, with shades of brown dominating the "brain coral landscapes." Nonetheless, I have a special place in my heart for the beautiful labyrinthine Caribbean *Diploria* species and the giant and magnificent *Colpophyllia natans*. Interestingly, *Colpophyllia* skeletons will float when dry—surprising for a coral that can be the size of a small car.

Cladocora species are very common in turbid, sandy reef areas and, in some senses, are the Atlantic equivalent to *Caulastrea curvata*. This genus also tends to be a "pioneer," and many of the aquacultured live rocks from Atlantic and Gulf of Mexico areas bear small colonies of this hardy faviid. I have also frequently found *Cladocora* attached to the base of Caribbean gorgonians.

Diploria labyrinthiformis (grooved brain coral): a common sight in the waters of the Caribbean, this species forms rounded heads. Collection is currently prohibited.

Trachyphyllia geoffroyi (open brain coral): easily identified, solitary corals.

Trachyphyllia radiata (Pacific rose coral): a durable but uncommon species.

FAMILY Trachyphylliidae Verrill, 1901

Pacific Genus: *Trachyphyllia.*

Trachyphyllia geoffroyi is very common and popular among aquarists, while *Trachyphyllia radiata* (formerly *Wellsophyllia radiata*) is both an unusual import and reported by some sources to be rare in nature. *Trachyphyllia radiata* has a colony shape different from *T. geoffroyi* even in juvenile stages, although the fusion of walls in *T. radiata* becomes more distinct in adult forms.

GENUS *Trachyphyllia* Milne-Edwards and Haime, 1848

(track'-ee-fill'-ee-ah)

Common Species: *T. geoffroyi, T. radiata.*

Common Names:

T. geoffroyi: open brain coral, folded brain coral, crater coral.

T. radiata: Pacific rose coral, open brain coral.

Identification: *Trachyphyllia* are unique solitary corals (occasionally colonial) with a flabello-meandroid skeleton. The free-living species (*Trachyphyllia geoffroyi*) may be quite convoluted with wide valleys and channels, though small specimens with a single folded channel have the most common shape and are most often seen in the aquarium trade. Their septa are thin, smooth, numerous, and very regular, imparting an even, ruffled look to the polyp tissue above. Paliform lobes are present. The bases of *Trachyphyllia* are normally cone-shaped, which helps specimens bury themselves in soft bottoms.

When *T. geoffroyi* corals are found (rarely) attached to hard substrates on the reef, the base does not have this characteristic shape. Attachment scars are often present. Polyp tentacles usually appear along the outer margin of the oral disc at night, occasionally during the day if food is present.

Trachyphyllia radiata are distinct in having fused walls of their adjacent and deep valleys. They are rounded and typically far more "folded" and meandroid than their relatives, though the septa and polyps look very much alike. *Trachyphyllia radiata* corals are always attached to hard substrate and are not reported as ever being free-living (Pichon, 1980).

Natural Location: *Trachyphyllia geoffroyi* are normally found on outer-reef margins and inter-reef areas with other free-living corals such as *Fungia* and their relatives. They are usually attached while immature and only become detached and free-living after some time. Some can be found on muddy bottoms in protected lagoons, in seagrass beds, and on sandy bottoms near the reef base. The more complex growth forms may be indicative of a coral needing protection from encrusting or boring organisms.

The natural locations of *T. radiata* are predominantly unknown—they are reportedly found in deeper water and under shaded overhangs.

Colors: *Trachyphyllia geoffroyi* are highly fluorescent corals that absolutely glow under actinic lighting. The polyps are brightly colored and most commonly green, red, pink, or brown. Blue morphs are rare and very beautiful. Walls and valleys may be of contrasting shades. The tissue above the septa may also be tinted or shaded in contrasting colors to give a finely striated appearance. The colors of *T. radiata* are similar to those of *T. geoffroyi*, often a very attractive green, although brown and drab tones are also common.

Captive Care: In the aquarium, *Trachyphyllia* are neither easy nor exceptionally difficult to maintain. Recession and failure of expansion are common problems. Some also tend to bleach, while others may be subject to tissue peeling. Corals must expend energy to remove accumulations of sediment and sand from their surfaces, and captive specimens can become weakened if

Trachyphyllia geoffroyi (open brain coral): requires good care to survive, including moderate water flow to wash away debris and occasional vitamin-enriched feedings.

they must constantly cope with aquarium substrate or debris covering them. Certain fishes, such as substrate-sifting gobies (e.g., *Valenciennea* species) may not be welcome additions in aquariums housing *Trachyphyllia*.

Red-colored *Trachyphyllia* reportedly come from shaded or turbid locations and require less light than the light-loving green and brown morphs. Iodine may be important in maintaining the light tolerance and the coloration of these corals and may also help to prevent recession. (This is an anecdotal observation by other authors and aquarists. As far as I am aware, there is no evidence to support this view.)

Water flow around *Trachyphyllia* should be moderate to help assist the coral in washing away debris that accumulates in its deep valleys and that may tend to cause localized tissue necrosis. *Trachyphyllia*, though strangely hardy in some aquariums, are

relentlessly finicky in others. Furthermore, these corals seem prone to a rapid disintegration of tissue (suggestive of rapid tissue necrosis seen in small-polyped corals), usually soon after acquisition. It is probable that *Trachyphyllia* do not tolerate stress well, and the combination of collection, shipping, handling, and changes in water chemistry are likely responsible for their oft-reported early demise. They are also quite susceptible to the chemicals released by certain soft corals—most frequently reported are encounters with *Sinularia* species.

Trachyphyllia may benefit dramatically from occasional feedings of vitamin-soaked foods. They are quite aggressive feeders and are even reported to be piscivorous (fish eating).

In terms of captive reproduction, polyp buds are frequently reported arising from the lower margins of the corallum.

Because they tend to attach to reef structures more often, *T.*

radiata corals may have less difficulty with sediment-caused problems. Their lack of bright colors indicates perhaps a broader tolerance of lighting conditions. Nonetheless, reasonably bright and indirect light have seemed appropriate for most reported examples in captivity.

Special Information: *Trachyphyllia* are well known for being nipped at or snacked on by certain tangs and angelfish species. Why this coral is so comparatively "tasty" to these fishes is not known.

Trachyphyllia radiata was formerly *Wellsophyllia radiata*. The *Wellsophyllia* genus has been eliminated (Borel Best and Hoeksema, 1987; Veron, 1989, 1992, 1993).

FAMILY Caryophylliidae Gray, 1847

Including many perennial favorites among reef aquarists, the Family Caryophylliidae consists of numerous genera of corals with similar skeletons but diverse appearance. They are some of the most interesting and unique stony corals known.

Pacific Genera: *Catalaphyllia, Euphyllia, Gyrosmilia, Montigyra, Nemenzophyllia, Physogyra,* and *Plerogyra.*

Of the above genera, *Catalaphyllia, Euphyllia, Nemenzophyllia, Physogyra,* and *Plerogyra* are commonly available in the aquarium trade, despite being somewhat uncommon in nature. Other nonreefal Pacific genera that may be found at moderate to very deep levels include *Conocyathus, Deltocyathus, Desmophyllum, Holcotrochus, Oryzotrochus, Paracyathus, Platytrochus,* and *Premocyathus.* Other genera are from very deep water (Veron, 1986).

Atlantic Genera: *Eusmilia* is the common Atlantic genus, with *Caryophyllia, Coenocyathus, Phacelocyathus, Rhizosmilia,* and *Thalamophyllia* being less common. There are many other genera from nontropical regions or ahermatypic tropicals from areas of highly reduced lighting or great depths—many of which may also be entirely aposymbiotic.

Thus this diverse family is composed of hermatypic, ahermatypic, symbiotic, and aposymbiotic tropical and temperate (unlisted) genera and species.

GENUS *Catalaphyllia* Wells, 1971

(cat-al'-ah-fill'-ee-ah)

Common Species: *C. jardinei.*

Common Names: elegance coral, elegant coral, wonder coral.

Identification: These beautiful corals have a skeleton that is almost identical to the flabello-meandroid species of *Euphyllia.* However, they have a cone-shaped base that helps them bury into soft bottoms where they are found in nature. The living polyp is determinant and is conspicuously different from any other coral. Polyps are extended during the day, exposing their vast oral disc

Catalaphyllia jardinei (elegance coral): captive colony warring with neighbors.

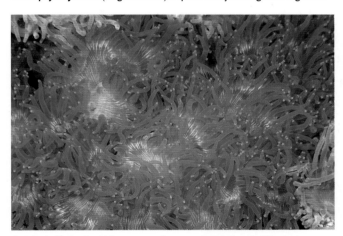

Catalaphyllia jardinei (elegance coral): group of pink-tipped wild colonies.

Proper placement of ***C. jardinei*** in sand and sea grass at Waikiki Aquarium.

Unidentified coral, possibly a highly unusual black morph of *Cataláphyllia jardinei*, recently photographed by Scott Michael while diving in Lembeh Strait, Sulawesi.

to the light. The tissue is almost fully retractable, but usually remains partially expanded at night. They are so distinctive that further descriptive identification is unnecessary. Their skeleton becomes more meandroid as it grows.

Natural Location: *Cataláphyllia* bury their base in soft substrate, and their hugely inflated polyps and tentacles wave on the bottom, making them all but indistinguishable from an anemone. Like *Trachyphyllia*, *Cataláphyllia* are often temporarily attached to substrate while young, but break away to become free-living when mature. *Cataláphyllia* are common in lagoonal areas with soft or muddy bottoms (though they may be found in other areas), and in inter-reef areas where they commonly share space with fungiids, seagrasses, and other lagoonal flora and fauna.

Colors: The colors of *Cataláphyllia* are nothing short of extraordinary. Their fluorescent qualities under actinic light are breathtaking. Bright fluorescent green with contrasting cream tentacles is a common variation. Brown examples are also common. More rarely, very desirable lime green specimens with blue-, orange-, or purple-tipped tentacles may be found. Contrasting colored tips on the tentacles are common; the species may have branched or bulb-shaped tips, as well.

Captive Care: *Cataláphyllia* are regularly offered at aquarium stores. They prefer a gentle current that does not lift them out of the substrate. Specimens are best placed on soft bottoms, since the dramatic tissue expansion can cause abrasion to the polyp if placed among live rock. Such abrasion can lead to recession or brown jelly infections. These corals can occasionally "bail out" of their skeletons, and may do so in response to poor water parameters or sudden changes in lighting and water quality. This is not a normal form of reproduction, but seems to be an escape reaction. The polyp will fortunately begin to calcify again, if conditions are appropriate. Small buds, similar to those of *Euphyllia*, are commonly produced in captive specimens with surprising regularity. They seem to possess a willingness to "swap" zooxanthellae in response to changed lighting, leading to the presumption of maladjustment, disease, or impending death. Remaining contracted, sometimes for months, they may suddenly "snap out of it" and again expand normally with subtle to dramatic color differences. They are sensitive to the presence of many soft corals, and may even be adversely affected by *Caulerpa* algae. They succumb to infection easily, are prone to bristleworm irritation, can be easily punctured or torn when inflated, may recede in aquariums with significant filamentous algae growth, and may require dietary supplementation to maintain long-term health. In short, they are quite frequently problematic.

Many years ago, *Catalaphyllia* were among the easiest corals to maintain, but the majority today are not surviving. They adopt an abnormal appearance, with an initially swollen polyp body and shriveled tentacles. Eventually, the polyp shrinks tight against the skeleton and succumbs by recession or opportunistic invasion. No environmental or treatment protocol seems to help. I cannot help but feel that collection, shipping, and transitional care has played a significant role in the number of injured or sick examples, and contributes to these recent failures.

Special Information: *Catalaphyllia* are willing feeders, and occasional feedings are encouraged. The strong nematocysts present in their many tentacles have the potential to ensnare small fishes, and they are certainly capable of raising welts on hobbyists' forearms and hands. In fact, the degree these corals can expand, coupled with their strong stinging cells, make any nearby coral susceptible to severe damage. Despite the formidable tentacles of *Catalaphyllia*, when near *Euphyllia ancora*, the latter is the dominant species. Even more surprising, I once witnessed damage to a *Catalaphyllia* after a specimen of *Pachyseris* (a virtually nonpolyped stony coral) fell on top of it with no collateral damage to the *Pachyseris*. The aggressive hierarchies in the corals are remarkable (and not always intuitive).

Certain clownfishes may adopt *Catalaphyllia* as a surrogate anemone. This may be detrimental to the coral: they are often rendered incapable of full expansion, become irritated, and may perish.

Collection Impact: *Catalaphyllia* is a solitary coral that must be taken in its entirety for collection. It is heavily collected and there are concerns that it may be subjected to local overharvesting.

GENUS *Euphyllia* Dana, 1846
(yoo-fill'-ee-ah)

Common Species and Common Names:
- *E. ancora:* hammer coral, anchor coral.
- *E. cristata:* grape coral.
- *E. divisa:* frogspawn coral, octopus coral.
- *E. glabrescens:* torch coral, branching hammer or branching anchor coral, pom-pom coral.
- *E. paradivisa:* branching frogspawn coral.
- *E. parancora:* branching hammer coral or branching anchor coral.

Identification: A unique feature of *Euphyllia* is that the identification of species is based to a large degree on the shape of the polyp and is not exclusively dependent on the skeleton. The colonies are often large and flabelloid, phaceloid, or meandro-phaceloid, depending on the species. The corallite walls are distinct, forming the outer edges of the colonies. Septa are very prominent, especially noticeable since the polyps of the species are completely retractable. The polyps are long and flowing and usually extend fully during the day and partially at night.

Euphyllia ancora is distinguished by having a solid flabello-meandroid skeleton with T-shaped or anchor-shaped tentacle tips. *Euphyllia parancora* is a phaceloid branching colony with T-shaped or anchor-shaped polyp tips extending from the ends of each branch. *Euphyllia divisa* has a slightly more solid skeleton than *E. ancora*, but is nearly identical in shape and form. Its polyps, however, are branched at the ends and have masses of round tips. This lends an appearance indicative of its common name, Frogspawn. *Euphyllia paradivisa* has a phaceloid branching skeleton with polyps similar to *E. divisa*. *Euphyllia glabrescens* has a phaceloid branching skeleton with polyps that have a single rounded tip and compact corallites, with inward projecting septa that do not extend much above the corallite wall. *Euphyllia cristata* and *E. yayamaensis* also have single round-tipped polyps and a phaceloid skeleton, but their corallites are more opened, and their larger septa project outward and above the walls.

Natural Location: As may be apparent from the multitude of common names for this genus, *Euphyllia* represent a significantly large fraction of aquarium imports. These corals are very common in the hobby, yet are surprisingly less than common in nature. None are considered to be hermatypic, though all are symbiotic. They occur in somewhat diverse habitats, but are most common on reef slopes in large colonies often clustered together on the same reef. *Euphyllia* are often found in deeper waters than many other species available within the hobby.

Colors: Most *Euphyllia* are pale brown or green, with a translucent quality to the tentacles. Pinkish brown to pink is relatively com-

Euphyllia ancora (hammer coral): note anchor or hammerlike polyp shape.

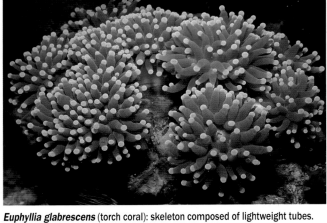

Euphyllia glabrescens (torch coral): skeleton composed of lightweight tubes.

Euphyllia cristata (grape coral): note crowded branches of phaceloid skeleton.

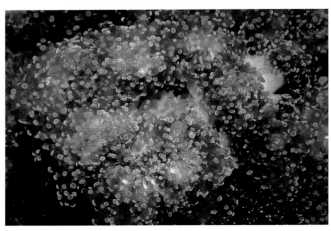

Euphyllia paradivisa (branching frogspawn coral): colors vary within species.

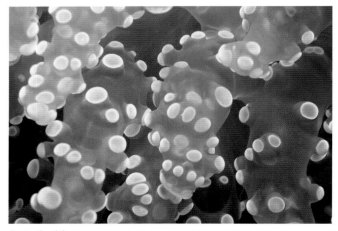

Euphyllia divisa (frogspawn coral): sensitive indicators of water quality.

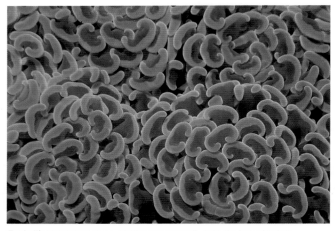

Euphyllia parancora (branching hammer coral): note clusters of polyps.

Euphyllia **sp.** (frogspawn coral): rare colony with clear tentacles. (Sulawesi)

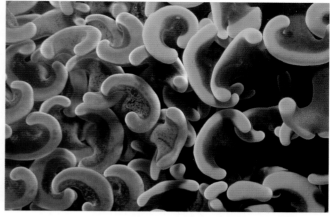

Euphyllia ancora (hammer coral): two color forms together on Indonesian reef.

Euphyllia parancora (branching hammer coral): note polyp rosettes.

Euphyllia divisa (frogspawn coral): can grow into large, spectacular colonies.

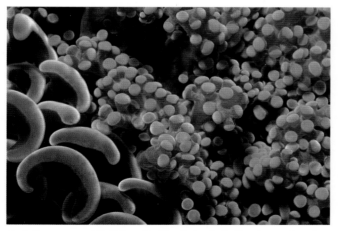

Euphyllia ancora and *E. divisa*: will aggressively attack other genera of corals.

Euphyllia paradivisa (branching frogspawn coral): polyps partially retracted.

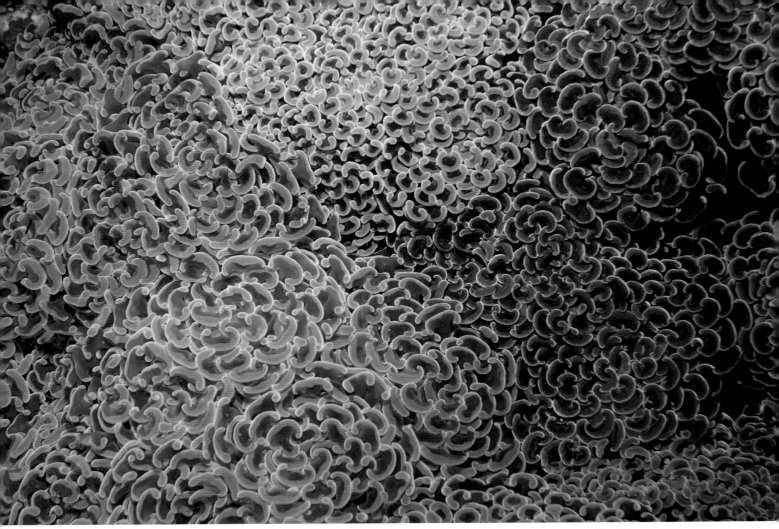

Euphyllia ancora (hammer coral) and *Euphyllia parancora* (branching hammer coral): observers worry that these corals may be overcollected in some areas.

mon. Fluorescent aqua and blue colonies are rare, but striking. Often, their tentacle tips may be of a contrasting shade to the tentacle "stems." This color trait is especially common in *E. ancora*.

Captive Care: In the aquarium, *Euphyllia* are good water-quality monitors. Though quite hardy, their failure to show good polyp expansion can indicate less-than-perfect water parameters. Colonies can tend to get brown jelly infections, and recession from the margins toward the center is also common. They seem unusually sensitive to extensive collections or large specimens of certain soft corals, notably certain *Sinularia* species. Budding via small groups of polyps with tiny calcified skeletons is common in captivity especially with *E. divisa, E. paradivisa,* and *E. glabrescens.* Like *Caulastrea,* the death of any individual branch of any of the phaceloid *Euphyllia* species does not affect the colony

as a whole. They prefer somewhat turbid locations in nature and will thrive with bright indirect light and a gentle current. Exceptionally strong water movement induces the formation of sweeper tentacles and should be avoided. Such forceful currents also prevent good tissue expansion, though constant gentle currents seem to enhance calcification rates dramatically. *Euphyllia* seem widely tolerant of lighting intensities but, strangely, seem to expand best in areas of the tank where the multiple parameters of water flow, lighting, and perhaps passing food sources are optimal. Some degree of trial and error in placement may be needed to determine their ideal location. All species accept food willingly, and their green, brown, or pinkish green tentacles quickly snatch passing food. It is quite astounding to watch fairly large food items slowly disappear into the mass of waving tentacles.

Special Information: The formation of long and very powerful sweeper tentacles is a daily occurrence with most *Euphyllia* species. The sting of *E. ancora*'s sweeper tentacles can actually be painful, and very few corals survive an aggressive attack by members of this genus. It has been reported on several occasions that sweeper tentacle tips of *E. ancora* may sometimes stick to substrate and break off, where they can then form new colonies. If this is true, it would be a totally novel and hither to undocumented form of asexual reproduction in the cnidarians and should be carefully verified. Furthermore, sometimes these tips are readily broken off in currents, having been completely pinched off by the animal prior to release. This does not seem to occur in stressed or weak corals, and it may be either an unreported form of asexual reproduction or a generalized defense mechanism. Tentacle tips with swollen acrospheres are more likely to become detached, and the drifting tips, completely sealed like neutrally buoyant water balloons, stick onto virtually any surface they encounter, often creating substantial damage to other sessile life, especially other corals.

Collection Impact: Unfortunately, questions arise about the wild harvest of *Euphyllia*. Their beauty and success in captivity is alluring, yet they are not reported as common in the wild, and the means of collection involves hammering or chiseling free pieces of larger colonies. Some sources report that regeneration occurs within two or three years, but there are concerns that imports of *Euphyllia* represent a disproportionately large number of corals collected for the aquarium trade. Again, it is important to remember that while the aquarium hobby as a whole is not responsible for significant degradation of natural reefs, we must understand our role as leaders and stewards of the reef, rather than merely takers.

GENUS *Nemenzophyllia* Hodgson and Ross, 1981
(neh-men'-zoh-fill'-ee-ah)

Common Species: *N. turbida*.

Common Names: fox coral, jasmine coral, ridge coral.

Identification: *Nemenzophyllia turbida* has appeared regularly as a species for sale within the aquarium trade for many years. Curiously, it is listed as uncommon by many references, and, until recently, it had not been observed in nature by some taxonomists. There is but one known species in this genus, and there was some question as to its taxonomic validity (Veron, pers. comm.). Obviously, this was an oversight, because there is no mistaking *Nemenzophyllia*. Its skeleton is flabello-meandroid and wafer thin. The walls are finely corrugated by costae on the outside, corresponding to the positions of the septa on the interior. A columella exists that extends continuously and is fused along the length of the valley centers. The interior is perforated by even and regular septa that all meet in the center. The result is the formation of small rectangular boxes within the skeleton. Polyps expand almost as dramatically as *Catalaphyllia*, especially considering the thin skeleton from which they originate—there seems to be no conceivable way that the graceful undulated polyps folded delicately outward could possibly come from such a skeleton. Thin striations in the tissue radiate outward to a puffed, ruffled edge.

Natural Location: *Nemenzophyllia turbida* is reported to be found under overhangs and in turbid water. However, scientific reports of general location and abundance of this coral are scarce. The original description of the species alluded to its presence in moderately deep water.

Colors: The polyps of *N. turbida* are generally cream to light green, occasionally turning brown with stronger light. Slight vari-

Nemenzophyllia turbida (fox coral): does best with moderate, indirect lighting.

Nemenzophyllia turbida (fox coral): green morphs are especially prized.

Physogyra lichtensteini (pearl coral): like *Plerogyra*, but with smaller vesicles.

Physogyra lichtensteini (pearl coral): most common member of this genus.

ations of shading may occur within an individual, though uniformity is the rule.

Captive Care: *Nemenzophyllia turbida* is a hardy coral that expands and calcifies best in dim to moderate indirect lighting in the presence of low currents. It tends to grow slowly, becoming more sinuous as it adds new skeletal material. Since this species has not been seen to produce feeding tentacles, is reported from turbid water, and is not subjected to intense light in nature, it probably obtains much nutrition by absorption from the surrounding water. Consequently, specimens are possibly better suited to aquariums without aggressive skimming or other highly efficient filtration. As with others in this family, brown jelly infections are possible, though reportedly less common than once thought. Occasionally, parts of the polyps may recede along the length of the skeleton, but this apparently does not affect the rest of the colony adversely. It may be that the "boxes" created by the skeleton serve to isolate the rest of the colony from localized injury or disease. Very pretty corals that seem neither to sting nor be stung, these are wonderful corals in any aquarium.

Special Information: *Nemenzophyllia turbida* was first recorded as a distinct species from the Philippines in 1981 and was named after Dr. Francisco Nemenzo, a pioneering researcher of Philippine corals. The origin of its common name, fox coral, is a mystery.

Collection Impact: Because of the lack of established data regarding the natural population numbers and range of this coral, there are questions about the abundance and collection pressures on *N. turbida*. Still, it has appeared prolifically in aquarium stores for many years, indicating that substantial collection sites exist. Contrary to some older sources, it has a fairly high reported rate of captive success with current reef-keeping methods.

GENUS *Physogyra* Quelch, 1884
(fie'-soh-jie'-rah)

Common Species: *P. lichtensteini.*

Common Names: pearl coral, grape coral, small bubble coral.

Identification: Closely related to *Plerogyra*, especially in its outward appearance, is the genus *Physogyra,* which displays smaller, more numerous bubbles that are also more retractable. The skeleton is meandroid and usually quite large. Valleys are widely separated, although their expanded polyp vesicles completely obscure the skeleton in living examples. The main skeletal difference is that the meanders of *Physogyra* are fused in a common corallite wall rather than having unbound lateral edges.

Natural Location: On the reef, they are found in the same type of protected and shaded areas favored by *Plerogyra,* although *Physogyra* may be more commonly found in shallower, higher-light environments in protected turbid water. *Physogyra* also tend to grow horizontally, in contrast to the vertical orientation of *Plerogyra.*

Colors: *Physogyra* are very similar to *Plerogyra* in color, although colonies that are not the typical ivory or cream color tend toward a greenish cast more frequently than toward the brownish cast of *Plerogyra.*

Captive Care: Strong light is not required to maintain these corals. Currents should be low. Like *Plerogyra,* these corals can form sweeper tentacles, are voracious feeders, and have a powerful sting. They have similar budding capabilities and are prone to the same brown jelly infections as their larger-vesicled relatives. Care should be taken when handling both *Plerogyra* and *Physogyra* to keep the delicate tissue that clings to the side of the skeleton from being damaged.

Special Information: Once an aquarium rarity, *Physogyra* is now

Physogyra lichtensteini (pearl coral): beautiful green specimen. (Indonesia)

Plerogyra sinuosa (bubble coral): delicately beautiful, but surprisingly tough.

much more frequently imported. Small pieces can grow into impressive colonies once established in a reef tank.

Collection Impact: As with *Plerogyra,* collection may involve breakage from large mother colonies. These should heal under good conditions, but the impact of ongoing heavy collection activities is of concern.

GENUS *Plerogyra* Milne-Edwards and Haime, 1848
(plee'-roh-jie'-rah)

Common Species: *P. sinuosa.*

Common Names: bubble coral, octobubble coral, bladder coral, grape coral, pearl coral.

Identification: These remarkable looking corals are quite uncommon in nature, yet they are one of the most commonly available species in the aquarium hobby. They form flat to round colonies with corallites raised on short, thick stalks. *Plerogyra* hardly need to be described by their phaceloid or flabello-meandroid skeleton with large, wide, prominent septa that extend well above the corallite walls. Rather, they can be immediately identified by their unique round, bubble-shaped polyp extensions. These vesicles are possibly modified tentacles, but are also zooxanthellate sacs—photosynthetic modulators capable of increasing light-exposed tissue by over 500%. They are hydrostatically inflated through a tube in the gastrovascular cavity of the polyp, with expanded vesicles having tissue as thin as the diameter of one zooxanthella. Expanded only during the day, the bubbles retract almost completely at night, when the tapered feeding tentacles emerge. Occasionally, these tentacles may appear from under the vesicles during the day. A common morph of this coral is known as Octobubble, having vesicles with curved, tapered fingers that project outward from each bubble. It is not known whether this version

is a subspecies or a distinct *Plerogyra* species. Its taxonomic status is currently synonymous with its oval-bubbled brethren, although Schumacher (pers. comm.) asserts that it is genus *Fusigyra.*

Natural Location: Occurring in nature in protected caves or under overhangs, these corals are usually in a vertical orientation under subdued light or even near-total shade. They may also be found occasionally in more highly lit shallower areas horizontally attached in turbid waters sometimes only 1 m (3 ft.) deep.

Colors: Ranging in color from ivory to cream to green, *Plerogyra* are often found with translucent streaks lending a striated appearance to the more opaque expanded bubbles.

Plerogyra sp. (bubble coral): nighttime appearance with bubbles deflated.

Plerogyra sinuosa (bubble coral): bubbles can sting if contacted.

Plerogyra sinuosa (bubble coral): naturally adapted to lower light situations.

Vir philippinensis (commensal shrimp): occurs exclusively with *Plerogyra*.

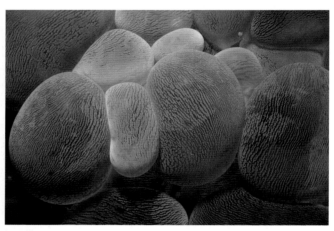

Plerogyra sinuosa (bubble coral): many color variations are seen.

Plerogyra simplex (bubble coral): phaceloid or torchlike species is less common.

Plerogyra simplex (bubble coral): feeding tentacles extended after dark.

Plerogyra sinuosa (bubble coral): two small colonies display color differences. Aquarium colonies can be long-lived and grow into show specimens if regularly fed.

Captive Care: Despite their common location in shady areas, *Plerogyra* do not seem to object to direct light at all. Nonetheless, low to moderate current is important in allowing the vesicles to expand fully. The bubble size naturally varies according to lighting intensity in order to maximize the exposure of the zooxanthellae. Larger vesicles will result from lower lighting conditions. The tentacles of *Plerogyra* are quite potent, and may form elongated sweeper tentacles that are more than capable of damaging almost any coral on contact. Feeding is eagerly welcomed by these large-polyped corals. They are remarkably durable aquarium additions that seem most likely to suffer from brown jelly infections. These infections are frequently brought about by a fall or mishandling that tears or punctures a bubble. *Plerogyra* are also susceptible to flatworm infestations, but the dark planaria are clearly visible on their surface and can be removed with a short freshwater dip. (See Chapter 11.) The living tissue of *Plerogyra* tends to grow out of its corallites and down the sides of the skeleton. This tissue frequently adheres to, and begins to encrust, nearby substrate. Occasionally, new skeletal material is formed in a type of budding.

Special Information: Shallow-water specimens can adapt to lower light conditions, but specimens adjusted to moderate lighting conditions can be shocked or killed if suddenly exposed to brighter light. Therefore, slow and careful acclimation and observation should be practiced. The pigment content of the animal varies dramatically, but the composition, size, and pigments of the photosynthetic apparatus remain constant. In other words, they do not photoadapt like most corals, seeming to use only their bubbles to modulate the light. In addition, *Plerogyra* seem to have a significantly higher density of zooxanthellae than most symbiotic corals studied.

Collection Impact: Reproduction by colony budding for both types of *Plerogyra* is fairly common in captivity. These corals are sometimes harvested by breakage from large colonies, despite the fact that small, whole colonies have a much better survival rate. *Plerogyra* are long-standing favorites in the aquarium trade, and may be subject to local overcollection.

FAMILY Dendrophylliidae Gray, 1847

Common Genera: *Balanophyllia, Cladopsammia, Dendrophyllia, Duncanopsammia, Heteropsammia, Tubastraea,* and *Turbinaria.*

Of the many species and genera in this family, only the Pacific genus *Turbinaria* is commonly considered a reef-building hermatypic genus. Along with the solitary coral *Heteropsammia* and the rather uncommon *Duncanopsammia*, it is one of the three genera in this family that have zooxanthellae.

Of the ahermatypic and aposymbiotic genera, *Tubastraea* is the only common import, and it occurs in both Atlantic and Pacific oceans as colonial forms. However, other common tropical genera are *Dendrophyllia, Cladopsammia,* and *Balanophyllia.* All three have both Atlantic and Pacific species, dwelling on reefs or in isolated nonreef areas. Other less-common genera present in one or both oceans and typically not associated with reefs include: *Psammoseris, Notophyllia, Thecopsammia, Endopsammia, Endopachys,* and *Leptopsammia* (Veron, 1986). Many of these genera form solitary or small groupings of isolated "cups" and single corallites that are quite similar in appearance at the gross level. Other genera and species of the Dendrophylliidae exist in nontropical regions as aposymbiotic, ahermatypic corals.

GENUS *Duncanopsammia* Wells, 1936

(dunk'-an-op-sam'-ee-ah)

Common Species: *D. axifuga.*

Common Name: whisker coral.

Identification: These green or blue-gray corals are deceptive. The dendroid skeleton possesses long tubular corallites that all face the top surface of the coral, and their polyps are extended day and night. Consequently, the long-bearded tentacles, often with contrasting tips, can obscure an otherwise distinctive skeleton. As such, these corals can somewhat resemble *Cataphyllia* when expanded. Even a cursory look at the skeleton will make the difference apparent. If noted carefully, the skeleton and extended tapered polyps look far more like fully expanded *Tubastraea micrantha*.

Natural Location: Generally small colonies are found in deep waters on soft and often muddy substrates or in shadowed locations in turbid shallows.

Colors: *Duncanopsammia* are normally green, blue-gray, or brownish.

Captive Care: These corals are reported to be very hardy and adaptive to almost all light conditions. Gentle currents typical of their deep-water or protected habitats allow for maximum expansion of the polyps. They are a rarity to find, but their uniqueness and reported hardiness would tend to make them excellent additions to an aquarium. Although they have zooxanthellae, feeding *Duncanopsammia* with pieces of fleshy marine foods is not only possible, but recommended for maximal growth. Reproduction occurs by budding from the lower edge of the corallites.

Special Information: Consisting of a single species, the genus *Duncanopsammia* is distributed in the waters of Australia, Papua New Guinea, and eastern Indonesia, and falls outside most current coral-collection areas.

Collection Impact: This is an uncommon genus not frequently encountered in nature or the aquarium trade. However, because it is available, its collection impact should be considered. Its reported survivability is very high, and its low collection numbers make it unlikely to affect natural populations to a significant degree despite its comparative rarity. Furthermore, it has a skeleton likely conducive to asexual fragmentation and captive breeding. Some effort has been made in this regard, mostly at local levels.

Duncanopsammia axifuga (whisker coral): a rarity with tubular corallites.

GENUS *Tubastraea* Lesson, 1829

(too'-bass-tree'-ah)

Common Species: *T. aurea, T. coccinea, T. diaphana, T. faulkneri, T. micrantha* (*T. micranthus, T. nigrescens*), and others.

Common Names:

T. faulkneri: orange cup coral or sun coral.

T. micrantha: black sun coral.

Identification: *Tubastraea* are possibly the most widely recognized corals in the world. Almost all coffee table books on coral reefs have a picture of these beautiful corals. They have a lightweight dendroid to submassive skeleton, with tubular corallites covered in bright orange tissue. The colonies tend to be about fist-sized, often forming large accumulations of small colonies. Their polyps are bright orange-yellow, and occasionally white. These corals have no zooxanthellae and are generally regarded as ahermatypic or non-reef-building; their polyps typically emerge at night when the plankton content of the reef is high. *Tubastraea micrantha* is a unique dendroid species with a markedly different coloration and skeletal pattern (see Colors, below).

Natural Location: *Tubastraea* are commonly found at the entrance to caves and under overhangs in nature where local nutrient levels are higher. However, many colonies can be found in diverse (sometimes surprising) locations—not always on reefs—and wherever high-nutrient or plankton populations exist. They may even be found in direct sunlight. *Tubastraea micrantha* colonies are found most often in areas of very strong water currents (up to 1 m/sec) at depths of 4-50 m (13-160 ft.), growing nearly 1 m (40 in.) tall among the company of normally present reef fauna and hermatypic corals, allowing them ready access to drifting zooplankton. Such currents tend to be laminar.

Colors: Most *Tubastraea* common to the aquarium trade have brilliant orange coenostea covering their "cups," and brilliant yellow or clear to white polyps. Yellow colonies from Fiji have become more common in recent years. *Tubastraea micrantha* has an olive green to brownish black coenosteum, with brownish cups and gray to greenish brown polyps. There is also a coral imported and sold as "black" *Tubastraea*. It shares a similar skeleton with the typical orange *Tubastraea* sp., but has greenish black to brownish black tissue sometimes mottled with orange to brownish orange splotches. It is probably *T. diaphana*.

Captive Care: Unable to rely on the benefits of photosynthesis, these corals *must* be fed in captivity. A responsible hobbyist who regularly feeds his/her *Tubastraea* polyps will probably soon be rewarded by rapid polyp budding, including the formation of detached polyps that start appearing throughout the aquarium. In nature, they capture fairly large planktonic organisms, so offering larger food sources—such as adult brine shrimp or

Tubastraea faulkneri (orange cup coral): aquarium hardy if properly fed.

Tubastraea diaphana: a relatively uncommon species with dark tissue.

***Tubastraea* sp.** (orange cup coral): several species share this common name.

Tubastraea aurea (golden cup coral): a more delicately colored relative of the common *T. faulkneri*. This genus demands heavy feeding and adequate water motion.

mysid shrimp—in the aquarium will be possible and perhaps preferred. Soaking food in a high-quality vitamin supplement before feeding seems to enhance the coral's reproduction. Well-fed polyps are often extended partially during the day, and they will adopt a "bloated" look that obscures the tubular corallites. Newly acquired colonies may need to be coaxed to feed by blowing food or brine shrimp juice across the closed cups for several nights in a row. Within days, they will extend as soon as the lights go off like a faithful pet waiting for dinner. If not regularly fed, *Tubastraea* will cease to open. Tissue recession begins on the coenosarc and rapidly spreads throughout the corallites. Starved corals show their cups clearly, with a thin veneer of orange tissue barely covering them. Algae overgrowth is also common.

Most aquarists place these corals under ledges or overhangs in an attempt to mimic their natural locale. Unfortunately, such placement often subjects them to areas of low current, contrary to the conditions they prefer in nature. The presence of light does not harm *Tubastraea*, and they may be kept in the open, exposed to full light. Adequate flow should be provided to keep the interstitial areas free of accumulated food and/or debris. Delbeek and Sprung (1994) note the occurrence of parasitic nudibranchs and predatory wentletrap snails on collected specimens, and colonies should be closely inspected for such tagalongs.

Tubastraea micrantha is not commonly available and has a notoriously poor record of survival—a fast current and large amounts of food are needed, but may still prove inadequate to ensure survival. With this, and with all species of *Tubastraea*, the required feedings must be done carefully so as not to overload the aquarium with nutrients and jeopardize water quality. These corals are best left to aquarists who have powerful protein skimmers or other means of efficient nutrient removal, including regular, substantial water changes. Even so, *Tubastraea* are fairly slow-growing corals, at about 4 cm/year (1.6 in./year) optimally.

Special Information: Although lacking zooxanthellae, the growth rate of *Tubastraea* in calcification studies is nothing short of amazing. It has been shown that, if provided with a good food source, these corals can calcify almost as fast as many hermatypic species. *Tubastraea micrantha* is known for having one of the densest skeletons of all corals, and may even be considered hermatypic by some because of its durability and persistence on reef formations where it exists. (It was previously known as *Dendrophyllia nigrescens*.) It has been found to be one of the only species that regularly resists the force of tropical cyclones and ty-phoons. *Tubastraea micrantha* is so tenacious and strong that it was one of the very few corals whose skeletons remained affixed following nuclear testings in the Pacific.

Tubastraea aurea, T. faulkneri, and probably other species have been shown to produce bioactive compounds similar to the soft corals. These corals were some of the first to have such substances isolated. One compound with anti-viral properties is called tubastrine. Other diterpenes are toxic to the larvae of other stony corals, inhibiting competition and settlement.

Collection Impact: *Tubastraea* are an excellent aquarium choice in terms of reef impact. Colonies are abundant in nature, and they commonly reproduce in captivity by asexual budding, but have also reproduced by the release of planula larvae. Their survival rate in captivity is less than it should be, simply because they are often not provided with adequate food. *Tubastraea micrantha* may also be a possible candidate for captive breeding.

Tubastraea micrantha (black sun coral): a poor prospect for most aquarists.

Tubastraea faulkneri (orange cup coral): will tolerate both shade and light.

Tubastraea coccinea (orange cup coral): common in some Caribbean locales.

Tubastraea micrantha (black sun coral): skeleton is exceptionally dense.

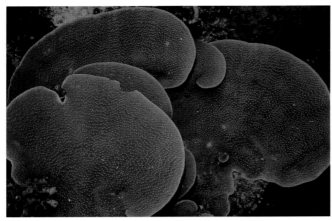

Turbinaria frondens (yellow cup coral): forms upright cups or flat fronds.

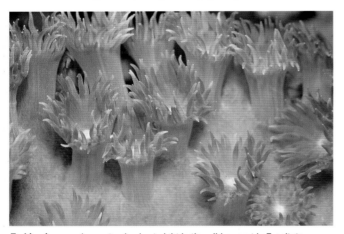

Turbinaria sp.: polyps extend only at night in the wild, except in *T. peltata*.

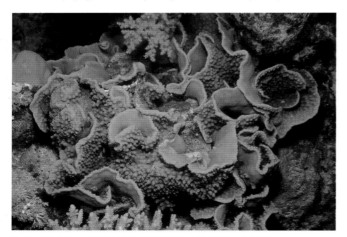

Turbinaria reniformis (scroll coral): flush free of detritus regularly.

GENUS *Turbinaria* Oken, 1815

(tur'-bin-air'-ee-ah)

Common Species and Names:

T. frondens: yellow cup coral.

T. mesenterina: pagoda coral.

T. patula: turban or cup coral.

T. peltata: turban or cup coral.

T. reniformis: scroll coral, vase coral, turban coral.

Identification: Consisting of many species with widely varied appearances and substantially environmentally induced growth patterns, *Turbinaria* are quite a handful to identify to the species level. The common names for this coral are often used to describe the shape of an individual colony, and may not provide an accurate or useful species identification.

Depending on the species, and the combination of depth, light, and water movement where they are found, *Turbinaria* can be massive, columnar, laminar, or foliaceous. Deep-water species tend to be flat, with mostly upward-facing polyps exposed to the light above them. These are commonly unifacial, having polyps only on one side of the plate.

Shallow-water species are more compact and upright, with polyps spaced across the colony. Colonies from areas of high water movement are usually twisted and convoluted. Colonies transplanted from one location to another type of location will alter their morphology greatly. All species have fairly porous and lightweight skeletons, this being more apparent in the thin, plate-like colonies. Although in nature only *T. peltata* extends its polyps during the day, many species may extend them day and/or night in captivity. The corallites of all *Turbinaria* species are fairly distinctive, being spaced apart from each other and separated by a coenosarc that is very membranous. These relatives of *Tubastraea* are the only hermatypic and symbiotic corals in the family.

Generalizations about shape are necessary, since even the corallites change according to their habitat. Polyps can often aid in identifications. Those of *T. reniformis* and *T. mesenterina* are like short tufts sprouting from the surface. *Turbinaria reniformis* has thin, unifacial plates and maintains widely spaced, small, almost flat, bumplike corallites with tiny polyps. The colors are yellowish or greenish brown, usually with bright yellow polyps and edges. This species is quite beautiful, especially when it forms graceful whorls or scrolls.

Turbinaria mesenterina is normally a shallow-water species comprised of folded and convoluted thin laminar plates, with corallites normally appearing on the sides of the plates facing the light. Deeper-water examples do not fold; they form plates or curved plates with unifacial polyps. The crowded corallites are substantially smaller than those of *T. reniformis* and are rarely

Turbinaria reniformis (scroll coral): note smooth surface, yellow margins.

Turbinaria peltata (turban coral): upright branching or columnar form.

Turbinaria peltata (turban coral): horizontal plating form.

Turbinaria reniformis (scroll coral): yellowish green color is typical for species.

Turbinaria peltata (turban coral): generally durable and long-lived in captivity.

Colangia immersa (lesser speckled cup coral): part of the Family Rhizangiidae, rather inconspicuous corals that sometimes hitchhike into the aquarium on live rock.

extended during the day. It is usually gray-green or gray-brown in color.

Turbinaria peltata and *T. patula* both have more fleshy, elongate polyps. *Turbinaria peltata* has generally fewer tubular corallites, and its calices are more uniform in the direction they face around the colony. It is usually gray or cream, and occasionally brownish. This species is the most likely to have its polyps greatly extended during the day, and they can somewhat resemble those of *Goniopora* sp.

Normally, *T. patula* is upright, convoluted, and gray in color, occasionally brownish or greenish. Its tubular corallites with somewhat tapering calices are long, and become upward-pointing toward the edges of a formation. It is not as common as *T.*

peltata. *Turbinaria frondens* is initially cup-shaped, though it matures into upright and often convoluted stands. Its corallites are tubular and tapering, with upward facing calices. The change of corallite, calice size, and shape, even within a single colony, is most similar to *T. patula*, though its calices are substantially smaller in diameter. It is usually brown or an olive greenish brown.

Natural Location: The locations of the various *Turbinaria* species are extremely varied. Growth patterns may provide the best clues (refer to Identification section, above).

Colors: Gray, brownish, gray-green, gray-brown, cream, yellowish or greenish brown, some with with bright yellow polyps and skeletal margins.

Captive Care: *Turbinaria* are highly variable in the care they require. Most species are quite hardy, although special attention should be focused on colony shape to suggest light and water-movement requirements. Most *Turbinaria* tolerate, even prefer, reduced light levels. Some are prolific mucus producers, especially *T. peltata* and *T. patula*, and they will shed mucus nets in response to the slightest touch. The regular production of this mucus is likely a method of trapping detritus or other nutritive material used by the corals. Though they appear delicate, most species are quite durable.

Highly convoluted and thin platelike specimens are among the most difficult to keep. For example, *T. reniformis* and *T. mesenterina* are notably harder to keep healthy, often eroding at the margins and showing chronic progressive tissue recession. They are susceptible to black-band and white-band disease as well. Cup-shaped specimens should be kept free of accumulations of detritus, which may settle in their folds and cause necrosis. (A regular flushing with a turkey baster or the output of a hand-held powerhead can prevent this problem.)

Fragmentation of colonies by simple breaking is possible as a means of asexual reproduction.

Special Information: This is a diverse group in terms of care and form. Some amount of observation and experimentation may be necessary to ensure their optimal placement and care in captivity. An excellent water-quality monitor, the polyps of *Turbinaria* can be used to gauge the overall health of the tank, with healthy polyps of certain species extending almost as far as those of some *Goniopora*.

Collection Impact: *Turbinaria* are great candidates for sustainable collection, as they are easily broken from colonies, leaving the mother colonies intact to heal and show complete regrowth. They are prolific in both number and type—normal collection for the aquarium trade should have an insignificant impact on most areas. They are successful in captivity, where they have reproduced sexually through the release of planula larvae. Fragmentation is possible, making captive propagation relatively simple.

FAMILY Rhizangiidae d'Orbigny, 1851

Pacific Genera: *Culicia, Oulangia,* and *Cladangia.*
Atlantic Genus: *Colangia.*
Atlantic and Pacific Genera: *Astrangia* and *Phyllangia.* (At least *Astrangia* also has temperate species.)

These are ahermatypic corals, many of which are also aposymbiotic. Small corallites are clustered in typically smallish colonies. They form cuplike clusters, often with deep pits leading to the oral opening. Colonies are normally encrusting, with rhizomelike stolons forming new buds from the base of parent polyps. In this way, they would seem to be the scleractinian equivalent of a stoloniferan or zoanthid colony. None are available in the aquarium trade, although many may be attached as incidental organisms on both Pacific and Atlantic aquacultured live rock.

FAMILY Flabellidae Bourne, 1905

This family consists of three genera of ahermatypic solitary corals from the Pacific: *Flabellum, Placotrochus,* and *Monomyces* (Veron, 1986). None of them are available to the aquarium trade, although it is conceivable that some species may be incidentally attached to live rock. The Atlantic genus is *Gardineria*, another solitary, aposymbiotic, ahermatypic cup-style coral that is found in caves and under rocks in both reef and nonreef areas. It is possible that this coral may also be found on some aquacultured live rock. There are many temperate species.

Phyllangia americana (hidden cup coral): sponges often surround corallites.

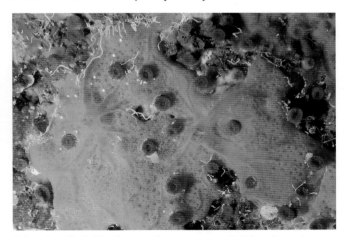

Astrangia solitaria (dwarf cup coral): may appear on Caribbean live rock.

CHAPTER 8

Husbandry

Captive Reef-keeping Approaches and Essentials

I started keeping reef aquariums in the late 1980s and was fortunate to get off on a good foot. I never had many of the problems that plague some newcomers, but I was—like everyone else—always looking for the latest gadgets and trying the newest products recommended by others. (At one point, I actually had 11 reef aquariums in my home.) For some reason, it took me years to step back and start thinking for myself, to use what I knew and what I had learned. I had trusted conventional wisdom and industry marketing rather than those things scholarly and experiential.

Over time, my aquariums became simpler and simpler. My current methods are so low-tech as to be outside the mainstream, but they prove that understanding the fundamental needs of the animals is more important than spending lavishly on equipment.

While it is possible to keep corals alive in a sterile, well-lit

> **"By the way, I know your path has been tried and so it might seem like the way to go.
> Me, I'd rather be found trying something new.
> And the bottom line in all this seems to say there's no right and no wrong way . . ."**
>
>
>
> *The Offspring, 1997*

laboratory-type setting, most people want their corals to be part of an appealing home reef aquarium display. The fundamentals of proper reef husbandry, the setup and maintenance of such systems, and other related topics have been thoroughly covered in a number of excellent references listed on page 326. This text will not attempt to describe the details of planning and creating a reef aquarium and will not advocate one approach over others. Indeed, there are few real "truths" in reef-aquarium methodology, and there is, in many cases, great flexibility in what works and what does not. There are certainly enough reef aquariums in existence now to demonstrate that corals can live, grow, and even reproduce under many types of care. What we do know is that captive corals absolutely require these six conditions:

1. unpolluted seawater (at the right temperature and salinity)
2. active water flow
3. light
4. food
5. bicarbonate
6. calcium.

Thriving 300-gallon reef aquarium designed by Wayne Shang of Fremont, California employs intense metal halide lighting, protein skimming, aggressive water circulation, and constant replenishment of calcium and bicarbonate.

One of the author's systems employing live rock, a deep sand bed, good light and circulation, heavy feeding of a plankton-substitute ration, and freshwater replacement with Kalkwasser (a saturated calcium hydroxide solution).

NATURAL METHODS

Over the relatively brief history of modern reef aquariums, various developments and methods have emerged to provide water conditions that suit the demands of many corals. In particular, great improvements in our ability to maintain nutrient-poor (oligotrophic) water have made possible the keeping of calcifying corals.

The first major step was the **Berlin method**, patterned after a methodology adopted by the Berlin Aquarium Society in the late 1970s and first popularized through the efforts of the Swiss aquarist and writer Peter Wilkens. The elements of this approach consist of an aquarium partially filled with live rock, strong lighting, and vigorous water movement. Foam fractionation, or protein skimming, is the only active filtration traditionally used in the Berlin method to supplement the natural functions of the live rock. Calcium-enriched water, often in the form of limewater, or what the Berliners call "Kalkwasser," (a saturated solution of calcium hydroxide or calcium oxide), is used to replace all evaporated water. Activated carbon is employed, either continuously or periodically, to remove dissolved organic matter from the water. The essence of the Berlin method forms the basis for a majority of reef aquariums kept today, and the details of its implementation are very well explained by other authors.

Another successful method of natural reef keeping, the **Jaubert method**, evolved from the systems developed by Dr. Jean Jaubert at the Musée Océanographique in Monaco during the 1980s. Filtration in these tanks is based almost entirely on arag-onite (calcium carbonate) reef sand and a limited amount of live rock. A thick layer of about 10 cm (4 in.) of mixed-grade sand is placed over a dead space of water at the bottom called a plenum. The plenum acts as an area of slightly higher oxygen content and is an area of flux, serving to create a concentration gradient through the substrate. This aspect theoretically helps prevent the formation of large areas of sulfate-reducing bacteria, which can produce potentially dangerous hydrogen sulfide in anaerobic conditions.

Thus the sand bed is designed to remain mostly hypoxic (having low oxygen conditions). Strong water movement, coupled with moderate use of live rock and intense lighting, are basic requirements of the methodology. Additionally, the true Jaubert method calls for the careful addition of planktonic and

A refugium tank with mangroves assembled by Julian Sprung showing the construction of a simple Jaubert-type plenum beneath a thick layer of substrate.

Lush 500-gallon reef aquarium created by New Yorker Gregory Schiemer illustrates the potential for captive coral growth that is now within reach of home aquarists.

meiofaunal organisms, which are allowed to proliferate long before the system is stocked with corals and fishes. The correct implementation thus demands patience, but allows for the advantages of increased denitrification within the sand community, along with greater biodiversity in the benthic (bottom) habitat. The Jaubert aquariums eventually gave rise to North American adaptations using sand beds (with or without plenums), live rock, and skimming in a type of hybrid Berlin system.

Algal turf scrubbers are yet another method of extracting nutrients from marine aquarium waters. First suggested and utilized by Dr. Walter Adey of the Smithsonian Institution in the early 1980s, algal turf scrubbing uses a brightly illuminated compartment where algal turfs can be segregated and cultured apart from the display aquarium. These turfs are very efficient consumers of the phosphorus and nitrate that reduce water quality and prevent successful growth of corals. Using various types of mechanisms or designs, algal turf scrubbers keep water from the display tank washing over the algae, which must be periodically harvested and removed from the system in order to accomplish the desired export of nutrients. Typically, the lights over the algal turf are operated during the period when the display tank lighting is off.

Today, aspects of these three "pure" methodologies are somewhat blurred and are frequently incorporated in various ways in contemporary reef aquarium systems. Rather than stamping one as "the best," I think it most important to recognize that the great advances in keeping reef organisms have come from better use of natural processes rather than new inventions.

In addition to live rock, sand beds, and algal turfs, other living "filters" being used by aquarists to remove nutrients from aquarium waters include sponges, macroalgae, seagrasses, mangroves, bivalves such as *Tridacna* clams, and even corals. All of these are now recognized as being able to uptake and assimilate considerable quantities of nutrients.

Concurrently, many aquarists are questioning the use of traditional filtration equipment such as skimmers, ozonizers, UV filters, and the like. Foam fractionators, in particular, have become so efficient that they can extract much of the particulate matter and plankton—already scarce in most aquariums—that can serve as an important food source for many corals. It is my belief, based on years of having used variations of all the methodologies listed above, that when such nutrient export mechanisms are used, they should be the least traumatic means available. The goal is to maintain nutrient-poor water without stripping the water column of all potential coral foods.

The whole subject of marine aquarium filtration is covered in depth by a number of other authors and is outside the scope of this book. Readers are urged to refer to such texts as *The Reef Aquarium, Vol. 1,* by J. Charles Delbeek and Julian Sprung (1994); *The Modern Coral Reef Aquarium, Vol. 1,* by Svein A. Fosså and Alf Jacob Nilsen (1996); and *Natural Reef Aquariums,* by John H. Tullock (1997).

A combination of HQI metal halide lamps and blue-actinic fluorescent lighting above a huge 35,000-liter (9,100 gallon) European home reef aquarium.

I especially like Tullock's appeal that we need "less technology, more biology," and feel that the natural approaches some reef keepers are now trying are much more appropriate than much of the electronic wizardry that has traditionally fascinated so many marine aquarists. Perhaps the lesson is not to seek the ultimate technological fix, but rather to concentrate on what is most likely to keep corals of all types healthy and prospering—even if it means using tactics that are as simple and biologically fundamental as possible.

However, there are two crucial requirements of captive corals that must be met mechanically in most home aquariums: lighting and water movement. Here we can thank advancing technology for making things much easier now than in the early days of reef keeping.

LIGHTING

Ultimately, almost every living thing on Earth needs light. Light is the energy source that causes primary production in the ocean, on land, and for life in general. The subject of lighting is obviously a very important topic for reef aquarists. Not only is it essential to maintain proper lighting for symbiotic corals, but all the other inhabitants of the aquarium depend upon it to some degree as well. The coralline algae, macroalgae, photosynthetic microorganisms, symbiotic sponges, and many invertebrates are all quite dependent on high-quality light. Nearly everyone eventually learns the importance of lighting to the reef hobby, but it is a source of considerable confusion to the newcomer.

It is also a major expense in the setup of a reef aquarium, and tends to become an area where many people try to cut costs. While shopping for a good price on lighting or engaging in a "do-it-yourself" project is admirable, not providing proper lighting to captive corals in the hopes that the light provided will turn out to be "adequate" is foolish. The loss of even two or three corals from improper light can easily negate any savings from using "cheap" lights. Light influences the growth patterns of corals, and inadequate lighting can easily prevent specimens from flourishing. Poor lighting conditions are a common cause of the decline and demise of captive corals, and the importance of light simply cannot be overstated.

Most coral specimens for the aquarium trade are collected from shallow waters. The majority of collection is done with a mask and fins, and scuba is often not even used. Therefore, corals from the protected lagoon and reef flat areas of leeward fringing reefs are the ones most likely to be offered in local stores. The sunlight impacting these shallow, tropical, protected areas can be very intense. In fact, on clear days the lighting is so powerful that it would be almost impossible to duplicate artificially. This is an important consideration when choosing lighting for the aquarium. Even though the multitude of pigments contained in the photosynthetic units of the zooxanthellae are very adept at converting various spectrums of light into usable energy for the corals, proper lighting is absolutely essential for their health.

Many reef keepers spend an extraordinary amount of time and discussion trying to determine a "best" light for their aquariums. Not only is light incredibly complex in its interactions in water, within the zooxanthellae, and in its effect on coral chemistry, biology, and physiology, but many aspects of these factors are as yet undetermined by science. To quote Dubinsky (1990), "Because of shadows cast by the calcium carbonate structure, reflection or back-scattering of light from the calcium carbonate of hermatypic corals or light focussing, and the occurrence of animal and algal pigments, it is extremely difficult to characterize, let alone generalize upon, the level of light to which zooxanthellae are exposed." He later adds, "Although there are many studies of various aspects of the effects of irradiance on corals, it is not possible to relate irradiance quantitatively to growth, or to the distributions of individual species." In short, we have much to learn about the photobiology of corals, especially under artificial light.

Direct sunlight is not available for most aquarists to use for their aquariums. Even if it were, the radiant energy of sunlight in a small closed system, without extensive cooling or infrared shielding apparatus, would tend to heat an aquarium like a tidepool, making it all but impossible to maintain a diversity of life. Sunlight through a window is not an effective solution either, and still poses many of the same negative attributes. Small amounts of sunlight in an aquarium are, however, attractive; this aesthetic function is feasible with proper consideration and management that prevents overheating, but most aquarists opt to keep their systems out of the reach of strong, direct sunlight. Artificial light sources, which are highly controllable, are almost universally employed for indoor home aquariums.

All aquarium bulbs have distinctive spectral characteristics, and the use of coatings, phosphors, glass, and other methods have allowed bulb manufacturers to deliver certain desirable spectra. A full-spectrum bulb should have relatively equal peaks of all the wavelengths of the visible light spectrum. Specialty bulbs have spectra corresponding to select wavelengths that maximally benefit certain organisms, at least in theory. Any marine aquarium bulb should at least provide strong spectral characteristics that correspond with the absorption peaks of chlorophyll a, the primary photosynthetic pigment of the zooxanthellae.

Taking the requirements for corals further, research indicates that photosynthesis, and hence the calcification rate in corals, is

Proliferating soft corals and an impressive shoal of anthias populate a section of the 35,000-liter home reef aquarium owned by Klaus Jansen of Germany.

enhanced by providing light primarily in the blue range, and secondarily in the white range (Kinzie, et al., 1984; Kinzie and Hunter, 1987; and others). Red and green spectra, despite being correlated with a shallower depth where one would expect to find many corals, do not have as pronounced a positive effect on coral growth. Red light has even induced bleaching. Thus, any lighting should optimally be concentrated in the blue and white light

QUALITIES OF LIGHT

Light is composed of infinitesimally small bundles of energy called photons. These photons behave like a wave, and give light characteristics that can be measured. Light can be measured by its spectrum, intensity, color temperature, and color rendition.

All the different wavelengths of light that correspond to certain colors together make up what is called the **spectrum**. The spectrum is measured by noting the relative strengths, or peaks, that a particular light displays when read by a spectrophotometer. Spectra are measured in terms of their wavelengths in units called nanometers (nm).

The **intensity** of light is a measurement of how much light energy, called photon flux, is available. Intensity can be measured in several ways. The first is a scientific measurement commonly read as microEinsteins per meter squared per second, or $\mu E/m^2/s$. This measurement is not too useful for those who are not scientists, so intensity is measured in terms of **irradiance**. Irradiance is the amount of light energy (photon flux) that strikes a given area over a period of time, and it is commonly described in units called **lumens**. The basic unit of measurement of the lumen is the **lux**, with one lux being the equivalent of 1 lumen per square meter. There are even more relevant measurements of light intensity known as **photosynthetically active radiation** (**PAR**) and **photosynthetically usable radiation** (**PUR**). These measurements, though fairly technical, are important since they correspond to the light that is potentially or actually usable by the zooxanthellae for photosynthesis, respectively. PAR is generally defined as the amount of radiation (quantum flux) between 400-700 nm wavelengths of light that zooxanthellae could potentially use in photosynthesis. PUR is the amount of radiation that, according to pigment concentration, water clarity, etc., is actually available to the zooxanthellae. Finally, there is **PSR**, or **photosynthetically stored radiation** which defines how much light is actually harvested and converted into chemical energy through photosynthesis. For what it is worth, PUR should most nearly equal PSR, the true radiation used by a photosynthesizing organism. The irradiance on the reef at the water surface averages over 75,000 lux, with intensity at midday without clouds exceeding 120,000 lux. At 5 m (15 ft.) of depth, the irradiance averages 20,000 lux. At 10 m (30 ft.), the value drops to an average of 10,000 lux. On the other hand, the light intensity that reaches corals is often substantially above the saturation rate for photosynthesis. *Acropora acuminata* collected from inshore reefs would be expected to be considered a very "high light" coral, yet the light saturation point for this coral occurs at 23,000 lux. Any irradiance beyond this level must be dealt with metabolically by the coral. *Montastraea annularis*, a "medium light" coral, has a light saturation value of only 5000-6000 lux. Most shallow-water stony corals saturate somewhere in the 20,000 to 30,000 lux range.

Light is also measured in terms of its **color temperature**. The units used to measure temperature are in degrees Kelvin (K). Sunlight has a color temperature of approximately 5500-6000 K. However, it is important to remember that the shorter

"Daylight" metal halide lighting (6500 K) over Michael Paletta's reef tank.

All-actinic fluorescent lighting on the same system shown at left.

wavelengths of red disappear a few feet underwater (discussed below). Therefore, the color temperature of light in water actually gets higher (hotter) as the depth gets greater.

Color rendition is a subjective measurement based on the perception of the human eye as to how accurately a light source renders the true color of an object. It is measured on a scale of 1-100, known as the color rendition index (CRI). An example of poor color rendition would be a dark blue light that makes a red object appear much less red than its actual color. The object, to the human eye, would not appear to be the same color at all. A crisp white light would have a much higher color rendition of the same object, making it appear very red. Color rendition is predominantly based on human perception, rather than being of photosynthetic importance. A CRI reading above 90 is thought to provide natural illumination approximating colors as displayed in sunlight.

Light on the reef is fairly complex. Within 5 m (15 ft.) of the surface in clear water, the spectrum of sunlight has been altered by the red and orange wavelengths that have been filtered out by the water. By 10 m (30 ft.), the yellow spectrum of light is gone. After 16 m (50 ft.), the greens disappear, leaving blue and violet to continue into the depths. Light of the wavelength 480 nm has the greatest depth penetration of all, with the light penetrating and creating a spectral light field in the open ocean near coral reefs of generally 440-490 nm, depending on water clarity. Ultraviolet light, once thought to be unable to penetrate deeply in water, is now known to penetrate very well to depths over 50 m (150 ft.). The greatest attenuation of light occurs within the first 3 m (10 ft.) below the surface, with 50% of light being attenuated at depths from 1-5 m (3-15 ft.), depending on water clarity and other factors (listed below). Corals typically thought of as "deep water" species rely on approximately 10-20% of the surface light levels, while most of the "shallow water" species receive approximately 50-60% of surface light levels. Corals with vertical positions on the reef receive only approximately 25% of the light that a horizontally positioned colony would receive at the same depth. Symbiotic corals remain common down to about the 1% PAR (photosynthetically active radiation) light level, though not all can adapt to such reduced light intensities and thrive.

Both the intensity and spectrum may be influenced by a variety of factors, from air quality, clouds, water surface conditions, water depth, and the optical density of the water, to the amount of plankton or particulate suspended matter and the relative orientation of the coral and substrate to the angle of light striking it. Plankton and algae, once decomposed, release yellow substances, called Gelbstoff, which also affect both the amount and quality of light passing through the water. This water yellowing, typically caused by refractory compounds such as organic acids, tends to be more pronounced in aquariums that do not employ activated carbon, foam fractionation devices, or other methods of organic uptake or decomposition. Upwelling light, or light that is reflected upward from particles in the water or from the sand bottom, may also be a significant source of light for corals. It is critical for corals that grow under other corals, and for illuminating the underside of coral colonies.

"Blue" metal halide lighting (20,000 K) gives an appearance favored by some.

Balanced lighting (6,500 K and 20,000 K halides; fluorescent actinics).

spectra. This is a bit of a misnomer, since white light theoretically encompasses all spectra of visible light. It may be more accurate to say that there should be a preponderance of blue-peaked spectra, with the remainder being made up of white, full-spectrum light devoid of sharp peaks or unbalanced spectral characteristics. While a mix of 50% blue and 50% white light has been generally promoted as a good mix of light spectra, I have found that mixes with from 60% to 75% blue light seem to give better results.

Fortunately, the numerous pigments in the zooxanthellae can make the most of the light provided in the aquarium. Still, the irradiance level is important. Irradiance can be measured in lumens, lux, PAR, PUR, and PSR. Because of the difficulty of measuring PAR, PUR, and PSR, these readings are not exceptionally relevant for most hobbyists (see "Qualities of Light," page 328). While they are conceptually and actually the most relevant measures of light to corals, they are not practically measured. This is especially true as lighting manufacturers do not publish these measurements, and access to such data entails following research and work by aquarium lighting experts (Joshi, 1998, 1999a, 1999b, et al.), field researchers, calculations, or specialized equipment.

Most lighting manufacturers do, however, publish the intensity of the bulbs measured in either **lumens** or **lux**. There are handy light measurement devices for aquariums, called lux meters, that do measure the intensity, in lux, of light sources. Lux meters, in my opinion, are very important tools that should be implemented by those keeping corals. Since light is so important to their success, there should be no reason why an aquarist is not informed as to the levels of lights to which he/she is exposing corals. If a lux meter cannot be borrowed, it is not extraordinarily expensive to purchase. If a lux meter is used for underwater measurements, care should be taken to silicone every area where water seepage could occur on the light collecting sensor. This includes the seams, screw holes, and cord connections.

There is a great deal of interest in debating relative merits of various bulb temperatures in degrees **Kelvin**. The "K" rating of a bulb has always been a hot topic. The higher the temperature rating in Kelvin, the more blue the bulb appears, and the greater the depth to which its color corresponds. Most lighting manufacturers provide very descriptive terms of color temperature with the bulbs they offer. It is best to provide corals with the proper spectrum of blue and white light, so bulbs with a correspondingly beneficial color temperature should be selected. As it stands, there are many unsupported opinions and claims of the superiority for some very unusual K values both from manufacturers and amateur proponents.

Sunlight is nearest to 5500-6000 K. It would seem that this would be the proper temperature for aquarium lighting. However, changes to sunlight occur dramatically as it passes through the air and water. The same holds true in aquariums, and the real answer as to which K rating is the best depends not only on the individual requirements of the coral species, but to the coral habitat as a whole. A bulb that provides ideal characteristics for a coral species may provide less than desirable characteristics for other photosynthetic animals and plants in the system, some of which the coral may be dependent upon. The interrelatedness of the community must be considered, as well as the individual needs of the species planned.

Metal halide lights above a reef aquarium: new bulbs, fixtures, and ballasts provide a constantly changing array of choices open to the marine aquarist.

A 4,500-liter (1,170-gallon) reef tank displays the realism of point-source illumination, which provides glitter lines that may benefit light-demanding corals.

Colorful stony corals dominate a 180-gallon (684-liter) reef created by Steve Tyree of Murrieta, California and lit with high-Kelvin (10,000-20,000 K) metal halide bulbs.

TYPES OF ARTIFICIAL LIGHTING

For all practical purposes, there are two types of lighting for aquariums containing corals: fluorescent and metal halide.

Fluorescent lighting is commonly available in three forms for the aquarium: normal output bulbs, very high output bulbs (VHO), and compact fluorescent bulbs. There are many different types of bulbs available to coral keepers, and no end of claims about which type, brand, or mix of different bulbs is superior. I think I have tried them all and can absolutely say that . . . I have tried them all. No further recommendation is possible, as most of them can be functional in the right circumstances.

Metal halide (HQI) lighting differs dramatically from fluorescent lighting. By comparison, it appears much more intense because it is a "point source" light. This means that all the irradiance of the light comes from a filament in a bulb rather than from the entire length of a tube. Consequently, it creates a very sharp crisp light that is not duplicated by any fluorescent fix-

ture. Metal halide bulbs also create strong **glitter lines** in the aquarium. These are caused by the point source light striking ripples on the surface. Ripples can act like moving lenses and magnify the light dramatically (up to 15x), creating very natural-looking patterns of rippling lines of shadow and brightness throughout the tank. These flashes are ubiquitous in nature, resulting from sunlight striking waves and ripples on the ocean surface. There is some research that suggests that the periodic amplification of light energy by the glitter lines is important in maintaining the health of light-demanding corals, as it serves to "punch" light deep into the coral tissue containing the zooxanthellae. The flashes typically amplify light energy by approximately 200% from 1-4 times per second for about 0.1 of that same second. Therefore, for up to one half of each second, corals receive greatly amplified light energy. Glitter lines certainly appear on the reefs, and even if there is no benefit to them, they are very natural and attractive looking in the aquarium.

Metal halide bulbs are commonly available to aquarists in several distinct temperatures: 5500 K, 6500 K, 10,000 K, 14,000 K, and 20,000 K. Early metal halide systems employed the 4200 or 5500 K bulb types, which produced a yellowish light that was generally offset for its poor color rendition by the use of actinic fluorescent supplements. To more closely approximate the color temperature of light directly under the water surface, 6500 K lamps soon replaced the 5500 K types as the bulbs of choice. Many aquarists prefer a whiter or bluer overall appearance, and the 10,000 K and 20,000 K bulbs are currently very popular with many coral keepers. The newest 14,000 K bulbs are intermediate in color between the 10,000 K and 20,000 K bulbs. There is no evidence to suggest that there is anything "magical" about this rating, though it is likely this bulb can be used quite successfully as well. As with the plethora of fluorescent bulbs available, metal halide choices are many and ever-changing, and it is impossible to make blanket recommendations about which are "best."

All metal halide bulbs emit substantial amounts of UV radiation, as do the VHO fluorescent bulbs. The use of a UV shield is recommended to prevent tissue damage to delicate organisms from excessive and potentially dangerous radiation—as well as to protect viewers if a bulb should explode. Normal levels of UV will not be likely to harm the corals. Care must be used in the selection of shielding material, because many materials, such as Plexiglas, do block UV light but may also substantially reduce the amount of beneficial light, despite their appearance of relative clarity. Riddle (1997) has suggested that type UG-4 Plexiglas is an effective shielding material.

As with any light source, the correct amount of light should be estimated for the tank size and depth, and in consideration of the requirements of the various types of corals. In the past, a general rule of thumb was to provide 3-5 watts of light per gallon. As with any such recommendation, there are problems with accepting this as absolute gospel. Not all light sources emit the same amount of irradiance, or PAR (photosynthetically active radiation), per watt, and the point source of metal halides penetrates deeper tanks much more effectively than fluorescent lights. Perhaps obviously to some, another reason that "watts per gallon" is a bad measurement is in terms of total irradiance. If a coral requires, say, 14,000 lux to reach its photosynthetic saturation level of light, it does not matter how many gallons of water it sits in—if a light source doesn't provide it, it doesn't provide it. This becomes especially true with the increase in the number of people keeping smaller reef tanks, or nanoreefs. Such small tanks still require large amounts of light if the aquarist plans on keeping light-demanding corals. Heat, obviously, will become an issue

in such small volumes of water receiving large amounts of irradiance. Therefore, success with corals depends greatly on the dimensions of the aquarium, the needs of the inhabitants within, and the types of lighting being used.

PUTTING LIGHT TO USE

It has been shown that, over time, the spectral integrity of light bulbs, both fluorescent and metal halide, tend to shift toward the red end of the spectrum. They also lose intensity over time. Despite the fact that the bulb appears to the human eye to be functioning well, the actual characteristics of the bulb may have changed dramatically. The length of time before replacement is usually given as the time when a bulb is functioning at 70% effectiveness or less. Based on this guideline, the maximum length of time that fluorescent bulbs will provide beneficial spectrums and intensities of light is 6 months, with many serious aquarists recommending replacement at 3 to 4 months. It has been shown that VHO bulbs may significantly shift their spectra even sooner than this. Therefore, all types of traditional fluorescent bulbs should be replaced at least twice a year, in my experience. There is some evidence that compact fluorescent bulbs may last substantially longer, perhaps a year or more. However, these data are not yet fully established or available, to my knowledge.

Metal halide bulbs may substantially change their intensity and spectra after approximately 1 year, and should be replaced after that time. Yearly changes have been a common practice in the past, though experience and some evidence seem to indicate that these bulbs can last significantly longer without being deleterious to the corals. It is important to consider that the use of bulbs of a higher color temperature may be warranted, since a shift toward the red end of the spectrum will still retain a comparatively acceptable color temperature, but may have less of an effect in stimulating problem algae. It is also important to keep lamps clean and free of dirt and salt spray, since even a thin buildup up of debris may dramatically decrease the amount of usable light that enters the aquarium. Similarly, all glass tops and shields should be maintained in an impeccably clean state to prevent loss of light transmission.

Another factor that may influence light transmission is the clarity of the water itself. Foam fractionation and granulated activated carbon (GAC) are two very effective means of maintaining water clarity. Finally, all high-intensity and high-wattage lighting systems should be fan-cooled to prolong the life of the bulbs, as well as to exhaust the heat produced by them. The heat from a single metal halide bulb alone can raise the aquarium water of a smallish system to unacceptable levels.

A combination of fluorescent and metal halide bulbs, with a total rating of more than 2,500 watts, lights Gregory Schiemer's splendid 500-gallon (1,900-liter) reef.

NATURAL VARIANCES IN THE LIGHT FIELD

Tropical sun is subjected to many factors over the course of an "average" day that serve to vary light intensity over the reef: passing clouds and storms, transient schools of fishes, plankton blooms, current changes, reef snow, and wave glitter.

Clouds and storms, for example, decrease irradiance, while simultaneously shifting light spectral qualities toward the blue end of the spectrum. A dramatic example of natural variances in sunlight can be demonstrated by placing a lux meter on the ground on a clear day. Even without visible clouds in the sky, atmospheric conditions, haze, and other factors create a never-ending pattern of "ups and downs" in the irradiance measured. Watching the meter on a partly cloudy day is even more fasci-

nating, as one can appreciate the different effects and durations of various cloud types on sunlight intensity. On coral reefs, because of their equatorial position, the sun is overhead fairly constantly in terms of duration and intensity. There is a period of approximately four hours from 11:00 a.m. to 3:00 p.m. when the sun's irradiance is particularly intense. The rate of irradiance falls off sharply, as do the spectral characteristics, before and after these hours.

The length of time in which lighting is "on" is termed the **photoperiod**. It is generally accepted that the photoperiod for the aquarium should be approximately 12 hours long, depending on the type of lighting used. By allowing the lights to remain on slightly longer, tanks with somewhat underilluminated conditions can provide (to a degree) a more normal "day" of photosynthesis. In the reef aquarium, it is common practice to stage a dusk and dawn simulation by having certain lights remain on for an hour or so before and after the complete set of lights are on. A typical example is using automatic timers to have fluorescent actinics that turn on at 8:00 a.m. and remain on until 8:00 p.m. Metal halide bulbs would then turn on at 9:00 a.m. and turn off at 7:00 p.m. This is a fairly accurate rendition of a reef, as well, since maximum photosynthesis in corals begins soon after sunrise and continues at a fairly consistent rate until about an hour before sunset. The recent availability of cloudcast dimming systems can now be used to automate this process beyond the common method of using automatic timers. These modules can be programmed to dim fluorescent and even metal halide bulbs to simulate dusk, dawn, thunderstorms, and passing cloud cover to create an extremely natural and beneficial lighting effect. Some of the devices even have computer-assisted programs to approximate meteorological conditions in certain reef areas of the world. In addition, they may be beneficial in reducing unnatural rates of photosynthesis, as discussed below.

The use of varying light intensities over the day has important implications. The consistently "clear" days over our aquariums is unnatural. Corals exposed to artificially intense and unrelenting light may begin to experience oxygen toxicity from the oversaturation of coral tissue with photosynthetic oxygen. In addition, corals that are exposed to sudden and dramatic increases in light can have their zooxanthellae produce more oxygen than can be consumed. These conditions can arise from the use of new bulbs, more powerful lights, the sudden use of ozone or large amounts of granular activated carbon (GAC), prolonged overly intense light, or sudden placement of species into new conditions without proper acclimation.

As discussed in Chapter 3, the production of enzymes such as superoxide dismutase and peroxidase may literally destroy coral tissue in an attempt to cope with the free oxygen radicals and peroxides endangering the corals. The enzymes secreted by the algae and the coral in an attempt to control these radicals can be overwhelmed, and light shock or oxygen toxicity is the result. Corals may then begin "bleaching," or expelling their zooxanthellae. It is strongly recommended that gentle acclimation of corals to new lighting systems be conducted, and that prolonged periods of very intense light be tempered with some "breaks" of intensity throughout the day.

Another consideration in lighting is the effect of moonlight. It is rarely totally dark on coral reefs, and the light produced by a full moon in clear tropical waters is substantial enough for divers to see fairly clearly even without supplemental lights. Still, the actual light irradiance of the moon is very low compared to sunlight, and its spectral qualities are blue or blue-white. The installation of low-wattage blue or white incandescent or actinic type bulbs may be a natural and aesthetically pleasant addition to lighting systems. It is also likely to be quite beneficial to the health of corals, if only in normalizing diurnal patterns. As mentioned in Chapter 5, mass coral spawnings in nature are triggered largely by the effects of moonlight and the time of year. If produced by manual dimming or through the use of a cloudcast dimming system, artificial moonlight may trigger spawning in captive corals, if other conditions are right. If nothing else, a small moon-simulating light lends a peaceful and pretty look to the reef aquarium at night.

In summary, artificial light loses intensity rapidly as it travels through water in even comparatively shallow tanks. There will be areas within a captive habitat that provide highly variant light intensity, based on shadows, reef growth, and reflections from the aquarium glass, the hood, and even the bulb itself. Understanding light, the needs of various species, and measuring the levels of light within the tank are infinitely more valuable to the individual aquarist than listening to claims for lights that promise miracles.

WATER MOVEMENT

Perhaps second only to lighting, in terms of importance to coral health, is water movement. Water movement profoundly affects both the function and structure of coral reefs. Several types of water movement have great effects on corals and coral reefs: currents, waves, surge, internal waves within the reef, tides, and thermoclines.

Currents are formed locally and regionally by prevailing winds and tides that result in large masses of moving water. They are predominantly unidirectional (laminar) over longer periods of time, and characterize water flow at depths below 15 m (50 ft.), although such currents can also be found in shallower waters. Major oceanic current patterns have dramatic effects on the distribution of coral reefs globally.

Waves affect coral growth mostly where the water becomes shallow, with the hydrodynamic energy creating great stresses that are important both in asexual fragmentation of corals and in controlling their growth forms. In deeper waters, the back and forth action of the water as waves pass overhead creates a rhythmic sway that not only causes very specific coral orientations, but also plays more obvious roles in selecting growth forms and nutrient/waste functions. While wave periodicity varies among locations and is dependent on the slope of the bottom in relation to sea level, waves average 3 to 5 seconds between crests. This type

System pumps on a 500-gallon reef include a 3/4 HP Hayward pool pump for circulation and 70 RLT Iwaki pump directed to a large protein skimmer.

A sump provides great flexibility in plumbing the components of a reef system, including pumps, heater/chiller, skimmer, calcium reactor, and other add-ons.

of water movement is known as oscillatory flow and is characteristic of water depths of 4.6-15 m (15-50 ft.).

Surge is the periodic rush of water created by waves as the mass of water rushes forward over and between physical objects. Clearly, the great and violent power of waves during storms and typhoons marks their pinnacle, at least in terms of their reef-shaping effects. Surge currents are common on reef crests and in shallower water, generally in depths of less than 4.6 m (15 ft.).

Finally, **internal waves** are created by moving water that careens off the structures of the reef itself.

Perhaps surprisingly, **tides** are the largest contributor to water-motion-induced changes to the reef. They are responsible for restoring salinity to rainfall or terrestrial freshwater-laden lagoons and flats, both exposing shallow water corals to air and resubmerging them, and creating sometimes rapid currents that cut deep grooves in the reef itself. Their effects on nutrient procurement and waste removal are self-evident.

Thermoclines are large mass water movements brought about by the movement of water layers of different temperatures. Nutrient-rich, cool water upwellings provide an important food source to corals in the wild.

Since corals are sessile animals, they depend on strong water movement to rid themselves of waste material. In addition, water flow can affect allelopathy and competition (removing toxins exuded by other corals), larval dispersal, predation, asexual fragmentation, and sedimentation. Proper water flow will also: increase efficiency and supply of plankton and particulate matter, increase metabolic gas exchange, increase the activities of antioxidant enzymes, increase availability of dissolved nutrients, and keep coral tissue free of debris, excess mucus, and algae.

Water motion seems to exert its influence over corals by changing the rate of exchange between the water and the coral tissue. In tests of high versus low water motion, more circulation resulted in potential increases of 60% in the rates of photosynthesis, respiration, and calcification, and a 25% increase in metabolism. Nighttime calcification is reduced in low water motion by up to 60% (Dennison and Barnes, 1988). It is likely that water movement, therefore, also plays a significant role in the oxygen and carbon limitation of coral colonies. Certain corals may even die if not exposed to sufficient water flow.

There is always a stagnant water area, called the coral surface microlayer, or CSM, immediately adjacent to coral skeletons. Such areas exist because of the hydrodynamics of water over the coral surface, but the thickness of the boundary is less with strong water movement. Thus, the transport of food, gas, and waste can occur more effectively when this layer is thinner, profoundly affecting growth rates. Corals with tightly packed polyps are somewhat less affected, but water flow is extremely important even in these corals.

In general, calcification rates are found to be significantly higher in more energetic water flow, though linear extension rates may be lower than in sheltered areas of reduced water flow. Areas of high water movement will also tend to favor hydrodynamically resistant, flattened, and compressed growth forms in corals. The shape of the corallites and the surface of the corallum is important in determining the type of flow conditions to which a coral is best adapted. Corals with smooth surfaces generally come from areas with lower flow rates, while those with irregular surfaces and raised corallites use their skeletal anomalies to "break" the normal turbulent water flow to which they are accustomed. Such adaptations maximize not only the transport of dissolved nutrients, but also the efficiency of prey capture.

Studies have shown that water movement contributes very significantly to the nutrient needs of many reefs in the wild. In fact, most natural reefs have what is termed "reef snow"—the drift of tiny, diverse particulate matter and plankton that is available to corals for food. Because most aquariums have a notoriously poor amount and diversity of plankton, water movement is even more important in providing corals with enough accessibility to the small amount of particulate matter that does exist.

Detritus, once thought of as a bane of aquarists, is an extremely important trophic food source. Proper water flow keeps detritus in circulation where it (and its attached algae, bacteria, and cyanobacteria) comprises an important energy source to feeding coral polyps. Areas of greater water flow provide even better access to these nutrients. The resulting higher growth rates and higher metabolic activity are largely due to this enhanced particulate availability. Increased water movement also allows for greater uptake of ammonium, phosphate, and other dissolved nutrients and aids in providing hydrostatic pressure to maintain the expansion of polyps. This may be absolutely critical in maintaining the turgor or fleshy expansion of some soft corals that have few supporting skeletal elements. Soft corals that are not exposed to sufficient water flow will often go limp or collapse; if left too long in such conditions they will shrink and eventually die.

Although good water flow has always been stressed for reef tanks, few aquarists have actually understood exactly what this really means. On a well-studied reef in Australia, 12,000 cubic meters of water flows over a 1 meter wide strip of reef during 24 hours (Ayukai, 1995). That's a lot of water flow. The Cabrillo Aquarium in Long Beach, California, has an intertidal surge tank populated by cold-water anemones. Every few seconds, a tremendous crash of water pounds directly down on these soft-bodied invertebrates. The amount of hydrodynamic energy is awesome, and the animals, incredibly, are thriving. Similarly, the reef environment, especially in shallow areas, can be a violently fluid place. Even at 15 m (50 ft.) of depth, the motion observed in polyps from currents and wave surge is dramatically greater than the flow present in most aquariums. The rhythmic back-and-forth movement is extremely pronounced, even in comparatively still water. Such oscillatory flow further reduces the thickness of the CSM, benefitting the health and growth of corals. Surging, or oscillatory turbulent water flow, prevents a steady-state boundary layer and allows the full colony to receive the benefits of the mixing water flow. Natural eddies are formed by the coral itself as water rushes across, around, and through a colony. There is an optimal flow rate and type of flow for every coral colony and, as with light, a colony can and does alter its morphology to maximize the beneficial aspects of water flow.

Sedimentation of detritus, sand, or other particulate matter in the tank can have serious consequences to corals. Stagnant water can lead to a 20-fold increase in bacterial populations, and the resultant hypersecretion of mucus can create pathogenic conditions or even suffocate the coral. Nonetheless, there are certain basic attributes and growth forms that predispose a species to a certain type of desirable water flow. Branched and stony corals tend to reject sediment easily. Flattened corals and soft corals, especially those with highly irregular or convoluted surfaces, can trap material easily. The anoxia that develops in such unwashed areas can lead to local tissue necrosis. Because of the action of microbes and other microorganisms, including sulfur-reducing bacteria that thrive in locally anoxic conditions, local necrosis can spread beyond the area of settling, potentially killing the entire coral. Good water flow, or at least periodic blasting of dead water areas, eliminates the likelihood of such depositions, as well as the problems associated with them. For the purposes of this book, and in relation to terminology developed by Sebens (1997), the following descriptives will be used:

Low flow	1-5 cm (0.5-2 in.)/sec.
Medium flow	6-20 cm (2.5-8 in.)/sec.
High flow	21-50 cm (8-20 in.)/sec.
Very high flow	>50 cm (>20 in.)/sec.

These rates can be compared to typical flow rates from various natural reef environments as detailed in the box on page 337.

Powerful, external Turbelle powerhead pumps controlled by a wavemaking timer provide essential circulation to a large European reef system.

MEASURING WATER FLOW

How does one know or measure the amount of water flow present in a given system? There are expensive devices made for measuring water flow called flow meters. Other methods of measuring water flow involve the construction of flumes and the injection of dyes. Neither of these are particularly convenient or necessary for use in aquariums, but given the importance of water flow to corals, having some idea of just how much flow is present in various areas and conditions is prudent.

Fortunately, there is a simple solution. Various rates of water flow within the tank can be estimated during feeding times when particles of food are present in the water column. What's necessary? A yardstick, some tape, a watch, and some food. The ruler can be placed at various points against the glass, and the length of time it takes an adult brine shrimp, say, to be carried a certain distance at various points in the tank will be a reasonable estimate of flow rates. (Fishes also tend to be less annoyed by humans feeding them while taping flat sticks to the outside of the tank than by having dyes or mechanical devices intrude upon their swimming areas.)

PROVIDING WATER MOVEMENT

In the aquarium, strong water flow is accomplished in several ways. Most common is the use of water pumps to direct return flow from a sump or filtering device into the tank. However, the **main pump** or system pump on most tanks housing corals typically does not provide adequate enough current to sustain a reef aquarium. (In many cases this pump is also feeding a skimmer and/or other devices, and may not be plumbed to maximize water flow.)

This one source of current is also only marginally effective as a method of creating a natural pattern of water movement, as the flow will tend to come only from a fixed point or two, and will be very laminar. Laminar, or linear, flow tends to be consistent and unidirectional. Although it is of some benefit in certain corals commonly exposed to constant current, it is an unnatural movement that many corals and tank inhabitants find irritating. It may even be destructive, depending on the flow rate. Some aquarists have used **spray bars** to diffuse the large flow of a water pump into many smaller flows. Despite their successful use in some applications, spray bars, especially in larger tanks, simply do not allow for enough mass movement of water. Rotating or oscillating nozzles (see below) that constantly shift the return of water to the tank show much more promise, but some models have high rates of mechanical failure.

Unfortunately, many of the pumps utilized for providing water motion are traumatic to plankton in the water column. While

WATER FLOW RATES IN CORAL REEF AREA HABITATS	
REEF AREA	**TYPICAL FLOW SPEED**
Reef crest, fast currents, wave surge	7-34 cm (3-13 in.)/sec. at times to 1 m (3 ft.)/sec.
Lagoon	1-16 cm (0.5-6 in.)/sec.
Deep fore-reef (deeper than 25 m [82 ft.])	5 cm (>2 in.)/sec.
Mid- to deep fore-reef	5-7 cm (2-3 in.)/sec. at times less
Shallow fore-reef	9-16 cm (3.5-6 in.)/sec.
(after Sebens, 1997; Sebens et al., 1998)	

certain in-hobby studies have shown plankton to be able to pass through standard magnetic impeller assemblies unharmed, others have been less positive. The data of Luckett et al. (1996), Small (1997, pers. comm.), and Adey (1998, pers. comm.) indicate a substantial loss of viable plankton, especially of certain types and sizes—notably fish and coral larvae and planulae. Bellows-type pumps, air-lift tubes, Archimedes screw pumps, and windshield wiper-type assemblies have all been used in various trials. These contraptions, while beneficial, unfortunately have notable drawbacks in cost, convenience, practicality, and/or availability. Perhaps most exciting is the potential use of disc-flow-style pumps, nontraumatic pumps already available in a wide range of industrial applications, which may be adapted or specially made for the aquarium industry in the future (Small, pers. comm., 1997).

Powerheads are small submersible water pumps that have generally lower flow rates than external water pumps. Multiple powerheads are frequently placed inside the tank, and are used to create various sources of water flow. While effective, these pumps also produce laminar or linear currents that can be damaging if not carefully positioned. It is best to aim powerheads so that the flow of water banks off glass walls and/or crashes into other powerhead currents to create a natural mass of water vortices and eddies. This type of chaotic, randomly shifting current is most effective at simulating natural conditions.

Admiring an exceptional German reef display is Kevin Gaines of Oceans, Reefs & Aquariums: corals can thrive in systems from the sophisticated to the very simple.

As with all electrical devices, substantial induced voltage may occur from magnetic impellers and submerged motor assemblies. The use of a commercially available grounding probe in all aquariums is highly recommended to eliminate any stray electrical charge that may cause disease, immune system dysfunction, stress—and potentially fatal shocks to the reef aquarists themselves!

The use of multiple powerheads may also tend to increase the temperature of the water column. Another common problem with powerheads is that many are attached to the inner walls of the aquarium with rubber suction cups. These cups tend to give out over time, and a fallen powerhead can easily end up blasting the tissue off nearby corals. Powerheads with attaching mounts that are affixed by hanging or clipping over the top edge of the aquarium are safer, though generally do not allow the flexibility of positioning afforded by the suction cup mounts.

The use of **wavemakers** has become a popular way to create natural currents. Wavemakers allow several powerheads to be plugged into them, and they oscillate electrical power on controllable timers so that a back and forth surge can be created that simulates the back and forth passage of waves. The units are quite functional, though the total amount of water flow in the tank at a given time is less than it would be without a wavemaker, as not all the powerheads are on at any one time. This can be compensated for by adjusting the size or number of powerheads to maintain a certain water flow (mass hydrodynamic flux). Many of the wavemakers currently available have timers that do not provide for the short duration of natural wave periodicity. As such, one bank of powerheads may remain on for a considerable length of time. Because of the short distance the flow has to travel in one direction before being dissipated on the side of the tank, these longer duration flows do not really replicate waves or create random currents. Rather, they merely simulate unidirectional currents in two alternating directions.

More recently, **powerhead oscillators** have appeared on the market. These devices rotate powerheads back and forth and so avoid the constant laminar flow created by static placement. They can be quite efficient at creating random flow in the tank, although they are, at present, somewhat expensive and failure-prone. Furthermore, the basic characteristic of strong, sometimes damaging, laminar flow inherent to normal powerhead output is still present. However, the overall effect on the currents occurring within the tank are much more random and beneficial.

The use of **dump buckets** is a highly efficient way of creating nonlaminar and natural flow in the aquarium. Water is pumped into a tiltable tray above the water surface. When the water in the tray reaches a certain level, the weight of the water causes the tray to tilt, and the water dumps into the tank. The effect is that of a standing wave, which causes coral polyps to wave back and forth very naturally. However, the total flow within the tank is not always ideal between dumps, and is contingent on the size of the tray, the strength of the pump, and the time between dumps. Furthermore, dump buckets are not convenient additions to most aquariums. They are not commonly available unless they are part of an algal turf scrubber filtration system or built as a do-it-yourself project. However, the hydrodynamic effects they cause are quite impressive, and they seem to have very healthy effects on corals.

Surge devices are similar to dump buckets, but are located above or beside the aquarium. Water is pumped into a reservoir, then released mechanically or by a siphon after reaching a certain level. The water then quickly empties out of the reservoir into the tank via a wide-diameter pipe or channel. The effect caused by surge devices is nothing short of dramatic. Billows of bubbles and a huge wash of water quickly enter the tank, giving the impression that a large wave has just passed over the reef. The water movement is random and quite strong, though not damaging. The drawbacks to surge devices include the inconvenience of their location, the noise of the siphon (which sounds like a toilet flush), large amounts of bubbles in the tank that may not be aesthetically pleasing for some, and the sudden increase in water level that comes with each surge. (The rise in water level may cause the tank to overflow if the volume of the surge is not given careful consideration.) There may also be some degree of difficulty in maintaining the constant siphon as flow rates change in the pipes and tubes over time. Finally, the salt creep resulting from spray as the mass of small bubbles breaks the surface may accumulate inside the lighting canopy, on the bulbs, on the exterior glass of the tank, the floor, the walls, etc. If the location permits, a surge tank is a terrific water movement device. If the tank is located on nice flooring in a formal living room, perhaps other methods would be best. I have designed a surge device that I believe minimizes at least some of the inconvenient aspects of traditional surge designs (Borneman, 1998c). The effects it has had on the health and growth of corals in my own tanks has been astonishing (see diagram and instructions, page 341). I have also discovered that if a strong powerhead is directed against an oncoming surge near the water surface, the water tends to roll over itself and create a visible eddy that looks almost exactly like a real wave passing overhead.

While each type of device available for creating water flow has its advantages and disadvantages, the fundamental importance of creating sufficient flow cannot be overstated. The nature of the currents is also very important. Realistically, most aquariums with proper water flow will have currents that are turbulent and variable, so that flow rates will vary greatly and will not be easily or accurately measurable. Having currents that are tumultuous and random will prove more important than the actual volume of water flow.

"Dead" or stagnant areas should be few or nonexistent in a healthy reef aquarium. Without adequate water flow, pockets of detritus can form in the live rock that may allow for the growth of problem algae. Such algae can encroach on living coral tissue, but its incidence is dramatically reduced with sufficient water movement. Some corals, such as *Euphyllia*, *Nemenzophyllia*, and *Cynarina* species, do not like very strong water movement. Other corals, such as *Pocillopora* species, prefer almost forceful currents. The requirements of individual species should be considered of primary importance. Experimentation with different placements and orientations of species within the aquarium, and with the devices used to create water movement, should be done to create beneficial water flow of various strengths throughout the tank. The installation of any—or all—of the devices used for creating natural currents and flow will help create a realistic looking and healthy aquarium that is ideal for coral growth.

"MYTHINFORMATION"

There is no "right" or "wrong" way to manage corals in an aquarium, except in fully admitting that Mother Nature does it right . . . and we often do it wrong. Still, while new technology will undoubtedly make things easier in the future, we do have an accumulation of some fairly successful guidelines for ensuring that our corals live and grow well over the long term.

The only wrong way to keep an aquarium is one that doesn't work, in which the health of the animals is quickly jeopardized or

A small Berlin-method reef aquarium in Europe: experience and an understanding of coral husbandry will serve the aquarist better than a large equipment budget.

compromised—or in which conditions decline over time. All aquarists should take it upon themselves to find the true nature of seemingly contradictory information and "mythinformation" (as Dr. Sanjay Joshi once phrased it) they may receive from various sources.

There are no "gurus"—holy possessors of sacred secrets— only those who seem to do it better. Without exception, these people have more knowledge than equipment, and I suspect that this is the reason for their success. Thankfully, most aquarists are more than happy to explain what they do. (Some of them are guilty of heartily endorsing theirs as *the* method of choice, but most do openly share their discoveries.)

For the newer aquarist who is confused by all the possibilities, it may help to recognize that relatively few people have the experience of keeping reef aquariums using several different methods. Fewer still are able to explain adequately *why* the system they use seems to work. Beware anyone who says that his or her system is "The Best." The most practical advice I can hope to offer, in regards to the massive overflow of information to which we are exposed, is simply to search out a method, through education and experience, that works for one's own style of aquarium keeping. The "experts" are many, but the truths are few. Biologist Rob Toonen offers the following view: "When we have stopped learning, we have stopped listening."

THE BORNEMAN FLUSH DEVICE

The importance of water flow to corals in a reef aquarium can hardly be overstated, and a number of devices have been created over the years to produce periodic surges of current in captive reef systems.

Several years ago, inspired by the ingenuity of the Carlson Surge Device (invented by Dr. Bruce Carlson, director of the Waikiki Aquarium), I began trying to develop a smaller, simpler mechanism for my own aquariums. I toyed with a number of designs, none of which seemed to function reliably or without filling the tank with bubbles. I was making little or no progress when, one day, a flash of inspiration appeared in the form of the everyday household noise of a manually forced surge "flush." A toilet!

All that is required to adapt an ordinary toilet flush mechanism into a nearly foolproof surge maker is a water container mounted above the water level of the display tank, some simple plumbing, and a pump. The device works automatically, with a float serving to lift the flapper valve when the water in the sump reaches a certain level, triggering a rush of water down into the aquarium.

An inexpensive powerhead is sufficient to run the unit, although faster surges will be possible with the use of a stronger pump. Noise is negligible, and as long as the siphon pipe is capable of flowing water out of the surge tank faster than it is being filled, any diameter pipe may be used. The design can easily be adapted to tanks large and small, and there is even a built-in overflow protector that prevents the surge tank from flooding.

The accompanying parts list and diagram show the basic approach to building this device. Everything should be readily available from local hardware or plumbing stores and aquarium shops. (A word of caution: assemble, test, and adjust this surger in a workshop or outdoors before mounting it on an aquarium filled with live organisms. Be sure to avoid overwhelming the aquarium with surges that are too voluminous or too frequent.)

This is an ideal project for do-it-yourselfers who may have been put off by the complexity of other surge devices. Many corals, even in small tanks, will respond positively to the new water motion created, and some hard-to-keep types may begin to thrive in the strong, chaotic currents.

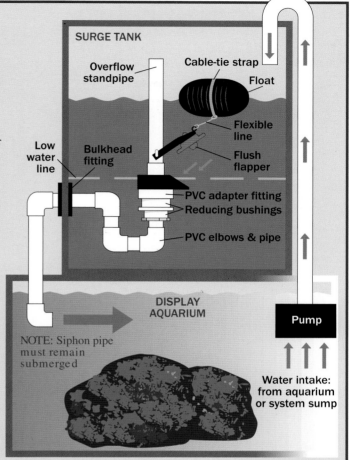

PARTS LIST

Surge tank: plastic or glass container drilled to accept a bulkhead fitting and to accommodate a standard toilet flush unit.

Toilet flush valve with 2" male pipe thread outlet, all plastic (Fluidmaster Flush Valve with Bullseye Flapper #507A).

Float: plastic toilet float ball or floats for boat rope.

Plastic cable ties and PVC primer and cement.

PVC adapter: 2" x 2" (female pipe thread x slip).

PVC reducing bushing: 2" x 1" (slip x slip). (Use additional reducing bushings if ½" or ¾" nozzle is desired.)

PVC pipe: diameter to match bushing; cut to length required.

90¡ PVC elbow: diameter to match pipe (slip x slip).

Water pump and clear water hose or PVC pipe.

CHAPTER 9

Water Chemistry

Parameters to Know and Maintain for Success with Corals

R eiki is the ancient Japanese art of healing based on simple touch. I recently took part in an introductory class to learn the methodology and basic techniques. In one memorable session, a fellow student told me she had seen some rather fiery visions of many of my past lives. I was still pondering her descriptions when she placed her hands on my face and head and told me I had finally escaped the fires of my past by being "born underwater."

> **"If there is magic on this planet, it is contained in water . . ."**
>
>
>
> Loren Eiseley,
> *The Immense Journey*, 1959

Born underwater. This part, at least, seemed to fit, considering my love for swimming, for having been around the ocean all my life, and for keeping an aquarium (or two or three) in every room. Past lives or not, I suspect that many of us who are involved in aquatic pursuits are innately drawn to water, for reasons that are not easily explained and that, in part, come from the mysteries that water holds.

Anyone determined to succeed in the husbandry of corals (and other marine organisms) has a real need to know some fundamentals of saltwater chemistry as well as the basic water conditions found on and around tropical coral reefs. No, we need not be

The model: waves break on a reef crest, creating powerful surges of clean, well-oxygenated water that are essential for the well-being of many corals.

chemists and we need not spend a great deal of time and money with test kits and monitoring equipment (although those who love chemistry invariably find reef aquarium water to be a fertile subject for testing, tracking, and experimentation). Knowing the basic requirements that must be met to keep corals alive and healthy is usually sufficient, and knowing how to maintain these parameters over time will help ensure the long-term success of any reef aquarium.

There are many kits, powders, vials, strips, meters, and even computers available to test aquarium water. Yet there is nothing that is a more-accurate reflection of water quality than the health of corals with their exquisitely sensitive polyps. With practice and observation, anyone keeping a reef tank will be able to judge overall water quality from the appearance of certain corals and their growth rates. Experienced reef keepers use test kits and meters, but they can often gauge, with reasonable accuracy, the chemical balance of their systems from the degree of polyp extension at a given time of day. Changes in colors, growth rates, skeleton shape in branching stony corals, and a host of other clues can signal just how well the aquarist is doing in keeping within the parameters of natural seawater.

In fact, corals are such good indicators of water quality that the presence of harmful chemicals and toxins, for which no simple tests are even available, can be ascertained merely by observing the corals. Of course, all of this requires an understanding of water quality and of the corals, a keen eye, and some years of day-to-day experience with these organisms. Even experts rely on test kits and equipment for regular checking of key measures, and newcomers should develop the habit of using good-quality water tests and monitoring equipment at least weekly.

The following factors should be followed and maintained within the given parameters or recommended levels:

AMMONIA

Ammonia (NH_3) is excreted by fishes and invertebrates and is produced in the breakdown of organic material by decomposers in the aquarium. It is highly toxic to most marine life and will damage or "burn" sensitive animal tissues, although most corals readily use it—in low concentrations—as a source of inorganic nitrogen for their zooxanthellae. (Most of the nitrogen present on coral reefs exists as ammonia, while most of the nitrogen in established aquariums exists as nitrate. Interestingly, nitrate, rather than ammonia, seems to be the preferred source of inorganic nitrogen in corals.) Low levels of ammonia are not immediately threatening to the health of corals, though the presence of ammonia when using a hobby-grade test kit usually indicates a problem with nitrification that may have other consequences.

Therefore, ammonia levels should remain effectively undetectable or near zero parts per million (ppm). It should be mentioned here that levels are never truly "zero," nor should they be. Extremely low levels of ammonia are present as a consequence of metabolic activities. "Zero" is used to describe a reading made by conventional, hobbyist-quality test kits, which do not provide for the accuracy of discriminating between zero and actual ammonia levels in a stable system. Pending unforeseen events, ammonia usually stays at a zero reading in stable tanks more than about 2 months old.

Levels up to about 20 μM (micromolar units; or 0.28 mg NH_3-N/L) of ammonia increase zooxanthellae growth, while 50 μM (0.7 mg NH_3-N/L) tend to show toxicity (Hoegh-Guldberg, 1994; Muller-Parker et al., 1994), but increases of zooxanthellae numbers may result in the symbionts overgrowing their coral host if such enrichment is continued over the long term. I make mention of this fact simply to illustrate what may be relatively safe or relatively unsafe levels in case of such events.

NITRITE

Nitrite (NO_2) is an intermediate product of nitrification, the conversion process of ammonia to nitrate. Nitrite is also toxic to marine life, although less so than ammonia. Nitrite is moderated largely by the bacteria *Nitrosomonas* spp., along with *Nitrosococcus mobilis* and *N. oceanus*. Corals will not utilize nitrite as a source of inorganic nitrogen. Nitrite is not immediately toxic to them, but its presence may indicate an instability in the aquarium itself that could be harmful. **Like ammonia, nitrite should remain effectively undetectable, or at "zero."** In a new aquarium, this is what is normally seen after live rock has cured and the tank has stabilized.

NITRATE

Nitrate is both the end product of nitrification (mediated at least partly by the bacteria *Nitrospira* spp.) and the starting product of denitrification, both processes being part of a complex and ideally balanced nitrogen cycle in the reef aquarium. Nitrate (NO_3) is not harmful in low amounts to most marine life, though its presence contributes to the growth of problem algae that readily assimilate it like fertilizer.

Despite the nitrogen-limited growth rate of most corals and their zooxanthellae, the presence of substantial and chronically elevated nitrate is not advisable and is highly unnatural. On coral reefs, nitrate levels are vanishingly low. **Nitrate levels in the aquarium should be well below 10 ppm (2.3 mg NO_3-N/L), preferably much lower or undetectable using conventional test kits.** Some aquarists believe that supplemental mechanical and chemical filtration devices, other than protein skimmers, are likely to cause higher nitrate levels in the tank. Many natural-method reef aquariums regularly have almost undetectable nitrate levels similar to ocean water, and such high-quality water is very desirable. Any excessive nitrate levels in natural systems (which already employ natural denitrification and nitrate uptake) are best managed through the use of water changes.

That said, at least some corals assimilate nitrate into both the polyp and the zooxanthellae by direct uptake from the water. The ability of corals to uptake nitrate seems to be related to the presence of nitrate reductase, an enzyme, in the coral and/or the zooxanthellae. It is present in both, although certain environmental conditions may stimulate its production, giving some corals a lag time in their ability to uptake substantial amounts of nitrate. Corals can be effective in reducing water nitrate levels to a degree that is, in many ways, equivalent to the use of other "denitrification" organisms within aquariums.

There seems to be a bit of confusion among those who have read about the results of nitrogen-enriched water on coral growth. Some studies have shown that nitrate enhancement has improved the growth of stony corals (Atkinson et al., 1995). While nitrogen is usually a limiting factor in the growth of both coral animal and zooxanthellae in the wild, the potential for

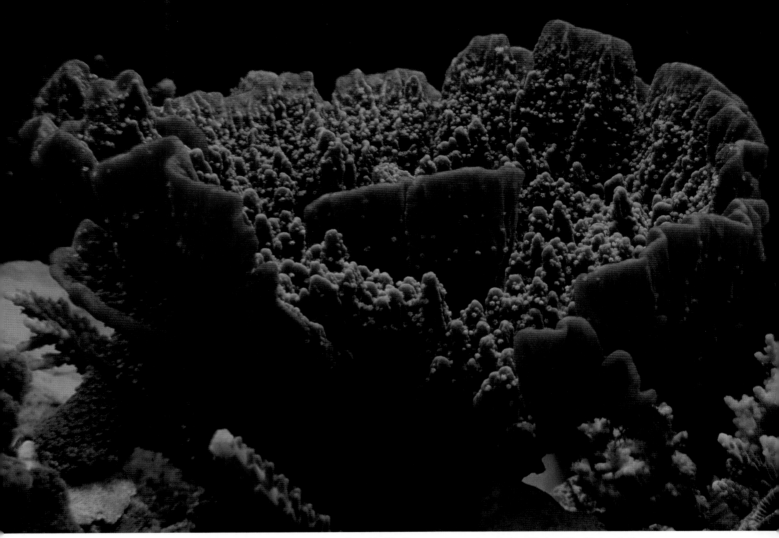

Excellent water parameters allow the keeping of exotic stony corals, such as this **Montipora sp.**, in a system designed by Leng Sy of Irvine, California.

misunderstanding this information is substantial. When the zooxanthellae have an enriched nitrogen environment, they do not translocate as much to the animal, and instead use it for their own growth. Nitrogen-enriched water, therefore, has an immediate effect of stimulating a larger zooxanthellae population, which, in turn, creates a higher demand for carbon dioxide that may not be met. Nitrogen enrichment can also directly block photosynthesis by interfering with photon absorption. While the information presented in such works is useful for the careful reader, there are also as many studies showing that nitrogen enrichment significantly reduces calcification, photosynthesis, and respiration rates, and even reduces skeletal density (Hoegh-Guldberg et al., 1997; Kinsey and Davies, 1979; Johannes et al., 1972;

Stambler et al., 1991; Dubinsky, 1990; Yamashiro, 1992; Stimson and Kinzie, 1991, Stimpson, 1992; and others).

In perhaps the most direct study on the subject, Marubini and Davies (1996) found that enriching water with only 1-5 μM (micromolar units, or 0.14-0.7 mg NO_3-N/L) nitrate for 30 days doubled the zooxanthellae population, reduced photosynthesis rates, and decreased skeletogenesis (skeleton-building) by 50%. Other studies show that at higher levels (approximately 40 ppm or 9 mg NO_3-N/L), there are toxic effects to corals. It is also very important to realize that even if nitrogen theoretically stimulates coral growth, there is usually no lack of nitrate in reef aquariums. Any aquarium is likely to have much higher levels than natural reef waters, even if readings are very low. Because of the complex and still somewhat unknown mechanisms of coral metabolism, it is essential that those keeping corals do not use studies suggesting nitrate-enhanced growth as an excuse to not maintain high-quality water. Corals will not benefit from an intentional disregard of high nitrate levels, and the other effects of nitrogen enrichment within a closed system may well become unmanageable.

PHOSPHATE

Phosphate (PO$_4$) is found in minute quantities in the waters on healthy coral reefs, and it is usually the limiting nutrient for reef biological processes. However, phosphate levels can become quite high in the aquarium because of the comparatively large bioload and food input, as well as phosphate import from make-up water.

Phosphate is thought to be a direct "poison" to calcification, and a significant factor in the proliferation of problem algae (Simkiss, 1959, et al.). It prevents normal calcium carbonate crystal formation, and although coral phosphate levels are normally controlled by uptake into the zooxanthellae, increased levels in the water column can cause substantial problems and negatively affect corals. Long-term phosphate enrichment can cause more than a 50% decrease in calcification. Phosphate also inhibits the deposition of strontium in the coral skeleton. It has not, however, been found to affect zooxanthellae metabolism or growth to any significant degree (Steven and Broadbent, 1997, et al.).

Corals are naturally adapted to extremely low phosphate levels, although they may deposit some excess within their limestone skeletons. They can also directly absorb it, if necessary. The zooxanthellae seem to be responsible for the uptake, as uptake is only significant during the day for most corals. As further proof, nonzooxanthellate (aposymbiotic) corals show an efflux of phosphate into the water. If phosphate levels are excessive, the symbiosis between coral and algae can go awry, in addition to reducing calcification directly. Some studies have shown that phosphate does not directly produce an increase in zooxanthellae populations; others have shown the opposite. Thus, to maximize coral calcification and minimize encroaching algae, **phosphate levels should remain extremely low, preferably at untestable levels.** Levels above 0.3 ppm are considered problematic in the aquarium and potentially disastrous in the wild.

Most test kits measure only inorganic phosphate, but sources from unprocessed organic waste (including uneaten food) can be significant. Kalkwasser (or a solution of calcium hydroxide) can be helpful in removing phosphates (usually bound with organic molecules) from aquarium waters, as it tends to help precipitate phosphates from the water column, at least temporarily. (Precipitated calcium phosphate salts may be redissolved into solution via nor-

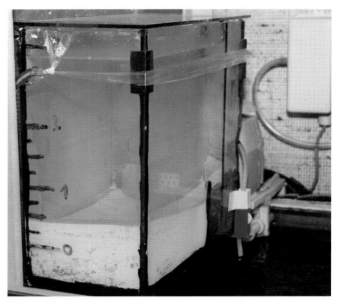

An early Kalkwasser-dosing system on a German reef tank, 1985: the highly basic solution of calcium hydroxide or calcium oxide must be added slowly.

mal biological processes.) Good circulation, along with foam fractionation or protein skimming, is also reported to be effective.

Phytoplankton, benthic algae, seagrasses, macroalgae, sponges, and other invertebrates may also be effective at removing excess nutrients from the water column. In addition to judicious feedings that maximize nutrient import without degrading water quality, regular water changes and the use of purified reverse osmosis (RO) or deionized sources of make-up water are very effective at managing phosphate levels.

The use of phosphate-removing commercial products are not generally recommended in tanks housing corals. Some of these aluminum-oxide products have been noted to have deleterious effects on soft corals, and may also have negative effects on stony corals and other tank inhabitants. Their use should be restricted to the pretreatment of make-up water, if used at all.

pH

pH is the measure of the relative concentration of hydrogen ions (H$^+$) and hydroxyl ions (OH$^-$), indicating a water sample's acidity or alkalinity. To be precise, a pH reading is actually the logarithm of the reciprocal of hydrogen-ion concentration in gram atoms per liter, using a scale of 0 (highly acidic) to 14 (highly basic), with a pH of 7 being neutral.

The pH of the coral reef aquarium should approximate natural seawater levels found on or around coral reefs. **The generally**

A contemporary calcium reactor filled with aragonite and dosed with carbon dioxide is one method of maintaining proper calcium and alkalinity levels.

accepted range for pH is 8.2-8.4 in reef aquariums. In many systems, there is a daily fluctuation of pH, with the highest pH shown during the day when bright sunlight is driving photosynthesis. On the reef, the daily cycle may take pH as high as 8.4-8.5 during the day and as low as 8.0 at night, and the aquarist should always note the time of day when taking pH readings before becoming alarmed.

Slightly higher-than-natural pH is not deleterious, and may be advantageous in helping prevent problem algae, which do not tolerate high pH water very well. The respiration and metabolism of bacteria and animals in the tank tends to produce acidic by-products such as carbon dioxide, humic acids, uric acids, organic acids, etc. Thus, an aquarium tends to become more acidic over time. The use of Kalkwasser or calcium hydroxide and the maintenance of proper buffering and alkalinity (below) are effective in countering this tendency.

ALKALINITY

A proper understanding of alkalinity and its role in water chemistry can provide a great deal of information about water parameters and overall tank conditions.

Alkalinity is very important in the coral reef aquarium because it reflects the capacity of the water to resist changes in pH (its buffering capacity). Higher alkalinity gives the solution more resistance to pH swings, a stability corals require. It is measured in either milliequivalents per liter (meq/L) or German degrees of carbonate hardness (dKH). Conversion from one measurement to the other is obtained by either multiplying meq/L or dividing dKH by the factor of 2.8.

The alkalinity of natural seawater is about 2.5 meq/L, although the comparatively high bioload of aquariums makes a slightly higher level of 3.2-4.5 meq/L beneficial to the system as a whole. (Carbonate hardness on the reef typically measures 7-8 dKH, with a range of 7-12 dKH generally recommended for aquarists.)

Alkalinity also affects the amount of calcium and other trace elements that can remain in solution. Higher alkalinity generally results in lower saturation levels of dissolved elements and vice versa. In seawater, most of the alkalinity is due to bicarbonate. Within coral tissue, carbon dioxide is turned into carbonic acid and then converted to bicarbonate and carbonate ions. This reaction is crucial in influencing the rate of calcification. (See "Calcification and Skeletal Growth," page 354.) In fact, calcification rates are generally measured in scientific communities by a technique called alkalinity depletion. The reaction raises the pH inside the coral's tissue, and it is then forced to precipitate calcium carbonate as skeletal growth to reduce the pH to normal levels. Thus, alkalinity plays an important role in the coral's health, growth, and photosynthesis.

Buffers are required in some systems, either on a regular or as-needed basis, to maintain alkalinity levels. (Aquarists using calcium hydroxide/Kalkwasser or two-part calcium and buffer additives [see page 354] may or may not need to use additional buffers in their tanks.) Most commercial aquarium buffers contain a mix of bicarbonates (sodium, magnesium, etc.), carbonates, and borates. Carbonates will usually equilibrate in seawater to their bicarbonate forms. Borates comprise a tiny fraction of the buffer component in both the commercial mixes and in seawater, and are not well-established to provide any significant influence on corals. For these reasons, standard sodium bicarbonate (baking soda) can be used cheaply, effectively, and safely as a buffer in marine aquariums. (Mix about 1 teaspoon per 25 gallons of system water in a container and add to the aquarium or sump. Repeat daily until the desired alkalinity is achieved. Do not attempt to correct an alkalinity deficiency in one dose, as harmful swings of pH can result.)

TEMPERATURE

Water temperature on the majority of coral reefs remains fairly constant throughout the year, although some reefs do have more temperature-tolerant corals, some being able to withstand prolonged extreme temperatures and others able to cope with large temperature swings. Some shallow areas of natural reefs do experience fairly significant and rapid temperature variations. Certain corals in the Red Sea (notably, the Gulf of Oman) are in waters that can fluctuate by up to 8°C (14°F) in a few hours. However, the life in these areas is adapted to this environment, and they are able to tolerate changes that would likely induce coral bleaching or mortality in other locations. Furthermore, other aspects of stress common to closed aquariums are generally not an issue in the ocean. Understanding that temperature changes are present in nature does not mean that the same vacillations in an aquarium are not stressful.

Other than through control of the ambient room temperature, aquarium thermal stability can be maintained by fan-assisted evaporative cooling, open tank tops (which I recommend), heaters, and chillers. Temperature shifts of a few degrees per day are stressful to all livestock, and especially to corals.

Although it has been recommended in the past that aquarium temperatures should be maintained between 24-27°C (75-80°F), the natural temperature of many Indo-Pacific reefs, especially in the shallow areas where most corals are collected, is higher than 27°C (80°F).

It had always been assumed that temperatures lower than natural levels prevented the rapid growth of unsightly algal films on the aquarium glass and lessened the proliferation of problem hair algae. **Recent trends favor maintaining somewhat more natural reef temperatures of 27-29°C (80-84°F).** The reasoning behind this increase is that the entire metabolism of the tank is raised, including those of the microbial community, detritus-processing organisms, and herbivores. Furthermore, it is a more natural temperature for many reef animals. The increased rates of calcification at these temperatures should, therefore, not be offset by increasing algae growth, unless the system is mismanaged.

There are some negative aspects to increased temperatures, however. Although higher ambient temperatures that are in line with normal reef temperatures may be beneficial, it has also been shown that increasing temperatures above those to which the corals are acclimated may decrease autotrophic abilities and trigger temperature-induced bleaching or death. Thus an accidental rise of a few degrees from a broken or misadjusted heater or chiller could have dire results. Even in nature, prolonged exposure to high or low temperatures can have serious consequences. Tropical corals live within about 2.8°C (5°F) of their upper lethal limit, yet temperatures below that range cause "profound physiological changes, notably in respiration and photosynthetic rates" (Davies, 1992). The oxygen-saturation level at higher temperatures is also lower, although good water movement and/or the use of a protein skimmer is sufficient to maintain oxygen levels at or near saturation.

Experienced aquarists are divided over the issue of ideal temperatures for maintaining corals. Some prefer to keep their systems at or close to the 29°C (84°F) upper limit, often in hopes of pushing coral growth. Those who are successful at maintaining consistently high temperatures typically have very reliable temperature control devices (high-quality heating and chilling equipment and accurate thermostatic controls). Others feel safer with their aquariums running near the lower end of the ideal range, 26-27°C (79-80°F), allowing themselves a comfortable margin of error. (Anecdotal reports by home aquarists suggest that corals normally kept at 26°C [79°F] may bleach at temperatures above 29°C [84°F], while those usually maintained at 29°C [84°F] may not bleach until the water exceeds 32°C [90°F].)

Reef aquarists are urged to track the temperature of their systems regularly and at various times during the day to be sure that lights, ambient room temperature, sunlight striking the tank, or other factors are not causing significant fluctuations in temperature. (Faltering equipment and seasonal variations can lead to problems; summer heat waves, particularly, can wreak havoc on reef tanks without adequate chilling capacity.)

As a footnote, the lethal temperatures for corals are 5°C (41°F) as a lower limit and 45°C (115°F) as an upper limit, although corals cannot sustain life at those temperatures for more than a few minutes, or in the case of extremely tolerate species, a few hours. In nature, coral reefs do not form where the average annual temperature is below 18°C (65°F).

Beautiful growth of corals in a German reef: note open-top aquarium and fan in background to alleviate possible overheating from lights or summer weather.

ENVIRONMENTAL AVERAGES AND EXTREMES FOR CORAL REEFS TESTED

VARIABLE	MINIMUM	MAXIMUM	AVERAGE
Temperature			
Average of all tested reefs	21°C (70°F)	30°C (86°F)	28°C (82°F)
Reef with lowest temperatures	16°C (61°F)	28°C (82°F)	25°C (77°F)
Reef with highest temperatures	25°C (77°F)	34°C (93°F)	30°C (86°F)
Salinity / Specific Gravity (SG)			
Reef with lowest salinities	23 ppt	40 ppt	34 ppt
	1.017 SG	1.030 SG	1.025 SG
Reef with highest salinities	31 ppt	42 ppt	35 ppt
	1.023 SG	1.031 SG	1.026 SG
Nutrients (for all tested reefs)			
NO_3 (nitrate)	0.00 ppm	3034 ppm	0.25 ppm
PO_4 (phosphate)	0.00 ppm	0.54 ppm	0.13 ppm
Max. depth of sunlight penetration			
Average	9 m (30 ft.)	81 m (266 ft.)	53 m (174 ft.)
Minimum	7 m (23 ft.)	72 m (236 ft.)	40 m (131 ft.)
Maximum	10 m (33 ft.)	91 m (298 ft.)	65 m (213 ft.)

Notes: Results represent data from approximately 1,000 reefs. Temperatures taken in degrees C, rounded to nearest degree. Salinity readings rounded to nearest whole number. Specific gravity (SG) equivalents are observable hydrometer readings (actually density measurements) obtainable using aquarium instruments. High temperature reefs are uncommon except in the Red Sea/Persian Gulf and in enclosed to semi-enclosed areas. The Philippines are unusually warm at 31°C (89°F). Ninety percent of all reef locations have less than 0.6 ppm NO_3 and less than 0.2 ppm PO_4.

(from Kleypas et al., 1999)

SALINITY

Salinity is a measure of the total dissolved solids (mostly salts) in water, and it is measured in parts per thousand (ppt). Natural seawater typically ranges from 34-37 ppt, with 35 ppt considered an average reading for reef environments.

Because equipment to measure salinity is rather expensive, and because true salinity is a complex measure, most marine aquarists measure specific gravity instead, using floating glass hydrometers or dip-and-read box-type hydrometers with floating plastic swing-arm indicators. Specific gravity is a measure of the density of a fluid (the reading is actually the ratio of the density of the measured sample to the density of pure water, at the same temperature). For our purposes, a good-quality hydrometer gives a reasonably good indication of the dissolved salt content or salinity of aquarium water. **The specific gravity of natural seawater with a salinity of 35 ppt is 1.027; this is a target to keep in mind for a reef aquarium.** (Note that readings from glass hydrometers calibrated at fixed temperatures must be corrected for temperature to obtain the true specific gravity.)

While marine fishes can be kept successfully at lower salinities, there is no evidence that corals should be maintained in anything other than natural seawater conditions. There are anecdotal reports of coral polyps failing to expand in systems with unusually high or low salinities, and many instances of corals being shocked or even killed by sudden, large changes of salinity.

While some corals can be found in areas with 26 ppt or 46 ppt salinities, these are colonies that have been adapted to hypersaline or hyposaline ranges over long periods of time. Corals in tidepools, shallow nearshore lagoons, reef flats, and near rivers can also experience significant increases or decreases in salinity during periods of rainfall or drought, and corals exposed to air at low tide may even experience direct rainfall. However, these salinity changes are generally temporary, and are usually largely corrected at the change of tides. There is a difference between the tolerance of corals to temporary salinity changes and chronic long-term stress due to salinities outside a "normal" range. Most corals will not tolerate salinities at 110% of normal levels for more than 2 weeks, and salinities of 150% of normal levels are usually lethal within 24 hours.

Extremely dilute seawater has similar effects, as the osmotic regulation ability of tissues is highly taxed. Despite the not-uncommon practice of keeping marine fishes at slightly lower salinities, it is not in the interest of corals, with soft corals and gorgonians most affected, according to field studies.

Reduced salinity also strongly affects species diversity and fertilization rates of invertebrates. For example, a 20% reduction in salinity can result in an 84% decrease in reproductive success (Richmond, 1992). This fact should be considered not only in terms of corals but in the overall health of an aquarium. Finally, low salinity can cause increased coral mortality under conditions of increased temperature, even those of short duration. If anything, slightly high salinities are less harmful than slightly low salinities, and may even impart a slight reduction in bleaching and thermal stress.

It is important to remember that glass hydrometer readings can vary with temperature, and it may be necessary to interpret an observed hydrometer reading to correct for water temperature. Most hydrometers sold in the marine aquarium trade are now calibrated for use in 24°C (75°F) water. Laboratory-grade saltwater instruments are often calibrated at 15°C (59°F), although most lab-supply stores have models calibrated at a variety of temperatures. A conversion chart must be consulted if the temperature of the water being tested differs from that at which the hydrometer is calibrated. (See *The Marine Aquarium Handbook*, Moe, 1992, page 111, for such a conversion chart.)

Hydrometers also vary in quality, so their accuracy should be calibrated against a known standard. The plastic swing-arm dip-and-read hydrometers common in the aquarium hobby can be highly variable in the readings they provide. They should, at the very least, be calibrated against a known standard to determine if a correction should be made. (To avoid getting an incorrect reading, tap the swing-arm with a pencil tip to dislodge any bubbles that might be clinging to its surface. Take the reading immediately after filling with water; evaporation can rather quickly increase the reading of a sample sitting in a small container. These units should always be rinsed with freshwater after use and cleaned with vinegar if they become encrusted with mineral deposits.) Manufacturers of the dip-and-read units claim they are self-compensating for temperatures in the typical tropical marine aquarium. Aquarists taking readings of water samples that vary significantly from 24°C (75°F) may want to adjust the water temperature before taking a reading.

A floating glass hydrometer should be used in a tall flask or other container of sample water, never left to bob around in the tank or sump. These units are very breakable, and are very difficult to read accurately when floating free in the aquarium. Always take the reading at eye level at the water's surface, but at the *bottom* of the meniscus (the small collar of water that creeps up the column of the hydrometer, owing to surface tension). Cheap glass hydrometers are just as prone to inaccuracy as the box-type units, and the serious aquarist may want to invest in a laboratory-grade instrument. Once again, be sure to note the temperature at which the hydrometer has been calibrated, so corrections can be made if necessary.

Other, more expensive options for measuring the salt content of water include electronic meters and salinity refractometers, both of which require careful, regular recalibration to maintain their accuracy.

In the end, avoiding dramatic shifts of salinity is surely more important than being able to make very precise specific gravity readings, and many successful coral keepers are able to maintain their systems with relatively inexpensive aquarium hydrometers. Care should be exercised to avoid a sudden change in salinity or a gradual progressions out of the normal range in which corals thrive.

DISSOLVED ORGANIC MATTER

Dissolved organic matter (DOM) is a general measure of the amount of nutrients, organic acids, and refractory compounds in the water column. German aquarists have called it Gelbstoff, as it typically causes a yellowing of the aquarium water (*gelb* in German means "yellow"). Humic acids and fulvic acids are typically constituents of the refractory compounds, and these are generally not utilized by corals. However, most corals are capable of utilizing DOM for nutrition, with some corals (xeniids, stoloniferans, corallimorphs) depending on it to a greater degree. Most corals from lagoons are quite capable of utilizing DOM, as local levels in lagoonal areas can be somewhat higher. In general, however, DOM is an indicator of water quality, with high levels being deleterious to coral growth. Algae often bloom and outcompete corals in such instances.

Although tests exist for DOM, an easy method to check for

Dark waste matter in a foam fractionator or skimmer "scum cup" illustrates the amount of dissolved organic matter (DOM) a heavily stocked reef can generate.

significant levels is to tape a white piece of paper on one end of the aquarium and view it lengthwise through the tank. If the paper does not appear white, DOM levels are significant. **Oceanic levels range from 0.5-3 ppm. If levels in the aquarium are much higher, some problems typical to nutrient-laden reefs may begin to occur.** The use of protein skimming and/or activated carbon, as well as water changes, can be used to reduce DOM to proper levels. The bacterial and algal flora of the water column, substrate surfaces, and (especially) sediments are all capable of removing significant quantities of DOM as well.

CALCIUM

Calcium is absorbed by coral polyps from seawater and is then transferred actively and passively across their cell membranes. Successive layers of calcium carbonate are then laid down as corals expand their limestone skeletons. Calcium, in effect, is a type of coral "food," and adequate levels must be maintained in order to keep up good rates of calcification. Of course, heavy calcification only occurs when other important factors for calcification (temperature, light, nutrients, water movement, alkalinity, etc.) are all ideal.

Tanks housing significant populations of rapidly calcifying coral species may deplete calcium levels in the water quickly enough that they need replenishing within a single day. Therefore, measurement of the calcium level is important to reef tanks housing corals. A 120-gallon reef tank of mine took nearly 5 gallons of Kalkwasser solution per day (1 teaspoon calcium hydroxide/gallon), and additional calcium through the addition of 20 ml/day of a popular two-part calcium additive. This gave a steady calcium level of nearly 450 ppm.

The ocean (especially in areas around coral reefs where significant amounts of aragonite sand and limestone are processed by water movement, bacteria, fishes, and small organisms) contains approximately 400-420 ppm of calcium. **Aquariums should probably be maintained at a minimum of 400 ppm, and ideally at levels of 450 ppm or higher.** In fact, calcium can be supersaturated to around 500 ppm in water of average alkalinity. It is not possible to have higher levels without corresponding changes in alkalinity, and additional calcium added to a saturated tank will simply not dissolve in the water. In fact, rapid addition of calcium to a saturated water column may cause a "snowstorm" in the tank, as calcium quickly precipitates out of solution. When levels are depleted, the calcium "fall out" will again redissolve in the water, unless it becomes converted to insoluble calcium compounds such as calcium carbonate.

There are several ways to add calcium to an aquarium. Each has its own benefits and disadvantages:

Kalkwasser, or saturated limewater, is one of the oldest and most widely established means of adding calcium to the reef aquarium. To make it, calcium hydroxide powder is dissolved to saturation in freshwater, causing a reaction that results in free calcium and hydroxide ions. This prepared Kalkwasser is stored in an airtight vessel and used to replace all evaporated water in the aquarium.

Besides providing calcium, Kalkwasser also increases the availability of hydroxide ions. These ions are useful in neutralizing acids, raising alkalinity, and adding to the buffering capacity. Furthermore, Kalkwasser has a naturally high pH that counters the aquarium's tendency toward decreasing pH and thus helps stabilize this aspect of water chemistry. There are no other ions present that can cause an imbalance in the water chemistry.

The disadvantages of Kalkwasser use are that it is fairly time-consuming to prepare and add to the system and must be dosed with care. Calcium hydroxide powder should be handled with caution to avoid inhalation of any of the fine dust that can be created. When freshly mixed, the milky solution is caustic and must be carefully dosed to avoid a precipitous and potentially lethal rise in pH. Furthermore, there is a limit to the amount of Kalkwasser that can be safely added to the aquarium, and it is ineffective at raising seriously depleted calcium levels. In tanks with low evaporation rates, it may be an inadequate method to replace all calcium lost to calcification.

Ideally, Kalkwasser should be made fresh every day. The level of calcium decreases in solution quickly, as does the pH of the solution. If several days' supply is being prepared, the container in which it is held should be tightly covered to prevent atmospheric carbon dioxide from reacting with the solution. Provided that ad-

ON CORAL GROWTH

It seems to be a preoccupation of some aquarists that they be able to grow corals at an exceedingly fast rate. I liken it to a sort of competition that doesn't have much biological merit.

Corals in captivity are already reported to produce a skeleton that is lighter and more fragile than those in the wild. Limited access to nutrients and/or light in nature allows the coral to regulate its use of energy, directing it toward various metabolic functions. It is obvious that corals producing a fast-growing skeleton are allotting a large percentage of their energy budget to growth. This may be contrary to normal metabolic processes. Growth may be favored, but other systems, including defense, immune, and reproductive systems, could be compromised. In fact, growth and reproductive viability are often a direct trade-off (Ward, 1995a, 1995b, et al.).

While trying to emulate natural growth rates is certainly worthwhile, the proliferation of gadgets, additives, and other growth enhancers seems to imply that some sort of race exists, that we can somehow do it "better than Mother Nature." If captive corals are not growing by leaps and bounds, aquarists often feel they are failing, somehow. This worry is usually unfounded.

For example, lighting and ambient nutrient levels vary from tank to tank. There are systemic calcification gradients that exist in branching corals that do not exist in massive ones. This is illustrated in studies of skeletal densities: massive and bushy corals are the most porous, foliaceous corals are the most dense, and some branching corals have porous, fast-growing ends but dense bases that are barely growing at all. There are noticeable differences in growth rates between, and even within, species—and even between colonies of the same species in similar environments.

Massive corals can calcify as quickly as branching ones, although they do so in a different manner, which may not be as obvious. Water flow rate, latitude, temperature, CO_2 availability, and countless other factors significantly affect calcification. Calcification mechanisms in corals are different from day to night, and there is even speculation of a possible third mechanism in aquariums using Kalkwasser. Branch density may be favored over linear growth, even though calcification rates remain the same. Some corals have a genetically predetermined maximum size that may or may not be environmentally affected.

The most rapidly extending corals ever measured are *Acropora cervicornis* and *A. formosa*, with branch-length growth rates of 14.5 and 18.5 cm (5.7 and 7.3 in.) per year, respectively. Yet these same species have also been reported in healthy wild reefs with linear extension rates of just 0.40 and 0.37 cm (0.16 and 0.15 in.) per year, respectively, with no indications of relative degrees of colonial "success," health, or viability.

In other words, growth rate is varied, even in the wild, and related to many factors. Trying to achieve some "standard" of growth in the aquarium is not valid, nor should it be sought. There is even a model, called Leslie's matrix, that predicts that in organisms exhibiting developmental plasticity, there is no con-

#1 *Acropora formosa* colony started from a fragment collected in Fiji. (November 24, 1991)

#2 Seven months later, showing rapid growth under the care of Alf Jacob Nilsen. (June 30, 1992)

#3 One year later, colony growth is accelerating. Note pink branch tips. (November 1, 1992)

sistent correlation between size and age (Hughes, 1984). A fascinating example of this can be seen in old collections of bonsai trees, with oak trees that are alive, growing and beautiful, more than 100 years of age but no more than 60 cm (24 in.) tall. Provided that corals polyps are expanding and healthy, no comparison of growth rates achieved by different aquarists is likely to have much meaning. More properly, the success of a well-planned reef community as a whole should be the aquarist's goal.

#4 Nineteen months later, the colony is beginning to stretch laterally and is becoming a dominant part of the tank aquascape. (May 15, 1993)

#5 Twenty-five months have elapsed, and the *Acropora formosa* is many times larger than the fragment from which it started. (January 1, 1994)

ditions are small and done daily, the clear Kalkwasser supernatant liquid can be added directly to the tank in a high-flow area without consequence. Milky fresh solutions, while providing higher amounts of calcium to the aquarium, are of a substantially high pH and must be added in a drip method. It is best to add Kalkwasser at night or early in the morning when the natural diurnal fluctuation of pH is at its lowest. A number of different dosing systems and precisely controllable metering pumps are available to automate the process of adding Kalkwasser. When used with a timer, these systems can be set to dose the tank during the dark hours when the addition will be most beneficial.

Calcium replacement with Kalkwasser offers many advantages, and this is an excellent method of regular calcium addition to reef aquariums. However, there is some evidence to suggest that the method of calcification used in tanks employing Kalkwasser may be of a different nature than normal carbonate depletion. This may be due to the significantly higher number of hydroxide (OH⁻) ions when Kalkwasser is used. They act as a buffer, of sorts, but not in the same manner as in the ocean where OH⁻ is normally almost nonexistent. Corals put in enclosed containers and measured for alkalinity depletion showed significantly reduced levels of bicarbonate uptake (Adey, 1998, pers. comm.; Small, 1997, pers. comm.). Clearly, there is adequate and obvious evidence that corals in aquariums can survive and grow well using Kalkwasser. However, the implications are that such growth may be occurring in a way that differs from what happens in the wild.

Two-part additives consist of a carbonate buffering component in one part and a highly concentrated composition of calcium ions in a second part, which is stored and dosed separately. The first solution is slowly added to the aquarium water, preferably in an area of high water flow, allowing the milkiness it produces to dissolve quickly and completely. The second part is then introduced. (The two parts must be stored and added separately to avoid a rapid precipitation of calcium carbonate.) These additives also typically provide a number of supplemental major, minor, and trace elements found in natural seawater.

These two-part additives are excellent at providing high levels of calcium, are easy to use, and maintain high alkalinity levels. Automatic dosing equipment is available for them. While somewhat expensive, they provide few disadvantages in their use as a calcium additive. They are highly effective in maintaining calcium levels that are quickly depleted by high rates of coral calcification. Although there is a possibility of trace elements accumulating or changed ionic composition of the aquarium water as result of their heavy use, many aquarists have reported good results, both short and long term. Regular partial water changes and monitoring of the specific gravity of the system should prevent any serious problems.

Calcium chloride is available either as a powder or liquid. It can be used to raise calcium levels rapidly, but its regular use results in the slow accumulation of chlorine atoms. It also tends to decrease alkalinity if overdosed and is not a particularly beneficial method of calcium addition compared to other methods. In severe cases of calcium depletion, calcium chloride may be used to increase calcium levels rapidly. However, such depletions can also be corrected easily, and with generally better results, using the two-part additives described above.

Calcium reactors are mechanical devices that provide calcium by bubbling acidic carbon dioxide through a calcium carbonate medium, dissolving it in a solution that is continuously fed into the aquarium. The calcium reactor is popular in Europe and is gaining popularity in the U.S. Some find it convenient, but the device is expensive to purchase and the use of carbon dioxide can lower the pH of the water, as well as fuel undesirable algae growth. The composition of the substrate material must be clean enough to prevent unwanted substances from being released into the water during dissolution.

Calcium reactors typically cause higher alkalinity and lower calcium levels (though calcium is maintained at saturation), and in some cases they have caused increases in phosphate levels. However, they make calcium replenishment convenient, maintain high alkalinity levels, and provide some additional trace elements as the calcareous material dissolves. A calcium reactor is not essential for the maintenance of healthy corals, but it may represent the most effective means of emulating natural processes and providing the two necessities for calcification—calcium and carbonate.

The addition of carbon dioxide to aquarium water poses both potential disadvantages and advantages. Additional carbon dioxide may be used for calcification, although it may throw off the normal conditions of the system. Especially at night, carbon dioxide levels (without photosynthesis) from respiration of high biomass can be significant even under ordinary circumstances, with oxygen levels concomitantly dropping. Even accidental leakage of carbon dioxide into tank water can create quite a problem in such a case, amplifying a frequently unnatural condition of closed systems. The use of an electronic pH controller, which shuts down the flow of carbon dioxide into the reactor when the pH of the system water reaches a certain point (8.4-8.5, for example), is strongly advised to avoid these problems.

Other calcium sources include: powdered coral, which dissolves poorly and has proved unable to keep up with the calcium demands of typical reef aquariums; calcium gluconate, a syrupy liquid that is a rich source of calcium but that has been implicated in algal blooms; and other proprietary products. Caution is recommended when selecting any new calcium product that has not passed the test of time and earned the recommendation of other marine aquarists.

CALCIFICATION AND SKELETAL GROWTH

Calcification is the complex process by which corals take calcium from seawater and form aragonite or calcite to be used in skeletogenesis. **Skeletogenesis** is the process by which the limestone (calcium carbonate) skeleton is formed. Calcification and skeletogenesis are intimately related, but are not the same, and may involve different processes.

Calcium carbonate ($CaCO_3$) is formed by corals in two primary forms: calcite and aragonite. Almost all stony corals create their skeletons solely of aragonite, although aragonite may, in time, be changed into calcite by geochemical processes. In addition, the presence of citrate, sulfate, and ammonium ions, as well as low pH, favors calcite formation over aragonite. This may have implications on the calcification of corals in aquariums, depending on the levels of these ions present. In contrast, the skeletal inclusions and supporting structures of octocorals and zoanthids are primarily made of calcite, although aragonite may also be present.

The basic compounds and ions needed to produce calcium carbonate are carbon dioxide (CO_2), calcium (Ca^{2+}), and carbonate (CO_3^{2-}), all of which are present in seawater. Normally, calcium is not limiting because of the large reserve of dissolved limestone in tropical seawater created by bioerosion and other processes. Instead, it is the carbon source that tends to limit calcification, especially as both bicarbonate (HCO_3^-) and carbon dioxide availability are closely coupled to photosynthesis, with both calcification and photosynthesis being strongly affected by the presence of sunlight. Calcification also allows extracellular sources of bicarbonate to be converted into carbon dioxide, which is then used by the zooxanthellae.

Calcification in zooxanthellate corals requires three basic biological processes:

Photosynthesis
$$CO_2 + H_2O \longrightarrow CH_2O + H_2O$$
Respiration
$$CH_2O + O_2 \longrightarrow CO_2 + H_2O$$
Calcification
$$Ca^{2+} + 2HCO_3^- \longrightarrow CaCO_3 + CO_2 + H_2O$$

The production of CO_2 in the last two reactions can conveniently be used to fuel photosynthesis.

Our current understanding of the process of calcification, as proposed by Ted McConnaughey (1991, 1996), is based on a model found in most other species, including algae and terrestrial

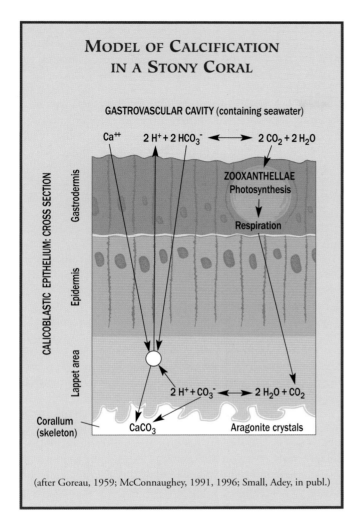

MODEL OF CALCIFICATION IN A STONY CORAL

GASTROVASCULAR CAVITY (containing seawater)

Ca^{++} $2H^+ + 2HCO_3^- \longleftrightarrow 2CO_2 + 2H_2O$

ZOOXANTHELLAE
Photosynthesis

Respiration

$2H^+ + CO_3^- \longleftrightarrow 2H_2O + CO_2$

$CaCO_3$ Aragonite crystals

CALICOBLASTIC EPITHELIUM: CROSS SECTION

Gastrodermis

Epidermis

Lappet area

Corallum (skeleton)

(after Goreau, 1959; McConnaughey, 1991, 1996; Small, Adey, in publ.)

---

biota. Known as *trans* calcification, this process generates protons (H^+ ions) that are pumped from the coral tissue into the body cavity of the polyp where they lower pH and cause the formation of CO_2 from bicarbonate. In this model, H^+ ions are swapped in a 2:1 ratio for calcium using the enzyme Calcium ATPase. Furthermore, the CO_2 released is then available to fuel photosynthesis by the zooxanthellae.

$$2H^+ + 2HCO_3^- \longleftrightarrow 2CO_2 + 2H_2O$$

In the process of pumping out protons, the area where calcification occurs maintains a high pH that favors the precipitation of skeletal material.

Calcification takes place in the lower epidermal tissue layer called the calicoblastic epithelium. This is the area where the outer polyp surface that is in contact with the water joins the skeleton. In order to calcify, the calcium and carbonate sources must be available to these epidermal cells. Water enters the body cavity through the mouth, where the needed components are then available for uptake.

Coral skeletons are grown outward as vertical plates or spires, occasionally joined by horizontal elements, resulting in a meshwork or layered stack of calcium carbonate. Contrary to what may be thought, corals do not produce solid limestone. Rather, they create variably porous skeletons.

At various rates and times of the day and night, and through possibly different processes, sections of the coral tissue at the calcification site are lifted up from the skeleton in small areas called lappets. To spaces within these tiny pockets, which are sealed to exclude seawater, calcium ions (Ca^{2+}) are brought in and hydrogen ions (H^+) are exported by the pumps in the coral membranes. The pH and the calcium ion concentrations rise substantially in the lappets, creating ideal conditions for the crystallization of calcium carbonate ($CaCO_3$). Through the complex series of enzymatic and biochemical processes, calcium and carbonate are precipitated on the external surface of the calicoblastic epithelial cells as aragonite.

Each hour, stony corals actively accrete all of the calcium from an amount of seawater that equals 50 to 100 times their own volume! There are daily variations in calcification, with the highest rates occurring shortly after sunrise and in late afternoon. Calcification at night seems to be a result of a separate process that relies on intracellular "getting ready," with actual skeletogenesis taking place in the daylight hours.

Night calcification does not seem to result in skeletogenesis. To quote Barnes and Crossland (1980): "It seems possible that the symbiotic association permits rapid growth because the coral can invest in flimsy scaffolding at night with the certainty that bricks and mortar will be available in the morning."

Under normal conditions, when a lappet is closed, the aragonite layer is pressed against the skeleton where it may combine with various organic and inorganic materials that are then incorporated into the skeleton. There are chitinous elements, trace elements, metals, and other organic materials within the skeletons of all corals in varying proportions. It is not known whether these "additions" are a by-product of the calcification process, required for crystal nucleation, formation, and growth, or simply added to the calcium carbonate matrix by relatively nonselective processes.

The following factors, in addition to those already mentioned, are important in favoring the precipitation of calcium carbonate in corals on reefs (Muscatine, 1971), resulting in skeletal growth (advice to aquarists follows each factor):

1. Increased temperature, within limits, that lowers the solubility product of calcium carbonate and the solubility of carbon dioxide, thereby increasing the carbonate ion concentration. (Aquarists note: Proper temperature regulation meets this condition in the aquarium.)

2. Ample calcium and carbonate concentration. (Aquarists note: Both conditions are met simply by the use of Kalkwasser, or other calcium or calcium/buffer additives.)

3. Movement of supersaturated water into a region where precipitation takes place. (Aquarists note: Good water flow, use of Kalkwasser or calcium additive and buffer, and healthy corals are all that are required to meet this condition.)

4. Photosynthesis, which lowers CO_2 concentration and concurrently increases carbonate concentration. (Aquarists note: Proper lighting is all that is required to meet this condition.)

5. Bacterial production of ammonia or other weak bases that increase the intracellular pH and, concurrently, the carbonate concentration. (Aquarists note: No special effort on the part of the aquarist is required to fulfill this condition.)

6. Various metabolic processes taking place intra- and extracellularly within the coral polyp that serve to accomplish increasing calcium or carbonate levels or catalytic events. (Aquarists note: These conditions will be met by healthy corals and good husbandry practices.)

MINOR ELEMENTS AND TRACE ELEMENTS

The use of chemical additives, liquid or powdered, to deliver minor or trace elements to reef aquariums is considered by some to be essential and by others as nothing more than a waste of money. It is an understatement to say that controversy surrounds the need for additives to replace minor elements and trace elements used by tank inhabitants, especially those involved in coral metabolism and calcification.

Evidence supporting the actual needs of corals for many commercially available aquarium products is unsubstantiated at best. In many systems, the use of these additives is unnecessary; at worst, it can actually be harmful. In the simplest terms, corals need light and food to meet their energy needs, and they require a carbon source and calcium for calcification. Other requirements are, for the most part, unknown, unstudied, or unneeded. We can hope that future research and experience in keeping aquarium corals will clarify the benefits and drawbacks of various popular additives.

Strontium is a prominent and widely used, or misused, trace element that is involved in coral skeletogenesis. Corals regularly replace and/or substitute calcium ions with strontium ions in their skeletons. Following normal calcium ion pathways, strontium competes with calcium; in studies of coral skeletons, strontium is most often found to be at levels equal, or nearly equal, to its concentration in seawater. Strontium is actively removed from polyp tissue, however, and is normally maintained by the coral at much lower levels than are found in seawater.

In any case, the actual requirements for strontium in corals are not at all clear. The fact that strontium is incorporated into coral skeletons does not establish that it is of any real significance. (Strontium has been found in several studies to be higher in aposymbiotic corals than in symbiotic ones, but aposymbiotic corals are also higher in uranium content and it is unlikely that weapons-grade additives are likely to be offered anytime soon in the reef aquarium business!) Although it has been suggested that calcification rates increase in the presence of enhanced strontium levels, it seems that the incorporation of strontium results in reduced or slower growth and increased skeletal density. Skeletal strontium content decreases as temperatures increase, but is seemingly unaffected by light intensity. In other words, there may be a seasonal influence to strontium incorporation, rather than it being a photosynthetically driven calcification response, but even this suggestion has proved conflicting and inconclusive in studies. In one study, calcification in synthetic seawater was significantly lower than in natural seawater, possibly from the significantly higher strontium levels in synthetic sea salt (Gattuso et al., 1998). Strontium has also been found to be a competitive inhibitor of calcification (Chalker, 1976; Ip and Krishnaveni, 1991).

Levels of strontium incorporation may depend on the mineralogy and adsorption properties of the skeleton, salinity, crystal formation, species or genetic differences, water depth, and possibly unknown metabolic effects. Studies have almost all shown strontium to be an anomaly of skeletogenesis, not required for calcification or growth. A number of commercially prepared supplements are available; free ionic solutions of strontium chloride result in more bioavailable strontium than similar chelated products.

Iodine is a trace element long thought to be required by many corals (Wilkens, 1992; Delbeek and Sprung, 1994; et al.). Soft corals were said to require it for their health and growth, and benefits to all corals were reported to include increased coloration and a degree of antiseptic protection against pathogens. For the most part, these conclusions are unsubstantiated. Although some red and brown macroalgae actually concentrate iodine from the surrounding seawater in their cells, the literature describing the exact use and merit of iodine to corals is sketchy at best. The axial cores of some gorgonians and "black" corals (antipatharians) contain significantly elevated levels of iodine. Nevertheless, while accurate information on species-specific iodine uptake rates by corals is lacking, many anecdotal reports in the aquarium community

Before: a portion of Gregory Schiemer's 500-gallon aquarium photographed in August 1998 with a variety of corals, *Tridacna* spp. clams, and fishes.

After: the same aquascape a year later (August 1999) dispels the myth that corals are slow-growing and shows that a realistic reef can be captively grown.

note the negative consequences of *not* adding iodine.

Iodine is commonly added as potassium iodide in any of a number of commercial preparations. It is also available as a combination of iodine and potassium iodide in a stronger product called Lugol's solution. (The potential uses of Lugol's solution for coral disease treatment are covered in Chapter 11, page 389.) Despite early rave reviews about the beneficial effects of Lugol's on the growth and coloration of certain coral and invertebrate species with regular use, many aquarists (including myself) have noted it to be quite deleterious to some coral species. Most notably, some *Xenia* species react favorably to Lugol's, while other *Xenia* species react as if it were a poison. *Pachyclavularia* and *Clavularia* species also frequently have a negative reaction to Lugol's. Potassium iodide, therefore, is recommended as an effective way to supplement iodine levels because it poses much less risk than Lugol's solution. Caution is in order, though: iodine is a powerful oxidant and is cytotoxic. Moderate and careful use is critical to prevent overdosing, and the use of a commercially available iodine/iodide test kit may be warranted in some cases.

Magnesium is deficient in some salt mixes, and **iron** is depleted from typical reef aquariums rather rapidly. However, it is not at all certain why this is occurring. One cannot assume biological uptake, unless an organism known to utilize a particular element is present; more is *unknown* about such aspects of reef systems than is *known*. At one time, **molybdenum** was thought to be quite important, but I have found no valid source showing it to be of value in any coral metabolic or calcification process. **Bromide** and **fluoride** have recently gained some attention as giving positive results with small-polyped corals. Bromide is actually used frequently as the halogen incorporated into many of

the bioactive and toxic chemical compounds produced by corals. Even the minute amounts of **vanadium** found in seawater are not without some benefit—in fact, some tunicates require it. However, any need for supplementing these various elements for corals has simply not been adequately established. Every day seems to bring out avid hobbyists proclaiming that a certain element is directly responsible for some wondrous effect. With no disrespect intended for such enthusiasm, I would point out that commercial salt mixes already provide most major and minor trace element constituents of seawater in amounts that far exceed the levels in natural seawater (Atkinson, 1998). Assuming that regular, partial water changes are being performed, replenishment of trace elements with additives is probably not justified and, in some cases, may even be poisonous. Overdosing can easily lead to ionic imbalances, blooms of nuisance algae, or even the death of corals. For those who choose to dose trace elements, I suggest careful use, and no more than is needed to maintain the bioavailability of these elements to any life forms that may require them.

REMEMBER THE BASICS

Some aquarists love the whole subject of water chemistry, while others find the topic mildly to wholly intimidating. In fact, the essentials are really not that complicated. Corals in captivity can be remarkably resilient and easy to attend. As with equipment, success in maintaining corals can be more easily attained by the "less is more" approach to water quality management.

To repeat, corals require an aquarium, seawater at the right temperature and salinity, water flow, light, food, bicarbonate/buffer, and calcium. Period. No other equipment, apparatus, magic potions, pills, voodoo, prayer, or other sacrifices are necessary.

CHAPTER 10

Care & Handling

Selecting, Acclimating, and Siting
Corals in the Reef Aquarium

The acquisition of a live coral never fails to be an exciting event—even for seasoned reef aquarists. For the neophyte bringing home a first coral, it is a momentous occasion— possibly the first step on the way to creating a captive coral reef.

However, there is some risk involved whenever corals are transported or moved from one system to another, and the initial attempts of inexperienced aquarists to keep corals are often met by failure. Many beginners are intimidated by the thought of buying and handling live corals, and there are some lessons to be learned. To avoid the unnecessary loss of life, not to mention the frustration and financial cost, it is best to review the requirements and characteristics of each coral species (or its family and genus) before making a purchase. Reef hobbyists are not known for restraint and patience, especially when confronted by a display of glorious coral specimens, all begging to be taken home. But, as everyone soon learns, it is a common and often expensive mistake to succumb to "love at first sight" when encountering an especially beautiful or interesting coral.

> "He who sees things grow from their beginnings shall have the finest view of them."
>
>
>
> Aristotle

Far too many aquarium corals are doomed by excited hobbyists who neglect to learn the basic requirements of the animals they are buying. Too often, the information provided by retail salespeople is superficial or even incorrect. Although most stores may attempt to provide good advice, individual sales staff members can easily be misinformed or, more typically, short on coral husbandry experience. When confronted with a coral whose identity or care requirements is unknown, a prudent aquarist will at least survey the reference books that every good aquarium shop should have on hand and available for use.

CORAL SELECTION

In the hands of an inexperienced aquarist, a new coral that is damaged, severely stressed, or diseased may have very limited chances of survival. Before buying any coral, it is essential to check carefully for signs of ill health. Especially noteworthy are signs of tissue recession or necrosis (torn or discolored sections of soft flesh or an abnormal shrinkage of a polyp or polyps that exposes the skeleton beneath). Patches of jelly-like material or thin tissue peeling from the skeleton are signs of potential quick demise for some corals.

Many corals will not be fully expanded in display tanks be-

Sweeper tentacles on a colony of **Plerogyra sinuosa** (bubble coral): aquarium specimens must be given room to expand without threatening other corals.

cause of shipping stress or less-than-ideal tank conditions, and it is important to know which corals are likely to respond well after being taken home. The difference between a truly ailing coral and a healthy, but currently "unhappy," coral is usually quite apparent to seasoned aquarists. Again, many corals are healthy but unexpanded in store displays or after shipping. Most of these will thrive once settled into a proper environment. The extremely low water flow in many retail facilities causes either a failure to expand or, in some cases, a hyperinflation of polyp tissue—a very unnatural condition.

Even some corals with potential problems may stand an excellent chance of recovery if given the right conditions and care, though it is best to avoid these specimens until one has the skill and experience to restore the coral to full health. Advanced, or compassionate, hobbyists can often get a good deal on a coral that is somehow flawed or "a little sick." (Some establishments routinely sell these as "scratch and dent" corals.) Even in nature, 60-80% of corals have sustained some degree of damage from one source or another, and the loss of some tissue, even barring complete recovery, is quite normal.

In short, for aquarium corals that are provided with a healthy environment, a little collateral damage is not something to be overly concerned about, as it happens to most corals over time. There is no need to abandon a reef-collected animal because it is less than a perfect "show winner." The best chance such ugly ducklings have is in the hands of a competent aquarist. It may be a stretch to call it the aquarium equivalent of a pound-puppy rescue, but I know that many such corals have rewarded their caretakers with similar "loyalty" in their hardiness and simple beauty.

Although the quarantine of new corals in a separate tank is highly recommended to prevent any diseases from being transmitted, the conditions of a quarantine tank must be at least as good as those of the main tank—not only to prevent stress, but to ensure that the quarantine procedure is more beneficial than harmful.

I use a 10-gallon tank with live sand, live rock, a pair of small powerheads and two 18-inch fluorescent bulbs as a quarantine tank for new corals. The tank is simple, inexpensive, and has high water quality. Water changes can be performed easily, if required, and the light and water flow are both adequate for temporary quarantine conditions. Corals should also be carefully inspected for parasites and other deleterious organisms that may be attached to, or residing within, the coral skeleton or the rock on which it is growing. Quarantine regimen, dipping procedures, and a list of potentially harmful organisms are covered in Chapter 11.

INTRODUCING CORALS TO THEIR HABITAT

After corals are purchased, it is imperative to oversee their proper introduction to the tank. Corals are anatomically delicate animals with relatively thin tissue layers, and they are very sensitive to changes in water chemistry. Even the best collectors, holding facilities, shippers, wholesalers, and retailers subject corals to an immensely stressful voyage from their natural environment to their final home in a reef tank. The adverse conditions they may endure include: exposure to air, rough handling, poor water conditions, changes in temperature, changes in salinity, lack of light, and lack of food for extended periods. Unpressurized cargo holds may also have an impact on corals in transport. The changes in temperature during transit may be especially significant, and the aquarist has no way of telling what fluctuations may have occurred. (I frequently test the shipping bag water for pH, salinity, and temperature before acclimating new corals.)

The important thing to remember is that the corals have been stressed and must now be properly acclimated. Acclimation is the term used to describe the gradual introduction of a species to its new environment. Some aquarists like to float new corals in their plastic shipping bags within the tank to allow for temperature equalization. (All aquarium lights should be turned off during this time, as intense lights can quickly overheat the bagged water.) This step is not altogether essential as long as the next step, which should not be skipped, is followed.

Whether the shipping bags have been floated or not, they should be nestled upright in buckets or other containers and the tops opened. A small portion—perhaps 20-25% of the shipping water—should be dipped out and replaced with an equal amount of tank water. This procedure should be repeated each 10-15 minutes over the course of 30 minutes to an hour or more. Another option is to add new tank water slowly and continuously. I like to drip water from the tank into the bags with an arrangement of flexible air-line tubing.

Corals do not have the same high oxygen requirements as fishes, so longer acclimation is not likely be deleterious to them. The very slow or periodic addition of tank water allows their tissues to adjust slowly to the new water chemistry. If this procedure is carried out in haste, many corals may refuse to open in the tank, or they may have an increased susceptibility to disease or bleaching. Once the acclimation period is finished, the coral may be gently removed from its bag or shipping container and placed in the quarantine aquarium. Discard all shipping and acclimation water—it may be contaminated with mucus, ammonia, nematocysts, and other undesirable contents; it should never be added to the aquarium.

Quarantine should be maintained for approximately a week

to watch for problems and to allow any preventive care or treatment that may be required. (These are always easier to carry out in a small tank, and any infectious problems can be safely isolated.) A week generally gives a coral ample time to begin adjusting to captivity, but is not so long that the transfer to the display aquarium will be another grossly traumatic event. During this time, the coral should have ample time to show its recovery from transit by exhibiting full polyp expansion.

Some corals, such as *Sarcophyton*, *Sinularia*, *Pachyclavularia*, and a few other species, will go through prolonged acclimation periods, especially following stress or long trips. This is to be expected, and the aquarist will, in time, learn what is normal and what is problematic when handling new specimens. The gradual addition of quarantine water to the main tank, and vice versa, is a technique that should be used for certain corals once it is established that they do not harbor disease.

PLACING NEW CORALS

Before introducing a new specimen to the main tank, it is necessary to consider the proper placement of the coral within the reef structure. Regardless of the type, all corals should be located temporarily in a low-light area of the tank if the aquarium is substantially more illuminated than the quarantine tank. (This is even more important if quarantine is not used.)

The sudden exposure to intense lighting, especially after days (or even weeks) in less-than-adequate light, can cause light-induced shock that can seriously harm coral tissue. It may result in either the rapid death of a colony or the expulsion of the zooxanthellae. (On the other hand, if the prior light regime of a new coral is known—in the case of a quick transfer or a captive-bred coral, for example—this will not be necessary, provided the new lighting is similar to the lighting from which the coral came.)

The coral can be gradually moved to higher irradiance over the course of a week or two, until the desired light intensity is reached. Corals that normally require higher irradiance levels should be attended to carefully in this regard. Continued exposure to low light levels may, in some cases, be a cause for low-light bleaching or become a stress that can lead to other problems. After this period of photoacclimation, the final siting of the coral can take place. Measures should be taken to ensure that the coral is in conditions of proper lighting and current for its genus or species, and that it is not within immediate proximity of potentially aggressive "neighbors."

Provisions for the coral's growth and tissue expansion should also be considered, as well as for the possible development of aggressive structures such as sweeper tentacles—either from the new coral or from existing specimens. It is important to realize

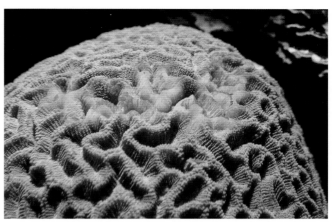

Oulophyllia sp. (brain coral): heals after suffering mechanical damage.

Favites abdita (brain coral): severe UV-C burns from a metal halide lamp.

Goniopora sp. (flowerpot coral): serious tissue loss in a wild colony. (Red Sea)

Catalaphyllia jardinei (elegance coral) stinging a too-close colony of zoanthids.

that once a coral becomes attached to the rockwork, relocation may be nearly impossible. Foresight, planning, and the preparation of a proper location should be made in advance of any final placement. The shape, color, and species of coral can provide important clues as to the type of conditions that it is accustomed to, or to those it prefers. For example, the skeletal features of stony corals, the shape of the branches of branched corals, the orientation of branches on flexible gorgonians, etc., can all give clues about their placement requirements.

During the period before final placement, great care should be taken to locate the new coral so it cannot fall onto or otherwise come into any contact with other corals. Damage from such accidents can be quick and long-lasting, or even fatal, to one or the other. Once in its desired position, the coral will soon make it apparent if the location is likely to work. The polyp or polyps should expand within a day or two in most cases. Excess mucus production may occur over the first several days, but should subside soon thereafter. Misjudgment of proper location is common with inexperienced coral keepers, and the animal will display its dissatisfaction by keeping itself retracted, even after several days of acclimation.

Allow at least several days (with careful observation) at any particular placement site to assess results. Testing the aquarium water frequently after introducing new specimens is good practice to ensure that conditions remain optimal. The constant touching and moving of corals is to be avoided. This will add stress and can result in poor expansion. Some corals will not expand fully for several weeks after being introduced to new conditions and/or being exposed to frequent handling. Even in the wild, transplanted corals can take up to a year to normalize their growth. Experience and judgment is often required to deter-

mine if a coral is poorly placed, sick, or just reacting and adapting to new conditions and/or handling stresses.

Prolonged retraction may also be a sign of health problems or poor water conditions. If several attempts at relocation—to areas of more or less light or current or away from offensive neighbors—give no improvement in appearance, or if the coral's health is worsening, it may be necessary to consult Chapter 11 for possible causes. Again, patience, understanding, and careful observations are among the best diagnostic tools. Drastic and fast reactions by the aquarist are rarely warranted. Familiarity with the parasites, predators, and diseases that can rapidly cause the death of a coral will help in making a choice between continued observation or action.

PERMANENT SITING

It is important to ensure that corals are carefully and firmly affixed to the rockwork when their permanent location is selected. Among the choices open to the aquarist are stable placement (wedging into the live rock structure) or using materials such as plastic bands, straps, or adhesives. Frequently, coral specimens fall within the rockwork of the tank, landing in a position where extraction is almost impossible. (These displacements can be caused by currents, fishes, brittlestars, shrimps, urchins, or accidental contact during maintenance.) The dismantling of significant portions of the reef may be required to save the coral. If a coral is not placed securely, it may be subjected to repeated falls, which can physically damage the coral itself or injure other specimens onto which it falls. All too common are coral deaths that result from a fall that lands one coral atop another. In such cases, the more-aggressive coral can quickly cause considerable damage to the weaker one. Any physical damage increases the opportunity for infection and/or other disease. (This is one instance where quick action by the aquarist in moving the corals apart may prevent terminal or permanent injuries.)

I have found that the average reef aquarist will endure at least three or four total "live rock avalanches" before heeding the advice to cement corals in place.

Some corals may be attached with the use of two-part underwater epoxy putties. These epoxies are very weakly adhesive (i.e., they are not very "sticky"), and their use is somewhat limited to creating molds that, when cured, can effectively secure corals to the rockwork. Some local necrosis may occur near the tissue/epoxy interface, but a coral usually recovers without incident. Anyone working with epoxies, though, should be forewarned of several potential pitfalls: there are many types of epoxy putties available, most of which are variably effective and safe to use. However, specialized two-part underwater epoxies are becoming more frequently available for plumbing and boating purposes and many contain fillers, such as copper and steel, that would not be suitable for use in aquarium applications housing invertebrates. Furthermore, most epoxies will cause protein skimmers to produce a great deal of effluent, which may not abate for several days or more.

I have found that the use of superglue (cyanoacrylate) gels to attach corals to rock is somewhat more effective. They are more strongly adhesive and allow for quicker overgrowth by the coral than the underwater epoxies. Superglues, however, become very brittle and are not as suitable for heavy items or those subjected to mechanical or gravitational stress. Once superglue is applied, fragments or colonies must be put in place fairly quickly or the saltwater forms a nonadhesive skin around the glue that prevents proper adhesion. These glues are also becoming more widely used in transplantation efforts on natural reefs.

Surprisingly, both epoxy and cyanoacrylate adhesives are quite innocuous in saltwater, and they may be used without much worry of toxicity. The use of hole saws, fragmentation, and cyanoacrylate adhesives, as well as attachment protocols for epoxies and substrate materials, can be found in Davies (1995). Readers will find that the methods of supergluing coral fragments to artificial substrate used within the aquarium hobby are the same ones being used in lab and field studies in the scientific community.

Some aquarists do not regularly use adhesives but rather try to wedge new corals securely into their aquascape. This works best with very irregularly shaped live rock, and it does take some experience to do it well.

With practice in the various ways of fastening, attaching, and placing corals with good stability, most aquarists will find that

Acropora sp. fragments cemented to rock using two-part epoxy that hardens underwater. Such putties can be extremely helpful in permanently siting corals.

Acropora sp. fragment attached to reefscape by coral farmer Bob Mankin encrusts its epoxy base, which is also being covered by coralline algae growth.

they soon attach to the reef rockwork through growth and/or cal-cification, and ill-fated falls will no longer be a cause for con-cern. Within the first few weeks to months, corals will adapt to tank conditions and begin what may prove to be a long life of growth and reproduction in captivity. However, they may also change a great deal from their original appearance. Depending on water flow, lighting, and water conditions, the relative growth rate of the coral may increase or decrease from previous or ex-pected levels, and many corals will change their color.

As an example, consider a beautiful blue-tipped *Acropora* species. It might not remain blue but may become brown, some-times quite quickly. It may start calcifying more rapidly as a brown species, and it may adopt a change in growth pattern. Lest the aquarist become dismayed, it is also very possible for a "boring" brown coral to begin to display vibrant and fluores-cent colors in response to a new set of aquarium conditions. It is virtually impossible to duplicate conditions in the tank that are even close to conditions from the wild area in which the coral was collected, and such changes are to be expected. Some branching corals may tend to encrust in certain tanks, and some encrust-ing corals may become branching. Thus it is nearly impossible to predict the growth rate, form, patterns, and colors of any coral in a given captive environment. As long as the coral's polyps are expanded and the coral is showing evidence of calcifying growth and is not "wasting," it can be considered a success.

Captive-propagated *Xenia* sp. (waving-hand coral) grown by LeRoy Headlee is an example of a coral that requires a quiet microhabitat with moderate currents.

CORAL ZONES AND THE REEF AQUARIUM

Just as corals are found in specific zones in nature, the establish-ment of zoned coral reef displays is also recommended for the aquarium. It is a common mistake to place anything and every-thing within the same display. Corals show a high degree of ag-gression toward each other, and careless purchase of incompatible species is easily avoided. Furthermore, corals are adapted to spe-cific environments, and a reef tank has a finite limit of habitats. To place corals with widely variant light, current, and water-qual-ity requirements together in the same system is folly.

In captivity, many of the natural factors that establish coral zones in the wild have shifted in importance. Predation is usu-ally lessened, physical stresses may be greater or lesser, but inter-actions with other corals are almost certainly increased. Natural calamities are nonexistent in aquariums (unless one considers live rock avalanches and clumsiness), yet many man-made influ-ences have been added. Still, using natural zonation cues in try-ing to create facsimiles of the conditions most appropriate to given species makes a great deal of sense.

The coral keeper will find greater chances of success when tailoring conditions favorable to particular types of corals, rather than trying to combine all the species of the reef within one tank. One example would be to create a display of predominantly stony corals found on the reef crest, where fish numbers are lim-ited to help maintain low nutrient levels. Such a microhabitat would be very brightly lit throughout, and water movement would be quite strong.

A second microhabitat possibility would be a lagoonal reef tank with many fishes, but fewer corals. This type of tank would tend to have higher nutrients, lower currents, and probably less light. Soft corals and a few hardy large-polyped stony corals may be the most appropriate selections for such a tank. Lagoon tanks are an easy habitat to create, as water movement can be reduced and higher nutrient levels will be tolerated.

While it is certainly possible to maintain a few microhabitats within a single tank, it is best to take the time to think about what species and overall effects are desired for any given setup. Although this may seem confining at first, it will also result in a more realistic and aesthetically pleasing design. The informa-tion provided in the genus descriptions in this book, coupled with the observation of actual reef environments in photographs or in person, will help the new coral keeper create healthy and lifelike displays that are a pleasure to view. In such circumstances, some corals can be expected to become impressively large, so the aquarium can avoid looking like a set of rock shelves with nu-merous small "specimens" placed like so many living knickknacks in a display case.

CAPTIVE-BRED CORALS

The shock of being moved from a tropical reef to a living room aquarium is eliminated when the aquarist chooses captive-bred or aquacultured corals rather than wild-harvested specimens. By virtue of having already proved adaptable to captive conditions, these corals tend to display far greater tolerance to light, water conditions, and other survival factors. They maintain their colors more easily and often adapt quickly to a new home aquarium. In part, captive-bred corals also tend to have a better survival rate than comparable wild-caught specimens because there is much less time spent in stressful transit to the retail store.

Many captive breds have been grown in, and are adapted to, lighting and water conditions that are easily matched—or even improved upon—in the well-managed home system. Most propagators are happy to provide information about conditions in which their corals were grown. Furthermore, wild-borne parasites and diseases are not present or are largely controlled at the propagating facility. In short, captive-propagated fragments and colonies are easier to acclimate to the home aquarium, with fewer risks and unknowns involved and a much-enhanced chance of success and survival.

Aquarists are often reluctant to purchase smaller captive-raised corals when they have the choice of larger ones from the wild. The quick acclimation of the captive corals, however, makes up for the size differences. In almost every case, I have had tiny captive fragments grow larger than full-size wild colonies within a year. After several years, the captive colonies dwarf the wild ones. For this and many other reasons, I highly recommend aquacultured corals whenever they are available.

UNEXPECTED MORTALITY

Even though corals are theoretically immortal, the average age of corals on a reef is rarely over 10 years. Reports of 1,000-year-old corals certainly exist, but mortality in such a competitive habitat is common. The average age of an *Acropora* colony on the Great Barrier Reef is between 4 and 7 years, while for massive corals like *Porites* it is between 7 and 11 years. Furthermore, most corals collected from the wild for aquariums are juvenile colonies or fragments, which even in nature are more prone to suffer mortality.

In the wild branching corals are likely to begin dying from the base up, as they do not appear "committed" to their base (Meesters and Bak, 1995). Both overall vigor and regenerative ability decrease strongly over distance from the tip of a branch, and the polyps near the base may even show signs of senescence. They frequently become weakened by boring organisms, lack of food availability, or lack of light. The same is true for the shaded

Small colonies or started fragments, such as this pink *Acropora* sp. farmed in the Solomon Islands, acclimate more readily to captive aquarium conditions.

underside of corals with other growth forms.

These considerations may be of some consolation to those aquarists who have lost corals to one thing or another; rest assured that competition, diseases, and coral mortality exist in nature, as well as in captive systems.

Perhaps the most important outcome of unexpected mortalities is that the aquarist can assess the cause and nature of the event. For me, no loss is frivolous. I don't think of life as simply replaceable, and the financial loss is not the greatest disappointment. There is a great deal that can be learned from such happenings, especially to avoid repetition of the same husbandry mistakes. Careful observation and reporting of the causes of mortality may be helpful in furthering coral aquaculture practices and even in assessing possible reasons for coral mortality in stressed wild reef communities.

CHAPTER 11

Coral Health

Recognizing, Preventing, and Treating Diseases,
Worrisome Conditions, and Pests

Anyone who has witnessed serious coral disease in the wild knows the helplessness of seeing majestic colonies of animals dying from conditions that are so often brought on by the workings of humankind. To see a 10-foot-wide head of brain coral eroded and dying brings forth the same feeling as watching an old growth sequoia being felled by loggers or a rugged mountainside blasted by miners.

As a one-time medical student and former cancer researcher, I have profound feelings about coral diseases that we are currently unable to stop. There are many pathologies we still don't fully understand, and we are very far from any solutions. I hate an unsolved mystery—or maybe I love one?—and anyone who attempts to keep corals is virtually assured of seeing a threatening coral malady sooner or later. When it happens, the aquarist suddenly finds himself sharing the emotion felt by marine biologists who see reefs in sudden decline. Fortunately, as aquarium owners, we have

> **"Our understanding of the intimate relationships of microorganisms with tropical marine flora and fauna, particularly those parasites causing disease, remains the world of the very unknown."**
>
>
>
> Esther Peters, 1988

greater control over our micro-environments and, at times, a better chance of stopping the progression of the disease. At the same time, the small volume of water can easily work against us, allowing a disease to overwhelm the system very quickly.

Keeping corals in aquariums is a two-edged sword. In some cases, the loss of a beautiful animal is a consequence of inexperience, a hit-or-miss accident, or avoidable neglect. However, at times corals become sick and die even with the best of care and seemingly perfect water and lighting conditions. This is the sharp edge of the sword.

The other side is that we are able to witness the growth and the condition of corals in great detail and can become familiar with the progression of their diseases and recoveries or demises. As painful as these experiences can sometimes be, we can at least gain insight into some coral diseases and their mechanisms, if not their causes and remedies. My hope is that serious coral keepers will be able to make a contribution to the woefully limited body of knowledge about coral disease—first to increase survivability of our own specimens and also to provide insights that may be of use to biologists studying the demise of corals on the world's reefs.

In a sight altogether too familiar in many places in the tropical western Atlantic and Caribbean, a colony of **Diploria labyrinthiformis** (grooved brain coral) stands eroded and in poor condition, attacked by various sponges and algae.

Coral Mortality

The factors leading to the death of a coral may be divided into five principal categories:

Physical damage may cause or initiate coral mortality. In the wild, this may be the result of natural or man-made physical perturbances ranging from violent storms to injuries inflicted by humans. As hurricanes and boat anchors are relatively rare in aquariums, physical damage usually occurs when corals are mishandled (during collection or shipping) or become dislodged from their placement sites (by tumbling rock, powerheads, other apparatus, or livestock). Commonsense and care can reduce the incidence of physical damage in the aquarium.

Sediment damage is a major cause of coral mortality in the wild. Sedimentation from storms, land-based runoff, flooding, and other sources is increasingly problematic. The cutting of forests on tropical shores and islands for development has resulted in dire consequences for many coral reefs. Not only does eroded soil run onto the reef, but the algae that proliferate in the nutrient-rich waters can be part of a damaging progression of events. In their blooming and crashing, these algal growths can throw an entire ecosystem off balance, impacting the natural populations of herbivores and creating vast amounts of detritus from the remains of dead and digested algae.

Physical damage, here caused by a fisherman s anchor in the Philippines, can weaken corals, paving the way for disease, decline, and, possibly, death.

Visibility and, therefore, light can be greatly reduced, affecting the health of photosynthetic animals, and corals may become inundated by sediments that they cannot adequately flush. Opportunistic algae can rapidly overtake the corals when they weaken or show any exposed skeleton or substrate. A coral reef community can very rapidly be replaced by an algal reef community.

The ability of corals to withstand sedimentation varies considerably between species, with growth form and mucus secretion being the primary factors in their ability to shed foreign materials. Recently, brown morphs of *Porites* were found to reject sediment better than green morphs, and it was discovered that they had a higher rate of mucus production (Gleason, 1998). It is not known to what degree this is true for other species, although the increased densities of zooxanthellae in brown corals may result in more mucus production from increased carbon translocation, conferring an adaptive edge.

In the aquarium, sedimentation can occur when water flow is not sufficient to remove particulate matter, food, or other detritus from the surface of sessile organisms. Corals placed on the bottom or in low-flow areas are more likely to accumulate sediments. Substrate-sifting gobies and other sand-stirring organisms can also create sedimentation problems, especially for corals placed on or near the bottom. Many corals can be partially or totally covered on a regular basis by the sifting actions of such animals. Strong currents can also blow "sand drifts" over the top of some bottom-dwelling specimens, like fungiids. Finally, powdery substrates, when introduced to an aquarium or stirred up, can cause a cloud of particulate matter that settles and becomes trapped on coral mucus.

Most corals, especially those from lagoon habitats and those with heavy mucus coats or branching skeletons, are capable of rejecting considerable amounts of surface sediment. However, sedimentation in the wild is primarily sand- or mineral-based and follows storms. Organic matter is largely composed of detritus. In the aquarium, organic matter that may settle on corals is often food-based and is quickly acted upon by bacteria. As such, the effects of food decomposition on a coral surface can pose a more immediate threat to the integrity of coral tissue than that of sand or mineral sediment. Both the increased number of bacteria and local anoxia (oxygen deprivation) can overwhelm corals or render them more susceptible to disease. Watching carefully for potentially troublesome detritus will allow the coral keeper to flush the waste material or sediment away with directed water flow from a powerhead, turkey baster, or syringe.

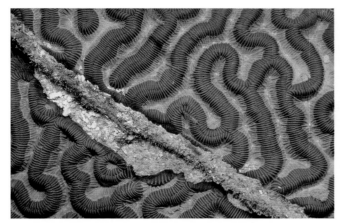

Sediment damage: foreign object traps detritus on injured brain coral.

Animal predation: hawksbill turtle grazes on *Euphyllia parancora*. (Papua NG)

Animal predation: parrotfishes eat tons of coral daily. (Bahamas)

Algal destruction: green hair algae overtaking *Tubipora musica*. (Indonesia)

The third category of coral mortality in the wild is **animal predation**. Many animals on the reef are **corallivores**, or coral-eaters. With the exception of plagues of corallivorous gastropods and *Acanthaster planci*, the Crown-of-Thorns Starfish, however, coral growth and coral predation are generally balanced. Even the grazing by parrotfishes, as substantial as it is, does not usually impact the net positive growth of coral reefs. In the aquarium, the closed environment allows coral predation to be controlled. Even with prudent avoidance of coral predators, however, some are occasionally introduced accidentally with live rock, live sand, or other material. Intervention on the part of the aquarist can be required to avoid significant losses.

The fourth category of coral mortality in the wild is **algal destruction**. Boring algae play a key role in the asexual reproduction of some coral species, but are largely incompatible with coral growth. These algae are also present in the captive environment. Corals that are damaged or weakened can become vulnerable to attack by various types of algae. (Some algae also contribute directly to coral disease and will be discussed further later in this chapter.)

The fifth and final cause of coral mortality is **disease**. Not long ago, very little was known of coral pathogens, or even if they existed. Stress factors (such as water quality conditions, sedimentation, and shifts in salinity, lighting, or temperature) were yet to be considered important triggers of coral disease. Today, there is a greatly heightened awareness of coral diseases in the wild, but there is still comparatively little known about their causes and origins (etiology) or mechanisms, much less how to treat them.

Recent coral reef epizootics (the animal kingdom equivalent to human epidemics), both disease and nondisease events, have devastated entire ecosystems. These include the widespread bleaching events in 1983 and 1987 and, in some areas, the loss of up to 95% of Atlantic *Acropora* species to white-band and black-band diseases. Some of the diseases being seen on coral reefs in the past few years had been previously unknown. In some cases, the problems appear directly related to unusually warm water temperatures, while in others it is suspected that anthropogenic (of human origin) influences may be at least partly responsible. Yet these natural tragedies have had some positive effects. They have alerted the public and coral researchers to the plight of the reefs. Through media coverage of such natural tragedies, the world has become more aware of the devastation occurring in these lush underwater landscapes.

DISEASE PROCESSES AND DEFENSES

Because of the symbiotic existences of many corals, understanding their disease processes can be exceedingly difficult. Fitt (1995) stated eloquently: "It is not clear at present whether coral death is solely a function of animal tissue death, or if lack or dysfunction of zooxanthellae may trigger or exacerbate events preceding host tissue sloughing and coral death." Simply put, it may be that some diseases affect coral polyps, while others strike the zooxanthellae.

Several definitions are useful in discussing disease. **Etiology** is the study or theory of the factors that cause a disease and the method of their introduction to a host. It is also the study of **pathogenesis**, or the cellular events, reactions, and mechanisms that occur in the development of the disease. **Disease**, strictly defined, is: "Any deviation from or interruption of the normal structure or function of any part, organ, or system (or combination thereof) that is manifested by a characteristic set of symptoms and signs and whose etiology, pathology, and prognosis may be known or unknown." Esther C. Peters (1997) uses the following characteristics to define coral disease:

1. an identifiable group of signs and/or
2. a recognized etiological or causal agent and/or
3. consistent structural alterations.

The pioneer researcher of coral disease, and an ongoing leader in the epizootiology field, is Arnfried Antonius. He is credited with the first descriptions of coral disease in 1973 and continues to be involved in helping to understand most of the major diseases that affect corals and coral reefs. Thanks to his work, the world has been alerted to many of these previously unknown maladies. The intensive efforts of Peters (and many others) have continued the ever-increasing investigation into coral disease, so that we may understand both the cause and effect of such maladies in the wild. More and more scientists are now looking into the alarming increases in coral diseases. There are now between 13 and 15 recognized, distinctive coral diseases reported in the wild, and only 4 positive identifications of cause. Disease is responsible for rapid loss of coral communities, both on the reef and in the aquarium.

Corals, according to present knowledge, have one primary defense against irritation and attack. This is the production of mucus. As we have seen, mucus is already the site of bacterial colonization, some types of which are likely pathogenic. For example, *Vibrio* species, implicated in some coral disease, may already comprise up to 20-30% of the normal bacterial population of the mucus of assessed corals.

Ritchie and Smith (1997) showed a shift in resident microbial populations in diseased corals to favor the proliferation of *Vibrio*. These bacteria are opportunistic and seem well adapted to utilize necrotic tissue as a substrate, though the degree to which they may play a causative role in coral disease is unknown at present. *Vibrio alginolyticus*, a normal component of coral mucus microbial flora, is closely related to a bacterium known to be pathogenic, and it shows a remarkable fondness for coral mucus. It is a rapid colonizer, is highly motile, and attacks the protein and sugar components of mucus. If a coral is stressed or injured, it will usually secrete excess mucus to cope with the stress, and the mucus composition and even the mucus-producing cells may change under such conditions. Despite being protective against many potential stressors in the wild, mucus alone can be a flimsy defense system. Furthermore, some corals are more proficient at mucus secretion than others. Repeated stress or serious tissue/skeletal trauma can lead to opportunistic algae encroaching on healthy coral tissue, or it can result in disease-causing bacteria and other microorganisms gaining a foothold and overtaking the coral.

As a next line of defense, corals display immunity. Researchers in invertebrate immunity have shown corals to possess all the requirements for a full-functioning immune system. Phagocytes (cells that attack bacteria and other invasive particles) have been found in corals. They are capable of mounting both directed and general responses to potential invaders. Corals do not possess the more advanced humoral (bodily fluid) immunity of vertebrates with true circulatory systems, nor do they possess many of the more "advanced" immunocompetent cell types, but they do have an effective system for dealing with the often intensive assaults of the marine environment. They possess many cell types and molecules analogous to the more well studied vertebrate systems. Some of these are considered the evolutionary precursors of vertebrate immunity. Others are virtually the same as in vertebrate models, as certain types of immunocompetence are found in all taxa of multicellular animals—

even in bacteria. Furthermore, corals secrete bioactive compounds, many of which have antibiotic effects. The soft corals and gorgonians are particularly well studied in this regard, although recent work by Esther Koh (1997) has shown that stony corals produce the same type of compounds. Some of these substances show antibiotic activity secondarily to their function in other roles. However, the specificity in other cases indicates they are most active against pathogens that are typically not native to their surface or their area.

CORAL BACTERIA

There is a great deal of confusion about the role of bacteria in aquarium coral maladies. Bacteria have not yet been found to play definitive roles in most of the coral diseases studied in the wild, though investigative work is still underway and microbiological studies have not been performed in many cases (Peters, pers. comm.).

Despite their reputation as a major source of disease in aquarium corals, bacteria are not all "bad." The phrase "bacteria-laden mucus" has been repeatedly cited as the explanation for many undiagnosed coral mortality events, with no evidence whatsoever that bacteria are the cause. Given that "bacteria-laden mucus" is an important trophic constituent for reef animals, such blanket pronouncements do little to further our understanding of the nature of coral disease. The presence of bacteria on coral surfaces is normal, and under healthy conditions and low stress, none known at present should become problematic pathogens. Normal coral bacterial flora found in the gastrovascular cavity and on the mucus may produce their own antimicrobial substances or anti-fungal substances that may serve both to protect the bacteria and to act as an agent of immunity for the coral. It is becoming recognized that these normal bacterial flora may have a symbiotic relationship with the corals (Kelman et al., 1998; Ferrier-Pages et al., 1998; and others). These bacteria are commonly gram-negative strains like *Pseudomonas* and *Vibrio* (Ritchie and Smith, 1995; Ducklow and Mitchell, 1979; and others)

However, infections from different bacteria and other organisms can and do occur in corals. Sometimes, the coral is able to recover completely or sustain comparatively minor damage after a brief or somewhat sustained trauma. Many other times, especially in the comparatively stressful captive environment, the loss of an entire colony is a result. The major bacterial components of coral mucus include the potential pathogens *Vibrio alginolyticus* and *V. parahaemolyticus*. While not proved to cause a single coral disease, these bacteria are known to cause gastroenteritis in humans—severe abdominal disorders resulting in sloughing of the inner tissue of the digestive tract that can result

Bacterial infections are often blamed for deaths of large-polyped stony corals, such as this *Cynarina lacrymalis*, although diagnosis is difficult. Note new buds.

in life-threatening diarrhea. These bacteria are present in large quantities in normal healthy coral mucus, along with a diverse microbial community that is critical to coral metabolism.

There are also opportunistic pathogens, such as the *Sphingomonas* sp., associated with a disease of wild corals known as white plague Type II and the various microbial associations in some of the so-called "band diseases." However, the presence of bacteria on coral surfaces is normal, and under healthy conditions and low stress, none known at present has been shown to become problematic as a virulent pathogen.

There is little doubt that any of a number of types of bacteria can cause disease in injured or stressed corals. It is, however, very important to recognize that bacteria are not coral enemies that must be exterminated. Using broad-spectrum antibiotics to kill all bacteria would lead to the loss of the productive and important microbial communities in the aquarium—a highly detrimental attack on the innocent and essential mediators of natural and captive community ecology.

RECOGNIZED CORAL DISEASES

There has been much misinformation in the aquarium literature as to what comprises coral disease. Aquarium hobbyists commonly refer to bleaching, recession events, infections, and rapid tissue necrosis (RTN) as "diseases." Some may, indeed, be diseases caused by pathogens (biotic factors), while others are diseases linked to physical stress, nutritional deficiencies, or other environmental problems (abiotic factors). Stressful conditions are both part and parcel of disease, and it is important for the new aquarist to realize that pathogens are far from universally responsible for disease processes. Corals have the ability to adapt to change and stress (homeostasis), but when various factors are beyond the limits of their adaptive mechanisms, impairment of function and disease results (Peters, pers. comm.). In fact, stressful conditions are probably the most significant contributor to coral mortality in captivity.

The following section contains descriptions of those conditions currently recognized as true coral diseases. Some have been reported for many years, while others have only recently been described. Low levels of disease may have always been present, although the increased frequency and types of coral disease on reefs has become a cause for concern. Future work will probably contribute greatly to the understanding of the etiology, nature, and occurrence of these diseases.

There is almost no information base for the treatment of coral disease. Suggestions below are based on the accumulated findings of those who have used a given method successfully and the small amount of data available on the subject. It is certain that there are far better methods of treatment yet to be discovered as knowledge is gained. A small degree of experimentation may not only save a coral in a captive reef, but may give rise to new methods for treating disease in the wild. Any disease treatment should be carried out in a quarantine treatment tank to avoid exposing healthy corals to further contact with potential pathogens or any stress-causing medications and chemicals that could be harmful to the tank community. Treatment tanks should be set up carefully with proper water flow, lighting, water quality and temperature. Just as sick people require pampering, so do unhealthy corals. Exposing an already weakened coral to the further stress of inhospitable conditions seriously and obviously lessens any chance for success.

Black-band disease (BBD) is a highly infectious and contagious disease thought to be caused primarily by the cyanobacterium *Phormidium corallyticum*, aided by a variable consortium of other opportunistic agents. The disease progression is marked by a characteristic black mat, beneath which coral tissue is dying and being digested by ectoenzymes of various attacking organisms. Within the band there may be ciliate protozoans, acoelate turbellarians, sulfide oxidizing bacteria (*Beggiatoa* species), sulfate-reducing bacteria (*Desulfovibrio* species), nematodes, a marine fungus, and small crustaceans that join in the "feast," creating a deadly dark line that moves slowly across the coral. Advancing at a rate of just millimeters per day, it slowly

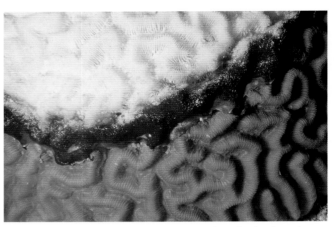

Black-band disease: note dark reddish cyanobacteria at the site of attack.

leaves a bare skeleton in its path, and this is quickly grown over by filamentous algae that trap silt and worsen local conditions. Originally reported in the Caribbean, black-band disease is now known to occur worldwide. It normally starts from a preexisting area of damaged tissue, possibly exacerbated by local conditions of active disease in other corals. In other words, the pathogens adapt to local conditions much the way viruses and bacteria form host population strains (Grosholz and Ruiz, 1997). BBD is also correlated to high nitrate and phosphate levels, perhaps related to the increase in problem algae that results from high nutrient levels. High temperatures—above 29°C (84°F)—increase the likelihood of BBD, while temperatures lower than 22°C (72°F) seem to inhibit the infection completely and halt progression of existent disease. Only alcyonarians, *Tubipora musica*, and the fungiids (which are heavy mucus producers) seem to be immune to this disease, although certain species are more susceptible than others. BBD occasionally halts on its own, and although recovery is possible in some cases, recession often continues even in the absence of the band. Gonadal development is also halted following BBD tissue loss.

In the aquarium, BBD is rarely seen (Richardson, pers. comm.) but if it does occur, early detection is crucial to prevent its spread. Any affected corals should be removed to a treatment tank. Because cyanobacteria are susceptible to antibiotics, a paste can be made of the antibiotic and saltwater. Neomycin sulfate is an excellent antibiotic that is very effective, though other broad-spectrum antibiotics may be used with varying degrees of success. The paste is lightly brushed onto the band area and allowed to remain in the treatment tank until at least several days after the black line is gone. The porosity of the coral skeleton allows sufficient antibiotic to remain on the coral even while immersed. High salin-

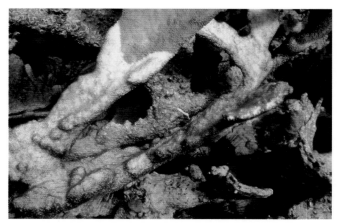

White-band disease: killing *Acropora palmata* (elkhorn coral). **(St. Croix)**

ity and/or 2-3 days of darkness are also somewhat effective in stopping the disease, albeit somewhat stressfully. Alternately, the coral may be broken off a centimeter or so ahead of the progressing band and the healthy part placed back into the aquarium. Harold Hudson developed a technique in which the band material is siphoned off and modeling clay applied to limit further bacterial and fungal infection with some success (Kuta, 1997).

White-band disease (WBD) was first described in 1977 and is sometimes incorrectly called white plague or white death. Such nomenclature is confusing because other diseases with separate etiologies have now been discovered and are known as white plague Types I and II. WBD occurs as two types also.

In WBD Type I, there is a clear and distinct margin of slowly advancing tissue necrosis. A progressive white band expands at a rate of several millimeters per day across the coral skeleton, leaving it bare. The tissue peels away from the skeleton in little balls (Gladfelter, 1982) with zooxanthellae largely intact. There is no consistent abnormal accumulation of organisms at the band, and analyses of microorganisms at local sites of infection reveal a host of bacteria, fungi, and other life. However, none of them are present at concentrations that would not ordinarily be expected on healthy specimens. One study did indicate the presence of gram-negative rod-shaped bacteria extracellularly (but surrounded by coral tissue) in WBD-affected *Acropora* colonies. Most recently, an absence of a microbial band was found, with ovoid bodies (possibly cellular and not microrganismal) in the basal tissue layers. The pathogenesis appears to occur from the basal tissues and may be a coral's response to stress (Guest et al., 1999; Le Tissier, pers. comm.; Borneman and Lowrie, 1998b).

WBD Type II is more virulent and results in a fast progres-

sion of necrosis across the coral skeleton. In WBD Type II, the disease line is variable and some tissue may bleach before becoming necrotic. A bacterium has been isolated from corals expressing WBD Type II: *Vibrio charcharii*. It is always present with an odd assortment of other bacteria, but it has not yet fulfilled the requirements of Koch's postulates as a causative agent. Its presence may be problematic or entirely benign.

WBD Type I remains among the most mysterious disease of coral, since no causative organism has yet been isolated in its long and well-studied history of occurrences. It is rarely, though occasionally, contagious to other corals, and seems to appear primarily at weakened areas of the coral (Peters, pers. comm.). Smith and Ritchie (1995) also reported a strain of *Vibrio charcharii* and *V. mediterranei* isolated from WBD samples, although their later work (Ritchie and Smith 1995, 1997) seems to indicate that *Vibrio*s are more adapted to utilizing the necrotic tissue than as a potential causative pathogen. White-band diseases can also serve as a starting point for black-band disease.

WBD almost always begins at the shaded base of corals (99% of the time by some accounts), and under overhangs, holes, or breaks in the skeleton. It has also been found to originate in the middle of branches in *Acropora cervicornis*. Although tissue may superficially appear normal at the time of purchase, degenerative changes and partial necrosis may be present in the coral's cells. Stress from collection is likely partly causal. Any further changes, including the relatively high nutrient levels commonly found in reef aquariums, may mark the beginning of a white-band-type condition in captive corals. Affected corals begin to lose tissue at varying rates in a recession area characterized by the presence of the white band. Some suggestion of an algae correlation has been made, and also one of temperature. Most recently, the corallivorous snail *Drupella cornus* has been associated with this disease (Antonius and Riegl, 1998). WBD is unaffected by antibiotics, which makes sense as there is no known causative microbial pathogen.

White-band disease, according to Peters, is confined to acroporid corals with a specific band of bare skeleton and bacterial aggregates. Antonius uses a broader definition, encompassing all species (including large-polyped corals) that lose tissue from the base of the colony and show the characteristic white band.

Treatment at present is limited. The use of antiseptic baths of Lugol's solution and/or chloramphenicol (see pages 389-391) may be somewhat useful in some cases. Fragmentation is often necessary to halt the spread of the disease and to prevent total colony loss. Proper water flow, lighting, and water conditions are most effective in preventing or halting WBD following fragmentation or remission.

Possible **shut-down reaction**: rapid, complete tissue loss in a wild *Acropora*.

Stress-related necrosis: note tissue loss on colony of *Montastraea cavernosa*.

Possible **white plague**: note blotches of dead tissue on *Montastraea* sp.

Shut-down reaction (SDR) is the most rapidly progressing disease ever reported in wild corals, and it was first described in 1977 by Antonius. In this malady, corals, often those with an existing case of noncontagious white-band disease, begin sloughing their tissue rapidly in response to continuing or acute stress (possibly temperature-related). It was found to be most prevalent in aquarium experiments, rare in the wild, and was described using terms that mimic the descriptions of the aquarium malady rapid tissue necrosis, or RTN (see page 381). No pathogen was identified, and definitive microbiological studies have not yet been done at this writing. Antonius's description of this disease has recently resurfaced in the scientific literature (Antonius and Riegl, 1998).

Shut-down reaction is described as highly contagious, with nearby corals showing signs within 5-10 minutes of exposure. Even a slight break in coral tissue can trigger SDR, which almost invariably begins at the lower part of the coral, proceeding upward and outward like an accelerated WBD. Corals under chronic or acute stress, often exemplified by chlorophyte overgrowth, are most likely to go into a shut-down reaction. Antonius says that it is always stressed corals that show SDR and that its fast progression makes it very difficult to observe, much less study, in the wild. He feels that this and other "white syndromes" are related, and notes that photographs of rapid tissue necrosis in aquarium corals appear similar to cases of SDR he has seen in the wild (Antonius, pers. comm.). It should be noted that not all coral researchers include shut-down reaction in their lists of generally recognized diseases.

OTHER DISEASES

The emergence of several new coral diseases has been reported in the past few years. These diseases, thus far, are not common in aquariums, although some have been reported from time to time.

Stress-related necrosis (SRN) is the label used by Peters for cases of tissue loss from the base of the colony upward in corals other than *Acropora* spp. The disease signs are similar to those of white plague (see below), but it is not known whether or not this disease has the same causative agent, because no microbiological studies have been performed on SRN (Peters, pers. comm.). SRN may be reversible.

White pox appears as randomly scattered pale blotches caused by patches of tissue loss. The description is "a white rash, as though bleach has been splattered on an otherwise healthy stand." (Bruckner and Bruckner, 1998). It is common to *Acropora palmata* (elkhorn coral) in the Florida Keys.

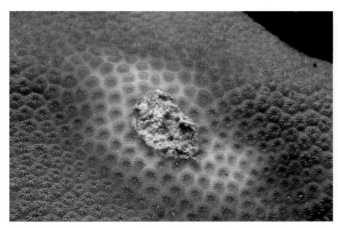

Yellow-blotch disease: a spreading problem on massive Caribbean corals, this disease kills tissue in patches, after which algae will colonize the skeleton.

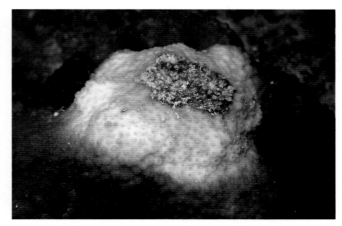

Rapid-wasting disease: scientists suspect that physical damage in the form of parrotfish bite marks may be associated with the onset of this disease.

White plague Type I has been known since the late 1970s and is characterized by the relatively rapid loss of tissue, especially in massive and encrusting coral species, leaving an exposed white skeleton behind. It was first reported in the Florida Keys but is now known to occur worldwide. No causative pathogen has been identified. (It resembles white-band disease but typically occurs at a faster rate.)

White plague Type II is a fast-progressing disease very similar to white plague Type I and seen in the Florida Keys in recent years. It spreads at up to 2 cm (0.75 in.) per day, while Type I typically advances at a rate of several millimeters (less than 0.25 in.) per day. A new species of bacterium of the genus *Sphingomonas* appears to be the sole cause of the disease. It is most common in the Caribbean elliptical star coral (*Dichocoenia stokesii)*, although the susceptibility of other corals, especially in aquariums, is unknown.

Yellow-blotch disease (YBD) primarily affects massive reef-building corals. First discovered in the Caribbean and Florida Keys, the disease is characterized by the appearance of yellow blotchy patches or rings on the upper surfaces or sides of corals. Necrosis occurs as the rings spread outward, and the coral is then attacked by filamentous algae. It has been seen in mid-depth to shallow-water corals in areas of pollution and runoff, but also in unspoiled reefs. There is some speculation that this disease may be a problem with the zooxanthellae rather than with the coral tissue, as the tissue appears fairly normal and the discoloration is from pigment lightening. This is rapidly becoming one of the more widespread diseases affecting corals in the Caribbean.

Rapid-wasting disease (RWD) was first noted in late 1996 and has been studied in the West Indies by coral researcher Ray Hayes. A filamentous fungus was reported to be associated with this blight (Cervino et al., 1997) and it may still be present in some samples. However, it is now known that this "disease" is actually caused by the repeat biting behavior of the Stoplight Parrotfish, *Sparisoma viride* (Bruckner & Bruckner, 1998, 2000). The bites may serve as introduction sites for other pathogens or algal encroachment, and the fungus originally reported may be a fungus associated with the parrotfish's teeth. Algae encroachment occurs rapidly on the denuded areas. The proliferation of algae communities in areas where it is found indicates that this "disease" is occurring where local nutrients are high. It affects mainly massive-type corals in mid-depth to shallow waters.

Aspergillosis is a fungal (*Aspergillus sydowii*) disease that affects sea fans (*Gorgonia* species) and is likely to affect other gorgonians. Oddly, this fungus is normally found in terrestrial soil, not in the marine environment. It does not sporulate in seawater, and its presence may be largely from terrestrial sedimentation (Nagelkerken et al., 1997a,b). Aspergillosis creates tissue lesions that result in coral mortality.

Red-band disease (RBD) affects gorgonians as well as certain stony corals in much the same way as black-band disease. It is also a cyanobacterially mediated affliction, although *Phormydium coralliticum* is not present. The cyanobacteria *Schyzothrix* sp. and *Oscillatoria* sp. are both present in the band. RBD, with a characteristic mat of reddish cyanobacteria, moves slower than black-band disease, advancing only during the day.

Brown-band disease was originally reported in 20 species of stony corals around the Great Barrier Reef. It has since been reported from other Pacific regions. The etiology of this disease has not been determined, though it may also be a cyanobacteria-mediated affliction. Some researchers have lumped it with red-band disease until more definitive studies have been completed.

Yellow-band disease was reported in 1998 in the Gulf of Oman. Corals most affected so far are various *Acropora* species, *Porites* species, *Turbinaria reniformis*, and *Cyphastrea* species. It is characterized by a broad yellow band that moves across the coral surface like BBD, but the denuded skeleton can remain yellow. It seems to progress faster in warmer temperatures, similar to other band-type diseases. It is suspected that this disease is pathogen-based, and investigations are continuing. This may also be known as yellow-line disease. Both names are occasionally used, erroneously, to describe yellow-blotch disease.

Patchy necrosis has been described as irregular necrosing areas on the surface of elkhorn coral (*Acropora palmata*). Tissue loss occurs quickly, spreading outward from localized, apparently random, points of origin across the coral surface. (Perhaps synonymous with white pox disease.)

Dark spots disease is characterized by small discolorations of the tissues of *Siderastrea* spp. and it has received much discussion in scientific Internet groups over the past year. Peters reports that the discolored areas can be quite extensive and might be seasonal in nature, based on her observations of corals in the Florida Keys. Tissue loss can result, but corals can recover with a regrowth of tissue and skeleton, leaving a "dimpling" effect on the surface of the colony (Peters, pers. comm.)

Purple-ring disease is a syndrome primarily affecting *Porites* species in the Pacific. It has been alternately called pink/purple spot/ring/blotch disease and does not represent a properly described disease at this point. Blotchy areas have been noted with some regularity in massive *Porites* species. The lesions are described as having algal encroachment and a distinctive pink-purple ring. Cervino (pers. comm.) describes a group of ovoid pink fungal hyphae raised above the lesion margins like filamentous warts. The remaining discoloration may be due to a common response of corals (especially *Porites* species) to become discolored, often purple, in response to stress or injury.

OTHER POSSIBLE DISEASE AGENTS

Bacteria: *Beggiatoa* are oxic (aerobic) bacteria that have been associated with coral necrosis in the Pacific and Caribbean. One case followed an oil spill in the Pacific, while Peters (1984) reported a whitish film of *Beggiatoa* filaments on a colony of *Porites astreoides* in the Caribbean. They are common components of BBD bacterial consortiums, but do not appear to be causative pathogenic organisms in coral disease. *Desulfovibrio* species are anaerobic sulfide-reducing bacteria that often accompany disease or band accumulations. Increased mucus production from stagnation, turbidity, irritants, and stress may create anoxia at the coral surface, which leads to the proliferation of these bacteria. They are commonly members of BBD consortiums.

Protozoans have also been found in coral tissue. *Nematopsis* sp., a sporozoan, has been associated with cell hypertrophy in *Porites*

Patchy necrosis: similar to white pox and seen here on *Acropora palmata*.

Dark spots disease: note discoloration spreading on this colony of *Siderastrea*.

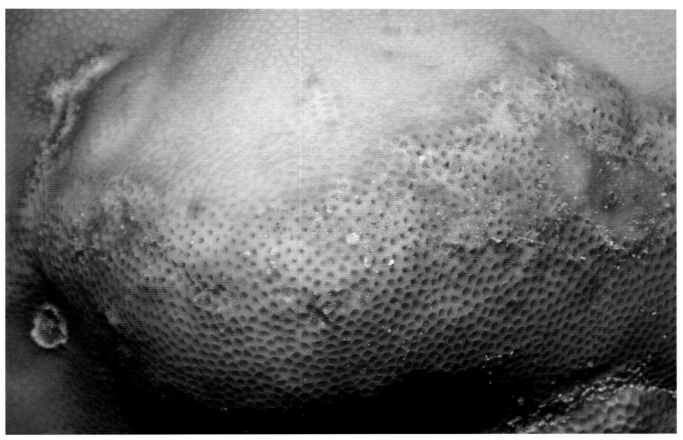

Purple-ring disease: this syndrome is seen primarily in *Porites* spp., which have a tendency to become discolored when injured or subjected to localized stress.

porites. This organism may involve mollusk or crustacean hosts in part of its life cycle. In 1986, a type of coccidean oocyst, ***Gemmocystis cylindrus***, was isolated from the mesenterial filaments of several stony corals after the colonies began displaying patchy bleaching, atrophy, and some tissue necrosis. **Ciliates** have been found associated with or embedded in both healthy and necrotic tissue of scleractinians in the Caribbean. Brown ciliates have been identified on "moribund" colonies of *Heteroxenia* species in the Red Sea (Gohar, 1940). **Amoebae** have also been found in large numbers in the calicoblast tissue of *Siderastrea* species.

Other organisms have been documented to cause disease or weakness in corals, but other than careful examination of a specimen to avert introduction of such pathogens, there is little that can be done to prevent such occurrences or to treat a preexisting case. Most treatment strategies depend on what organism is causing the problem, but freshwater dips of tolerant corals may be advised for infestations of externally parasitic animals.

ABNORMAL GROWTHS ("TUMORS")

Abnormal growths are occasionally seen on various species of stony corals and some gorgonians. Although commonly described as "tumors," some of these are true neoplasms (uncontrolled proliferations), while others are areas of localized accelerated growth (hyperplasms) or tumorous lesions growing in response to algal or fungal agents.

Tumors reported in *Acropora* spp. and *Montipora* spp. by Bak, Cheney, and Peters et al. (1983) were defined as "superficial calcified protuberances showing an abnormal arrangement of calcicular and polypary elements" that result in gigantism, corallite distortion, and other malformations. They have been reported for over 30 years. There have been other reports of abnormal tissue growth in *Madrepora kauaiensis, Agaricia lamarcki,* and *Diploria strigosa.* I have also seen a large growth on a *Diploria clivosa* in the Caribbean.

The effect of true tumors on coral tissue is much the same

Abnormal growth: note giant corallites on this *Echinophyllia* sp. (Indonesia)

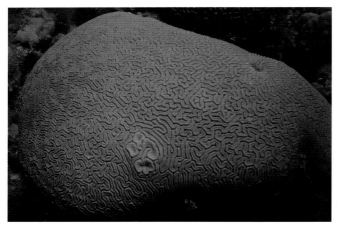

Abnormal growth: unusual skeletal development on *Diploria labyrinthiformis.*

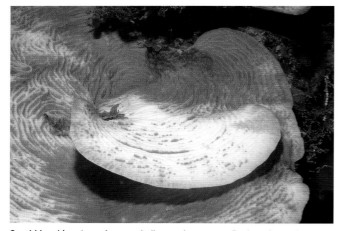

Coral bleaching: loss of zooxanthellae or pigments on *Pachyseris speciosa.*

as with neoplasms in higher animals. Pronounced change in both skeletal corallite and tissue appearance is present, along with decreased function. Rapid or abnormal growth is often present. The tumors may metastasize (spread), are nutrient-dependent on the host tissue, and are invasive. Normal polyp tissue is destroyed, with the polyps replaced by tumor tissue and skeleton. Calcification is abnormal (although the aragonite crystal structure may remain the same), and tumors are typically lighter colored or white, due to decreased or abnormal zooxanthellae populations.

Other types of unusual growths include "gigantism," in which a section of a colony grows rapidly, expanding with normal cellular structures (not tumorous tissue). In *Madrepora,* a crustacean symbiont is known to cause the development of lesions, and algae and fungi are also known as etiologic agents in the development of tumors on some gorgonians (Goldberg et al., 1984; Nagelkerken et al., 1997a,b; Peters, pers. comm.).

There are no known cures for abnormal growths, but these are seldom reported as the cause of coral losses in aquarium settings.

VIRUSES

There is very little known about specific viruses related to coral diseases, but their occurrence in marine habitats and their pathogenicity makes them likely contenders as disease-causative organisms. These tiny, highly mutable organisms, which have received so much attention in the mass media and scientific literature, deserve increased attention for their possible involvement in cnidarian disease processes. Their possible role in some of the observed abnormal growths in some corals has yet to be established.

OTHER CONDITIONS & EVENTS

Several other types of events (which may or may not represent true disease processes) can result in coral mortality.

Bleaching: Probably the most likely problem to be encountered with corals, both in the wild and in aquariums, is bleaching. Bleaching is defined as the mass expulsion of zooxanthellae or their pigments from the coral, which typically appears white or abnormally light in color. (It is important to note that a bleached coral is still very much alive, albeit with translucent or slightly pigmented tissue. A coral that has been denuded of its tissue will also appear white at first, but it is no longer living.)

Bleaching is a regular occurrence on natural reefs, and some level of bleaching is almost always present in some species. In fact, as the zooxanthellae divide by mitosis, the expulsion of old, degenerate, or extra algae cells is always happening as part of the natural growth and regeneration of a coral.

However, recent widespread bleaching events in the wild

have raised concern about possible causes and possible prevention. Bleached corals, as well as those under other stressed conditions, become nutritionally compromised. Without the energy provided by a full complement of zooxanthellae, corals must meet their needs through other means. Frequently falling short of needed energy, stressed and bleached corals begin metabolizing their lipid reserves, which normally comprise from 20-90% of the dry weight of coral tissue (Glynn, 1985). Levels may fall precipitously—by 50% in as little as a few weeks. Concurrent with lipid metabolism is a significant decrease in mucus production. Without the protective and immunological function of mucus, disease resistance is reduced; protective symbiotic crabs that depend on mucus often leave the coral, opening up the potential for predation. There is no single causative agent in most bleaching events, and it can happen under a number of circumstances (see box, "Causes of Bleaching"). Interestingly, a new species of gram-negative bacteria, *Vibrio shiloi*, has recently been fingered as a causative agent in some unusual (blotchy) bleaching events in *Oculina patagonica* on the Mediterranean coast of Israel. Thus far, this is the only known example linking a bacterium with bleaching, and more work is needed to examine other species of bleaching corals for bacterial pathogens (Rosenberg and Loya, 1999).

While most attention has been focussed on zooxanthellae loss in stony corals, soft corals are no less vulnerable to bleaching. While members of the Xeniidae may be more resistant, they will disintegrate very quickly when bleached. Alcyoniids can quickly lose volume and become fouled by algae. The fact that many are highly dependent on their zooxanthellae for nutrition may be partly responsible for their often severe reaction (Fabricius, 1999).

Bleaching: stark white colonies of wild *Acropora* sp. (Australia)

CAUSES OF BLEACHING

Among the agents or factors that can singly, or in combination, cause a coral to bleach are:

bacteria
chemicals
ciliates
coccideans
darkness
fungi
heavy metals
higher temperature
hypersalinity
hyposalinity
lack of water movement (doldrums)
light
medications
noxious agents
physical stress
red spectral light
sedimentation
starvation
stress
temperature change
ultraviolet radiation (suddenly increased or prolonged exposure)

In part, bleaching occurs when the symbiosis between the coral and its zooxanthellae spins out of control, with an overproduction of oxygen radicals and peroxide that can cause the coral to expel its algae in order to survive.

It is now known that **heat shock proteins** (**hsps**) or "stress" proteins play a role in thermoregulation, and under the normal stress of elevated temperatures, these proteins are capable of reducing the likelihood of bleaching by preventing damage to important cellular proteins. However, it is likely that the formation of hsps is severely altered under extreme stress, possibly leading to a bleaching event. Recently, a calcium trigger was found to cause the production of heat shock proteins under elevated temperature conditions.

It has also been proposed that bleaching offers a competitive edge to corals, allowing them the opportunity to adopt a strain of zooxanthellae that may be better adapted to new conditions. This theory is supported by the fact that corals which have partially bleached in the past show a higher resistance to subsequent bleaching conditions. While this may be the case in nature when large and numerous colonies are affected, bleaching seriously compromises the integrity of the coral. Without the proper number of zooxanthellae in their tissues, corals must rely almost entirely on dissolved nutrient uptake and heterotrophic feeding to meet their energy needs. Without their symbionts, the corals' ready carbon source produced by zooxanthellae photosynthesis is severely, if not totally, reduced. Furthermore, there is no guarantee that a bleached coral can or will adopt new zooxanthellae. Without the uptake of new symbionts, it will then likely perish. At the least, metabolic activity becomes abnormal while the coral is in a bleached or partially bleached state, leading to changes in reproduction, reduced growth, and possible tissue degeneration.

A rise of several degrees over a relatively short period of time, including constant ambient temperatures from 29-32°C (85-89°F), can induce bleaching in corals accustomed to lower water temperatures, possibly by lowering their resistance to pathogenic organisms. (It is also possible that the zooxanthellae, which can also suffer from temperature shifts, may induce the bleaching.) Higher temperatures also decrease the concentrations of UV-absorbing substances and increase photoinhibition.

(Aquarists can sometimes prevent bleaching if it is known that water temperatures are temporarily elevated—for example, in accidental heater/chiller failures or heat waves. If light levels are reduced significantly, corals can tolerate higher temperatures for a period without bleaching.)

Zooxanthellae densities in bleached corals are reduced by 50-90% under normal bleaching patterns. (Up to 50% loss may occur without any visible change in appearance of the coral.) Provided that the bleaching is not too severe and that the causative stressors can be removed, normal zooxanthellae populations can be regained in a few weeks to a few months. Wild bleached corals generally take a few months to a year to recover as zooxanthellae migrate or are taken up to replace those that are lost. However, a bleached coral is severely limited nutritionally and may be prone to necrosis, disease, predation, or starvation. Even after zooxanthellae populations are normalized, recovery of lost tissue biomass and energy stores can take some time. Growth rates may be slowed for a considerable period after recovery of zooxanthellae populations as the coral will have utilized its own tissues (lipids, etc.) during the time of bleaching/nutritional compromise.

Decalcification:

Decalcification: Skeletal dissolution occurs naturally in several fungiids as a normal means of asexual reproduction. However, other corals may begin to degenerate spontaneously despite a fairly healthy appearance and good polyp expansion. The

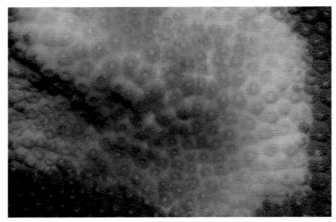

Bleaching with recovery: note return of zooxanthellae at center of white patch.

skeleton progressively dissolves from within, often continuing until the coral finally dies. Decalcification occurs more rapidly than would be expected if the denuded skeleton were simply exposed to normal reef decomposition processes. This may indicate an active role by the coral (Ikeda et al., 1992).

The mechanism by which corals are able to decalcify is somewhat of a mystery, but it appears that at least some species have biochemical control over the process. It is likely that the energy or nutrients liberated by the decalcification process are needed by the coral, whether to satisfy carbonate, internal pH, zooxanthellae needs, inadequate respiration, or other factors. The most likely external cause is a fluctuation in calcium, in which the level present in the surrounding water is lower than saturation, resulting in a net outward flux of calcium from the coral itself.

Boring sponges, worms, and algae may exacerbate the process or be entirely responsible in some cases, and bacteria can also be responsible for the intraskeletal dissolution of aragonite. In some cases, such decalcification is deleterious to the integrity of the coral, though it may also play a role in the asexual spread of corals by fragmentation, as well as in ensuring biodiversity and available substrate for natural colonization.

The most common cause of problematic decalcification in captivity is the lack of bioavailable calcium, carbon sources, or other elements required for skeletogenesis in the water. Usually, the addition of these elements to the water will reverse the process, provided other tank conditions are adequate. Sometimes, however, the decalcification continues despite efforts to stop it, and the coral will slowly lose mass until it perishes.

Polyp bail-out: Polyp bail-out is a regular occurrence in several coral species, notably the pocilloporids. These species have gained

Dying *Catalaphyllia jardinei*: a common victim of brown jelly infections.

an advantageous ability to withdraw their coenosarc and systematically dislodge entire polyps, zooxanthellae intact, from their limestone encasement. The freed polyp may drift considerable distances and settle in an environment that may or may not be better than the one it has escaped. Two slightly adhesive filaments are retained by the polyp to facilitate a successful settlement. Under natural conditions, less than 5% of such bailed polyps will settle successfully after a nonattached state that typically lasts 7-9 days.

Polyp bail-out almost always occurs in response to a disease or stress. Although corals that are undergoing a bail-out may appear to be bleaching, close examination shows that small round balls are occasionally floating out from the skeleton and are intact. By contrast, the expelled zooxanthellae of a bleaching coral occur in strands and masses of brown pigment and/or tissue.

In the aquarium, the removal of environmental stress or disease is necessary to stop bail-out from progressing completely. Although some new settlement may occur, aquariums with strong circulation and efficient protein skimmers will reduce this likelihood. Removing the bailing coral to another aquarium with less stressful conditions or one that will better allow for settlement may be helpful.

AQUARIUM MALADIES

A number of conditions have been observed to cause coral mortality or "sickness" in the aquarium. In some cases, I think of these as "dis-ease," for the ailments often spontaneously vanish. Alternatively, they can progress until a loss of polyps or entire colonies has occurred. Although these conditions show a loss or interruption of normal function, this does not necessarily imply that a pathogen is involved. (Faulty nutrition or water-quality

problems are common suspects.) Most of these conditions seem, so far, to be limited to aquarium-kept corals.

Until now, aquarists have described such conditions superficially: "It died on me." "It failed to thrive." But this is increasingly unsatisfactory. Our understanding of the captive reef environment is reaching a level where we should be able to sustain the life of most corals.

Brown jelly or protozoan infections are commonly seen by aquarists, notably in certain large-polyped corals such as *Galaxea*, *Euphyllia*, *Catalaphyllia*, *Xenia*, and others. The infection is often initiated by tissue trauma or accidental damage to the coral specimen. At such times, opportunistic protozoans (e.g., *Helicostoma* sp.) and a host of other organisms begin to digest the injured tissue. Ectoenzymes and further digestion of the tissue by the feeding organisms perpetuate the infection until the coral tissue is consumed. Brown jelly infections may progress fairly rapidly, often leading to the loss of the entire colony. In addition, nearby colonies may be affected, and the infection may spread across an entire tank.

Higher temperatures and poor water quality are the most important contributors to an increased likelihood of brown jelly infections.

To treat an afflicted specimen, as much of the digested tissue (jelly) should be siphoned or brushed off the unhealthy coral as possible. Ideally, this should occur outside of the main tank. The mix of dead tissue and microorganisms should be considered a contagious agent, as the jelly can initiate infections in nearby corals. Once cleansed of the excess slough, the coral can be given a freshwater dip for several minutes to kill many of the microorganisms present. An antibiotic paste on the infected areas or a Lugol's dip may also be advised as alternative or additional treatments. It is best to use the least stressful methods first and see if the result is satisfactory. Excessive treatment or stress may cause a coral to become susceptible to other infection, or may result in bleaching or the loss of the entire coral. If it appears that none of the above methods are halting the progress of the infection, the coral should be cut, snipped, or cleaved slightly ahead of the progressing jelly and the healthy piece or pieces placed in a quarantine tank. In some cases, the coral will be able to heal in such an environment.

Rapid tissue necrosis (RTN) or rapid tissue degeneration (RTD) has been the source of tremendous concern—and controversy—among reef aquarists in recent years. As the number of coral keepers and the importation of some sensitive genera such as *Acropora* have increased, a new perceived disease has been noticed with alarming regularity. It has been dubbed RTN (rapid tissue necrosis) within the reef-keeping community.

(Some coral scientists argue that the term "necrosis"—which means "the sum of the morphological changes indicative of cell death and caused by the progressive degradative action of enzymes"—is inaccurate, unless histological analyses confirm that necrosis is or is not actually present. Rapid tissue degeneration [RTD] might be a more-appropriate label for this condition.)

In a typical case, a newly introduced specimen of acroporid or pocilloporid coral begins peeling (sloughing its tissue rapidly) usually from the base up. In many cases, a coral with RTN can lose all of its tissue within a period of hours or days, leaving a stark white skeleton and absolutely no chance of recovery. The same signs sometimes spread from the afflicted coral to well-established, healthy acroporid and pocilloporid corals nearby or in the same system. In some reported cases, large, long-healthy collections of corals have been lost in a single episode of RTN. Equally often, a newly introduced coral can trigger tissue sloughing in other corals, while remaining unaffected itself.

Among the North American community of small-polyped-stony coral keepers, the "great RTN scare" began in the mid-1990s. Within a short time, Craig Bingman (enlisting the microbiological expertise of Beverly Dixon) felt he had isolated a causative pathogen, *Vibrio vulnificus,* based on samples taken from the shipping water of a number of RTN-affected corals There is little doubt of the virulence of this bacterium in humans, and it may initiate the RTN reaction in some cases. However, there have been many reports and studies done on corals that exhibit rapid tissue sloughing in the wild and in the laboratory. In many cases, no pathogen at all has been found (Peters, Antonius, Glynn, Lowrie, et al.). As Peters notes, "There are only so many ways for a coral to die" (pers. comm., 1997).

In fact, rapid tissue loss is frequently the mode of coral death, especially in thin-tissued corals, and has been reported in numerous studies on the effects of various stressors on coral populations. The observation of *Pocillopora* and *Acropora* in rapid overnight deaths has been documented, very similar to Antonius's shut-down reaction in many studies of stressed, fragmented, or injured corals (Bak and Criens, 1981; Chesher, 1985). No pathogens have been identified as causative agents, but sophisticated microbiological studies were not done in most of the cases cited (Peters, pers. comm.).

Lowrie (1992-7) induced RTN through the use of different stressors, such as sedimentation with diatomaceous earth, temperature changes, and chemicals, in *Acropora* and *Pocillopora* colonies. In my own work with Lowrie, we did bacterial platings from more than 400 separate cases of RTN and found no

Rapid tissue necrosis (RTN): *Acropora* sp. with typical bottom-first tissue loss.

consistent or obvious bacterial population at the genus level (Borneman and Lowrie, 1998a; 1998b).

It is my strong opinion that RTN will prove to be synonymous with shut-down reaction (SDR), described on page 374. In my view, RTN does not represent a new disease but rather is very likely to be, at least in part, a response to stress. It is possible, in fact, that this response results in self-rejection or autolysis—the digestion by the coral of its own tissue.

Coral desmocytes are cells that attach coral tissue to the skeleton. These cells may play a role in this and other behaviors/maladies of corals where tissue sloughing, loss of host-cell adhesion, or the bail-out of living tissue is involved. In some cases, the enzyme carbonic anhydrase may play a role in the initial onset of a tissue sloughing event (Muller et al., 1984).

Investigation of the process of tissue necrosis indicates that host-cell immune function is severely compromised. The "contagion" seen, the reaction of the affected coral, the lack of a confirmed pathogen, the lack of consistent effectiveness of antibiotic therapy, the known aspects of invertebrate immunity, and the times involved in the reaction all correspond very closely with what would be expected in a nonpathogenic, stress-related model.

It is also suspected that histoincompatibility following the addition of new coral specimens to established systems may be a key stressor in producing the reaction in certain instances. The ability of corals to detect "self" and "non-self" is very acute, and copious numbers of as-yet-unidentified allelochemical, allomone, and pheromone markers, including glycoproteins and toxic organic compounds could be involved. There have been numerous studies showing and suggesting that cytotoxic effector molecules are present in necrotic tissue or produced by dying

Rapid tissue necrosis (RTN): *Pocillopora* species are commonly vulnerable.

corals. Certainly such substances would explain the "contagion" that is a part of RTN.

There have been other terms, in addition to SDR, that also seem to describe the sudden-death reaction of RTN. "Bacteriosis" and "pull-in-of-polyps," was used to describe the reaction of corals to stress: the polyps would retract and cease to be active, with tissue falling off in strips after several days, resulting in the coral's rapid death (Sorokin, 1995). "Autolysis" was the term used by Muller et al. (1984) and Glynn (1985) to describe stress-related mortality in stony corals, and "acute toxic syndrome" was used to describe the lethal stress effects of salinity that resulted in cell changes and mortality in acroporids and pocilloporids (Glazebrock and VanWoesik, 1992). "Host cell detachment" has also been used to describe tissue death under extreme stress (Gates, Baghdasarian, and Muscatine, 1992; Buddemier and Fautin, 1993; Brown, Le Tissier, and Bythell, 1995).

The RTN reaction is most prevalent in certain species of stony corals. By far the two most affected coral types are pocilloporids and *Acropora* species, with the latter being especially susceptible. Other coral types have been observed to undergo sudden tissue loss reactions in captivity as follows:

Very Common: *Acropora* spp.
Common: *Pocillopora* spp.; *Seriatopora hystrix; Galaxea* spp.; *Cladocora* spp.; *Trachyphyllia geoffroyi*
Less Common: *Turbinaria reniformis; Stylophora pistillata; Hydnophora* spp.
Uncommon: *Lobophyllia hemprichii; Pectinia paeonia; P. alcicornis; Pachyseris* spp. (though easily induced); *Montipora digitata, M. capricornis.*

The frequency of RTN observed in predominantly wild-collected *Acropora* upon recent introduction might have a great deal to do with abnormally high stress levels to which corals are subjected in transit and in holding facilities. *Acropora* are known to be among the most-sensitive species to environmental stresses. I suspect that the high rate of mucus production in these corals, coupled with the stagnant water in shipping containers, creates an environment where both gas exchange and bacterial populations become abnormal enough to create metabolic changes that result in tissue sloughing. This has also been seen in similar corals with heavy mucus production.

This explanation may work for cases following shipping, but not for other events. RTN is also frequently reported to occur after precipitous drops in redox levels (usually following heavy sedimentation, sand stirring, etc.). Once again, it is a highly stressful event that seems to bring about the RTN response. Perhaps most interesting is the frequency with which total tissue loss occurs overnight. The implications to photosynthesis and calcification, along with the variances in the availability of CO_2 are thought-provoking. The earlier quotation by Fitt (1995) should be restated here: "It is not clear at present whether coral death is solely a function of animal tissue death, or if lack or dysfunction of zooxanthellae may trigger or exacerbate events preceding host tissue sloughing and coral death."

Indeed, there are only so many ways for a coral to die. These are only some of the common observations, and it is important to restate that the exact nature of the stress, tissue loss, or mechanism of RTN has yet to be conclusively determined.

As for treatment, there has been some indication from anecdotal reports that the use of Lugol's solution or other "SPS dip" treatment is effective in preventing the occurrence of RTN in newly introduced specimens. It is not likely that such treatments are directly responsible for the prevention, though secondary sterilization of potentially lethal numbers of mucus-cultured bacteria may ease the stress on a coral, preventing a sloughing event.

It is anecdotally reported that tank-raised RTN-susceptible species have a dramatically reduced occurrence of sloughing their tissues, though they are by no means immune. In any case, the nature of the response and the physiologic nature of these corals suggests that the following protocol will be effective in preventing an initial outbreak of RTN: all new coral specimens should be placed in a quarantine tank with strong circulation and cool (mid-20s C [70s F]) fresh seawater after a slow, drip-type acclimation period of an hour or longer. The water from the specimen container should not be added to the quarantine facility. Activated carbon and or a Poly Filter absorbent pad should be placed in a small power filter serving the quarantine tank. The specimen should remain in the quarantine container, with moderate lighting, for at least 72 hours. After this time, another slow, drip-type acclimation should be done before the coral is added to its final position in the display aquarium. None of the quarantine water should be added to the display aquarium. The coral should then be subjected to moderate photoperiods for the next several days with strong turbulent water flow around the colony. Fresh activated carbon and/or Poly Filters should also be used in the filtration system of the main aquarium for at least a week after final placement. I have found these chemical absorbents to be fairly effective in the temporary absorption of unknown biochemical compounds.

If RTN is detected in any specimen in the display aquarium, it should be removed from the tank as soon as possible to avoid triggering further RTN reactions in healthy corals. Some aquarists report success at halting the progress of RTN in individual coral colonies with repeated daily—or twice-daily—dips in Lugol's solution (see page 389), but this is far from a surefire "cure."

Another protocol established by Bingman, involving the antibiotic chloramphenicol, is effective for some *Acropora* with RTN. It offers the possibility of arresting the tissue sloughing before it consumes the coral. However, the unpredictability of this drug in saving corals tends to indicate multiple causative factors. Chloramphenicol-sensitive cases may have bacteria as a more important agent than those cases in which the drug is ineffective. Pocilloporids seem less tolerant of the procedure, tending to engage in polyp bail-out soon after being immersed in the treatment water. (The chloramphenicol procedure is outlined on page 391.)

If chloramphenicol is not available, then the coral branches may be broken off, or fragmented, well ahead of the area where tissue loss has begun. The healthy-looking fragments should be removed to a quarantine facility for at least several days before being returned to the tank. The remainder of the affected coral should be discarded entirely. RTN is almost invariably fatal, and its presence should be acted on quickly. It is one of the few times where fast action is required by the aquarist to prevent the loss of one or many corals.

OTHER AQUARIUM CONDITIONS

I include the following conditions, with working names only, in hopes that other aquarists will add their own findings and observations, and that we will eventually determine causes, reasons, and possibly cures to limit the losses of these corals both in the aquarium and in the wild.

Zoanthid condition 1 occurs when zoanthid colonial polyps stop opening for prolonged periods of time. No amount of wa-

ter changing or addition of chemical absorbents/adsorbents, additives, or food has a noticeable direct effect. The removal of potential sources/organisms of questionable chemical makeup or predatory behavior has no direct or apparent effect. Polyps may spontaneously begin to slowly open after days or weeks for no obvious reason. Occasionally, wasting and isolated polyp loss may result. Other times, there is no loss. Polyps in such a state may show some cyanobacterial growth on their surface, or may succumb to zoanthid condition 2.

Zoanthid condition 2 is characterized by zoanthid polyps closing up and becoming soft and mushy. Most often, there is a white "cheesy" deposit or film that appears on the outer surface of the polyps. This almost invariably results in the death of the animal and is almost certainly caused by *Beggiatoa* sp. A new disease of *Palythoa caribaeorum* (which may be the same as this condition) has been described and positively correlated with higher temperatures, low salinities, freshwater inputs (sediments), and maximal gonad development. No pathogen has yet been found (Acosta, 1999).

Mushroom condition 1 affects corallimorphs, primarily from the genus *Actinodiscus* (= *Discosoma*), which fail to thrive. They shrink, their tissue becomes mottled and pale, and they seem unable to regain the ability to expand. This behavior seems remarkably like the wasting of certain anemones, and the similarities in the biology of corallimorphs and anemones may be relevant. As in zoanthid condition 1, no amount of water chemistry manipulation seems to have a pronounced effect. The en-

Zoanthid condition 2: note "cheesy" deposits on the outer surface of the polyps. The pathogen is almost certainly *Beggiatoa* sp. (Florida Keys)

vironment of the corallimorphs may have remained virtually unchanged in terms of normal additions, lighting, and water flow for long periods of time when this condition occurs. Individual mushrooms or whole colonies can be affected. Affected mushrooms may remain in such a state for many months, or they may die fairly quickly. Occasionally, individuals or colonies may spontaneously recover, though this is rare. This condition is different from the common "unhappy mushroom" that fails to expand under intense light or lack of proper conditions.

Large-polyp recession condition 1 is most common in large-polyped corals such as faviids (*Favia, Favites,* etc.), mussids (*Lobophyllia, Symphyllia,* etc.), *Trachyphyllia, Cataphyllia, Nemenzophyllia,* etc. An apparently healthy coral with good expansion begins to display a loss of tissue from the margins, exposing septa and the rest of the skeleton. The condition may or may not be accompanied secondarily by *Ostreobium* algae or protozoan brown jelly infections. The tissue recession seems "forced," as even marginal tissue at the edges of recession appears healthy, though slightly shrunken or "stretched." The coral may experience a certain amount of tissue loss, and then have the progression halt as quickly as it began. At other times, the entire coral is lost through a slow wasting.

Again, the coral seems unresponsive to normal courses of action. It may well be that a nutritional deficit is being experienced, as other massive corals show tissue atrophy and necrosis in a similar manner when starved. In most anecdotal observations, salinities lower than those of natural seawater seem to increase the incidence of this syndrome. The separation of the polyp from the skeleton in *Cataphyllia* may be related to this condition.

Xeniid condition 1 is no stranger to anyone who has kept soft corals from the Family Xeniidae. It is commonly described as "melting" or "crashing." Colonies that are healthy one day become a degenerating, melting mass of tissue on the next. The rate of tissue degeneration can be quicker than almost any other coral disease, including RTN. Xeniids are very sensitive to water-quality changes and can react in a similar fashion to temporary stressors. (Rarely do xeniids slowly "fade away.")

Nutritional status may play an important role in the health of these corals, as they have few of the typical structures involved with the digestion of prey. This may be relevant in some cases. However, it is quite interesting that colonies which are growing well and are thriving will suddenly just crash. Is it that the colonies have exhausted a needed nutrient from the water column? Is this perhaps why they seem to thrive in higher-nutrient water? What is responsible for the rapid growth of certain

colonies followed by a growth stasis in virtually unchanged conditions? Is it a problem brought about by long-term stress to unknown tank conditions that reaches a critical level?

It is also interesting that, like the unseparated pedal progeny of certain anemones (*Aiptasia,* etc.), the basal tissue of *Xenia* and *Heteroxenia* maintains a high degree of resistance to noxious stimuli or parent-colony pathogens. In other words, small fragments or "stumps" of basal stem tissue may remain after the rest of the colony has "melted." This tissue can reform new (sometimes numerous) parent colonies, despite the fact that no other obvious changes have occurred in the captive conditions.

Goniopora condition 1 describes the slow wasting of *Goniopora* and *Alveopora.* It is, unfortunately, an occurrence that is more a rule than an exception. The pattern of death is quite predictable: lower marginal polyps stop expanding, then die, leaving a bare skeleton behind. This process progresses gradually up the branch or colony until all polyps have degenerated and disappeared. Opportunistic infections common to these corals, such as protozoan brown jelly, are often secondary. Although many theories have been given to explain this commonly seen demise, none have proved completely tenable.

One positive observation involving *Goniopora* is the high rate of success and even recovery of ailing specimens reported in aquariums at Inland Aquatics in Terre Haute, Indiana. Morgan Lidster, the manager of the facility, has claimed an approximately 95% success rate with these corals in his tanks, which are run with algal turf scrubbers. These systems are also set up to have a very low impact on plankton populations. It is also thought-provoking that similar successes are reported there for several other notoriously difficult-to-keep corals and invertebrates, including *Dendronephthya* species and *Heteractis malu,* the delicate, or sebae, anemone.

Whether it is the use of the algal turf scrubbers—with the substances they add or extract from the water—the presence of certain live plankton, or perhaps another factor or factors remains to be determined.

Soft coral collapsing condition is sometimes seen in stalked soft corals with arboreal growth patterns. Typically, a colony will fail to maintain cellular turgor and will collapse like a fallen tree or a wilted deciduous herb. With an herb, all that may be necessary is simply to add water and the plant will perk up again. This is not the case with these octocorals, which may never be revived.

Although in some cases, the colony may become turgid and erect again, in most cases the "deflation" of tissue is irreversible and the colony rapidly deteriorates. It is now well known that cer-

Sudden collapse and death of this *Sarcophyton* specimen is attributed by photographer Alf Jacob Nilsen to the release of toxins by a blue reef sponge.

tain corals that are affected (*Dendronephthya*, *Nephthea*, etc.) require large amounts of food and/or water flow to survive. Most aquariums are incapable of providing the volume and type of appropriate nutritive support required. However, there are other soft corals (*Litophyton*, *Capnella*, *Lemnalia*, etc.) that are highly photosynthetic and may still collapse for no apparent reason, even after long terms in captivity. These occasions seem unprovoked, with the corals being subjected to very consistent conditions of proper water flow and lighting. Salinity may play a role in this inexplicable collapse, although this has not yet been carefully investigated, to my knowledge.

Tissue trauma, such as cutting, excision, or injury, may also cause a collapse in certain species prone to this problem. Many such corals are propagated by the cutting method, but the loss

of water from the colony and the resultant loss of internal static pressure can sometimes cause susceptible coral types to collapse and never recover.

Leather coral condition 1 may happen separately from or in conjunction with the regular surface-sloughing sessions seen in the genera *Sinularia*, *Sarcophyton*, *Lobophytum*, etc. Although many new hobbyists become needlessly worried when a leather coral begins a normal shedding period that makes it appear that the coral is dying, this condition is potentially a serious problem. The polyps and tissue of the coral stop expanding and turn a darker color. At some point, after a prolonged unexpanded state that may last several weeks, the tissue becomes cheesy and degenerates, rather than renewing. The coral exhibits local areas where holes and rotting tissue begin to appear on the capitulum or stalks, and these progress outward. This condition occasionally occurs in healthy, fully expanded corals, usually of the *Sarcophyton* genus.

Although the explanation in otherwise healthy specimens is harder to validate, it may be that a prolonged sloughing period is a result of poor tank conditions or stagnant water flow. With a protracted period of time in which the coral does not feed or photosynthesize in a normal manner because of its shrunken state, the nutritive/energy status of the coral becomes compromised and allows degenerative areas to develop. There may also be specific chemical or mechanical stimuli such as detritus, debris, or additives that create a locally noxious or anaerobic area. In such an area, tissue stress would be followed by necrosis caused by bacteria or other agents. Fortunately, this condition is treatable in many cases. Lugol's and freshwater dips may be of value in some cases, as the superficial necrosis is susceptible to the antiseptic properties of the dips. Simple excision of the affected areas and reliance on the remarkable healing powers of these particular leather-type soft corals is also quite successful in stopping the progression of the malady. Although these procedures may work well, they have the disadvantage of treating the outward signs and not the cause.

Gorgonian condition 1 describes the general loss of tissue from branches and the exposure of the central rod, or axis. It is fairly common in many species of symbiotic and aposymbiotic gorgonians. Sometimes, this is accompanied or exacerbated by the proliferation of undesirable cyanobacteria or filamentous algae and their encroachment on healthy tissue.

This condition is often treatable by excision of the afflicted branch, cutting slightly ahead of the problem and into healthy tissue. This may work, or the tissue loss may continue in a steady progression. It seems that improper lighting, water quality, or (especially in the case of aposymbiotic gorgonians) lack of food, may be a common starting point for this condition.

Gorgonian condition 2 occurs when the cortical layer of tissue becomes soft and spongy and separates from the inner core. The outer tissue looks like latex paint that has bubbled up from poor adhesion. The tissue may get darker in color, resembling a leaf of spinach that has been bruised. This reaction occurs spontaneously in the absence of local stressors and seems most frequent near the base, or holdfast. Thick-branched gorgonians and encrusting gorgonians seem more prone to this problem. Sometimes, the tissue seems to heal itself and reattach to the core. In other cases, there may be localized degeneration resulting in an exposed skeleton that may cause the colony to break free. In rarer cases, the condition is progressive, and tissue loss continues up the coral, possibly from secondary bacterial, protozoan, algal, or other infections. In such cases, excision ahead of the advancing tissue loss can be effective. I have also seen the same type of discoloration in wild Caribbean sea fans (*Gorgonia* species), although tissue loss was not yet apparent. This is known to be a precursor condition to the sea fan disease aspergillosis.

FALSE ALARMS
A number of coral conditions are frequently thought to be signs of disease, when, in fact, they are normal or common occurrences. Sometimes, the perceived affliction is brought about by tank conditions, including lighting, current, and water quality. Every effort has been made to address these issues in the general coral care sections of the book, or under species-specific information. Nonetheless, these problems are so commonly thought to indicate an ailing coral that some description in this chapter seems appropriate:
 • The regular shedding behavior of *Sarcophyton* species, and other leather corals, which is healthy in most instances. The corals may close up and remain closed for prolonged periods of time
 • The cessation of pulsing behavior in *Xenia* species and related species. This is common, and though mostly not understood, is normally not a cause for concern.
 • The shrinking of mushroom corals. This normally occurs when tank conditions do not provide the environment the particular mushrooms need to thrive. Check all water parameters and tank conditions.
 • The periodic purging by large-polyped corals such as *Discosoma, Cataláphyllia, Cynarina,* etc. These corals, capable of ingesting large prey, must purge their gastrovascular cavities of waste by expelling it back through the oral opening. After large meals, these corals may shrink, deflate, darken, and look generally "sick." The condition normally passes within a day. The material that is often seen around the oral opening of coral polyps (*Fungia,* etc.) is usually such waste. The waste may also be acted upon by local populations of cyanobacteria, making the coral appear to be "under attack" by slime algae. These occurrences are normal.
 • Excessive mucus secretion. While this may be a sign of irritation, many corals such as *Turbinaria* and *Acropora* produce copious mucus nets that are part of the excretory or feeding response. Unless the coral tissue looks unhealthy under the prolific mucus, it is usually not a cause for concern. Corals may also hypersecrete mucus after being handled or after the additions of food or chemicals to the aquarium. (The mucus of some species can sometimes damage other colonies it contacts, however.)
 • The waxy shed of *Porites* and many gorgonians. These corals regularly shed a layer of film from their surface. During such times, the polyps will not expand and the coral will appear "sick." The shed will usually last from a day to a week. Strong currents expedite the process.
 • Polyps that don't come out after introduction or new placement of a coral. Touching or handling corals, especially some soft corals, will result in the polyps remaining closed for what can be a considerable length of time. Constant repositioning, without giving a coral a chance to acclimate, may prolong this behavior and result in true disease.
 • Nightly soft coral collapse. Many, if not most, soft corals deflate, shrivel and/or collapse at night until the lights come back on. This is normal behavior.
 • Zoanthid colonies are closed. Many mats of colonial anemones may react in unison to food or water conditions in which some or all of a group close up together. This is common and typical behavior.
 • Brown strands of material seen coming from the oral opening. Frequently, corals may release excess zooxanthellae from their oral openings. This may or may not be indicative of a normal bleaching event. It frequently occurs in response to new tank or lighting conditions. Upon introduction, a brown mucuslike discharge may be seen floating away from the oral opening in long strands. When corals purge zooxanthellae, they often do so by a mechanism of transport from gastrodermal cells into the gastrovascular cavity. I find it fascinating because zooxanthellae may also be taken up into coral tissue through the gastrovascular cavity. It is not yet known how a coral distinguishes between zooxanthellae to be "admitted" versus those to be "expelled," although historecognition has been suggested. No matter the explanation, it is a fairly normal occurrence.

TROUBLESHOOTING

Frequently, the first sign that a coral is truly ailing is a prolonged lack of expansion or poor polyp extension. In other words, the coral is not "opening up." Next, areas of degenerating and receding tissue may begin to appear at the margin or base of the coral and these then progress slowly across or up the colony.

It is important to remember that many corals go through regenerative, excretory, or simple cyclical periods, where poor expansion may appear be an ailment, when in fact it is a normal behavior or process. Parasites and predation are notable exceptions, and it is worth mentioning that many coral predators choose to dine on corals at night. An occasional midnight examination may locate any potential "wrongdoers." Obvious irritation and predation during the day are much easier to assess, of course.

The following checklist may be useful in isolating the cause of a coral ailment, with treatment suggestions to follow each item. Procedures for each of the treatments begins on page 389. A complete assessment or list of potential causative agents or environments is impossible, but corals that fail to thrive are most often "unhappy" for one or more of the reasons listed here:

Water chemistry: All water parameters should be within acceptable limits as outlined in Chapter 9 (page 343). Specifically, check temperature, specific gravity, pH, alkalinity, ammonia, nitrite, nitrate, and calcium levels. If any of them vary significantly from the recommended levels, corrective action should begin. Water changes using good-quality salt mix and a purified freshwater source are usually the easiest and safest way to correct water chemistry problems, though any changes that may significantly alter pH, temperature, and salinity should be done gradually so as not to shock the corals or the other tank inhabitants. The application of various chemicals, drugs, or "wonder cures" is not advised unless the problem can be directly attributed to something that requires an addition.

Lighting: The light used should obviously be appropriate and adequate for the coral being kept. Often, the growth of other corals or the misplacement of a specimen may alter the amount of light reaching the ailing coral. At other times, and especially with newly introduced corals, the light may initially be too intense. New bulbs or recently upgraded lighting are a frequent cause of the usually temporary poor expansion of established colonies. On the other hand, old bulbs may not be properly stimulating zooxanthellae photosynthesis, and a tankful of corals may go into gradual decline as the output of aging bulbs drops off.

Water movement: Corals need variable but healthy levels of random and continuous current around them. Powerheads tend to become clogged with debris and calcium deposits over

Zooxanthellae release: *Euphyllia* being purged of brown strands of algae.

time, reducing their flow. Suction cups often fail, and powerhead flow may be inadvertently misdirected. Over time, the ideal water flow for existing corals may be altered, or it may not be correct for new specimens from the beginning.

Other water quality aspects: The use of aerosol cleaners, pesticides, or other airborne toxins, or the accidental dumping of a toxic substance into the water are often causes for coral contraction and even death. In the event of such contamination, water changes, foam fractionation, Poly Filters, and activated carbon should all be used to eliminate the substance as quickly as possible. There is always the possibility of inadvertent aerosol introduction, especially if painting, neighborhood mosquito spraying programs, or in-house pesticide treatments occur without the aquarium owner's knowledge. Herbicides, pesticides, and oils are reported in many studies as causing significant coral mortality.

Irritations by other organisms, including other corals:

The presence of hard corals (especially aggressive ones) and large, numerous, or nearby soft corals and corallimorpharians should be noted to be sure that ones adjacent to or "upstream" of the ailing coral are not a factor. In general, large and numerous allelopathic organisms may be responsible for the demise of certain species, with some corals less tolerant than others. Encroaching algae and *Aiptasia* species anemones are especially common coral irritants.

Coral disease: Shock, stress, and a captive environment take their toll on many corals, allowing disease to take advantage of susceptible specimens. Most often, coral disease occurs within the first few weeks after introduction to a new tank, or after some substantial modification of the captive environment. Some stressful changes include: the complete breakdown of a tank for any reason, including large disturbances of an established sand bed system; the addition or subtraction of live rock and/or live sand; the introduction of disease from a newly introduced coral; large water changes; extended losses of power; the failure of certain equipment; and rapid or prolonged temperature variations.

The recognition of disease, especially white-band disease, tissue sloughing (SDR, RTN), brown jelly infections, and other infections should prompt quick action to prevent loss of the colony and possible transmission of infection to other corals in the tank. Any diseased corals should be removed—if possible—to a proper quarantine tank for treatment (see below) to prevent further losses.

TREATMENT PROCEDURES

Freshwater dips: Some corals, mostly certain species of large-polyped stony corals and some soft corals (alcyonarians, mainly) may be subjected to a brief 1-3-minute freshwater dip, usually without consequence. This procedure is useful in eliminating certain parasites such as flatworms, brown jelly infections, and cyanobacterial overgrowth. Anytime a freshwater dip is attempted, the water should be of the same temperature and pH as the tank from which the coral is taken. (Tap water should be free of chlorine and buffered with sodium bicarbonate/baking soda or an aquarium buffering agent that sets the pH at about 8.2.) **Important:** Most small-polyped corals and xeniids do not tolerate freshwater dips to any degree.

Lugol's dips: Over the past years, Lugol's solution (iodine in potassium iodide) has become a touted "panacea" for many coral ills. Iodine does have an astringent, antiseptic, and bacteriostatic effect, and it is this property that is possibly exploited when dipping corals in a dilute Lugol's solution. While new coral specimens may indeed benefit from such dips (since some potentially pathogenic microorganisms may be reduced before they become problematic) iodine is a strong oxidant and is not a chemical with which any invertebrate appreciates being in prolonged contact. It is also quite toxic. Certain corals do not tolerate Lugol's dips and may begin bleaching or bailing out of their skeleton almost immediately upon contact. Others tolerate extended Lugol's dips with seemingly no ill effect. If a Lugol's dip is done as a pretreatment for new specimens or as treatment for any number of diseases or parasites, the coral should be closely monitored for the entirety of the treatment and removed immediately if signs of zooxanthellae expulsion or polyp bail-out begin to occur.

The procedure for standard Lugol's dips is 5-10 drops of 5% Lugol's solution per liter (per quart) of freshly made, circulating seawater for 10-20 minutes. If in doubt about a coral's ability to tolerate this treatment, use the 10-minute dip. The length of the dip or concentration of the solution can be altered depending on the tolerance of the coral.

Some aquarists administer several drops of Lugol's solution to the tank (1 drop per 75-150 L [20-40 gal.] of water) directly over the affected area of the coral. (In extreme cases, pure or very concentrated Lugol's solution can be carefully applied directly to the coral, at the boundary between healthy and affected tissue. This should be done outside the aquarium to prevent overdosing the aquarium with iodine.) Depending on the sensitivity of certain species to Lugol's and the potentially high levels of tank iodine which may result (including species which may not tolerate it at all, including certain *Xenia, Anthelia, Pachyclavularia*, etc.), this procedure can be risky.

There are now a plethora of other coral "dips" in the aquarium market. Their exact composition and effectiveness is unknown. Until such time as effectiveness studies can be done, their use falls into the category "miracle cures."

Coral "surgery": Often, the easiest way to prevent or remove necrotic or diseased areas of coral is to use the coral's innate regenerative abilities. Simple excision of the damaged or diseased area is often possible with many nonmassive corals. On soft corals, areas of disease, necrosis, or recession may be cut away and, in most cases, the coral will heal without incident. For stony corals, breaking or cutting the skeleton using scissors, shears, or other cutters will be effective. When excising such areas on corals, it is best to perform the procedure in a separate container of saltwater with the coral submerged. (Discard this water, which is likely to become contaminated.) This is especially true for the soft corals that "leak" when cut. The coral should be cut or broken off ahead of the area to be removed, slightly into the healthy tissue area to ensure complete removal of the problem

Corallivorous fish: obligatory coral feeders include the Longnose Filefish.

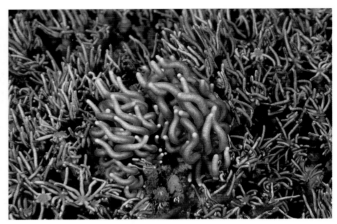
Corallivorous nudibranch: two well-disguised aeolids graze *Tubipora* polyps.

area. The broken edge or tissue will heal rapidly in most cases provided that a healthy environment is maintained. It's often best to reattach the coral to the substrate with the broken or cut edge cemented or tied to the reef structure to allow the coral to rapidly attach to a suitable location. I have used the product Liquid Bandage on cut coral fragments with some degree of success. Superglue also seems to seal broken tissue quite well.

Antibiotics (pastes, powders, and solutions):
Several diseases of corals can be effectively treated using antibiotic pastes, including cyanobacterial band diseases and brown jelly infections. This has a relatively good success rate with a relatively low degree of risk or toxicity. Neomycin sulfate, Kanamycin, and several other broad-spectrum human or veterinary antibiotics that affect gram-positive and gram-negative bacteria are commercially available and can be used effectively in saltwater. The pill or capsule can be made into a powder and then a paste by a small addition of seawater. The paste can be applied to the affected area of the coral using a soft brush like an artist's paint brush. The coral's skeleton is porous and absorbent, assuring that enough antibiotic will remain at locally high concentrations to affect any pathogenic organisms. Additionally, the local and somewhat absorptive application prevents the antibiotic from significantly affecting the biological filter bacteria or other beneficial microorganisms as would occur with antibiotic treatments applied generally to the system water.

Tetracycline at a dose level of 10 mg/L (10 mg/1 qt.) has been used to prevent necrosis in sedimentation stresses in corals (Hodgson, 1990). This antibiotic has a fairly low toxicity to corals and is active against a broad range of gram-positive and gram-negative bacteria, including opportunistic natural flora of corals, such as *Vibrio* spp., and sulfur-oxidizing bacteria associated with coral mortality and black-band disease (Mitchell and Chet, 1975, et al.). *Artemia* nauplii (brine shrimp) can also be "enriched" with antibiotics and fed to coral polyps. (Live brine shrimp will feed on particulate antibiotic material, particulate food soaked in antibiotic, or on medicated powdered flake foods. This may provide one of the safest and most effective methods of administering such drugs to aquarium corals.)

A product known as Marin OOmed, by Tetra, is a broad-range antibiotic and antiparasitic treatment that has a fairly low degree of toxicity in marine environments. The dosages are listed at three levels, the lowest of which is claimed to be safe for all invertebrates. It is unlikely that any medication effective in treating most coral disease is entirely "reef safe," but Marin OOmed does provide a significant amount of antimicrobial/antiparasitic activity considering its low toxicity. In several courses of treatment for ich outbreaks among the fishes in my own tanks, no adverse effects were seen in any invertebrate or coral in over 2 weeks of treatment. Marin OOmed is useful in treating fishes in reef aquariums, and it is possible that this product may be used with a reasonable amount of safety and efficacy in treating certain coral diseases, though cautionary experimental trials are highly advised.

Some words of caution regarding antibiotics: First, be sure that the use of antibiotic therapy is warranted. Given the fact that very few problems are conclusively or obviously caused by bacteria, such treatments should rarely be necessary. Second, the use of antibiotics can very easily result in the development of resistant strains of bacteria. This has profound implications, not only to the aquarium, but to bacterial ecology in general. Finally, antibiotics should never be improperly dumped back into the environment. They should be inactivated with household

Voracious predator: Crown-of-Thorns Starfish feeds on stony corals. (Hawaii)

Soft coral predator: *Nardoa* sp. starfish feeding on a patch of *Anthelia* sp.

bleach before being disposed of in household waste water (see chloramphenicol, below).

UV sterilizers and ozone: The use of ultraviolet sterilization and ozonation may be of benefit in treating and/or preventing the spread of certain coral pathogens. All pathogens must of course be waterborne to be killed as they pass through the UV filter or the chamber where ozone is administered. This means that any biotic disease already present on the coral's surface will likely remain unaffected. Ozone, especially, has a long list of potential hazards and side effects that may be detrimental to aquarium inhabitants. It is likely that neither of these techniques is as effective as other methods in treating coral maladies, and each has possible negative consequences resulting from its use (especially on a continuous basis). Their use in quarantine conditions may be more acceptable.

Chloramphenicol: There has been widespread discussion about the use of chloramphenicol in the treatment of rapid tissue necrosis (RTN). Bingman said in a 1997 online speech, "It works like voodoo." Indeed, this drug has proved very effective in many cases to preclude, prevent, arrest, and even aid in the healing of corals with this condition. Unfortunately, some corals with RTN fail to respond. In some cases, coral death can actually occur from its use. Chloramphenicol is an old antibiotic that has been used in the veterinary industry (and human medicine) for decades. Today, it is used very little except in the treatment of certain ocular diseases in small animals and for gram-negative meningitis and rickettsia. This is because of the widespread use of safer, more effective modern antibiotics (none of which has thus far proved effective in treating RTN). Nonetheless, its effect on many corals

can be quite remarkable, and most veterinarians seem willing to sell or part with the drug quite willingly. Aquarists requests are often met with more than a bit of interest and amusement.

Nonetheless, chloramphenicol is not without contraindications. It is not currently approved for aquacultural use, nor is it legal to obtain without a prescription. **Important:** Mere contact with this drug can trigger a rare form of aplastic anemia in sensitive individuals. This is a condition that can be fatal. Fortunately, only one in 40,000 people is sensitive, but the use of gloves and/or masks is advisable when preparing a treatment bath or coming in any contact with chloramphenicol. It is also noteworthy that some corals do not tolerate the treatment well, and colonies of *Stylophora, Madracis,* and *Pocillopora* have all been observed either bleaching or in polyp bail-out within minutes of contact with chloramphenicol-treated water. On the other hand, *Acropora* species seem especially tolerant. Chloramphenicol does not dissolve well in water, but is almost completely soluble in alcohol. The pure grain alcohol sold in liquor stores works well for this purpose. Chloramphenicol is soluble at 100 mg/ml of ethanol, so a few drops of ethanol is enough to dissolve enough of this drug to dose a small quarantine tank. The procedure for a typical chloramphenicol procedure is as follows (Bingman, 1997):

To a separate quarantine or treatment tank, 20mg/L of dissolved chloramphenicol is added to the circulating seawater. The coral is left in the tank for 24 hours after which time it can be removed and replaced in the main tank. A Lugol's dip for 15 minutes or the addition of a few drops of Lugol's to the quarantine tank may be useful and a second 24-hour chloramphenicol bath may be needed. It has been my own experience that neither of these additional treatments has been necessary for corals that are going to respond to the chloramphenicol, and they may be an

Soft coral predator: nudibranch (*Phyllodesmium longicirra*) on leather coral.

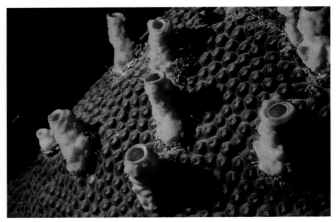

Boring sponge: sponges invade colony of *Montastraea* sp. (boulder star coral).

unneeded additional stress. The treated coral should recover easily after being replaced in the main tank.

Cautionary notes:

1. The use of chloramphenicol in display aquariums is not recommended, except in extreme emergencies. The antibiotic will effectively decimate beneficial bacteria populations, and the aquarist must be prepared to deal with a massive die-off of these organisms and to restore biological filtration promptly. The sudden decomposition of dead bacteria can consume oxygen and quickly lead to the death of fishes, corals, and other organisms in the system. (Aquarists rarely realize that the biomass of bacteria in their systems, despite being largely unseen, may be greater than the entirety of other living organisms present. Rapid loss of this biomass will have serious implications on water quality.)

2. Water treated with chloramphenicol must be inactivated with a small amount of bleach (at a rate of 1/4 cup per 5 gal. of treated water) or by using an activated carbon filter for 24 hours before the water is discarded. The release of such antibiotics into the environment is blamed for the spread of resistant strains of bacteria, and aquarists should have no part in this ominous trend.

QUARANTINE TANKS

In most circumstances where an actual disease is present, or when a treatment will involve medications or compounds that may be detrimental to the aquarium's biologic filter or other tank inhabitants, the use of a quarantine tank is advisable. The establishment of a separate treatment area allows for careful observation of the affected coral colony, facilitates water changes and additions, allows for other corals to receive care if they begin showing signs of disease, prevents further spread of disease, and lowers the cost of treatment due to the smaller amounts of water, salt, and treatment products used.

In all cases, it is important that the quarantine tank not be a haphazardly established container of water. It should be like a hospital, providing a stable, stress-free environment that facilitates healing. This may include a small heater for thermostability, a small powerhead for adequate gas and waste exchange, stable and proper water parameters, and regular water changes. It is usually not necessary to provide lighting to corals in treatment provided that their medication period is not prolonged for more than a few days. Even while in treatment, low lighting levels may lower the stress of the coral animal by reducing its metabolic rate. In any event, a treatment tank is a simple and beneficial way to handle most coral problems and is recommended if set up with diligence and care.

PREDATORS AND PARASITES

Many aquarists have returned home with a new coral, only to find it has unknown "beasties" dwelling within. All too often, panic ensues. What is it? Will it kill my coral? Should I get rid of it? are typical questions that arise.

Up to several hundred different species can be associated with a single coral head in nature. These organisms are often known as **cryptofauna**. Most of these animals are commensal: they seek refuge within the safety of their coral habitats. Many use corals only as temporary refuge, while others are permanent associates. Some are parasitic or predatory, feeding or existing on corals. As a general rule, however, aquarists tend to worry needlessly about many strange newcomers, and the majority of hangers-on that arrive with corals are harmless—or even beneficial. A complete survey and coverage of all the animals and organisms that can predate or associate with corals would constitute a book of its own. The following handful of plants and animals include only those that most commonly cause problems for aquarium corals.

Anemones: Whether intentionally introduced or not, anemones can cause serious problems in reef aquariums housing corals. All anemones are motile and can move into contact with corals. In some cases, they are sufficiently dominant in their stinging capabilities to seriously damage the corals. If the competition from the coral is strong, the anemone may simply move away. Generally, corals that can be moved out of the way of an anemone that seems reasonably "happy" in its position should be moved. If the coral cannot be relocated, placing an object between the anemone and the coral or gently moving the anemone by detachment or sufficient irritation (shading, water flow, etc.) may be required.

Aiptasia species: These infamous small anemones will sting and outcompete corals for space, and many species can and will grow to plague proportions in the tank. These are highly regenerative and prolifically reproductive organisms that are a nemesis to many marine aquarists. Injecting them with either boiling water, supersaturated calcium hydroxide, dilute hydrochloric acid, dilute sodium hydroxide, hydrogen peroxide, vinegar, or capsicum ex-

Stinging anemone: *Bartholomea annulata* (corkscrew anemone) kills surrounding tissue of *Montastraea annularis* (boulder star coral). (Caribbean)

tract all have moderate rates of success in killing them. Use of a Water Pik dental cleaning tool to blast *Aiptasia* tissue from pieces of rock or the base of corals is also effective (do this in a separate tank to avoid regeneration of pieces within the main tank).

A predatory nudibranch, *Berghia verrucicornis*, is available to control *Aiptasia* populations. This nudibranch is found on coral rubble in areas commonly populated by *Aiptasia pallida*. I have finally succeeded in breeding these nudibranchs, and they have rapidly eliminated my *Aiptasia* populations (Borneman, 1998). After many years of fruitless attempts to rid myself of these spawn of Satan, I took almost sadistic pleasure in watching the *Berghia* voraciously consume these anemones, often ganging up in "packs" of four or five. I can say through experience that several breeding *Berghia* adults should be allowed to eat *Aiptasia* in a separate tank and to multiply and grow before being placed in a fully stocked aquarium. Additions of tiny *Berghia* nudibranchs to an aquarium will result in their almost immediate disappearance. I suspect that predation may be the cause.

The Pacific anemone *Aiptasia pulchella* is preyed on by the nudibranch *Berghia major*. Two other nudibranchs (which may be misidentified or the same species as *Berghia*) also prey on *Aiptasia*. One is *Phidiana lynceus*, an inhabitant of rocky intertidal and rubble areas. The other is *Dondice occidentalis*, found in mangroves and rubble areas (frequent haunts of *Aiptasia pallida*). It preys on numerous cnidarians, storing nematocysts in its cerata as reported for *Berghia*.

Lysmata wurdemanni (the Caribbean Peppermint Shrimp) has drawn mixed reports of success in the predation of *Aiptasia*. Certain other predators, such as the Raccoon Butterflyfish (*Chaetodon lunula*) and various other fishes and crustaceans are known to eat invertebrates without hesitation. The Threadfin, Teardrop, and Copperband Butterflyfishes (*Chaetodon auriga, C. unimaculatus*, and *Chelmon rostratus*, respectively), are also known to consume *Aiptasia*. Such treatment methods must usually take place outside the coral aquarium, because collateral damage to any attached invertebrate life will be likely. Other reported biological controls, such as brushing with *Catalaphyllia* or *Euphyllia* species, are not very effective, in my experience.

Anemonia species: These small anemones have also been reported to plague certain aquariums. Removal may be necessary in such events, although I have not found them to multiply at anywhere near the rate of certain *Aiptasia* species.

Crustaceans: Crustaceans are ubiquitous associates of corals. The small commensal crabs and shrimps found with many corals, especially branching ones, are known as **crustacean guards**. They play an important role to the corals and increase their survivorship in several ways: protecting corals from predators, combing and grooming the coral surface of debris and excess mucus, and increasing water flow within the coral branches through their activities and respiratory currents. These symbionts should be welcomed.

Commensal and reef-safe crabs: Commensal crabs often are commonly found in the branches of ramose coals, frequently *Pocillopora* and *Acropora* species. In fact, there are close to 500 species of brachyuran crabs associated exclusively with coral reefs, some dwelling in the lower dead part of coral colonies, while others associate with the living parts. Many have brushes on their legs that they use to "comb" the coral mucus for food. However, they may modify the coral's growth patterns by their activities. They seem to induce various modifications to the coral skele-

> ## CORAL PREDATORS AND POTENTIAL PESTS
>
> Algae (some species)
> Anemones (esp. *Aiptasia* spp.)
> Amphipods, Copepods, Isopods, Ostracods
>   (some species)
> Barnacles (some species)
> Bivalves (some boring species)
> Bristleworms (esp. *Nereis, Eunice*, and
>   *Hermodice* spp.)
> Coral, Murex, Rapa, and Sundial Snails
> Cowries
> Flatworms (some species)
> Nudibranchs (some species)
> Sea Spiders
> Sea Stars (many species; exceptions: *Linckia,
>   Fromia*, and *Astropecten* spp.)
> Shrimps (esp. *Saron* spp., Rhynchocinetidae spp.,
>   and *Lysmata* spp.)
> Sponges (esp. *Cliona* spp.)
> Wentletraps

ton, changing the patterns of radial corallites, forcing the anastomosis of branches, and thus creating cyst or gall-like areas on the skeleton. Not surprisingly, these crabs are often called **gall crabs**. Such formations seem to offer protection to the crabs that dwell within the branches. In return, the coral is kept free of parasites and predators that would seek to damage or harm

Skeletal gall: swollen *Pocillopora* branch houses a live gall crab (see right).

Gall crab: female *Hapalocarcinus marsupialis* is exposed by opening the gall.

Pyrgomatid barnacle: note feeding limbs of these small, harmless crustaceans.

Predatory shrimp: *Saron marmoratus* is one of several species that eat corals.

the crab's "custom" home. Gall crabs do not seem to injure the coral or have any real deleterious effect. Other symbiotic crabs and reef-safe crabs include the porcelain crabs (Porcellanidae), anemone crabs, herbivorous *Mithrax* crabs, and certain herbivorous hermit crabs.

Unsuitable crabs: Many other species of crabs prey on corals. Even "safe" hermit crabs, decorator crabs, and the frequently-mislabeled-as-reef-safe Sally Lightfoot Crab (*Percnon* sp.) may eat corals (and will definitely eat coralline algae). Some commensal crabs have predatory mimics, and the exact determination of any such species found living among coral is advised. Of course, if associated crabs are actually predatory, it will become obvious over time as coral tissue disappears. Still, the sighting of a crab doesn't necessarily need to be a signal or panic. Most species of swimming crabs (Portunidae) and box crabs (Callapidae) are carnivorous, and may prey on corals, although it does not seem to be their food of choice. Some small portunid swimming crabs are actually commensals of alcyonarian corals.

Removal of crabs can be difficult. They are very quick and smart, rapidly recognizing traps and threats. The use of baited nets and commercial traps may be the best solution, although manual removal of single offenders hiding in coral heads is sometimes possible, using a pair of tweezers or a sharp, spearlike object. Obviously, no predatory crabs should ever be intentionally introduced to a reef aquarium. Most harmful crabs are accidentally introduced as incidentals on live rock and coral specimens. Careful examination of such additions will help in preventing the introduction of predatory crabs. (For hard-to-catch parasitic species, freshwater dips of tolerant corals may be advisable.)

Shrimps: Many small shrimps make fine additions to reef aquariums, but several genera seen in the aquarium trade are known to graze upon or constantly irritate corals. Especially to be avoided are *Saron* species, some *Lysmata* species, and shrimps from the Family Rhynchocinetidae.

Worms: Many thousands of species of worms can inhabit corals and coral reefs. Most of them are commensal. Almost all worms and their larvae can be important food sources to corals, and should be regarded as a functional part of a coral aquarium community. There are comparatively few that are problematic.

Some polychaetes may infest gorgonians and cause malformation of their spicules. However, most polychaetes seen near or associated with corals may be feeding on mucus, bacteria, detritus, or other plankton and debris that forms the coral infracommunity. As such, they are not detrimental. But they are also likely to move into any area where there is tissue damage, so corals in the process of healing may be impeded in this regard.

Bristleworms (one category of polychaete worms) are primarily beneficial detritus eaters, but larger specimens of a few genera may be carnivorous and may eat and/or irritate corals, invertebrates, clams, and even some echinoderms and fishes. Bristleworms are also highly reproductive, are regenerative, and may reach high densities in the aquarium. This is not necessarily problematic, and their larvae provide an important food source for corals and other filter-feeding invertebrates. Carnivorous bristleworms, while quite rare, can and will prey on coral tissue. These larger specimens (especially some of those in the genera *Nereis*, *Eunice*, and *Hermodice*) can either burrow into corals or actively feed on their surface. Many are venomous and can grow longer than 1 m (3 ft.). Some have powerful jaws with venom glands and each of the bristles (setae) has small poison glands at its base. Great care must be taken when handling these *taeniourus*), arrow crabs (*Stenorhynchus* spp.), banded coral shrimps (*Stenopus* spp.), and lizardfishes from the genus *Parapercis*. Unfortunately, most fanworms, spaghetti worms, and other beneficial polychaete-type worms will also be eaten by the fishes and crustaceans that snack on the relatively few offending species. No reef tank is ever likely to be completely free of bristleworms, nor are they usually harmful to corals.

ALGAE

A number of algae commonly disturb the sanity of aquarium keepers. Most are not immediately harmful to corals, but some encroach on living coral tissue. Corals that are fragmented, injured, or produce a lot of mucus may tend to have localized areas of filamentous algae growing on the high nutrient areas of damaged tissue. Such growth may cause further recession and damage to the coral and allow for other disease to ensue.

Some sediment-trapping filamentous algae (*Bryopsis* spp., *Derbesia* spp., and others) can form on areas of dead skeleton where the porosity of the corallum traps particulate matter. The filaments trap further sediments, which then foul the tissue of the coral at the edge where algae is encroaching. This allows for the spread of the algae across the coral surface.

Caulerpa species and other forms of macroalgae may also cause problems when grown in proximity to corals, especially stony corals. Many produce anti-predatory compounds. *Caulerpa*, *Laurencia*, and *Halimeda* species, in particular, may produce volatile organics, terpenes, and phenols that can cause the demise of stony corals. *Dictyota* species, *Microdictyon marinum*, and *Halimeda* species are also capable of simple overgrowth, smothering and killing corals in the process. (Some coral keepers have been experimenting with growing *Caulerpa* and

worms. The major boring polychaetes are from the families Eunicidae, Lumbrineridae, Dorvilleidae, Spionidae, Cirratulidae, and Sabellidae. Those with well-developed grinding teeth probably erode the coral skeleton mechanically, while those with poorly developed teeth may use chemical dissolution.

Larger carnivorous specimens may be caught using a commercial tube-type trap found in most aquarium shops. Manual removal with tweezers is also possible. Smaller specimens can be controlled biologically. The Red Sea dottyback fishes (*Pseudochromis* spp., especially *P. springeri*) seem fond of the smaller worms. Other biologic controls are some species of butterflyfishes, including the Big Longnose (*Forcipiger longirostris*), Copperband (*Chelmon rostratus*), and Raccoon (*Chaetodon lunula*), all of which may also eat many beneficial reef inhabitants, including coral polyps and polychaete tube and fanworms. Other potential polychaete predators are wrasses from the genera *Macropharyngodon* and *Halichoeres*, the Marine Betta or Comet (*Calloplesiops altivelis*), the Rockmover Wrasse (*Novaculichthys*

Boring worms: burrows of marine worms pit the surface of a *Goniastrea* sp.

Parasitic flatworms: harmless shrimp shares turbellarian-infested *Heliofungia*.

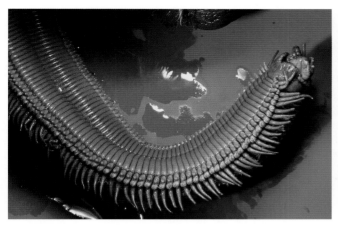

Coral-eating worm: this 1.5 meter (5-foot) *Palolo* sp. worm, imported on live rock, was discovered in a German tank, where it fed on soft corals.

Filamentous algae: a newly established reef aquarium, intentionally allowed to mature without herbivorous fishes or invertebrates, is overtaken by *Bryopsis*.

other macroalgae in lighted refugiums, without apparent harm to the stony corals in their display aquariums.)

To discourage algae, all light bulbs should be replaced as scheduled to prevent spectrum shifts and intensity drops that may preferentially select for algae growth over calcareous growth. All types of filters providing highly aerobic surface areas, such as canister, wet/dry, fluidized bed, cartridge, wheel-type, and undergravel units, tend to act as nutrient traps and need to be cleaned frequently. They will almost inevitably lead to an increase in nitrate and phosphate levels within the aquarium. In-tank circulation should be high to avoid localized pockets of waste and detritus that cultivate problem algae. Protein skimming is another excellent method of lowering nutrient levels and consequently lowering algae growth. Alkalinity and pH should be at proper levels, perhaps even increasing them slightly if algae blooms occur.

Water changes are one easy and effective way to alleviate short- and long-term water parameter problems (excess nitrate or phosphate, for example) that may fuel the growth of problem algae. Reverse osmosis, deionized, or other pretreated water is sometimes necessary, as tap water may have high levels of contamination and/or nutrients.

However, even in tanks with very good water conditions, algae will grow. For systems with proper filtration and water management, nutrient levels may be less important in controlling nuisance algae than was once thought. Grazing by macrograzers (fishes, urchins, etc.) and micrograzers (amphipods, etc.) may serve as the crucial check on algae growth (see box, page 396). Biocontrols commonly introduced by the reef aquarist (snails, small herbivorous hermit crabs, and fishes) are extremely useful—if not essential—in keeping algae in check.

SUMMARY

The management of aquarium coral diseases, pests, and other troublesome conditions, while still in the proverbial dark ages, does not present hopeless problems.

It is interesting that many hypotheses about the cause of diseases in aquarium corals involve suspicions that there is an elemental or nutritional absence in the corals that aquarists have difficulty maintaining. As a whole, reef hobbyists strive to maintain nutrient-poor conditions through the use of increasingly sophisticated water purification devices and compounds, coupled with limited nutrient import.

Again, we must look at the biology of coral reefs for clues: these animals have become highly evolved over millions of years to survive in otherwise very harsh conditions, in high densities and species numbers, and are highly and often specifically heterotrophic. Preventing many diseases and degenerative conditions in the future may well demand that we supply the critical nutrients that corals normally obtain through food capture and absorption from the water medium.

The careful treatment of diseased corals by those of us maintaining them in aquariums is well worth the effort and respect for life involved. Most corals, once cured of problems, recover easily and will regrow some areas of denuded skeleton. At the very least, new growth can continue. While it is never advisable to treat a problem randomly or rashly, a certain amount of judicious experimentation with treatment programs, once some experience is gained, will allow us to judge the merits and flaws of certain protocols. We can hope that such work by amateur coral keepers may help in discovering treatments that can be used not only with captive corals, but perhaps those in the wild.

CHAPTER 12

Conservation

Endangered Reefs and the
Ethical Coral Keeper

It remains to be seen whether corals will have the adaptability to outlive the human race, but there is no doubt that reefs as we know them are in serious trouble today. The worries began to be voiced several decades ago, as in this 1973 warning signal by author and marine naturalist Gilbert L. Voss:

"An unprejudiced observer might well be fearful that in the not too distant future our children may be able to learn about the coral reefs only from books and documentary films, for one of nature's most unique habitats will have vanished from the face of the Earth."

Today, more than half of the world's reefs are considered to be threatened by human activities and encroachment, according to a World Resources Institute report (Bryant et al., 1998). According to this analysis, 27% of all shallow-water coral reefs are considered to be at high risk. An additional 30% are classified as under medium risk of human disturbance in the foreseeable future. Only about 40% of living shallow-water coral reefs are considered stable and at low risk, with many of these in the vast, undeveloped Pacific.

Outside the Pacific region, an estimated 70% of reefs are at

> ## "The palm tree grows, the coral spreads, but man shall vanish."
>
>
>
> Polynesian saying

risk, while 56% of reefs in Southeast Asia, encompassing the Philippines and Indonesia, two areas that supply the majority of livestock for marine aquariums, are threatened. Despite increasing public awareness of the problem and some efforts at protection and recovery, the successes are too few and far between, with deterioration continuing and even increasing.

Mass population explosions and movements to coastal areas have fueled much of the coral reef degradation already recorded. In most Caribbean island nations, the population has quadrupled in the past 30 years, with 75% of the people living near a coastline.

Along with increased human population come the problems inherent to overfishing. Though shallow coral reefs occupy about 0.2% of the world's oceans, more than 10% of the worldwide fish harvest comes from these areas. Once prolific, the conch, groupers, turtles, top predator game fishes, lobsters, and other fishes, crustaceans, and shellfishes have become scarce in many areas, if not locally endangered or extirpated. With the loss of such animals, the entirety of the food chain, and indeed the reef community itself, can become unbalanced and jeopardized.

New roads, buildings, and airport runways are built using blasted coral limestone. Entire reefs are destroyed to make room for shipping channels and new cruise ship docks and oil rigs.

Cnidarian recycling: a discarded soda can is colonized by a small *Xenia* sp. in North Sulawesi. Coral reefs worldwide are threatened by human activities.

Bleaching events are often linked to unusually high water temperatures.

Dying Caribbean reef: more than half of the world's reefs are threatened by human activities, including deforestation, waste generation, and development.

Net and drag fishing, improper boat anchoring, and increasing numbers of careless divers can all damage or destroy large areas of a reef.

Pesticides, fertilizers, sewage, toxic chemicals, cyanide, overfishing, and agricultural runoff are overwhelming many tropical coastlines and eliminating reef habitats through poisoning and eutrophication. Fish-collecting chemicals, such as rotenone, arsenic, quinaldine, urethane, bleach, gasoline, cyanide, and cresol, are routinely used to harvest food and aquarium fishes and can cause damage or kill corals and other flora and fauna. Dynamite and electric shock are also commonly used in unsustainable and highly destructive fishing practices.

DIRE SCENARIOS

Coral researcher C.M. Yonge had already listed threats to the conservation of coral reefs in 1969 as follows: geomorphological changes brought by civil or military installations, pollution of all types, mining of coral rock, dynamiting and poisoning of fishes, indiscriminate collection, and divers. Nearly 30 years have passed since this observation, and, without question, none of these problems have been alleviated; rather they have largely been exacerbated, and certainly compounded with new threats.

We must also add global climate changes—notably atmospheric degeneration and warming trends—that are extremely worrisome to many scientific observers and researchers. Geologist Dr. Robert Buddemeir, in a recent analysis of factors affecting coral reefs ("Is it Time to Give Up?," 1999), pointed out that four major global variables are now outside their normal ranges and increasing at an unprecedented rate: atmospheric carbon dioxide, nitrogen cycle flux, carbon cycle flux, and the population of humans.

Some scientists fear that it may already be too late to prevent mass declines of coral reefs in the near-term future. Some predictions call for mass extinctions of many corals in the twenty-first century, with a wholesale loss of current reefs within a single human generation.

In the gloomiest of scenarios, coral reef devastation would fuel increasing levels of atmospheric carbon dioxide (from the massive loss of the normal carbon-binding activities of corals in calcification). If coupled with increasing deforestation, this could dramatically impact all of life as we know it. The importance of coral reefs to us and to the future of the Earth is profound, and the effect of their looming loss is almost incomprehensible.

Already, recent climatic overheating events have contributed to widespread coral bleaching and the appearance of coral diseases in formerly healthy reef areas. The sense of urgency to map, assess, and protect those reef areas that can still be saved is mounting, and there is a clear consensus among the experts that the leaders of the world must begin to act immediately and decisively if we are to avoid a global disaster of unprecedented proportions.

Getting people and politicians to act will not be an easy matter. Buddemeir believes that "political, social, and economic considerations" have been allowed to outweigh the laws of nature and are being used to minimize the warnings and conclusions of leading scientists who have tried to alert the world's leaders to the potential calamity that lies ahead.

The message, when fully explained, can be complex, especially in view of the fact that corals and coral reefs have existed on this planet for hundreds of millions of years, and have endured a number of serious global climate-changing events. While their prospects in a near-future, man-made mass extinction are certainly grim, it is likely that many will endure. Buddemeir and Smith (1999) describe the current situation as a need to resolve "the 'most ingenious paradox' of organisms that appear biologically fragile but geologically robust."

A primary question to be asked is "What constitutes a healthy reef?" Is the rate of decline and multi-faceted and potentially synergistic global change creating an event of which there is no precedent? To eliminate the problem involved with human time frames, Kinzie (1999) states, "It is clear that the definition of a healthy reef as 'what it looked like when I started diving' is fraught not only with hubris, but strong temporal bias." At the very least, reefs may persist in some form structurally or functionally, but even in the very near future they will almost assuredly be very different from what we have come to associate with the species-diverse coral assemblages that have captured our hearts.

REEF EXPLOITATION

Easier to grasp for those of us who dive, snorkel, and keep marine aquariums are issues involving current overexploitation of reef resources.

Global tourism is increasing tremendously, further subjecting natural reefs to human exposure. With burgeoning tourist traffic in formerly out-of-the-way places comes increased damage from sewage, clearing of land for development, boat traffic and anchorage, contamination by pesticides, and pollution from fossil fuels.

Furthermore, popular reefs can suffer from the often uncontrolled collection of curio specimens, coral skeletons, and mollusk shells to supply the demand for travel souvenirs and the needs of craftspeople making semiprecious art and artifacts. Heavy dive traffic, damage from anchors, and other direct effects of a worldwide growth in underwater exploration has led

to the decline of certain reefs. Unfortunately, marine protection programs and sanctuaries are few and conservation laws poorly enforced, for the most part. Many organizations and individuals are working to improve this situation, and wherever possible we should encourage and assist their efforts.

We should also be asking what role the aquarium industry is playing in determining the state—and the future—of tropical reefs.

There can be no one who looks at a successful reef aquarium, replete with the bounty of the coral reef, who will not stand in awe, mesmerized by its staggering beauty. Increasingly, however, viewers and aquarists themselves are asking probing questions:

Appreciation or impact: Australian divers on coral reef with *Cypraea* sp. (tiger cowrie). Heavy tourist traffic has caused the decline of some reef areas.

tanks. A number of writers have suggested that such collected organisms are doomed to a shortened lifespan in captivity (Tsuroka, 1993; Nash, 1996; Wood, 1985).

For both corals and fishes, the fact is that captive survival rates and longevity have improved dramatically in recent years, thanks to much better husbandry techniques, as well as improved handling and shipping of organisms before they reach the aquarist.

Nonetheless, the number of live corals being collected for aquarium keepers is substantial and is increasing each year. For example, Indonesia is annually exporting nearly one million pieces of stony coral to the United States (Bentley, 1998).

A disproportionate number of these corals are of the large-polyped varieties, such as *Euphyllia*, *Plerogyra*, *Fungia*, and *Catalaphyllia* (Shoup, 1995; Bentley, 1998). These corals have long been mainstays of the retail aquarium coral trade, despite being some of the less-common genera in the wild (Carlson, 1989). Conversely, some corals, such as *Nemenzophyllia* and the coral-limorpharians, are almost unreported in the scientific literature (Veron, 1986) and yet they have appeared in large retail quantities for well over a decade. Whether or not collection for the aquarium trade is having a detrimental effect in the areas of harvest is unknown at this time. Although the effect on the environment is minimal compared to other reef-degrading influences (Wheeler, 1996), local depletion is occurring in some areas.

Currently, all stony corals and black corals are listed as Appendix II species by the Convention on International Trade in Endangered Species of Wild Flora and Fauna (CITES). Trade in Appendix II species is legal and (theoretically) regulated by a permit system. While we have great concerns about the future of reef systems as a whole, individual coral species are not now re-

Curio trade: the uncontrolled collection and killing of corals to provide travel souvenirs and decorative pieces has had negative impacts on many reefs.

Yachties trail: recreational boaters dropping anchor on live corals is a problem being faced by many tropical countries now working to preserve their reefs.

"Where does all of this come from . . . and does it harm the reef?"

It is extremely difficult to know the true impact of livestock collection for the aquarium trade because of poor recordkeeping, lack of data about reef populations and biodiversity, and unknown levels of sustainable harvest in most Third World collection areas. Some observers have a negative opinion of the aquarium industry, largely fueled by images of cyanide-poisoned fishes and corals dead or dying during shipment, sale, or in home

Aquarium corals: some question the collection of live corals for the aquarium trade, while aquarists counter that they bring many people face-to-face with reef life.

garded as endangered. CITES provides some measure of control and protection against overexploitation, but the lack of information on wild populations and the actual numbers being collected make any sort of regulation very difficult.

Very few studies have investigated the nature and potential loss of non-CITES-listed marine species, specifically various invertebrates and nonscleractinian corals. The octocorals and zoanthids, along with still-unclassified Indo-Pacific corallimorpharians have, in fact, long been the standard coral types stocked in retail stores.

SUSTAINABLE HARVESTS

While some critics can find little benefit to the aquarium livestock trade, there are obvious economic reasons for its continuation, in terms of both importing and exporting countries. It is a large industry employing thousands of individuals around the globe (Weber, 1993). It is also one method of giving a tangible value to coral reefs being harvested (Wheeler, 1996).

There are many aquarium clubs, stores, and individual aquarists who make great efforts in teaching and education.

Much work has been done in the public aquarium world to help educate the general public about coral reefs (Greco, 1997; Cubie, 1998; Yates and Carlson, 1992; et al.).

The success of modern reef-keeping methods has made quantum leaps forward from the old, artificial systems that provided, admittedly, little chance of captive corals surviving for a year or more. The dedication and understanding of amateurs keeping reef organisms in closed systems has astonished and impressed many scientists in the fields of marine biology and ecology, and coral scientists and marine hobbyists have found many points of common interest and concern. However, there is a need for more hobbyists to document their anecdotal reports and thus make them of real value to others.

There is much to be said about being in the presence of live corals and reef organisms 24 hours a day. Being able to observe, measure, and experience these systems continually is something that no amount of underwater research can duplicate. Many behaviors never reported in the scientific literature are observed on a daily basis by a worldwide community of avid marine aquarists. These behaviors include competitive methods, asexual reproduction, and physiological changes based on varied environmental parameters, many of which have never before been reported. Studies on growth rates in captivity have also resulted, along with estimates of biodiversity (Bates, 1997; Bingman, 1998; Small et al., 1998).

Aquaculture and breeding data has been accumulated by aquarists at a rapidly increasing rate. Many techniques used to improve the water quality of closed systems now being used in many public aquariums have come directly from the methods discovered by private aquarists.

Perhaps most importantly, reef hobbyists learn to appreciate the subtleties, dynamics, beauty, and fragility of nature. I must admit that, even with years of diving experience, I have become a much better observer of corals and reef dynamics since starting to keep reef aquariums. Proper reef husbandry almost inevitably teaches new respect for these wonderful organisms and the wild ecosystems that provide them.

For some, reef aquariums are their only likely contact with a natural reef environment. Certainly the marine aquarium can be an invaluable educational tool for many who will never have a chance to see the tropical underwater world through a dive mask. A well-managed reef aquarium can be a powerful tool for teaching awareness, respect, and admiration for a rare and increasingly threatened environment.

Sustainable harvest? A collector frees **Sarcophyton elegans** from a shallow reef in Fiji. Exporters argue that careful collection causes no permanent harm.

FUTURE IMPROVEMENTS

Fortunately, many individuals and groups are attempting to put their newfound knowledge into action. Concerned aquarists, in fact, are part of the current push to reform harvesting methods, eliminate cyanide usage in fish collection, and promote responsible, sustainable gathering of corals and other reef organisms. In addition to its toxic effects on fishes, cyanide has been shown to cause the loss of zooxanthellae in corals, leading to bleaching and the death of seriously damaged colonies (Jones and Hoegh-Guldberg, 1999).

The Marine Aquarium Council (MAC) has been established as part of a joint group to establish responsible and sustainable collection of marine organisms. The American Marinelife Dealers Association (AMDA) is a group dedicated to the informed and ethical buying and selling of live marine organisms.

There is also a growing motivation to take our success with captive systems and use it to propagate corals that not long ago were thought impossible even to keep alive. Coral farming in a few short years has leapt from a strange fantasy to a very real phenomenon. Pioneering aquaculture operations are succeeding in producing cultured corals both in tropical Third World settings and in indoor facilities in developed countries.

In North America, numerous commercial and amateur or hobbyist propagators are taking small cuttings or fragments of soft and stony corals and growing new specimens or colonies that are in great demand by aquarists. They are typically disease-free and are provided to the aquarist without the stress of collection, long-distance shipping, and traumatic periods spent in holding facilities. They do not have to endure the many shocks of long flights and frequent and drastic environmental changes. And most importantly, with captive-grown livestock there is no negative impact on natural coral reefs.

At the present time, there are hundreds of captive-bred coral species commercially available. The possibility of hundreds more being propagated is already within sight, in farflung locales from the Solomon Islands to the suburbs of Detroit, Michigan. Other initiatives are putting in place procedures to certify that fishes and other reef organisms sold in the aquarium trade have been collected in a legal, responsible, and sustainable way. The Breeder's Registry provides great services to anyone interested in marine ornamental aquaculture through the dissemination of statistics and data regarding captive propagation.

It is my hope that all of us involved with the keeping of marine aquariums will support ethical coral farmers, collectors, and sellers, even if it means sometimes paying more for the livestock. In time, and with proper support, the prices of corals and fishes sustainably harvested or propagated can become lower as the

Farmed corals: a tankful of captive-propagated corals at the Geothermal Aquaculture Research Foundation in Idaho suggests the exciting potential of coral farming.

demand for cheap, low-quality, and poorly collected organisms disappears. It is, after all, folly to want a large head of rare coral that was hacked off a reef with a crowbar (and subjected to intolerable handling conditions) just because it is inexpensive. Many of us have learned that it is far wiser—and infinitely more satisfying—to purchase a well-cared-for and properly shipped smaller coral colony (or fragment) that was either captive grown or harvested responsibly; one that can be nurtured as it grows; one with a high likelihood not only of surviving, but possibly of becoming a source of new corals for other hobbyists.

In time, and with the proper motivation, there is even the exciting possibility that the reef hobby and coral propagation facilities would be able to help in providing the stock to repopulate or replenish wild reefs that have been damaged by other means (Borneman and Lowrie, 1999). While many would say this is wishful thinking, there is no doubt that those growing and reproducing corals in their homes and businesses are already doing much toward developing methods of keeping corals healthy and finding methods of reproducing them efficiently.

In fact, it is my view that the reef aquarium hobby has the potential to be of tangible benefit to the tropical coral reefs of the world. I also hope that growth in our understanding of the animals we keep and the habitats they come from becomes an ever greater motivating force. There is no excuse for destroying the bounty of our Earth, and no profit worth the loss of the coral reefs. We, as keepers of the captive reef, must be examples of informed stewardship rather than bioconsumerism. I am personally honored and grateful to have the beauty of living corals around me every day, and I hope we as aquarists can spread the astonishment and joy brought by observing these magnificent creatures.

Contacts

CORAL REEF AND AQUARIUM CONSERVATION GROUPS

The following organizations are active in protecting and preserving coral reefs, in educating the public about environmental issues, and in promoting reef stewardship in the aquarium trade and among aquarists. Many of their Web sites have links to more contacts.

The American Marinelife Dealers Association (AMDA)
569 32 Road, Suite 7B #241
Grand Junction, CO 81504
Web site: www.execpc.com/~jkos/amda

Australian Institute of Marine Science (AIMS)
PMB 3
Townsville MC
Townsville, Queensland 4810
Australia
Web site: www.aims.gov.au

The Breeder's Registry
P.O. Box 255373
Sacramento, CA 95865-5373
Web site: www.breeders-registry.gen.ca.us

CEDAM International
1 Fox Road
Croton-on-Hudson, NY 10520
Web site: www.cedam.org

Center for Marine Conservation (CMC)
1725 DeSales Street NW, Suite 500
Washington, DC 20036
Tel: (202) 647-0239
Web site: www.cmc-ocean.org

Coral Gardens Initiative
Foundation for the Peoples of the South Pacific
P.O. Box 14447
Suva, Fiji Islands
Tel: (679) 300-392-314-160

Convention on International Trade in Endangered Species (CITES)
15 Chemin des Anémones
CH-1219 Chatelaine-Genève
Suisse
Tel: (4122) 917-8139

The Coral Reef Alliance
64 Shattuck Square, Suite 220
Berkeley, CA 94704
Tel: (510) 848-0110
Web site: www.coral.org

Coral Cay Conservation, Ltd.
154 Clapham Park Road
London SW4 7DE, UK
Tel: 44-0-171-498-6248
Web site: www.coralcay.org

Cousteau Society
870 Greenbrier Circle, Suite 402
Chesapeake, VA 23320
Tel: (800) 441-4395
Web site: www.cousteausociety.org

Crusoe Reef Society
P.O. Box 890
Port of Spain, Trinidad and Tobago
Tel: (809) 628-2207

Earthwatch Institute
680 Mount Auburn Street
P.O. Box 9104
Watertown, MA 02471
Tel: (617) 926-8200
Web site: www.earthwatch.org

Environmental Defense Fund
257 Park Avenue South
New York, NY 10010
Tel: (800) 684-3322
Web site: www.edf.org

Environmental Solutions International
13826 Castle Cliff Way
680 Mt. Auburn
Silver Spring, MD 20904
Tel: (301) 989-1731

Global Coral Reef Alliance
324 Bedford Road
Chappaqua, NY 10514
Tel: (914) 238-8788

Great Barrier Reef Marine Park Authority (GBRMPA)
P.O. Box 1379
Townsville, Queensland, 4810
Australia
Tel: (61) 7-4750-0770

Greenpeace USA
1436 U Street NW
Washington, D.C. 20009
Tel: (202) 462-1177
Web site: www.greenpeace.org

International Coral Reef Initiative
c/o ICRI Coordinator
OES/ETC, Room 4325
Department of State
Washington, DC 20520
Web site: www.iucn.org/themes/icri

International Marinelife Alliance (US)
2800 4th Street North, Suite 123
St. Petersburg, FL 33704
Tel: (813) 896-8626
Web site: www.imamarinelife.org

The Coral Disease Page
Web site:
ourworld.compuserve.com/homepages/
mccarty_and_peters/coraldis.htm

IUCN (The World Conservation Union)
219c Huntingdon Road
Cambridge CB3 ODL, UK
Tel: 44-1223-277894
Web site: www.iucn.org

Marine Aquarium Council
3035 Hibiscus Drive
Honolulu, HI 96815
Tel: (808) 923-3254
Web site: www.aquariumcouncil.org

Marine Aquarium Societies of North America (MASNA)
P.O. Box 508
Penns Park, PA 18943
Web site: www.masna.org

Marine Conservation Group
c/o Nature Society
601 Sims Drive
#04-04 Bam-I Complex
S (1438) Singapore
Tel: 65-7412036

Marine Conservation Society
9 Gloucester Road
Ross-on-Wye
Herefordshire HR9 5BU, UK
Tel: 01989-566017

The Nature Conservancy
Asia/Pacific Regional Office
1116 Smith Street #201
Honolulu, HI 96817
Tel: (808) 537-4508

NYZS/Wildlife Conservation Society
2300 Southern Blvd.
Bronx, NY 10460
(212) 861-6030
Web site: www.wcs.org

Ocean Voice International
Box 37026
3332 McCarthy Road
Ottawa, ON K1V 0W0 Canada
Web site: www.ovi.ca

Reefkeeper International
2809 Bird Avenue, Suite 162
Miami, FL 33133
Tel: (305) 358-4600
Web site: www.reefkeeper.org

Reef Relief
P.O. Box 430
Key West, FL 33041
Tel: (305) 294-3100
Web site: www.reefrelief.org

ReefsUK
Kings Walk
5 Durham way
Rayleigh, Essex SS69RY, UK
Tel: (44) 0-973-310603
Web site: www.reefsuk.org

Reefwatch
Tropical Marine Research Unit
Dept. of Biology, University of York
York Y01 5DD, UK
Tel: (44) (904) 432930

Saba Conservation Foundation
P.O. Box 18
The Bottom
Saba, Netherlands Antilles

Singapore Underwater Federation
c/o Dept. of Zoology, National
University of Singapore
10 Kent Ridge Crescent
Singapore 0511
Tel: (65) 7723863

Tubbataha Foundation
83A Harvard Street
Cubao, Quezon City
Philippines

World Resources Institute
10 G Street NE, Suite 800
Washington, DC 20002
Tel: (202) 729-7600
Web site: www.wri.org

World Wide Fund for Nature (WWF-UK)
Panda House
Weyside Park
Godalming, Surrey GU7 1XR, UK
Tel: 44-1483-426-444
Web site: www.wwf-uk.org

World Wildlife Fund US
1250 24th Street NW
P.O. Box 97180
Washington, DC 20007
Tel: (202) 293-4800
Web site: www.worldwildlife.org

Coral Propagators

The following companies and organizations are part of a rapidly burgeoning international body of aquaculturists dedicated to propagating and/or marketing corals, both in captivity and in waters on or near coral reefs.

Aquatic Wildlife
5200 North Lee Highway
Cleveland, TN 37412-4519
Tel: (423) 559-9000
Web Site: www.aquaticwildlife.com

Coral Farms
10270 Alpine Drive #3
Cupertino, CA 95014
Tel: (408) 735-8439
Web site: www.coralfarms.com

Coral Reef Aquarium
1464 Fall River Avenue
Seekonk, MA 02771
Tel: (508) 336-0904
Web site: www.inverts.com

C-Quest
P.O. Box 1162
Salinas, PR 00751
Tel: (787) 845-2160
Web site: www.c-quest.com

Dynamic Ecomorphology
39525 Los Alamos Road, Suite A143
Murrieta, CA 92562
Tel: (909) 677-0073
Web site: www.masla.com/home000.htm

Geothermal Aquaculture Research Foundation, Inc.
1321 Warm Springs Avenue
Boise, ID 83712
Tel: (208) 344-6163
Web site: www.garf.org

Indo-Pacific Sea Farms
P.O. Box 1206
Kailua-Kona, HI 96745
Tel: (808) 334-1709
Web site: www.ipsf.com

Inland Aquatics
10 Ohio Street
Terre Haute, IN
Tel: (812) 232-9000
Web site: www.inlandaquatics.com

Oceans, Reefs & Aquariums (ORA)
5600 US 1 North
ACTED Building
Fort Pierce, FL 34946
Tel: (561) 468-7008
Web site: www.orafarm.com

Scientific Corals
850 Dogwood Road, Suite A400-489
Lawrenceville, GA 30044
Tel: (770) 736-9220
Web site: www.scientificcorals.com

Sea Critters
1005 Sea Critter Lane
Dover, FL 33527
Tel: (813) 986-6521
Web site: petsforum.com/seacritters

Something Fishy
16 Nor Bath Boulevard
Northampton, PA 18067
Tel: (610) 502-9760
Web site: www.toofishy.com

A Splash of Life
43W484 Burlington Road
Elgin, IL 60123
Tel: (847) 464-0306
Web site: www.splashoflife.com

Tropicorium
20080 Inkster Road
Romulus, MI 48174
Tel: (734) 782-2622
Web site: www.tropicorium.com

Author and Publisher

Readers with comments about this book or suggestions for future editions may contact:

Eric H. Borneman
2222 North Fountain Valley
Missouri City, TX 77459
e-mail: EricHugo@aol.com

Microcosm Ltd.
Attn: James M. Lawrence, Editor
P.O. Box 580
Shelburne, VT 05482
e-mail: jml@microcosm-books.com

Glossary

These definitions relate to the contents of this book and, primarily, to corals. Many of these words have other meanings in general etymology or in different branches of science.

Pronunciation Note: The pronunciations given are in a common-sense format and do not follow formal phonetic standards. Furthermore, the rules of nomenclature and foreign pronunciations allow for different pronunciations across cultures. In general, it is a rule of scientific nomenclature that in the absence of cues or other standardization, the following is to be standard: In words containing five or more syllables, the primary accent will be on the third-to-last syllable. In words containing four or fewer syllables, the accent lies on the second-to-last syllable. In multisyllabic words, alternating minor inflections of accent/nonaccent exist.

accessory pigments: various pigment molecules contained within the photosynthetic unit (PSU) and within chloroplasts that aid in photosynthesis.

acclimatization: compensatory change in the metabolism and physiological response of an organism exposed to temporal variation(s) in its environment.

acontial filament: (ah-kon'-tee-ul) a threadlike extension of a septal filament that extends into the gastrovascular cavity, used in digestive functions and aggressive attacks; may be expelled under stress.

acrorhagus (sing.)/acrorhagi (pl.): (ak'-ro-rah'-gus/ak'-ro-rah'-gee) specialized raised areas with high densities and special types of cnidocytes, found on sweeper tentacles and on some anthozoan columns.

acrosphere: (ak'-ro-sphere) swollen tip of a cnidarian tentacle, heavily equipped with nematocysts.

aerobic: occurring in the presence of oxygen.

ahermatypic: (ay'-her-mah-tip'-ik) describing a type of coral that does not contribute substantially to building the matrix or calcareous framework of a coral reef; nonreef-building.

alkalinity: the measurement used to describe water's resistance to pH changes (its buffering capacity); also known as carbonate hardness.

allelopathy: (uh-lee'-luh-path'-ee) a process by which biomanufactured chemicals directly influence the development of another organism; primarily competitive.

ammonia (NH$_3$): a chemical that is the primary nitrogen-containing end-product of protein metabolism and the breakdown of living or formerly living matter. Corals and their zooxanthellae can use small amounts of ammonia as a nitrogen food source; large concentrations are toxic to corals and fishes.

ampulla (sing.)/ampullae (pl.): (am-pue'-lah/am-pue'-lee) a pore or dilated portion of a duct found in certain calcareous hydrozoans that produce medusae from internal self-fertilization.

anaerobic: occurring without the presence of oxygen.

anecdotal: evidence or information based on individual example or informal case report, not from scientific or controlled study.

anastomosis: (an-as'-tuh-moe'-sis) the fusion between branches or columns of a coral.

anthocodia (sing.)/anthocodiae (pl.): (an'-thoe-koe'-dee-ah/an'-thoe-koe'-dee-ee) the upper or distal end of an octocoral polyp, including the mouth and eight tentacles.

anthocauli: (an'-thoe-call'-ee) daughter colonies formed by asexual reproduction in some members of the genus *Fungia*, where decalcification of the parent colony results in self-sufficient clones that develop on the skeleton of the parent before being separated to become free-standing colonies.

anthostele: (an'-thoe-steel) stiffened polyp base or stalk from which the anthocodia arises and into which it may be withdrawn (see **calyx**).

apertures: (ap'-er-tchoors) openings, especially those in the rind surface of gorgonians, from which the polyps emerge.

aposematic coloration: (a'-puh-sih-mat'-ik) the use of conspicuous colors to warn off predators.

aposymbiotic: (a'-puh-sim-bee-ah'-tik) describing corals that do not contain the mutualistic algae commonly known as zooxanthellae (equivalent to **azooxanthellate**).

arboreal: (ar-bor'-ee-ul) growth form of certain corals (equivalent to **branching** or **ramose**).

aragonite: (ah-rag'-oh-nite) a crystalline form of calcium carbonate ($CaCO_3$) produced by corals. It is commonly used to describe the composition of coral skeletons and coral reef sand.

asexual reproduction: any reproduction resulting in a new coral that occurs without the exchange of gametes (sexual cells, a.k.a. sperm and eggs).

ATP: adenosine triphosphate; the biochemical compound that is the basic energy source for organisms.

atrich: (ay'-trik) unbarbed, smooth, threadlike nematocyst common to corallimorphs, but also found in other corals.

ATS: algal turf scrubber; trademark name for an aquarium methodology that uses turf algae to control water quality by means of nutrient uptake by the algae.

autotroph: (aw'-toe-trof') an organism capable of manufacturing all necessary organic compounds from inorganic sources using photosynthesis as source of energy (compare to **heterotroph**).

autozooid: (aw'-toe-zoe'-id) a primary feeding polyp type of an octocoral, having eight pinnate tentacles. It is the only polyp type in monomorphic species, the larger polyp type in dimorphic species (see **siphonozooid**).

axial: (ak'-see-all) pertaining to, associated with, or in reference to a central core or axis.

axial corallite: the specialized elongated terminal corallite found at the tip of a branch, primarily of the genus *Acropora*.

axis: (ak'-sis) the central core of a gorgonian that provides rigid support; also known as the core.

azooxanthellate: (ay'-zoe-zan'-thuh-late) lacking symbiotic zooxanthellae (equivalent to **aposymbiotic**).

Berlin method: an approach to reef aquarium operation employing the use of live rock, foam fractionation, strong water movement, and strong lighting.

benthic: related to or occurring at the bottom of a body of water.

binomial nomenclature: a system of naming in which an organism is identified by its genus and species.

biofilm: a coating on a surface composed of microscopic plants and animals and their metabolic products.

black-band disease: an infectious, progressive disease caused primarily by the cyanobacterium *Phormidium corallyticum*, characterized by an advancing black band of necrotic tissue that results in the death of affected stony corals and some gorgonians.

bleaching: the process in which a coral expels some or all of its zooxanthellae in response to stress, resulting in the coral appearing white or less intensely colored.

brachycnemic: (brake'-ee-snee'-mik) a characteristic arrangement of mesenteries of some colonial polyps in the Order Zoanthidea; having an imperfect fifth mesentery (compare to **macrocnemic**).

branching: a growth form of corals in which skeletal extensions of the corallum or the tissue/supportive elements form offshoots or divisions from a main stem (also known as **arboreal** or **ramose**).

brooders: corals that are hermaphroditic and self-fertilize within the gastrovascular cavity to form planulae (free-swimming planktonic larval corals).

brown jelly: a coral infection characterized by tissue breakdown and the appearance of a gelatinous substance at the site of active degeneration; thought to result from attack by numerous microorganisms, especially protozoans, which cause extracellular tissue digestion.

budding: a form of asexual reproduction in corals in which a polyp gives rise to one or more daughter polyps by forming a tissue extension. There are many types of budding common to corals; some types of buds form entire small colonies before their release from the parent.

calcification: (cal'-si-fi-kay'-shun) the process by which coral polyps build a skeleton or skeletal elements by precipitating calcium carbonate through complex processes and biochemical reactions.

calcium (Ca): an inorganic element that may be complexed in various forms. It is the predominant building block for many corals and calcareous reef organisms.

calice (sing.)/calices (pl.): (kay'-liss/kay'-lih-sees) in stony corals, the opening of a corallite or the rim of the cuplike skeletal structure in which a coral polyp resides.

calyx (sing.)/calyces (pl.): (kay'-lix/kay'-lih-sees) in soft corals, a raised area on the surface of many octocorals forming an opening, or cup, into which the polyps may be withdrawn.

capitate: (kah'-pih-tate) referring to unbranched corals having a broad "head" arising from the base or stalk.

capitulum: (kah-pit'-yoo-lum) the flat, broad, upper surface of certain octocorals from which the polyps arise (also called the **polypary** or **polyparium**).

captive breeding: the propagation of marine organisms in aquariums or aquaculture facilities.

catkin: see **lappet**.

cerioid: (seh'-ree-oyd) a type of stony coral colony formation where adjacent corallites share fused walls.

chloramphenicol: (klor'-am-fen'-ih-kawl) a broad-spectrum antibiotic used to treat some of the rapid tissue loss diseases of corals.

chlorophyll: (klor'-o-fill) the primary green pigment in plants and algae, including zooxanthellae, essential in the production of carbohydrates during photosynthesis.

cilia: (sill'-ee-ah) short hairlike processes or structures that are cellular extensions capable of motility in a jointly coordinated back and forth movement. Corals use their cilia for various purposes, including the transport of particulate matter across the surface of the polyp.

clade: (klayd) a taxonomic unit used in the science of cladistics; that is, groupings based on similar characters as defined by phylogeny.

closed systems: used to describe captive or aquarium environments that are free from natural oceanic water inputs.

cnidocyte: (nie'-doh-site) the general term used to describe a specialized cell that contains stinging or other specialized functional cellular organelles. Nematocysts are located within cnidocytes.

cnidom: (nie'-dum) the portion of a tentacle that contains the cnidocytes.

coenenchyme: (see'-nehn-kyme) the stiff, gelatinous tissue matrix of certain soft corals that serves to anchor and support the stalk of polyps and that may be embedded with particulate matter or sclerites. Sometimes referred to as the **mesoglea**, as this intracellular layer is the source of its formation.

coenosarc: (see'-no-zark') the soft tissue that lies over the stony coenosteum of a coral, usually linking the tissue between adjacent polyps.

coenosteum (sing.)/coenostea (pl.): (see'-no-stee'-um/see'-no-stee'-uh) the calcium matrix of the skeleton that lies between and fuses adjacent corallites.

color rendition: a measurement of the subjective accuracy of a light source at portraying the true color of an object.

color temperature: a measurement used to describe the color of a light source, measured on the Kelvin temperature scale.

columella: (call'-uh-meh'-luh) a vertical pillarlike skeletal structure in the center of the corallite of certain stony corals; formed by inward-projecting skeletal septa becoming intertwined and fused.

columnar: a growth form of corals in which the corallum forms columns or pillars from the substrate.

commensalism: (cuh-men'-suh-liz'-um) a type of symbiosis in which one species benefits and the other species receives neither benefit nor harm.

coral: a sessile polyp animal or colony of polyp animals, with or without a calcareous skeleton, that is a member of the Classes Anthozoa or Hydrozoa within the Phylum Cnidaria.

corallite: (ko'-rah-lite) the basic skeletal unit of a stony coral that contains the polyp, which secretes the corallite around itself.

coralline algae: (ko'-rah-lin) a generic term for the many species of red algae that incorporate calcium carbonate into their encrustations; primary constituents of coral reef structure and sand; also known as calcareous or crustose algae.

corallum (sing.)/coralla (pl.): (ko-ral'-lum/ko-ral'-luh) the skeletal matrix of a stony coral colony.

coral surface microlayer (CSM): a thin region adjacent to a coral surface that is characterized by still or stagnant water resulting from the hydrodynamics of water flow across surfaces.

core: see **axis**.

costa (sing.)/costae (pl.): (koss'-tuh/koss'-tee) thin skeletal plates that protrude outward from the walls of a corallite, away from the center of the calice.

cryptofauna: animals concealed by their habitat; in corals, animals associated with corals that use them for concealment and protection.

curing: a process of preparing live rock for use in a reef aquarium. Decaying organisms are broken down by microfauna, along with a concomitant increase in nitrifying and denitrifying bacterial populations, resulting in a relatively stable microenvironment on and within the rock.

cuticle: (cue'-tih-kul) the protective, leathery skin of colonial polyps.

cyanoacrylate: (sigh'-a-no-ah-kril'-ate) a quick-setting adhesive that displays a low bond strength, high adhesion properties, and relatively low toxicity in marine applications. Also known as superglue.

cyclosystem: (sye'-kloh-sis'-tehm) the interconnected canal system that allows for communication and nutrient exchange within the skeleton of certain corals, notably some calcareous hydrozoans.

dactylopores: (dak-til'-oh-porz) small openings in the skeletons of calcareous hydrozoans that contain the dactylozooids.

dactylozooids: (dak-til'-oh-zoe'-id) hairlike nematocystic extensions of a hydrozoan polyp, used in prey capture.

decalcification: (dee-kal'-sih-fih-kay'-shun) the dissolution of calcified skeletal matter by some corals.

dendroid: (den'-droyd) a type of stony coral colony formation in which corallites spread away from each other like the branches on a tree.

denitrification: (dee-nie'-trih-fih-kay'-shun) the reduction of nitrate to nitrite, ammonia, nitrous oxide, nitrogen gas, or other nitrogen-containing compounds, usually by processes mediated by bacteria or algae.

detritus: (deh-try'-tuss) flocculent drifting material composed primarily of dead algae, coral mucus, and animal waste material and coated with bacteria and cyanobacteria. Also known as particulate organic matter (POM), suspended organic matter (SOM), reef snow, and pseudoplankton. It is an important food source for corals and for other organisms that participate in nutrient recycling.

dichotomous: (dye-kah'-toe-muss) splitting in a y-shaped formation; a form of branching or repeated forking of a branch or stem.

dimorphic: (dye-more'-fik) describing octocorals that have both autozooid- and siphonozooid-type polyps.

dinoflagellate: (die'-no-flaj'-eh-late) a photosynthetic protozoan characterized by golden brown coloration and motile flagella; their characteristics as phytoplankton allow for their common consideration as algae.

dissolved organic matter (DOM): organic compounds dissolved in water and used as a food source by corals.

diurnal: (die-ur'-null) active by day; occurring daily; of or pertaining to daytime.

ecomorphs: (ee'-koh-morfs') groups of genetically similar individuals that may have dissimilar morphologic appearances due to genetic or environmental factors.

ecotypes: (ee'-koh-types') groups of genetically dissimilar individuals that may share similar morphologic appearances due to genetic or environmental factors.

encrusting: a growth form of certain corals (and other reef organisms) in which the tissue and/or skeleton grows outward across the substrate, adhering closely to it.

epidermis: (eh-pih-dur'-mis) the outermost layer of coral tissue.

epizoon: (ep'-ee-zoe'-on) an animal that lives on the exterior surface of another organism (adjective: **epizoic**).

epoxy: a two-part manufactured adhesive with relatively low toxicity, used for various marine applications, particularly the cementing of coral fragments to substrate.

etiology: (ee'-tee-ahl'-oh-jee) the study of the factors that cause disease.

eutrophic: (you-troh'-fik) describing a body of water characterized by high levels of nutrients and low levels of dissolved oxygen.

exsert: (ek'-surt) protruding.

extracoelenteric: (ek'-strah-see-len'-tehr-ik) occurring outside the body cavity.

fecundity: (feh-kun'-dih-tee) the ability to produce large numbers of offspring successfully.

fission: (fizh'-un) a generic term for several types of asexual reproduction in which tissue and/or skeletal division occurs, either laterally or longitudinally, through a section or sections of a coral, resulting in one or more daughter colonies.

fissure: (fish'-ure) a form of asexual reproduction in corallimorphs, similar to fission, in which a polyp divides across itself and splits, resulting in two new polyps.

flabellate: (fla'-buh-late) a type of stony coral colony formation in which corallites form short valleys with separate walls.

flabello-meandroid: (fla'-bell-oh-me'-an-droid) a type of stony coral colony formation in which corallites form long, meandering valleys with separate walls.

fluorescing proteins: fluorescent pigments produced by the polyp; thought to assist in photosynthesis by turning unusable light wavelengths into usable ones through reflection.

foliaceous: (foe-lee-ay'-shus) a growth form of corals exhibiting leaflike sheets and plates, sometimes curved or folded.

fragmentation: a form of asexual reproduction in which parts of a parent coral colony are accidentally or purposely detached and allowed to grow into separate colonies.

gastrodermis: (gas'-troh-dur'-mis) the layer of coral tissue lying underneath, or interior to, the epidermis.

gastropore: (gas'-troh-pore) a small opening in the skeleton of a calcareous hydrozoan containing the gastrozooids.

gastrozooid: (gas'-troh-zoe'-id) a short, fuzzy nematocystic extension of a specialized feeding polyp of calcareous hydrozoans.

genotype: (jee'-nuh-type) the genetic makeup of an organism.

genus: (jee'-nuss) a taxonomic group of individuals with substantially similar characteristics and the first part of standard **binomial nomenclature**.

glitter lines: intensifications of light energy seen in shallow water, resulting from the refraction of light striking a rippled surface.

gonochoric: (go'-no-kore'-ik) opposite of hermaphroditic; possessing normal separate development of male and female sex organs/gonads.

gorgonin: (gore'-goe-nihn) a horny proteinaceous compound made and used by gorgonians to produce rigid support structures.

heat shock proteins (HSPS): highly specific protein chains that prevent the denaturation of metabolically important cellular proteins when corals are exposed to thermal stress.

hermaphroditic: (her-maf'-roh-dit'-tik) having both male and female sex organs/gonads within the same organism.

hermatypic: (her'-mah-tip'-ik) describing a type of coral that contributes substantially to the matrix or calcareous framework of a coral reef; reef-building.

heterotroph: (heh'-ter-oh-trof') an organism incapable of manufacturing organic substances from inorganic sources, thus requiring nutrition from its environment.

hexacoral: a coral with polyps whose tentacles number six or multiples of six. The true stony corals (scleractinians) are all hexacorals.

histocompatible: capable of being accepted and remaining functional across genotypic differences.

holdfast: the specialized and flared basal portion of a gorgonian that aids in its attachment to the substrate.

holotrichus isorhizas: (ho-lo-trick'-us eye'-so-rye'-zus) a type of nematocyst used for prey capture, predominantly in night-feeding corals.

hybridization: the process of producing an organism from dissimilar parents (species, strain, etc.).

hydnophore: (hid'-no-for') a conically raised skeletal bump between corallites, especially in the stony coral genus *Hydnophora*.

hydnophoroid: (hid-nah'-for-oyd) a type of stony coral colony formation characterized by the presence of hydnophores.

hydrocoral: (hie'-dro-koh'-ral) a colonial calcifying hydrozoan that is not a "true" stony coral.

hypostome: (high'-poh-stome) a mouth or oral opening that is raised from the surface of the oral disc.

hypoxia: (hye-pox'-ee-ah) the state of having extremely low oxygen concentrations.

inorganic compounds: chemical compounds not containing carbon; also not derived from living sources.

iodine: a trace element in seawater that has an as yet unfounded, yet anecdotally beneficial, role in the health of corals and other marine organisms. Utilized primarily as potassium iodide by aquarists, it also has antiseptic, bacteriostatic, and oxidative uses or effects.

irradiance: (ih-ray'-dee-ance) the intensity of light or the amount of light energy striking a certain area over time; measured in lumens.

isomones: (eye'-soh-mohns) bioproduced chemicals that control growth patterns between and within species.

Jaubert method: (zhah-bare') an approach to reef aquarium operation employing the use of a deep bed of substrate over a plenum, with strong water movement and strong lighting. Foam fractionation is not used.

Kalkwasser: (kulk'-vos-ser) a term coined by German aquarists for a saturated solution of calcium hydroxide or calcium oxide in water. Informally, Kalkwasser is also used to describe commercial preparations of calcium hydroxide powder used to prepare Kalkwasser solutions.

Kelvin: a standard scientific temperature scale; also used to indicate measurements of "color temperature" of light in degrees K.

laceration: (lass'-er-ay'-shun) a form of asexual reproduction in corallimorphs, also common to anemones, where tissue lost from the pedal attachment separates or tears away from the parent to form a new daughter organism.

laminar: (lam'-ih-ner) a growth form of corals typified by flat, horizontal plates that are often unifacial. Laminar may also refer to currents that occur in a continuous planar or unidirectional manner.

lappet: (lap'-it) a group of polyps given support by a bundle of sclerites; their contracted appearance is cauliflower-like. Characteristic of the Family Nephtheidae. Also an area of tissue uplifting between the calicoblastic epithelium and the skeleton where calcification and skeltogenesis processes are active.

lateral: pertaining to, associated with, or in reference to a side; moving away from the midline of a body or structure.

light shock: stress in corals resulting from a rapid change of lighting conditions; a potential cause of bleaching.

live rock: aquarium aquascaping material of biological calcareous origin replete with associated and attached marine life, collected from reef areas and shipped wet or damp to preserve life forms.

LPS: large-polyped stony or large-polyped scleractinian coral. An informal and imprecise aquarium-hobby term, typically used to group corals in such genera as *Alveopora, Blastomussa, Catalaphyllia, Euphyllia, Cynarina, Goniopora, Fungia, Heliofungia, Lobophyllia, Nemenzophyllia, Symphyllia, Trachyphyllia, Tubastraea,* and others (compare to **SPS**).

lumen: (loo'-men) a unit measurement of irradiance or luminous flux; the amount of light emitted by a single candle and reaching one square foot of a surface placed so that all points are one linear foot from the source of light (see **lux**). 1 lumen = 10.76 lux.

lux: the international measurement of light intensity; equal to one lumen per square meter (see **lumen**). 1 lux = 0.0929 lumens.

MAAs: mycosporine-like amino acids. Clear UV-protectant substances produced by either coral polyps or their zooxanthellae to protect their cells against harmful ultraviolet radiation.

macrocnemic: (mak'-roh-snee'-mik) a characteristic arrangement of mesenteries of some colonial polyps in the Order Zoanthidea; having a complete fifth mesentery (compare to **brachycnemic**).

marginal: pertaining to, associated with, or in reference to a border or edge in coral anatomy.

massive: a growth form of coral that is boulderlike.

mat polyps: octocorals in the Suborder Stolonifera that have a network or solid mat of polyps connected by runners, known as stolons; stoloniferans.

meandroid: (mee-an'-droyd) a type of stony coral colony formation in which the corallites are longitudinally fused to form sinuous hills and valleys.

medusa: a free-swimming umbrella-shaped juvenile form of some cnidarians, especially hydrozoans.

"melting": an informal term used to describe the rapid collapse and degeneration of some soft corals, notably nephtheids and xeniids.

mesenterial filaments: (mez'-ehn-tare'-ee-al) the extensions of the mesenteries, primarily used in digestion and aggression; includes the septal and acontial filaments.

mesenteries: (mez'-ehn-tear'-ees) longitudinal sheets of tissue that penetrate the symmetrical skeletal compartments in scleractinians and divide the body cavity of all polyps into sections.

mesoglea: (mez'-oh-glee'-ah) a mostly empty connective tissue space between the epidermis and the gastrodermis where immune cells and other cell types can be found in loose arrangement. May also refer to the coenenchyme of colonial polyps.

microbasic mastigophore: (my'-kro-bay'-sik mas-tig'-oh-for) a type of nematocyst common to day-feeding corals, used for prey penetration and substrate adhesion. The two most common types are microbasic p-mastigophores (found mainly in normal tentacles) and microbasic b-mastigophores (found mainly in specialized tentacles).

microvilli: (my'-kro-vill'-ee) cylindrical protrusions on the outer surface of cells that increase their absorptive surface area.

monomorphic: (mah'-noe-more'-fik) describing octocorals that have only autozooid-type polyps.

monostomatous: (mahn'-oh-stoh-ma'-tuss) having a single mouth.

morphologic: (more'-foe-lah'-jik) dealing with the physical structure or form of an organism or its parts.

mouth: the opening into the gastrovascular cavity of a polyp. Also know as the oral opening.

mucus: (myu'-kuss) a polysaccharide-rich substance secreted by corals as an adhesive, protectant, lubricant, and food-capture mechanism.

mucus tunic: a sloughed surface layer of mucus fouled by algae, bacteria, and other material; produced by certain corals.

mucus web: the flocculent release of mucus by some coral species; used to trap particulate material for food.

mutualism: (myu'-choo-uh-li'-zum) a type of symbiosis in which both species benefit from their association with each other. The relationship of a coral polyp and its zooxanthellae is one of mutualism.

necrosis: (neh-kroe'-sis) death of a circumscribed portion of coral tissue.

nematocyst: (ne-mat'-oh-sist) a cell organelle that contains a sac and a harpoon-type structure that is used to ensnare and sting in coral defensive or feeding behavior. Held within cnidocytes.

nitrate (NO$_3$): a chemical ion that is the end product of nitrification and the beginning source of denitrification. Corals may use nitrate as a nitrogen source for themselves and their zooxanthellae.

nitrification: (nie'-trih-fih-kay'-shun) the aerobic process in which bacteria mediate the conversion or oxidation of ammonia into nitrite, and then nitrite into nitrate.

nitrite (NO$_2$): (nie'-trite) the intermediate nitrogen-containing ion of nitrification and some forms of denitrification. Corals have not been shown to utilize nitrite as a nitrogen source.

nomenclature: (no'-men-klay'-chur) a system of names or terms, usually following a regular pattern of order.

NNR: natural nitrate reduction; aquarium-hobby term for the use of substrate materials (often sand) to aid in the process of denitrification in closed systems.

nutrient export: a method by which organic inputs to a system, such as an aquarium, are removed to prevent their accumulation.

octocoral: any of a number of corals, mostly lacking rigid calcium skeletons, whose polyps have eight tentacles. Gorgonians and soft corals are the primary constituents of the octocorals.

oligotrophic: (ah'-lig-oh-troh'-fik) describing a body of water having abundant dissolved oxygen but relatively devoid of nutrients and stratification.

ontogeny: (on-tah'-jeh-nee) the development of an organism.

oozooid: (oh'-oh-zoe'-id) a modified polyp found on sea pens (Order Pennatulacea), which constitutes the main polyp axis.

open systems: used to describe captive or natural environments where outside oceanic inputs are received constantly.

oral disc: the usually flat area of tissue around the mouth of a coral polyp, the edges or surface of which may bear tentacles.

organic compounds: chemical compounds containing carbon; also compounds derived from living organisms.

Ostreobium: (oss'-tree-oh'-bee-um) a commensal and sometimes parasitic boring alga that is harbored within the skeleton of most stony corals.

overgrowth: the means by which some corals compete for space by physically growing over the top of adjacent species.

overtopping: the means by which some corals compete for space by shading photosynthetic species below them, compromising their ability to harness light energy.

oxygen toxicity: the damaging effects of excessive oxygen levels as oxygen radicals poison or cause cellular damage in zooxanthellate corals.

paliform lobe: (pal'-i-form) a feature of some stony coral skeletons; an upward-pointed and usually rounded protrusion from the septa, near the center of the calice, adjacent to the columella. Paliform lobes are important skeletal cues in determining the species of many scleractinians.

palytoxin: (pal'-ee-tox'-in) a potent neurotoxin found in the mucus and gonads of most zoanthids and all palythoids.

papillae: (pap-ih'-lee or pap-ih'-lie) small bumpy protuberances on the surface of many corallimorphs; they are vestigial tentacles armed with nematocysts.

PAR: photosynthetically active radiation. The radiation, or light energy, that is theoretically available to a photosynthetic organism.

parasitism: (pair'-ah-si-tiz'-um) a type of symbiosis in which one species exists at the expense of the other.

parazoon: (pair'-uh-zoe'-on) an animal that lives on or within another organism, usually parasitically (see **epizoon**).

pedal disc: the specialized and thickened disc-like basal attachment of anemones and certain corals.

peduncle: (peh-dunk'-ull) the thick muscular foot of sea pens that anchors them to soft substrates.

"peeling": the term used to describe the tissue-sloughing characteristic of rapid wasting diseases in stony corals.

pelagic: (peh-laj'-ik) living or occurring in open ocean water.

peroxidase: (purr-ox'-ih-days) one of the protective enzymes produced by polyps to destroy oxygen radicals and prevent cellular damage. Also known as hydrogen peroxidase.

pH: a measurement of the concentration of hydrogen ions in a solution; the relative acidity or alkalinity of a solution.

phaceloid: (fa'-seh-loyd) a type of stony coral colony formation where tall separate corallites rise upward from the skeleton (corallum).

phenotype: (fee'-no'-type) the physical characteristics expressed by genotype.

pheromones: (fere'-oh-mownz) chemical substances released by organisms to affect other organisms; among corals, little-understood chemicals thought to be used in species recognition, alloattraction, and as settlement cues, all involved with sexual reproduction.

phosphate: a nutrient and waste by-product that, in small quantities, is important to coral health; in higher concentrations, it acts as a crystalline inhibitor to calcification. Normally found only in trace amounts on coral reefs.

photoadaptation: (foe'-toe-a'-dap-tay'-shun) the process by which zooxanthellate corals become adjusted to changing levels of light to maximize photosynthesis.

photoinhibition: (foe'-toe-in'-hi-bi'-shun) the process by which light slows or stops the metabolic processes of zooxanthellate corals.

photoperiod: the duration of time during a 24-hour day in which light energy is available for photosynthesis.

photosynthate: (foe'-toe-sin'-thate) a generic term used to describe all the products of photosynthesis.

photosynthesis: (foe'-toe-sin'-thuh-sis) the process by which plants and some single-celled animals catalyze the building of organic products using light as the primary energy source.

phototaxis: (foe'-toe-tak'-sis) the movement of an organism toward or away from a source of light.

phylogeny: (fie-lah'-jeh-nee) the evolution of genetically related groups of organisms.

phytoplankton: (fie'-toe-plank'-tun) microscopic algae found in the light zones of the water column; plankton containing chlorophyll (compare to **zooplankton**).

pinna (sing.)/pinnae (pl.): (pin'-nuh/pin'-nee) the featherlike extensions of the tentacles of some corals, especially octocorals and stoloniferans.

pinnate: (pin'-nayt) having a feathery appearance.

pinnitomy: (pin-nit'-oh-me) a form of asexual reproduction in which pinnules fall from the polyps, attach to the substrate, and begin a new colony.

pinnule: (pin'-yool) the feathery side branches of an octocoral polyp's tentacle.

plankton: (plank'-tun) small organisms, both plants and animals, that drift in the sea; composed of zooplankton, phytoplankton, bacterioplankton, etc. Plankton is an important constituent food for corals.

planula (sing.)/planulae (pl.): (plan'-yu-lah/plan'-yu-lee) the free-swimming planktonic larval stage of corals, produced sexually or asexually.

plasticity: (plas-tiss'-ih-tee) the quality or state of being transformable in appearance or form.

plenum: (pleh'-num) with reference to the **Jaubert method**, an enclosed water space located under a bed of substrate at the bottom of an aquarium.

plocoid: (ploe'-soyd) a type of stony coral colony formation where the corallites have separate and well-defined walls.

pocilloporin: (poe-sill'-oh-pore'-in) a pigment of unknown function responsible for the pink or blue coloration in some genera of corals, most notably *Pocillopora* and some species of *Acropora*.

polyp: (pah'-lip) the smallest whole living unit of a coral or cnidarian. A polyp can be extremely diverse in its morphology, from the huge solitary polyp of *Cynarina*, to the fused polyps of stony corals, to the colonial but mostly separate polyps of the zoanthids.

polypary or **polyparium:** see **capitulum**

polyp bail-out: a form of asexual reproduction, usually in response to stress, in which a polyp ejects itself from its corallite; in some cases, such polyps will resettle successfully in another location.

polyp expulsion: a form of asexual reproduction similar to polyp bail-out, but with some or all of the corallite remaining attached to the ejected polyp.

polystomatous: (pah'-lee-sto-ma'-tus) having more than one mouth.

polytrophic: (pah'-lee-troh'-fik) obtaining nutrition from multiple sources; mixotrophic.

prostaglandins: (prah'-stah-gland'-ihnz) a unique group of fatty acids produced by some gorgonians; widely used in human medicines.

pseudoplankton: see **detritus**.

PSR: photosynthetically stored radiation; the amount of light radiation actually used by a coral in the production of chemical energy from photosynthesis.

PSU: photosynthetic unit; the term used to describe the parts of a cell with all associated cellular components involved in photosynthesis, including chloroplasts, pigments, electron transport chains, etc.

PUR: photosynthetically usable radiation; the amount of photosynthetically active radiation (PAR) that is able to be utilized by a photosynthetic organism.

purse-string closure: a form of prey capture utilized by some corallimorphs in which the disc is rapidly lifted and closed to form a saclike enclosure.

quarantine: the procedure of isolating organisms in a separate area for observation and treatment before introduction into a new system; used to prevent exposure of resident populations to potential antigens, pathogens, or other problematic organisms.

quenching: the process by which excess light energy is dissipated by photoprotective pigments to prevent photoinhibtion or cellular damage.

rachis: (ray'-kiss) the upper portion of the main polyp of a sea pen; it is attached to the peduncle, or muscular "foot," that anchors the animal in substrate.

ramose: (rah-mose') see **branching**.

rapid tissue necrosis (RTN): an aquarium-hobby term, possibly the same as **shut-down reaction (SDR)**.

reef: a positive topographic structure in a marine environment of biogenic origin or built by corals, calcareous algae, and other hermatypic invertebrates and able to resist the forces of the ocean.

refugium: (reh-fyoo'-gee-um) a designated or separate area within the confines of an aquarium or connected to an aquarium that allows for the proliferation of small food organisms, free from constant predation by fishes or other animals.

regeneration: the regrowth or replacement of a lost or injured body part by an organism. Most corals are highly regenerative animals.

rind: the tissue layer that surrounds the axis of gorgonians. There may be inner and outer rinds that contain various sclerites, pigments, and the polyps.

salinity: a measurement of the total amount of dissolved solids, mostly salts, in water. Expressed in ppt (parts per thousand); natural sea water on coral reefs typically measures 34-35 ppt.

scleractinian: (sklehr-ack-tin'-ee-an) a stony or hard coral; a member of the Order Scleractinia.

sclerite: (sklehr'-ite) a small (usually microscopic) calcium body or spicule that aids in supporting the body structure of soft corals. Sclerites have varied and distinctive shapes and aid in the taxonomic distinction of many species (see **spicule**).

sea pens: a group of unique substrate-dwelling octocorals of the Order Pennatulacea.

septum (sing.)/septa (pl.): (sep'-tum/sep'-tah) a thin skeletal plate in stony corals that protrudes from the corallite wall inward, toward the center of the calice.

septal filament: an extension of the mesentery in scleractinians, used in digestive functions and aggressive attacks (compare to **acontial filament**).

septo-costae: (sep'-toe-koss'-tee) skeletal teeth in stony corals, composed of septa and costae, that form radial partitions of the corallite.

shut-down reaction (SDR): a rapidly progressing degenerative condition in stony corals, perhaps synonymous with **rapid tissue necrosis (RTN)**.

siphonozooid: (sye-fah'-no-zoe'-id) a reduced secondary polyp of dimorphic octocorals that aids in colonial water circulation (see **autozooid**).

siphonoglyph: (sye-fah'-no-glif') a grooved opening of the mouth of colonial polyps that is ciliated to aid in food procurement, water exchange, and excretion.

skeletogenesis: the process by which the products of calcification are laid down to create coral skeletons.

slough: (sluf) detaching or necrotic tissue that is in a process of being shed and separated from healthy tissue, especially in certain soft corals.

soft coral: an informal descriptive term that includes all corals which do not precipitate an external calcium skeleton. Usually meant to include the many soft-bodied members of the Subclass Octocorallia.

solenium (sing.)/solenia (pl.): (so -lee'-nee-um/so-lee'-nee-ah) tube-like connections that link the gastrovascular canals of polyps in a colony; also called stem canals.

solitary: a growth form of corals in which single polyps exist without a colonial association or formation.

spatial heterogeneity: variances in the complexity of surfaces that result in the formation of niche habitats.

spawning: the release of sperm, eggs, and/or planulae into the water by one or many organisms.

species: the largest unit of reproductive capability and the fundamental individual unit of taxonomic classification.

specific gravity: an indirect measurement of the salinity of water, actually the ratio of the density of a given solution to the density of pure water. The specific gravity of natural seawater on a coral reef is typically 1.025-1.026.

species richness-energy hypothesis: the theory that the diversity of species contributes to the relative health and energy of a habitat in a synergistic fashion, and that the loss of one species affects many others.

spectrum: a measurement of the wavelengths or colors present in a particular source of light.

sphincter: (sfink'-tur) a ring of muscle tissue that, when contracted, closes an opening (such as a mouth).

spicule: (spik'-yule) a small skeletal inclusion or calcium body that aids in supporting the body structure of soft corals (see **sclerite**).

spinule: (spin'-yool) a small, spiny, conical outgrowth of the coenosteum in a stony coral skeleton.

spirocyst: (spy'-roh-sist) a type of nematocyst common in coral tentacle tips, used mainly for prey capture and substrate adhesion.

SPS: small-polyped stony or small-polyped scleractinian coral. An informal and imprecise aquarium-hobby term, typically used to group corals in the genera *Acropora, Montipora, Leptoseris, Pachyseris, Pavona, Pectinia, Pocillopora, Porites, Psammocora, Seriatopora, Stylophora,* and others (compare to **LPS**).

stolon: (stoe'-lahn) rootlike runners from the polyps of certain soft corals that aid in substrate adhesion, asexual reproduction, and inter-colonial communication.

stolon plates: calcified **stolons**.

stress response: the physiological reaction of a coral to environmental variables that results in a reduction in fitness of structure and/or function.

strontium: (strahn'-tee-um) a trace element that is, in some cases, concentrated by corals from natural seawater levels. It replaces calcium in the skeleton and may result in the formation of a denser skeleton.

substrate: a generic term used to describe the base of an environment used to provide support or foundation. In aquarium usage, substrate may mean the sand or gravel bottom, or the rock or reef base on which corals make their attachments. Also, the medium on which organisms can grow.

sulcus: (sull'-kuss) a shallow depression or groove.

superoxide dismutase: (soo'-purr-ox'-ide diz'-myu-tays') one of the protective enzymes produced by polyps to destroy oxygen radicals and prevent cellular damage.

surge: a periodic increase in water flow.

sweeper tentacles: elongate tentacles with stinging (cnidocytic) capabilities; normal tentacles adapted for use in aggressive or defensive interactions.

symbiosis: (sim'-bee-oh'-sis) the living together of two dissimilar species (see **commensalism, mutualism, parasitism**).

symbiotic: (sim'-bee-ah'-tik) describing corals that contain the microscopic dinoflagellate algae commonly known as zooxanthellae (equivalent to **zooxanthellate**).

tabular: (tab'-yoo-lahr) stony corals that exhibit flat tabletop growth formations.

taxon (sing.)/taxa (pl.): (taks'-on/taks'-uh) a taxonomic category, such as a genus or species.

taxonomy: (taks-ah'-no-me) the science or technique of classifying organisms into hierarchical groups or taxa; identifying and naming organisms in a systematic way.

tentacle: (tent'-uh-kul) a simple or complex extension of a coral's body tissue in a bumplike to filamentous protrusion that aids the coral in food capture and defense.

terpene: (tur'-peen) one of a class of chemical compounds commonly manufactured and released by corals, most notably octocorals; biochemical compounds used for anti-predation protection, settlement cues, and competition.

totipotent: (toe'-tee-poh'-tent) cells or tissue having the potential, under appropriate external or internal stimuli, to differentiate in various ways.

trace element: a minor constituent element found naturally in seawater that may be required for certain biochemical roles. Iodine, strontium, molybdenum, vanadium, etc. are all trace elements.

translocation: (tranz'-low-kay'-shun) the process by which the products of zooxanthellate photosynthesis are passed on to the coral animal.

tubercles: (too'-burr-culls) raised and rounded protuberances on sclerites, giving them distinctive shapes.

turbinate: (ter'-bi-net) a growth form of corals in which colonies take a cone or vaselike shape, sometimes convoluted.

turf algae: general term used to describe species of algae that form dense filamentous mats on substrates.

unifacial: (yoo-nih-fay'-shul) describing stony corals in which all corallites are on one side of the plate.

verrucae: (veh'-roo-see) evaginations or bumps on a corallimorph's oral disc that form short, often bifurcated tentacles laden with nematocysts. They are longer than papillae and usually account for the common names associated with "hairy" mushrooms. Also, nodules or wartlike growths on the skeleton of *Pocillopora* spp. stony corals.

Vibrio: (vih'-bree-oh) one of the most common genera of marine bacteria; actively motile gram-negative rods, some of which have been implicated as coral pathogens, as well as food sources.

wall: the outer skeletal sides of a corallite.

water column: the body of freely mobile water in a particular environment and not trapped or contained within any organism or mechanically contrived area.

white-band disease: progressive and noncontagious recession of the tissue of a stony coral. Of unknown cause. Often incorrectly called white plague or white death.

zonation: (zoe-nay'-shun) the distribution of characteristic organisms within different regions of a defined area, each region or zone having its own environmental parameters.

zooplankton (zoe'-uh-plank'-tun) small or microscopic organisms and larval forms found suspended in the water column; plankton without chlorophyll (compare to **phytoplankton**).

zooxanthellae: (zoh'-zan-thel'-ee) microscopic, single-celled marine algae or dinoflagellates that live in mutualistic symbiosis with corals (and other organisms, such as tridacnid clams).

zooxanthellate: (zoe-zan'-thuh-late) describing corals that contain the symbiotic single-celled algae commonly known as zooxanthellae (equivalent to **symbiotic**).

References

Abdel-Salam, H. A., and J.W. Porter. 1988. Physiological effects of sediment rejection on photosynthesis and respiration in three Caribbean reef corals. *Proc. 6th Int. Coral Reef Symp.* 2: 285-9.

Achituv, Y., and Y. Benayahu. 1990. Polyp dimorphism and functional, sequential hermaphroditism in the soft coral *Heteroxenia fuscescens* (Octocorallia), *Mar. Ecol. Prog. Ser.* 64: 263-9.

Achituv, Y., and Z. Dubinksy. 1990. Evolution and zoogeography of coral reefs. In: *Coral Reefs: Ecosystems of the World, Vol. 25* (Z. Dubinsky, ed.). Elsevier Scientific Publishing Co. Inc. New York: 1-9.

Acosta, A. 1999. A new disease infecting *Palythoa caribaeorum* (Cnidaria: Zoanthidea): Dynamics in Space and Time. Proceedings: NCRI International Conference on Scientific Aspects of Coral Reef Assessment, Monitoring, and Restoration. April14-16, Fort Lauderdale, FL: 43-4.

Adey, W.H. 1983. The microcosm: A new tool for reef research. *Coral Reefs* 1: 193-201.

Adey, W.H. 1987. Marine microcosms. In: *Restoration Ecology. A Synthetic Approach to Ecological Research* (W.R. Jordan III, M.E. Gilpin, and J.D. Aber, eds.) Cambridge University Press, Cambridge: 133-49.

Adey, W.H. 1998. Personal communications.

Adey, W.H. 1998. Coral reefs: algal structured and mediated ecosystems in shallow, turbulent, alkaline waters. *J. Phycol.* 34: 393-406.

Adey, W.H. 1998. Coral reefs: conservation by valuation and the utilization of pharmaceutical potential. In: *Coral Reefs: Challenges and Opportunities for Sustainable Management; Proceedings of an Associated Event of the Fifth Annual World Bank Conference on Environmentally and Socially Sustainable Development*, World Bank, Washington, D.C. October 9-11, 1997. Pp. 72-5.

Adey, W.H., and K. Loveland. 1991. *Dynamic Aquaria: Building Living Ecosystems*. Academic Press, San Diego. 643 pp.

Adey, W.H., and K. Loveland. 1998. *Dynamic Aquaria: Building Living Ecosystems*, 2nd ed. Academic Press, San Diego. 498 pp.

Adjerhoud, M., and B. Salvat. 1996. Spatial patterns in biodiversity of a fringing reef community along Opunohu Bay, Moorea, French Polynesia. *Bull. Mar. Sci.* 59: 175-87.

Alino, P.M., P.W. Sammarco, and J.C. Coll. 1988. Studies on the feeding preferences of *Chaetodon melannotus* (Pisces) for soft corals (Coelenterata; Octocorallia). *Proc. 6th Int. Coral Reef Symp.* 3: 31-7.

Alino, P.M., P.W. Sammarco, and J.C. Coll. 1992. Competitive strategies in soft corals (Coelenterata, Octocorallia). IV. Environmentally induced reversals in competitive superiority. *Mar. Ecol. Prog. Ser.* 81: 129-45.

Allemand, D., S. Al-Moghrabi, and J. Jaubert. 1992. Fatty acids of the scleractinian coral *Galaxea fascicularis* and its symbiont: effect of lighting and feeding. *Proc. 7th Int. Coral Reef Symp.* 1: 379.

Allen, Dr. G.R., and R. Steene. 1994. *Indo-Pacific Coral Reef Field Guide*. Tropical Reef Research, Singapore. 378 pp.

Allison, N. 1996. Geochemical anomalies in coral skeletons and their possible implications for paleoenvironmental analysis. *Mar. Chem.* 55: 367-79.

Al-Moghrabi, S., D. Allemand, and J. Jaubert. 1992. Neutral amino acid uptake by the symbiotic coral *Galaxea fascicularis*: effect of light and feeding. *Proc. 7th Int. Coral Reef Symp.* 1: 397.

Al-Moghrabi, S., D. Allemand, and J. Jaubert. 1993. Valine uptake by the scleractinian coral *Galaxea fascicularis:* characterization and effect of light and nutritional status. *J. Comp. Physiol. Biol.* 163: 355-62.

Andrews, J.C., and G.L. Pickard. 1990. The physical oceanography of coral-reef systems. In: *Coral Reefs: Ecosystems of the World, Vol. 25* (Z. Dubinsky, ed.). Elsevier Scientific Publishing Co. Inc. New York: 11-48.

Anthony, K.R.N. 1999. Coral suspension feeding on fine particulate matter. *J. Exp. Mar. Biol. Ecol.* 232: 85-106.

Anthony, S.L., J.C. Lang, and B. Maguire. 1997. Causes of stony coral mortality of a central Bahamian reef: 1991-95. *Proc. 8th Int. Coral Reef Symp.* 2: 1789-94.

Antonius, A. 1977. Coral mortality in reefs: a problem for science and management. *Proc. 3rd Int. Coral Reef Symp.* 617-23.

Antonius, A. 1981. The "Band" diseases in coral reefs. *Proc. 4th Int. Coral Reef Symp.* 2: 7-13.

Antonius, A. 1981. Coral reef pathology: a review. *Proc. 4th Int. Coral Reef Symp.* 2: 3-6

Antonius, A. 1985. Coral diseases in the Indo-Pacific: a first record. *Mar. Ecol.* 6: 197-218.

Antonius, A. 1985. Black band disease infection experiments on hexacorals and octocorals. *Proc. 5th Int. Coral Reef Symp.* 6: 155-61.

Antonius, A. 1988. Black band disease behavior on Red Sea reef corals. *Proc. 6th Int. Coral Reef Symp.* 3: 145-50.

Antonius, A. 1988. Distribution and dynamics of coral diseases in the Eastern Red Sea. *Proc. 6th Int. Coral Reef Symp.* 2: 293-7.

Antonius, A., and B. Riegl. 1998. Coral diseases and *Drupella cornus* invasion in the Red Sea. *Coral Reefs* 17: 48.

Antozzi, W.O. 1997. The developing live rock aquaculture industry. *Natl. Mar. Fish. Ser.* SERO-ECON-98-10. 11 pp.

Appukuttan, K.K. 1972. Coral-boring bivalves of Gulf of Mannar and Palk Bay. In: *Proc. Symp. Corals Coral Reefs* (C. Mukundan and C.S. Gopinadha Pillai, eds.) Marine Biological Ass'n. of India, Cochin: 379-98.

Armstrong, P.B., and J.P. Quigley. 1996. Comparative biology of the a2-macroglobulin-based immune system. In: *Advances in Comparative and Environmental Physiology, Vol. 24: Invertebrate Immune Responses: Cell Activities and the Environment* (E.L. Cooper, ed.) Springer-Verlag Berlin Heidelberg: 9-27.

Ates, R. 1995. Colonial anemones—Zoantharia: a review for the seriously interested marine aquarist. *Aquarium Frontiers* 2(2): 10-13.

Atkinson, M.J. 1998. Presentation, Western Marine Conference, Seattle.

Atkinson, M.J., B. Carlson, and G.L. Crow. 1995. Coral growth in high-nutrient, low-pH seawater: a case study of corals cultured at the Waikiki Aquarium, Honolulu, Hawaii. *Coral Reefs* 14: 215-23.

Atkinson, M.J., and R.W. Bilger. 1992. Effects of water velocity on phosphate uptake in coral reef-flat communities. *Limnol. Oceanogr.* 37: 273-9.

Atwood, D.K., et al. 1992. An assessment of global warming stress on Caribbean reef ecosystems. *Bull. Mar. Sci.* 51: 118-30.

Auberson, B. 1982. Coral transplantation: an approach to re-establishment of damaged reefs. *Kalikasan* 11: 158-172.

Austin, A.D., S.A. Austin, and P.F. Sale. 1980. Community structure of the fauna associated with the coral *Pocillopora damicornis* (L.) on the Great Barrier Reef. *Aust. J. Mar. Freshwater Res.* 31: 163-74.

Ayre, D.J., J.E.N. Veron, and S.L. Duffy. 1991. The corals *Acropora palifera* and *Acropora cuneata* are genetically and ecologically distinct. *Coral Reefs* 10: 13-18.

Ayre, D.J., and B.L. Willis. 1988. Population structure in the coral *Pavona cactus*: clonal genotypes show little phenotypic plasticity. *Mar. Biol.* 99: 495-505.

Ayukai, T. 1991. Standing stock of microzooplankton on coral reefs: a preliminary study. *J. Plankton Res.* 13: 895-9.

Ayukai, T. 1995. Retention of phytoplankton and planktonic microbes on coral reefs within the Great Barrier Reef, Australia. *Coral Reefs* 14: 141-7.

Babcock, R.C. 1984. Reproduction and distribution of two species of *Goniastrea* (Scleractinia) from the Great Barrier Reef Province. *Coral Reefs* 2: 187-95.

Babcock, R.C. 1988. Age-structure, survivorship and fecundity in populations of massive corals. *Proc. 6th Int. Coral Reef Symp.* 2: 625-30.

Bak, R.P.M. 1983. Neoplasia, regeneration and growth in the reef-building coral *Acropora palmata*. *Mar. Biol.* 77: 221-7.

Bak, R.P.M. et al. 1998. Bacterial suspension feeding by coral reef benthic organisms. *Mar. Ecol. Prog. Ser.* 175: 285-8.

Bak, R.P.M., and J.L.A. Borsboom. 1984. Allelopathic interaction between a reef coelenterate and benthic algae. *Oecologia* 63: 194-8.

Bak, R.P.M., and S.R. Criens. 1981. Survival after fragmentation of colonies of *Madracis mirabilis, Acropora palmata*, and *A. cervicornis* (Scleractinia) and the subsequent impact of a coral disease. *Proc. 4th Int. Coral Reef Symp.* 2: 221-7.

Bak, R.P.M., and J.H.B.W. Elgershuizen. 1976. Effects of oil-sediment rejection in corals. *Mar. Biol.* 37: 105-13.

Bak, R.P.M., and M.S. Engel. 1979. Distribution, abundance and survival of juvenile hermatypic corals (Scleractinia) and the importance of life history strategies in the parent coral community. *Mar. Biol.* 54: 41-52.

Bak, R.P.M., and E.H. Meesters. 1998. Coral population structure: the hidden information of colony size-frequency distributions. *Mar. Ecol. Prog. Ser.* 162: 301-6.

Bak, R.P.M., and E.H. Meesters. 1999. Population structure as a response of coral communities to global change. *Amer. Zool.* 39: 56-65.

Bak, R.P.M., R.M. Termaat, and R. Dekker. 1982. Complexity of coral interactions: influence of time, location of interaction and epifauna. *Mar. Biol.* 69: 215-22.

Bak, R.P.M., and G. Van Eys. 1975. Predation by the sea urchin *Diadema antillarum* Phillipi on living coral. *Oecologia* 20: 111-15.

Baker, A.C., and R. Rowan. 1997. Diversity of symbiotic dinoflagellates (zooxanthellae) in scleractinian corals of the Caribbean and Eastern pacific. *Proc. 8th Int. Coral Reef Symp.* 2: 1301-6.

Baker, A.C., R. Rowan, and N. Knowlton. 1997. Symbiosis of two Caribbean acroporid corals. *Proc. 8th Int. Coral Reef Symp.* 2: 1295-1300.

Bakus, G.J. 1981. Chemical defense mechanisms on the Great Barrier Reef, Australia. *Science* 211: 497-9.

Bakus, G.J., N.M. Targett, and B. Schulte. 1986. Chemical ecology of marine organisms: and overview. *J. Chem. Ecol.* 12: 951-87.

Banaszak, A.T., et al. 1998. Relationship between ultraviolet (UV) radiation and mycosporine-like amino acids (MAAS) in marine organisms. *Bull. Mar. Sci.* 63: 617-28.

Bang, F.B. 1973. Immune reactions among marine and other invertebrates. *BioScience* 23: 584-9.

Barlocher, F., J. Gordon, and R.J. Ireland. 1988. Organic composition of seafoam and its digestion by *Corophium volutator* (Pallas) *J. Exp. Mar. Biol. Ecol.* 115: 179-86.

Barnes, D.J. 1972. The structure and formation of growth-ridges in scleractinian coral skeletons. *Proc. Roy. Soc. Lond.* B 182: 331-50.

Barnes, D.J. 1973. Growth in colonial scleractinians. *Bull. Mar. Sci.* 23: 280-98.

Barnes, D.J. 1985. The effect of photosynthetic and respiratory inhibitors upon calcification in the staghorn corals, *Acropora formosa*. *Proc. 5th Int. Coral Reef Symp.* 2: 23.

Barnes, D.J., and B.E. Chalker. 1990. Calcification and photosynthesis in reef-building corals and algae. In: *Coral Reefs: Ecosystems of the World, Vol. 25* (Z. Dubinsky, ed.). Elsevier Scientific Publishing Co. Inc. New York: 109-32.

Barnes, D.J., and D.L. Taylor. 1973. *Helgo wiss Meers* 24: 284-91.

Barnes, D.J., B.E. Chalker, and D.W. Kinsey. 1986. Reef metabolism. *Oceanus* 29:20-6.

Barnes, D.J., and C.J. Crossland. 1980. Diurnal and seasonal variations in the growth of a staghorn coral measured by time-lapse photography. *Limnol. Oceanogr.* 25: 1113-17.

Barnes, D.J., and M.J. Devereaux. 1988. Variations in skeletal architecture associated with density banding in the hard coral *Porites*. *J. Exp. Mar. Biol. Ecol.* 121: 37-54.

Barnes, D.J., and J.M. Lough. 1989. The nature of skeletal density banding in scleractinian corals: fine banding and seasonal patterns. *J. Exp. Mar. Biol. Ecol.* 126: 119-34.

Barnes, D.J., and J.M. Lough. 1990. Computer simulations showing the likely effects of calix architecture and other factors on retrieval of density information from coral skeletons. *J. Exp. Mar. Biol. Ecol.* 137: 141-64.

Barnes, D.J., and J.M. Lough. 1992. Systematic variations in the depth of skeleton occupied by coral tissue in massive colonies of *Porites* from the Great Barrier Reef. *J. Exp. Mar. Biol. Ecol.* 159: 113-28.

Barnes, D.J., and J.M. Lough. 1993. On the nature and causes of density banding in massive coral skeletons. *J. Exp. Mar. Biol. Ecol.* 167: 91-108.

Barnes, D.J., J.M. Lough, and R.B. Taylor. 1992. Coral density banding—the mist is clearing. *Proc. 7th Int. Coral Reef Symp.* 1: 221.

Barrington, E.J.W. 1979. *Invertebrate Structure and Function.* John Wiley & Sons: NY. 765 pp.

Bates, J. 1997. Growth rate study of *Acropora cervicornis* at the Smithsonian's exploring marine ecosystem's microcosm. *Aquarium Frontiers*, July issue. http://www.aquariumfrontiers.com/archives.

Battey, J.F., and J.W. Porter. 1988. Photoadaptation as a whole organism response in *Montastrea annularis. Proc. 6th Int. Coral Reef Symp.* 3: 79-82.

Bayer, F.M. 1956. Octocorallia. In: *Treatise on Invertebrate Paleontology. Part F. Coelenterata* (R.C. Moore, ed.) Geological Society of America and University of Kansas Press: F166-F231.

Bayer, F.M. 1957. Recent octocorals. In: *Treatise on Marine Ecology and Paleontology Vol 1.* (J.W. Hedgepeth, ed.), University of California, Scripps Institute of Oceanography, La Jolla, CA. *Geol. Soc. America Memoir* 67: 1105-8.

Bayer, F.M. 1961. *The Shallow-Water Octocorallia of the West Indian region: A Manual for Marine Biologists.* Martinus Nijhoof, The Hague, Netherlands. 375 pp.

Bayer, F.M. 1973. Colonial organization in octocorals. In: *Animal Colonies. Development and Function through Time* (R.S. Boardman, A.H. Cheetham, and W.A. Oliver, Jr., eds.). Dowden, Hutchinson & Ross, Inc., Stroudsberg, Pennsylvania: 63-93.

Bayer, F.M. 1981. Key to the genera of Octocorallia exclusive of Pennatulacea (Coelenterata: Anthozoa) with diagnoses of new taxa. *Proc. Biol. Soc. Wash.* 94: 902-47.

Bayer, F.M. 1992. The helioporacean octocoral *Epiphaxum*, recent and fossil: A monographic iconography. *Stud. Trop. Oceanogr. Miami* 15: vii + 76 pp.

Bayer, F.M. 1996. New primnoid gorgonians (Coelenterata: Octocorallia) from Antarctic waters. *Bull. Mar. Sci.* 58: 511-30.

Bayer, F.M., and M. Grasshoff. 1994. The genus group taxa of the Family Ellisellidae, with clarification of the genera established by Gray (Cnidaria: Octocorallia). *Senck biol.* 74: 21-45.

Bayer, F.M., and H.B. Owre. 1968. *The Free-Living Lower Invertebrates. Phylum Coelenterata.* The Macmillan Company, NY. 25-125.

Beck, J.W., et al. 1992. Sea-surface temperature from coral skeletal strontium/calcium ratios. *Science* 257: 644-7.

Becker, L.C., and E. Mueller. 1999. The culture, trasplantation and storage of *Montastrea faveolata, Acropora cervicornis* and *A. palmata*: what we learned so far. Proceedings: NCRI International Conference on Scientific Aspects of Coral Reef Assessment, Monitoring, and Restoration. April 14-16, 1999. Fort Lauderdale, FL: 171.

Bell, J.L., and C.J. Hurlbut. 1992. Recruitment of *Epitonium ulu* onto the solitary coral *Fungia scutaria. Proc. 7th Int. Coral Reef Symp.* 2: 861.

Benayahu, Y. 1985. Faunistic composition and patterns in the distribution of soft corals (Octocorallia Alcyonacea) along the coral reefs of Sinai Peninsula. *Proc. 5th Int. Coral Reef Symp.* 2: 28+ a.

Benayahu, Y. 1992. Onset of zooxanthellae acquisition in course of ontogenesis of broadcasting and brooding soft corals. *Proc. 7th Int. Coral Reef Symp.* 1: 500

Benayahu, Y. 1997. Developmental episodes in reef soft corals: Ecological and cellular determinants. *Proc. 8th Int. Coral Reef Symp.* 2: 1213-1218.

Benayahu, Y. 1998. Lobe variation in *Sinularia nanlobata* Verseveldt, 1977 (Cnidaria: Alcyonacea). *Bull Mar Sci* 63:229-40.

Benayahu, Y., Y. Achituv, and T. Berner. 1989. Metamorphosis of an octocoral primary polyp and its infection by algal symbiosis. *Symbiosis* 7: 159-69.

Benayahu, Y., Y. Achituv, and T. Berner. 1988. Embryogenesis and acquisition of algal symbionts by planulae of *Xenia umbellata* (Octocorallia: Alcyonacea). *Mar. Biol.* 100: 93-101.

Benayahu, Y., T. Berner, and Y. Achituv. 1989. Development of planulae within a mesogleal coat in the soft coral *Heteroxenia fuscescens. Mar. Biol.* 100: 203-10.

Benayahu, Y., and Y. Loya. 1977. Space partitioning by stony corals, soft corals, and benthic algae on the coral reefs of the northern Gulf of Eilat (Red Sea). *Helgo wiss Meers* 30: 362-82.

Benayahu, Y., and Y. Loya. 1981. Competition for space among coral reef sessile organisms at Eilat, Red Sea. *Bull. Mar. Sci.* 31: 514-22.

Benayahu, Y., and Y. Loya. 1983. Surface brooding in the Red Sea soft coral, *Paraerythropodium fulvum fulvum* (Forskal, 1775). *Biol. Bull.* 165: 353-69.

Benayahu, Y., and Y. Loya. 1984. Life history studies on the Red Sea soft coral *Xenia macrospiculata* Gohar 1940. II. Planulae shedding and post larval development. *Biol. Bull.* 166: 44-53.

Benayahu, Y., and Y. Loya. 1984. Life history studies on the Red Sea soft coral *Xenia macrospiculata* Gohar 1940. I. Annual dynamics of gonadal development. *Biol. Bull.* 166: 32-41.

Benayahu, Y., and Y. Loya. 1985. Settlement and recruitment of a soft coral: Why is *Xenia macrospiculata* a succesful colonizer? *Bull. Mar. Sci.* 36: 177-88.

Benayahu, Y., and Y. Loya. 1986. Sexual reproduction of a soft coral: Synchronous and brief annual spawning of *Sarcophyton glaucum* (Quoy & Gaimard, 1833). *Biol. Bull.* 170: 32-42.

Benayahu, Y. and M.H. Schleyer. 1998. Reproduction in *Anthelia glauca* (Octocoralli: Xeniidae). II. Transmission of algal symbionts during planular brooding. *Mar. Biol.* 131: 433-42.

Benayahu, Y. 1990. Xeniidae (Cnidaria: Octocorallia) from the Red Sea, with the description of new species. *Zool. Med. Leiden.* 64: 113-120.

Benayahu, Y., D. Weil, and Z. Malik. 1992. Entry of algal symbionts into oocytes of the coral *Litophyton arboreum. Tissue and Cell* 24: 473-82.

Ben-David-Zaslow, B., et al. 1999. Reproduction in the Red Sea coral *Heteroxenia fuscescens*: seasonality and long-term record (1991 to 1997). *Mar Biol* 133: 553-9.

Bentley, N. 1998. An overview of the exploitation, trade and management of corals in Indonesia. *TRAFFIC Bulletin* 17(2): 67-78.

Benzie, J.A.H. 1999. Genetic structure of coral reef organisms: ghosts of dispersal past. *Amer. Zool.* 39: 131-45.

Benzie, J.A.H., A. Haskell, and H. Lehman. 1995. Variation in the genetic composition of coral (*Pocillopora damicornis* and *Acropora palifera*) populations from different reef habitats. *Mar. Biol.* 121: 731-9.

Bigger, C.H., and W.H. Hildemann. 1982. Cellular defense systems of the Coelenterata. In: *The Reticuloendothelial System: A Comprehensive Treatise, Volume 3: Phylogeny and Ontogeny* (N. Cohen and M.M. Sigel, eds.): pp. 59-87.

Bil', K.Y., P.V. Kolmakov, and L. Muscatine. 1985. Photosynthetic products of zooxanthellae of the reef-building corals *Stylophora pistillata* and *Seriatopora coliendrum* from different depths of the Seychelles islands. The Ecology of Reefs: Symposia Series for Underseas Research, *NOAA* 3: 1-7.

Bilger, R.W., and M.J. Atkinson. 1995. Effects of nutrient loading on mass-transfer rates to a coral-reef community. *Limnol. Oceanogr.* 40: 279-89.

Bingman, C. 1995. Limewater, Part I. Precipitation of phosphate in limewater and in the aquarium. *Aquarium Frontiers* 2(4) 6-9.

Bingman, C. 1995. Green-fluorescent protein: a model for coral host fluorescent proteins? *Aquarium Frontiers* 2(3) 6-9.

Bingman, C. 1996. Presentation: MACNA VII. Kansas City, MO.

Bingman, C. 1997. Bacterial diseases of corals: perspectives and "cures." Online chat, April 6, 1997. members.aol.com/reefchat/ index.html

Bingman, C. 1998. Calcification rates in several tropical coral reef aquaria. *Aquarium Frontiers*, March issue. http://www.aquariumfrontiers.com/ archives

Birkeland, C. 1976. An experimental method of studying corals during early stages of growth. *Micronesica* 12: 319-22.

Birkeland, C., ed. 1997. Geographic differences in ecological processes on coral reefs. In: *Life and Death of Coral Reefs* (C. Birkeland, ed.). Chapman & Hall, New York: 273-97.

Bischof, B. 1998. State of the reef: cities beneath the sea. *Nat. Hist.* 106: 39-45.

Bischof, B. 1998. Status report: reefs in crisis. *Nat. Hist.* 106: 46-8.

Black, K.P., et al. 1990. Residence times of neutrally buoyant matter such as larvae, sewage or nutrients on coral reefs. *Coral Reefs* 9: 105-14.

Black, N.A., R. Voellmy, and A.M. Szmant. 1995. Heat shock protein induction in *Montastrea faveolata* and *Aiptasia pallida* exposed to elevated temperatures. *Biol. Bull.* 188: 234-40.

Blank, R.J. 1987. Cell architecture of the dinoflagellate *Symbiodinium* sp. inhabiting the Hawaiian stony coral *Montipora verrucosa*. *Mar. Biol.* 94: 143-55.

Blank, R.J., and R.K. Trench. 1985. Speciation and symbiotic dinoflagellates. *Science* 229: 656-8.

Blank, R.J., and R.K. Trench. 1986. Nomenclature of endosymbiotic dinoflagellates. *Taxon* 35(2): 286-94.

Blythell, J.C. 1990. Nutrient uptake in the reef-building coral *Acropora palmata* at natural environmental concentrations. *Mar. Ecol. Prog. Ser.* 68: 65-9.

Blythell, J.C., E.H. Gladfelter, and M. Blythell. 1993. Chronic and catastrophic natural mortality of three common Caribbean reef corals. *Coral Reefs* 12: 143-52.

Blythell, J., and C. Sheppard. 1993. Mass mortality of Caribbean shallow corals. *Mar. Poll. Bull.* 26: 296-7.

Boots, K., and R. Ates. 1995. Ejection seat coral *Oulophyllia crispa*. *Aquarium Frontiers* 2(1) 2-5.

Borel-Best, M. and B.W. Hoeksema. 1987. New observations on scleractinian corals from Indonesia: 1. Free-living species belonging to the Faviina. *Zoologische Mededelingen* 61(27): 387-403

Borel-Best, M., and Suharsono. 1991. New observations on scleractinian corals from Indonesia 3. Species belonging to the Merulinidae with new records of *Merulina* and *Boninastrea*. *Zool. Med. Leiden.* 65: 333-42.

Borneman, E.H. 1996. Montipora and the trouble with taxonomy. *Aquarium Net*, November issue. http:/www.aquarium.net

Borneman, E.H. 1996. The Fire Corals. *Aquarium Net*, October issue. http://www.aquarium.net.

Borneman, E.H. 1996. *Dendronephthya*: a seduction of allusions and illusions. *Aquarium Net*, December issue. http://www.aquarium.net

Borneman, E.H. 1997. The striking sunflower coral—*Tubastraea*. *Aquarium Net*, July issue. http://www.aquarium.net.

Borneman, E.H. 1997. Is leather optional? *Aquarium Net*, June issue. http://www.aquarium.net.

Borneman, E.H. 1997. The elusive blue-tipped *Acropora*. *Aquarium Net*, May issue. http://www.aquarium.net.

Borneman, E.H. 1997. Bird's nest coral: feathers not included. *Aquarium Net*, April issue. http://www.aqualink.com

Borneman, E.H. 1997. *Pocillopora* and the beginnings of coloration. *Aquarium Net*, March issue. http://www.aquarium.net.

Borneman, E.H. 1997. Sweeping beauty: a tale of anchors, hammers, and other things. *Aquarium Net*, January issue. http://www.aquarium.net.

Borneman, E.H. 1998. Successful raising of the *Aiptasia* predator *Berghia verrucicornis*. *Journ. Maqua*. 6: 49-54

Borneman, E.H. 1998. Do you need a little extra help? *Practical Fishkeeping*.August 82-5

Borneman, E.H. 1998. To surge or not to surge. *Freshwater and Marine Aquarium* 21(5) 158-66.

Borneman, E.H., and J. Lowrie. 1999. Advances in captive husbandry: an easily utilized reef replenishment means from the private sector? Proceedings: NCRI International Conference on Scientific Aspects of Coral Reef Assessment, Monitoring, and Restoration. April14-16, Fort Lauderdale, FL.

Borneman, E.H., and J. Lowrie. 1998a. The immune response of corals: Part 1: The invertebrate immune system. *Aquarium Net*. http://www.aquarium.net.

Borneman, E.H., and J. Lowrie. 1998b. The immune response of corals: Part 2: Models for "RTN." *Aquarium Net*. http://www.aquarium.net.

Borneman, E.H., and J. Lowrie. 1999. The aquarium malady, rapid tissue necrosis: implications for stony coral mortality and its relation to coral disease. Manuscript #158, in submission, *Diseases of Aquatic Organisms*.

Borneman, E.H., and E. Puterbaugh. 1996. *A Practical Guide to Corals for the Reef Aquarium*. Crystal Graphics, Inc., Lexington, KY. 112 pp.

Boschma, H. 1948. The species problem in *Millepora*. *Zool. Verh. Mus Leiden* 13: 1-49.

Boschma, H. 1956. Milleporina and Stylasterina. In: *Treatise on Invertebrate Paleontology. Part F. Coelenterata* (R.C. Moore, ed.) Geological Society of America and University of Kansas Press: F90-F106.

Bosscher, H., and E.H. Meesters. 1992. Depth related changes in the growth rate of *Montastrea annularis*. *Proc. 7th Int. Coral Reef Symp.* 1: 507-11.

Bothwell, A.B. 1981. Fragmentation, a means of asexual reproduction and dispersal in the coral genus *Acropora* (Scleractinia: Astrocoenida: Acroporidae)—a preliminary report. *Proc. 4th Int. Coral Reef Symp.* 2: 137-44.

Bowden, B.F., et al. 1978. Studies of Australian soft corals. IV. A novel bicyclic diterpene from *Lobophytum hedleyi*. *Aust. J. Chem.* 31: 163-70.

Bowden, B., et al. 1985. Some chemical aspects of spawning in Alcyonacean corals. *Proc. 5th Int. Coral Reef Symp.* 2: 46.

Bowden, B.F., J.C. Coll, and S.J. Mitchell. 1980. Studies of Australian soft corals. XVIII. Further cembranoid diterpenes from soft corals of the genus *Sarcophyton. Aust. J. Chem.* 33: 879-84.

Bowden, B.F., J.C. Coll, and S.J. Mitchell. 1980. Studies of Australian soft corals. XIX. Two new sesquiterpenes with the nardosinane skeleton from a *Paralemnalia* species. *Aust. J. Chem.* 33: 879-84.

Bowden-Kirby, A. 1999. The "Johnny Coral Seed" approach to coral reef restoration: new methodologies appropriate for lower energy reef areas. NCRI International Conference on Scientific Aspects of Coral Reef Assessment, Monitoring, and Restoration. April 14-16, 1999. Fort Lauderdale, FL: 148.

Bowen, H.J.M. 1966. The elementary composition of living matter. In: *Trace Elements in Biochemistry,* Academic Press, London: 66-97.

Bradbury, R.H., and P.C. Young. 1981. The race and the swift revisited, or is aggression between corals important? *Proc. 4th Int. Coral Reef Symp.* 2: 351-6.

Brakel, W.H. 1977. Corallite variation in *Porites* and the species problem in corals. *Proc. 3rd Int. Coral Reef Symp.* 1: 457-62.

Brakel, W.H. 1983. Depth-related changes in the colony form of the reef coral*, Porites astreoides*. The Ecology of Deep and Shallow Coral Reefs: Symposia Series for Undersea Research, *NOAA* 1: 21-25.

Brawley, S.H., and W.H. Adey. 1982. *Coralliophila abbreviata*: a significant corallivore! *Bull. Mar. Sci.* 32: 595-9.

Brazeau, D.A., and H.R. Lasker. 1989. The reproductive cycle and spawning in a Caribbean gorgonian. *Biol. Bull.* 176: 1-7.

Brazeau, D.A., and H.R. Lasker. 1990 Sexual reproduction and external brooding by the Caribbean gorgonian *Briareum asbestinum. Mar. Biol.* 104: 465-74.

Bright, T.J., et al. 1992. Mass spawning of reef corals at the Flower Garden Banks, NW Gulf of Mexico. *Proc. 7th Int. Coral Reef Symp.* 1: 500.

Brockman, D., and A.J. Nilsen. 1995. A critical comparison of methods for dosing calcium in sea aquariums, Part 1. *Aquarium Frontiers* 2(3) 2-25.

Brockman, D., and A.J. Nilsen. 1995. A critical comparison of methods for dosing calcium in sea aquariums, Part 2. *Aquarium Frontiers* 2(4) 2-27.

Bronikowski, E.J. 1982. The collection, transportation, and maintenance of living corals. *AAZPA 1982 Annual Proceedings*: 65-70.

Brown, B.E. 1997. Disturbances to reefs in recent times. In: *Life and Death of Coral Reefs* (C. Birkeland, ed.) Chapman & Hall, New York: 354-79.

Brown, B.E., R. Hewit, and M.D. Le Tissier. 1983. The nature and construction of skeletal spines in *Pocillopora damicornis* (Linnaeus). *Coral Reefs* 2: 81-9.

Brown, B.E., and L.S. Howard. 1985. Assessing the effects of "stress" on reef corals. *Advances in Marine Biology* 22: 1-63.

Brown, B.E., and M. Le Tissier. 1992. Quantification of coral bleaching. *Proc. 7th Int. Coral Reef Symp.* 1: 70.

Brown, B.E., M.D.A. Le Tissier, and J.C. Bythell. 1995. Mechanisms of bleaching deduced from histological studies of reef corals sampled during a natural bleaching event. *Mar. Biol.* 122: 655-74.

Brown, B.E., and Suharsono. 1990. Damage and recovery of coral reefs affected by El Nino related seawater warming in the Thousand Islands, Indonesia. *Coral Reefs* 8: 163-70.

Bruce, A.J. 1972. A review of information upon the coral hosts of commensal shrimps of the subfamily Pontoninae, Kingsley, 1878 (Crustacea, Decapoda, Palaemonidae). In: *Proc. Symp. Corals Coral Reefs* (C. Mukundan and C.S. Gopinadha Pillai, eds.) Marine Biological Ass'n of India, Cochin: 399-419.

Bruce, A.J. 1976. Coral reef *Caridea* and "commensalism." *Micronesica* 12: 83-98.

Bruce, A.J. 1977. *Periclimenes kororensis* n. sp., an unusual shrimp associate of the fungiid coral, *Heliofungia actiniformis. Micronesica* 13: 33-43.

Bruce, A.J. 1998. New keys for the identification of Indo-West Pacific coral associated Pontoniine shrimps, with observations on their ecology. *Ophelia* 49: 29-46.

Bruckner, A.W. 1999. Personal communications.

Bruckner, A.W., and R.J. Bruckner. 1997. Outbreak of coral disease in Puerto Rico. *Coral Reefs.* 16: 260.

Bruckner, A.W., and R.J. Bruckner. 1997. The persistence of black-band disease in Jamaica: impact on community structure. *Proc. 8th Int. Coral Reef Symp.* 1: 601-6.

Bruckner, A.W., and R.J. Bruckner. 1998. Emerging infections on the reefs. *Nat. Hist.* 12/97-1/98: 48.

Bruckner, A.W., and R.J. Bruckner. 1998. Rapid Wasting Syndrome or coral predation by stoplight parrotfish? *Reef Encounter* 23: 18-22.

Bruckner, A.W., and R.J. Bruckner. 2000. Predation of *Sparisoma viride* and relationships with coral disease. *Proc. 9th Int. Coral Reef Symp.* Bali: 280.

Bruno, J.F., and P.J. Edmunds. 1998. Metabolic consequences of phenotypic plasticity in the coral *Madracis mirabilis* (Duchassaing and Michelotti): the effect of morphology and water flow on aggregate respiration. *J. Exp. Mar. Biol. Ecol.* 229: 187-95.

Brusca, R.C., and G.J. Brusca. 1990. *Invertebrates.* Sinauer Associates Inc., Sunderland, Massachusetts: 217-61.

Bryant, D., L. Burke, J. McManus, and M. Spalding. 1998. *Reefs at risk: a map-based indicator of threats to the world's coral reefs.* A joint publication by WRI, ICLARM, WCMC and UNEP. 56 pp.

Bucher, D.J., V.J. Harriott, and L.G. Roberts. 1998. Skeletal micro-density, porosity and bulk density of acroporid corals. *J. Exp. Mar. Biol. Ecol.* 228: 117-36.

Buchsbaum, R., et al. 1987. *Animals Without Backbones,* 3rd ed., University of Chicago Press, Chicago. 572 pp.

Budd, A.F. 1988. Large-scale evolutionary patterns in the reef—coral *Montastrea*: the role of phenotypic plasticity. *Proc. 6th Int. Coral Reef Symp.* 3: 393-7.

Buddemeir, R.W. 1999. Is it time to give up? Plenary Address: NCRI International Conference on Scientific Aspects of Coral Reef Assessment, Monitoring, and Restoration. April14-16, Fort Lauderdale, FL.

Buddemeir, R.W., and D. Fautin. 1993. Coral bleaching as an adaptive mechanism: a testable hypothesis. *Bioscience* 43: 320-6.

Buddemeir, R.W., R.C. Schneider, and S.V. Smith. 1981. The alkaline earth chemistry of corals. *Proc. 4th Int. Coral Reef Symp.* 2: 81-5.

Buddemeir, R.W., and S.V. Smith. 1999. Coral adaptation and acclimatization: a most ingenious paradox. *Amer. Zool.* 39:1-9.

Burke, M. 1994. Phosphorous fingered as coral killer. *Science* 263:1086.

Burkholder, P.R., and L.M. Burkholder. 1958. Antimicrobial activity of horny corals. *Science* 127: 1174-5.

Burnett, W.J., J.A.H. Benzie, J.A. Beardmore, and J.S. Ryland. 1997. Zoanthids (Anthozoa, Hexacorallia) from the Great Barrier Reef and Torres Strait, Australia: systemics, evolution and a key to the species. *Coral Reefs* 16: 55-68.

Burris, J.E., J.W. Porter, and W.A. Laing. 1983. Effects of carbon dioxide concentration on coral photosynthesis. *Mar. Biol.* 75: 113-16.

Bythell, J.C. 1988. A total nitrogen and carbon budget for the elkhorn coral *Acropora palmata. Proc. 6th Int. Coral Reef Symp.* 2: 535-40.

Cairns, S. 1977. *Guide to the Commoner Shallow-Water Gorgonians (Sea Whips, Sea Feathers and Sea Fans) of Florida, the Gulf of Mexico, and the Caribbean Region.* University of Miami Sea Grant Program, Miami.

Cairns, S.D. 1978. *Distichopora (Haplomerismos) anceps,* a new stylasterine coral (Coelenterata: Stylasterina) from deep water off the Hawaiian Islands. *Micronesica* 14: 83-7.

Cairns, S.D. 1983. A generic revision of the Stylasteridae (Coelenterata: Hydrozoa). Part 1: description of genera. *Bull. Mar. Sci.* 33: 427-508.

Cairns, S.D. 1988. Asexual reproduction in solitary Scleractinia. *Proc. 6th Int. Coral Reef Symp.* 2: 641-5.

Cairns, S.D. 1991. Common and scientific names of aquatic invertebrates from the United States and Canada: Cnidaria and Ctenophora. *American Fisheries Society Special Publication* 22, Bethesda, Maryland.

Cairns, S.D. 1995. *The Marine Fauna of New Zealand: Scleractinia (Cnidaria: Anthozoa).* New Zealand Oceanographic Institute Memoir 103, National Institute of Water and Atmospheric Research (NIWA), 146 pp.

Campbell, D.G. 1977. Bahamian chlorine bleach fishing: a survey. *Proc. 3rd Int. Coral Reef Symp.* 3: 593-5.

Carleton, J.H., and P.W. Sammarco. 1987. Effects of substratum irrefularity on success of coral settlement: quantification by techniques by comparative geomorphological techniques. *Bull. Mar. Sci.* 40: 85-98.

Carlgren, O. 1942. *Actiniaria and Zooantharia of the Danmark Expedition.* Pt. 2 Bd3 nr: 9. XIX.

Carlgren, O. 1949. *A survey of the Ptychodactiaria, Corallimorpharia, and Actinaria.* Kungl Svenska Vetenskapsakademiens Handlingar, Fjarde Serien, Almqvist & Wiskels Boktryckeri AB, Stockholm 1: 1-17.

Carlon, D.B., T.J. Goreau, N.I. Goreau, R.K. Trench, R.L. Hayes, and A.T. Marshall. 1996. Calcification rates in corals. *Science* 274: 117-.

Carlson, B.A. 1987. Aquarium systems for living corals. I*nt. Zoo. Yb.* 26: 1-9.

Carlson, B.A. 1989. Living coral in the aquarium. *AAZPA 1989 Annual Proceedings:* 237-41.

Carlson, B. 1996. Presentation, MACNA VIII. Kansas City, MO.

Carlson, B.A. 1999. Organism responses to change: what aquaria tell us about nature. *Amer. Zool.* 39: 44-55.

Carpenter, R.C. 1997. Invertebrate predators and grazers. In: *Life and Death of Coral Reefs* (C. Birkeland, ed.) Chapman & Hall, New York: 198-229.

Carroll, D.J., and S.C. Kempf. 1990. Laboratory culture of aeolid nudibranch *Berghia verrucicornis* (Mollusca, Opisthobranchia): some aspects of its development and life history. *Biol. Bull.* 179: 243-53.

Carter, R.W. 1999. Coral fluorescence and fluorescent compounds, University of Miami, personal communications.

Castro, P. 1976. Brachyuran crabs symbiotic with scleractinian corals: a review of their biology. *Micronesica* 12:99-110.

Castro, P. 1996. Eastern Pacific species of *Trapezia* (Crustacea, Brachyura: Trapeziidae), sibling species symbiotic with reef corals. *Bull. Mar. Sci.* 58: 531-54.

Cervino, J. 1999. Personal communications.

Cervino, J. 1999. Coral reef diseases and bleaching: applications for monitoring and sample collection. NCRI International Conference on Scientific Aspects of Coral Reef Assessment, Monitoring, and Restoration. April 14-16, 1999. Fort Lauderdale, FL: 66.

Cervino, J., T. Goreau, G. Smith, K. DeMeyer, I. Nagelkerken, and R. Hayes. 1997. Fast-spreading new Caribbean coral disease.*Reef Encounter*22:16-18.

Cervino, J.M., and Dr. G. Smith. 1997. Corals in Peril. *Ocean Realm,* Summer issue: pp. 33-5.

Chadwick, N.E. 1988. Competition and locomotion in a free-living fungiid coral. *J. Exp. Mar. Biol. Ecol.* 123: 189-200.

Chadwick-Furman, N., and B. Rinkevich. 1994. A complex allorecognition system in a reef-building coral: delayed responses, reversals and nontransitive hierarchies. *Coral Reefs* 13: 57-63.

Chalker, B.E. 1976. Calcium transport during skeletonogenesis in hermatypic corals. *Comp. Biochem. Physiol.* 54A: 455-9.

Chalker, B.E. 1977. Daily variation in the calcification capacity of *Acropora cervicornis. Proc. 3rd Int. Coral Reef Symp.* 1: 417-23.

Chalker, B.E. 1981. Simulating light-saturation curves for photosynthesis and calcification by reef-building corals. *Mar. Biol.* 63: 135-41.

Chalker, B.E. 1995. Calcification by corals and other animals on the reef. In: *Perspectives on Coral Reefs* (D.J. Barnes, ed.) AIMS, Brian Clouston Publisher: 29-46.

Chalker, B.E., and W.C. Dunlap. 1981. Extraction and quantitation of endosymbiotic algal pigments from reef-building corals. *Proc. 4th Int. Coral Reef Symp.* 2: 47-50.

Chalker, B., and D.L. Taylor. 1975. Light enhanced calcification, and the role of oxidative phosphorylation in calcification of the coral *Acropora cervicornis. Proc. Roy. Soc. Lond. B* 190: 323-331.

Chamberlain, J.A. Jr., and R.R. Graus. 1975. Water flow and hydromechanical adaptations of branched reef corals. *Bull. Mar. Sci.* 25: 112-25.

Chang, S.S., B.B. Prezelin, and R.K. Trench. 1983. Mechanisms of photoadaptation in three strains of the symbiotic dinoflagellate, *Symbiodinium microadriaticum. Mar. Biol.* 76: 219-29.

Chapman, D.M. 1969. The nature of cnidarian desmocytes. *Tissue and Cell* 1: 619-32.

Chappell, J. 1980. Coral morphology, diversity and reef growth. *Nature* 286: 249-52.

Chen, C.A., et al. 1995. Systematic relationships within the Anthozoa (Cnidaria: Anthozoa) using 5'-end of the 28S rDNA. *Mol. Phyl. Evol.* 4: 175-83.

Chen, C.A., et al. 1995. Spatial variability of size and sex in the tropical corallimorpharian *Rhodactis* (=*Discosoma*) *indosinensis* (Cnidaria: Corallimorpharia) in Taiwan. *Zool. Stud.* 34: 82-7.

Chen, C.A., et al. 1995. Sexual and asexual reproduction of the tropical corallimorpharian *Rhodactis* (=*Discosoma*) *indosinensis* (Cnidaria: Corallimorpharia) in Taiwan. *Zool. Stud.* 34: 29-40.

Chen, C.A., and D.J. Miller. 1996. Analysis of ribosomal ITS1 sequences indicate a deep divergence between *Rhodactis* (Cnidaria: Anthozoa: Corallimorpharia) species from the Caribbean and the Indo-Pacific/Red Sea. *Mar. Biol.* 126: 423-32.

Chen, C.A., B.L. Willis, and D.J. Miller. 1996. Systematic relationships between tropical corallimorpharians (Cnidaria: Anthozoa: Corallimorpharia): utility of the 5.8S and internal transcribed spacer (ITS) regions of the rRNA trancription unit. *Bull. Mar. Sci.* 59: 196-208.

Cheney, D.P. 1975. Hard tissue tumors of scleractinian corals. In: *Immunologic Phylogeny* (W.H. Hildemann, and A.A. benedict, eds.). Plenum, NY: 77-87.

Chesher, R. 1985. Practical problems in coral reef utilitzation and management: a Tongan case study. *Proc. 5th Int. Coral Reef Symp.* 4: 213-18.

Chetail, M., and J. Fourni. 1969. Shell-boring mechanism of the gastropod, *Purpura* (*Thais*) *lapillus*: a physiological demonstration of the role of carbonic anhydrase in the dissolution of $CaCO_3$. *Am. Zool.* 9: 983-90.

Chornesky, E.A. 1983. Induced development of sweeper tentacles on the reef coral *Agaricia agaricites*: a response to direct competition. *Biol. Bull.* 165: 569-81.

Chornesky, E.A. 1989. Repeated reversals during spatial competition between corals. *Ecology* 70: 843-55.

Chornesky, E.A. 1991. The ties that bind: inter-clonal cooperation may help a fragile coral dominate shallow high-energy reefs. *Mar. Biol.* 109: 41-51.

Chornesky, E.A. 1992. The development of sweeper tentacles in direct competitive encounters among reef corals. *Am. Zool.* 32: 960.

Chornesky, E.A., and S.L. Williams. 1985. Distribution of sweeper tentacles on *Montastrea cavernosa*. The Ecology of Coral Reefs: Symposia Series for Undersea Research, *NOAA* 3: 61-7.

Chou, L.M., and S.T. Quek. 1992. Planulation in the scleractinian coral, *Pocillopora damicornis* in Singapore waters. *Proc. 7th Int. Coral Reef Symp.* 1: 500-1.

Claereboudt, M.R. 1988. Spatial distribution of fungiid coral population on exposed and sheltered reef slopes in Papua New Guinea. *Proc. 6th Int. Coral Reef Symp.* 2: 653-7.

Clark, S., and A.J. Edwards. 1995. Coral transplantation as an aid to reef rehabilitation: evaluation of a case study in the Maldive Islands. *Coral Reefs* 14: 201-13.

Clark, T. 1997. Tissue regeneration rate of coral transplants in a wave exposed environment, Cape D'Aguilar, Hong Kong. *Proc. 8th Int. Coral Reef Symp.* 2: 2069-74.

Clayton, W.S. Jr., and H.R. Lasker. 1982. Effects of light and dark treatments on feeding by the reef coral *Pocillopora damicornis* (Linnaeus). *J. Exp. Mar. Biol. Ecol.* 63: 269-79.

Coates, A.G. 1973. Coloniality on zoantharian corals. In: *Animal Colonies. Development and Function through Time* (R.S. Boardman, A.H. Cheetham, and W.A. Oliver, Jr., eds.) Dowden, Hutchinson & Ross, Inc., Stroudsberg, Pennsylvania: 3-27.

Coffroth, M.A. 1984. Ingestion and incorporation of coral mucus aggregates by a gorgonian soft coral. *Mar. Ecol. Prog. Ser.*.17: 193-9.

Coffroth, M.A. 1988. The function and fate of mucous sheets produced by reef coelenterates. *Proc. 6th Int. Coral Reef Symp.* 2: 15-19.

Coffroth, M.A. 1990. Mucus sheet formation on poritid corals: an evaluation of coral mucus as a nutrient source on reefs. *Mar. Biol.*105: 39-49

Coffroth, M.A. 1991. Cyclical mucus sheet formation on poritid corals in the San Blas Islands, Panama. *Mar. Biol.* 109: 35-40.

Coffroth, M.A., and H.R. Lasker. 1998. Larval paternity and male reproductive success of a broadcast-spawning gorgonian, *Plexaura kuna. Mar. Biol.* 131: 329-37.

Cohen, A.L., P.S. Lobel, and G.L. Tomasky. 1997. Coral bleaching on Johnston Atoll, Central Pacific Ocean. *Biol. Bull.* 193: 276-9.

Coles, S.L. 1969. Quantitative estimates of feeding and respiration for three scleractinian corals. *Limnol. Oceanogr.* 14: 949-53.

Coles, S.L. 1997. Reef corals occurring in a highly fluctuating temperature environment at Fahal Island, Gulf of Oman (Indian Ocean). *Coral Reefs* 16: 269-72.

Coles, S.L., and Y.H. Fadlallah. 1991. Reef coral survival and mortality to low temperatures in the Arabian Gulf: low species-specific lower temperature limits. *Coral Reefs* 9: 231-7.

Coles, S.L., and P.L. Jokiel. 1977. Effects of temperature on photosynthesis and respiration in hermatypic corals. *Mar. Biol.* 43: 209-16.

Coles, S.L., and P.L. Jokiel. 1978. Synergistic effects of temperature, salinity and light on the hermatypic coral *Montipora verrucosa. Mar. Biol.* 49: 187-95.

Coles, S.L., and D.G. Seapy. 1998. Ultra-violet absorbing compounds and tumerous growths on acroporid corals from Bandar Khayran, Gulf of Oman, Indian Ocean. *Coral Reefs* 17: 19508.

Colin, Dr. P.L. 1988. *Marine Invertebrates and Plants of the Living Reef.* T.F.H. Publications, Neptune City, New Jersey. 512 pp.

Colin, P.L., and C. Arneson. 1995. *Tropical Pacific Invertebrates.* Coral Reef Press, Beverly Hills, California. 296 pp.

Coll, J.C., et al. 1986. Studies of Australian Soft Corals XXXX: The natural products chemistry of alcyonacean soft corals with special reference to the genus *Lobophytum. Bull. Soc. Chim. Bel.* 95: 815-34.

Coll, J.C., et al. 1987. Algal overgrowth of alcyonacean soft corals. *Mar. Biol.* 96: 129-35.

Coll, J.C., B.F. Bowden, and D.M. Tapiolas. 1982. In situ isolation of allelochemicals released from soft corals (Coelenterata: Octocorallia): a totally submersible sampling apparatus. *J. Exp. Mar. Biol. Ecol.* 60: 293-9.

Coll, J.C., B.F. Bowden, D.M. Tapiolas, R.H. Willis, P. Djura, M. Streamer, and L. Trott. 1985. Studies of Australian Soft Corals XXV: The terpenoid chemistry of soft corals and its implications. *Tetrahedron* 41: 1085-92.

Coll, J.C., G.B. Hayes, N. Liyanage, W. Oberhansli, and R.J. Wells. 1977. Studies of Australian soft corals. I* A new cembrenoid diterpene from a *Sarcophyton* species. *Aust. Chem.* 30: 1305-9.

Coll, J.C., and D. Kelman. 1997. Possible locations for sperm chemo-attractants in the eggs of the soft coral *Lobophytum crassum. Proc. 8th Int. Coral Reef Symp.* 2: 1251-1254.

Coll, J.C., S. LaBarre, P.W. Sammarco, W.T. Williams, and G.J. Bakus. 1982. Chemical defenses in soft corals (Coelenterata: Octocorallia) of the Great Barrier Reef: a study of comparative toxicities. *Mar. Ecol. Prog. Ser.* 8: 271-8.

Coll, J.C., and P.W. Sammarco. 1983. Terpenoid toxins of soft corals (Cnidaria, Octocorallia): their nature, toxicity, and ecological significance. *Toxicon Suppl.* 3: 69-72.

Coll, J.C., and P.W. Sammarco. 1986. Soft corals: chemistry and Ecology. *Oceanus* 29: pp. 33-7.

Coll, J.C., and P.W. Sammarco. 1988. The role of secondary metabolites in the chemical ecology of marine invertebrates: a meeting ground for biologists and chemists. *Proc. 6th Int. Coral Reef Symp.* 1: 167-73.

Colley, N.J., and R.K. Trench. 1985. Cellular events in the reestablishment of a symbiosis between a marine dinoflagellate and a coelenterate. *Cell. Tiss. Res.* 239:93-103.

Connell, J.H. 1976. Competitive interactions and the species diversity of corals. In: *Coelenterate Ecology and Behavior* (G.O. Mackie, ed.). University of Victoria, British Columbia: pp. 51-8.

Connell, J.H., T.P. Hughes, and C.C. Wallace. 1997. A 30-year study of coral abundance, recruitment, and disturbance at several scales in space and time. *Ecol. Monogr.* 67: 461-88.

Cook, C.B., and C.F. D'Elia. 1987. Are natural populations of zooxanthellae ever nutrient-limited? *Symbiosis* 4: 199-212.

Cook, C.B., G. Muller-Parker, and C.F. D'Elia. 1992. Factors affecting nutrient sufficiency for symbiotic zooxanthellae. *Proc. 7th Int. Coral Reef Symp.* 1: 379-80.

Cooke, W. J. 1976. Reproduction, growth, and some tolerances of *Zoanthus pacificus* and *Palythoa vestitus* in Kaneohe Bay, Hawaii. In: *Coelenterate Ecology and Behavior* (G.O. Mackie, ed.). University of Victoria, British Columbia: pp. 281-8.

Cooper, E.L. 1996. Introduction. In: *Advances in Comparative and Environmental Physiology, Vol. 23: Invertebrate Immune Responses: Cells and Molecular Products* (E.L.Cooper, ed.). Springer-Verlag Berlin Heidelberg: 1-5.

Cope, M. 1981. Interspecific coral interactions in Hong Kong. *Proc. 4th Int. Coral Reef Symp.* 2: 357-62.

Cox, E.F. 1992. Fragmentation in the Hawaiian coral *Montipora verrucosa*. *Proc. 7th Int. Coral Reef Symp.* 1: 513-17.

Craik, W., R. Kenchington, and G. Kelleher. 1990. Coral-reef management. In: *Coral Reefs: Ecosystems of the World, Vol. 25* (Z. Dubinsky, ed.). Elsevier Scientific Publishing Co. Inc. New York: 453-68.

Cramphorn, I. 1996-7. Personal communications.

Crossland, C. 1939. Some coral formations. In: Reports on the Preliminary Expedition for the Exploration of the Red Sea. *Publ. Mar. Biol. St. Gha.* 1: 21-33.

Crossland, C.J. 1987. In situ release of mucus and DOC-lipid from the corals *Acropora variabilis* and *Stylophora pistillata* in different light regimes. *Coral Reefs* 6: 35-42.

Crossland, C.J. 1995. Dissolved nutrients in coral reef waters. In: *Perspectives on Coral Reefs* (D.J. Barnes, ed.). AIMS, Brian Clouston Publisher: 56-69.

Crossland, C.J., and D.J. Barnes. 1977. Gas-exchange studies with the staghorn coral *Acropora acuminata* and its zooxanthellae. *Mar. Biol.* 40: 185-94.

Crossland, C.J., D.J. Barnes, and M.A. Borowitzka. 1980. Diurnal lipid and mucus production in the staghorn coral *Acropora acuminata*. *Mar. Biol.* 60: 81-90.

Cubie, D.B. 1998. Coral reefs: rain forests of the sea. *The Rotarian*, Sept. issue: 30-3.

Cumming, R.L., and D. McCorry. 1998. Corallivorous gastropods in Hong Kong. *Coral Reefs* 17: 178.

Curry, N. 1996-7. Personal communications.

Custodio, H.M. III, and H.T. Yap. 1997, Skeletal extension rates of *Porites cylindrica* and *Porites (Synarea) rus* after transplantation to two depths. *Coral Reefs* 16: 267-8.

D'A, M., and A. Le Tissier. 1988. Diurnal patterns of skeleton formation in *Pocillopora damicornis* (Linnaeus). *Coral Reefs* 7: 81-8.

Dahan, M., and Y. Benayahu. 1997. Clonal propagation by the zooxanthellate octocoral *Dendronephthya hemprichi*. *Coral Reefs* 16: 5-12.

Dahan, M., and Y. Benayahu. 1997. Reproduction of *Dendronephthya hemprichii* (Cnidaria: Octocorallia): year round spawning in an azooxanthellate soft coral. *Mar. Biol.* 129: 573-9.

Darwin, C. 1889. *On the Structure and Distribution of Coral Reefs*. Ward, Lock & Co., Ltd., London. 549 pp.

Daumas, R., R. Galois, and B.A. Thomassin. 1981. Biochemical composition of soft and hard coral mucus on a New Caledonian lagoonal reef. *Proc. 4th Int. Coral Reef Symp.* 2: 59-67.

Daumas, R., and B.A. Thomassin. 1977. Protein fractions in coral and zoantharian mucus; possible evolution in coral reef environments. *Proc. 3rd Int. Coral Reef Symp.* 517-23.

Davies, P.S. 1984. The role of zooxanthellae in the energy requirements of *Pocillopora eydouxi*. *Coral Reefs* 2: 181-6.

Davies, P.S. 1991. Effect of daylight variations on the energy budgets of shallow-water corals. *Mar. Biol.* 108: 137-44.

Davies, P.S. 1992. *Endosymbiosis in Marine Cnidarians. Plant-Animal Interactions in the Marine Benthos* (D.M. John, S.J. Hawkins, and J.H. Price, eds.). Clarendon Press, Oxford. pp 511-40.

Davies, P.S. 1995. Coral nubbins and explants for reef assessment and laboratory ecotoxicology. *Coral Reefs* 14: 267-9.

Dayton, L. 1995. The killing reefs. *New Scientist* 148: 14-15.

de Kruijf, H.A.M. 1977. Individual polyp behavior and colonial organization in the hydrocorals *Millepora complanata* (Milleporina) and *Stylaster roseus* (Stylasterina). *Proc. 3rd Int. Coral Reef Symp.* 445-51.

Debelius, H. 1996. *Nudibranchs and Sea Slugs: Indo-Pacific Field Guide*. IKAN—Unterwasserarchiv, Frankfurt, Germany. 321 pp.

Debrot, A.O., et al. 1998. Recent declines in the coral fauna of the Spaanse Water, Curacao, Netherland Antilles. *Bull. Mar. Sci.* 63: 571-80.

Delbeek, J.C. 1987. The care and feeding of mushroom anemones (suborder: Corallimorpharia). *Freshwater and Marine Aquarium* 10(10): 4-6. http://nic2.hawaii.edu/~delbeek

Delbeek, J.C. 1987. The role of symbiotic algae in marine invertebrates. *Freshwater and Marine Aquarium* 10(11): 41-4. http://nic2.hawaii.edu/~delbeek

Delbeek, J.C. 1990. Keeping corals: fact or fiction? *Atoll* 3(5): 13-18. http://nic2.hawaii.edu/~delbeek

Delbeek, J.C. 1990. Reef aquariums part 6: coral aggression. *Aquarium Fish* 2(7): 26-32. http://nic2.hawaii.edu/~delbeek

Delbeek, J.C. 1990. Stocking the reef aquarium: Coral compatibility. *Aquarium Fish*. download from http://www.delbeek. com

Delbeek, J.C. 1994. Corals in the reef tank: what they are and how they live. *Aquarium USA* 1995: 68-85.

Delbeek, J.C., and J. Sprung. 1994. *The Reef Aquarium, Volume 1*. Ricordea Publishing, Coconut Grove, Florida. 544 pp.

Delbeek, J.C., and J. Sprung. 1997. *The Reef Aquarium, Volume 2*. Ricordea Publishing, Coconut Grove, Florida. 546 pp.

DelFavero, C. 1993-7. Personal communications.

D'Elia, C.F. 1977. The uptake and release of dissolved phosphorous by reef corals. *Limnol. Oceanogr.* 22: 301-15.

D'Elia, C.F., and K.L. Webb. 1977. The dissolved nitrogen flux of reef corals. *Proc. 3rd Int. Coral Reef Symp.* 1: 325-30.

D'Elia, C.F., and W.J. Wiebe. 1990. Biogeochemical nutrient cycles in coral-reef ecosystems. In: *Coral Reefs: Ecosystems of the World, Vol. 25* (Z. Dubinsky, ed.). Elsevier Scientific Publishing Co. Inc. New York: 49-74.

Demmig-Adams, B. 1990. Carotenoids and photoprotection in plants: a role for the xanthophyll zeaxanthin. *Bioch. et Biophys. Acta* 1020: 1-24.

den Hartog, J.C. 1977. The marginal tentacles of *Rhodactis sanctithomae* (Corallimorpharia) and the sweeper tentacles of *Montastrea cavernosa* (Scleractinia): their cnidom and possible function. *Proc. 3rd Int. Coral Reef Symp.* 463-9.

den Hartog, J.C. 1980. Caribbean shallow water Corallimorpharia. *Zool. Verh.* 176: 83pp.

Dennison, W.C., and D.J. Barnes. 1988. Effect of water motion on coral photosynthesis and calcification. *J. Exp. Mar. Biol. Ecol.* 115: 66-77.

Derr, M. 1992. Raiders of the reef. *Audobon* 94: 48-56.

De Ruyter van Steveninck, E.D., L.L. Van Mulekom, and A.M. Breeman. 1988. Growth inhibition of *Lobophora variegata* (Lamaroux) Womersly by scleractinian corals. *J. Exp. Mar. Biol. Ecol.* 115: 169-78.

Devlin, M. 1999. Personal communications. Great Barrier Reef Marine Park Authority, Townsville, Queensland.

d'Hondt, M.J. 1977. Some Octocorallia from Australia. *Aust J. Mar. Freshwater Res.* 28: 241-59.

Dineson, Z.D. 1983. Patterns in the distribution of soft corals across the central Great Barrier Reef. *Coral Reefs* 1: 229-36.

Dineson, Z.D. 1985. Aspects of the life history of a stolon-bearing species of *Efflatounaria* (Octocorallia: Xeniidae). *Proc. 5th Int. Coral Reef Symp.* 6: 89-94.

DiSalvo, L.H. 1969. Isolation of bacteria from the corallum of *Porites lobata* (Dana) and its possible significance. *Am. Zool.* 9: 735-40.

DiSalvo, L.H. 1969. On the existence of a coral reef regenerative sediment. *Pac. Sci.* 23: 129.

Ditlev, H. 1978. Zonation of corals (Scleractinia: Coelenterata) on intertidal reef flats at Ko Phuket, Eastern Indian Ocean. *Mar. Biol.* 47: 29-39.

Dodge, R.E., and G.W. Brass. 1984. Skeletal extension, density, and calcification of the reef coral, *Montastrea annularis*: St. Croix, U.S. Virgin Islands. *Bull. Mar. Sci.* 34: 288-307.

Dodge, R.E., R.C. Aller, and J. Thompson. 1974. Coral growth related to resuspension of bottom sediments. *Nature* 247: 574-7.

Done, T.J. 1977. A comparison of units of cover in ecological classifications of coral communities. *Proc. 3rd Int. Coral Reef Symp.* 1: 9-14.

Done, T.J. 1995. Coral zonation: Its nature and significance. In: *Perspectives on Coral Reefs* (D.J. Barnes, ed.). AIMS, Brian Clouston Publisher: 107-48.

Done, T.J. 1999. Coral community adaptability to environmental change at the scales of regions, reefs and reef zones. *Amer. Zool.* 39: 66-79.

Douglas, A.E. 1988. Alga-invertebrate symbiosis. In: *Biochemistry of the Algae and Cyanobacteria* (L.J. Rogers and J.R. Gallon, eds.). Clarendon Press: Oxford: pp. 297-309.

Dove, S.G., M. Takabayashi, and O. Hoegh-Guldberg. 1995. Isolation and partial characterization of the pink and blue pigments of pocilloporid and acroporid corals. *Biol. Bull.* 189: 288-97.

Drew, E.A. 1972. The biology and physiology of alga-invertebrate symbioses. II. The density of symbiotic algal cells in a number of hermatypic hard corals and alcyonarians from various depths. *J. Exp. Mar. Biol. Ecol.* 9: 71-5.

Drollet, J.H., P. Glaziou, and P.M.V. Martin. 1993. A study of mucus from the solitary coral *Fungia fungites* (Scleractinia: Fungiidae) in relation to photobiological UV adaptation. *Mar. Biol.* 115: 263-6.

Dubinsky, Z. 1990. *Coral Reefs: Ecosystems of the World.* Vol. 25. Elsevier Scientific Publishing Co. Inc. New York.

Dubinsky, Z., P.G. Falkowski, J.W. Porter, and L. Muscatine. 1984. Absorption and utilization of radiant energy by light- and shade-adapted colonies of the hermatypic coral *Stylophora pistillata*. *Proc. Roy. Soc. Lond. B* 222: 203-14.

Dubinsky, Z., P. G. Falkowski, and D. Sharf. 1984. Aspects of adaptation of hermatypic corals and their endosymbiotic zooxanthellae to light. *Bull. Inst. Oceanogr. Fish* 24:124-34.

Dubinsky, Z., and P.L. Jokiel. 1994. Ratio of energy and nutrient fluxes regulates symbiosis between zooxanthellae and corals. *Pac. Sci.* 48: 313-24.

Dubinsky, Z., N. Stambler, M. Ben-Zion, L.R. McCloskey, L. Muscatine, and P.G. Falkowski. 1989. The effect of external nutrient resources on the optical properties and photosynthetic efficiency of *Stylophora pistillata*. *Proc. Roy. Soc. Lond. B* 239: 231-46.

Ducklow, H.W. 1990. The biomass, production and fate of bacteria in coral reefs. In: *Coral Reefs: Ecosystems of the World, Vol. 25* (Z. Dubinsky, ed.). Elsevier Scientific Publishing Co. Inc. New York: 265-90.

Ducklow, H.W., and R. Mitchell. 1979. Composition of mucus released by coral reef coelenterates. *Limnol. Oceanogr.* 24: 706-14.

Ducklow, H.W., and R. Mitchell. 1979. Bacterial populations and adaptations in the mucus layers on living corals. *Limnol. Oceanogr.* 24: 715-25.

Dunlap, W.C., and B.E. Chalker. 1986. Identification and quantitation of near-UV absorbing compounds (S-320) in a hermatypic scleractinian. *Coral Reefs* 5: 155-9.

Dunlap, W.C., B.E. Chalker, and W.M. Bandaranayake. 1988. Ultraviolet light absorbing agents derived from tropical marine organisms of the Great Barrier Reef, Australia. *Proc. 6th Int. Coral Reef Symp.* 3: 89-93.

Dunn, D.F., and W.M. Hamner. 1980. *Amplexidiscus fenestrafer* n. gen., n. sp. (Coelenterata: Anthozoa), a tropical Indo-Pacific corallimorpharian. *Micronesica* 16: 29-36.

Dustan, P. 1977. Vitality of reef coral populations off Key Largo, Florida: recruitment and mortality. *Env. Geol.* 2: 51-8.

Dustan, P. 1979. Distribution of zooxanthellae and photosynthetic chloroplast pigments of the reefbuilding coral *Montastrea annularis* (Ellis and Solander) in relation to depth on a West Indian coral reef. *Bull. Mar. Sci.* 29: 79-95.

Dustan, P. 1982. Depth-dependent photoadaption by zooxanthellae of the reef coral, *Montastrea annularis*. *Mar. Biol.* 68: 253-64.

Dykens, J.A., and M. Shick. 1982. Oxygen production by endosymbiotic algae controls superoxide dismutase activity in their animal host. *Nature* 297: 579-80.

Eakin, C.M. 1996. Where have all the carbonates gone? A model comparison of calcium carbonate budgets before and after the 1982-1983 El Nino at Uva Island in the eastern Pacific. *Coral Reefs* 15: 109-19.

Eakin, C.M. 1996. Low tidal exposures and reef mortalities in the eastern pacific. *Coral Reefs* 15: 120.

Edmunds, P.J., and P.S. Davies. 1989. An energy budget for *Porites porites* (Scleractinia), growing in a stressed environment. *Coral Reefs* 8: 37-43.

Eldridge, L.G., and R.K. Kropp. 1981. Decapod crustacean-induced skeletal modification in Acropora. *Proc. 4th Int. Coral Reef Symp.* 2:115-20.

Endean, R. 1976. Destruction and recovery of coral reef communities. In: O.A. Jones and R. Endean (eds.), *Biology and Geology of Coral Reefs. III. Biology 2*, Academic Press, New York: 215-54.

Endean, R., and A.M. Cameron. 1990. Trends and new perspectives in coral-reef ecology. In: *Coral Reefs: Ecosystems of the World, Vol. 25* (Z. Dubinsky, ed.). Elsevier Scientific Publishing Co. Inc. New York: 469-92.

Entsch, B., et al. 1983. Indications from photosynthetic components that iron is a limiting nutrient in primary producers on coral reefs. *Mar. Biol.* 73: 17-30.

Erez, J., et al. 1992. Plankton is a major source of nutrients in coral reef ecosystems. *Proc. 7th Int. Coral Reef Symp.* 1: 345.

Erez, J. 1990. On the importance of food sources in coral-reef ecosystems. In: *Coral Reefs: Ecosystems of the World, Vol. 25* (Z. Dubinsky, ed.). Elsevier Scientific Publishing Co. Inc. New York: 411-18.

Fabricius, K.E. 1995. Nutrition and community regulation in tropical-reef inhabiting soft corals (Coelenterata:Octocorallia) Ph.D. thesis, Universitat München, Verlag Shaker Aachen. 132 pp.

Fabricius, K.E. 1997. Soft coral abundance on the central Great Barrier Reef: effects of *Acanthaster planci*, space availability, and aspects of the physical environment. *Coral Reefs* 16: 159-67.

Fabricius, K. 1999. Tissue loss and mortality in soft corals following mass bleaching. *Coral Reefs* 18: 54.

Fabricius, K.E., Y. Benayahu, and A. Genin. 1995. Herbivory in asymbiotic soft corals. *Science* 268: 90-2.

Fabricius, K.E., and G. De'ath. 1997. The effects of flow, depth and slope on cover of soft coral taxa and growth forms on Davies Reef, Great Barrier Reef. *Proc. 8th Int. Coral Reef Symp.* 2: 1071-6.

Fabricius, K.E., A. Genin, and Y. Benayahu. 1995. Flow-dependent herbivory and growth in zooxanthellae-free soft corals. *Limnol. Oceanogr.* 40: 1290-1301.

Fabricius, K.E., and D.W. Klumpp. 1995. Widespread mixotrophy in reef-inhabiting soft corals: the influence of depth, and colony expansion and contraction on photosynthesis. *Mar. Ecol. Prog. Ser.* 125: 195-204.

Fadlallah, Y.H. 1983. Sexual reproduction, development and larval biology in scleractinian corals. *Coral Reefs* 2: 129-50.

Fadlallah, Y.H. 1996. Sychronous spawning of *Acropora clathrata* coral colonies from the Western Arabian Gulf (Saudi Arabia). *Bull. Mar. Sci.* 59: 209-16.

Fadlallah, Y.H., et al. 1995. Mortality of shallow reef corals in the western Arabian Gulf following aerial exposure in winter. *Coral Reefs* 14: 99-107.

Fadlallah, Y.H., and R.T. Lindo. 1988. Contrasting cycles of reproduction in *Stylophora pistillata* from the Red Sea and the Arabian Gulf, with emphasis on temperature. *Proc. 6th Int. Coral Reef Symp.* 3: 225-9.

Fadlallah, Y.H., R.T. Lindo, and D.J. Lennon. 1992. Annual synchronous spawning event in *Acropora* spp. from the Western Arabian Gulf. *Proc. 7th Int. Coral Reef Symp.* 1: 501.

Fagerstrom, J.A. 1987. *The Evolution of Reef Communities.* Wiley, New York, 600 pp.

Falkowski, P.G., and Z. Dubinsky. 1981. Light-shade adaptation of *Stylophora pistillata*, a hermatypic coral from the Gulf of Elat. *Nature* 289: 172-4.

Falkowski, P.G., Z. Dubinsky, L. Muscatine, and L. McCloskey. 1993. Population control in symbiotic corals. *Bioscience* 43: 606-11.

Falkowski, P.G., Z. Dubinsky, L. Muscatine, and J. Porter. 1984. Light and the bioenergetics of a symbiotic coral. *Bioscience* 34: 705-9.

Falkowski, P.G., P.L. Jokiel, and R.A. Kinzie III. 1990. Irradiance and Corals. In: *Coral Reefs: Ecosystems of the World, Vol. 25* (Z. Dubinsky, ed.). Elsevier Scientific Publishing Co. Inc. New York: 89-108.

Falkowski, P.G., and J.A. Raven. 1997. Zooxanthellae: a case study in unbalanced growth. In: *Aquatic Photosynthesis.* Blackwell Science. p. 257.

Fan, T.Y., and C.F. Dai. 1992. Reproductive cycles of *Echinophyllia aspera* in Southern and Northern Taiwan. *Proc. 7th Int. Coral Reef Symp.* 1: 501.

Fandian, T.J. 1975. Heterotrophy: feeding responses. In: *Marine Ecology* (Otto Kinne, ed.). John Wiley & Sons, London: 64-71.

Fang, L.S., Y.W. Chen, and C.S. Chen. 1989. Why does the white tip of stony coral grow so fast without zooxanthellae? *Mar. Biol.* 103: 359-63.

Fang, L., S. Huang, and K. Lin. 1997. High temperature induces the synthesis of heat-shock proteins and the elevation of intracellular calcium in the coral *Acropora grandis. Coral Reefs* 16: 127-31.

Fankboner, P.V. 1976. Accumulation of dissolved carbon by the solitary coral *Balanophyllia elegans*—an alternative nutritional pathway? In: *Coelenterate Ecology and Behavior* (G.O. Mackie, ed.). University of Victoria, British Columbia: pp. 111-16.

Farrant, P.A., M.A, Borowitzka, R. Hinde, and R.J. King. 1987. Nutrition of the temperate Australian soft coral *Capnella gaboensis. Mar. Biol.* 95: 575-81.

Faust, M.A., J.C. Sager, and B.W. Meson. 1982. Response of *Prorocentrum maraie-lebouriae* (Dinophycae) to light of different spectral qualities and irradiances: growth and pigmentation. *J. Phycol.*18: 349-56.

Fautin, D. 1999. Personal communications.

Fautin, D.G., and J.M. Lowenstein. 1992. Phylogenetic relationships among scleractinians, actinians, and corallimorpharians (Coelenterata: Anthozoa). *Proc. 7th Int. Coral Reef Symp.* 2: 665-70.

Feingold, J.S. 1988. Ecological studies of a cyanobacterial infection of the sea plume *Psuedopterogorgia acerosa* (Coelenterata: Octocorallia). *Proc. 6th Int. Coral Reef Symp.* 3: 157-62.

Feingold, J.S., and L.L. Richardson. 1999. Impact of Plague Type II disease on populations of *Dichocoenia stokesii* in southeast Florida. NCRI International Conference on Scientific Aspects of Coral Reef Assessment, Monitoring, and Restoration. April 14-16, 1999. Fort Lauderdale, FL: 85.

Fenical, W. 1978. Diterpenoids. In: *Marine Natural Products: Chemical and Biological Perspectives, Vol. II* (P.J. Scheuer, ed.). Academic Press, London: 173-246.

Fenner, D. 1999. Personal communications.

Fenner, D. 1999. New observations on the stony coral (Scleractinia, Milleporidae, and Stylasteridae) species of Belize (Central America) and Cozumel (Mexico). *Bull. Mar. Sci.* 64: 143-54.

Ferrer, L.M., and A.M. Szmant. 1988. Nutrient regeneration by the endolithic community in coral skeletons. *Proc. 6th Int. Coral Reef Symp.* 3: 1-4.

Ferrier-Pages, C., et al. 1998. Release of dissolved organic carbon and nitrogen by the zooxanthellate coral *Galaxea fascicularis. Mar. Ecol. Prog. Ser.* 172: 265-74.

Fishelson, L. 1970. Littoral fauna of the Red Sea: the population of nonscleractinian anthozoans of shallow waters of the Red Sea (Eilat). *Mar. Biol.* 6: 106-16.

Fishelson, L. 1973. Ecological and biological phenomena influencing coral-species composition on the reef tables at Eilat (Gulf of Aqaba, Red Sea). *Mar. Biol.* 19: 183-96.

Fitt, W.K., et al. 1993. Recovery of the coral *Montastrea annularis* in the Florida Keys after the 1987 Caribbean "bleaching event." *Coral Reefs* 12: 57-64.

Fitt, W.K., et al. 1999. Monitoring the physiology of reef corals: tissue biomass and zooxanthellae. NCRI International Conference on Scientific Aspects of Coral Reef Assessment, Monitoring, and Restoration. April 14-16, 1999. Fort Lauderdale, FL: 87.

Fitt, W.K., and M.E. Warner. 1995. Bleaching patterns of 4 species of Caribbean reef corals. *Biol. Bull.* 189: 298-307.

Fitzgerald, L.M., and A.M. Szmant. 1988. Amino acid metabolism: adaptations to low nutrient conditions? *Proc. 6th Int. Coral Reef Symp.* 3: 5-9.

Fitzhardinge, R.C. 1988. Coral recruitment: the importance of interspecific differences in juvenile growth and mortality. *Proc. 6th Int. Coral Reef Symp.* 2: 673-7.

Flynn, K.J., and K. Flynn. 1998. Release of nitrite by marine dinoflagellates: development of a mathematical simulation. *Mar. Biol.* 130: 455-70.

Fontaine, M., A. Momzikoff, R. Taxit, M. Bernadec, and G. Chennebault-Gondry. 1981. Riboflavin content in corals and release of this vitamin in the ecosystem. *Proc. 4th Int. Coral Reef Symp.* 2: 75-80.

Fork, D.C., and A.W.D. Larkum. 1989. Light harvesting in the green alga, *Ostreobium* sp., a coral symbiont adapted to extreme shade. *Mar. Biol.* 103:381-5.

Fosså, S.A., and A.J. Nilsen. 1996. *The Modern Coral Reef Aquarium, Volume 1.* Birgit Schmettkamp Verlag, Bornheim, Germany. 362 pp.

Fosså, S.A., and A.J. Nilsen. 1998. *The Modern Coral Reef Aquarium, Volume 2.* Birgit Schmettkamp Verlag, Bornheim, Germany. 362 pp.

Foster, A.B. 1983. The relationship between corallite morphology and colony shape in some massive reef-corals. *Coral Reefs* 2: 19-25.

Fox, D.L. 1972. Pigmented calcareous skeletons of some corals. *Comp. Biochem. Physiol.* 43B: 919-27.

Fox, D.L. 1976. *Animal Biochromes and Structural Colors: Physical, Chemical, Distributional & Physiological Features of Colored Bodies in the Animal World.* University of California Press, Berkeley: 82-91, 390-3.

Fox, J.P., C.E. Hall, and L.R. Elveback. 1980. *Epidimiology: Man and Disease.* MacMillan Publishing Co. Inc., New York. 339 pp.

Fox, D.L., and C.F.A. Pantin. 1944. Pigments in the coelenterata. *Biol. Rev.* 19: 121-34.

Fox, D.L., and D.W. Wilkie. 1970. Somatic and skeletally fixed carotenoids of the purple hydrocoral, *Allopora californica. Comp. Biochem. Physiol.* 36: 49-60.

Frakes, T. 1995. Salinity measurement in review. *Aquarium Frontiers* 3(1) 32-43.

Frank, U., and B. Rinkevich. 1994. Nontransitive patterns of historecognition phenomena in the Red Sea hydrocoral *Millepora dichotoma. Mar. Biol.* 118: 723-9.

Fraser, R.H., and D.J. Currie. 1996. The species richness-energy hypothesis in a system where historical factors are thought to prevail: coral reefs. *Am. Nat.* 148: 138-59.

Fretter, V., and A. Graham. 1976. *A Functional Anatomy of Invertebrates.* Academic Press, London. 589 pp.

Froelich, A.S. 1985. Functional aspects of nutrient cycling on coral reefs. The Ecology of Coral Reefs: Symposia Series for Undersea Research, *NOAA* 3: 133-9.

Gamble, S. 1996-7. Personal communications.

Garrett, P., and H. Ducklow. 1975. Coral diseases in Bermuda. *Nature* 253: 349-50.

Gates, R.D., et al. 1999. The influence of an anthozoan "host factor" on the physiology of a symbiotic dinoflagellate. *J. Exp. Mar. Biol. Ecol.* 232: 241-59.

Gates, R.D., G. Baghdasarian, and L. Muscatine. 1992. Temperature stress causes host cell detachment in symbiotic cnidarians: implication for coral bleaching. *Biol. Bull.* 182: 324-332.

Gates, R.D., and P.J. Edmunds. 1999. The physiological mechanism of acclimitization in tropical reef corals. *Amer. Zool.* 39: 30-43.

Gattuso, J.P., et al. 1998. Effect of calcium carbonate saturation of seawater on coral calcification. *Glob. Planet Change* 18: 37-46.

Gattuso, J.P., et al. 1999. Photosynthesis and calcification at cellular, organismal and community levels in coral reefs: a review on interactions and control by carbonate chemistry. *Amer. Zool.* 39: 160-83.

Gattuso, J.P., D. Yellowlees, and M. Lesser. 1993. Depth- and light-dependent variation of carbon partioning and utilization in the zooxanthellate coral *Stylophora pistillata. Mar. Ecol. Prog. Ser.* 92: 267-76.

Genin, A., et al. 1995. Vertical mixing and coral death in the Red Sea following the eruption of Mount Pinataubo. *Nature* 377: 507-10.

Gerhardt, D.J. 1983. The chemical systematics of colonial marine animals and estimated phylogeny of the order Gorgonacea based on terpenoid characteristics. *Biol. Bull.* 7: 71-81.

Gilmore, M.D., and B.R. Hall. 1976. Life history, growth habits, and constructional roles of *Acropora cervicornis* in the patch reef environment. *J. Sed. Petr.* 46: 519-22.

Gil-Turnes, S., and J. Corredor. 1981. Studies of photosynthetic pigments of zooxanthellae in Caribbean hermatypic corals. *Proc. 4th Int. Coral Reef Symp.* 2: 51-3.

Gladfelter, E.H. 1982. Skeletal development in *Acropora cervicornis*: I. Patterns of calcium carbonate accretion in the axial corallite. *Coral Reefs* 1: 45-51.

Gladfelter, E.H. 1983. Skeletal development in *Acropora cervicornis*. II. Diel patterns of calcium carbonate accretion. *Coral Reefs* 2: 91-100.

Gladfelter, E.H. 1984. Skeletal development in *Acropora cervicornis*. III. A comparison of monthly rates of linear extension and calcium carbonate accretion measured over a year. *Coral Reefs* 3: 51-7.

Gladfelter, E.H., and R.K. Monahan. 1977. Primary production and calcium carbonate deposition rates in *Acropora palmata* from different positions in the reef. *Proc. 3rd Int. Coral Reef Symp.* 1: 389-94.

Gladfelter, W.B. 1982. White-band disease in *Acropora palmata*: implications for the structure and growth of shallow reefs. *Bull. Mar. Sci.* 32: 639-43.

Glazebrock, J.S., and R. VanWoesik. 1992. Effects of low salinity on the tissues of hard corals *Acropora* spp., *Pocillopora* sp., and *Seriatopora* sp. from the Great Keppel region. *Proc. 7th Int. Coral Reef Symp.* 1: 307-8.

Gleason, D.F. 1998. Sedimentation and distributions of green and brown morphs of the Caribbean coral *Porites asteroides* Lamarck. *J. Exp. Mar. Biol. Ecol.* 230: 73-89.

Gleason, D.F., and D.A. Brazeau. 1999. Can selfing coral species be used to enhance restoration of damaged reefs? Proceedings: NCRI International Conference on Scientific Aspects of Coral Reef Assessment, Monitoring, and Restoration. April 14-16, 1999. Fort Lauderdale, FL: 92-3.

Gleason, D.F., and G.M. Wellington. 1993. Ultraviolet radiation and coral bleaching. *Nature* 365: 836-8.

Glynn, P.W. 1976. Some physical and biological determinants of coral community structure in the eastern Pacific. *Ecol. Monogr.* 46: 431-56.

Glynn, P.W. 1984. Widespread coral mortality and the 1982-83 El Nino warming event. *Env. Cons.* 11: 133-46.

Glynn, P.W. 1985. El Nino-associated disturbance to coral reefs and post-disturbance mortality by *Acanthaster planci. Mar. Ecol. Prog. Ser.* 26: 295-300.

Glynn, P.W. 1990. Feeding ecology of selected coral-reef macroconsumers: patterns and effects on coral community structure. In: *Coral Reefs: Ecosystems of the World, Vol. 25* (Z. Dubinsky, ed.). Elsevier Scientific Publishing Co. Inc. New York: 365-400.

Glynn, P.W. 1997. Bioerosion and coral-reef growth: A dynamic balance. In: *Life and Death of Coral Reefs* (C. Birkeland, ed.). Chapman & Hall, New York: 68-94.

Glynn, P.W., et al. 1984. The occurrence and toxicity of herbicides in reef building corals. *Mar. Poll. Bull.* 15: 370-4.

Glynn, P.W., et al. 1994. Reef coral reproduction in the eastern Pacific: Costa Rica, Panama, and Galapagos Islands (Ecuador). II. Poritidae. *Mar. Biol.* 118: 191-208.

Glynn, P.W., and M.W. Colgan. 1992. Sporadic disturbances in fluctuating coral reef environments: El Nino and coral reef development in the Eastern Pacific. *Amer. Zool.* 32: 707-18.

Glynn, P.W., and L. D'Croz. 1990. Experimental evidence for high temperature stress as the cause of El Nino-coincident coral mortality. *Coral Reefs* 8: 181-91.

Glynn, P.W., and D.A. Krupp. 1986. Feeding biology of a Hawaiian sea star corallivore, *Culcita novaguineae* Muller & Troschel. *J. Exp. Mar. Biol. Ecol.* 96: 75-96.

Glynn, P.W., M. Perez, and S.L. Gilchrist. 1985. Lipid decline in stressed corals and their crustacean symbionts. *Biol. Bull.* 168: 276-84.

Glynn, P.W., E.C. Peters, and L. Muscatine. 1985. Coral tissue microstructure and necrosis: relation to catastrophic coral mortality in Panama. *Dis. Aquat. Org.* 1: 29-37.

Glynn, P.W., and A.M. Szmant, et al. 1989. Condition of coral reef cnidarians from the Northern Florida reef tract: pesticides, heavy metals, and histopathological examination. *Mar. Poll. Bull.* 20: 568-76.

Goad, L.J. 1978. The sterols of marine invertebrates: composition, biosynthesis, and metabolites. In: *Marine Natural Products: Chemical and Biological Perspectives Vol II* (P.J. Scheuer, ed.). Academic Press, New York: 76-165.

Gohar, H.A.F. 1940. Studies on the Xeniidae of the Red Sea: Their ecology, physiology, taxonomy and phylogeny. *Publ. Mar. Biol. Sta. Al-Gha* 2: 25-116.

Gohar, H.A.F. 1940. A revision of some genera of the Stolonifera. *Publ. Mar. Biol. Sta. Al-Gha* 3: 3-23.

Gohar, H.A.F. 1940. The development of some Xeniidae (Alcyonaria). *Publ. Mar. Biol. Sta. Al-Gha* 3: 27-69.

Gohar, H.A.F. 1948. A description and some biological studies of a new alcyonarian species *Clavularia hamra* Gohar. *Publ. Mar. Biol. Sta. Al-Gha* 6: 1-35.

Gohar, H.A.F., and H.M. Roushdy. 1959. The neuromuscular system of the Xeniidae (Alcyonaria) I. Histological. *Publ. Mar. Biol. Sta. Al-Gha* 10: 64-81.

Gohar, H.A.F., and H.M. Roushdy. 1959. On the physiology of the neuromuscular system of *Heteroxenia* (Alcyonaria). *Publ. Mar. Biol. Sta. Al-Gha* 10: 92-143.

Gohar, H.A.F., and H.M. Roushdy. 1961. On the embryology of the Xeniidae (Alcyonaria). *Publ. Mar. Bio. Sta. Al-Gha* 11: 45-73.

Gohar, H.A.F., and G.N. Soliman. 1963. On the biology of three coralliophilids boring in living corals. *Publ. Mar. Biol. Sta. Al-Gha* 12: 100-27.

Goldberg, W. 1973. Ecological aspects of salinity and temperature tolerances of some reef-dwelling gorgonians from Florida. *Carib. J. Sci.* 13: 173-7.

Goldberg, W.M. 1976. Comparative study of the chemistry and structure of gorgonian and antipatharian coral skeletons. *Mar. Biol.* 35: 253-67.

Goldberg, W.M. 1977. Radioiodine as an indicator of skeletogenesis in gorgonian and antipatharian corals. *Proc. 3rd Int. Coral Reef Symp.* 512-16.

Goldberg, W.M., J.C. Makemson, and S.B. Colley. 1984. *Entocladia endozoica* sp. nov., a pathogenic chlorophyte: Structure, life history, physiology, and effect on its coral host. *Biol. Bull.* 166: 368-83.

Gordon, H.R., and J. Dera. 1969. Irradiance attenuation measurements in sea water off Southeast Florida. *Bull. Mar. Sci.* 19: 279-85.

Goreau, N.I., and R.L. Hayes. 1977. Nucleation catalysis in coral skeletogenesis. *Proc. 3rd Int. Coral Reef Symp.* 439-45.

Goreau, T.F., and N.I. Goreau. 1959. The physiology of skeleton formation in corals. II. Calcium deposition by hermatypic corals under various conditions in the reef. *Biol. Bull.* 117: 239-50.

Goreau, T.F., and N.I. Goreau. 1973. The ecology of Jamaican coral reefs. II. Geomorphology, zonation, and sedimentary phases. *Bull. Mar. Sci.* 23: 399-464.

Goreau, T.F., N.I. Goreau, and C.M. Yonge. 1971. Reef corals: autotrophs or heterotrophs? *Biol. Bull.* 141: 247-60.

Goreau, T.F., and W.D. Hartman. 1966. Sponge: effect on the form of reef corals. *Science* 151: 343-4.

Goreau, T.J. 1977. Seasonal variations of trace metals and stable isotopes in coral skeleton: physiological and environmental controls. *Proc. 3rd Int. Coral Reef Symp.* 426-30.

Goreau, T.J., and A.H. MacFarlane. 1990. Reduced growth rate of *Montastrea annularis* following the 1987-1988 coral-bleaching event. *Coral Reefs* 8: 211-15.

Gosliner, T.M., D.W. Behrens, and G.C. Williams. 1996. *Coral Reef Animals of the Indo-Pacific*. Sea Challengers, Monterey, California. 314 pp.

Goulet, T.L., and M.A. Coffroth. 1997. A within colony comparison of zooxanthella genotypes in the Caribbean gorgonian *Plexaura kuna*. *Proc. 8th Int. Coral Reef Symp.* 2: 1331-4.

Grant, A.J., M. Remond, and R. Hinde. 1998. Low molecular-weight factor from *Plesiastrea versipora* (Scleractinia) that modifies release and glycerol metabolism of isolated symbiotic algae. *Mar. Biol.* 130: 553-7.

Grasshoff, M. 1979. Zur bipolaren Verbreitung der Oktokoralle *Paragorgia arborea* (Cnidaria: Anthozoa: Scleraxonia). *Senckenbergiana marit.* 11: 115-37.

Grasshoff, M. 1992. Die Flachwasser—Gorgonarien von Europa und Westafrika (Cnidaria: Anthozoa). *Courier Forschunginstitut Senckenberg* 149: 1-35.

Grasshoff, M., and H. Zibrowius. 1983. Kalkkrusten auf Achsen von Hornkorallen, rezent und fossil. *Senckenbergiana marit.* 15: 111-45.

Greco, F. 1994. Coral propagation chat. Fishchat: America Online. Library archives.

Greco, F. 1995-6. Personal communications.

Greco, F. 1997. The marine aquarium hobby—a second opinion. *Bull. of the Aquatic Cons. Network* 2(2): 14 pp.

Green, E., and F. Shirley. 1999. The global trade in coral. WCMC Biodiversity Series No. 9. 70 pp.

Grigg, R.W., and S.J. Dollar. 1990. Natural and anthropogenic disturbance on coral reefs. In: *Coral Reefs: Ecosystems of the World, Vol. 25* (Z. Dubinsky, ed.). Elsevier Scientific Publishing Co. Inc. New York: 439-52.

Grosholz, E.D., and G.M. Ruiz. 1997. Evidence for regional adaptation of black band disease at Carrie Bow Cay, Belize. *Proc. 8th Int. Coral Reef Symp.* 1: 579-82.

Grygier, M.J., and S.D. Cairns. 1996. Suspected neoplasms in deep-sea corals (Scleractinia: Oculinidae: *Madrepora* spp.) reinterpreted as galls caused by *Petrarca madreporae* n. sp. (Crustacea: Ascothoracida: Petrarcidae). *Dis. Aquatic Org.* 24(1):61-69.

Guest, J.R., M.D.A. Le Tissier, and J.C. Blythell. 1999. A novel method for investigating the histo-pathology of coral "band diseases." Presentation: NCRI International Conference on Scientific Aspects of Coral Reef Assessment, Monitoring, and Restoration. April14-16, Fort Lauderdale, FL.

Gunthorpe, L., and A.M. Cameron. 1990. Toxic exudate from the hard coral *Goniopora tenuidens*. *Toxicon* 28: 1347-50.

Gutierrez, S., and J. Sprung. 1992. Still more on lighting. *Freshwater and Marine Aquarium* 15: 136-212.

Guzman, H.M., et al. 1990. Coral mortality associated with dinoflagellate blooms in the eastern Pacific (Costa Rica and Panama) *Mar. Ecol. Prog. Ser.* 66: 299-303.

Guzman, H.M., and D.R. Robertson. 1989. Population and feeding responses of the corallivorous pufferfish *Arothron meleagris* to coral mortality in the eastern Pacific. *Mar. Ecol. Prog. Ser.* 55: 121-31.

Habicht, G.S., and G. Beck. 1996. Evidence for invertebrate inflammatory cytokines. In: *Advances in Comparative and Environmental Physiology, Vol. 24: Invertebrate Immune Responses: Cell Activities and the Environment* (E.L. Cooper, ed.). Springer-Verlag Berlin Heidelberg: 29-47.

Hadfield, M.G. 1976. Animal associates on coral reefs: introductory remarks. *Micronesica* 12: 67-8.

Hadfield, M.G. 1976. Molluscs associated with living tropical corals. *Micronesica* 12: 133-48.

Halldal, P. 1968. Photosynthetic capacities and photosynthetic action spectra of endozoic algae of the massive coral *Favia*. *Biol. Bull.*.134: 411-24.

Hall, V.R. 1997. Interspecific differences in the regeneration of artificial injuries on scleractinian corals. *J. Exp.Mar. Biol. Ecol.* 212: 9-23.

Hallock, P. 1997. Reef and reef limestones in earth history. In: *Life and Death of Coral Reefs* (C. Birkeland, ed.). Chapman & Hall, New York: 43-67.

Hamner, W.M., and D.F. Dunn. 1980. Tropical Corallimorpharia (Coelenterata: Anthozoa): Feeding by envelopment. *Micronesica* 16: 37-41.

Hamner, W.M., et al. 1988. Zooplankton, planktivorous fish, and water currents on a windward reef face: Great Barrier Reef, Australia. *Bull. Mar. Sci.* 42: 459-79.

Hand, C. 1966. On the evolution of the Actiniaria. *Proc. Symp. Zool. Soc. Lond.* 16: 135-46.

Haramaty, L., Y. Achituv, and Z. Dubinsky. 1997. Morphology, photoadaptation and autotrophy in hermatypic corals. *Proc. 8th Int. Coral Reef Symp.* 1: 855-60.

Harriott, V.J. 1985. Mortality rates of scleractinian corals before and during a mass bleaching event. *Mar. Ecol. Prog. Ser.* 21: 81-8.

Harriott, V.J. 1988. Coral transplantation as a reef management option. *Proc. 6th Int. Coral Reef Symp.* 2: 375-9.

Harriott, V.J. 1998. Growth of the staghorn coral *Acropora formosa* at Houtman Abrolhos, Western Australia. *Mar. Biol.* 132: 319-25.

Harrison, P.L. 1988. Psuedo-gynodioecy: an unusal breeding system in the scleractinian coral *Galaxea fascicularis. Proc. 6th Int. Coral Reef Symp.* 2: 699-704.

Harrison, P.L., and C.C. Wallace. 1990. Reproduction, dispersal, and recruitment of scleractinian corals. In: *Coral Reefs: Ecosystems of the World, Vol. 25* (Z. Dubinsky, ed.). Elsevier Scientific Publishing Co. Inc. New York: 133-208.

Harriss, R.C. 1964. *The transfer of strontium, iron, and magnesium from sea water to skeletal carbonate material.* Geology Thesis: Rice University. 43 pp.

Harriss, R.C., and C.C. Almy, Jr. 1964. A preliminary investigation into the incorporation and distribution of the minor elements in the skeletal material of scleractinian corals. *Bull. Mar. Sci.* 14: 418-23.

Hart, S.R., A.L. Cohen, and P. Ramsay. 1997. Microscale analysis of Sr/Ca and Ba/Ca in *Porites. Proc. 8th Int. Coral Reef Symp.* 2: 1701-12.

Harvell, C.D., et al. 1993. Local and geographic variation in the defensive chemistry of a West Indian gorgonian coral (*Briareum asbestinum*). *Mar. Ecol. Prog. Ser.* 93: 165-73.

Harvell, C.D., et al. 1999. Emerging marine diseases—climate links and anthropogenic factors. *Science* 285:1505-1510.

Harvey, H.W., ed. 1955. *The Chemistry and Fertility of Sea Waters.* University Press, Cambridge: pp. 131-52.

Hatcher, B.G. 1997. Organic production and decomposition. In: *Life and Death of Coral Reefs* (C. Birkeland, ed.). Chapman & Hall, New York: 140-74.

Hawkins, J.P., and C.M. Roberts. 1993. Effects of recreational scuba diving on coral reef: trampling on reef-flat communities. *J. Appl. Ecol.* 30: 25-30.

Hay, M.E. 1999. Basic processes structuring coral reefs: do we know what to monitor or why? Plenary talk: NCRI International Conference on Scientific Aspects of Coral Reef Assessment, Monitoring, and Restoration. April 14-16, 1999. Fort Lauderdale, FL: 41.

Hayes, R.L., and P.G. Bush. 1990. Microscopic observations of recovery in the reef-building scleractinian coral, *Montastrea annularis*, after bleaching on a Cayman reef. *Coral Reefs* 8: 203-9.

Hayes, R.L., and N.I. Goreau. 1977. Cytodynamics of coral calcification. *Proc. 3rd Int. Coral Reef Symp.* 433-45.

Hayes, R.L., and T.J. Goreau. 1992. Histology of Caribbean and South Pacific bleached corals. *Proc. 7th Int. Coral Reef Symp.* 1: 71.

Haywick, D.W., and E.M. Mueller. 1997. Sediment retention in encrusting *Palythoa* spp.—a biological twist to a geological process. *Coral Reefs* 16: 39-46.

Heidelberg, K.B., K.B. Sebens, and J.E. Purcell. 1997. Effects of prey escape behavior and water flow on prey capture by the scleractinian coral, *Meandrina meandrites. Proc. 8th Int. Coral Reef Symp.* 2: 1081-6.

Helmuth, B., and K. Sebens. 1993. The influence of colony morphology and orientation to flow on particle capture by the scleractinian coral *Agaricia agaricites* (Linnaeus). *J. Exp. Mar. Biol. Ecol.* 165: 251-78.

Helmuth, B.S.T., E.F. Stockwell, and D.R. Brumbaugh. 1997. Morphological and environmental determinants of mass flux to corals. *Proc. 8th Int. Coral Reef Symp.* 2: 1103-8.

Helmuth, B.S.T., B.E.H. Timmerman, and K.P. Sebens. 1997. Interplay of host morphology and symbiont microhabitat in coral aggregations. *Mar. Biol.* 130: 1-10.

Hendler, G., et al. 1995. *Sea Stars, Sea Urchins, and Allies.* Smithsonian Institution Press, Washington, D.C. 390 pp.

Hendricks, N. 1997-8. Personal communications. Manager, Guam Mariculture facility.

Herndon, T. 1997-9. Personal communications.

Hertwig, R. 1882. *Die Actinien der Challenger Expedition.* Jena Verlag Gustav Fischer.

Heyward, A.J., and J.A. Stoddart. 1985. Genetic structure of two species of *Montipora* on a patch reef: conflicitng results from electrophoresis and histocompatibility. *Mar. Biol.* 85: 117-21.

Hickson, S.J. 1924. *An Introduction to the Study of Recent Corals.* Manchester: At The University Press, London. 257 pp.

Hidaka, M. 1985. Tissue compatibility between colonies and between newly settled larvae of *Pocillopora damicornis. Coral Reefs* 4: 111-16.

Hidaka, M. 1985. Nematocyst discharge, histoincompatability, and the formation of sweeper tentacles in the coral *Galaxea fascicularis. Biol. Bull.* 168: 350-8.

Hidaka, M. 1988. Surface structure of skeletons of the coral *Galaxea fascicularis* formed under different light conditions. *Proc. 6th Int. Coral Reef Symp.* 3: 95-9.

Hidaka, M. 1991. Deposition of fusiform crystals without apparent diurnal rhythm at the growing edge of septa of the coral *Galaxea fascicularis*. *Coral Reefs* 10: 41-5.

Hidaka, M. 1992. Skeletal growth rate and surface structure of the coral *Galaxea fascicularis* kept in darkness for various lengths of time. *Proc. 7th Int. Coral Reef Symp.* 1: 521-5.

Hidaka, M., et al. 1997. Contact reactions between young colonies of the coral *Pocillopora damicornis*. *Coral Reefs* 16: 13-20.

Hidaka, M., A. Uechi, and K. Yamazato. 1981. Effects of certain factors on budding of isolated polyps of a scleractinian coral, *Galaxea fascicularis*. *Proc. 4th Int. Coral Reef Symp.* 2: 229-31.

Hidaka, M., and K. Yamazato. 1984. Intraspecific interactions in a scleractinian coral, *Galaxea fascicularis*: induced formation of sweeper tentacles. *Coral Reefs* 3: 77-85.

Highsmith, R.C. 1980. Passive colonization and asexual colony multiplication in the massive coral *Porites lutea* (Milne, Edwards, and Haime). *J. Exp. Mar. Biol. Ecol.* 47: 55-67.

Highsmith, R.C. 1982. Reproduction by fragmentation in corals. *Mar. Ecol. Prog. Ser.* 7: 207-26.

Highsmith, R.C., A.C. Riggs, and C.M. D.'Antonio. 1980. Survival of hurricane-generated coral fragments and a disturbance model of reef calcification/growth rates. *Oecologia* 46: 322-9.

Hinde, R.1986. Symbioses between aquatic invertebrates and algae. In: *Parasitology—Quo Vadit?* (M.J. Howell, ed.) Austr. Acad. Sci. Canberra, Australia. pp. 383-90.

Hinde, R.1987. Animals with photosynthetic symbionts. *Ann. NY Acad. Sci.* 503: 348-54.

Hinde, R. 1987. Control of translocation in some associations between invertebrates and algae. *Ann. NY Acad. Sci.* 503: 355-8.

Hinde, R. 1988. Symbiotic nutrition and nutrient limitation. *Proc. 6th Int. Coral Reef Symp.* 1: 199-204.

Hinde, R. 1988. Factors produced by symbiotic marine invertebrates which affect translocation between the symbionts. In: *Cell to Cell Signals in Plant, Animal and Microbial Symbiosis* (S. Scannerini et al., eds.). pp. 311-24.

Hinrichsen, D. 1997. Coral reefs in crisis. *BioScience* 47: 554-8.

Hixon, M.A. 1997. Effects of reef fishes on corals and algae. In: *Life and Death of Coral Reefs* (C. Birkeland, ed.). Chapman & Hall, New York: 230-48.

Hodgson, G. 1985. A new species of *Montastrea* (Cnidaria: Scleractinia) from the Philippines. *Pac. Sci.* 39(3): 283-90.

Hodgson, G. 1988. Potential gamete wastage in synchronously spawning corals due to hybrid inviability. *Proc. 6th Int. Coral Reef Symp.* 2: 707-11.

Hodgson, G. 1990. Tetracycline reduces sedimentation damage to corals. *Mar. Biol.* 104: 493-6.

Hodgson, G. 1994. Coral reef catastrophe. *Science* 266: 1930-1

Hodgson, G. 1997. Resource use: conflicts and management solutions. In: *Life and Death of Coral Reefs* (C. Birkeland, ed.). Chapman & Hall, New York: 386-410.

Hodgson, G., and M.A. Ross. 1981. Unreported scleractinian corals from the Philippines. *Proc. 4th Int. Coral Reef Symp.* 2: 171-5.

Hoegh-Guldberg, O. 1994. Population dynamics of symbiotic zooxanthellae in the coral *Pocillopora damicornis* exposed to elevated ammonium $\{(NH_4)_2SO_4\}$ concentrations. *Pac. Sci.* 48: 263-72.

Hoegh-Guldberg, O. 1999. Climate change, coral bleaching and the future of the world's coral reefs. Personal communications.

Hoegh-Guldberg, O., L.R. McCloskey, and L. Muscatine. 1987. Expulsion of zooxanthellae by symbiotic cnidarians from the Red Sea. *Coral Reefs* 5: 201-4.

Hoegh-Guldberg, O., and G.J. Smith. 1989. Influence of the population density of zooxanthellae and supply of ammonium on the biomass and metabolic characteristics of the reef corals *Seriatopora hystrix* and *Stylophora pistillata*. *Mar. Ecol. Prog. Ser.* 57: 173-86.

Hoegh-Guldberg, O., and G.J. Smith. 1989. The effect of sudden changes in temperature, light and salinity on the population density and export of zooxanthellae from the reef corals *Stylophora pistillata* (Esper) and *Seriatopora hystrix* (Dana). *J. Exp. Mar. Biol. Ecol.* 129: 279-303.

Hoegh-Guldberg, O., M. Takabayashi, and G. Moreno. 1997. The impact of long-term nutrient enrichment on coral calcification and growth. *Proc. 8th Int. Coral Reef Symp.* 1: 861-6.

Hoegh-Guldberg, O., and J. Williamson. 1999. Availability of two forms of dissolved nitrogen to the coral *Pocillopora damicornis* and its symbiotic zooxanthellae. *Mar Biol* 133: 561-70.

Hoeksema, B.W. 1983. Excavation patterns and spiculate dimensions of the boring sponge *Cliona celata* from the SW Netherlands. *Senckenbergiana marit.* 15: 55-85.

Hoeksema, B.W. 1988. Mobility of free-living fungiid corals (Scleractinia), a dispersion mechanism and survival strategy in dynamic reef habitats. *Proc. 6th Int. Coral Reef Symp.* 2: 715-19.

Hoeksema, B.W. 1989. Taxonomy, phylogeny and biogeography of mushroom corals (Scleractinia: Fungiidae). *Zool. Verh.* 24: 295 pp.

Hoeksema, B.W. 1991. Control of bleaching in mushroom coral populations (Scleractinia: Fungiidae) in the Java Sea: stress tolerance and interference by life history strategy. *Mar. Ecol. Prog. Ser.* 74: 225-37.

Hoeksema, B.W. 1993. Mushroom corals (Scleractinia: Fungiidae) of Madang Lagoon, northern Papua New Guinea: an annotated check-list with the description of *Cantharellus jebbi* spec. nov. *Zool. Med. Leiden.* 67: 1-19.

Hoeksema, B.W. and M. Borel-Best. 1984. *Cantharellus noumeae* (Gen. nov., spec. nov.), a new scleractinian coral (Fungiidae) from New Caledonia. *Zool. Med. Leiden.* 58(9): 323-28.

Hoeksema, B.W., and M. Borel-Best. 1991. New observations on scleractinian corals from Indonesia: 2. Sipunculan-associated species belonging to the genera *Heterocyathus* and *Heteropsammia*. Zool. Med. Leiden. 65: 221-45.

Holden, C. 1997. New Caribbean coral killer. *Science* 276: 1979.

Holiday, L. 1989. *Coral Reefs*. Tetra Press, Morris Plains, New Jersey. 204 pp.

Houck, J.E., and R.W. Buddemeir. 1977. The response of coral growth rate and skeletal strontium content to light intensity and water temperature. *Proc. 3rd Int. Coral Reef Symp.* 1: 425-31.

Hubbard, J.A.E.B. 1972. *Diaseris distorta*, an "acrobatic" coral. *Nature* 236: 457-8.

Hubbard, J.A.E.B. 1973. Sediment-shifting experiments: a guide to functional behavior in colonial corals. In: *Animal Colonies. Development and Function through Time* (R.S. Boardman, A.H. Cheetham, and W.A. Oliver, Jr., eds.). Dowden, Hutchinson & Ross, Inc., Stroudsberg, Pennsylvania: 31-41.

Hudson, J.H. 1981. Response of *Montastrea annularis* to environmental change in the Florida Keys. *Proc. 4th Intl. Coral Reef Symp.* 2:233-40.

Hudson, J.H., et al. 1989. Building a coral reef in Southeast Florida: Combining technology and aesthetics. *Bull. Mar. Sci.* 44: 1067-8.

Hughes, T.P. 1984. Population dynamics based on individual size rather than age: a general model with a reef coral example. *Am. Nat.* 123: 778-95.

Hughes, T.P. 1987. Skeletal density and growth form of corals. *Mar. Ecol. Prog. Ser.* 35: 259-66.

Hughes, T.P. 1994. Catastrophes, phase shifts, and large-scale degradation of a Caribbean coral reef. *Science* 265: 1547-54.

Hughes, T.P., and J.H. Connell. 1987. Population dynamics based on size or age? A reef-coral analysis. *Am. Nat.* 129: 818-29.

Hughes, T.P., and J.B.C. Jackson. 1980. Do corals lie about their age? Some demographic consequences of partial mortality, fission, and fusion. *Science* 209: 713-15.

Hughes, T.P., and J.B.C. Jackson. 1985. Population dynamics and life histories of foliaceous corals. *Ecol. Monogr.* 55: 141-56.

Humann, P. 1992. *Reef Creature Identification*. New World Publications, Inc., Jacksonville, Florida. 240 pp.

Humann, P. 1993. *Reef Coral Identification*. New World Publications, Inc., Jacksonville, Florida. 239 pp.

Hunter, C.L. 1988. Environmental cues controlling spawning in two Hawaiian corals, *Montipora verrucosa* and *M. dilitata*. *Proc. 6th Int. Coral Reef Symp.* 2: 727-31.

Hutchings, P. 1986. Bioerosion of coral reefs. *Oceanus* 29: 71.

Hutchings, P.A. 1986. Biological destruction of coral reefs. *Coral Reefs* 4: 239-52.

Hutchings, P. 1995. Cryptofaunal communities of coral reefs. In: *Perspectives on Coral Reefs* (D.J. Barnes, ed.) AIMS, Brian Clouston Publisher: 200-9.

Hutchings, P., and M. Peyrot-Clausade. 1988. Macro-infaunal boring communities of *Porites*: a biological comparison. *Proc. 6th Int. Coral Reef Symp.* 3: 263-8.

Iglesias-Prieto, R. 1997. Temperature-dependent inactivation of Photosystem II in symbiotic dinoflagellates. *Proc. 8th Int. Coral Reef Symp.* 2: 1313-18.

Iglesias-Prieto, R., et al. 1992. Photosynthetic response to elevated temperature in the symbiotic dinoflagellate *Symbiodinium microadriaticum* in culture. *Proc. Natl. Acad. Sci. USA* 89: 10302-10305.

Iglesias-Prieto, R., and R.K. Trench. 1994. Acclimation and adaptation to irradiance in symbiotic dinoflagellates. I. Responses of the photosynthetic unit to changes in photon flux density. *Mar. Ecol. Prog. Ser.* 113: 163-75.

Iglesias-Prieto, R., and R.K. Trench. 1997. Acclimation and adaptation to irradiance in symbiotic dinoflagellates. II. Response of chlorophyll-protein complexes to different photon-flux densities. *Mar. Biol.* 130: 23-33.

Iglesias-Prieto, R., and R.K. Trench. 1997. Photoadaptation, photoacclimation and niche diversification in invertebrate-dinoflagellate symbioses. *Proc. 8th Int. Coral Reef Symp.* 2: 1319-24.

Ikeda, Y., T. Maruyama, and S. Miyachi. 1992. Decalcification by a solitary coral, *Fungia* sp., in the medium with calcium ion concentration lower than aragonite saturation. *Proc. 7th Int. Coral Reef Symp.* 2: 1157-60.

International Coral Reef Initiative. 1996. *State of the Reefs Report*. Downloaded from America Online, Fish and Marine Life Forum, Marine and Reef Library.

Ip, Y.K., and P. Krishnaveni. 1991. Incorporation of strontium ($^{90}Sr^{2+}$) into the skeleton of the hermatypic coral *Galaxea fascicularis*. *J. Exp. Zool.* 258: 273-6.

Ireland, C.M., et al. 1987. Natural product peptides from marine organisms. In: *Bioorganic Marine Chemistry, Vol. 3* (P.J Scheuer, ed.). Springer Verlag, Berlin: 33-6.

Isdale, P. 1977. Variation in growth rate of hermatypic corals in a uniform environment. *Proc. 3rd Int. Coral Reef Symp.* 2: pp.403-8.

Isdale, P.J. 1986. Coral rings give clues to past climate. *Oceanus*: p. 29: 31.

Jaap, W.C., and J. Wheaton. 1975. Observations on Florida reef corals treated with fish-collecting chemicals. *Fl. Mar. Res. Publ.* 10: 17 pp.

Jackson, J.B.C. 1991. Adaptation and diversity of reef corals. *BioScience* 41: 475-82.

Jackson, J.B.C., and L. Buss. 1975. Allelopathy and spatial competition among coral reef invertebrates. *Proc. Nat. Acad. Sci.* 72: 5160-3.

Jamieson, G.S. 1993. Marine invertebrate conservation: evaluation of fisheries over-exploitation concerns. *Amer. Zool.* 33: 551-67.

Jaubert, J., 1989. An integrated nitrifying-denitrifying biological system capable of purifying sea water in a closed circuit aquarium. Second International Aquariology Congress (1988), Monaco. *Bulletin de l'Institute Oceanographique, Monaco*. Special #5, 101-106.

Jaubert, J., et al. 1992. Productivity and calcification in a coral reef mesocosm. *Proc. 7th Int. Coral Reef Symp.* 1: 363.

Jeffrey, S.W., and F.T. Haxo. 1968. Photosynthetic pigments of symbiotic dinoflagellates (zooxanthellae) from corals and clams. *Biol. Bull.* 135: 149-65.

Jeffrey, S.W., M. Sielicki, and F.T. Haxo. 1975. Chloroplast pigment patterns in dinoflagellates. *J. Phycol.* 11: 374-84.

Jensen, P.R., et al. 1996. Antimicrobial activity of extracts of Caribbean gorgonian corals. *Mar. Biol.* 125: 411-19.

Jeyasuria, P., and J.C. Lewis. 1987. Mechanical properties of the axial skeleton in gorgonians. *Coral Reefs* 5: 213-19.

Jindal, A., et al. 1995. Bacterial ecology of selected corals following the 1994 South Central Pacific bleaching event. 27th Meeting Assoc. Mar. Labs. Carib.

Johannes, R.E., S.L. Coles, and N.T. Kwenzel. 1970. The role of zooplankton in the nutrition of some scleractinian corals. *Limnol. Oceanogr.* 15: :579-86.

Johannes, R.E., et al. 1972. The metabolism of some coral reef communities: a team study of nutrient and energy flux at Eniwetok. *BioScience* 22: 541-3.

Johansen, J.E., W.A. Svec, and S. Liaaen-Jensen. 1974. Carotenoids of the dinophycae. *Phytochemistry* 13: 2261-71.

Johansson, M.W., and K. Soderhall. 1996. The prophenoloxidase activating system and associated proteins in invertebrates. In: *Progress in Molecular and Subcellular Biology: Invertebrate Immunology* (B. Rinkevich and W.E.G. Muller, eds.). Springer-Verlag Berlin Heidelberg: 46-65.

Johnson, A.S., and K.P. Sebens. 1993. Consequences of a flattened morphology: effects of flow on feeding rates of the scleractinian coral *Meandrina meandrtites*. *Mar. Ecol. Prog. Ser.* 99: 99-114.

Johnson, C.R., et al. 1997. Bacterial induction of settlement and metamorphosis in marine invertebrates. *Proc. 8th Int. Coral Reef Symp.* 2: 1219-24.

Johnson, K.G. 1988. Size, meander pattern, and behavior in the Caribbean free-living meandroid coral *Manicina areolata* (Linnaeus). *Proc. 6th Int. Coral Reef Symp.* 3: 403-7.

Johnson, M.S., and R.L. Cumming. 1995. Genetic distinctness of three widespread and morphologically variable species of *Drupella* (Gastropoda, Muricidae). *Coral Reefs* 14:71-8.

Johnston, I.S. 1977. Aspects of the structure of a skeletal organic matrix, and the process of skeletogenesis in the reef coral, *Pocillopora damicornis*. *Proc. 3rd Int. Coral Reef Symp.* 1: 447-53.

Jokiel, P.L. 1978. Effects of water motion on reef corals. *J. Exp. Mar. Biol. Ecol.* 35: 87-97.

Jokiel, P.L. 1980. Solar ultraviolet radiation and coral reef epifauna. *Science* 207: 1069-71.

Jokiel, P.L. 1985. Lunar periodicity of planula release in the reef coral *Pocillopora damicornis* in relation to various environmental factors. *Proc. 5th Int. Coral Reef Symp.* 2: 196.

Jokiel, P.L. 1988. Is photoadaptation a critical process in the development, function and maintenance of reef communities? *Proc. 6th Int. Coral Reef Symp.* 1: 187-92.

Jokiel, P.L., and R.H. York, Jr. 1982. Solar ultraviolet photobiology of the reef coral *Pocillopora damicornis* and symbiotic zooxanthellae. *Bull. Mar. Sci.* 32: 301-15.

Jokiel, P.L., and R.H. York. 1984. Importance of ultraviolet radiation in photoinhibition of microalgal growth. *Limnol. Oceanogr.* 29: 192-9.

Jones, R.J., and O. Hoegh-Guldberg. 1999. Effects of cyanide on coral photosynthesis: implications for identifying the cause of coral bleaching and for assessing the environmental effects of cyanide fishing. *Mar. Ecol. Prog. Ser.* 177: 83-91.

Joshi, S., and D. Morgan. 1998. Spectral analysis of metal halide lamps used in the reef aquarium hobby. Part 1: new 400-watt lamps. November. *Aquarium Frontiers Online.*

Joshi, S., and D. Morgan. 1999a. Spectral analysis of metal halide lamps used in the reef aquarium hobby. Part 2: used 400-watt lamps. January. *Aquarium Frontiers Online.*

Joshi, S., and D. Morgan. 1999b. Spectral analysis of metal halide lamps used in the reef aquarium hobby. Part 3: 250-watt metal halide lamps. January. *Aquarium Frontiers Online.*

Juilllet-LeClerc, A., et al. 1997. Seasonal variation of primary productivity and skeletal ∂^{13}C and ∂^{18}O in the zooxanthellate coral *Acropora formosa*. *Mar. Ecol. Prog. Ser.* 137: 109-17.

Kaplan, E.H. 1982. *A Field Guide to Coral Reefs of the Caribbean and Florida.* Houghton Mifflin Company, Boston, Massachusetts.

Karlson, R.H. 1980. Alternative competitive strategies in a periodically disturbed habitat. *Bull. Mar. Sci.* 30: 894-900.

Karlson, R.H. 1981. Reproductive patterns in *Zoanthus* spp. from Discovery Bay, Jamaica. *Proc. 4th Int. Coral Reef Symp.* 2: 700-4.

Karlson, R.H., and H.V. Cornell. 1999. Integration of local and regional perspectives on the species richness of coral assemblages. *Amer. Zool.* 39: 104-112.

Kawaguti, S. 1969. Effect of the green fluorescent pigment on the productivity of the reef corals. *Micronesica* 5: 313.

Kawaguti, S. 1985. Skeletal pigments of a scleractinian coral *Oulastrea crispata*.

Kawaguti, S. 1966. Electron microscopy on the fluorescent green of reef corals with a note on mucous cells. *Biol. J. Okayama Univ.* 12: 11-21.

Kayanne, H., et al. 1995. Diurnal changes in the partial pressure of carbon dioxide in coral reef water. *Science* 269: 214-17.

Kelman, D., et al. 1998. Antimicrobial activity of a Red Sea soft coral, *Paraerythrpodium fulvum fulvum*: reproductive and developmental considerations. *Mar. Ecol. Prog. Ser.* 169: 87-95.

Kelman, D., Y. Benayahu, and Y. Kashman. 1999. Chemical defence of the soft coral *Paraerthyropodium fulvum fulvum* (Forskal) in the Red Sea against generalist reef fish. *J. Exp. Mar. Biol. Ecol.* 238: 127-37.

Keough, M.J., and P.T. Raimondi. 1995. Responses of settling invertebrate larvae to bioorganic films: effects of different types of films. *J. Exp. Mar. Biol. Ecol.* 185: 235-53.

Kerr, J.Q. 1992. Animal-plant association defense: the soft coral *Sinularia* sp. protects algae from herbivory. *Proc. 7th Int. Coral Reef Symp.* 2: 876.

Kim, K. 1994. Antimicrobial activity in gorgonian corals (Coelenterata, Octocorallia). *Coral Reefs* 13: 75-80.

Kim, K., and H.R. Lasker. 1997. Flow mediated resource competition in the suspension feeding gorgonian *Plexaura homomalla* (Esper). *J. Exp. Mar. Biol. Ecol.* 215: 49-64.

Kingsley, R.J., and N. Watabe. 1987. Role of carbonic anhydrase in calcification in the gorgonian *Leptogorgia virgulata*. *J. Exp. Zool.* 241: 171-80.

Kinne, O. 1980. *Diseases of Marine Animals. Vol. 1: General Aspects, Protozoa to Gastropoda.* John Wiley and Sons: pp. 167-239.

Kinsey, D.W. 1978. Alkalinity change and coral reef calcification. *Limnol. Oceanogr.* 23: 989-91.

Kinsey, D.W. 1991. Can we resolve the nutrient issue for the reef? *Search* 22: 119-21.

Kinsey, D.W. 1991. The coral reef: an owner-built, high-density, fully-serviced, self-sufficient housing estate in the desert—or is it? *Symbiosis* 10: 1-22.

Kinsey, D.W., and P.J. Davies. 1979. Effects of elevated nitrogen and phosphorous on coral reef growth. *Limnol. Oceanogr.* 24: 935-40.

Kinsman, D.J.J. 1964. Reef coral tolerance of high temperatures and salinities. *Nature* 202: 1280-2.

Kinzie, R.A. 1993. Effects of ambient levels of solar ultraviolet radiation on zooxanthellae and photosynthesis of the reef coral *Montipora verrucosa*. *Mar. Biol.* 116: 319-27.

Kinzie, R.A., III. 1999. Sex, symbiosis, and coral reef communities. *Amer. Zool.* 39: 80-91.

Kinzie, R.A., and T. Hunter. 1987. Effect of light quality on photosynthesis of the reef coral *Montipora verrucosa*. *Mar. Biol.* 94: 95-109.

Kinzie, R.A., P.L. Jokiel, and R. York. 1984. Effects of light of altered spectral composition on coral zooxanthellae associations and on zooxanthellae in vitro. *Mar. Biol.* 78: 239-48.

Kinzie, R.A., and T. Sarmiento. 1986. Linear extension rate is independent of colony size in the coral *Pocillopora damicornis*. *Coral Reefs* 4: 177-81.

Kitano, Y., N. Kanamori, and T. Oomori. 1971. Measurements of distribution coefficients of strontium and barium between carbonate precipitate and solution—abnormally high values of distribution coefficients measured at early stages of carbonate formation. *Geochem. J.* 4: 183-206.

Kittredge, J.S., et al. 1974. Chemical signals in the sea: Marine allelochemicals and evolution. *Fishery Bulletin* 72(1): 1-11.

Kleppel, G.S., R.E. Dodge, and C.J. Reese. 1989. Changes in pigmentaton associated with the bleaching of stony corals. *Limnol. Oceanogr.* 34: 1331-5.

Kleypas, J.A., J.W. McManus, and L.A.B. Menez. 1999. Environmental limits to coral reef development: where do we draw the line? *Amer. Zool.* 39: 146-59.

Knauer, G.A., and J.H. Martin. 1981. Introduction. In: *Trace Metals in Sea Water* (Boyle, C.S., et al., eds.) Plenum Press, Oxford.

Knop, D. 1997. Artificial propagation of corals—the soft corals. *Aquarium Frontiers*, October issue. http://www.aquariumfrontiers.com/archives.

Knop, D. 1998. Artificial propagation of corals—the stony corals. *Aquarium Frontiers*, February issue. http://www.aquariumfrontiers.com/archives.

Knowlton, M., et al. 1992. Sibling species in *Montastrea annularis*, coral bleaching, and the coral climate record. *Science* 255: 330-3.

Knowlton, N. 1999. Who are the players on coral reefs and does it matter? Plenary address, NCRI International Conference on Scientific Aspects of Coral Reef Assessment, Monitoring, and Restoration. April 14-16, 1999. Fort Lauderdale, FL: 42.

Koehl, M.A.R. 1977. Water flow and the morphology of zoanthid colonies. *Proc. 3rd Int. Coral Reef Symp.* 1: 437-44.

Koh, E.G.L. 1997a. Do scleractinian corals engage in chemical warfare against microbes? *J. Chem. Ecol.* 23: 379-98.

Koh, E.G.L. 1997b. Secretion of bioactive compounds by a scleractinian coral. *Proc. 8th Int. Coral Reef Symp.* 2: 1263-6.

Kojis, B.L., and N.J. Quinn. 1984. Seasonal and depth variation in fecundity of *Acropora palifera* at two reefs in Papua New Guinea. *Coral Reefs* 3: 165-72.

Koop, K., and A.W.D. Larkum. 1987. Deposition of organic material in a coral reef lagoon, One Tree Island, Great Barrier Reef. *Est. Coast Shelf Sci.* 25: 1-9.

Korrubel, J.L., and B. Riegl. 1998. A new coral disease from the southern Arabian Gulf. *Coral Reefs* 17: 22.

Korrubel, J.L., and B. Riegl. 1999. Yellow-blotch disease outbreak on reefs of the San Blas Islands, Panama. *Coral Reefs* 18: 97.

Kramarsky-Winter, E., M. Fine, and Y. Loya. 1997. Coral polyp expulsion. *Nature* 387: 137.

Kruger, A., M.H. Schleyer, and Y. Benayahu. 1998. Reproduction *in Anthelia glauca* (Octocorallia: Xeniidae). I. Gametogenesis and larval brooding. *Mar. Biol.* 131: 423-32.

Krupp, D.A. 1983. Sexual reproduction and early development of the solitary coral *Fungia scutaria* (Anthozoa: Scleractinia). *Coral Reefs* 2: 159-64.

Krupp, D.A. 1984. Mucus production by corals exposed during and extreme low tide. *Pac. Sci.* 38: 1-11.

Krupp, D.A. 1985. An immunochemical study of the mucus from the solitary coral *Fungia scutaria* (Scleractinia, Fungiidae). *Bull. Mar. Sci.* 36: 163-76.

Kuhlmann, D.H.H.; translated from German by Sylvia Furness. 1985. *Living Coral Reefs of the World*. Arco Publishing Inc., New York. 185 pp.

Kuhlmann, D.H.H. 1988. The sensitivity of coral reefs to environmental pollution. *Ambio* 17: 13-21.

Kurosawa, Y., and K. Hashimoto. 1996. The immunoglobulin superfamily: where do invertebrates fit in? In: *Advances in Comparative and Environmental Physiology, Vol. 23: Invertebrate Immune Responses: Cells and Molecular Products* (E.L. Cooper, ed.). Springer-Verlag Berlin Heidelberg: 151-84.

Kushmaro, A., et al. 1997. Bleaching of the coral *Oculina patagonica* by *Vibrio* AK-1. *Mar. Ecol. Prog. Ser.* 147: 159-65.

Kushmaro, A., et al. 1998. Effect of temperature on bleaching of the coral *Oculina patagonica* by *Vibrio* AK-1. *Mar. Ecol. Prog. Ser.* 171: 131-7.

Kushmaro, A., Y. Loya, and M. Rosenberg. 1996. Bacterial infection causes bleaching of the coral *Oculina patagonica*. *Nature* 380:396.

Kuto, K.G., and L.L. Richardson. 1997. Black band disease and the fate of the diseased coral colonies in the Florida Keys. *Proc. 8th Int. Coral Reef Symp.* 1: 575-8.

LaBarbera, M. 1984. Feeding currents and particle capture mechanisms in suspension feeding animals. *Amer. Zool.* 24: 71-84.

LaBarre, D., and J.C. Coll. 1982. Movement in soft corals: an interaction between *Nephthea brassica* (Coelenterata: Octocorallia) and *Acropora hyacinthus* (Coelenterata: Scleractinia). *Mar. Biol.* 72: 119-24.

LaBarre. S.C., J.C. Coll, and P.W. Sammarco. 1986a. Defensive strategies of soft corals (Coelenterata: Octocorallia) of the Great Barrier Reef. II. The relationship between toxicity and feeding deterrence. *Biol. Bull.* 171: 565-76.

LaBarre, S.C., J.C. Coll, and P.W. Sammarco. 1986b. Competitive strategies of soft corals (Coelenterata: Octocorallia): III. Spacing and aggressive interactions between alcyonareans. *Mar. Ecol. Prog. Ser.* 28: 147-58.

Lagziel, A., J. Erez, B. Lazar, and Z. Dubinsky. 1992. Contribution of zooplankton feeding to the symbiotic association of two hermatypic corals. *Proc. 7th Int. Coral Reef Symp.* 1: 381.

Lamberts, A.E. 1982. The reef coral *Astreopora* (Anthozoa, Scleractinia, Astrocoeniidae): a revision of the taxonomy and description of a new species. *Pac. Sci.* 36: 83-105.

Lamberts, A.E. 1984. The reef corals *Lithactinia* and *Polyphyllia* (Anthozoa, Scleractinia, Fungiidae): a study of morphological, geographical, and statistical differences. *Pac. Sci.* 38: 12-27.

Lang, J., 1971. Interspecific aggression by scleractinian corals. 1. The rediscovery of *Scolymia cubensis* (Milne, Edwards, and Haime). *Bull. Mar. Sci.* 21: 952-9.

Lang, J. 1973. Interspecific aggression by scleractinian corals. 2. Why the race is not only to the swift. *Bull. Mar. Sci.* 23: 260-79.

Lang, J.C., et al. 1992. Spatial and temporal variability during periods of "recovery" after mass bleaching on Western Atlantic coral reefs. *Amer. Zool.* 32: 696-706.

Lang, J.C., and E.A. Chornesky. 1990. Competition between scleractinian reef corals—a review of mechanisms and effects. In: *Coral Reefs: Ecosystems of the World, Vol. 25* (Z. Dubinsky, ed.). Elsevier Scientific Publishing Co. Inc. New York: 209-52.

Lang, J.C., R.I. Wicklund, and R.F. Dill. 1988. Depth- and habitat-related bleaching of zooxanthellate organisms at Lee Stocking Island, Exuma Cays, Bahamas. *Proc. 6th Int. Coral Reef Symp.* 3: 269-73.

Lankester, E.R., ed. 1900. *A Treatise on Zoology: The Anthozoa*. Adam & Charles Black, London: 1-84.

Lankester, E.R., ed. 1900. *A Treatise on Zoology. Part II. The Porifera and Coelenterata*. Adam & Charles Black, London: 1-80.

LaPointe, B.E. 1989. Caribbean coral reefs: are they becoming algal reefs? *Sea Frontiers* 39: 82-91.

Lasker, H.R. 1976. Intraspecific variability of zooplankton feeding in the hermatypic coral *Montastrea cavernosa*. In: *Coelenterate Ecology and Behavior* (G.O. Mackie, ed.). University of Victoria, British Columbia: pp. 101-110.

Lasker, H.R. 1977. Patterns of zooxanthellae distribution and polyp expansion in the reef coral *Montastrea cavernosa*. *Proc. 3rd Int. Coral Reef Symp.* 1: 607-13.

Lasker, H.R. 1980. Sediment rejection by reef corals: the roles of behavior and morphology in *Montastrea cavernosa* (Linnaeus). *J. Exp. Mar. Biol. Ecol.* 47: 77-87.

Lasker, H.R. 1981. Phenotypic variation in the coral *Montastrea cavernosa* and its effects on colony energetics. *Biol. Bull.* 160: 292-302.

Lasker, H.R. 1981. A comparison of the particulate feeding abilities of three species of gorgonian soft coral. *Mar. Ecol. Prog. Ser.* 5: 61-7.

Lasker, H.R. 1983. Vegetative reproduction in the octocoral *Briareum asbestinum* (Pallas). *J. Exp. Mar. Biol. Ecol.* 72: 157-69.

Lasker, H.R. 1988. The incidence and rate of vegatative propagation among coral reef alcyonareans. *Proc. 6th Int. Coral Reef Symp.* 2: 763-7.

Lasker, H.R., and M.A. Coffroth. 1999. Responses of coral reef taxa to environmental change. *Amer. Zool.* 39: 92-103.

Lasker, H.R., M.D. Gottfried, and M.A. Coffroth. 1983. Effects of depth on the feeding capabilities of two octocorals. *Mar. Biol.* 73: 73-8.

Lasker, H.R., K. Kim, and M. A. Coffroth. 1998. Production, settlement, and survival of plexaurid gorgonian recruits. *Mar. Ecol. Prog. Ser.* 162: 111-23.

Lasker, H.R., K. Kim, and M.A. Coffroth. 1996. Reproductive and genetic variation among Caribbean gorgonians: the differentiation of *Plexaura kuna*, a new species. *Bull. Mar. Sci.* 58: 277-88.

Lasker, H.R., E.C. Peters, and M.A. Coffroth. 1984. Beaching of reef coelenterates in the San Blas Islands, Panama. *Coral Reefs* 3: 183-90.

Le Campion-Alsumard, T., S. Golubic, and K. Preiss. 1995. Fungi in corals: Symbiosis or disease? Interaction between polyps and fungi causes pearl-like skeleton biomineralization. *Mar. Ecol. Prog. Ser.* 117:137-147.

Leclerc, M. 1996. Humoral factors in marine invertebrates. In: *Progress in Molecular and Subcellular Biology: Invertebrate Immunology* (B. Rinkevich and W.E.G. Muller, eds.). Springer-Verlag Berlin Heidelberg: 1-9.

Leletkin, V.A., and V.I. Zvalinsky. 1981. Photosynthesis of coral zooxanthellae from different depths. *Proc. 4th Int. Coral Reef Symp.* 2: 33-7.

Lesser, M.P. 1997. Oxidative stress causes coral bleaching during exposure to elevated temperatures. *Coral Reefs* 16:187-92.

Lesser, M.P., W.R. Stochaj, D.W. Tapley, and J.M. Shick. 1995. Bleaching in coral reef anthozoans: effects of irradiance, ultraviolet radiation, and temperature on the activities of protective enzymes against active oxygen. *Coral Reefs* 8: 225-32.

Lesser, M.P., V. Weis, M. Patterson, and P. Jokiel. 1992. The effects of water flow on carbon delivery and productivity in *Pocillopora damicornis* from Hawaii. *Proc. 7th Int. Coral Reef Symp.* 1: 363-4.

Lesser, M.P., and J.M. Shick. 1989. Effects of irradiance and ultraviolet radiation on photoadaptation in the zooxanthellae of *Aiptasia pallida*: primary production, photoinhibition, and enzymatic defenses against oxygen toxicity. *Mar. Biol.* 102: 243-55.

Lesser, M.P., and J.M. Shick. 1990. Effects of visible and ultraviolet radiation on the ultrastructure of zooxanthellae (*Symbiodinium* sp.) in culture and in situ. *Cell Tiss. Res.* 261: 501-8.

Lesser, M.P., V.M. Weis, M.B. Patteson, and P.L. Jokiel. 1994. Effects of morphology and water motion on carbon delivery and productivity in the reef coral, *Pocillopora damicornis* (Linnaeus): diffusion barriers, inorganic carbon limitation, and biochemical plasticity. *J. Exp. Mar. Biol. Ecol.* 178: 153-79.

Lessios, H.A., P.W. Glynn, and D.R. Robertson. 1983. Mass mortalities of coral reef organisms. *Science* 222: 715.

Le Tissier, M. 1999. Personal communications.

Leversee, G.J. 1976. Flow and feeding in fan-shaped colonies of the gorgonian coral, *Leptogorgia*. *Biol. Bull.* 151: 344-56.

Lewis, D.H., and D.C. Smith. 1971. The autotrophic nutrition of symbiotic marine coelenterates with special reference to hermatypic corals. I. Movement of photosynthetic products between the symbionts. *Proc. Roy. Soc. Lond. B* 178: 111-29.

Lewis, J.B. 1974. The importance of light and food upon the early growth of the reef coral *Favia fragum* (Esper). *J. Exp. Mar. Biol. Ecol.* 15: 299-304.

Lewis, J.B. 1976. Experimental tests of suspension feeding in Atlantic reef corals. *Mar. Biol.* 36: 147-50.

Lewis, J.B. 1977. Suspension feeding in Atlantic Reef Corals and the importance of suspended particulate matter as a food source. *Proc. 3rd Int. Coral Reef Symp.* 1: 405-408.

Lewis, J.B. 1981. Coral reef ecosystems. In: *Analysis of Marine Ecosystems* (A.R. Longhurst, ed.). Academic Press, New York: pp. 127-58.

Lewis, J.B. 1982. Feeding behavior and feeling ecology of the Octocorallia (Coelenterata: Anthozoa) *J. Zool. Lond.* 196: 371-84.

Lewis, J.B. 1989. Spherical growth in the Caribbean coral *Siderastrea radians* (Pallas) and its survivial in disturbed habitats. *Coral Reefs* 7: 161-7.

Lewis, J.B. 1989. The ecology of *Millepora*: a review. *Coral Reefs* 8: 99-107.

Lewis, J.B., and R.E. Crooks. 1996. Foraging cycles of the amphinomid polychaete *Hermodice carunculata* preying on the calcareous hydrozoan *Millepora complanata*. *Bull. Mar. Sci.* 58: 853-6.

Lewis, J.B., and W.S. Price. 1976. Feeding mechanisms and feeding strategies of Atlantic reef corals. *J. Zool. Lond.* 176: 527-44.

Lewis, J.B., and P.V.R. Snelgrove. 1990. Corallum morphology and composition of crustacean cryptofauna of the hermatypic coral *Madracis mirabilis*. *Mar. Biol.* 106: 267-72.

Liaaen-Jensen, S. 1978. Marine carotenoids. In: *Marine Natural Products: Chemical and Biological Perspectives, Vol. II* (Paul J. Scheuer, ed.). Academic Press, New York: 2-70.

Liberman, T., A. Genin, and Y. Loba. 1995. Effects on growth and reproduction of the coral *Stylophora pistillata* by the mutualistic damselfish *Dascyllus marginatus*. *Mar. Biol.* 121: 741-6.

Libes, S.M. 1992. *An Introduction to Marine Biogeochemistry*. John Wiley & Sons, Inc., New York: pp. 30-6.

Licuanan, W.Y., and G.J. Bakus. 1992. Coral spatial distributions: The ghost of competition past roused? *Proc. 7th Int. Coral Reef Symp.* 1: 545-50.

Liddle, M.J., and A.M. Kay. 1987. Resistance, survival and recovery of trampled corals on the Great Barrier Reef. *Biol. Cons.* 42; 1-18.

Lidster, Morgan. 1996-7. Facility Manager, Inland Aquatics. Personal communications.

Lindahl, U. 1998. Low tech rehabilitation of degraded coral reefs through transplantation of staghorn corals. *Ambio* 27: 645-50.

Linley, E.A.S., and K. Koop. 1986. Significance of pelagic bacteria as a trophic resource in a coral reef lagoon, One Tree Island, Great Barrier Reef. *Mar. Biol.* 92: 457-64.

Lipschultz, F. 1992. Assimilation of NH_4 by host and zooxanthellae of *Pocillopora damicornis*. *Proc. 7th Int. Coral Reef Symp.* 1: 381.

Littler, D. S., et al. 1989. *Marine Plants of the Caribbean*. Smithsonian Institute Press, Washington D.C., 263 pp.

Livingston, H.D., and G. Thompson. 1971. Trace element concentrations in some modern corals. *Limnol. Oceanogr.* 16: 78-96.

Logan, A. 1985. Intraspecific immunological reposes in five species of corals from Bermuda. *Proc. 5th Int. Coral Reef Symp.* 6: 63-8.

Logan, A., K. Halcrow, and T. Tomascik. 1990. UV excitation-fluorescence in polyp tissue of certain scleractinian corals from Barbados and Bermuda. *Bull. Mar. Sci.* 46: 807-13.

Lopez, J.V., et al. 1999. Molecular determination of species boundaries in corals: genetic analysis of the *Montastraea annularis* complex using amplified fragment length polymorphisms and a microsatellite marker. *Biol. Bull.* 196: 80-93.

Lough, J.M., and D.J. Barnes. 1992. Comparisons of skeletal density variations in *Porites* from the Central Great barrier Reef. *J. Exp. Mar. Biol. Ecol.* 155: 1-25.

Lovell, E.R., and M. Tumuri. Provisional environmental impact assesment for the extraction of coral reef products for the marine aquarium curio trade in Fiji. A Report Prepared for the Fisheries Division, Government of Fiji. 125 pp.

Lowrie, J. 1992-7. Unpublished research.

Lowrie, J. 1996-8. Personal communications.

Lowrie, J., and E.H. Borneman. 1999. Positive and negative impacts of the marine aquarium trade on coral reefs. Proceedings: NCRI International Conference on Scientific Aspects of Coral Reef Assessment, Monitoring, and Restoration. April14-16, Fort Lauderdale, FL.

Loya, Y. 1976. Recolonization of Red Sea corals affected by natural catastrophes and man-made perturbations. *Ecol.* 57: 278-89.

Loya, Y. 1976. Effects of water turbidity and sedimentation on the community structure of Puerto Rican corals. *Bull. Mar. Sci.* 26: 450-66.

Loya, Y. 1976. Settlement, mortality and recruitment of a Red Sea scleractinian population. In: *Coelenterate Ecology and Behavior* (G.O. Mackie, ed.). University of Victoria, British Columbia: pp. 89-100.

Loya, Y. 1976. Skeletal regeneration in a Red Sea scleractinian coral population. *Nature* 261: 490-1.

Loya, Y. 1976. The Red Sea coral *Stylophora pistillata* is an r-strategist. *Nature* 259: 478-80.

Loya, Y., G. Bull, and M. Pichon. 1984. Tumor formation in scleractinian corals. *Helgo wiss Meers* 37: 99-112.

Luckett, C., W.H. Adey, J. Morrissey, and D.M. Spoon. 1996. Coral reef mesocosms and microcosms—successes, problems, and the future of laboratory models. *Ecol Engineering* 6: 57-72.

Luoma, J.R. 1996. Reef madness. *Audubon* 67: 461-3.

Lyons, M.M., et al. 1998. DNA damage induced by ultraviolet radiation in coral-reef microbial communities. *Mar. Biol.* 130: 537-43.

Mackie, G.O., ed. 1976. *Coelenterate Ecology and Behavior*. Plenum Press, New York: 751 pp.

Madigan, N. Dec. 24, 1996. Key West reefs dying of mysterious disease. *The New York Times* C11.

Maguire, L.A., and J.W. Porter. 1977. A spatial model of growth and competitive strategies in coral communities. *Ecol. Monogr.* 3: 249-71.

Maida, M., P.W. Sammarco, and J.C. Coll. 1995. Effects of soft corals on scleractinian coral recruitment. I. Directional allelopathy and inhibition of settlement. *Mar. Ecol. Prog. Ser.* 121: 191-202.

Manfried, L.J., et al. 1996. Interspecific interactions and competitive ability of the polymorphic reef-building coral *Montastrea annularis*. *Bull. Mar. Sci.* 58: 792-803.

Mankin, B. 1998. Personal communications.

Marchioretti, M., and J. Jaubert. 1992. Ecophysiology of growth forms and ecotypes of the reef corals *Stylophora pistillata* (Esper, 1797). *Proc. 7th Int. Coral Reef Symp.* 2: 679.

Mariscal, R.N., and C.H. Bigger. 1977. Possible ecological significance of octocoral epithelial ultrastructure. *Proc. 3rd Int. Coral Reef Symp.* 127-33.

Mariscal, R.N. 1971. Effect of a disulfide reducing agent on the nematocyst capsules from some coelenterates, with an illustrated key to nematocyst classification. In: *Experimental Coelenterate Biology* (H.M. Lenhoff, L. Muscatine, and L.V. Davis, eds.). University of Hawaii Press, Honolulu: 157-68.

Mariscal, R.N., and H.M. Lenhoff. 1968. The chemical control of feeding behavior in *Cyphastrea ocellina* and in some other Hawaiian corals. *J. Exp. Mar. Biol. Ecol.* 49: 689-99.

Marsden, J.R. 1962. A coral-eating polychaete. *Nature* 193: 598.

Marshall, A.T. 1996. Calcification in hermatypic and ahermatypic corals. *Science* 271: 637-9.

Marshall, N. 1972. Notes on mucus and zooxanthellae discharged from coral reefs. In: *Proc. Symp. Corals Coral Reefs* (C. Mukundan and C.S. Gopinadha Pillai, eds.). Marine Biological Ass'n of India, Cochin: 59-67.

Marubini, F., and P.S. Davies. 1996. Nitrate increases zooxanthellae population denisty and reduces skeletogenesis in corals. *Mar. Biol.* 127: 319-28.

Massin, C. 1988. Boring coralliophilidae (Mollusca, Gastropoda): coral host relationship. *Proc. 6th Int. Coral Reef Symp.* 3: 177-82.

Masuda, K., et al. 1992. Photoadaptation of solitary corals, *Fungia repanda, F. echinata*, and their zooxanthellae. *Proc. 7th Int. Coral Reef Symp.* 1: 373-8.

Masuda, K., et al. 1993. Adaptation of solitary corals and their zooxanthellae to low light and UV radiation. *Mar. Biol.* 117: 685-91.

Mate T., J.L. 1992. Variations in chlorophyll concentration and zooxanthellae density with depth in Caribbean reef corals of Panama. *Proc. 7th Int. Coral Reef Symp.* 1: 382.

Mate T., J. L. 1997. Experimental responses of Panamanian reef corals to high temperature and nutrients. *Proc. 8th Int. Coral Reef Symp.* 1: 515-20.

Mather, P., and I. Bennett, eds. 1993. *A Coral Reef Handbook*. Surrey Beatty & Sons Pty Limited, Queensland, Australia. 250 pp.

Matz, M.V., et al. 1999. Fluorescent proteins from nonbioluminescent Anthozoa species. *Nat. Biotech.* 17: 969-73.

Mazel, C. 1988. Optical magic: underwater fluorescence. *Sea Frontiers* 38: 274-9.

McConnaughey, T. 1989. ^{13}C and ^{18}O isotopic disequilibrium in biological carbonates: I. Patterns. *Geochim. Cosmochim. Acta* 53: 151-62.

McConnaughey, T. 1989. ^{13}C and ^{18}O isotopic disequilibrium in biological carbonates: II. In vitro simulation of kinetic isotopic effects. *Geochim. Cosmochim. Acta* 53: 163-71.

McConnaughey, T. 1991. Calcification in *Chara corallina*: CO_2 hydroxylation generates protons for bicarbonate assimilation. *Limnol. Oceanogr.* 36: 619-28.

McConnaughey, T.A., et al. 1997. Carbon isotopes in biological carbonates: respiration and photosynthesis. *Geochim. Cosmochim. Acta* 61: 611-22.

McConnaughey, T.A., and J.F. Whelan. 1996. Calification generates protons for nutrient and bicarbonate uptake. *Earth Sci. Rev.* 967: 1-23.

McFadden, C.S. 1986. Colony fission increases particle capture rates of a soft coral: advantages of being a small colony. *J. Exp. Mar. Biol. Ecol.* 103: 1-20.

McField, M.D. 1999. Coral responses during and after mass bleaching in Belize. *Bull. Mar. Sci.* 64: 155-72.

McKenna, S.A. 1997. Interactions between the boring sponge, *Cliona lampa* and two hermatypic corals from Bermuda. *Proc. 8th Int. Coral Reef Symp.* 2: 1369-74.

McManus, J.W., and M.C.A. Ablan. 1997. Reefbase: a global database of coral reefs and their resources. *Proc. 8th Int. Coral Reef Symp.* 2: 1541-4.

Meesters, E.H., and R.P.M. Bak. 1995. Age-related deterioration of a physiological function in the branching coral *Acropora palmata*. *Mar. Ecol. Prog. Ser.* 121: 203-9.

Meesters, E.H., A. Bos, and G.J. Gast. 1992. Effects of sedimentation and lesion position on coral tissue regeneration. *Proc. 7th Int. Coral Reef Symp.* 2: 671-8.

Meesters, E.H., I. Wesseling, and R.P.M. Bak. 1996. Partial mortality in three species of reef-building corals and the relation with colony morphology. *Bull. Mar. Sci.* 58: 838-52.

Meglitsch, P.A., and F.R. Schram. 1991. *Invertebrate Zoology, 3rd ed.* Oxford University Press, Oxford: 69-96.

Meikle, P., G.N. Richards, and D. Yellowlees. 1988. Structural investigations on the mucus from six species of coral. *Mar. Biol.*. 99: 187-93.

Mestel, R. 1999. Drugs from the sea. *Discover* 20: 70-4.

Miller, D.J., and D. Yellowlees. 1989. Inorganic nitrogen uptake by symbiotic marine cnidarians: a critical review. *Proc. Roy. Soc. Lond. B* 237: 109-25.

Miller, I. 1996. Black band disease on the Great Barrier Reef. *Coral Reefs* 15: 58.

Miller, K.J. 1992. Morphologic variation in the scleractinian coral *Platygyra daedalea* (Ellis and Solander, 1786)—genetically or environmentally determined? *Proc. 7th Int. Coral Reef Symp.* 1: 550-6.

Mills, M.M., and K.P. Sebens. 1997. Particle ingestion efficiency of the coral *Siderastrea siderea* and *Agaricia agaricites*: effects of flow speed and sediment load. *Proc. 8th Int. Coral Reef Symp.* 2: 1059-64.

Misc. 1992. Aquaria Archive: reefs Reproduction Coral asexual From: fs-smith@venus.lerc.nasa.gov (G. Smith) Date: 22 Apr 1992 11:34 EDT Newsgroups: rec.aquaria,alt.aquaria Subject: Re: [M] More on MH lighting.

Misc. 1994. Distribution and frequency patterns of Black band disease in the Northern Florida Keys. *Bull. Mar. Sci.* 54: 1078.

Misc. 1996. Subject: Temp and Water Movement / Temp and Water Motion Section 8 Advanced Reefkeeping pt. 1. CompuServe: Fishnet thread, library archives.

Misc. 1996. Subject: Temp and Water Movement / Temp and Water Motion Section 8 Advanced Reefkeeping pt. 2. CompuServe: Fishnet thread, library archives.

Misc. 1997. *Aiptasia* question br@kplace.monrou.com. *Aquarium Net*, June issue. http://www.aquarium.net

Misc. 1997. Popping polyps. In : Breakthroughs in science, technology and medicine: biology. *Discover*, Sept.: 15.

Misc. 1998. Scientists figure out the coral-killing culprit. Florida Keys Online, Associated Press, *Miami Tribune*.

Misc. 1998. Diseases of reef-building corals. Fact sheet released by the Bureau of Oceans and International Environmental and Scientific Affairs, Washington DC.

Misc. 1999. ISRS Statement on Diseases on Coral Reefs.

Mitchell, N.D., et al. 1993. Colony morphology, age structure, and relative growth of two gorgonian corals, *Leptogorgia hebes* (Verrill) and *Leptogorgia virgulata* (Lamarack), from the Northern Gulf of Mexico. *Coral Reefs* 12: 65-70.

Mitchell, R., and I. Chet. 1975. Bacterial attack of corals in polluted seawater, *Microb. Ecol.* 2: 227-33.

Moe, M.A. Jr., 1992. *The Marine Aquarium Handbook: Beginner to Breeder*. Revised edition. Green Turtle Publications, Plantation, FL.

Mokady, O., et al. 1992. Settlement, metamorphosis and bioerosion rate of *Lithopaga simplex*. *Proc. 7th Int. Coral Reef Symp.* 1: 438.

Mokady, O., Y. Loya, and B. Lazar. 1998. Ammonium concentration from boring bivalves to their coral host—a mutualistic symbiosis? *Mar. Ecol. Prog. Ser.* 169: 295-301.

Moll, H., and M. Borel-Best. 1984. New scleractinian corals (Anthzoa: Scleractinia) from the Spermonde Archipelago, South Sulawesi, Indonesia. *Zool. Med. Leiden*. 58(4): 47-58.

Montebon, A.R.F., and H.T. Yap. 1992. Metabolic responses of *Porites cylindrica* Dana to water motion. *Proc. 7th Int. Coral Reef Symp.* 1: 381-2.

Moore, R.C., ed. 1956. *Treatise on Invertebrate Paleontology: Part F: Coelenterata*. Geologic Society of America and Kansas City Press, F1-F498.

Morin, J.G. 1976. Probable functions of bioluminescence in the Pennatulacea (Cnidaria, Anthozoa). In: *Coelenterate Ecology and Behavior* (G.O. Mackie, ed.). University of Victoria, British Columbia: pp. 629-38.

Morris, P.A. 1975. *A Field Guide to Shells*. Houghton Mifflin Company, Boston. 330 pp.

Morrissey, J., M.S. Jones, and V. Harriot. 1988. Nutrient cycling in the Great Barrier Reef Aquarium. *Proc. 6th Int. Coral Reef Symp.* 2: 563-7.

Morse, A,N.C. 1992. Unique patterns of substratum selection by distinct populations of *Agaricia humilis* contribute to opportunistic distribution within the Caribbean. *Proc. 7th Int. Coral Reef Symp.* 1: 501-2.

Morse, A.N, et al. 1999. The use of a novel chemo-inductive substrate to determine species-specific factors that influence successful recruitment of corals. Proceedings: NCRI International Conference on Scientific Aspects of Coral Reef Assessment, Monitoring, and Restoration. April14-16, 1999. Fort Lauderdale, FL: 141.

Morse, D.E., A.N.C. Morse, and H. Duncan. 1977. Algal "tumors" in the Caribbean sea-fan, *Gorgonia ventalina*. *Proc. 3rd Int. Coral Reef Symp.* 623-9.

Morse, D.E., and A.N.C. Morse. 1991. Enzymatic characterization of the morphogen recognized by *Agaricia humilis* (Scleractinian coral) larvae. *Biol. Bull.* 181: 104-22.

Morse, D.E., and A.N.C. Morse. 1992. Sulfated polysaccharide induces settlement of metamorphosis of *Agaricia humilis* larvae on specific crustose red algae. *Proc. 7th Int. Coral Reef Symp.* 1: 502.

Mueller, E.M. 1992. *Palythoa caribaeorum*: an indicator of coral reef perturbation. *Proc. 7th Int. Coral Reef Symp.* 1: 72.

Mueller, E. [undated]. Aquarium Myths and Legends: Professor Jaubert's Microcean System. Dept. of Marine Sciences, University of South Alabama (until 1 Sept.) Mobile, AL. downloaded from America Online, Fish and Marine Life Forum, Marine and Reef Library.

Muirhead, A., and J.S. Ryland. 1985. a review of the genus *Isaurus* Gray, 1828 (Zoanthidea), including new records from Fiji. *J. Nat. Hist.* 19: 323-35.

Muller-Parker, G. 1984. Dispersal of zooxanthellae on coral reefs by predators on cnidarians. *Biol. Bull.* 167: 159-67.

Muller-Parker, G., et al. 1994. Effect of ammonium enrichment on animal and algal biomass of the coral *Pocillopora damicornis*. *Pac. Sci.* 48: 273-83.

Muller-Parker, G., C.F. D'Elia, and C.B. Cook. 1992. Elemental composition of corals exposed to elevated seawater NH_4^+. *Proc. 7th Int. Coral Reef Symp.* 1: 382.

Muller-Parker, G., and C.F. D'Elia. 1997. Interactions between corals and their symbiotic algae. In: *Life and Death of Coral Reefs* (C. Birkeland, ed.). Chapman & Hall, New York: 96-113.

Muller, W.E.G. 1983. Histoincompatibility reactions in the hydrocoral *Millepora dichotoma*. *Coral Reefs* 1: 237-41.

Muller, W.E.G., et al. 1984. Intraspecific recognition system in scleractinian corals: morphological and cytochemcial description of the autolysis mechanism. *J. Hist. Cyto.* 32: 285-8.

Mundy, C.N., and R.C. Babcock. 1998. Role of light intensity and spectral quality in coral settlement: Implications for depth-dependent settlement? *J. Exp. Mar. Biol. Ecol.* 223: 235-55.

Munoz-Chagin, R.F. 1997. Coral transplantation program in the Paraiso coral reef, Cozumel Island, Mexico. *Proc. 8th Int. Coral Reef Symp.* 2: 2075-8.

Murdock, G.R. 1978. Digestion, assimilation, and transport of food in the gastrovascular cavity of a gorgonian octocoral (Cnidaria; Anthozoa). *Bull. Mar. Sci.* 28: 354-62.

Murdock, G.R. 1978. Circulation and digestion of food in the gastrovascular system of the gorgonian octocorals (Cnidaria; Anthozoa). *Bull. Mar. Sci.* 28: 363-70.

Muscatine, L. 1971. Calcification in corals. In: *Experimental Coelenterate Biology* (H.M. Lenhoff, L. Muscatine, and L.V. Davis, eds.). University of Hawaii Press, Honolulu: 227-38.

Muscatine, L. 1973. Nutrition of corals. *Biology and Geology of Coral Reefs* 2: 77-115.

Muscatine, L. 1990. The role of symbiotic algae in carbon and energy flux in reef corals. In: *Coral Reefs: Ecosystems of the World, Vol. 25* (Z. Dubinsky, ed.). Elsevier Scientific Publishing Co. Inc. New York: 75-88.

Muscatine, L., et al. 1989a. The effect of external nutrients resources on the population dynamcis of zooxanthellae in a reef coral. *Proc. Roy. Soc. Lond. B* 236: 311-24.

Muscatine, L., and E. Cernichiari. 1969. Assimilation of photosynthetic products of zooxanthellae by a reef coral. *Biol. Bull.* 137: 506-23.

Muscatine, L., P.G. Falkowski, J.W. Porter, and Z. Dubinsky. 1984. Fate of photosynthetic fixed carbon in light- and shade-adapted colonies of the symbiotic coral *Stylophora pistillata*. *Proc. Roy. Soc. Lond. B* 222: 181-202.

Muscatine, L., and H.M. Lenhoff. 1974. *Coelenterate Biology: Reviews and New Perspectives*. Academic Press, NY: 501 pp.

Muscatine, L., and J.W. Porter. 1977. Reef corals: Mutualistic symbioses adapted to nutrient poor environments. *BioScience* 27: 454-60.

Muscatine, L., J.W. Porter, and I.R. Kaplan. 1989b. Resource partitioning by reef corals as determined from stable isotope composition. I. $\partial^{13}C$ of zooxanthellae and animal tissue vs. depth. *Mar. Biol.* 100: 185-93.

Muscatine, L., E. Tambutte, and D. Allemand. 1997. Morphology of coral desmocytes, cells that anchor the calicoblastic epithelium to the skeleton. *Coral Reefs* 16: 205-13.

Muszynski, F.Z., et al. 1998. Within-colony variations of UV absorption in a reef building coral. *Bull. Mar. Sci.* 63: 589-94.

Nagelkerken, I., et al. 1997a. Widespread disease in Caribbean sea fans: I. Spreading and general characteristics. *Proc. 8th Int. Coral Reef Symp.* 1: 679-82.

Nagelkerken, I., et al. 1997b. Widespread disease in Caribbean sea fans: II. Patterns of infection and tissue loss. *Mar. Ecol. Prog. Ser.* 160:255-263.

Nair, S., and U. Simidu. 1987. Distribution and significance of heterotrophic marine bacteria with antibacterial activity. *Appl. Env. Microb.* 53: 2957-2952.

Nakaya, S., and K. Yamazato. 1985. Intra- and inter-specific interactions in a scleractinian coral *Porites*. *Proc. 5th Int. Coral Reef Symp.* 2: 261.

Nash, M. 1996. Wrecking the reefs. *Time* Sept 30: 60-62.

Ne'eman, I., L. Fishelson, and Y. Kashman. 1974. Sarcophine—a new toxin from the soft coral *Sarcophyton glaucum* (Alcyonaria). *Toxicon* 12: 593-8.

Neigel, J.E., and J.C. Avise. 1983. Clonal diversity and population structure in a reef-building coral, *Acropora cervicornis*: self recognition analysis and demographic interpretation. *Evolution* 37: 437-53.

Newman, W.A., P.A. Jumars, and A. Ross. 1976. Diversity trends in coral-inhabiting barnacles (Cirripedia, Pyrgomatinae). *Micronesica* 12: 69-82.

Nilsen, A.J. 1998. Mass coral spawning in a captive reef tank. *Aquarium Frontiers*, January issue. http://www.aquariumfrontiers.com/archives

Nilsen, A.J. 1996. Presentation: MACNA VIII. Kansas City, MO.

Nishihira, M. 1981. Interactions of Alcyonaria with hermatypic corals on an Okinawan reef flat. *Proc. 4th Int. Coral Reef Symp.* 1: 722.

Ocana, O., A. Brito, and J. Nunez. 1992. A new species of *Sarcodictyon* (Anthozoa: Stolonifera) from Tenerife, Canary Islands. *Zool. Med. Leiden*. 66: 423-28.

Ogawa, K., and K. Matsuzaki. 1992. Do coral-barnacles select their host corals or not? *Proc. 7th Int. Coral Reef Symp.* 2: 863.

Ogden, J.C. 1997. Ecosystem interactions in the tropical coastal seascape. In: *Life and Death of Coral Reefs* (C. Birkeland, ed.). Chapman & Hall, New York: 288-97.

Ogden, J.C., and J.C. Zieman. 1977. Ecological aspects of coral reef-seagrass bed contacts in the Caribbean. *Proc. 3rd Int. Coral Reef Symp.* 1: 377-82.

Ohde, S., and Y. Kitano. 1981. Behavior of minor elements in the transformation of coral aragonite to calcite. *Proc. 4th Int. Coral Reef Symp.* 2: 91-4.

Olafsen, J.A. 1996. Lectins: models of natural and induced molecules in invertebrates. In: *Advances in Comparative and Environmental Physiology, Vol. 24: Invertebrate Immune Responses: Cell Activities and the Environment* (E.L. Cooper, ed.). Springer-Verlag Berlin Heidelberg: 49-76.

Oliver, A.P.H. 1975. *The Hamlyn Guide to Shells of the World*. Hamlyn Publishing Group, Ltd, London. 320 pp.

Oliver, J.K. 1984. Intra-colony variation in the growth of *Acropora formosa*: extension rates and skeletal structure of white (zooxanthellae-free) and brown-tipped branches. *Coral Reefs* 3: 139-47.

Oliver, J. 1985. Commercial coral collecting on the Great Barrier Reef. *Proc. 5th Int. Coral Reef Symp.* 2: 274.

Oliver, J.K., et al. 1988. Geographic extent of mass coral spawning: Clues to ultimate causal factors. *Proc. 6th Int. Coral Reef Symp.* 2: 803-7.

Ott, B., and J.B. Lewis. 1972. The importance of the gastropod *Coralliophila abbreviata* (Lamarck) and the polychaete *Hermodice carunculata* (Pallas) as coral reef predators. *Can. J. Zool.* 50: 1651-6.

Ounais, N. 1997. Head of the Aquarium, Musee d'Oceanographique, Monaco. Personal communications.

Pajaro, M. 1992. Alternatives to cyanide use in aquarium fish collection: A community based approach. *Proc. 7th Int. Coral Reef Symp.* 2: 1039-40.

Pandian, T. 1975. Heterotrophy. In: *Marine Ecology: A Comprehensive, Integrated Treatise on Life in Oceans and Coastal Waters* (O. Kinne, ed.). John Wiley and Sons, London: pp. 64-75.

Parker, G.M. 1984. Dispersal of zooxanthellae on coral reefs by predators on cnidarians. *Biol. Bull.* 167: 159-67.

Pascal, H., and E. Vacelet. 1981. Bacterial utilization of mucus on the coral reef of Aqaba (Red Sea). *Proc. 4th Int. Coral Reef Symp.* 1: 669-77.

Pass, M.A., et al. 1989. Stimulation of contractions in the polyps of the soft coral *Xenia elongata* by compounds extracted from other alcyonacean soft corals. *Comp. Biochem. Physiol.* 94C: 677-81.

Patterson, M.R. 1991. Passive suspension feeding by an octocoral in plankton patches: empirical test of a mathematical model. *Biol. Bull.* 180: 81-92.

Patterson, M.R. 1991. The effects of flow on polyp-level prey capture in an octocoral, *Alyconium siderium*. *Biol. Bull.* 180: 93-102.

Patterson, M.R., and K.P. Sebens. 1989. Forced convection modulates gas exchanges in cnidarians. *Proc. Nat. Acad. Sci. USA* 86: 8833-8836.

Patterson, M.R., K.P. Sebens, and R.R. Olson. 1991. In situ measurements of flow effects on primary production and dark respiration in reef corals. *Limnol. Oceanogr.* 36: 936-48.

Paul, J.H., M. DeFlaun, and W.H. Jeffrey. 1986. Elevated levels of microbial activity in the coral surface microlayer. *Mar. Ecol. Prog. Ser.* 33: 29-40.

Paul, V.J. 1992. Chemical defenses of benthic marine invertebrates. In: *Ecological Roles of Marine Natural Products* (V.J. Paul, ed.). Comstock Publishing Associates, Ithaca: 164-89.

Paulay, G. 1997. Diversity and distribution of reef organisms. In: *Life and Death of Coral Reefs* (C. Birkeland, ed.). Chapman & Hall, New York: 298-354.

Pawlik, J.R. 1992. Induction of marine invertebrate larval settlement: evidence for chemical cues. In: *Ecological Roles of Marine Natural Products* (V.J. Paul, ed.). Comstock Publishing Associates, Ithaca: 189-237.

Pawlik, J.R. 1993. Marine invertebrate chemical defenses. *Chem. Rev.* 93: 1911-22.

Pawlik, J.R., M.T. Burch, and W. Fenecal. 1987. Patterns of chemical defense among Caribbean gorgonian corals: a preliminary study. *J. Exp. Mar. Biol. Ecol.* 108: 55-66.

Peach, M.B., and O. Hoegh-Guldberg. 1999. Sweeper polyps of the coral *Goniopora tenuidens* (Scleractinia: Poritidae). *Invert. Biol.* 118: 1-7.

Pearce. F. 1994. A paler shade of coral . . . *New Scientist* 142: 19.

Pearse, V.B. 1971. Sources of carbon in the skeleton of *Fungia scutaria*. In: *Experimental Coelenterate Biology* (H.M. Lenhoff, L. Muscatine, and L.V. Davis, eds.). University of Hawaii Press, Honolulu: 239-45.

Pecheaux, M. 1995. *Review on Coral Reef Bleaching*. Internal report for the Observatoire Oceanologique European, Monaco. 300+ pages.

Pecheaux, M. 1998. Personal communications.

Pennings, S.C. 1997. Indirect interactions on coral reefs. In: *Life and Death of Coral Reefs* (C. Birkeland, ed.). Chapman & Hall, New York: 249-72.

Perrin, D. 1995-6. Personal communications.

Peters, E.C., et al. 1981. Bioaccumulation and histopathological effect of oil on a stony coral. *Mar. Poll. Bull.* 12: 333-9.

Peters, E.C. 1984. A survey of cellular reactions to environmental stress and disease in Caribbean scleractinian corals. *Helgo wiss Meers* 37: 113-37.

Peters, E.C. 1988. Symbiosis to pathology: are the roles of microorganisms as pathogens of coral reef organisms predictable from existing knowledge? *Proc. 6th Int. Coral Reef Symp.* 1: 205-10.

Peters, E.C. 1992. The role of environmental stress in the development of coral diseases and micro-parasite infestations. *Amer. Zool.* 32: 960.

Peters, E.C. 1993. *Advances in Fisheries Science: Pathobiology of Marine and Estuarine Organisms* (J.A. Couch and J.W. Fournie, eds.). CRC Press: pp. 400-49.

Peters, E.C. 1997. Diseases of coral reef organisms. In: *Life and Death of Coral Reefs* (C. Birkeland, ed.) Chapman & Hall: pp. 114-39.

Peters, E.C. 1997-9. Personal communications.

Peters, E.C., J.C. Halas, and H.B. McCarty. 1986. Calicoblastic neoplasms in *Acropora palmata* with a review of reports of anomalies of growth and form in corals. *J. Nat. Cancer Inst.* 76(5):895-912.

Peters, E.C., and H.B. McCarty. 1996. Carbonate crisis? *Geotimes* 41: 20-3.

Peters, E.C., J.J. Oprandy, and P.P. Yevich. 1983. Possible causal agent of "white band disease" in Caribbean scleractinian corals. *J. Inv. Path.* 41: 394-6.

Peters, E. C., and M.E.Q. Pilson. 1985. A comparative study of the effects of sedimentation on symbiotic and asymbiotic colonies of the coral *Astrangia danae* (Milne, Edwards, and Haime, 1849). *J. Exp. Mar. Biol. Ecol.* 92: 215-30.

Phillips, J.H. 1963. Immune mechanisms in the phylum Coelenterata. In: *The Lower Metazoa: Comparative Biology and Phylogeny*. University of California Press, Berkeley: 425-31.

Pichon, M. 1980. *Wellsophyllia radiata* n. gen., n. sp., a new hermatypic coral from the Indonesian region (Cnidaria: Anthozoa, Scleractinia). *Revue Suisse Zool.* 87(1): 253-59.

Picken, L.E.R., and R.J. Skaer. 1953. A review of researches on nematocysts. *Symp. Zool. Soc. Lond.* 16: 19-50.

Pinker, R.T., and I Laszlo. 1992. Global distribution of photosynthetically active radiation as observed from satellites. *J. Climate* 5: 56-65.

Pinker, R.T., and I. Laszlo. 1992. Modeling surface solar irradiance for satellite applications on a global scale. *J. Appl. Met.* 31: 194-211

Pinto, S.M., and M.J.C. Belem. 1997. On desmoidal processes in Discosomatidae (Cnidaria: Corallimorpharia). *Proc. 8th Int. Coral Reef Symp.* 2: 1587-90.

Pires, D.O., and C.B. Castro. 1997. Scleractinia and Corallimorpharia: an analysis of cnidae affinity. *Proc. 8th Int. Coral Reef Symp.* 2: 1581-6.

Pitcock, A.B. 1999. Coral reefs and environmental change: adaptation to what? *Amer. Zool.* 39: 10-29.

Plucer-Rosario, G., and R.H. Randall. 1987. Preservation of rare coral species by transplantation and examination of their recruitment and growth. *Bull. Mar. Sci.* 41: 585-93.

Porter, J.W. 1976. Autotrophy, heterotrophy, and resource partitioning in Caribbean reef-building corals. *Amer. Naturalist* 110: 731-42.

Porter, J.W. , et al. 1989. Bleaching in reef corals: physiological and stable isotopic responses. *Ecology* 86: 9342-9346.

Porter, J.W., et al. 1999. Patterns and distribution and spread of coral disease in the Florida Keys. NCRI International Conference on Scientific Aspects of Coral Reef Assessment, Monitoring, and Restoration. April 14-16, 1999. Fort Lauderdale, FL: 155.

Porter, J.W., and O.W. Meier. 1992. Quantification of loss and change in Floridian reef coral populations. *Amer. Zool.* 32: 625-40.

Porter, J.W., L. Muscatine, Z. Dubinsky, and P. G. Falkowski. 1984. Primary production and photoadaptation in light- and shade-adapted colonies of the symbiotic coral, *Stylophora pistillata. Proc. Roy. Soc. Lond. B* 222: 161-80.

Porter, J.W., and N.M. Targett. 1988. Allelochemcial interactions between sponges and corals. *Biol. Bull.* 175: 230-9.

Potts, D.C. 1976. Growth interactions among morphological variants of the coral *Acropora palifera.* In: *Coelenterate Ecology and Behavior* (G.O. Mackie, ed.). University of Victoria, British Columbia: pp. 79-88.

Potts, D.C., R.L. Garthwaite, and A.F. Budd. 1992. Speciation in the coral genus *Porites. Proc. 7th Int. Coral Reef Symp.* 2: 679.

Powers, D. 1970. A numerical taxonomic study of Hawaiian reef corals. *Pac. Sci.* 24: 180-6.

Prota, G. 1980. Nitrogenous pigments in marine invertebrates. In: *Marine Natural Products: Chemical and Biological Perspectives, Vol. III* (P.J. Scheuer, ed.). Academic Press, New York: 141-80.

Raftos, D.A. 1996. Histocompatability reactions in invertebrates. In: *Advances in Comparative and Environmental Physiology, Vol. 24: Invertebrate Immune Responses: Cell Activities and the Environment* (E.L. Cooper, ed.). Springer-Verlag Berlin Heidelberg: 77-121.

Rahav, O., Z. Dubinsky, Y. Achituv, and P.G. Falkowski. 1989. Ammonium metabolism in the zooxanthellate coral *Stylophora pistillata. Proc. Roy. Soc. Lond. B* 236: 325-37.

Rand, G.M., and S.R. Petrocelli, eds. 1985. *Fundamentals of Aquatic Toxicology: Methods and Applications.* Taylor & Francis, Bristol, Pennsylvania. 666 pp.

Randall, R.H. 1976. Some problems in reef coral taxonomy. *Micronesica* 12: 151-6.

Randall, R.H. 1981. Morphological diversity in the scleractinian genus *Acropora. Proc. 4th Int. Coral Reef Symp.* 2:158-63.

Randall, R.H., and L.G. Eldredge. 1976. Skeletal modification by a polychaete annelid in some scleractinian corals. In: *Coelenterate Ecology and Behavior* (G.O. Mackie, ed.). University of Victoria, British Columbia: pp. 453-66.

Rands, M.L., et al. 1992. Avoidance of hypoxia in a cnidarian symbiosis by algal photosynthetic oxygen. *Biol. Bull.* 182: 159-62.

Rasmussen, C.E. 1988. The use of strontium as an indicator of anthropogenically altered environmental parameters. *Proc. 6th Int. Coral Reef Symp.* 2: 325-30.

Raymundo, L.J., and A.P. Maypa. 1999. Using cultured coral to rehabilitate a degraded reef in the central Philippines. NCRI International Conference on Scientific Aspects of Coral Reef Assessment, Monitoring, and Restoration. April 14-16, 1999. Fort Lauderdale, FL: 160.

Reed, J.K., and P.M. Mikkelson. 1987. The molluscan community associated with the scleractinian coral *Oculina varicosa. Bull. Mar. Sci.* 40: 99-131.

Rees, J.T. 1972. The effect of current on growth form in an octocoral. *J. Exp. Mar. Biol. Ecol.* 10: 115-23.

Reimer, A.A. 1971. Observations on the relationships between several species of tropical zoanthids (Zoanthidea, Coelenterata) and their zooxanthellae. *J. Exp. Mar. Biol. Ecol.* 7: 207-14.

Reimer, A., 1971. Uptake and utilization of 14C-Glycine by *Zoanthus* and its coelenteric bacteria. In: *Experimental Coelenterate Biology* (H.M. Lenhoff, L. Muscatine, and L.V. Davis, eds.). University of Hawaii Press, Honolulu: 209-17.

Ricart y Menendez, F.O., and G.M. Friedman. 1977. Morphology of the axial corallite of *Acropora cervicornis. Proc. 3rd Int. Coral Reef Symp.* 1: 453-6.

Rice, M.E. 1976. Sipunculans associated with coral communities. *Micronesica* 12: 119-132.

Richardson, C.A., P. Dustan, and J.C. Lang. 1979. Maintenance of living space by sweeper tentacles of *Montastrea cavernosa,* a Caribbean reef coral. *Mar. Biol.* 55: 181-6.

Richardson, L.L. 1998. Coral diseases: what is really known? *TREE* 13: 438-43.

Richardson, L.L., et al. 1997. Ecology of the black band disease microbial consortium. *Proc. 8th Int. Coral Reef Symp.* 1: 597-600.

Richardson, L., et al. 1998. Florida's mystery coral-killer identified. *Nature* 392: 557-8.

Richardson, L.L., et al. 1999. Status of the health of coral reefs: an update. Presentation at USGCRP Seminar, Washington, DC.

Richardson, L. 2000. Personal communications.

Richmond, R.H. 1985. Reversible metamorphosis in coral planula larvae. *Mar. Ecol. Prog. Ser.* 22:181-5.

Richmond, R.H. 1987. Energetic relationships and biogeographical differences among fecundity, growth and reproduction in the reef coral *Pocillopora damicornis. Bull. Mar. Sci.* 41: 594-604.

Richmond, R.H. 1988. Competency and dispersal potential of planula larvae of a spawning versus a brooding coral. *Proc. 6th Int. Coral Reef Symp.* 2: 827-32.

Richmond, R.H. 1992. Fertilization in corals: Problems and Puzzles. *Proc. 7th Int. Coral Reef Symp.* 1: 502.

Richmond, R.H. 1993. Coral reefs: present problems and future concerns resulting from anthropogenic disturbance. *Amer. Zool.* 33: 524-36.

Richmond, R.H. 1997. Reproduction and recruitment in corals: Critical links in the persistence of reefs. In: *Life and Death of Coral Reefs* (C. Birkeland, ed.). Chapman & Hall, New York: 175-97.

Richmond, R.H., and C.L. Hunter. 1990. Reproduction and recruitment of corals: comparisons among the Caribbean, the Tropical Pacific, and the Red Sea. *Mar. Ecol. Prog. Ser.* 60: 185-203.

Richmond, R.H., and P.L. Jokiel. 1984. Lunar periodicity in larva release in the reef coral *Pocillopora damicornis* at Enewetak and Hawaii. *Bull. Mar. Sci.* 34: 280-7.

Richmond, R.H., S. Romano, and S. Leota. 1999. Coral cultivation and its application to reef restoration, environmental assessment, monitoring and the aquarium trade. Proceedings: NCRI International Conference on Scientific Aspects of Coral Reef Assessment, Monitoring, and Restoration. April 14-16, 1999. Fort Lauderdale, FL: 161-2.

Riddle, D. 1995. *The Captive Reef: A Concise Guide to Reef Aquaria in the Home*. Energy Savers Unlimited, Inc. 297 pp.

Riddle, D. 1996. Zonation: an important concept for the reef aquarium hobbyist? *Aquarium Net*, December issue. http://www.aquarium.net

Riddle, D. 1997. Water motion in the reef aquarium, part II. *Aquarium Frontiers* 4(1): 12-24.

Riddle, D. 1997. Personal communications.

Riegl, B. 1995. Effects of sand deposition on scleractinian and alcyonean corals. *Mar. Biol.* 121: 517-26.

Riegl, B. 1999. Corals in a non-reef setting in the southern Arabian Gulf (Dubai, UAE): fauna and community structure in response to recurring mass mortality. *Coral Reefs* 18: 63-73.

Riegl, B., W.E. Piller, and M. Rasser. 1996. Rolling stones: first report of a free living *Acropora anthocercis* (Brook) from the Red Sea. *Coral Reefs* 15: 149-50.

Rinkevich, B. 1995. Restoration strategies for coral reefs damaged by recreational activities: the use of sexual and asexual recruits. *Restoration Ecology* 3: 241-251.

Rinkevich, B., U. Frank, R.P.M. Bak, and W.E.G. Muller. 1994. Alloimmune responses between *Acropora hemprichii* conspecifics: nontransitive patterns of overgrowth and delayed cytotoxicity. *Mar. Biol.* 118: 731-7.

Rinkevich, B., and Y. Loya. 1983. Oriented translocation of energy in grafted reef corals. *Coral Reefs* 1: 243-7.

Rinkevich, B., and Y. Loya. 1983. Intraspecific competitive networks in the Red Sea coral *Stylophora pistillata*. *Coral Reefs* 1: 161-72.

Rinkevich, B., and Y. Loya. 1984. Does light enhance calcification in hermatypic corals? *Mar. Biol.* 80: 1-6.

Rinkevich, B., and Y. Loya. 1984. Coral illumination through an optical glass-fiber: incorporation of 14C photosynthates. *Mar. Biol.* 80: 7-15.

Rinkevich, B., and Y. Loya. 1985. Intraspecific competition in a reef coral: effects on growth and reproduction. *Oecologia* 66: 100-5.

Rinkevich, B., and Y. Loya. 1985. Coral isomone: a proposed chemical signal controlling intraclonal growth patterns in a branching corals. *Bull. Mar. Sci.* 36: 319-24.

Rinkevich, B., N. Shashar, and T. Liberman. 1992. Nontransitive interactions between four common Red Sea sessile invertebrates. *Proc. 7th Int. Coral Reef Symp.* 2: 833-9.

Risk, M.J., P.W. Sammarco, and E.N. Edinger. 1995. Bioerosion in *Acropora* across the continental shelf of the Great Barrier Reef. *Coral Reefs* 14: 79-86.

Ritchie, K.B., and G.W. Smith. 1995. Preferential carbon utilization by surface bacterial communities from water mass, normal, and white-band diseased *Acropora cervicornis*. *Mol. Mar. Biol. Biotech* 4: 345-52.

Ritchie, K.B., and G.W. Smith. 1995. Carbon-source utilization patterns of coral associated marine heterotrophs. *J. Marine Biotechnol.* 3: 107-9.

Ritchie, K.B., and G.W. Smith. 1997. Physiological comparison of bacterial communities from various species of scleractinian corals. *Proc. 8th Int. Coral Reef Symp.* 1: 521-26.

Roberts, J.M., P.S. Davies, and L.M. Fixter. 1999. Symbiotic anemones can grow when starved: nitrogen budget for *Anemonia viridis* in ammonium-supplemented seawater. *Mar. Biol.* 133: 29-35.

Robertson, J.D. 1957. Osmotic and ionic regulation in aquatic invertebrates. In: *Recent Advances in Invertebrate Physiology: A Symposium*. University of Oregon Publishing: Eugene: pp. 229-46.

Robertson, R. 1970. Review of the predators and parasites of stony corals, with special reference to symbiotic prosobranch gastropods. *Pac. Sci.*: 24: 43-51.

Robson, E.A. 1976. Locomotion in sea anemones: the pedal disk. In: *Coelenterate Ecology and Behavior* (G.O. Mackie, ed.). University of Victoria, British Columbia: pp.479-90.

Roch, P. 1996. A definition of cytolytic responses in invertebrates. In:*Advances in Comparative and Environmental Physiology, Vol. 23: Invertebrate Immune Responses: Cells and Molecular Products* (E.L. Cooper, ed.). Springer-Verlag Berlin Heidelberg: 116-50.

Rogers, C.S. 1983. Sublethal and lethal effects of sediments applied to common Caribbean reef corals in the field. *Mar. Poll. Bull.* 14: 378-82.

Romano, S.L. 1990. Long-term effects of interspecific aggression on growth of the reef-building corals *Cyphastrea ocellina* (Dana) and *Pocillopora damicornis* (Linnaeus). *J. Exp. Mar. Biol. Ecol.* 140: 135-46.

Ronneberg, H., D.L. Fox, and S. Liaaen-Jensen. 1979. Animal carotenoids—carotenoproteins from hydrocorals. *Comp. Biochem. Physiol.* 64b: 407-8.

Rosenberg, E., and Y. Loya. 1999. *Vibrio shiloi* is the etiological (causative) agent of *Oculina patagonica* bleaching: General implications. *Reef Encounter* 25:8-10.

Ross, D.M. 1966. The receptors of the Cnidaria and their excitation. *Proc. Symp. Zool. Soc. Lond.* 16: 413-18.

Roth, A.A., et al. 1982. Some effects of light on coral growth. *Pac. Sci.* 36; 65-81.

Rowan, R., N. Knowlton, A. Baker, and J. Javier. 1997. Landscape ecology of algal symbionts creates variation in episodes of coral bleaching. *Nature* 388: 265-9.

Rowan, R., and N. Knowlton. 1995. Intraspecific diversity and ecological zonation in coral-algal symbiosis. *Proc. Natl. Acad. Sci. USA* 92: 2850-4.

Rowan, R., and D.A. Powers. 1991. A molecular genetic classification of zooxanthellae and the evolution of animal-algal symbioses. *Science* 251: 1348-51.

Rublee, P.A., H.R. Lasker, M. Gottfried, and M.R. Roman. 1980. Production and bacterial colonization of mucus from the soft coral *Briarium asbestinum*. *Bull. Mar. Sci.* 30: 888-93.

Ruppert, E.E., and R.D. Barnes. 1994. *Invertebrate Zoology*. Saunders College Publishing, Ft. Worth, Texas. 1056 pp.

Ryland, J.S., and R.C. Babcock. 1991. Annual cycle of gametogenesis and spawning in a tropical zoanthid, *Protopalythoa* sp. *Hydrobiologia* 216/217: 117-23.

Sadovy, Y. 1992. A preliminary assessment of the marine aquarium export trade in Puerto Rico. *Proc. 7th Int. Coral Reef Symp.* 2: 1014-22.

Sakai, R., and T. Higa. 1987. Tubastrine, and new guanidostyrene from the coral *Tubastrea aurea*. *Chem. Lett.* 1: 127-8.

Samarri. F. 1995. Helping urchins may benefit coral. *Sea Frontiers* 41(4): 16-18.

Sammarco, P.W. 1981. Escape response and dispersal in an Indo-Pacific coral under stress: "polyp bail-out." *Proc. 4th Int. Coral Reef Symp.* 2: 194.

Sammarco, P.W. 1982. Polyp bail-out: an escape response to environmental stress and a new means of reproduction in corals. *Mar. Ecol. Prog. Ser.* 10: 57-65.

Sammarco, P.W., J.C. Coll, S. LaBarre, and B. Willis. 1983. Competitive strategies of soft corals (Coelenterata: Octocorallia): allelopathic effects on selected scleractinian corals. *Coral Reefs* 2: 173-8.

Sammarco, P.W., J.C. Coll, and S. LaBarre. 1985. Competitive strategies of soft corals (Coelenterata: Octocorallia). II. Variable defensive responses and susceptibility to scleractinian corals. *J. Exp. Mar. Biol. Ecol.* 91: 199-215.

Sammarco, P.W., and J.C. Coll. 1987. The chemical ecology of alcyonarian corals. In: *Bioorganic Marine Chemistry Vol. 2* (P.J. Scheuer, ed.). Springer-Verlag, Berlin: 87-116.

Sammarco, P.W., and J.C. Coll. 1990. Lack of predictability in terpenoid function: multiple roles and integration with related adaptations in soft corals. *J. Chem. Ecol.* 16: 273-89.

Sammarco, P.W., and J.C. Coll. 1992. Chemical adaptation in the Octocorallia: evolutionary considerations. *Mar. Ecol. Prog. Ser.* 88: 93-104.

Sammarco, P.W., and J.C. Coll. 1997. Secondary metabolites—or primary? Re-examination of a concept through a marine example. *Proc. 8th Int. Coral Reef Symp.* 2: 1245-50.

Sammarco, P.W., S. LaBarre, and J.C. Coll. 1987. Defensive strategies of soft corals (Coelenterata: Octocorallia) of the Great Barrier Reef. III. The relationship between ichthyotoxicity and morphology. *Oecologia* 74: 93-101.

Santavy, D.L., and E.C. Peters. 1997. Microbial pests: coral diseases in the Western Atlantic. *Proc. 8th Int. Coral Reef Symp.* 1: 607-12.

Santavy, D.L., E.C. Peters, C. Quirolo, J.W. Porter, and C.N. Bianchi. 1999. Yellow-blotch disease outbreak on reefs of the San Blas Islands, Panama. *Coral Reefs* 18:97.

Sathyendranath, S., and T. Platt. 1989. The light field in the ocean: its modification and exploitation by pelagic biota. II. Physics of Light in the Sea. In: *Light and Life in the Sea* (P.J. Herring, et al., eds.). Cambridge University Press, Cambridge. pp: 3-19.

Sawada. T., and S. Tomonaga. 1996. The immunocytes of protostomes and deuterostomes as revealed by LM, EM, and other methods. In: *Advances in Comparative and Environmental Physiology, Vol. 23: Invertebrate Immune Responses: Cells and Molecular Products* (E.L. Cooper, ed.). Springer-Verlag Berlin Heidelberg: 9-40.

Scelfo, G. 1985. The effects of visible and ultraviolet solar radiation on a UV-absorbing compound and chlorophyll *a* in a Hawaiian zoanthid. *Proc. 5th Int. Coral Reef Symp.* 6: 107-12.

Scheuer, P.J., ed. 1983. *Marine Natural Products.* Academic Press, New York . 429 pp.

Schiller, C., and G.J. Herndi. 1989. Evidence of enhanced microbial activity in the interstitial space of branched corals: possible implications for coral metabolism. *Coral Reefs* 7: 179-84.

Schlichter, D. 1973. The integument of the lower invertebrates. In: *The Integument: A Textbook of Skin Biology* (R.I.C. Spearman, ed.) Cambridge Press, Cambridge, MA: pp. 20-58.

Schlichter, D. 1982. Nutritional strategies of cnidarians: the absorption, translocation and utilization of dissolved nutrients by *Heteroxenia fuscescens. Amer. Zool.* 22: 659-69.

Schlichter, D. 1982. Epidermal nutrition of the alcyonarian *Heteroxenia fuscescens* (Ehrb.): absorption of dissolved organic material and lost endogenous photosynthates. *Oecologia* 53: 40-9.

Schlichter, D., H.W. Fricke, and W. Weber. 1986. Light harvesting by wavelength transformation in a symbiotic coral of the Red Sea twilight zone. *Mar. Biol.* 91: 403-7.

Schlichter, D., and G. Liebzit. 1991. The natural release of amino acids from the symbiotic coral *Heteroxenia fuscescens* (Ehrb.) as a function of photosynthesis. *J. Exp. Mar. Biol. Ecol.* 150: 83-90.

Schlichter, D., A. Svoboda, and B.P. Kremer. 1983. Functional autotrophy of *Heteroxenia fuscescens* (Anthozoa: Alcyonaria): carbon assimilation and translocation of photosynthates from symbionts to host. *Mar. Biol.* 78: 29-38.

Schneider, R.C., and S.V. Smith. 1982. Skeletal Sr content and density in *Porites* spp. in relation to environmental factors. *Mar. Biol.* 66: 121-31.

Schoenberg, D.A., and R.K. Trench. 1976. Specificity of symbioses between marine cnidarians and zooxanthellae. In: *Coelenterate Ecology and Behavior* (G.O. Mackie, ed.). University of Victoria, British Columbia: pp. 423-32.

Schonwald, H., Z. Dubinsky, and Y. Achituv. 1997. Diel carbon budget of the zooxanthellate hydrocoral *Millepora dichotoma. Proc. 8th Int. Coral Reef Symp.* 1: 939-46.

Schumacher, H. 1977. Ability in fungiid corals to overcome sedimentation. *Proc. 3rd Int. Coral Reef Symp.* 1: 503-9.

Schumacher, H. 1984. Reef-building properties of *Tubastraea micranthus* (Scleractinia, Dendrophyliidae), a coral without zooxanthellae. *Mar. Ecol. Prog. Ser.* 20: 93-9.

Schumacher, H. 1992. Impact of some corallivorus snails on stony corals in the Red Sea. *Proc. 7th Int. Coral Reef Symp.* 2: 840-5.

Schumacher, H. 1997. Soft corals as reef builders. *Proc. 8th Int. Coral Reef Symp.* 1: 499-502.

Schumacher, H., and M. Plewka. 1981. The adaptive significance of mechanical properties versus morphological adjustments in skeletons of *Acropora palmata* and *Acropora cervicornis* (Cnidaria, Scleractinia). *Proc. 4th Int. Coral Reef Symp.* 2: 122-8.

Schumacher, H., and H. Zibrowius. 1985. What is hermatypic?: a redefinition of ecological groups in corals and other organisms. *Coral Reefs* 4: 1-9.

Schwarz, J.A., et al. 1999. Late larval development and onset of symbiosis in the scleractinian coral *Fungia scutaria. Biol. Bull.* 196: 70-9.

Scoffin, T.P., et al. 1992. Patterns and possible environmental controls of skeletogenesis of *Porites lutea*, South Thailand. *Coral Reefs* 11: 1-11.

Sebens, K.P. 1976. The ecology of Caribbean sea anemones in Panama: utilization of space on a coral reef. In: *Coelenterate Ecology and Behavior* (G.O. Mackie, ed.). University of Victoria, British Columbia: pp. 67-78.

Sebens, K.P. 1977. Autotrophic and heterotrophic nutrition of coral reef zoanthids. *Proc. 3rd Int. Coral Reef Symp.* 1:397-404.

Sebens, K.P. 1984. Water flow and coral colony size: interhabitat comparisons of the octocoral *Alcyonium siderium. Proc. Natl. Acad. Sci. USA* 81: 5473-5477.

Sebens, K.P. 1992. Water flow, growth form and distribution of scleractinian corals; Davies Reef (GBR), Australia. *Proc. 7th Int. Coral Reef Symp.* 1: 557-60.

Sebens, K.P. 1994. Biodiversity of coral reefs: what we are losing and why? *Amer. Zool.* 34: 115-33.

Sebens, K.P. 1997. Adaptive responses to water flow: morphology, energetics, and distribution of reef corals. *Proc. 8th Int. Coral Reef Symp.* 2: 1053-8.

Sebens, K.P., et al. 1998. Water flow and prey capture by three scleractinian corals, *Madracis mirabilis, Montastrea cavernosa,* and *Porites porites,* in a field enclosure. *Mar. Biol.* 131: 347-60.

Sebens, K.P., and A.S. Johnson. 1991. Effects of water movement on prey capture and distribution of reef corals. *Hydrobiologia* 216/217: 247-8.

Sebens, K.P., and A.S. Johnson. 1991. Effects of water movement on prey capture and distribution of reef corals. *Hydrobiologia* 226: 91-101.

Sebens, K.P., and J.S. Miles. 1988. Sweeper tentacles in a gorgonian octocoral: morphological modifications for interference competition. *Biol. Bull.* 175: 378-87.

Sebens, K.P., J. Witting, and B. Helmuth. 1997. Effects of water flow and branch spacing on particle capture by the reef coral *Madracis mirabilis* (Duchassaing and Michelotti). *J. Exp. Mar. Biol. Ecol.* 211: 1-28.

Segel, L.A., and H.W. Ducklow. 1982. A theoretical investigation into the influence of sublethal stresses on coral-bacterial ecosystem dynamics. *Bull. Mar. Sci.* 32: 919-35.

Sepers, A.B.J. 1977. The utilization of dissolved organic compounds in aquatic environments. *Hydrobiologia* 52: 39-54.

Serene, R. 1972. On the brachyuran fauna of the Indo-Pacific coral reefs. In: *Proc. Symp. Corals Coral Reefs* (C. Mukundan and C.S. Gopinadha Pillai, eds.). Marine Biological Ass'n of India, Cochin: 419-25.

Shanks, A.L., and J.D. Trent. 1979. Marine snow: microscale nutrient patches. *Limnol. Oceanogr.* 24: 850-4.

Sheppard, C.R.C. 1979. Interspecific aggression between reef corals with reference to their distribution. *Mar. Ecol. Prog. Ser.* 1: 237-47.

Sheppard, C.R.C. 1981. Illumination and the coral community beneath tabular *Acropora* species. *Mar. Biol.* 64: 53-8.

Sheppard, C.R.C. 1981. "Reach" of aggressively interacting corals, and relative importance of interactions at different depths. *Proc. 4th Int. Coral Reef Symp.* 2: 363-8.

Shibata, K. 1969. Pigments, and a UV-absorbing substance in corals and a blue-green alga living in the Great Barrier Reef. *Plant & Cell Physiol.* 10: 325-35.

Shick, M.J., 1990. Diffusion limitation and hyperoxic enhancement of oxygen consumption in zooxanthellate sea anemones, zoanthids, and corals. *Biol. Bull.* 179: 148-58.

Shick, J.M., and J.A. Dykens. 1985. Oxygen detoxification in algal-invertebrate symbioses in the Great Barrier Reef. *Oecologia* 66: 33-41.

Shick, M.J., M.P. Lesser, and W.R. Stochaj. 1991. Ultraviolet radiation and photooxidative stress in zooxanthellae anthozoa: the sea anemone *Phllodiscus semoni* and the octocoral *Clavularia* sp. *Symbiosis* 10: 145-73.

Shimada, H., and H. Yokochi. 1992. Coral spawning and its synchrony at Irimote Island, Southern Ryukyus. *Proc. 7th Int. Coral Reef Symp.* 1: 502.

Shimek, R.L. 1995. What benefit does strontium supplementation offer the reef aquarium? *Aquarium Frontiers* 2(1) 7-13.

Shimek, R.L. 1997. Feed your corals. It is the natural way. *Aquarium Net,* January issue. http://www.aquarium.net.

Shimek, R.L. 1997. Why and what: foods and feeding in aquarium coral husbandry. *Aquarium Net,* February issue. http://www.aquarium.net.

Shimeta, J., and P.A. Jumars. 1991. Physical mechanisms and rates of particle capture by suspension feeders. *Oceanogr. Mar. Biol. Ann. Rev.* 29: 191-257.

Shinn, E.A. 1989. What is really killing the corals? *Sea Frontiers* 39: 72-81.

Shinn, E.A. 1996. No rocks, no water, no ecosystem. *Geotimes* 41: 16-19.

Shoup, C.O., and A.L. Gaski. 1995. Trade in CITES-listed hard corals, 1989-1993: a preliminary report. *TRAFFIC USA,* Washington, DC. 14 pp.

Shreve, J. 1996. Are algae—not coral—reef's master builders? *Science* 271: 597-8.

Siebeck, O. 1988. Experimental investigation of UV tolerance in hermatypic corals (Scleractinia). *Mar. Ecol. Prog. Ser.* 43: 95-103.

Sier, C.J.S., and P.J.W. Olive. 1994. Reproduction and reproductive variability in the coral *Pocillopora verrucosa* from the Republic of Maldives. *Mar. Biol.* 118: 713-22.

Simkiss, K. 1976. Cellular aspects of calcification. In: *The Mechanisms of Mineralization in the Invertebrates and Plants* (N. Watabe and K.M. Wilbur, eds.). Univ. South Carolina Press, Columbia, South Carolina: pp. 1-29.

Slattery, M., et al. 1999. Chemical signals in gametogenesis, spawning, and larval settlement and defense of the soft coral *Sinularia polydactyla. Coral Reefs* 18: 75-84.

Small, A. 1997. Smithsonian Institution. Personal communications.

Small, A., and W.H. Adey. 1998. Reef corals, zooxanthellae & free-living algae: interactions that optimize calcification and primary production. In submission: *Ecological Engineering.*

Small, A.M., W.H. Adey, and D. Spoon. 1998. Are current estimates of coral reef biodiversity too low? The view through the window of a microcosm. *Atoll Research Bulletin* 458:1-20.

Smith, G.W., and K.B. Ritchie. 1995. Bacterial studies on white-band disease of *Acropora cervicornis. Eur. Mtg. Int. Soc. Reef Stud. ISRS.*

Smith, L.D., et al. 1999. Experimental assessment of the factors affecting the settlement and survival of reseeded coral spat in the field. NCRI International Conference on Scientific Aspects of Coral Reef Assessment, Monitoring, and Restoration. April 14-16, 1999. Fort Lauderdale, FL: 180-1.

Smith, L.D., and T.P. Hughes. 1999. An experimental assessment of survival, re-attachment and fecundity of coral fragments. *J. Exp. Mar. Biol. Ecol.* 235: 147-64.

Smith, N., and H.M. Lenhoff. 1976. Regulation of frequency of pedal laceration in a sea anemone. In: *Coelenterate Ecology and Behavior* (G.O. Mackie, ed.). University of Victoria, British Columbia: pp. 117-26.

Smith, S.V. 1978. Coral-reef area and the contributions of reefs to processes and resources to the world's oceans. *Nature* 273: 225-6.

Smith, S.V. 1984. Phosphorous versus nitrogen limitation in the marine environment. *Limnol. Oceanogr.* 29: 1149-60.

Smith, S.V. 1995. Coral Reef Calcification. In: *Perspectives on Coral Reefs* (D.J. Barnes, ed.). AIMS, Brian Clouston Publisher: 240-8.

Smith, S.V., and D.W. Kinsey. 1978. Calcification and organic carbon metabolism as indicated by carbon dioxide. In: *Coral Reefs: Research Methods.* UNESCO Monographs on Oceanographic Methodology. pp. 469-84.

Smith, V.J. 1996. The prophenoloxidase activating system: a common defense pathway for deuterostomes and protostomes? In: *Advances in Comparative and Environmental Physiology, Vol. 23: Invertebrate Immune Responses: Cells and Molecular Products* (E.L. Cooper, ed.). Springer-Verlag Berlin Heidelberg: 75-114.

Snidvongs, A., and R.A. Kinzie III. 1994. Effects of nitrogen and phosphorous enrichment on in vivo symbiotic zooxanthellae of *Pocillopora damicornis. Mar. Biol.* 118: 705-11.

Snyderman, M., and C. Wiseman. 1993. *Guide to Marine Life: Caribbean, Bahamas, Florida*. Aqua Quest Publications, New York.

Soong, K. 1992. Reproduction and coral size of reef coral species. *Proc. 7th Int. Coral Reef Symp.* 1: 503.

Soong, K. 1993. Colony size as a species character in massive reef corals. *Coral Reefs* 12: 77-83.

Soong, K., et al. 1999. A very large poritid colony at Green Island, Taiwan. *Coral Reefs* 18:42.

Soong, K., and L.C. Cho. 1998. Synchronized release of medusae from three species of hydrozoan fire corals. *Coral Reefs* 17: 145-54.

Sorokin, Y.I. 1973. Trophical role of bacteria in the ecosystem of the coral reef. *Nature* 242: 415-17.

Sorokin, Y.I. 1973. On the feeding of some scleractinian corals with bacteria and dissolved organic matter. *Limnol. Oceanogr.* 18: 380-5.

Sorokin, Y.I. 1981. Aspects of the biomass, feeding and metabolism of common corals of the Great Barrier Reef, Australia. *Proc. 4th Int. Coral Reef Symp.* 2: 27-32.

Sorokin, Y.I. 1981. Microheterotrophic organisms in marine ecosystems. In: *Analysis of Marine Ecosystems* (A.R.Longhurst, ed.). Academic Press, New York: pp. 293-311.

Sorokin, Y.I. 1990. Plankton in the reef ecosystems. In: *Coral Reefs: Ecosystems of the World, Vol. 25* (Z. Dubinsky, ed.). Elsevier Scientific Publishing Co. Inc. New York: 291-328.

Sorokin, Y.I. 1990. Aspects of trophic relations, productivity and energy balance in coral-reef ecosystems. In: *Coral Reefs: Ecosystems of the World, Vol. 25* (Z. Dubinsky, ed.). Elsevier Scientific Publishing Co. Inc. New York: 401-10.

Sorokin, Y.I. 1991. Biomass, metabolic rates and feeding of some common zoantharians and octocorals. *Aust. J. Mar. Freshwater Res.* 42: 729-41.

Sorokin, Y.I. 1991. Parameters of productivity and metabolism of coral reef ecosystems off Central Vietnam. *Est. Coast Shelf Sci.* 33: 259-80.

Sorokin, Y.I. 1995. *Ecological Studies: Coral Reef Ecology Vol. 102*. Springer-Verlag, Berlin. 564 pp.

Spalding, M. and A.M. Grenfell. 1997. New estimates of global and regional coral reef areas. *Coral Reefs* 16:225-30.

Sparks, A.K. 1972. *Invertebrate Pathology*. Academic Press, NY.

Sparks, A.K. 1985. *Synopsis of Invertebrate Pathology: Exclusive of Insects*. Elsevier Science Publishers B.V.: Amsterdam: pp. 2-8, 311-12.

Spearman, R.I.C. 1973. *The Integument: A Textbook of Skin Biology*. University Press, Cambridge: pp. 20-58.

Spokes, L.J., and P.S. Liss. 1996. Photochemically induced redox reactions in seawater. II. Nitrogen and iodine. *Mar. Chem.* 54: 1-10.

Squires, D.F. 1965. Neoplasia in a coral? *Science* 148: 503-5.

Stafford-Smith, M.G. 1992. Mortality of the hard coral *Leptoria phrygia* under persistent sediment influx. *Proc. 7th Int. Coral Reef Symp.* 1: 289-99.

Stambler, N., N. Popper, Z. Dubinsky, and J. Stimson. 1991. Effect of nutrient enrichment and water motion on the coral *Pocillopora damicornis. Pac. Sci.* 45: 299-307.

Stambler, N., and Z. Dubinsky. 1992. Effects of light and eutrophication on coral-algae association. *Proc. 7th Int. Coral Reef Symp.* 1: 347.

Stearn, C.W., and R. Riding. 1973. Forms of the hydrozoan *Millepora* on a recent coral reef. *Lethaia* 6: 187-200.

Steen, R.G., and L. Muscatine. 1984. Daily budgets of photosynthetically fixed carbon in symbiotic zoanthids. *Biol. Bull.* 167: 477-87.

Stephens, G.C. 1962. Uptake of organic material by aquatic invertebrates. I. Uptake of glucose by the solitary coral *Fungia scutaria. Biol. Bull.* 123: 648-59.

Steven, A.D.L., and A.D. Broadbent. 1997. Growth and metabolic responses of *Acropora palifera* to long term nutrient enrichment. *Proc. 8th Int. Coral Reef Symp.* 1: 867-72.

Stimson, J.S. 1976. Reproduction of some common Hawaiian reef corals. In: *Coelenterate Ecology and Behavior* (G.O. Mackie, ed.). University of Victoria, British Columbia: pp. 271-80.

Stimson, J. 1985. The effect of shading by the table coral *Acropora hyacinthus* on understory corals. *Ecology* 66: 40-53.

Stimson, J. 1992. The effect of ammonium addition on coral growth rate. *Proc. 7th Int. Coral Reef Symp.* 1: 383.

Stimson, J. 1996. The annual cycle of density of zooxanthellae in the tissues of field and laboratory-held *Pocillopora damicornis* (Linnaeus). *J. Exp. Mar. Biol. Ecol.* 214: 35-48.

Stimson, J. 1996. Wave-like outward growth of some table- and plate-forming corals, and a hypothetical mechanism. *Bull. Mar. Sci.* 58: 301-13.

Stimson, J., and R.A. Kinzie. 1991. The temporal pattern and rate of release of zooxanthellae from the reef coral *Pocillopora damicornis* (Linnaeus) under nitrogen-enrichment and control conditions. *J. Exp. Mar. Biol. Ecol.* 153: 63-74.

Stoddart, D.R., and R.E. Johannes. 1978. *Coral Reefs: Research Methods*. UNESCO Monographs on Oceanographic Methodology. 581 pp.

Steitwieser, A., and C.H. Heathcock. 1981. *Introduction to Organic Chemistry*. MacMillan Publishing Co., Inc., New York, 1258 pp.

Stromgren, T. 1976. Skeleton growth of the hydrocoral *Millepora complanata. Limnol. Oceanogr.* 21: 156-60.

Stromgren, T. 1987. The effect of light on the growth rate of intertidal *Acropora pulchra* (Brook) from Phuket, Thailand, lat. 8°N. *Coral Reefs* 6: 43-7.

Styan, C.A. 1997. Inexpensive and portable sampler for collecting eggs of free-spawning marine invertebrates underwater. *Mar. Ecol. Prog. Ser.* 150: 293-6.

Suchanek, T.H. 1981. Interspecific competition between *Palythoa caribaeorum* and other sessile invertebrates on St. Croix reefs, U.S. Virgin islands. *Proc. 4th Int. Coral Reef Symp.* 2: 679-84.

Swart, P.K., et al. 1996. The origin of variation in the isotopic record of scleractinian corals: II. Carbon. *Geochim. Cosmochim. Acta* 60: 2871-28885

Szmant, A.M. 1997. Nutrient effects on coral reefs: a hypothesis on the importance of topographic and trophic complexity to reef nutrient dynamics. *Proc. 8th Int. Coral Reef Symp.* 2: 1527-32.

Szmant, A.M., et al. 1997. Hybridization within the species complex of the scleractinian coral *Montastrea annularis. Mar. Biol.* 129: 561-72.

Szmant, A.M., and N.J. Gassman. 1990. The effects of prolonged "bleaching" of the tissue biomass and reproduction of the reef coral *Montastrea annularis. Coral Reefs* 8: 217-24.

Szmant-Froelich, A. 1974. Structure, iodination and growth of the axial skeletons of *Muricea californica* and *M. fructicosa* (Coelenterata: Gorgonacea). *Mar. Biol.* 27: 299-306.

Szmant-Froelich, A., and M.E.Q. Pilson. 1984. Effects of feeding frequency and symbiosis with zooxanthellae on nitrogen metabolism and respiration of the coral *Astrangia danae*. *Mar. Biol.* 81: 153-62.

Takabayashi, M., and O. Hoegh-Guldberg. 1995. Ecological and physiological differences between two colour morphs of the coral *Pocillopora damicornis*. *Mar. Biol.* 123: 705-14.

Tambutte, E., D. Allemand, E. Mueller, and J. Jaubert. 1996. A compartmental approach to the mechanism of calcification in hermatypic corals. *J. Exp. Bio.* 199: 1029-41.

Tanner, J.E. 1992. Experimental analysis of digestive hierarchies in coral assemblages. *Proc. 7th Int. Coral Reef Symp.* 1: 569-74.

Tanner, J.E. 1996. Seasonality and lunar periodicity in the reproduction of pocilloporid corals. *Coral Reefs* 15: 59-66.

Tanner, J.E. 1997. Interspecific competition reduces fitness in scleractinian corals. *J. Exp. Mar. Biol. Ecol.* 214: 19-34.

Taylor, D.L. 1983. The coral-algal symbiosis. In: *Algal Symbiosis: A Continuum of Interaction Strategies* (L.J. Goff, ed.). Cambridge University Press, Cambridge: pp. 19-35.

Taylor, D.L. 1974. Symbiotic marine algae: taxonomy and biologic fitness. *Symbiosis in the Sea* (W.B. Vernberg, ed.) Univ. of S. Carolina Press, Columbia. pp. 245-58.

Taylor, D.L. 1977. Intra-colonial transport of organic compounds and calcium in some Atlantic reef corals. *Proc. 3rd Int. Coral Reef Symp.* 1: 431-6.

Teai, T., et al. 1997. Widespread occurrence of mycosporine-like amino acid compounds in scleractinians from French Polynesia. *Coral Reefs* 16: 169-76.

Tentori, E., J.C. Coll, and B. Fleury. 1997. ENCORE: Effects of elevated nutrients on the C:N:P ratios of *Sarcophyton sp.* (Alcyonacea). *Proc. 8th Int. Coral Reef Symp.* 1: 885-90.

Thomas, F.I.M., and M.J. Atkinson. 1997. Ammonium uptake by coral reefs: effects of water velocity and surface roughness on mass transfer. *Limnol. Oceanogr.* 42:81-88.

Thomas, P.A. 1972. Boring sponges of the reefs of Gulf of Mannar and Palk Bay. In: *Proc. Symp. Corals Coral Reefs* (C. Mukundan and C.S. Gopinadha Pillai, eds.). Marine Biological Ass'n. of India, Cochin: 333-63.

Thompson, G., and H.D. Livingston. 1970. Strontium and uranium concentrations in aragonite precipitated by some modern corals. *Earth Planet Sci. Let.* 8: 439-42.

Titlyanov, E.A. 1981. Adaptation of reef-building corals to low light intensity. *Proc. 4th Int. Coral Reef Symp.* 2: 39-43.

Titlyanov, E.A., M.G. Shaposhnikova, and V.I. Zvalinskii. 1980. Photosynthesis and adaptation of corals to irradiance 1. Contents and native state of photosynthetic pigments in symbiotic microalga. *Photosynthetica* 14: 413-21.

Titlyanov, E.A., T.V. Titlyanova, Y. Loya, and K. Yamazato. 1998. Degradation and proliferation of zooxanthellae in planulae of the hermatypic coral *Stylophora pistillata*. *Mar. Biol.* 130: 471-7.

Tomascik, T., and F. Sander. 1985. Effects of eutrophication on reef-building corals. I. Growth rate of the reef building coral *Montastrea annularis*. *Mar. Biol.* 87: 143-55.

Tomascik, T., and F. Sander. 1987. Effects of eutrophication on reef-building corals. III. Reproduction of the reef-building coral *Porites porites*. *Mar. Biol.* 94: 77-94.

Toonen, R. 1997. A reefkeeper's guide to introductory invertebrate zoology: Part 3: Cnidarians (Anthozoa). *Aquarium Net*, January issue. http://www.aquarium.net

Toonen, R. 1997. Reefkeeper's Guide to Invertebrate Zoology: Part 8: Phylum Annelida—Polychaetes, "the bristleworms." *Aquarium Net*, June issue. http://www.aquarium.net.

Toonen, R.J. 1997-8. Personal communications.

Toren, A., et al. 1998. Effect of temperature on the adhesion of *Vibrio* AK-1 to *Oculina patagonica* and coral bleaching. *Appl. Environ. Microbiol.* 64: 1379-84.

Torreton, J.P. 1999. Biomass, production and heterotrophic activity of bacterioplankton in the Great Astrolabe Reef lagoon (Fiji). *Coral Reefs* 18: 43-53.

Travis, J. 1996. Bleaching power: marine bacteria rout coral's colorful algae. *Sci. News* 149: 379.

Trench, R.K. 1974. Nutritional potentials in *Zoanthus sociatus* (Coelenterata, Anthozoa). *Helgo wiss Meers* 26: 174-216.

Trench, R.K. 1988. Specificity in dinomastigote-marine invertebrate symbioses: an evaluation of hypotheses of mechanisms involved in producing specificity. In: *Cell to Cell Signals in Plant, Animal and Microbial Symbiosis* (S. Scannerini et al., eds.). 325-46 pp.

Trench, R.K. 1997. Diversity of symbiotic dinoflagellates and the evolution of microalgal-invertebrate symbioses. *Proc. 8th Int. Coral Reef Symp.* 2: 1275-86.

Tsien, R.Y. 1999. Rosy dawn for fluorescent proteins. *Nat. Biotech.* 17: 956-7.

Tsuroka, D. 1993. Vanishing coral refs. *Far East Econ. Rev.* Jan. 7: 24-25.

Tuckova, L., and M. Bilej. 1996. Mechanisms of antigen processing in invertebrates: are there receptors? In: *Advances in Comparative and Environmental Physiology, Vol. 23: Invertebrate Immune Responses: Cells and Molecular Products* (E.L. Cooper, ed.) Springer-Verlag Berlin Heidelberg: 41-72.

Tudhope, A.W., et al. 1992. Growth characteristics and susceptibility to bleaching in massive *Porites* corals, South Thailand. *Proc. 7th Int. Coral Reef Symp.* 1: 64-9.

Tullock, J.H. 1997. *Natural Reef Aquariums*. Microcosm Ltd. Shelburne, Vermont. 336 pp.

Tunnicliffe, V. 1981. Breakage and propagation of the stony coral *Acropora cervicornis*. *Proc. Natl. Acad. Sci., USA* 78: 2427-2431.

Tursch, B., et al. 1978. Terpenoids from coelenterates. In: *Marine Natural Products: Chemical and Biological Perspectives, Vol. II* (P.J. Scheuer, ed.). Academic Press, New York: 247-95.

Tursch, B., and A. Tursch. 1982. The soft coral community on a sheltered reef quadrat at Laing Island (Papua New Guinea). *Mar. Biol.* 68: 321-332.

Tyree, S. 1992. Aquaria Archive: reefs Reproduction Coral moonlight. From: steve@celia.UUCP (Steve Tyree) Date: 16 Apr 92 18:34:54 GMT Newsgroups: rec.aquaria Subject: Re: [M] Hard coral spawning continued...

Tyree, S. 1992. From: steve@celia.UUCP (Steve Tyree) Date: 30 Nov 92 21:23:07 GMT Newsgroups: rec.aquaria Subject: Re: Liverock organisms.

Tyree, S. 1992. Tropical Coral Reef Environment Rhythmicity and Techniques for Inducing Captive Coral Spawning. Aquaria Archive: reefs Reproduction Coral tyree_rhythms92.

Tyree, S. 1993. Aquaria Archive: reefs Corals acropora From: steve@rhythm.com (Steve Tyree) Date: Mon, 25 Oct 1993 08:57:43 GMT Newsgroups: rec.aquaria.

Tyree, S. 1994. Sexual reproduction and recruitment of the stony coral *Pocillopora verrucosa* with discussion of spawning induction techniques. *Aquarium Frontiers* 1(1) 13-29.

Upton, S.J., and E.C. Peters. 1986. A new and unusual species of coccidium Apicomplexa: Agammococcidorida from Caribbean scleractinian corals. *J. Invertbe. Pathol.* 47:184-193.

U.S. Department of State. Dec. 26, 1994. Fact Sheet: *The International Coral Reef Initiative.* U.S. Department of State Dispatch Vol. 5 (52): 859.

Vago, R. et al. 1998. Colony architecture of *Millepora dichotoma* Forskal. *J. Exp. Mar. Biol. Ecol.* 224: 225-35.

Vallejo, B.M. Jr. 1997. An overview of the Philippine marine aquarium fish industry. *Proc. 8th Int. Coral Reef Symp.* 2: 1981-6.

Van Alstyne, K.L., C.R. Wylie, and V.J. Paul. 1992. Differential feeding deterrence generated by asymmetrical defense production in Indo-Pacific soft corals. *Proc. 7th Int. Coral Reef Symp.* 2: 877.

Van Alstyne, K.L., and V.J. Paul. 1988. The role of secondary metabolites in marine ecological interactions. *Proc. 6th Int. Coral Reef Symp.* 1: 175-85.

Vandermuelen, J.H., and L. Muscatine. 1974. Influence of symbiotic algae on calcification in reef corals: critique and progress report. *Symbiosis in the Sea.* 1-8.

Van Treeck, P., and H. Schumacher. 1997. Initial survival of coral nubbins transplanted by a new transplantation technology—options for reef rehabilitation. *Mar. Ecol. Prog. Ser.* 150: 287-92.

Van Veghel, M.L.J. 1992. Reproductive aspects of *Montastrea annularis* morphotypes. *Proc. 7th Int. Coral Reef Symp.* 2: 679.

Vareschi, E., and H. Fricke. 1986. Light responses of a scleractinian coral *Plerogyra sinuosa. Mar. Biol.* 90: 395-402.

Veron, J.E.N. 1981. The species concept in "Scleractinia of Eastern Australia." *Proc. 4th Int. Coral Reef Symp.* 2: 183-6.

Veron, J.E.N. 1986. *Corals of Australia and the Indo-Pacific.* University of Hawaii Press, Honolulu, Hawaii. 644 pp.

Veron, J.E.N. 1986. Distribution of reef-building corals. *Oceanus* 29: pp. 27-31.

Veron, J.E.N. 1992. *Hermatypic Corals of Japan.* AIMS, Townsville. 234 pp.

Veron, J.E.N. 1993. *A Biogeographic Database of Hermatypic Corals: Species of the central Indo-Pacific genera of the world.* Australian Institute of Marine Science Monograph Series Vol. 10, AIMS, Townsville. 433 pp.

Veron, J.E.N. 1995. *Corals in Space and Time: The Biogeography and Evolution of the Scleractinia.* Comstock/Cornell, Cornell University Press, New York.

Veron, J.E.N. 1996-7. Personal communications.

Veron, J.E.N., et al. 1996. Reassessing evolutionary relationships of scleractinian corals. *Coral Reefs* 15: 1-9.

Veron, J.E.N. and P.R. Minchin. 1989. Annotated checklist of the hermatypic corals of the Philippines. *Pacific Science* 43(3): 234-87.

Verseveldt, J. 1977. Octocorallia from various localities in the Pacific Ocean. *Zool. Verh.* 15: 50 pp.

Verseveldt, J. 1977. Australian Octocorallia (Coelenterata). *Aust, J. Mar. Freshwater Res.* 28: 171-240.

Verseveldt, J. 1977. On two new *Sinularia* species (Octocorallia: Alcyonacea) from the Moluccas. *Zool. Med. Leiden.* 50(20): 303-07.

Verseveldt, J. 1978. Alcyonaceans (Coelenterata: Octocorallia) from some Micronesian Islands. *Zool. Med. Leiden.* 53(5): 49-55.

Verseveldt, J. 1978. On some Telestacea and Alcyonacea (Coelenterata: Octocorallia) from the West Indian region. *Zool. Med. Leiden.* 53(4): 41-7.

Verseveldt, J. 1980. A revision of the genus *Sinularia* May (Octocorallia, Alcyonacea). *Zool. Verh.* 179: 1-128.

Verseveldt, J. 1982. A revision of the genus *Sarcophyton* Lesson (Octocorallia, Alcyonacea) *Zool. Verh.* 192: 1-99.

Verseveldt, J. 1983. A revision of the genus *Lobophytum* von Marenzeller (Octocorallia, Alcyonacea). *Zool. Verh.* 200: 1-103.

Verseveldt, J. 1988. Revision of the genera *Bellonella, Eleutherobia, Nidalia* and *Nidaliopsis* (Octocorallia: Alyconiidae and Nidalliidae), with descriptions of two new genera. *Zool. Verh.* 245: 1-131.

Verseveldt, J., and Y. Benayahu. 1978. Descriptions of one old and five new species of Alcyonacea (Coelenterata: Octocorallia) from the Red Sea. *Zool. Med. Leiden.* 53(6): 57-74.

Verseveldt, J., and Y. Benayahu. 1983. On two old and fourteen new species of Alcyonacea (Coelenterata, Octocorallia) from the Red Sea. *Zool. Verh.* 208: 1-31.

Vervoort, W., and H. Zibrowius. 1981. Annotations on H. Boschma's work on hydrocorals (Milleporina, Axoporina, Stylasterina), with additions to his list of the described species of Stylasterina. *Zool. Verh.* 181: 1-39.

Vosburgh, F. 1977. The response to drag of the reef coral *Acropora reticulata. Proc. 3rd Int. Coral Reef Symp.* 477-82.

Wahbeh, M.I., and A.M. Mahasner. 1988. Composition and bacterial utilization of mucus of corals from Aqaba (Red Sea), Jordan. *Proc. 6th Int. Coral Reef Symp.* 2: 53-7.

Wahle, C.M. 1980. Detection, pursuit, and overgrowth of tropical gorgonians by milleporid hydrocorals: perseua and medusa revisited. *Science* 209: 689-91.

Wainwright, S.A., and J.R. Dillon. 1969. On the orientation of sea fans (Genus *Gorgonia*). *Biol. Bull.* 136: 130-9.

Wainwright, S.A., and M.A. Koehl. 1976. The nature of flow and the reaction of benthic Cnidaria to it. In: *Coelenterate Ecology and Behavior* (G.O. Mackie, ed.). University of Victoria, British Columbia: pp. 5-22.

Walker, D.I., and R.F.G. Ormond. 1982. Coral death from sewage and phosphate pollution at Aqaba, Red Sea. *Mar. Poll. Bull.* 13: 21-5.

Walker, T.A., and G.D. Bull. 1983. A newly discovered method of reproduction in gorgonian coral. *Mar. Ecol. Prog. Ser.* 12: 137-43.

Wallace, C.C., R.C. Babcock, P.L. Harrison, J.K. Oliver, and B.L. Willis. 1986. Sex on the reef: mass spawning of corals. *Oceanus* 29: 38-42.

Ward, F. 1990. Florida's coral reefs are imperiled. *Natl. Geog.* 178 (1): 115-32

Ward, S. 1995a. Two patterns of energy allocation for growth, reproduction and lipid storage in the scleractinian coral *Pocillopora damicornis. Coral Reefs* 14: 87-90.

Ward, S. 1995b. The effect of damage on the growth, reproduction and storage of lipids in the scleractinian coral *Pocillopora damicornis* (Linnaeus). *J. Exp. Mar. Biol. Ecol.* 187: 193-206.

Warner, J. 1996. Personal communication.

Webb, K.L., and W.J. Wiebe. 1978. The kinetics and possible significance of nitrate uptake by several algal-invertebrate symbioses. *Mar. Biol.* 47: 21-7.

Weber, J.N. 1973. Incorporation of strontium into reef coral skeletal carbonate. *Geochim. Cosmochim. Acta* 37: 2173-2190.

Weber, P. 1993. Reviving coral reefs. *State of the World 1993: A Worldwatch Institute Report on Progress Toward a Sustainable Society.* W.W. Norton & Company, New York: 42-60.

Weber, P.K. 1993. Saving the coral reefs. *The Futurist*, July/August: 28-33.

Weis, V.M., G.J. Smith, and L. Muscatine. 1989. A "CO_2" supply mechanism in zooxanthellate cnidarians: role of carbonic anhydrase. *Mar. Biol.* 100: 195-202.

Wellington, G.M. 1980. Reversal of digestive interactions between Pacific reef corals: mediation by sweeper tentacles. *Oecologia* 47: 340-3.

Wellington, G.M. 1982. An experimental analysis of the effects of light and zooplankton on coral zonation. *Oecologia* 52: 311-20.

Wells, J.W. 1956. Scleractinia. In: *Treatise on Invertebrate Paleontology. Part F. Coelenterata* (R.C. Moore, ed.). Geological Society of America and University of Kansas Press: F328-F438.

Wells, J.W. 1966. Evolutionary development in the scleractinian family Fungiidae. The Cnidaria and their evolution. *Proc. Symp. Zool. Soc. Lond.* 16: 223-46.

Wells, J.W. 1969. Aspects of Pacific coral reefs. *Micronesica* 5: 317-22.

Wells, J.W., and D. Hill. 1956. Zoantharia—general features. In: *Treatise on Invertebrate Paleontology. Part F. Coelenterata* (R.C. Moore, ed.). Geological Society of America and University of Kansas Press: F231-2.

Wells, J.W., and D. Hill. 1956. Zoantharia, Corallimorpharia, and Actiniaria. In: *Treatise on Invertebrate Paleontology. Part F. Coelenterata* (R.C. Moore, ed.). Geological Society of America and University of Kansas Press: F232-3.

Wells, S.M. 1981. International trade in ornamental corals and shells. *Proc. 4th Int. Coral Reef Symp.* 1: 323-30.

Wells, S., and N. Hanna. 1992. *The Greenpeace Book of Coral Reefs*. Sterling Publishing Co., Inc., New York. 160 pp.

Wells, S. M., R. M. Pyle, and N. Mark Collins. 1983. *The IUCN Invertebrate Red Data Book*. ICUN, Gland, Switzerland: i-33.

Wells, S., and E.M. Wood. 1991. The marine curio trade: conservation guidelines and legislation. A Report for The Marine Conservation Society. 23 pp.

Wesseling, I., et al. 1999. Damage and recovery of four Philippine corals from short-term sediment burial. *Mar. Ecol. Prog. Ser.* 176: 11-15.

West, D.A. 1976. Aposematic coloration and mutualism in sponge-dwelling tropical zoanthids. In: *Coelenterate Ecology and Behavior* (G.O. Mackie, ed.). University of Victoria, British Columbia: pp. 443-52.

West, J.M., et al. 1993. Morphological plasticity in a gorgonian coral (*Briareum asbestinum*) over a depth cline. *Mar. Ecol. Prog. Ser.* 94: 61-9.

Wethey, D.S., and J.W. Porter. 1976. Sun and shade differences in productivity of reef corals. *Nature* 262: 281-2.

Wethey, D.S., and J.W. Porter. 1976. Habitat-related patterns of productivity of the foliaceous reef coral *Pavona praetorta* Dana. In: *Coelenterate Ecology and Behavior* (G.O. Mackie, ed.). University of Victoria, British Columbia: pp. 59-66.

Wheeler, J.A. 1996. The marine aquarium trade: a tool for coral reef conservation. A Report for the Sustainable Development and Conservation Biology Program. University of Maryland, College Park. 47 pp.

Whittaker, R.H., and P.P. Feeny. 1971. Allelochemicals; chemical interactions between species. *Science* 171: 757-70.

Wiebe, W.J., C.J. Crossland, R.E. Johannes, and D.W. Rimmer. 1981. High latitude (Abrolhos Islands) reef community metabolism: what sets latitudinal limits on coral reef development? *Proc. 4th Int. Coral Reef Symp.* 1: 72.

Wijsman-Best, M. 1976. Biological results of the Snellium expedition. XXVII. II. The genera *Favites, Goniastrea, Platygyra, Oulophyllia, Leptoria, Hydnophora,* and *Caulastrea. Zool. Med. Leiden.* 50(4): 45-61.

Wijsman-Best, M. 1977. Indo-Pacific coral species belonging to the subfamily Montastreinae Vaughan & Wells, 1943 (Scleractinea-Coelenterata) Part I. The genera *Montastrea* and *Plesiastrea. Zool. Med. Leiden.* 52(7): 81-97.

Wijsman-Best, M. 1977. Intra- and extratentacular budding in hermatypic reef corals. *Proc. 3rd Int. Coral Reef Symp.* 1: 471-5.

Wijsman-Best, M. 1980. Indo-Pacific coral species belonging to the subfamily Montastreinae (Scleractinea-Coelenterata) Part II. The genera *Cyphastrea, Leptastrea, Echinopora,* and *Diploastrea. Zool. Med. Leiden.* 55(21): 235-63.

Wilbur, K.M. 1976. Recent studies of invertebrate mineralization. In: *The Mechanisms of Mineralization in the Invertebrates and Plants* (N. Watabe and K.M. Wilbur, eds.). Univ. South Carolina Pres, Columbia, South Carolina.

Wilkens, P. 1992. *Marine Invertebrates: Stony Corals, Mushroom and Colonial Anemones*. Karl-Heinz Dahne Publishing: Wuppertal, Germany. 136 pp.

Wilkens, P., and J. Birkholz. 1992. *Marine Invertebrates: Organ-pipe and Leather Corals, Gorgonians*. Karl-Heinz Dahne Publishing: Wuppertal, Germany. 134 pp.

Wilkinson, C.R. 1986. The nutritional spectrum of coral reef benthos. *Oceanus* 29: 68-75.

Wilkinson, C.R. 1992. Coral reefs of the world are facing widespread devastation: can we prevent this through sustainable management practices? *Proc. 7th Int. Coral Reef Symp.* 1: 11-15.

Wilkinson, C.R., et al. 1988. Nutritional spectrum of animals with photosynthetic symbionts—corals and sponges. *Proc. 6th Int. Coral Reef Symp.* 3: 27-30.

Williams, E.H., and L. Bunkley-WIlliams. 1988. Coral reef bleaching. *Sea Frontiers*, March-April: 81-7.

Williams, E.H., and L. Bunkley-Williams. 1990. The world-wide coral reef bleaching cycle and related sources of coral mortality. *Caribbean Aquatic Animal Health Project* 1-63.

Williams, E.H., and L. Bunkley-Williams. 1990. Coral reef bleaching alert. *Nature* 346: 225.

Williams, E.H., Jr., L. Bunkley-Williams, J.M. Grizzle, E.C. Peters, D.V. Lightner, J. Harshbarger, A. Rosenfield, and R. Reimschuessel. 1993. Epidemic misuse. Nature 364:664.

Williams, E.H., C. Goenaga, and V. Vicente. 1987. Mass bleachings on Atlantic coral reefs. *Science* 238: 877-8.

Williams, G.C. 1992. Biotic diversity, biogeography, and phylogeny of pennatulacean octocorals associated with coral reefs in the Indo-Pacific. *Proc. 7th Int. Coral Reef Symp.* 2: 729-35.

Williams, G.C. 1992. Biogeography of the octocorallian coelenterate fauna of southern Africa. *Biol. J. Linn. Soc.* 46: 351-401.

Williams, G.C. 1993. *Coral Reef Octocorals: An Illustrated Guide to the Soft Corals, Sea Fans, and Sea Pens Inhabiting the Coral Reefs of Northern Natal*. Dep't. of Invertebrate Zoology and Geology, California Academy of Sciences, San Francisco, California. 64 pp.

Willis, B.L. 1985. Phenotypic plasticity versus phenotypic stability in the reef corals *Turbinaria mesenterina* and *Pavona cactus. Proc. 5th Coral Reef Symp.* 2: 406.

Willis, B.L., et al. 1992. Experimental evidence of hybridization in reef corals invovled in mass spawning events. *Proc. 7th Int. Coral Reef Symp.* 1: 504.

Willis, B.L., and D.J. Ayre. 1985. Asexual reproduction and genetic determination of growth form in the coral *Pavona cactus*: biochemical genetic and immunogenetic evidence. *Oecologia* 65: 516-25.

Wilson, E.O. 1988. The current state of biological diversity. In: *Biodiversity* (E.O. Wilson, ed.). National Academy Press, Washington DC. 521 pp (3-18).

Wilson, R., and P.L. Harrison. 1998. Settlement competency periods of larvae of three species of scleractinian corals. *Mar. Biol.* 131: 339-45.

Winiarski, K. 1998. Coral in peril as reefs suffer worldwide. *USA Today,* October 19, 1998: 4A.

Wisniewski, J. 1990. Fireworms in the marine aquarium, *Marine Fish Monthly,* p. 22. Downloaded from rec. aquaria newsgroup.

Witman, J.D. 1988. Effects of predation by the fireworm *Hermodice carunculata* on Milleporid hydrocorals. *Bull. Mar. Sci.* 42: 446-58.

Wood, E.M. 1983. *Corals of the World*. T.F.H. Publications Ltd., NJ. 256 pp.

Wood, E.M. 1985. Exploitation of coral reef fishes for the aquarium trade. Report to the Marine Conservation Society. 121 pp.

Woodland, D.J., and J.N.A. Hooper. 1977. The effect of human trampling on coral reefs. *Biol. Cons.* 11: 1-4.

Wylie, C.R., and V.J. Paul. 1989. Chemical defenses in three species of *Sinularia* (Coelenterata, Alcyonacea): effects against generalist predators and the butterflyfish *Chaetodon unimaculatus* Bloch. *J. Exp. Mar. Biol. Ecol.* 129: 141-60.

Yamashiro, H. 1992. Skeletal dissolution by scleractinian corals. *Proc. 7th Int. Coral Reef Symp.* 2: 1142-6.

Yamashiro, H., and M. Nishihira. 1995. Phototaxis in Fungiidae corals (Scleractinia). *Mar. Biol.* 124: 461-5.

Yamashiro, H., and K. Yamazato. 1996. Morphologic studies of soft tissues involved in skeletal dissolution in the coral *Fungia fungites*. *Coral Reefs* 15(3): 177-80.

Yamazato, K., and T. Ito. 1981. Dynamics of colonial growth in a zoanthid, *Palythoa tuberculosa* (Esper). *Proc. 4th Int. Coral Reef Symp.* 2: 760.

Yamazato, K., M. Sai, and Y. Nakano. 1992. Sexual reproduction of Okinawan corals, *Stylophora pistillata* (Esper) and *Seriatopora hystrix* (Dana). *Proc. 7th Int. Coral Reef Symp.* 1: 504.

Yamazato, K., M. Sato, and H. Yamashiro. 1981. Reproductive biology of an alcyonarian coral, *Lobophytum crassum* Marenseller. *Proc. 4th Int. Coral Reef Symp.* 2: 671-8.

Yaiullo, J. 1994. Spawning *Tubastraea coccinea*. *Aquarium Frontiers* 2(3): 2-17.

Yap, H.T., et al. 1998. Physiological and ecological aspects of coral transplantation. *J. Exp. Mar. Biol. Ecol.* 229: 69-84

Yap, H.T., P.M. Alino, and E.D. Gomez. 1992. Trends in growth and mortality of three coral species (Anthozoa: Scleractinia), including effects of transplantation. *Mar. Ecol. Prog. Ser.* 83: 91-101.

Yap, H.T., and E.D. Gomez. 1981. Growth of *Acropora pulchra* (Brook) in Bolinao, Pangasinan, Philippines. *Proc. 4th Int. Coral Reef Symp.* 2: 210-13.

Yap, H.T., and E.D. Gomez. 1985. Growth of *Acropora pulchra*. III. Preliminary observations on the effects of transplantation and sediment on the growth and survival of transplants. *Mar. Biol.* 87: 203-9.

Yates, K.R., and B.A. Carlson. 1992. Corals in aquariums: how to use selective collecting and innovative husbandry to promote reef conservation. *Proc. 7th Int. Coral Reef Symp.* 2: 1091-5.

Yonge, C.M. 1963. The biology of coral reefs. In: *Advances in Marine Biology* (F. Russel, ed.). Acad. Press, New York. pp. 209-60.

Yonge, C.M. 1968. Living corals. *Proc. Roy. Soc. Lond. B* 169: 329-44.

Yonge, C.M. 1969. Conservation of coral reefs. *Micronesica* 5: 307-10.

Yoshino, T.P., and G.R. Vasta. 1996. Parasite-invertebrate host immune interactions. In: *Advances in Comparative and Environmental Physiology, Vol. 24: Invertebrate Immune Responses: Cell Activities and the Environment* (E.L. Cooper, ed.). Springer-Verlag Berlin Heidelberg: 125-67.

Yoshioko, P.M., and B.B. Yoshioko. 1989. Effects of wave energy, topographic relief and sediment transport on the distribution of shallow-water gorgonians of Puerto Rico. *Coral Reefs,* 8:145-52.

Yoshioko, P.M., and B.B. Yoshioko. 1991. A comparison of the survivorship and growth of shallow-water gorgonian species of Puerto Rico. *Mar. Ecol. Prog. Ser.* 69: 252-60.

Young, S.D. 1971. Organic matrices associated with $CaCO_3$ skeletons of several species of hermatypic corals. In: *Experimental Coelenterate Biology* (H.M. Lenhoff, L. Muscatine, and L.V. Davis, eds.). University of Hawaii Press, Honolulu: 260-4.

Zankl, H., and H.G. Multer. 1992. Cavalites: facies indicators in a high-energy reef environment. *Proc. 7th Int. Coral Reef Symp.* 1: 439.

Zann, V.P., and L. Bolton. 1985. Zone distribution, abundance, and ecology of the blue coral *Heliopora coerulea* (Pallas) in the Pacific. *Coral Reefs* 4: 125-34.

Zilderberg, C., and P.J. Edmunds. 1999. Patterns of skeletal structure variability in clones of the reef coral *Montastraea franksi*. *Bull. Mar. Sci.* 64: 373-81.

Zorpette, Glenn. 1995. More coral trouble. *Sci. Amer.* 273: 37-8.

Photography Credits

Scott W. Michael

Front cover (center inset), 37(T, B), 41, 56, 58, 66(R), 73, 88, 96(T), 100(B), 102(L), 103(L), 107, 108(T), 112, 115, 116(TL), 117(TL, BL), 119(C, B), 120(TL, BL), 122(TL, TR, BR), 126(B), 127(T), 128(TL, TR, BL), 130(TL, TR, BL), 131(L), 133(TL, CR, BR), 134(T, B), 135(L), 138(BR), 139(TL, CR, BL, BR), 140(TL, TR, BR), 141, 142(C, B), 143, 146(TL, BL, BR), 147(TR, BL, BR), 149(BR), 152(B), 154, 156(BR), 160(B), 161(T), 163(R), 174(L), 175(R), 176, 183(B), 186, 187(R), 190(C), 192, 194, 195, 199(TR, BL, BR), 200, 202(TL, CR, BR), 203, 204(R), 207(TL, CL, CR, BL), 209(TL, TR, BR), 214(BL), 216(B), 217(T, C) 218(TL, BR), 219(BR), 221, 223(BR), 224(BR), 227(TR), 229(B), 230(CR, BR) 232(CL), 233(BL, BR), 235, 236(TR, CL, BL), 238(B), 239, 240(BL, BR), 241(T, B), 242(BL, BR), 243(B), 247(L), 249, 251(TR), 252, 254(CL, BL), 255(BR), 256(TR, BL, BR), 259(TR, BL), 261(L), 262, 264(BR), 266(TR, CL), 268(L), 269(BL), 271(T, B), 272(T, B), 273, 274, 275(BL), 276(TL, CR), 278(TR, BR), 279, 280(TR, BL), 282(BR), 283(T, C), 284, 285, 286(BL), 288(BL), 289, 290(TL, TR, CL, BR), 291(L), 292(T, BL), 293, 298, 301(L), 302, 303(C), 304, 306(TR, BL), 307(CL, CR), 309, 310(R), 311(TR, B), 312(TR), 313, 317(TR, BR), 318(C, B), 319(CL, BR), 358, 361(B), 362, 363(B), 366, 369(BR), 375(R), 377, 378(T), 381, 384, 390(R), 392(L), 395(L), 396, 400(T)

Janine Cairns-Michael

Front cover (background and left inset), 16(TR), 36(T, B), 37(C), 59, 66(L), 84, 105(T, C), 116(TR, BL, BR), 120(TR, BR), 121, 127(C, B), 129, 130(BR), 131(R), 133(CL), 134(C), 135(R), 137, 138(TL, TR, CL), 139(TR, CL), 140(BL), 144(TR, BL), 145, 147(TL), 151(C), 152(T, C), 156(TL, TR, CL, CR, BL), 158(TL), 160(C), 162, 182(B),

183(T, C), 188, 189(C), 198(T, B), 199(TL), 207(BR), 208, 209(BL), 213(R), 214(TL, TR, CL, BR), 218(BL), 219(TL, TR, BL) 222, 223(TL), 224(CL, CR, BL), 225(TL, TR, CL, BR), 227(TL, CL, CR, BR), 228, 229(T, C), 230(TL, TR, CL, BL), 232(TL, CR, BR), 233(TL, CL), 234, 236(TL, CR, BR), 237(C), 240(TL, TR) 241(C), 244(CL, BL, TR), 245(C, B), 247(R), 248(TL, BL, BR), 251(TL, BL), 253, 254(TL, TR, CR), 255(TL), 256(TL, CR), 257, 258, 259(TL, CR, BR), 260, 261(R), 263, 264(BL), 266(TL, BL, BR), 267(L), 268(R), 269(TL, TR), 271(C), 275(TL, TR, CL, CR, BR), 276(BR), 277, 278(TL, BL), 280(TL), 281(BL), 282(TL, TR), 283(B), 288(CL, CR, BR), 290(CR, BL), 292(BR), 294, 295(C), 296, 297(R), 299(TR, BL), 306(TL, CL, CR, BR), 307(TL, TR, BL, BR), 308, 310(L), 311(TL), 312(TL, CL, CR, BL), 315(T, B), 316, 317(TL), 318(T), 319(TL, TR), 374(T), 391(R), 398, Back cover(T, B)

Alf Jacob Nilsen

14(BR), 16(TL, B), 17, 26(TL, BL), 27, 28, 30(L), 31(L), 32(T), 34, 36(C), 38, 46, 48(L), 50, 51(L), 52, 61, 70, 74, 76, 79, 80, 85, 86, 87, 102(R), 103(R), 104(CL), 108(BL, BR), 110, 114, 117(R), 119(T), 122(BL), 123, 124, 125, 126(T, C), 128(BR), 132, 133(TR, BL), 136, 138(CR, BL), 142(T), 144(TL, BR), 146(TR), 149(L, TR), 151(T, B), 153, 158(BL), 161(B), 172(B), 173(C), 174(R), 175(L, C) 178, 180, 181, 184(B), 185, 189(T), 202(TR, BL), 204(L), 207(TR), 214(CR), 216(T), 220, 223(TR, CR), 224(TR), 233(CR), 242(TR), 244(TL), 246(L), 248(TR), 250, 255(BL), 265, 269(BR), 272(C), 276(TR, BL), 280(BR), 281(TL), 282(BL), 286(T, BR), 288(TL, TR), 295(T, B), 297(L), 303(T, B), 312(BR), 314, 315(C), 324(R), 326, 327, 330, 336, 340, 346, 351, 352, 353, 361(T, C), 363(T), 371, 386, 388, 394, 395(R), 397, 402(R), 403

PAUL HUMANN

18, 21(BL, BR), 26(BR), 29, 30(R), 31(R), 32(B), 33, 48(R), 55, 60, 72, 90, 93, 96(BCR, BR), 97(3rd row L, BL, BR), 98, 100(T, C), 101, 104(TL, TR, CR), 105(B), 106, 118, 158(R), 159, 160(T), 161(C), 163(L), 164, 165, 166, 167, 168, 169, 170, 171, 172(T, C), 173(L, R), 182(T), 184(T), 187(L), 189(B), 190(T, B), 191, 198(C), 205, 210, 211, 213(L), 216(C), 223(CL), 224(TL), 225(CR, BL), 226, 232(TR), 233(TR), 242(TL), 243(T, C), 245(T), 246(R), 251(BR), 264(TL, TR), 270, 281(R), 291(R), 299(TL), 300, 317(BL), 319(BL), 320, 321, 342, 372, 374(B), 378(B), 392(R)

NORBERT WU/www.norbertwu.com

20, 26(TR), 78, 82, 215, 267(R), 287, 299(BR), 368, 369(TL, TR, BL), 391(L)

KELVIN AITKEN

21(T), 24, 32(C), 83, 94, 217(B), 232(BL), 379, 390(L), 401, 402(L)

GREGORY SCHIEMER

51(R), 196, 201, 237(B), 325, 333, 335, 347, 357, 382, 383, Back cover(C)

LARRY JACKSON

223(BL), 227(BL), 231, 238(T), 244(BR), 254(BR), 255(TR), 256(CL), 266(CR), 393

DR. ESTER C. PETERS

373, 374(C), 375(L), 376, 378(C), 380

STEVE TYREE

14(BL), 53, 237(T), 331, 345

SALLY JO HEADLEE/www.garf.org

202(CL), 364, 365, 405

JEFFREY TURNER/Oceans, Reefs & Aquariums

14(TL, TR), 15, 338, 348

ROBERT M. FENNER

Front cover (right inset), 113, 404

MICHAEL S. PALETTA

150, 328, 329

WAYNE SHANG/www.underseadiscovery.net

12, 218(TR), 322

ERIC H. BORNEMAN

324(L)

MARK CONLIN/www.norbertwu.com

400(B)

JIM GARDNER

67

AVI KLAPPER/www.norbertwu.com

68

DOUG PERRINE/www.norbertwu.com

81

J.E.N. VERON

92

JOSHUA HIGHTER

All illustrations

Special Thanks

The publisher wishes to acknowledge the support, participation, and encouragement
of the following individuals and organizations during the production of this book:

**Microcosm Authors, Field Editors
& Contributors**
Robert M. Fenner, author
    The Conscientious Marine Aquarist
Larry Jackson, Fishnet marine advisor
    (Compuserve)
Scott W. Michael, author *Reef Fishes*
Wayne Shang, reef aquarist
    (www.underseadiscovery.com)
Michael S. Paletta, author
    The New Marine Aquarium
Ronald L. Shimek, Ph.D., author
    *The PocketExpert™ Guide to
    Marine Invertebrates*
John H. Tullock, author
    Natural Reef Aquariums

Aqua Marines
Dennis & Kathleen Reynolds
614 Vincent Street
Redondo Beach, CA 90277
(310) 379-2581

Aquarium Systems
Edwin Mowka, Thomas A. Frakes,
Rand Kollman
8141 Tyler Boulevard
Mentor, OH 44060
(800) 822-1100
www.aquariumsystems.com

Bioquatic Photo
Alf J. Nilsen
N-4432
Hidrasund, Norway
www.aquariumworld.com/
    bioquaticshop
e-mail: bioquatic@aquariumworld.com

CoralFarms.com
Bob Mankin
10270 Alpine Drive
Cupertino, CA 95014
(800) 877-CORALS1
www.coralfarms.com

CPR (Creative Plastic Research)
Suk Choo Kim
P.O. Box 1111
Arcata, CA 95518-1111
(800) 357-2995
www.cprusa.com

Dynamic Ecomorphology
Steve Tyree
39525 Los Alamos Road, Suite A143
Murrieta, CA 92562
(909) 677-0073
www.dynamicecomorphology.com

Ecosystem Aquarium
Leng Sy
17775 Main St., Suite D
Irvine, CA 92714
(949) 851-6880
www.ecosystemaquarium.com

E.S.V. Co., Inc.
Bob Stark
38 Varick Street
Brooklyn, NY 11222
(718) 387-7839

**Geothermal Aquaculture Research
Foundation, Inc.**
LeRoy & Sally Jo Headlee
1321 Warm Springs Avenue
Boise, ID 83712
(208) 344-6163
www.garf.org

Hamilton Technology Corp.
14902 South Figueroa Street
Gardena, CA 90248
(800) 447-9797
www.hamiltontechnology.com

Harbor Aquatics
Joy & Gary Meadows
927 N. 200 W.
Valparaiso, IN 46385
(219) 764-4404
www.harboraquatics.com

IceCap, Inc.
Andrew S. Howard
9-B South Gold Drive
Hamilton, NJ 08691
(800) 742-3227
www.icecapinc.com

Marine Center
Randy Walker
P.O. Box 61250
Dallas, TX 75261
(817) 295-3988
www.flash.net/~rarefish

Marine Technical Concepts, Inc.
225 Godwin Avenue
Midland Park, NJ 07432
(201) 444-7165
www.marinetechnical.com

ORA (Oceans, Reefs & Aquariums)
Jeffrey Turner
112 North County Road
Palm Beach, FL 33480
(561) 835-4992
e-mail: clownfish@aol.com

Scientific Corals
Noel Curry
850 Dogwood Road, Suite A400-489
Lawrenceville, GA 30244
(770) 736-9220
www.scientificcorals.com

Sea Critters
Roy & Teresa Herndon
13005 Sea Critter Lane
Dover, FL 33527
(813) 986-6521

Splash of Life
Glenn Campbell
43W484 Burlington Road
Elgin, IL 60123
(847)464-0306
www.splashoflife.com

Tropicorium, Inc.
Dick Perrin
20080 Inkster Road
Romulus, MI 48174
(313) 782-2622
www.tropicorium.com

Index

Numbers in **boldface** indicate photographs.
Numbers in **boldface with an asterisk** (*) indicate the main entry for that genus.

About the Author

Eric H. Borneman is an aquarist, researcher, and author who writes frequently on marine subjects for various periodicals, including *Freshwater and Marine Aquarium, Tropical Fish Hobbyist, Practical Fishkeeping* and others. He is co-author of *A Practical Guide to Corals* and speaks nationally and internationally at aquarium-related and scientific conferences, events, and societies, and teaches classes on coral propagation and other reef issues.

Eric is co-founder of the Marine and Reef Society of Houston. His personal home aquariums include a multihabitat system of more than 500 gal-

lons that links a seagrass habitat, an intertidal habitat, and a large coral reef that runs without mechanical filtration devices.

With 20 years' experience diving on and photographing coral reefs, he is an active member of ReefCheck and provides coral survey data to various institutions. He is actively involved with reef conservation efforts, aquarium trade sustainability issues, investigations of coral diseases in captivity, and is creating a large searchable database of coral-related literature. Eric has a degree from Rice University and resides in suburban Houston, Texas.